SLAVERY, RESISTANCE AND ABOLITIONS
A PLURALIST PERSPECTIVE

This book is published with the financial assistance of the Office of the High Commissioner for Human Rights and the support of the UNESCO Slave Route Project. The views expressed in this book are those of the author(s) and do not necessarily reflect the views of the United Nations.

The Editors would like to express their gratitude to Mr. Mactar Ndoye, Human Rights Officer, Office of the United Nations High Commissioner for Human Rights, for his invaluable guidance and personal involvement in the preparation and publication of this book.

They also thank Mr. Yury Boychenko, Claudie Fioroni, Christina Saunders, Gloria Nwabuogu, Niraj Dawadi and all the Anti-Racial Discrimination Section of the Office of the United Nations High Commissioner for Human Rights for their contributions to this book.

The Editors and authors would also like to thank the translators for their efforts and personal dedication to the translation of texts into English: Eduardo António, Véronique Bergeron, Patrick Campbell, N. Maureen Conley, Carlos Costa Cox, Kathleen Fingleton, Magdalena Lopez Gorritxo, Adam K. Graham, Maud Marchand, Leonor Michelsen, Bonaventure Ntwari, Vincente Rafael, Júlia Rosa and Kate de Zillie.

Likewise, the Editors and authors wish to thank the UNV editors and proofreaders who contributed their efforts: Timo Knäbe, Aleksandra Król, Johanna R. Wallner and Michele Howe.

Special thanks are also extended to the lead editor, N. Maureen Conley (Editors Canada) and to Peter Greenhill and Patricia Valentine (True to Type, Claremont, Canada) for the care they bestowed on every detail of this book.

To quote this book or an excerpt, please indicate:
Ali Moussa Iye, Nelly Schmidt, Paul E. Lovejoy, Eds., *Slavery, Resistance and Abolitions: A Pluralist Perspective*, Africa World Press, Inc., 2019.

Slavery, Resistance and Abolitions
A Pluralist Perspective

Edited by

Ali Moussa Iye, Nelly Schmidt, Paul E. Lovejoy

A Contribution to
The United Nations International Decade
for People of African Descent
2015–2024

AFRICA WORLD PRESS

TRENTON | LONDON | CAPE TOWN | NAIROBI | ADDIS ABABA | ASMARA | IBADAN | NEW DELHI

AFRICA WORLD PRESS
541 West Ingham Avenue | Suite B
Trenton, New Jersey 08638

Cover:
Laura Facey, Their Spirits Gone Before Them, 2006.
Photograph © Donnette Zacca

Designed and typeset by True to Type Inc., Claremont,
Canada

Cataloging-in-Publication Data may be obtained from the
Library of Congress.

ISBNs: 978-1-56902-665-6 HB
       978-1-56902-666-3 PB

Contents

Foreword

The African slave trade and slavery were a global phenomenon that involved all continents, provoked profound transformations and became part of the foundation of our modern world. Through the capital accumulated during the trade and invested in the industrialisation of Europe and the Americas, through the cultural interactions that nurture most modern artistic creations, and through the fight for emancipation, which redefined the very concepts of human dignity and freedom, this history has deeply shaped our world. It is troubling to notice that it was only at the beginning of the third millennium that the slave trade and slavery were recognised as a Crime against Humanity at the World Conference against Racism, Racial Discrimination, Xenophobia and Related Intolerance, held in Durban, South Africa, in September 2001. Had this tragedy been duly taken into account, it would have enriched the debate on the 'duty to remember' and reinforced the universality of the responses given to this fundamental request. This recognition has opened new perspectives on the struggle of people of African descent for their rights.

It is to better understand this global history that UNESCO launched the Slave Route Project in 1994. For the first ten years – 1994 to 2004 – the UNESCO Slave Route Project focused on the magnitude of the research that was required and on the methods that were needed to combat ignorance and the avoidance of the topic of slavery and the slave trade. During this period, scientific research expanded dramatically, including the publication of scholarly studies and the production of educational and audio-visual tools. The resulting public discussion went some way towards meeting the expectations of the UNESCO initiative. For example, slavery was now permanently on the international scholarly agenda, and it was increasingly made clear that the tragedy affected all of humanity, not just people of African descent. The Project highlighted the contradiction between the accepted humanist principles that underpin the United Nations and the barbarity that allowed societies claiming the privilege of civilisation to treat people as commodities.

An International Scientific Committee has guided the Project in establishing goals, maintaining its cross-sectoral and multidisciplinary perspective, and addressing new issues and geographic areas. This scientific guidance has helped the Project by reinforcing research, by developing various materials and by mobilising marginalised Afro-descent populations for better recognition of the African presence in the world. The Slave Route Project, together with the Office of the High Commissioner for Human Rights (OHCHR), and the Working Group of Experts on People of African Descent actively contributed to the discussions that led to the proclamation by the General Assembly of the United Nations of the International Year for People of

African Descent in 2011 and of the International Decade for People of African Descent: 'Recognition, Justice and Development' (2015–2024) in December 2014.

Today, more than twenty-five years after the launch of the Slave Route Project, research on slavery and the slave trade has expanded to a level never before seen. Moreover, there has been a multiplication of efforts to insert the history of slavery into public discourse through remembrance activities and memorials.

The scholarly and public debate that now prevails has challenged a new generation of researchers and students to confront the increasing complexity of the topic, the overwhelming availability of primary documentation and sources of information, and the demanding and often ambiguous requests from policy makers and the public. Researchers and activists now face situations that vary considerably depending upon the different regions and countries in which they work. In Africa there is sometimes reluctance to discuss and examine complicity, while in the Middle East there are efforts to circumvent historical reality through denial, and in Asia, there is generally a lack of knowledge about this history. Hence the efforts at breaking the chain of silence today have to manage controversies that have emerged and to deal with the reluctance around repentance and also with false competition among victims of history. The focus has to be on unravelling diaspora and the legacy of slavery it is confronted with and on highlighting the enormous contributions of people of African descent to contemporary culture and society in the Americas, the Caribbean and globally, despite the gravity of the crime that was committed.

A review of the Durban Declaration and Programme of Action and the International Year for People of African Descent (2011) demonstrated the magnitude of the task at hand. It was noted that progress on assuring the rights of people of African descent could not, in a single year, produce results that satisfied the high expectations, despite the great number of activities undertaken by some countries, various international organisations and civil society. After a debate about the usefulness, relevance and goals of this recognition of the African past and its global influence, the UN General Assembly agreed that the proclamation of a Decade for People of African Descent dedicated to the recognition of the African past and its global influence would enable Member States to fulfil their commitments. The Decade offers a framework and a supportive operational platform to encourage Member States to implement policies to reduce historically inherited social injustices which still victimise people of African descent. The intention is to fight racism, racial prejudice and discrimination through education and thereby to promote cultural pluralism as the driving force enabling people to live together. Rather than stigmatising people through a past identified with slavery, the aim is to enhance an appreciation of the tangible and intangible heritage resulting from the cultural interaction of Africans in a global context despite being born of the slave trade and slavery. In recognition of the weight of history, the programme of activities articulates the aspiration for Recognition, the necessity of Justice, and the promise of Development.

The present publication is intended to be an academic contribution to this International Decade by addressing the concerns expressed by people of African descent for greater awareness of their history, their culture and their contributions to modern society.

The issues addressed in this publication are of extreme importance in better understanding our contemporary societies and many of our collective and individual behaviours. The essays are not meant to provide a survey of the research that has been undertaken,[1] but rather to provide a framework for highlighting the insights of members of the International Scientific Committee of the Slave Route Project and of other researchers. In this manner, the aim is to highlight the progress of research into the struggle for freedom and abolition and thereby to identify and preserve the heritage from this history, with the intention of giving a voice to the victims of this tragedy.

The articles in this publication concern all geographic areas affected by slavery: Africa, the Caribbean and the Americas, the Mediterranean, the Middle East, the Indian Ocean, the Red Sea, the Pacific Ocean and the Andean regions. This publication offers readers a diverse corpus of scientific knowledge and a pluralist perspective on the history of the trade in human beings. It addresses slavery and the resistance that was triggered and the resulting abolition. It examines the decisive debates which this history has unleashed, assesses the extensive data that has been recovered and suggests new topics that require further research. Its purpose is not only to reveal important results but also to demonstrate the magnitude of the work still to be done.

The necessity of offering a holistic perspective on the slave trade and slavery is also the purpose of this publication. It brings together a wide range of expertise from different regions and different disciplines to shed light on various aspects of this history. Only a rigorous and pluralistic knowledge of what has happened in the past, what is being perpetuated in the present and what threatens our future can help us transcend the legacies of slavery and the slave trade. This publication is a path towards that end and offers new insights into this history.

In the Caribbean, North America and South America, as well as in the Indian Ocean and Red Sea, historical research concerning people of African descent has achieved significant milestones in the last four decades. The many publications, which for a long time were entangled in a restrictive colonial historiography, have now evolved a new degree of political awareness since the Second World War. The debate shifted, as reflected in the work of Eric Williams and the emergence of econometric historical methodology. This body of research created a renewed analysis and understanding of colonial economies based on the slavery system and also opened new perspectives with regard to the impact of Western economies on this system of exploitation.

---

1 An initial summary of two decades of work can be accessed on the UNESCO Slave Route Project website, as well as on the DVD *Slave Routes: A Global Vision* published by UNESCO in 2010, which contains a film, a booklet, educational resources and bibliographic instructions.

The scholarship has made important contributions to understanding resistance and the means of survival under slavery. The enslavement of the workforce in the Caribbean and the maintenance of a slave trade internal to the Caribbean raise questions about the sources of information used by historians and social scientists. New themes have emerged in relation to the contributions of persons of African descent to different fields of knowledge, and to the acknowledgement, finally, of the traumatic impact generated by this history and the resulting discrimination. The consequences of the political discussion that relegated slavery to oblivion have not been completely identified and certainly not fully measured to date.

Over the last two decades, the focus of research has shifted, introducing new questions and reference materials that inform the educational world and cultural stakeholders. The significant progress in the generation of pedagogical content on slavery and its effects has important implications for understanding memory – what is remembered, what is forgotten, and how the historical record has been altered – and addresses the issue of 'reparations' for the damages caused by centuries of slavery and the resulting social disparities and racism. Historians and legal experts have an extensive agenda of study and collaboration with respect to correcting past social injustices and accepting the need for reconciliation.

The celebration of the 200th anniversary of the Haitian Revolution marked an important milestone because the emergence of Haiti as an independent country was a decisive moment in the history of the Americas and in the process of eliminating slavery. The many events that commemorated the role of Haiti in the struggle to end slavery encouraged a renewal of energy directed at addressing the history of slavery, including different approaches and many publications.

The presence of people of African descent in Asia, which has become a subject of research only recently, allows comparison of different systems of servitude (Atlantic and Indian Ocean models of slavery, Asian slavery, and indentured and forced labour). Some implications of this comparison are discussed in this book. The comparison of contemporary forms of slavery with historical slavery makes it possible to understand continuities and discontinuities in human trafficking that neither the proliferation of international campaigns nor socio-economic progress has managed to eradicate. Clearly, the study of ways of combating modern servitude is especially useful within a historical perspective.

Transmission of past knowledge on human trafficking and slavery in the world and an understanding of the indelible marks that have been left take on new significance in examining both tangible and intangible heritage. The museums of the world have a vital role to play in informing the public at large as well as researchers and educators of the invaluable – and often rare – evidence of a crime against humanity that lasted for centuries. Museums take people on the memory road to places throughout the world for them to see the landscape of this history. The written record alone does not tell everything but delivers only a version of history, which is why the collection of oral traditions is essential to expose another perspective on this history. They inform us about how the victims themselves and their descendants have managed to keep alive the memory of the tragic events. Each generation makes its contribution: creators, artists, writers seize this history and memory to create works recounting the untold and hidden experiences of various participants, stakeholders, players and protagonists.

The present publication reflects on these multiple approaches, perspectives and themes. It highlights the vigorous efforts that have been made in public outreach arising from the research endeavour, not only for the Caribbean and the Americas but also globally. By questioning this multifaceted history, and by deconstructing the ignorance that prevails with regard to it, this publication provides an intellectual contribution to the International Decade for People of African Descent.

Ali MOUSSA IYE
Chief – History and Memory for Dialogue Section
Social and Human Sciences Sector
UNESCO

Nelly SCHMIDT
Research Director at the CNRS (French National Centre for Scientific Research), Sorbonne University. Former President of the International Scientific Committee of the UNESCO Project, The Slave Route: Resistance, Freedom, Heritage

Paul E. LOVEJOY
Distinguished Research Professor. Former Director of the Harriet Tubman Institute for Research on the Global Migrations of African Peoples, York University, Toronto, Canada. Former member of the International Scientific Committee of the UNESCO Project, The Slave Route: Resistance, Freedom, Heritage

Africa and Slavery in a Global Context

Toyin Falola

BIOGRAPHY

Dr Toyin Falola is currently the Frances Higginbotham Nalle Centennial Pro-
fessor at the University of Texas at Austin, where he has been a professor of
African history for several years. His research interests are African history
since the nineteenth century, with a concentration on West Africa, Nigeria and
the Yoruba-speaking people. He has been Vice President of the International
Scientific Committee of the UNESCO Project 'The Slave Route: Resistance,
Liberty, Heritage' (2011–2013). Recently he has authored and co-edited
Globalization and Sustainable Development in Africa (Rochester, NY: University of Rochester Press, 2011); *The Women's War of 1929: A History of
Anti-Colonial Resistance in Eastern Nigeria* (Durham, NC: Carolina Academic Press, 2011); *Africa, Empire and Globalization: Essays in Honor of A.
G. Hopkins* (Durham, NC: Carolina Academic Press, 2011); and *Yoruba Fiction, Orature, and Culture: Oyekan Owomoyela and African Literature and
the Yoruba Experience* (Trenton, NJ: Africa World Press, 2011).

Introduction

No topic illustrates the African location in the international system better than
slavery, both as an institution and as a system of commerce. While chattel slavery is virtually dead in most parts of the world, new categories and processes of
exploitation have emerged in ways that bring us back to the characteristics that defined slavery in the past. The transatlantic slave trade, colonialism, the cold war
and the lingering economic status of Africa as a dependent continent are some of
the most critical historical developments that tie Africa to the rest of the world.
Of those ties, slavery and the slave trade remain the most compelling, their impact lingering to this day. A social institution connected with commerce produced
a culture that manifested the intricacies and dangers of globalisation. In any discussion of slavery, the transatlantic slave trade looms large. No other cases of
human trafficking compare with the transatlantic slave trade in its magnitude and
impact. Many will agree with David Northrup's summary of its centrality:

First, it brought many millions of Africans to the Americas (four times the
number of European immigrants who settled there down to about 1820), leav-

ing a permanent cultural and genetic imprint on many parts of the New World. Second, the creation of slave labour systems in the New World was associated with the first phase of European expansion and the rise of capitalism. Third, the end of the slave trade was the subject of a massive abolitionist campaign that scholars widely have seen as one of the great turning points in Western moral consciousness. Finally, the Atlantic slave trade has been seen not only as affecting Africa during the four centuries of its existence but also as leading to the later European takeover of the continent and causing its present-day under development.[1]

The transatlantic slave trade and the Americas' experience of slavery shape the way we look at the subject, and they dominate much of the space on writing about the African diaspora.

To work backward from the present to the past: the development of an Afrocentric paradigm in the United States, especially by Professor Molefi Kete Asante and his disciples,[2] and the assertive demands for area studies are tied to a strong belief among blacks that the academy cares little about them and their concerns; that if they do not develop alternatives to mainstream knowledge, topics such as slavery and the slave trade will either be ignored or treated with levity or duplicity. In his combative memoir, Asante even attributes the creation of an alternative PhD programme at Temple University to the politics of race and what he sees as the deliberate undermining of issues relating to minorities in mainstream disciplines. In this programme, Africa takes centre stage. As he closes his memoir, he exudes confidence, declaring that:

> The real work of this century is not going to be about race, colour or Black Studies but rather about the deep quest for African identity, liberated from mental enslavement on the continent and in the diaspora, and gaining United Africa based on democratic power and founded on the realisation of the dreams of Marcus Garvey, DuBois, Kwame Nkrumah, Muammar Gaddafi and Cheikh Anta Diop.[3]

Asante's 'quest for African identity' is hard to separate from race, colour and the very history of the slave trade that defined the Atlantic World for centuries. As he noted, until that legacy of 'mental enslavement' is eradicated, moving forward may be too difficult. The names he invoked, all controversial figures in one way or another, reveal his support for the kinds of struggles the men had, all

---

1 David Northrup (ed.), *The Atlantic Slave Trade* (Boston: Houghton Mifflin, 2002), xiii.
2 Molefi Kete Asante, *As I Run Toward Africa* (Boulder, CO: Paradigm, 2011), 269–81.
3 Ibid., 310.

linked by a desire to create a powerful solidarity among blacks in different parts of the world.

Before the rise of the Afrocentric paradigm that Asante popularised, the pan-Africanist movement developed as a diaspora organisation by descendants of slaves who wanted to transcend the limitations of slavery and colonial exploitation, overcome dependence on other races and create a new African world. Pan-Africanism responded to the earlier consolidation of racist ideologies and regimes, arising in part from the slave trade. By the nineteenth century, the West had imbibed an attitude of utter disrespect for Africa, and this has carried over to the present. Many argue that this lack of respect is due to the transatlantic slave trade, when the idea of racism was consolidated in ways that were very much tied to slavery. Various arguments over the era of the slave trade continue to be repackaged today, often disguised in elegant language and theories to mask the ideologies: Africa remains the primitive 'Other'; the continent that requires rescue missions; a people without a worthy past or significant future. An 'impending anarchy' is in the horizon, we have been told many times, and many pessimistic analysts have concluded that projects of colonisation, similar to those of the nineteenth century, deserve to be pursued.

What the analysts forget to mention, not because they are ignorant, but because it is convenient to forget, is that Africa's problems, in many of their forms and ramifications, are due both to the inadequacies of its political leaders and to the limited imagination of its planners, on the one hand, as well as to Africa's role in the larger world, on the other. Slavery represents one reason for underdevelopment. Africa is a huge continent, but its total population of less than 800 million is rather small. The slave trade is in part responsible for this, and the gains of the first half of the twentieth century that led to population increases are being wiped out in some places by the ravages of AIDS.

I hope I have mentioned a few points to indicate that the legacies of slavery do remain. It is this theme that I intend to explore in this chapter, focusing on the globalisation generated by slavery and its aftermath. We all know that the issues are many, the complications too countless to mention, and that controversies abound. I will focus on three major ideas: how slavery has impacted African history; the continued existence of slavery in the modern world; and the current discussions on new categories of exploitation.

The Past and Its Troubles

The starting point is how slavery created a diaspora and what this means to us today. European expansion after the fifteenth century was impressive, part of the achievements of the Renaissance and the Industrial Revolution. Technological improvements and the consequences of the creation of nation-states as projects empowered Europe in ways that devastated Africans, with the transatlantic slave trade as one major outcome. Contacts established by the Portuguese were not sustained for long through trade in gold, raw products and weapons, but in humans, following the heavy demand for labour in the New World. The establishment of small forts and the seizure of places along the coast to create trading colonies in the mid-fifteenth century established patterns that increased in scale and intensity over the years.[4] In later years, the trade in slaves became large, highly professionalised and truly global in its operations.[5] The encounter was forceful and fatal, changing many aspects of the continent and its institutions in profound ways. It is now difficult, and nearly impossible in some cases, to comprehend African political and economic institutions before the rise of the transatlantic slavery. While Africans continued to keep some traditions of old, it was clear that many had to be adjusted to the needs of slavery and the global trade in slaves. At the same time, they had to accept new ideas from abroad and to Africanise many of them in order to survive. Slavery became an established social institution in various parts of the world. Practices of enslavement acquired notions of racism in some places, and contributed to laws and ideas that allowed one person to own, inherit and sell fellow human beings. Ethical and moral codes arose to justify enslavement and wars to enslave and sell; and rules were established on rights and duties between masters and slaves.

To be sure, Europe cannot claim to have pioneered all things connected with slavery. Arab slave traders and recruiters had been active for many years before the fifteenth century, moving Africans across the Indian Ocean and the Red Sea to different parts of Asia. We cannot accurately calculate the number of slaves that were also moved across the Sahara Desert to North Africa and the Middle East, and the Mediterranean Sea to southern Europe, especially during the eighth century. Arabs and Europeans sold Islam and Christianity to Africans, but not the sects that saw slavery as an assault on human rights. The Arabs connected the jihad with slavery, and the holy wars became an opportunity to turn war captives into slaves; consequently, the wars and captives multiplied in number as Islam spread into various parts of North, East and West Africa. Africans in the savanna, those in the eastern and central parts, and in the Horn suffered the most in what is now called by some the 'oriental slave trade'. Africans were used to serve in the army and

---

4 On a recent study of these forts and their impact, see Edmund Abaka, *House of Slaves and 'Door of No Return': Gold Coast/Ghana Slave Forts, Castles and Dungeons and the Atlantic Slave Trade* (Trenton, NJ: Africa World Press, 2012).

5 See, for instance, Hugh Thomas, *The Slave Trade: The Story of the Atlantic Slave Trade, 1440–1870* (New York: Simon and Schuster, 1997).

state administrations, and as domestics. Women and children were preferred. In the Horn where the women were portrayed as obedient, honest and beautiful, thousands of Oromo, Ethiopians and Nilotic women suffered a great deal, as they were relocated to other lands to become concubines and domestics. With respect to male slaves, Arab merchants who stayed within the continent, as with the plantation owners along the East African coast, needed them for intensive farm work. Raiding expeditions were many, devastating various areas.

The Arab slave dealers have been less scrutinised by African scholars.[6] For one thing, Islam is presented in many parts of Africa as an indigenous religion; Christianity as external; Islam as pro-protest; Christianity as pro-Western. Elements of this historical presentation have led to the marginalisation of oriental slavery, such that we talk more of the transatlantic than the trans-Saharan. The literature on the Indian Ocean slave trade is poorly connected to the larger body of literature on slavery. Even assertive demands for reparations leave Islamic areas out. As if slavery and the slave trade had some redeeming values, oriental slavery is sometimes defended because it involved fewer victims (under five million compared to about thirteen million from the transatlantic slave trade), and emancipation was easier to obtain, thus promoting integration with society. While some of the comparisons are valid, the context of the economic systems must be borne in mind: expansive economic systems did not emerge in most parts of the Arab world as intensely as in the American plantation economies. Neither did many slave communities emerge. But racism and exploitation were not foreign to the system. Today, Sudan represents the survival of elements of Islamic slavery. It was through the Arab connection that Africans found themselves in Arabia, India and the Far East, travelling great distances as slaves carried across the Sahara Desert, the Red Sea, the Mediterranean Sea and the Indian Ocean. Surviving as minorities, communities of descendants of African slaves can be found today in Iraq, Iran, India and Pakistan.

Nothing, however, can compare to the heinous transatlantic slave trade. In attempting to underplay its damages and spread the blame, two issues have always been debated. One is the existing indigenous slavery before, during and after the transatlantic slave trade. The other is the role of Africans within it. With respect to the nature of indigenous slavery, three points are relevant. It is abundantly clear that indigenous slavery in the nineteenth and twentieth centuries was a response to the external demands for raw materials on a large scale. Harvesting palm oil,

---

6 A number of new studies are in print on Islam and slavery. Among others, see Behnaz A. Mirzai, Ismael Musah Montana and Paul E. Lovejoy (eds.), *Slavery, Islam and Diaspora* (Trenton, NJ: Africa World Press, 2009); Paul E. Lovejoy (ed.), *Slavery on the Frontiers of Islam* (Princeton, NJ: Marcus Wiener, 2004).

palm kernel, peanuts, cocoa and others was labour intensive. Thus, slavery during that era must be connected to a global economic system, with Africa playing the role allocated to it in the international division of labour. Between the fifteenth and nineteenth centuries, what we call indigenous slavery was also transformed by the transatlantic slave trade. The external trade injected violence into the system, and relationships of power were sharply defined, with a widening gap between those who managed the state and the poor producers. Definitions of social relationships increasingly responded to external pressures. As to the nature of slavery before the fifteenth century, we actually do not have substantial evidence on various practices, and some scholars such as Walter Rodney have denied that it existed in ways that we define for the nineteenth century.[7] The definition of indigenous slavery continues to pose problems, as some are inclined to regard it as mild form of servitude. Some scholars have warned that we may be confusing a slave with a serf.

Problems arise, too, from the characteristics of slavery in Africa when they are compared and contrasted with transatlantic slavery, with African practices not similar to those of slavery in American plantation economies. No one denies that slavery was practised in one form or another in various places, representing a major way to accumulate assets and expand the labour force.[8] The real issue that is always ignored is clear: domestic slavery did not instigate the external slave trade, nor did it establish the conditions for the transatlantic slave trade. Existing institutions of dependence could have been modified to take care of the external demand for slaves, in the process turning servants, political clients and war captives into slaves.

As to the second issue of African complicity, one must make a distinction between people and states, between the poor and the rich, strangers and citizens, the continent and the ethnic units. Slavery and the slave trade involved the massive use of violence, in wars and military expeditions; markets protected by the state; and the power to make criminals and punish them. The tiny political class associated with the state saw benefits in the trade: the acquisition of resources to build and consolidate the state; self-enrichment and aggrandisement; and competition with fellow chiefs and neighbouring states. This tiny political class collaborated with those who instigated and sustained the demands for slaves. When a greedy political class saw the opportunity to connect indigenous slavery with the external trade in slaves, the scale of brutality became boundless, with wars – even those justified on the basis of state forma-

---

7 Walter Rodney, 'African Slavery and Other Forms of Social Oppression on the Upper Guinea Coast in the Context of the Atlantic Slave Trade', *Journal of African History*, 7/5 (1966), 431–43.

8 Discussions on a variety of practices can be found in Jay Spalding and Stephanie Beswick (eds.), *African Systems of Slavery* (Trenton, NJ: Africa World Press, 2010).

tion – converting innocent war victims into slaves. Economic gain motivated African chiefs, just as it motivated those who approached them for slaves. In a complex global economy, Africans were asked to supply the labour, Europe the capital, and the Americas the land to produce sugar cane, cotton and tobacco. The African chiefs, no matter how much blame is apportioned to them, neither created this global economy nor served as its main financial managers.

Treating the slave trade as nothing but business tends to downgrade its human costs, its far-reaching consequences. When Philip Curtin came up with an estimated figure of 11.5 million as having left Africa, with 9.5 million actually reaching the Americas,[9] the data generated controversy, the political side of which saw it as one effort to underplay the significance of the slave trade. Critics ignored Curtin's remark that a reduction in the estimate of the number of enslaved Africans did not lessen the harm caused by the trade. Statistics are one thing; their interpretation is another. The overall impact on Africa's population has also been a subject of contention: while no one disputes the fact that the slave trade contributed to a population decrease, some point to other reasons such as wars, droughts, epidemics and other forms of disaster. The population structure in some areas was altered in negative ways, in large part because of the enslavement of adult males.[10] And millions of people suffered in the process of being captured, stored, transported and exploited. More men than women left the continent as slaves, and the women left behind became intensely exploited for their productive labour, especially as farm workers.[11] Africa became the labour basket that sustained the economic enterprises of European settlers in the New World. The price it paid is incalculable. Violence spread, as slaves were obtained mainly through wars and raiding expeditions. The most devastated areas were Angola and areas north of the Congo River and the Gulf of Guinea, and large areas in their hinterlands. After the eighteenth century, south-eastern Africa was drawn into the slave trade, thus spreading the devastation.

The slave trade scattered blacks to various parts of the world, in large part a consequence of centuries of slave trafficking. Thus, we have blacks on various continents, as part of both forced and voluntary migrations.[12] The origins of the blacks

9 Philip D. Curtin, *The Atlantic Slave Trade* (Madison: University of Wisconsin Press, 1969).

10 Patrick Manning, 'Contours of Slavery and Social Change in Africa', *American Historical Review*, 88/4 (October 1983), 835–57.

11 Claire C. Robertson and Martin A. Klein (eds.), *Women and Slavery in Africa* (Madison: University of Wisconsin Press, 1983).

12 See, for instance, Vincent Bakpetu Thompson, *The Making of the African Diaspora in the Americas, 1441–1900* (London: Longman, 1987).

in diaspora approximate to the main sources of slave supply: West Africa supplied the majority, and others were drawn from south-west and central Africa (areas of Cameroon, Congo, Angola, Gabon and Zaire). Many slaves from East Africa went to the islands in the Indian Ocean and Brazilian plantations. So entrenched are blacks in these various places that not many see the connections to Africa or understand its history; and some do not have clusters that are powerful enough to construct politics around those connections. An articulate minority has always pointed to the connections in the diaspora, using it to build political movements.

Many have argued that the contributions of Africans and diasporan Africans to Western economies and civilisation have been ignored, maligned or underrepresented. Yet certain things are not at all controversial. Slavery made it possible for the New World to become part of a global economy, facilitated by the Europeans who recruited the slaves from Africa and sent them to the Western Hemisphere where they became the major labour force. Why Africans constituted such a significant portion of the labour force has been a subject of contention: economic reasons combined with racialist ones, and as David Eltis argues, they also combined with the belief that Europeans should not enslave one another, thus making Africans the most desired slaves.[13]

Due to slavery, the Atlantic region became an active trading network that united four continents in the exchange of people, goods and services. Credit and capital also developed as a result of slave trade. European merchants invested large sums of money in ships and goods; guns and other goods were produced in large quantities to sell in exchange for slaves. All the participants were affected: the New World produced commodities that were traded to Europe in ways that affected the economies of such countries as Great Britain, the Netherlands, Portugal and France.[14] Slaves contributed to the colonisation and development of the Americas, enabled Brazil to become the leading producer of sugar, and made it possible for the Dutch to create successful sugar plantations in the West Indies and for the English to do the same in Jamaica and Barbados, and for the French to do the same in Saint Domingue. Slavery also shaped the identities of blacks and whites and con-

---

13 For various arguments relating to why Africans were enslaved, see, for instance, Eric Williams, *Capitalism and Slavery* (Chapel Hill: University of North Carolina Press, 1972; 1st edn., 1944); Winthrop D. Jordan, *White Over Black: American Attitudes Toward the Negro, 1550–1812* (Chapel Hill: University of North Carolina Press, 1968); David Brion Davis, *Slavery and Human Progress* (Oxford: Oxford University Press, 1984); and David Eltis, *The Rise of African Slavery in the Americas* (New York: Cambridge University Press, 2000).

14 See, for instance, Barbara L. Solow (ed.), *Slavery and the Rise of the Atlantic System* (New York: Cambridge University Press, 1991).

tributed to defining the character of European imperialism. The legacies of racism and contrasting identities remain in various parts of the world.[15]

Trying to show the varied impact of blacks on the creation of Western civilisation has become a major academic industry that partly led to the emergence of the combative Afrocentric framework. The gentle side of the paradigm looks at issues from the 'African perspectives', writing history from the bottom up, focusing on issues of slave resistance and rebellion, African anti-abolitionism and the various contributions of Africans to the development of other places. The 1944 survey by Eric Williams lays the foundation: he shows the crucial role of the slave trade in building commercial capitalism, and he argues that the abolition of slavery in the nineteenth century also had to do with the emergence of a new generation of industrial capitalists who could profit by other means. Some of Eric Williams' conclusions have been modified or rejected, but they remain widely influential. A major recent achievement of the historiography more aligned to the views of Williams is the brilliant book by Joseph E. Inikori who shows – with relentless energy, massive data and mastery of the economic history of Britain – that the Atlantic commerce and the role of African labour in it contributed to the completion of the industrialisation process between the mid-seventeenth and mid-nineteenth centuries.[16]

The contributions are not limited to the economies. Various studies have shown profound black imprints on American religions, music and cuisines.[17] With cultural survival and adaptation at work, a spirit of 'double consciousness' and cultural hybridity was put in place: African slaves and their successors would keep those elements of African cultures that were possible while integrating into new environments. Africa enabled them to create an identity while their host societies made possible the creation of new ways to live. Something new emerged in the process: the 'modernity and double consciousness' that Paul Gilroy presents in *The Black Atlantic.*[18]

The less aggressive side of the Afrocentric paradigm sees the beginning of the decline of Africa from the slave trade era, an idea widely popularised by Walter

15 See, for instance, Jose C. Curto and Paul E. Lovejoy (eds.), *Enslaving Connections: Changing Cultures of Africa and Brazil During the Era of Slavery* (New York: Humanity Books, 2004).

16 Joseph E. Inikori, *Africans and the Industrial Revolution in England: A Study in International Trade and Economic Development* (Cambridge, UK: Cambridge University Press, 2001).

17 See, for instance, John Thornton, *Africa and Africans in the Making of the Atlantic World, 1400–1800*, 2nd edn. (New York: Cambridge University Press, 1998).

18 Paul Gilroy, *The Black Atlantic: Modernity and Double Consciousness* (Cambridge, MA: Harvard University Press, 1993).

Rodney.[19] In spite of the challenges offered to Rodney, most recently by John Thornton,[20] Afrocentrists keep the argument alive. To continue with Rodney's schema, the slave trade era was followed by colonialism, which incorporated the continent into a global economy in an exploitative manner. Decolonisation did not bring about the much-anticipated changes, as the colonialists handed over power to a political class with values not different from theirs. The logic of exploitation was perpetuated, as the postcolonial leaders did not pursue a serious agenda of development. Rather, they merely facilitated neo-colonial dependence, the marginalisation of Africa and the impoverishment of their own people. The failure to dismantle the institutions constructed around slavery and colonialism has created problems at a time when the technologies of global domination have become more efficient and more threatening.

Legacies and Lingering Problems

Slavery also has its recent history, a dirty aspect of the so-called modern twentieth century. Slavery and the slave trade survived the nineteenth century, as Brazil and Cuba did not enact laws to end slavery until the late 1880s. Abolition of the transatlantic slave trade in the early nineteenth century, however, did not translate into the abolition of slavery in Africa. In many parts of Africa, practices associated with slavery and other forms of servility continued well into the twentieth century.[21] While contributing to its abolition on the one hand, European colonial governments contributed to the survival of slavery on the other hand. The international demand for African products led to the extensive use of slave labour to produce and carry raw materials to the coastal cities. As a result, slavery had a slow death, surviving in some places till the 1930s.[22]

The need for labour to work on the creation of new infrastructures encouraged colonial officers to tap into various relations of servitude, notably forced labour. In the early decades of the colonial era, the need to sustain an economy based on cash

19 Walter Rodney, *How Europe Underdeveloped Africa* (Washington, DC: Howard University Press, 1972).

20 Thornton, *Africa and Africans in the Making of the Atlantic World*.

21 See, for instance, Roger Sawyer, *Slavery in the Twentieth Century* (London: Routledge and Kegan Paul, 1986); Martin A. Klein (ed.), *Breaking the Chains: Slavery, Bondage, and Emancipation in Modern Africa and Asia* (Madison: University of Wisconsin Press, 1993); and Joel Quirk, *Unfinished Business: A Comparative Survey of Historical and Contemporary Slavery* (Paris: UNESCO, 2009).

22 Paul E. Lovejoy and Jan S. Hogendorn, *Slow Death for Slavery: The Course of Abolition in Northern Nigeria* (Cambridge, UK: Cambridge University Press, 1993).

crops allowed for the toleration of slavery.[23] The demand for raw materials also meant that many colonial officers overlooked abuses and cared less about the consolidation of social hierarchies. Many colonial governments also used labour in ways not different from slavery, such as forced labour, poorly remunerated labour and semi-slave workers.[24] Pawnship consolidated itself in many areas, in ways not too different from slavery, largely to create cheap labour for cash crops.[25] A fascinating case study has been done on the island of Fernando Po, which developed a plantation economy in the late nineteenth century. The migrant labour upon which the economy of Fernando Po relied worked in conditions not much different from slavery. Ibrahim Sundiata shows how free and contract labour had many things in common, concluding that free labour did not always triumph over slavery.[26] As he concludes, 'Far from collapsing, traditional slaving networks interdigitated with the new traffic in "contract laborers"'.[27] In some other areas where raw materials were profitable, there were various ways to bind workers to the land to the benefit of landlords and rich merchants. Wage labour could exist, but it did not necessarily mean that its conditions produced freedom and a higher standard of living. To return to the Fernando Po experience, the failure 'to produce a self-replicating population created policies which made the distinction between slave and contract workers at times no more than nominal'.[28] Slavery was compatible with imperialism: 'the triumph of British-imposed abolition and emancipation coincided with the increasing exploitation of the worker and the tying of the laborer to the plantation'.[29] Women have probably suffered more, staying much longer in socioeconomic conditions akin to slavery than men who could opt for wage-sector jobs.

In precolonial African formations where land was plentiful, the struggle was to obtain the means to obtain labour. In colonial economies, both land and labour be-

---

23 See, for instance, John Grace, *Domestic Slavery in West Africa* (London: Frederick Muller, 1975), 159–219.

24 See, for instance, Suzanne Miers and Richard Roberts (eds.), *The End of Slavery in Africa* (Madison: University of Wisconsin Press, 1988); Frederick Cooper, *Decolonization and African Society: The Labor Question in French and British Africa* (New York: Cambridge University Press, 1996).

25 Toyin Falola and Paul E. Lovejoy (eds.), *Pawnship in Africa. Debt Bondage in Historical Perspective* (Boulder, CO: Westview, 1994).

26 Ibrahim K. Sundiata, *From Slaving to Neoslavery: The Bight of Biafra and Fernando Po in the Era of Abolition, 1827–1930* (Madison: University of Wisconsin Press, 1996).

27 Ibid., 8.

28 Ibid., 7.

29 Ibid., 8.

came necessary to have in abundance in order to benefit from the modern economies. Wealth had to be extracted from both land and labour. As slavery declined in importance, alternative forms of servitude were either invented or improved upon, many in relation to debt. Pawnship of crops, of trees and of the poor used debts to create access to cheap labour. Unlike the slaves with their outsider status, the new pawn could be an insider, even with well-known, visible kinship connections. A number of the aspects of the ideology that sustained slavery in the past[30] are similar to those that maintain contemporary relations of dependence. For instance, the apartheid system that existed in South Africa until the early 1990s was seen by many as the continuation of slavery by other means.

Mauritania and Sudan remain in the news as places where slavery continues in one form or another. Both Mauritania and Sudan have complicated racial problems, even when denied by the government, tied to the trade in slaves and the impact of Islam. In Mauritania, the French prohibited slavery in 1905, but it has continued nevertheless. Racial categories have been defined around slavery, land and power. At the top are the Beidan, the Berber/Arab, called by some as 'white Moors', who own land, big businesses, power and slaves. The Beidan construct themselves as superior to blacks and control the Abid, the black slaves either bought or born into slavery. The Abid are regarded as chattel slaves, owned by Beidan masters and exploited on land and used to rear livestock. The third category, sandwiched between the Abid and Beidan, are the Haratin, the descendants of local populations and freed slaves. They can use land given to them by the Beidan, own their own businesses, and marry and raise their children. The Haratin are not allowed to be equal to their former masters or enjoy similar social standing as the Beidan. The Haratin and Abid are collectively known as the Black Moors, and they regard themselves as an oppressed category. The droughts and economic decline of the 1970s and 1980s brought the interracial tension to a head, with various conflicts over the rights to land and payment of tributes by slaves to their masters and landlords. In the 1970s, various protest movements by the Black Moors to overcome their status were violently suppressed.

President Mauusa ould Si' Ahmed declared in 1997 that opposition to slavery was against the spirit of his so-called democratic regime. Professor Cheikh Saad Bouth Kamara and four other leaders were arrested in the following year for so-called anti-government activities that involved the internationalisation of the problems of slavery and human rights' abuses. The government argued that the Universal Declaration of Human Rights did not apply to the Islamic Republic of Mauritania. The argument came as a rude shock to political activists and many in

---

30 Paul E. Lovejoy (ed.), *The Ideology of Slavery in Africa* (Beverly Hills, CA: Sage, 1981).

the world community; after all, the country claimed to have abolished slavery in 1981 and inserted many liberal and democratic clauses in its 1991 Democratic Constitution. Professor Kamara later received an award in 1998 from the United Nations for his activist role,[31] but his struggles and those of others have yet to transform Mauritania. Relations of dependence are established, justified by the force of history and traditions, and sustained by the dominant class in power. The freed slaves (Haratin) do not believe that freedom has given them much economic and political power, although they are no longer slaves in legal terms. Many have been granted freedom but are still required to be part of former slave estates or pay dues to former masters. And the Abid remain legally defined as slaves with masters enjoying their power.[32]

Turning to the Sudan,[33] the external and internal slave trade has a long history in this country. Current cases of slavery evoke conditions of violence reminiscent of the long-dead transatlantic and trans-Saharan slave trade and merit more space than most others. Slave raiding to supply external markets began in some parts of the Sudan in the late eighteenth century, doing much damage to the society at large.[34] The wars associated with countless slave-raiding expeditions and other problems have created a 'memory of war and blood'.[35] Stephanie Beswick has analysed the dangerous psychology of this experience, 'emotions that are attached to the memories of previous wars, killings and misdeeds'. During the 1980s, an alliance of slave merchants and government officials conducted slave-raiding expeditions that were accompanied by the rape and abuse of women and children. In spite of various statements to the contrary, these expeditions have yet to end.[36] Even today, there are still cases of 'predatory attacks' between groups, prompted by the fears associated with the domination of the south by the north, unending ethnic clashes and slave raiding.

31 Desmond Davies, 'Mauritania Anti-Slavery Campaigner Wins Award', *PANA* (London), 18 November 1998.

32 See, for instance, C. S. Kamara, 'Narratives of the Past, Politics of the Present: Identity, Subordination and the Haratines of Mauritania', PhD diss. (University of Chicago, 1997).

33 This essay was completed before Sudan was split into two countries, North and South, because of unresolvable conflicts driven by a host of reasons, including identity politics and resource allocation.

34 Stephanie Beswick, *Sudan's Blood Memory: The Legacy of War, Ethnicity and Slavery in Southern Sudan* (Rochester, NY: University of Rochester Press, 2004), 29–42.

35 Ibid., 198.

36 Baroness Cox, Slavery in Sudan (Christian Solidarity International US Congress House Committee on International Relations, Wednesday 13 March 1996).

The 1990 report by Human Rights Watch on Sudan was (and still is) highly disturbing.[37] In addition to detailing a variety of abuses committed in the conduct of wars, the report devoted attention to slavery, implicating both the army and the government in episodes where thousands of Dinka women and children were enslaved and dragged to other places to work as domestic and farm labour. Due to the international exposure of the slavery cases, the Sudanese government was put on the defensive, saying that kidnapping was different from slavery, and that captive-taking was part of a long history of ethnic hostility between the Baggara and the Dinka. A government controlled by the north blamed the leaders of the south for trashing the name of the country. To the south, the Baggara and northerners of Arab descent have always exploited them, capturing their citizens and turning them into slaves.

In 1996, another report on Sudan concluded that slavery was still prevalent and linked to the ongoing war. To the compilers of the report, the Sudanese government could no longer call the widespread occurrence of slavery 'hostage-taking'. The denial is often expressed by those who support it, as government officials and soldiers are known to have participated in kidnapping and selling people.[38] The situation in Sudan has energised more than a few in the anti-slavery movements such as the American Anti-Slavery Group (AASG) and Anti-Slavery International. In 2001, the AASG appeared before the US Congress to ask that trade in gum arabic produced in the Sudan should stop because it was being produced by slaves, and to ask Americans and others not to buy stocks linked to oil in Sudan. The AASG also took with it to the Congress a freed slave, Francis Bok, who narrated his sufferings and enslavement in ways similar to the slave narratives Olaudah Equiano had written two centuries earlier[39]:

I was born in southern Sudan near Nyamillel. When I was seven, my mother sent me to the market to sell eggs and beans. I never saw my mother again.

At the market, the militia soldiers attacked. Hundreds of Arabs on horses came into the market shouting. They shot people in the head. And they cut off heads with their swords. And the streets were a river of blood.

They took me and many children as slaves. They put me in a big basket tied to a donkey, and they took us north.

37 Africa Watch, *Denying 'The Honor of Living': Sudan, A Human Rights Disaster* (New York: Human Rights Watch, 1990).
38 Human Rights Watch, *Behind the Red Line: Political Repression in Sudan* (New York: Human Rights Watch, 1996), 307–14.
39 Olaudah Equiano, *The Interesting Narrative of the Life of Olaudah Equiano, or Gustavus Vassa, the African* (London: Author, 1789).

One girl had seen her parents killed, and she would not stop crying. So they shot her in the head. Her younger sister started crying. So they cut her foot off. I was quiet.

In the north, I was given as a slave to Giema Abdullah. He took me to his family, and he beat me with sticks. All of them – the women and children too – they called me 'abeed, abeed' meaning black slave.

For ten years, they beat me every morning. They made me sleep with animals. And they gave me very bad food. They said I was an animal. For ten years I had no one to laugh with. For ten years nobody loved me. But every day I prayed to God.

One day I asked my master a question: 'Why do you call me abeed? And why do you feed me bad food all the time and make me sleep with animals? Is it because I am black?' My master was very angry. 'Where did you learn to ask me this question?' he said. 'Never ask me again.' And he beat me and beat me. When I was 17, I decided to escape. I would rather die than be a slave.

I ran away, and I came to a police station. 'Please help me,' I told the police. But they kept me as their slave and made me do work for them all day. After two months, I ran away. An Arab truck driver helped me escape. He hid me in his lorry, and he helped me to get to Khartoum, the capital.[40]

More suffering followed, with an arrest by the Sudanese secret police and five months in jail. He later escaped to Cairo where the United Nations Refugees Office arranged his relocation to Iowa in the United States. His story, packaged and popularised by anti-slavery groups, is one of many that have brought attention to the continuity of slavery in modern Africa.

Anti-Slavery International has also been relentless in popularising the atrocities in the Sudan and pressuring its government to abolish slavery. The organisation has noted that the Sudanese government is not sincere, and it keeps mounting international pressure to free those in bondage and prevent new enslavement.[41]

The cases of Sudan and Mauritania have long attracted international attention. The two countries and various cases of human rights abuse have led to the creation of many non-governmental organisations (NGOs) to attack slavery and related forms of dependency and labour injustice. Also, within the United Nations, a

---

40 Senate Committee on Foreign Relations, *Slavery Throughout the World: Hearing before the Committee on Foreign Relations*, 106th Congress, 2001. Text version, http://purl.access.gpo.gov/GPO/LPS11447, 18.

41 For all their various efforts, see the website of Anti-Slavery International, www.anti-slavery.org.

working group emerged in 1975,[42] with varying levels of success over the years, to address issues of slavery, pawnship (popularly known as debt bondage), various abuses to children (traffic in children, child pornography, child prostitution, involvement of children in warfare and criminal activities, sweatshops, etc.), various abuses to women (prostitution, genital mutilation) and the deliberate killing of people in order to sell their body parts. The new anti-slavery movements have given us a new definition of the institution of exploitation, limited no longer to the ownership and domination of a person, but expanded to include cases of 'forced exploitation of labor', the control of one person by another and severe restrictions to individual freedom that deprive people of their liberty. In the process, indigenous people have been allowed to speak, to provide extensive data on a wide range of age-old abuses of forced labour, servitude and debt bondage. Various governments have been forced to respond to criticisms and challenges offered by international organisations, although not all have been sincere, using all sorts of excuses, if not outright denial, to justify various practices. More astute governments simply make promises or even send delegations to international meetings without necessarily reforming their societies.

While it may be misleading to compare modern abuses to the chattel slavery of old, and while it is certain that no country in the world now relies on slavery to sustain its economy, it is not wrong to emphasise contemporary relations of subservience akin to the slavery of old. It is also important to question the ideology of free labour and how poor wages affect millions of people in different parts of the world. The desire of those who seek labour and those who seek the means to survive converge in ways that create servile conditions. Modern forms of slavery exhibit three tendencies: 'control by another person, the appropriation of labour power and the use or threat of violence'.[43] A few serious forms of contemporary slavery are identified below. First, young African girls have been shipped to Europe to work as prostitutes, later abandoned by their 'madams' or 'masters' when they are no longer active or when they become independent. An underworld economy, sometimes connected with crime and drugs, is hard to root out. Second, the rise of so-called illegal aliens in Western countries is often tied to bondage. Syndicates recruit migrants in order to exploit their labour. Afraid of the police and immigration authorities, illegal aliens cooperate with recruiters, making it difficult to arrest and punish the criminals. Third, within many African countries, young chil-

---

42 Suzanne Miers, *Slavery in the Twentieth Century: The Evolution of a Global Economy* (New York: AltaMira Press, 2003), 445–56.

43 Kevin Bales and Peter T. Robbins, 'No One Shall Be Held in Slavery or Servitude: A Critical Analysis of International Slavery Agreements and Concepts of Slavery', *Human Rights Review*, 2/2 (January–March 2001), 18–45.

dren, instead of going to schools, can be found hawking goods or working as domestics in poor conditions and in exploitative situations. 'UNICEF estimates that human trafficking is more lucrative than any other trade in West Africa except guns and drugs,' declared Allan Little, a BBC correspondent in Nigeria who reported in 2004 the alarming trend in child trafficking in Nigeria. He added that,

> The streets of Nigeria are teeming with trafficked children. Of the hundreds of thousands of street kids living rough in Nigeria's oil rich cities, perhaps 40 percent have been bought and sold at some time. The girls are most frequently sold into domestic service, or prostitution, the boys into labour on plantations, or to hawk fruit and vegetables for 12 hours a day in an open-air market. Some work as washers of feet.[44]

Although we are not sure that Little's usage of 'bought and sold' is correct, what is more common is the parents collecting the wages on behalf of their children. A way of socialising children to adulthood in the past has now become an avenue to make small amounts of money for parents to survive. In Madagascar, child traffic rings have emerged to steal new babies, selling them abroad for adoption. A few parents with many children have been accused of dumping newer ones on street corners because they have no resources to take care of them. In addition, the tradition of pawning continues in various ways. Poor people use themselves or children as collateral for loans, using their labour to pay off debts. The relationship between money lenders and pawns is unequal, leading to gross abuses. And finally, cheap or poorly remunerated labour is a common feature in many parts of Africa.

Reparations and the Politics of Power

One of the main issues in recent years has been that of reparations, in some ways reviving some of the ideas of the pan-Africanist ideology shaped by W. E. B. Du Bois. Since the nineteenth century, slavery and the diaspora have combined to create a black transnationalist ideology. For the greater part of the twentieth century, transnationalism was expressed in pan-Africanism, a political movement that advocated the end of colonialism in Africa and the political and economic empowerment of all blacks irrespective of where they lived. Black transnationalism has enabled Africa to reassert its glory as the homeland, for blacks in various parts of the world to fashion their identity from African roots and the legacies of slav-

44 This was broadcast on Saturday, 17 April 2004 at 11:30 BST on BBC Radio 4 and reported on http://news.bbc.co.uk/2/hi/programmes/from_our_own_correspondent /36322 03.stm.

ery, and to engage multiple ways of survival in various places. The consciousness of Africa fuels the vigorous search for creative means to move forward and solidify a non-Western way of living. Ideas such as those of Negritude represent ways of seeking new paths in a modern world. Pan-Africanism's connection to socialism was identifying a non-capitalist route to development, if capitalism was regarded as the source of slavery and colonialism.

The successors of slaves now demand compensation on various grounds. Some countries are being called upon to start with an apology. In making the case, activists are exposing the ruthlessness and brutality of slavery. No one can deny the violence associated with slavery, the loss of relations and friends, the horrors of the Middle Passage and the exploitation in the plantations. Even on the ground of suffering alone, an apology is justified. But apology is very much tied to domestic politics. Where racism persists, as in the United States, an apology is difficult for politicians looking for votes.

The aggressive demand for reparations is linked with black radicalism, most especially in the United States. African American scholars and politicians of the radical-nationalist persuasion have called on their members to calculate the debt – that is, the principal and accrued interest – and negotiate their collection from Western countries. Treating the slave trade as a case of war, robbery and genocide against blacks, the radical-nationalists point to cases of compensation to Jews, American Indians and Japanese for offences committed against them in the past.[45] The various costs that advocates have demanded, calculated by different people using different criteria, are staggering. In the late 1980s, Africans joined in the demands for reparations. A host of organisations emerged, and the Organization of African Unity (later known as the African Union) accepted the idea. Not only would African Americans receive compensations, Africans, too, would receive a share. The late Chief M. K. O. Abiola, a prominent Nigerian businessman and politician, adopted the cause of reparations and donated time and money to it. Reparations can never do full justice to the victims, Abiola notes, but it is a principle that 'wrongs must be righted, injuries compensated'.[46] His arguments are similar to those expressed in the United States: Africa deserves to be compensated for the brutality and losses associated with the slave trade, colonialism, neocolonialism and apartheid. To Abiola, Africa suffered for five hundred years and continues to suffer in recent time because of 'apartheid, debt burden and unequal exchange'.[47] As with African

45 Clarence J. Munford, *Race and Reparations: A Black Perspective for the 21st Century* (Trenton, NJ: Africa World Press, 1996), 393–439.

46 Muyiwa Philips (ed.), *Reparations: A Collection of Speeches by M. K. O. Abiola* (Lome, Togo: Linguist Service, 1992), 233.

47 Ibid., 234.

American advocates, Abiola sees reparations as crucial to Africa's development. 'To a productive Africa', he concludes, $250 billion in debt will be onerous but manageable. So, the solution being humbly proffered is that reparations should take the form of massive infusions of investments in infrastructures, manufactures, machine-tools, power, telecommunications, education, health, advanced agricultural technology and support for political democracy in the motherland.[48]

The demands for reparations have to confront the Afro-pessimist views of a continent whose tragedy can disappear only with recolonisation. It was when the movement for reparations was about to gather steam that some began to call for the return of colonialism. Recolonisation became the antithesis of reparations. While the view is not solely his, Paul Johnson, writing in the *New York Times Magazine*, doubted the capacity of many African countries to govern themselves and suggested recolonisation in order to overcome problems of corruption, civil wars, ethnic conflicts and famine.[49] In an imagined second round of colonisation, independence should be off the table until the world is assured that a particular country is able to govern itself. This primitive suggestion undercuts the demands to transfer wealth to a so-called tragic continent.

Conclusion

In drawing this chapter to a close, I would like to make a number of points that tie the subject of slavery to contemporary realities in Africa. The connection between the past and present is not a stretch, at least not in this case. The thread is clear to see: the use of cheap labour has made it possible to build and manage states, centralise power and accumulate wealth. Servitude is linked to power and accumulation. The slaves of old and the pawns of the present share a number of things in common: marginalisation, poverty, ownership by a master, social domination and the difficulty of redemption. The case of Sudan also shows that violence remains a defining characteristic of slavery even today.

First, the violence and criminality of the slave trade era bear close resemblance to contemporary politics and warlordism. Violence underpins the exercise of political power in Africa: in the slave trade era, it was to capture people, now it is to dominate and suppress the poor and the marginalised. Chiefs of old and warlords of the moment connect power with obtaining resources; whether they are after slaves or diamonds, the two groups behave similarly. The political classes that supplied slaves are the predecessors of contemporary leaders who act as collaborators and com-

48 Ibid., 237.
49 Paul Johnson, 'Colonialism's Back – and Not a Moment Too Soon', *New York Times Magazine,* 18 April 1993, 43–44.

pradors to bring together internal repressive forces and external profit seekers to prevent putting authentic development on the agenda of the state. Thus, as Africans complain about slavery and its legacies, we must also complain about the decadent and corrupt political leadership that promotes cultures of dependence and poverty. Those who want to help the oppressed and those in conditions resembling slavery may have to ignore the argument that the sovereignty of every nation is sacrosanct. Supranational institutions may acquire the power to deal with abusive political regimes.

Second, African governments, especially in Mauritania and Sudan, must stamp out slavery. Elsewhere, all ways in which slavery affects democratic institutions or the growth of liberal politics must be reformed. Many governments will deny a connection between modern-day politics and past histories of social stratification. Some connections are clear to see, as in the case of gender relations or ethnicity. Many are difficult to see and are disguised under so-called traditional practices, such as the male domination of women. Embedded in traditional practices may be relations of dependence such as slavery and pawnship, which affect the practice of politics. Traditional practices do affect what we define as political ideologies and do shape politics in ways that empower some established 'traditional aristocracies' and disempower families related to the poor of old. Sudan and Mauritania show that established social hierarchies and the history of slavery affect political contests at the local and national levels. Even where the meanings of slaves and slavery are contested, there are attempts by those seeking power to manipulate the definitions to gain power and exclude others.

Third, conditions that resemble slavery must be eliminated. Today, this includes practices such as child trafficking, child labour and child prostitution, trafficking in women, debt bondage and various coercive aspects of the sex industry. Such cases continue, sometimes on a staggering scale, as part of underground economies, leisure business and the production of goods for an international market. Moral appeals to stop servile conditions will not work, just as moral appeals did not end slavery and the slave trade. Inducement in terms of cash payments for the enslaved to become free has been tried, but the success, in both the short- and long-term, has been limited.[50] Those who use cheap labour regard attacks on their practices as attempts to weaken them, to destroy their privilege. Child labour, like slavery, may not be efficient, but it does work in terms of the ability of masters to maximally exploit labour, reduce maintenance costs and operate without sanctions. The child or the displaced prostitute, like the slave of old, may be rootless, which makes them subject to a variety of abuses. Those who treat children or pros-

---

50 On the practice of assisting slaves, prostitutes and child labourers to regain freedom, see Kwame Anthony Appiah and Martin Bunzl (eds.), *Buying Freedom: The Ethics and Economics of Slave Redemption* (Princeton, NJ: Princeton University Press, 2007).

titutes as free agents miss the connection between poverty and servility, and between servility and the ambiguous meaning of freedom in highly stratified and complex societies. Slaves were able to use force and resistance to negotiate power relations, even in some cases creating an independent power base and communities.[51] Children are unable to build alliances to free themselves, and prostitutes are not likely to be able to turn reproductive power to advantage. Governments and NGOs have to intervene to protect the weak, releasing the servile from their bondage. Access to credit and land will go a long way in preventing many people from surrendering their lives and futures to a greedy system.

Fourth, irrespective of the position one takes on reparations, I very much doubt that anyone can argue that the West owes no responsibility to Africa, if only to ensure that politics and economies develop in a sustainable manner. Involvement in the slave trade and the ruthless colonial exploitation are more than enough justification. This responsibility is not all about aid in the form of money. Even reducing the transfer of wealth from poor Africa to the developed West will go a long way in solving many problems. The strengthening of NGOs and various social movements will contribute to the expansion of democratic space, the training of leaders at various levels and the empowering of many in positive ways. Africa is an integral part of the world, and its problems and promises must be included in global politics and economy. The continent has contributed to the development of other continents, gaining and suffering in the process.

The negative legacies of slavery and colonialism will disappear if Africa marches toward a better future. This is possible if conditions of democracy, good governance, sound economic management and responsible political leadership are created in a sustainable manner.

Three examples demonstrate how African cultures are manifested in the African diaspora, including the survival of medicinal and healing practices, the rapid spread of Nollywood movies to other parts of the world, and the work of a new generation of diaspora artists living and working in the Western world. These three and many more topics illustrate how various aspects of African culture are spreading to other parts of the world, despite the legacy of slavery.

African Medicine

The example of Yoruba gods and goddesses demonstrates the importance of medicine. Healing practices, including ideas and the uses of plants, were part of what

---

51 Studies on resistance and their impact are extensive. Among others, see Rosalyn Howard, *Black Seminoles in the Bahamas* (Gainesville: University Press of Florida, 2002).

they brought with them, including divination and the incantations to make them work. Various studies have shown how Africans carried their cultural ideas to the Americas. In a recent book by James Sweet, he uses the case of Domingos Álvares, a prominent healer and diviner, to illustrate how many African ideas of healing survived and spread during the era of the Atlantic slave trade.[52] Álvares was originally from Benin in West Africa. Forced into slavery in 1730, he worked on a sugar plantation in Pernambuco, and was later exiled to Portugal as a prisoner. In his various locations until his death in 1750, Álvares converted his spiritual and healing power as a vodun priest into service to the needy, thus acquiring fame and prestige in the process. Curing illnesses and diseases, Álvares also made speeches and remarks that upset slave owners as well as attacking imperialism and the capitalist system. Although Sweet's study is located in the Lusophone world, it was not peculiar to this part of the world. As he shows, Álvares's knowledge and practices were acquired in Africa. In the Atlantic World, he had an audience, those who subscribed to his faith and world view. In the United States, many similar practices have been noted in different parts of Louisiana, South Carolina and Virginia. For example, reference has been made to Caesar's cure for poison published in the *South Carolina Gazette* of 9 May 1750 recorded by a wealthy slave owner, Richard Jordan, and his successors from about 1620 to 1687.[53] The remedy gained widespread fame, and his inventor, an African slave, was able to use his medical knowledge and healing power to attain freedom. We cannot know how many Álvares and Caesars existed in different parts of the African diaspora, bringing various ideas from Africa and introducing them to new lands, not just in medicine but also in all aspects of culture. The nameless had enabled the transfer of various aspects of African cultures to different parts of the world.[54] During the era of the transatlantic slave trade, migrations moved people and their knowledge, ideas, skills and mindsets. They were also able to reproduce their knowledge, using socialisation within families to transfer what they knew to their children.

As Linda M. Heywood and John K. Thornton show, slaves from Central Africa, as early as the first hundred years of the Atlantic slave trade, laid the basis of an

52 James H. Sweet, *Domingos Álvares, African Healing, and the Intellectual History of the Atlantic World* (Chapel Hill: University of North Carolina Press, 2011).

53 This can be found in the archives of the Virginia Historical Society, labelled as Jordan, 'Commonplace Book', Virginia Historical Society, Mss 5: 5J7664.

54 Among others, see Don C. Ohadike, *Sacred Drums of Liberation: Religions and Music of Resistance in Africa and the African Diaspora* (Trenton, NJ: Africa World Press, 2007); and James Sweet, *Recreating Africa: Culture, Kinship and Religion in the African-Portuguese World* (Chapel Hill: University of North Carolina Press, 2004).

African American identity, one that included aspects of religion, languages and material culture.[55] And as Marie Jenkins Schwartz also shows,[56] children born into slavery had opportunities, even in cruel plantation settings, to learn useful ideas from their parents, enabling cultural retention. Various aspects of the contributions to science, technology and medicine have been underexplored. Botanical and food ideas were developed and transmitted from one generation to another.[57] For instance, with respect to medicine, we see the creativity in adapting African herbs and knowledge to new situations not just at the time of Álvares and Caesar but even today.

Healing in Africa and its recreation in the African diaspora reveals several issues: the knowledge of plants and animals, the poetic incantations to manipulate symbolism to prevent and cure, divination and 'magic'. No disease escapes the imagination to find an answer to cure it. Where the original plant used in Africa could not be found, new ones were sought, as in the case of Brazil and Chesapeake plantations during slavery. Without the knowledge of science and pharmacology, there could be no medicine. Kay Moss, who examined some of the documents relating to the eighteenth and nineteenth centuries, points to the combination of herbs, incantations and witchcraft to cure many diseases.[58]

Whereas these are often wrongly presented as 'primitive', they demonstrate incredible knowledge, great insights into people and the forces that shape their lives, and prescriptions for many health problems as complicated as smallpox and barrenness to simpler ones such as cough. The authority and relevance of these healers have been written about in different parts of the African diaspora to suggest that Caesar of Virginia was not alone or unique.[59]

As to medicine itself, studies have confirmed the impressive knowledge contained in what indigenous ideas have created. In Brazil, where African medicine

55 Linda M. Heywood and John K. Thornton, *Central Africans, Atlantic Creoles, and the Foundation of the Americas, 1585–1660* (Cambridge: Cambridge University Press, 2007).

56 Marie Jenkins Schwartz, *Born in Bondage: Growing Up Enslaved in the Antebellum South* (Cambridge, MA: Harvard University Press, 2000).

57 Judith A. Carney and Richard Nicholas Rosomoff, *In the Shadow of Slavery: Africa's Botanical Legacy in the Atlantic World* (Berkeley: University of California Press, 2009).

58 Kay K. Moss, *Southern Folk Medicine, 1750–1820* (Columbia: University of South Carolina Press, 1999).

59 See, among others, Richard A. Roeks, *Sacred Leaves of Candomble: African Magic, Medicine and Religion in Brazil* (Austin: University of Texas Press, 1997); and Karol K. Weaver, *Medical Revolutionaries: The Enslaved Healers of Eighteenth Century Saint Domingue* (Urbana: University of Illinois, 2006).

and religions are more intermeshed, research has shown that the Yoruba have a profound knowledge of the uses of plants and animals to cure various ailments, minor
and major. Pierre Fatumbi Verger has done the most comprehensive study ever conducted on the use of plants among the Yoruba.[60] A scholar and a practitioner, his
long book of well over 700 pages describes over 2,000 remedies and practices,
3,529 Yoruba plant names, and the Yoruba names and equivalences for 1,086 scientific names. A careful observer, Verger provides dense elaboration in five forms:
(a) the parts of plants that are used for medication, that is, the leaves, barks and
roots; (b) how the leaves are prepared, that is, boiled, burnt into ashes, pounded;
(c) how they are used internally and externally; (d) the Ifa divination sign that makes
the remedy work; and (e) the incantations that give power to the plants.[61] Verger collected his recipes from established practitioners who combined the knowledge of
herbs with divination 'based on 256 signs called odu under which traditional medical practices are classified. These 256 odulfa are double signs derived from sixteen
single ones and paired, either with themselves to form sixteen primary odu, or with
one of the fifteen other single signs to form the 24 secondary ones'.[62] Spoken words
expressed in the odu acquire power (ase), which makes the plant work. The knowledge of plants and signs become the 'creative force' that can heal and cure. He
demonstrates the plants used in various remedies, linking specific ones to medicine, magical formulae and pharmacology. 'The medicinal virtues and values of a
plant', concludes Verger, 'are not easy to find out, because rarely is a plant used on
its own. In general, formulae are made up of three to six different plants.'[63] He continues: 'A plant may be compared to a letter of a word. On its own it is insignificant, but when joined with other letters it contributes to the meaning of the word.'[64]
His recipes, numbering thousands, are classified into six categories:

1. 237 formulae for medicinal remedies (oogun) which tally, to some extent, with
   similar ideas in Western medicine;
2. 32 formulae for remedies relating to pregnancy and birth (ibimo);
3. 33 formulae for 'magical works' relating to the worshipping of Yoruba deities
   (orisa);

60 Pierre Fatumbi Verger, *Ewe: The Use of Plants in Yoruba Society* (São Paulo, Brazil:
Companhia das Letras, 1995).
61 The incantations, known as ofo, have been the subject of an earlier book by the same
author, Awon Ewe Osanyin, *Yoruba Medicinal Leaves* (Ile-Ife: Institute of African Studies,
University of Ife, 1967).
62 Ewe, 13.
63 Ewe, 16.
64 Ibid.

4. 91 formulae for 'beneficent works' (awure);
5. 32 formulae for 'evil works' (abilu);
6. 41 formulae for 'protective works' (idaabobo).[65]

Verger points to the difficulty of demarcating the difference between magic and scientific knowledge: 'This stems from the importance ... given to the notion of an incantation (ofo) spoken during the preparation or application of the medicinal formulae (oogun).'[66] As he further explains:

> If Western medicine prioritises a plant's scientific name and its pharmacological characteristics, then traditional societies prioritise the knowledge of ofo. Countless remedies from around the world were originally extracted from plants and later replaced by chemically reconstituted drugs, which had the same curative effects on the human body. But in traditional societies, it is the knowledge of the ofo (incantation), which is essential, as it contains the 'power-to-alter' the formula's pharmacological effect.[67]

From the ofo, the medicinal effect of the plant is revealed. When an ofo changes, the action of the plant may also change. Verger considers ofo as definitions: 'The incantations are often based on a particular reasoning being used for a particular situation or remedy. They also serve as evidence of the continuity in the traditional archive of data transmitted from one generation of babalawo to the next.'[68]

Examining the thousands of entries in Ewe and their ofo, it is clear that there is an established knowledge of pathology. Diseases are named in various ways. Some are merely descriptive, as in diarrhoea (igbegburu) and dysentery (igbeorin), with the use of medicine that requires no ofo, rituals or reference to any supernatural forces.

No society can have this rich, extensive and expansive knowledge without an understanding of chemistry, biology and related sciences. The knowledge cannot be accumulated and transmitted without an education and socialisation process in place. The consumption of the products of the knowledge requires that social and political institutions be in place to mediate interpersonal and intergroup relations. And without the means for a class to extract resources, it would be much harder for politics to function and to sustain social stratification where it does exist.

---

65 Ibid.
66 Ewe, 17.
67 Ibid.
68 Ewe, 19.

Different forms of creativity and knowledge reveal the nature of society with regard to power and control, relationships among individuals, work and leisure. References made to magic and poison may also allude to fear by those in power that those under them can kill them. Connections have been made between magic and resistance,[69] and between slave medicine and social control.[70] If Álvares and many diviners had power in Africa (and they still do), we can imagine that Africans with the knowledge to heal and create new meanings from new plants and other resources would also have power. If Caesar had the power to invent an antidote for poison, we should also assume that he had the power to make poison to kill. Thus, in combining both, we see how his status among his peers and slave owners would be enhanced. The ability to create music and dance, and to acquire spiritual relevance is to convert low status into social status and political agency within the community. Caesar, a contemporary of Álvares, through his discovery, the testimonies that it worked, and his consent to reveal the elements, was able to obtain his freedom in 1750 and given a moderate sum of money for the rest of his life. He was able to convert knowledge into freedom. That whites sought the means to neutralise poison was not new by 1750 – in earlier years, seeking bezoar (organic materials found in ungulate animals) and 'Goa Stones' (substances of herbal medicine) to neutralise poison was not uncommon, drawing not a few to Africa and parts of the Indian Ocean region.

New forms of knowledge were created on many aspects of human endeavour. Knowledge circulated over a wider region, and some was carried from Africa to Europe and the Americas, as in the examples of healing and plant species, the knowledge of divination and herbs, and food cultivation as in the example of rice.[71] Spirituality and religions have received prominent treatment in books on Candomble and Santeria by scholars and practitioners.[72] Healing and praying were connected in religious beliefs. What they created and repackaged have served as the basis of new identities.[73] These identities and their meanings are different from those of other races with regard to aspects of living, interactions with others and

---

69 Roeks, *Sacred Leaves*.

70 Gwendolyn Midlo Hall, *Social Control in Slave Plantation Societies: A Comparison of St. Domingue and Cuba* (Baltimore: Johns Hopkins University Press, 1971).

71 Judith Carney, *Black Rice: The African Origins of Rice Cultivation in the Americas* (Cambridge, MA: Harvard University Press, 2001).

72 See, for instance, Sweet, *Recreating Africa*.

73 See, among others, Michael A. Gomez, *Exchanging Our Country Marks: The Transformation of African Identities in the Colonial and Antebellum South* (Chapel Hill: University of North Carolina Press, 1998); John Thornton, *Africa and Africans in the Atlantic World* (Cambridge, 1998); James Sidbury, *Becoming African in America: Race and Nation in the Early Black Atlantic* (Oxford: Oxford University Press, 2007); and Patrick Manning, *The African Diaspora: A History Through Culture* (New York: Columbia University Press, 2009).

even death. Álvares and Caesar would be confused if their remedies were dismissed as irrelevant or not medicine, or if the knowledge to cure was separated from the one to kill. And as Sweet points out, preaching and healing were also political statements that had the capacity to rupture society.

While Álvares and Caesar were two remarkable men, they probably were not alone in the knowledge they possessed, and their skills and ideas were grounded in communal traditions that originated in Africa. Today, such traditions are being revived and extended in different parts of the Western world where a new generation of African priests, healers and diviners practises non-Western medicine in the context of African religious traditions.

Nollywood

The second example to illustrate the spread of African culture is a Nollywood production, *Virginia Is for Lovers*.[74] A story of love and the complications of marriage, the film portrays the life of contemporary Africans in an American setting. The description on the DVD's cover gives a summary without revealing the answers:

> The issue of a man and a woman as best friends has always been on our minds. In other words, can a man and a woman be close friends without being in love? Or is there any such thing as a platonic relationship? Now before you say anything please enjoy this romantic drama between Michael Collins (Desmond Elliot) and Stacey Thompson (Ginnefine Kanu) who are both raised in Virginia (United States), have been friends since childhood and had always helped each other. Now eventually how does Michael's wife Chobis (Hassanatu Kanu) and her best friend Kim (Veeda Darko) feel about this and how it relates to their marriage, friends and family relations?

Africa is dragged into it, creating a hybridity of ideas on multiple issues: romance, marital responsibility, imagined kinship, the impact of money, etc. *Virginia Is for Lovers* is targeted to a younger generation of Africans living in the West. It is part of a growing body of work in which the signifier in black profane discourse is being rejected and replaced with something positive. A way of life, as captured in *Virginia Is for Lovers*, attempts to use a language where the range of meanings keeps to standard English usage. The relationship between the signifier and the signified is less complex, and the text lacks rhetorical strength. If signifying in black speech is to reveal the tension in society and racial and class divisions, serious and mundane issues in *Virginia Is for Lovers* are presented in the language of a rising middle class.

74 DVD, James Oddoye's Production, Black Star Entertainment, 2009.

Africa and the experience of immigrants are not presented as esoteric, but as real, not intellectualised as a past heritage but as a living culture. Western values are not being rejected but appropriated and adapted, thereby rejecting the binary opposition between the values to be encouraged in being black and those to be repudiated by imitating whiteness. Tensions are mediated by popular culture and the market rather than by race and class. The images of the 1970s are gone: there is no revolutionary talk of the past, nor the dirty characterisation of blacks as wig-wearing whores and konk-haired hipsters.

Virginia Is for Lovers reveals how creativity can capture a moment, and allows us to compare and contrast peoples of different generations as well as the different historical eras that shape their attitudes. The black middle class represented in the creative work of the Harlem Renaissance is not the one in *Virginia Is for Lovers*. The rage of the class and racial wars of the past involved statements about Africa, the Atlantic slave trade, slavery, the trauma of emancipation and the sufferings during the civil rights movement. If in the past many had to reject their origins because of the trauma of slavery, many of the present are affirming their origins. The suffering and pains of the past required confrontation with the heritage of slavery, which included accepting or rejecting Africa. In *Virginia Is for Lovers*, assimilation is celebrated, and the Western conception of romance is accepted. The trope of success and failure can become repetitive, as in the annual repetition of festivals and rituals, but such repetition should not be confused with the lack of theoretical sophistication or creative imagination. A film or work can be mediocre, but the repetition in its theme is not responsible for the mediocrity. On the issue of repetition, I am reminded of the statement by James A. Snead:

> In any case, let us remember that, whenever we encounter repetition in cultural forms, we are indeed not viewing 'the same thing' but its transformation, not just a formal ploy but also often the willed grafting onto culture of an essentially philosophical insight about the shape of time and history.[75] *Virginia Is for Lovers* weaves the trope of friendship and love into a repetitive cultural form, using the signifier of affection and marriage to narrate the experience of contemporary migrants.

Aderonke Adesanya's Time Traveller

My third and final illustration is the paintings and poetry of Dr Aderonke Adesanya of James Madison University, Harrisonburg, Virginia. If Caesar illustrates

---

75 James A. Snead, 'Repetition as a Figure of Black Culture', in Henry Louis Gates Jr. (ed.), *Black Literature and Literary Theory* (London: Methuen Press, 1990), 59–60.

the transfer of culture and its repackaging from Africa to the Americas, and *Virginia Is for Lovers* presents the love lives of transnationalists, the third illustration takes us back to Africa to relate art and poetry to culture, indigenous and modern. In her most recent painting, *Time Traveller*, Adesanya takes motifs from different African culture groups, notably the Yoruba and Fulani, to create a complex work on mythologies that link the world of the living with the spiritual, and the environment with the people. In this complicated work, she wades into the murky, controversial world of terrestrial travels and spatial fractures, with thoughtful lines imposed above unreadable minds and fragmented bodies. The very heart of the painting is rather intensive, highlighting the pivotal minds of a hidden he and a disguised she. The he manifests a double identity, a sort of a guru with an undefined race but invoking the apparati of the Yoruba cult of secrecy (ogboni). The staff made of iron is both a figuration and signification of power – how a metal whose production is ritualised becomes further embedded in a religious system where everything is explained in spiritual terms. Denis Williams is right when he made the statement that 'Power inherent in the unfamiliar and intractable metal is to be controlled not so much by means of analyzing the process of its operation as by propitiation and prayer addressed to the orisa, or god, who has been able to tame such power.'[76] Ogun, god of metal from needle to airplane, is the work of science and technology. But in Adesanya's work, Ogun is the spirit, the god to be invoked. Artefact and mental fact become blended to reveal a philosophy.

The woman in *Traveller Time* is reflective, with ideas refracted from an empty space, drawing energy from the spiritualised man behind her, with an arrogant gaze into what appears to be a predictable future. In the woman emerges an elephant, a metaphor on strength, but one in which the elephant can metamorphose into a woman, and the woman, when energy is needed, sheds her human flesh to become the strongest persona in the jungle. Her strength is not destructive, like that of the lions and tigers eating their neighbours, but a gentle force walking quietly and merely grazing. The elephant tusk symbolises energy, while a decorated calabash floats in air. The imagery, presented in a disguised form, may have tapped into Adesanya's unconscious, represented in poems on women where she deploys a similar combination of Yoruba and English words to portray a strong woman who is ready to spring into action on rather short notice: Formidable foe.

---

76 Quoted in Biodun Jeyifo, 'Wole Soyinka and the Tropes of Disalienation', in Wole Soyinka, *Art, Dialogue and Outrage: Essays on Literature and Culture* (Ibadan: New Horn Press, 1988), xxii.

Wrapped in Riotous Tornado

Both man and woman appear to defy gravity and her levitating to the sky (before the womb in which they are imprisoned breaks into a world under), where the mutable boundaries above seem cautioned by the subtle faded envelope opened on two wide sides. They are, forever unclosed, becoming an ideological metaphor of the complex interplay of those overwhelming forces that shape movements. Adesanya endorses ritualistic and essentialist beliefs, thus bringing the value of African indigenous spirituality and theology back to the forefront at a time of rising Christian fundamentalism. Set in a modernist context, the man and his ritual objects are not primitive, but forward-looking, actually appearing to be intellectualising a body of ideas. We are left guessing about the outcome of his introspection.

In previous paintings,[77] Adesanya has depicted women in various activities in work and leisure, while her cartoons, running into three thousand over a ten-year period, have made many social and political statements on gender and politics. The cartoons stratify society and culture into high and low, but also create a parody of urbanised women.

Her poems[78] are critical of patriarchy and politicians, affirming the statement that scholarship for black women is an opportunity to make political statements about society and male domination. While drawing on the indigenous idioms, she is aware of the larger currents in the West, and seems to combine them, as in a painting of women on horseback playing polo. Amilcar Cabral, in *Unity and Struggle*, written at a time of both anger and hope – anger directed at the Portuguese brutalities and exploitation of his people, and hope at the possibility of a new future following decolonisation – admonished Africans that part of the strategy for obtaining freedom is also to fully understand the positive contributions that the oppressor's culture has to offer, and that liberation is an 'act of culture'.[79] Women on horseback playing polo is, no doubt, an 'act of culture' in a Cabralian notion of liberation.

The combination of culture and ideology represented in Adesanya's art and poems is the signification of contemporary reality in Africa and the emerging nature of change. I think that she is searching for effective tropes of disalienation in aesthetics to transform gender relations and make national politics more representative, responsible and responsive. Her predecessors, in framing modernity, as

77 See http://www.flickr.com/photos/toyinfalola/sets/72157611525063119/
78 Toyin Falola and Aderonke Adesola Adesanya, *Etches on Fresh Waters* (Durham, NC: Carolina Academic Press, 2008).
79 Amilcar Cabral, *Unity and Struggle*, ed. Michael Wolfers (London: Heinemann, 1980).

in the work of Ben Enwonwu,[80] dealt with the tropes of modernity and alienation. If Wole Soyinka settles for Ogun, the Yoruba god of iron, using him to frame an African-tragic/tragic-Africa discourse,[81] Adesanya seems to have settled for Oya, the river goddess, and in her cartoons of well-dressed sophisticated urban women to frame issues of modernity. The cartoons may appear postmodernist to the neo-traditionalists, and her assumption of the possibility of cultural autonomy for women may be misplaced in view of the media being deployed to communicate her message and of the Western impact on society.

However, Adesanya is not alone in the problem of seeking cultural autonomy as a solution to some aspects of Africa's problems, in her case that of reconciling women's place to postcolonial situations. Great thinkers such as Frantz Fanon, Amilcar Cabral and Agostinho Neto have had to address similar problems in the larger context of development and the minimisation of dependence on the West. In an extraordinary essay, Professor Olaoba F. Arasanyin, also of James Madison University, has related the difficulty of creating a language policy in Africa to the way in which colonisation left Africa with 'an alien political character' which makes it vulnerable to powerful pressures outside of its boundaries.[82] Wole Soyinka is dismissive of the presentation of African reality in narrower forms, as in his attack on Negritude. Cultural autonomy for Africans may be elusive in the context of globalisation, just as cultural autonomy is hard for women in the con-text of patriarchy, indigenous traditions, Christianity and Islam.

Furthermore, Adesanya's work seems to be advocating an agenda of liberal hu-manism. I use 'liberal humanism' intentionally and critically to point to the inad-equacies of 'liberalism' to confront violence and inequality. The recall of past Yoruba traditions, especially the representation and invocation of Orisa, is a state-ment on the continuity of the past. But as we combine her paintings, poetry and cartoons, we see some acts of subversion and transgression. Her 'truth' is not anti-colonial, but anti-postcolonial, although I must point out that 'postcolonial' does not have a straightforward meaning in the body of her work. If the images can be read as 'texts', the mythological patterns of figuration stress the role of moderni-sation on women, but not in terms of any complete break with the past.

80 Sylvester Ogbechie, *Ben Enwonwu: The Making of an African Modernist* (Rochester, NY: University of Rochester Press, 2008).

81 Wole Soyinka, *Myth, Literature and the African World* (Cambridge: Cambridge University Press, 1976).

82 Olaoba F. Arasanyin, 'Africa and Language-Policy Inertia: The Historical Genesis', in Toyin Falola and Salah M. Hassan (eds.), *Power and Nationalism in Modern Africa: Essays in Honor of Don Ohadike* (Durham, NC: Carolina Academic Press, 2008), 281–308.

The open-endedness that her creativity suggests invokes a Bakhtinian concept of indeterminacy of dealing with an 'evolving contemporary reality' where art operates in a 'zone of contact with the present in all its open-endedness, a zone that was first appropriated by the novel'.[83] Her paintings are fresh, like her poetry, and the trajectory of what they represent is clear in terms of cultural and gendered significations of the postcolonial moment.

Creativity, Politics and Empowerment

I now want to combine and collapse the three entry points to 'shift the map of innovation and reason', the elegant phrase coined by Dr. Besi Brillian Muhonja of James Madison University, to invite us to reflect on the 'Africana world'. I will do so in a holistic framework set in the context of changing historical eras. The first entry allows us to talk about Africanisation and re-Africanisation, while the second and third encourage us to talk about transnationalisation and globalisation.

In the African diaspora, identity emerged in the context of slavery, race and migration. The voices speaking for members of the diaspora of slavery, represented in the emergence of African American identity in the United States and related ones in Europe, Asia, Latin America and the Caribbean, have had to link creativity with this context. Derek Walcott makes the connections in his well-cited essay 'The Muse of History':

In the New World servitude to the muse of history has produced a literature of recrimination and despair, a literature of revenge written by the descendants of slaves or a literature of remorse written by the descendants of masters. Because this literature serves historical truth, it yellows into polemic and evaporates into pathos. The truly tough aesthetics of the New World neither explains nor forgives this history. It refuses to recognise it as a creative and culpable force. This shame and awe of history possesses poets of the Third World, who think of language as enslavement and who in a rage of identity, respect only incoherence and nostalgia.[84]

Walcott attempts a creative exorcism in *Dream on Monkey Mountain and Other Plays*,[85] where a lead character, Makak, who lives as a 'wild beast in hiding', gains his freedom after wandering through the landscape of oppression and subjugation and ending in Africa, where he makes a symbolic execution of all those who had subjugated and oppressed his people.

83   M. M. Bakhtin, *The Dialogic Imagination: Four Essays*, ed. and trans. Michael Holquist and Caryl Emerson (Austin: University of Texas Press, 1986), 7.

84   Derek Walcott, 'The Muse of History: An Essay', in Orde Coombs (ed.), *Is Massa Day Dead?* (New York: Anchor and Doubleday, 1974).

85   *Dream on Monkey Mountain and Other Plays* (London: Jonathan Cape, 1972).

In seeking the means for liberation and emancipation, cultural and political ideas and actions found expression in black empowerment, black power and black capitalism. Whether in Brazil or the United States, Africa – a place, a home, a race, an ethnicity, a civilisation, etc. – becomes central to the formation of ideas and activism, as various people become like Makak. Africa is used to capture the imagination of people of African descent. Many writers see Africa as a source of black dignity and pride. When Africa was under colonial rule, the desire to free Africa merged into a global pan-Africanist network to free the continent, to end apartheid, and to turn the continent into the leading place of pride for all blacks irrespective of where they lived. The pan-Africanist agenda of creating the United States of Africa was rooted in the assumptions of shared cultural heritage and the common history of domination and exploitation by Europe.

A 'manifesto' had emerged by the turn of the twentieth century: all blacks should unite to end oppression, exploitation and discrimination; they must free themselves of foreign control; they must be economically and politically strong. If blacks outside of Africa understood Africans and vice versa, progress, it was believed, would surely come. African Americans have always been urged to be interested in African affairs, and to derive their pride from there, while Africa is advised to reach out to them to acquire skills. To cement the collaboration and the interactions, projects of cultural celebration were to be embarked upon. Marcus Garvey, one of the best-known activists in the articulation of this comprehensive networking, put the unity of black people as entering 'into common partnership to build up Africa in the interest of our race'.[86] W. E. B. DuBois refined many of these ideas, elevating them to higher political heights. Of course, not everyone accepted that the connections were possible, as some, like James Baldwin, point to different historical struggles that have to be resolved differently:

> The African has not yet endured the utter alienation of himself from his people and his past. His mother did not sing, 'Sometimes I Feel Like a Motherless Child', and he has not all his life ached for acceptance in a culture which pronounced straight hair and white skin the only acceptable beauty. They face each other, the Negro and the African, over a gulf of three hundred years – an alienation too vast to be conquered in an evening's goodwill.[87]

Being caught in different struggles does not mean that the journeys are too far apart in their sources, paths and destinations. Indeed, many embarked on the 'trip'

---

86 Marcus Garvey, 'Africa for the Africans', in Jacob Drachler (ed.), *Black Homeland/Black Diaspora* (New York: National University Publication, 1975).

87 James Baldwin, 'Colloquium in Paris', in Jacob Drachler (ed.), *Black Homeland/Black Diaspora* (New York: National University Publication, 1975), 105.

to Africa, even as the cynical and critical Baldwin presaged that they would not find the answers they wanted but instead more questions. One reason to start from Africa is to understand the origin and context of many ideas, the milieus that produced them and the mindset that shapes the imagination. We can understand how ideas travel, and how these ideas are reformulated in other places. If the ideas of survival and health were linked to a spiritual universe, it is not hard to understand why the worship of gods and goddesses would spread in other parts of the world, why Christianity would be redefined to include ideas drawn from African religions, why the use of herbs and incantations to solve health problems would not just go away and why Nollywood cannot thrive if it eliminates beliefs in juju and witchcraft.

Not all new inventions and ideas are owing to Africa, as borrowing and adaptations also occur to modify the template, to apply new technologies and concepts to older ideas, to substitute new materials for older ones that are not available or adaptable. From the very moment of encounter with the West, even in plantation economies, innovations have always been part of the negotiation of interaction and survival. In creating new products and ideas, the enslaved mixed Amerindian, European and African traditions. In colonial Africa, Africans were clever agents in translating received ideas to meet local needs. Several works have been published on the creation of an African American identity and the contributions of the enslaved to Western cultures, all providing data about the human agency to adapt to new environments and conditions.[88] Today, such innovations continue in all aspects, from cuisine to attire, from the use of language and communication devices to the use of technologies to create new cultural meanings.

The possession of knowledge opens up opportunities to use capital for social and political purposes. For instance, healers and priests have always been respected. During slavery, slaves and slave masters could be afraid of conjurors whom they believed had the poison to kill, and in awe of those with the love portion to win women's affection, and the remedies to cure. Where knowledge was a threat or became connected with resistance,[89] there were efforts to ban practitioners, conjurors, use of certain lyrics in music, herbs and poison. Those with literary skills

---

88 Among others, see Sidney W. Mintz and Richard Price, *Birth of African-American Culture: An Anthropological Perspective* (Boston: Beacon, 1992); Melville J. Herskovits, *The New World Negro: Selected Papers in Afro-American Studies* (Bloomington: Indiana University Press, 1966); and Joseph E. Holloway (ed.), *Africanisms in American Culture* (Bloomington: Indiana University Press, 1990; 2nd edn., 2005).

89 See, for instance, such episodes in Michael Mullin, *Africa in America: Slave Acculturation and Resistance in the American South* (Urbana: University of Illinois Press, 1992); Joao J. Reis, *Slave Rebellion in Brazil: The Muslim Uprising of 1835 in Bahia* (Baltimore: Johns Hopkins University Press, 1993).

could acquire public acclaim. If associated with radical ideas, they could be perceived as a threat, as in the case of socialist-oriented activists of the twentieth century who were labelled 'communists' in order to impose sanctions on them. Celebrations, notably of funeral ceremonies, even turned death into victory,[90] bluntly revealing to hegemonic power that the end would come to all and glories await the weak and marginalised in the world that counts the most – the next!

The second and third examples reveal the new currents in contemporary global forces. Millions of contemporary African migrants are agents and couriers of cultures. As constant travellers, they have enormous capital to innovate, to tap into the social power embedded in their difference. Many can be found at the crossroads of change and innovation; millions generate hybrid knowledge in all aspects of life; their skills are varied, multilateral, drawing from many sources and ideas. Contrary to what many people think, Africans have created spaces of cultural innovation and expression all over the world, represented in scholarship, politics, inventions, music, dance, food, honour and much more. Moving back and forth from Africa represents social power in the age of globalisation where voices and beliefs can be carried. By demonstrating African cultures outside of Africa, migrants become powerful agents of communication. By recreating and producing new ideas that blend African inheritances with others, they become innovators. By taking ideas back to Africa, they are brokers, agents of globalisation with the skills to announce and communicate new things, some borrowed. Without the large immigrant population, there would have been no *Virginia Is for Lovers*, and without the global academic marketplace, Dr Adesanya would not be at James Madison University.

We are now at a moment where the frontiers of knowledge must include the understanding of these transnational beings both in Africa and the West. Indeed, our teaching must begin to respond to what they represent. Powerful forces have submerged the African states into the bigger space of the marketplace, of invisible forces, of virtual space, of imagined spaces and of denationalised geographies in relation to identity, authority and power. A new set of connections is derived from alternative spaces and global networks. The ties between Lagos and London are much stronger than people think. Both are global cities with many functions and institutions that are regional, national and international. The managers of the leading sectors of the economy think in terms of transborder networks; the communication infrastructures they deploy have global outreach. So, also are the ties between villages and the cities part of a regional network that connects to many other countries. The cell phone is a point of contact between all parts of the world.

90 Vincent Brown, *The Reapers Garden: Death and Power in the World of Atlantic Slavery* (Cambridge, MA: Harvard University Press, 2008).

The cell phone, the Internet and the spread of technology have created a more connected world where economic and social ties are very dense. The reality is that the world has become intimately connected. The European Union is a case of creating 'borderless' countries where citizens travel from one country to another without a visa and where they can actually work. The Euro is a currency that almost 500 million people can use for transactions.

The intensity of migrations within and across borders (driven by a host of factors such as war, political instability, famine, persecution, social disintegration, poverty, etc.[91]) have created millions of people whose nationality cannot be understood within the framework of just one nation-state. Diasporas of migrants are now many, intentional and voluntary, unlike those of the transatlantic and trans-Saharan. These migrants reflect the opportunities in globalising cities and strong economies, while also showing the consequences of troubling politics and economies in their original homelands.

Movements, mixed marriages and constant travel have produced transnationalists who live in multiple countries.[92] As the concept of 'home' becomes harder to define or shifts, they can be detribalised or denationalised. They can be citizens of everywhere and nowhere. Or they can think in terms of 'double consciousness',[93] a sense of being in one place and thinking of another place as the homeland. Consciousness can be triple or more, suggesting a notion of both mental and physical deterritorialisation. Within a state, people also move, changing jobs and locations, selling their houses and changing their addresses on a permanent basis. The distance between the place of birth and the place of death can be separated by thousands of miles.

The understanding of contemporary innovations and cultures can no longer be limited to the peculiar identities of the local. Popular culture spreads so fast and widely.[94] The superstars of music and sports are global icons. The cultural exchange of books, music, films and others have globalised cultures so that we can even point to elements of 'global culture' in consumption and leisure.

We are confronted with a set of opportunities and challenges. The marketplace is ever extending, circulating goods from Dubai to Kaduna, from Lagos to New

91   Aaron Segal, *An Atlas of International Migration* (London: Hans Zell, 1993).

92   Toyin Falola and Aribidesi Usman (eds.), *Movements, Borders, and Identities in Africa* (Rochester, NY: University of Rochester Press, 2009).

93   This term is borrowed from W. E. B. Du Bois, although I have given it a different usage. He describes it as 'the sense of always looking at one's self through the eyes of others'. *The Souls of Black Folk* (Greenwich: Fawcett, 1961), 16–18.

94   Toyin Falola and A. Agwuele (eds.), *Africans and the Politics of Popular Culture* (Rochester, NY: University of Rochester Press, 2009).

York. As legitimate commodities spread, so too do illegal ones such as forged currencies and drugs. The use of cocaine, marijuana and other drugs is global, connecting the desire of youth in Chicago with those of Dar es Salam. Sexual practices are glamorised and globalised. Inequalities in economies and access to opportunities and consumption are among the reasons that instigate the desire to migrate. The pace keeps accelerating. There is competition to seek places; there is competition to seek markets. A new economic elite is benefiting from free borders. A generation of transnationalist imperialists has emerged, using the markets available to them anywhere in the world to make money. The new elite sees state barriers as hindrances to market expansion.

This new elite is also developing the culture that reinforces deterritorialisation. They tend to study similar economic principles in elite schools, consume similar food items in similar restaurants, watch similar movies and engage in similar vacation culture. Common culture creates common politics in a virtual space that keeps expanding.[95] Aspiring people try to imitate the culture of the new elite.[96]

Globalisation brings its gains and pains. There are such disasters as the spread of AIDS and environmental degradation with incalculable consequences for societies and cultures. Changing world politics impacts local and global cultures. The cultural might of Islam is treated with fear in the West where it influences military budgets and the conduct of foreign policy. The rise of China is leading to discussion in Africa about possible new forms of Asian imperialism. There is controversy about the choice between war and peace, as the strategy divided the United States and Europe during the George Bush administration. There are fears of cultural clashes and conflicts over a variety of issues. Popular markets and cultures threaten local ones. The tradition of moonlight stories cannot survive the onslaught of the television and the Internet. Home-made meals are giving way to fast food. African youth are attracted by the charms of Western artists. Seeing what they do not like or are afraid of, defenders of tradition attack the youth for their deviations. One defender of religious/cultural values can attack the other, as in the condemnation of the hosting of Miss World in Nigeria. A panic measure can be triggered to protect against the inroad of foreign cultures as in the implementation of the Sharia in some countries (e.g. Sudan), even if there are political calculations added to the motive.

95 Richard Rosecrance, *The Rise of the Virtual State: Wealth and Power in the Coming Century* (New York: Basic Books, 2000).

96 New studies are emerging on their character, culture and politics. Among others, see Mark Leibovich, *The New Imperialists* (New York: Prentice Hall, 2002); and Richard Rosecrance, 'The Rise of the Virtual State', *Foreign Affairs* (July–August 1996), 59–60.

Islam will surely dominate the central attention in the West, and will continue to be of importance in African politics and cultures. With respect to Africa, a number of people will continue to argue that ideas should be drawn from Islam to replace or reform the secularist state. A few may argue that using Islam to reform capitalism may lead to transformation. The clerics will continue to insist that the best way to counter Western wasteful consumerism is to turn to the values of modesty in Islam. Regarding Islam and the West, the linkage between religion and terrorism will continue to generate resentment among Muslims who already think that they are being persecuted. Islam still has scores to settle: the humiliation caused by imperialism, the crises in the Middle East, the power of the West, etc. In settling the scores, Islam will reinvigorate itself, and various elements will align the religion to various political ideologies, from the moderate to the revolutionary.

What is the place of African migrants in Western societies in all this? First, they serve as the connectors in taking Africa to the West by way of migration, travels, exchange of ideas, cultural transmission and much more. African migrants in the West take with them African ideas, African cultures and African attitudes[97]. When they build churches and mosques, markets and stores, they alter the landscape. When they wear their clothes, they alter the marketplace of attire and costumes. No one can but notice the headgear, colourful flowing robes, caps, etc. When they speak, they enrich the language with their accents and sentences. When they talk, they show their attitude, as in the loud and argumentative communication style of Nigerians.[98]

Second, the African migrants take the West to Africa through the same process of travel, migration and the information highway. Following the principle of either you make it or fake it, they lend credence to the mythology that the West is a land of opportunities. Gambians who did not finish high school eulogise the welfare system in Sweden; Nigerian cab drivers in Chicago or New York describe themselves as businessmen who make money as land pilots; and Senegalese carriers of small wares in the marginalised zone of Paris call themselves business tycoons in the making. Of course, there are many stories of success, and African migrants represent one of the most successful in many places. The professionals occupy solid middle-class status. Hard currencies and Western goods are sent to Africa, adding to capital assets.

Third, Africans allow us to study the activities of transnationalists and the impact of globalisation. Many have created new nationalities on the Internet, as in so

---

97   Alusine Jalloh and Toyin Falola (eds.), *The United States and West Africa: Interactions and Relations* (Rochester: University of Rochester Press, 2008).

98   Toyin Falola, Niyi Afolabi and Aderonke Adesanya (eds.), *Migrations and Creative Expressions in Africa and the African Diaspora* (Durham, NC: Carolina Academic Press, 2008).

many ethnic associations such as the Igbo Progressive Unions. In drawing on a network of new friends, kinship has been redefined, in which the fictional performs a similar role as in the original African variant. The celebration of the rites of passage in elaborate form shows how powerful fictional kinship has become. Social parties, with all the paraphernalia of live bands, excess food and drink and gorgeous attire show how ideas of success and public display can be transferred from Africa to the West.

Cultural presentations, while affirming difference, can also create an entry point to problems of stigmatisation, racism and ethnocentric attacks. To ultra-nationalists in the West, those who live among them must assimilate. Thus, veiling has been banned in some European countries, restrictions imposed on marriage practices, tough child-raising cultures have been criticised, activities associated with child-rearing are labelled as child labour, etc. As ultra-nationalists argue, those who do not want to assimilate should leave so that the hegemonic culture is not diluted. Where Christian fundamentalists join in the discussion, they want a country where other religions, especially Islam, will have a limited role and significance.

Fourth, the migrants complicate the notions of the state and nation in Africa. They can be from Ghana or Nigeria, but the power of such states is curtailed in dealing with their own citizens. For many of them, the states mean little. They would rather focus on their ethnicities which they consider important since they represent building blocks for identity and by which they formulate associations. Their towns and cities are also important, since these are where they build houses and are buried should their bodies return home. And their parents and relations do count, but not the state. Those who are firmly committed to ethnic identities have even called for secession.

Finally, the migrants widen the discourse on race. Of paramount importance in private discussions is the topic of race, which they confront through daily realities with ordinary people and with institutions and structures of society.[99] Racism can be both overt and covert, open and disguised. There are two dimensions: the first is specific, the second general. The specific one is on the collaboration and conflicts between continental Africans and African Americans, two separate identities united by colour. The bridge between both is weak.

---

99 Research is just emerging on contemporary African immigrants in the West. See, for instance, Toyin Falola and Niyi Afolabi (eds.), *African Minorities in the New World* (New York: Routledge, 2007); Toyin Falola and Niyi Afolabi (eds.), *Trans-Atlantic Migration: The Paradoxes of Exile* (New York: Routledge, 2008); and Toyin Falola and Niyi Afolabi (eds.), *The Human Cost of African Migrations* (New York: Routledge, 2007).

As to the general, Africans are used to the politics of ethnicity and religion in Africa. As cruel and exploitative as the colonial system was,[100] the majority of Africans outside of South Africa read about racism and apartheid in textbooks and from stories told by a dying generation. In the West, they face that of race which they may understand or misread. Thus, it is not unusual for Africans to regret exile, to present exile as a condition of shame, to express disillusionment. Where some have gone to Europe or America looking for quick success and opulent living, they may have become disappointed, seeing the promises of high culture and prestige as a mirage. Migration dreams may become dampened, unfulfilled, as people experience difficulties or alienation. Disappointments may lead to trauma, painful feelings of profound cultural dislocation and mental agonies, among others. The very suspicion of their presence can generate visceral reactions.

Encounters with the homeland may produce suspicions in which migrants feel a sense of loss in all spaces – a being neither here nor there, an African who cannot relate to Africa nor the West. Not being African Americans, they may not be black enough. When they are black enough, the narratives of their experience are reported by others, narrators who feel neither pain nor anguish.

Racism, like ethnicity, can attach categories to people on the basis of difference. In the case of racism, on the basis of colour, which is then associated with deficiencies in intelligence, trust, efficiency and ability. Whether in racism or ethnicity, the invention of difference, real (as in different colour or different location) or imaginary (as in the crude determination of intelligence) and the values attached to that difference are to achieve a set purpose. One is to obtain and keep privileges of wealth and power. Thus, a group in power can resort to cultural and biological difference to separate itself from others and then argue that those who are different are inferior. Second, the division enables the use of violence to create and sustain divisions and privileges. In racialised societies, attitudes and exercises of ethnocentrism and xenophobia are robbed of guilt, and the deadly apparatus of violence can be visited on the underprivileged race. Albert Memmi, a sophisticated analyst, uses the concept of 'ethnophobia' to characterise what I just called 'attitudes', saying that biological differences are astutely deployed to ground social and physical assault and hostility.[101] Racism then becomes an alibi for domination.[102] For Africans who leave Africa because of the problems of ethnicity, they have to confront another reality of cleavage: racism. They may have exaggerated

---

100 Toyin Falola, *Colonialism and Violence in Nigeria* (Bloomington: Indiana University Press, 2009).

101 Albert Memmi, *Racism* (Minneapolis: University of Minnesota Press, 2000).

102 Steve Martinot, 'Introduction: The Double Consciousness', in Memmi, *Racism*, xxvi.

the cleavage, attributing their own inadequacies and limitations to it. Or they may be dealing with structures and institutions that impose boundaries. Many are successful, so successful that they also generate envy.

The movements of people and global interactions will continue to instigate discontents in politics and cultures. Uneven global development will mean that rich and poor people will create different cultures, that those who feel excluded from resources will grumble and formulate resistance cultures. The production and manufacture of goods will impact the environment, most especially forest depletion, which in turn might lead to rural-urban migrations. Population increase and urbanisation will produce new urban cultures. Marginalised people will produce expressions of disappointment in words and actions. Such political expressions will empower ethnic movements and religious associations, thereby allowing a limitless number of organisations and millions of people to have allegiances in opposition to the state and such supra-state organisations as the World Bank.

Conclusion

One conclusion unites all the three entry points: creativity has an agenda that overcomes any legacy of slavery and racism. Various expressions are connected with identity. Self-definition enables the rejection of imposed ones, changing the paradigm of negativity to the positive. Self-definition gives power to colour and supplies the energy to fight stereotypes, humiliations and rejection. Creativity puts breaks and checks on the process of 'deculturation' that encounters with others can produce, enabling us to revalorise and reappropriate elements of cultures that have been discarded. Where religion and spirituality are involved, they allow beliefs to be used as cultural therapy. Creativity provides the opportunity to create a counter discourse to hegemonic representations of blackness. Be they artists, singers or poets, creativity allows black people to fight back with disdain, anger and rationalisation. They provide evidence of the civilisation of the past, as in works by W. E. B. Du Bois and Cheikh Anta Diop, and evidence of the possibilities of the present.

Creativity preaches the need for dignity, provides an identification with blackness, produces criticism of racism and dehumanisation and gives nationalistic support for the emergence of powerful black nations. Creativity announces success and pride: it puts on stage the richness of black cultures, the talents and skills of writers, poets, artists and others. As the works are enjoyed and appreciated, the masters and the audience all become worthwhile collaborators in the project of progress and race uplift.

Creativity refutes racial prejudices and affirms blackness. The large body of work in black literature and African history combines to say that the black race is not infantile and inferior, that black people are intelligent and talented, and do have a common identity, a rich heritage and a long history. Not denying the contributions of other races, black scholars assert that all races, nationalities and ethnicities have their geniuses, make original contributions to world heritage and civilisation. Rather than support an ideology and bureaucracy to facilitate a monolithic system, the originality expressed in black creative endeavours points to diverse cultures and shows us the way out of totalitarian and repressive modes of thinking.

Creativity is a statement that blacks are beyond labour, that is, people defined just in terms of manual exploitation, irrespective of the economic system. While some do have character flaws (as with all groups of people in any part of the world), the race cannot be stereotyped as foolish and mediocre. Richard Wright attempts in *Black Boy* to say that even the characterisation of being foolish can be rejected by small acts of violence, and that ambition and identity should not be caged. As Wright attempts to aspire to greater heights, he is pulled back by negative characterisation, his humanity dehumanised, his personality depersonalised, until he can stand it no more:

> I could not make subservience an automatic part of my behaviour. I had to feel and think out each tiny item I brought to the whole of my life. While standing before white men, I had to figure out how to perform each act and how to say each word. I could not help it. I could not grin. In the past I had always said too much, now I found that it was difficult to say anything at all. I could not reach as the world in which I lived expected me to; that world was too baffling, too uncertain.[103]

Ralph Ellison's[104] *Invisible Man* adopts a similar connection of creative use of violence for individual liberation. Disengagement and withdrawal or silence have been represented as yet other ways out, in countless examples of blues music, religious tracts and poems. Even Richard Wright gestures at the use of this strategy as he withdraws deeper and deeper, agonising that: 'I grew silent and reserved as the nature of the world in which I lived became plain and undeniable; the bleakness of the future affected my will to study'.[105]

I am reminded of the warning by Frantz Fanon about the need to avoid intellectual dependency. What creativity has done to many poets, artists, filmmakers, etc. is to meet this Fanonian injunction, although there are also, of course, too

103 Richard Wright, *Black Boy* (New York: Harper and Row, 1966), 215.
104 Ralph Ellison, *Invisible Man* (New York: Random House, 1952).
105 Ibid., 181.

many examples of mere imitation. As new knowledge, objects and ideas are created, it becomes much harder to ridicule representation, to say that others must always speak for oneself. The monologic frame of universalism gives way to a dialogic form of diversity which, to cite Michel Foucault, 'ultimately matters, a discourse against power, the counter-discourse of prisoners and those we call delinquents'.[106]

As the vibrant Nollywod industry has demonstrated, Africa is a major site of creative innovations. Whether it is Candomble in Brazil or Blues music in the United States, we see examples of creativity in all parts of the African diaspora – abundant, limitless, boundless, vibrant and energetic. European domination of Africa did not succeed in killing the music and dance, the stories and festivals, the aesthetics, etc. They have continued in various forms and been reinvented into others. Migrations have created new opportunities. The characters in the *Virginia Is for Lovers* seem to be echoing an old statement by George Lamming in *The Pleasures of Exile*[107] where the individuals belong to wherever they are, but without forgetting their homeland in both the subliminal, psychical and physical connections they still maintain.

Creativity, in whatever form it is expressed, is not politically neutral. It is identity seeking, defining oneself and creating the boundaries of difference and meaning. Identity asserts the self – the individual, the nation, the ethnicity, the religion, the race – all with a goal of attaining recognition, visibility and purpose. There have been literary schools and devices (such as Negritude, for instance) to generate pride for blackness and practical devices to bring creative minds together to generate unity (e.g. Festival of Black Arts and Cultures). In the musical talents of such figures as Miriam Makeba, Michael Jackson, King Sunny Ade, Fela Anikulapo Kuti, Hugh Masekela, Asa, Sade, etc., Ellison's 'invisible man' acquires visible names. In the leading actors and actresses in Nollywood, Le Roi Jones Clay[108] has become not one thunderbolt but many thunderbolts. In Nelson Mandela, Julius Nyerere and Barack Obama, Richard Wright's *Black Boy* has now become a man, the epitome of power, dignity and nobility.

---

106 Michel Foucault, *Language-Counter-Memory Practice*, ed. and trans. Donald F. Bouchard (Oxford: Basil Blackwell, 1977), 209.

107 George Lamming, *The Pleasures of Exile* (London: Michael Joseph, 1960).

108 The reference here is to LeRoi Jones (Imamu Amiri Baraka), *Dutchman* (London: Faber and Faber, 1964).

Work, Power and Society in Pharaonic Egypt

Alain Anselin

BIOGRAPHY

Founder of the periodical *Cahiers Caribéens d'Égyptologie* (1999) and of the electronic papyrus *i-Medjat* (2007), Alain Anselin (alain.anselin@gmail.com) taught ancient Egyptian at the Antilles-Guyane University until 2012. His publications include a hundred articles on Egyptology (periodicals, conference and seminar proceedings) and several books, including *La Troisième Île. L'émigration antillaise en France* (1991) and *Le Refus de l'Esclavitude. Résistances africaines à la traite négrière* (2009).

ABSTRACT

The titles of the officials in the Annales and the Old Egyptian Kingdom's biographies have outlined and highlighted the political economy of the Pharaonic state apparatus. From a few words linked together in a title emerges a meaningful picture of a 'combination of classical production factors': capital (land, tools), labour (manpower, techniques and skills) in the domains and workshops, and raw materials (mineral, vegetable, animal). Using well-demonstrated sociological parallels from classical antiquity, as well as a rigorous lexicographical, semantic and comparative approach extended to the Nile Valley's hinterland, the author shows that the Egyptian vocabulary of work reflects *social relationships* between those who used and benefited from the system and those who were affected by it. Social movements that punctuated the history of Ancient Egypt are inscribed in the ever-fluid history of these relationships, which are threaded throughout the biographical, administrative and legal texts of Ancient Egypt.

Introduction

'In the collective consciousness, the words "slavery" and "Egypt" are often associated with the images evoked by Hollywood blockbusters, sparked by the enormous effort' that the building of the pyramids seems to have required. 'Most of the modern writers who have worked on the institutions of Pharaonic Egypt have immediately admitted the existence of slavery as a premise', taking Rome as the standard measure for simplistic historical scenarios (Menu 2000).

In reality, 'the issue of work and social status in ancient societies, particularly in Pharaonic Egypt' (Menu 1998) is anything but simple. The 'official discourses (royal inscriptions and monuments), rules of public organisation (royal decrees, circulars and administrative notes) and texts from daily life (established practice, memoranda, accounting)', which represent most of the available sources, are not sufficient to cover every aspect of the issue. In fact, 'the written sources have been steeped in a state vision, classifying and describing the rural society with terms usable by the State, without necessarily giving a faithful report of the complexity or all the productive activities that took place in the rural society' (Moreno-Garcia 1998, 104).

Throughout the three millennia of a never-motionless history, declarations of land ownership, successions, marriages, work benefit systems, work assignment methods, remuneration, administrative archives, and legal trials have outlined a quite complex reality.

If one considers that a language is the black box of a civilisation, the rich and varied Egyptian vocabulary used in all these texts offers an appropriate framework for reflection prior to the study of those official acts and social practices that have left written records and of the depiction of the mechanisms of palatial, domain and village work systems.

Therefore, what is called work in ancient Egyptian? Who works? At what? For what? How? And for whom: who owns the work (on behalf of whom does someone own it)? Who benefits from the work (or who benefits from the work done)? What are the areas of society, domains, workshops, village lands where the concrete reality of work is ordered?

Hence, it is by studying words and the definition of their semantic field (placed in the appropriate economic and social context) that we will deal with the issue.

Questioning the Words Related to Work

As in every society, the Egyptian terminology of work reflects social relationships between those who benefit from the work and those who are assigned to it.

Starting from the top of the social pyramid, the titles so well identified by Naguib Kanawati for the Old Kingdom outline nothing less than the political economy of the Pharaonic state apparatus.

Some high-ranking officials' titles of the 4th and 5th Dynasties during the Old Kingdom, and the words they employ, suffice to clearly express the conception of the mechanisms of work within Egyptian society: Pepy-Seneb is *imy-r₃ wpt mrt* (*3ḫt*), an intendant or supervisor of the *mrt* and of divine offerings in the estates: from the assignment (*wpt*) of work (the *mrt*) to the land capital (the *3ḫt*), as well as the provision of products, the offerings, to the temples. Khnoum-Hotep is the '*intendant of deeds relative to royal documents of the palace, to the mrt and to the fields*'.

In the Egyptian capital, the title of *director* (*imy-r3*) of *all the projects* (*k3.t*) *of the king* (*nswt*) is characteristic of the '*vizier*' or *prime minister*. The most important titles of the provincial administration are no less significant: *director* (*imy-r3*) *of the missions (wp.(w)t)*, (or *of the delivery of the offerings*); *directors of new cities, of the city of the pyramid (nwt mr), of monuments, of royal dependents*. Also significant are the innumerable *administrators* (*ḥk3*) *of domains* (*ḥw.t*), domains whose foundation by the Pharaonic power invests in and progressively and unequally shapes the rural areas (*niwt*) from which the Pharaonic power recruits most of its workers – modelling in return the customs of the village communities (Kanawati 1974, Menu 1995, Moreno-Garcia 2008[1]).

Therefore, in just a few words linked together in a title, there appears 'a combination of classical production factors': capital (land, tools), labour (manpower, techniques and skills) in the domains and workshops, and raw materials (mineral, vegetable, animal).

21. The word ⩓ ⵣ , *imy-r3*

The first word on which we focus here is a key title (but it is not the only one: *ḥk3* and *ḥrp* administer and manage; the *ḥtmw* manage by the *seal, ḥtm,* and by writing).

The generic nature of the title ⩓ ⵣ , *imy-r3*, is a reminder that '*the one who is in the mouth*' (of the king) gives the orders, that speaking, like writing, is a political good. It also underlines his influence in the forms of authority, scars of a more

---

1 We owe to Juan Carlos Moreno-Garcia a precious synthesis of the management of a rural landscape spread across a huge delta and two thousand kilometres of valley by the Pharaonic State, which gives a context to the distribution of titles, status and words: 'On the one hand, the State contributed to the creation of local elites, thanks to marriage alliances, to the integration of rural elites in the administration and to the opening of new ways of social promotion in the margins of power local bases [...]. On the other hand, the foundation (by the State) of agricultural domains or temples disrupted the organisation of the rural space, the exploitation of local resources and working times and patterns [...]. Finally, the State's tax requirements, both in terms of work and specific agricultural products, led to a deterioration of the farmers' productive choices, of their agricultural cycles and of the area's organisation and exploitation' (Moreno-Garcia 2008, 141).

ancient time, conveyed since 3000 BC by the era of writing – or rather in the forms of writing in Ancient Egypt: hieroglyphic for the discourses of power and cursive for administrative tasks.

The *imy-r3* orders the ones who have to listen to him, in a language in which *sḏm,* to *listen to,* also means *to obey* (Wb IV 384,4-387,14).

Those who listen, in this case, are the recipients of the orders to work, *b3k.w* and *ḥm.w, mrt* and then *ḥsb.w* – as well as the craftsmen, *ḥmw.wt,* recruited for the construction of monuments and pyramids, often accommodated in new cities near the main sites.

Here is listed the vocabulary from across the sociological spectrum of Ancient Egypt, *wp.wt, k3.t, mr.t, b3k.w, ḥm.w.*

We will now study their semantic fields in their historical, economic and social context.

22. The word 𓏏𓏜𓂝𓀁, 𓎡𓏏, *wp.wt*

As given, working implies *an order.* The word 𓏏𓏜𓂝𓀁, 𓎡𓏏, OK *wp(w)t, missions,* is based on the Egyptian: *ip* < **lep, send,* with the *l* being a phonetic value of / *i* /, *ip.wt* > *wp.wt, message, mission, task* (Wb I 303-304). The determinatives are those of **oral** communication, 𓀁, A2, and **written**, 𓏜, Y1. The *Message – oral and/or written order –* and the *work* are one and the same thing in ancient Egyptian, as outlined by the history of words from Egyptian to Coptic: *h3b, send (a letter, a message),* Coptic: r-**hob,** *to perform work,* ti-**hob,** *to give work, employ* (Wb II 479,13-481,1); *wpw.t, ipw.t (send) message, mission, affair (business),* Coptic: **eiope,** *craft, art, occupation.*

The archaeology of each Egyptian word will be carried out using the comparative sociological approach made possible by modern methods of etymological research. The Egyptian word *ip.wt* > *wp.wt, message, mission,* finds its best cognates in West Chadic, particularly in angas-sura: ***lep,** *send,* angas : *lep,* **leplep,** *send* sura: *lɔp, message,* **la-lèp,** *servant,* literally: *child* **of the message** (Takacs 1999, 88; 2004, 228).

23. The word 𓏠𓂝𓀀, *k3.t*

The word 𓏠𓂝𓀀, pyr *k3.t,* is first and foremost a generic term expressing the notion of work (Kothay 2010) and has connoted, ever since the Old Kingdom, the physical aspect of a form of work, *load, carry* (Wb IV 98,2-101,7), dedicated to the fields and to the building of monuments. The word implies the notion of *load* (cf. Chadic: *kɔrɔ, carry, load*) (Newman 1977, 1–42), of drudgery; its written form can even be abridged to the only hieroglyph A9 of the man carrying a basket on his head, which always gives its determinative: 𓀀.

A text owed to the high priest Heqanakht during the 11th Dynasty shows that the persons who worked for him (*k3.t*), who were given *orders* by him, are Egyptians, ⌒𓈖𓀀𓏤, *rmṯ.w*, and that they were paid (Allen 2002, 17, 233, II.29-30).

In Central Chadic: kotoko: **k-l-*, *duty, service,* gives an acceptable cognate to *k3.t*, with /l/ phonetic value of /ɜ/ (Takacs 2005, 331; 1999, 37, 62–63)—as well as in Berber: **a-kli, i-kl-an, slave,* whose reduction in the semantic field bears the scar of the tran-Saharan and Oriental slave trade developed in the course of the last two millennia. Bantu could also supply some rarer cognates, yaka: *-kele,* 'slave', teke: *-kere* (Johnstone 1919, 558), ending up in the vocabulary of the history of the second half of the last millennium's Atlantic slave trade.

24. The word 𓈖𓀀𓏤, *mr.t*

Still in the Old Kingdom, another word, 𓈖𓀀𓏤, OK*mr.t*, actually a collective, *mr.yt*, refers to *work teams*[2]. The *mrt* figure among the productive forces (fields, livestock) granted by the king to an institution (or sometimes transferred to private individuals) and appears in the titles of the Pharaonic high administration.

These are periodic work teams, to which African cultures hold up a recent lexicographical mirror, in this case also marked by the competing and parallel development of the Western and Oriental slave trades of the last millennium: '*zenaga*' (Berber): *u-mūr-ä(y)n, worker,* Cushitic: *rendille: mir, persons working in groups,* West Chadic: **mar(i), slave, daffo-butura: mōòr,* pl. *mwāār, north-bauchi:* **mar* (Takacs 2008, 378–80)'. 'Central Chadic: zulgo : *mor, worker,* mbuko : *mer, work,* compares best with the Egyptian *mr.t*' (Anselin 2012).

Juan Carlos Moreno Garcia highlights the fact that the *mrt* are 'comparable to the *rmṯ* and to the *rḥyt* in Egyptian sources, which are ordinary Egyptians'.

The *mrt* were indeed 'Egyptians living in their villages and who could acquire and transfer land properties' (Moreno-Garcia 1998, 81). Enrolled on a periodic basis by the Pharaonic administration, they were provided by the village leaders, who received lists of them in order to carry out the chores needed to develop the domains of the State. After the 6th Dynasty, the word disappeared from the vocabulary, while a term like *ḥsb.w*, has been more generally used to designate as 'listed' those workers used periodically for menial labour in the royal domains and temples.

---

2 It is necessary to distinguish the OK*mr.t*, workers of the Old Kingdom, from the 𓊌𓀀𓏤, NK*mr.t*, weavers of the Ramesside period in the New Kingdom (Allam 2010).

25. The word 𓅠𓄿𓏛, *b3k*

In a team, 𓅠𓄿𓁐𓏥, *b3k.wt*, *Dienerschaft* [servants] (Wb I 430,11) or alone, 𓅠𓄿𓏛, *b3k, servant,* 𓅠 𓂝 𓏛, *b3k.t, maid,* 𓅠 𓂝 𓁐𓏥, ᴼᴷ*b3k.w, the workers* (Wb I 429,6-430,3-10): several words derived from the same very productive root, *b3k*, this time take as a model the form of the *activity* itself.

The series of words refers to an *agent* and to an *action* because the word admits as a determinative the forearm ⌐ (hieroglyph D40), the standing man 𓀜 (A24), holding a stick, metaphors for the *action obtained by the use of force,* or a *directive* illustrated by the papyrus hieroglyph ⊟ Y1, a metaphor for writing.

All the vocabulary derived from this root presents work as an *obligated effort*, involving social hierarchy. In this case, too, this is a service owed to the king by the teams he had ordered enrolled, *hsb*, in their villages in collaboration with village leaders and councils, [and] by his officials, often literate, who assigned them to works in nearby domains and temples.

From the Middle Kingdom, taxes, duties, and usage fees, together with the government and the management, are measured in terms of this service: 𓅠𓏛, ᴹᴷ*b3k, work,* 𓅠𓏛𓀜, ᴹᴷ*b3k, work, tax, service* (Wb I 426). And 𓅠 𓏛𓏥, ᴹᴷ,ᴺᴷ *b3k.t,* ends up meaning *to work, to tax and to govern* (Wb I 429,16). Governing the Egyptian people is mainly done by governing them through *taxes and work,* the latter determining the amount of tax.

Finally, the same word, *b3k*, is used to designate the fact of *imposing tribute* on foreign peoples which implies that, in Egyptian thought, the captives from war could be rapidly assimilated into the domestic tributaries, the *b3k.w.*

Gabor Takacs considers the Egyptian word *b3k* closer to West Chadic: bauchi: boghom: *ḇiyak*, polchi: *ḇiyɔk*, from Central Chadic: lame: *bʸek, bèk*, matakam : *beke,* mofu, moloko: *bèké*; musgu: *begé,* fem., *bagai,* girvidik: *bakay, slave.* The Hungarian linguist adds the Yemeni: *byk, to engage a workman, bāyik, engaged workman* (Takacs 2005, 326–27).

The semantic reduction of the notion of work in Chadic languages has evidently occurred in the context of the Oriental slave trade, involving a good deal more than submission to authority: the loss, pure and simple, of freedom and personality; and, in the context of the western slave trade, for the Bantu series established by Sigismund Koelle from the middle of the nineteenth century, bangante: *-bega,* luyi: *-peka, slave,* kikongo : *mu.bika, servant, war prisoner, mvika, servitude* (Koelle 1854). The series was completed at the beginning of the twentieth century by Sir Harry Johnstone: luyi : *mu.bika* and *mpeka,* luba : *mu.pika,* nkoya : *mu.bike,* vili : *nvika,* yaka, pende : *mu.hika, slave* (Johnstone 1919, 341, 371, 385, 402, 558).

26. The word ⌷𓎡, ḥm

Another word, **ḥm,** has been very successful throughout the centuries and across social classes. Written with the hieroglyph U36, a club, and completed with hieroglyph N35, water, it firstly refers to the ⌷𓎡, *ḥmww, the launderer* (Wb III 87,7-8). The widespread use of the term soon places the **authority** at the centre of the semantic dispositive and is used in a cascading hierarchy: 𓏤𓃾 , *ḥm, Majesty,* if the stick icon has the determinative of royalty, hieroglyph A42 (Wb III 91,1-92,11) – or in the expression *ḥm.f, His Majesty,* litt. *'slave'* (sic) *of himself;* 𓏤 , *ḥm(w) nṯr, priest of the god* ; 𓏤 , *ḥm k3, priest of k3, priest of the dead* (Wb III 90,8-14 ; Kahl 2004, 304–306); and finally with the gender determinative, hieroglyph A1, 𓏤𓀀, *ḥm(w), slave, servant,* and B1, 𓏤𓁐, ᴼᴷ*ḥm(w).t, slave, maid, collective:* 𓏤𓁐 (Wb III 87,13-88,8). Therefore, the semantic value attributed to *ḥm* varies according to the determinative and the position of authority, from the royal majesty to the slave, creating two questionable translations, particularly the one of *ḥm* by *slave.*

Indeed, 'legally, the *ḥm.w* and the *b3k.w* are free men: they can have a family, secure a contract, testify; they also exploit for themselves a plot of land and pay taxes, as such they are directly linked to tax administration and hence with royal power, relayed by the temples, basic economic units' (Menu 1970).

The statement of a sandal maker, Penyun, at the end of the Ramesside period, New Kingdom, illustrates the status of the *ḥm* at this time: 'The citizen (*ꜥnḫ n niwt*) - Shedese "a slave" (*ḥm*) of mine, came to me saying: take care of me while I am alive and you shall find (*gm*) the land (*p3 t3 n 3ḥt*) belonging to me' (Bakir 1952, 85–87). By what sociological contortion a slave can be a citizen and own land and vice versa – unfathomable mysteries of the past century's translations… As for the royal barber Sibastit, 'he gives as a spouse to the "slave" (*ḥm*) Amenyoui, won by the strength of his arm, alongside pharaoh in the war, Takamenet, the daughter of his sister, Nebet-ta, turning him into one of his heirs' (de Linage 1939).

27. The word 𓈖𓎛𓅱, nmḥw

During the Middle Kingdom, texts distinguish a last category, the *nmḥw*, from *b3k.w*, the powerful, *wr.w*, and the nobles, *wsr.w*.

A prayer to Amun illustrates this opposition: '*Ô Amun, give thy ear to one who is alone in the ḳnbt, who is pauper (nmḥ) and is not powerful (wsr)!*' (Bakir 1952, 51; cf. Vycichl 1983, 175).

The word *nmḥ*, means *being a pauper, orphan,* 𓈖𓌰𓏤𓀀, *nmḥw, the pauper*; ME*nmḥw, pauper, free, private* (Wb II 268,4-16). We can translate '*nmḥ* ... as a private and independent person, meaning deprived of hierarchical or familial ties'. From an economic point of view, the '*nmḥ.w* are ... holders of agricultural tenures' without 'any obligation except the payment of a low income to the institution owning the fields' (Menu 2000, 59 et seq.).

But things are complex. Often opposed to *bȝk* for that reason, the *nmḥ* is likely to become *bȝk* himself, during a contract concluded with a notable, in return for payment, in grain and in money (Menu 2000, 76–79).

From a legal point of view, the *nmḥw* have *the right of citizenship* of all the *rmṯ.w,* and the expression *nmḥyy.t n.t niw.t* in a text from the Middle Kingdom is **usually** translated by '*citizen of the city*' (Bakir 1952, 51).

The Egyptian word originally meaning *orphan, deprived of family* has several sociological comparison points with vocabularies in African, European and Asian societies. Bantu: the *mu.hega pende* is the *poor, the man without protection, the man without parents, the orphan*; the *u.fumu* being *the condition of lord, the u.hega, condition of the person without protection,* here is opposed to the *u.higa, condition of the slave* (Gusimana 1972). Nilo-Saharan: mursi: *bhoga: poor people, orphan* (Turton, Yizegu & Olibui 2008). Indo-European: **orbho < orphans,* Old Indian: *arbhah, orphan,* German: *Arbeit, work* (Satzinger 2005, 321).

Social Movements at the End of the Old Kingdom

31. A context of crisis…

The end of the Old Kingdom is marked by a serious economic and social crisis, fuelled by the worsening of the climate; the famines are devastating; revolts of the peasants, too heavily taxed, are not rare (Hassan 2007).

32. The Lamentations of Ipuwer

The *Admonitions of Ipuwer*, written near the 12th Dynasty in the classical Egyptian rhetoric format of order and chaos, illustrates the crisis. The chosen format alludes to the turbulence at the end of the Old Kingdom. There is a litany of lamentations by the elites, victims of the revolt of those they had oppressed. The scribes who travel with their register are the symbol of the State and of its abuses of power. Their writings (accounts, land registers) are stolen, destroyed, they themselves sometimes killed. 'The wealthy are in mourning; the poor man is full of joy. Every town says: let us suppress the powerful among us…!' The poor serve themselves in the shops (Gardiner 1909, 26, 2.7-8; 61, pl.6, l.8-9).

33. The story of the Eloquent Peasant

A little older, the *Story of the Eloquent Peasant* considers the realities of power from a peasant viewpoint and gives a voice to the *social mutes* that are the *sḥtyw*, the peasant masses, traditionally suppliers of *bꜣkw* and *ḥmw*, enrolled for chores related to taxation.

We follow a peasant, coming from an oasis with his goods in the Nile Valley, in a social odyssey punctuated by complaints and renewed beatings. An employee of a royal domain's *superintendent* accuses his donkey of grazing there and confiscates it; the peasant complains to the *superintendent* himself; the latter passes on his grievances to the king Nebkaourê Kheti – 19th Dynasty, around 2100 BC (Le Guilloux 2002, B1 103-118). Stolen, beaten – listened to and whipped during each of his defence speeches – the peasant does not stay quiet, quite the opposite. Speaking is a political good. *It can both enact power and contest it.*

In fact, the author of the story of the Eloquent Peasant, a scholar, puts in the mouth of a peasant a picture of the society as it is and as it should not be: *magistrates act wrongfully, the truth of speaking is put aside* (B129), *the judges steal* (B1 130), plus a rebel indictment that the theatre of Césaire or the *Wretched of the Earth* of Fanon would not have disowned forty centuries later. It calls out power in the following terms: 'your territory is infected with crocodiles (B 161), you are a bird of prey living on the plovers, the most miserable birds (B1 204-206), you are as a policeman who steals, a governor who sacks (B1 223)'.

Social Movements during the New Kingdom

41. A context of prosperity...

A millennium later, at the end of the 18th Dynasty, Pharaoh Horemheb made a decree displayed in Karnak. He cut taxes, fees and chores, [and] reformed justice, as he wanted it to be 'respectful of the palace's instructions and laws of the tribunal, free, acceptable and incorruptible' (Valbelle 1998, 285). The economic context of the New Kingdom is thus propitious. The State draws its resources from the extension of its domains, from their exploitation, from the imposed tributes, *bꜣk*, from foreign countries during domination, and from the incorporation of an increasing number of prisoners of war into its economy after victorious campaigns, as for instance those of Thutmose III and Amenhotep I in Palestine (Menu 2004, 187 et seq.). Never before was commercial trade with Asian neighbours as developed as it was then, nor [so many] technological transfers decided by Egyptian sovereigns [regarding] shipyards for seagoing vessels, *mnš*, and high-warp looms, often accompanied by their qualified workforce, ship's carpenters and weavers, who were encouraged to settle in – or came from as booty – the closest countries of the East.

In this context of prosperity, captive manpower is distributed to royal domains and temples and may also be allocated to private individuals. Bernadette Menu presents some examples of jobs *ʿ3m.wt,* assigned by private individuals to Syrians, such as *ḥm.wt* and *b3k.wt* , notably the case of a weaver, Irinefert, the wife of a district leader, who trains an apprentice coming from Syria and then rents out her services as a *ḥm.t* and *b3k.t,* to other persons for remuneration (Menu 1998, 199). Subcontracting of services, often done by herdsmen, is convenient at the time: the temporary rental of servants' workdays against cattle in transit (of which they had charge) between the temple and the offering ritual (Menu 1998, 204–205).

42. Protests against conscription

The services of the *ḥmw* acquired by one or several private individuals for pay could be requested by officials for menial chores controlled by officials or even transferred during the carrying out of a 'chore' from one institution to another, depending on the rank of the officials in charge.

Therefore, during the 20th Dynasty, Djehoutyemheb, the chief of the record keepers of the royal granary in Memphis, wrote 'a letter of protest against the conscription for obligatory work', contesting that eight members of his staff (the ⟨hieroglyphs⟩, *rmṯw,* Egyptians), assigned to the fields of the temple of Thot, had been requisitioned without authorisation by the scribe of a priest, Bakenptah, to carry stones to the temple of another god in the same city (Trapani 2004). What a pity the letter does not indicate the attitude of the eight staff members, *rmṯ.w,* 'moved around' during a job. It feeds the *historiography* of the elites' protest, but the *historicity* of those without a voice, without hagiography, is eluded. But not always…

43. The Place of the Truth

During the 18th Dynasty, Thutmose I created on the Theban mountain, on the west bank of the Nile, a village to gather together all the craftsmen needed for the construction of royal necropolises: quarry workers, masons, sculptors, draughtsmen, painters…: it was called Set Mâat, *the Place of the Truth,* today named *Deir el-Médineh.* From 1500 to 1080 BC, from the 18th to the 20th Dynasty, generations of craftsmen, organised in two teams, and their families lived there, except during the village's move to Tell El-Amarna under Akhenaton (1359–1342 BC). Come to power at the end of the Amarnian era, Horemheb reorganised the village according to the *Institution of the Tomb.* Ramses III added a more complete *archives service,* making historians of today quite happy. But the last decades of the New Kingdom's prosperous centuries were characterised by the worsening economic crisis and the corruption of the institutions. During the reign of Ramses XI (1098–1080 BC), the power crumbled, the scribe of the Tomb directly collected the taxes required to pay the craftsmen; the latter were soon dispersed when the pharaohs abandoned the Theban necropolises (Valbelle 1998).

44. The word 𓏤𓂝𓏛, *ḥmw.t* .

The craftsmen employed at Deir el Medineh, the 𓏤𓂝𓏛, *ḥmw.t* (Wb III 83-84), formed a category of qualified professionals, not work conscripts, in the service of the elites. The word *ḥmwt, arts and crafts, production* (Wb III 84,9-21), 𓏤𓂝𓏛 , *ḥmww, the skilful, the expert, the craftsmen* (plural) (Wb III 83,5-84,8). The written form of their name is made of a specialist's tool, a drill bit, 𓏤 , differentiating itself from the ones of the 𓏏𓂝𓏛 *ḥmw.t*. They sometimes employed *ḥm* and *bȝk* in their houses.

In Deir el Medinah, the *ḥmw.t* left several hundreds of votive steles – a goldmine of socio-historical documentation. And the scribes who lived there allocated abundant administrative records to them, such as the registers of absences from work.[3]

Perfectly organised, the *ḥmw* had their own patron, Ptah, *Lord of the Truth*, to which they devoted a popular cult, distinct from the official worship practiced by their hierarchy; it served Ptah, *the Creator, imy rȝ ḥmwt – Supervisor of the Craftsmen* – and elected a delegate, *idnw*, who represented them at institutions.

All these points suggest that the craftsmen's village of Set Maât cannot be considered a fair representation of all the workers of the Egyptian New Kingdom (Exell 2006, I, 42). From a sociological point of view, the Egyptian word can be compared to notions known in every society where craftsmen are present, for instance, the Indo-European: *uerg-, to do,* English: *to work,* Greek: *to ergon, opus, work* and Latin: *opera, opus,* vocabulary also implying a notion of savoir-faire (Satzinger 2005).

45. Work stoppage in the Necropolis
Now we have the outline of the social, economic and political context for the first strike attested by world historiography. It is in the reign of Ramses III that the scribe Amenakhte, already the author of the indictment against team leader Paneb

---

3 Register of absences to work (ostracon around 1239 BC: Year 39 and the beginning of Year 40 of Ramses III). Out of 40 workers, only 2 have never missed one day of work. The organisation of the work is not very constraining and absenteeism is flourishing: 2 ˈ absences are due to drinking sessions, 117 absences for personal reasons (mother and sons ill, spouse and daughter indisposed, unspecified illnesses), 29 for religious reasons (worship, beer brewing, libations, funerals, mourning, embalming of a relative); a hundred for services rendered (building of his own house [1], of the house of a leader [55], of a scribe [10], of colleagues [22]… Cf. Cerny, Exell). Otherwise, the workers are on leave the last two days of every decade; if no work can be given to them, they are on paid leaves.

(accused of corruption, thefts and rapes), tells the facts on a papyrus dated to the 20th Dynasty (1190–1080 BC), today exhibited at the Museum of Turin.

The workers employed at the royal necropolis of Set Maât (Deir el Medineh) protested because they were no longer receiving the food rations due them. The object of their claim was therefore their remuneration, guaranteed in bread, fabrics, beers; their method was a *sit-in* behind a temple beyond numerous police stations. 'Year 29, second month of winter, day 10', recounts Amennakhte: 'The team went by the five control positions of the Necropolis saying "We are hungry! Already 18 days have passed this month" and the men sat behind the mortuary temple of Menkheperrê [Thutmose III]'.

The conciliation failed; the strike continued. 'The cause of this strike is hunger and thirst, there are no more clothes, unguent, fishes, vegetables: write to the Pharaoh, our good lord, [...] write to the vizier, our superior, in order to get the provisions needed' (Gardiner 1948, 45–58).

The authorities granted 'rations from the first month of winter'.

But scarcity and food shortages reigned, the pharaoh's granaries were empty (the king no longer protected from *chaos,* contrary to the ideology legitimating his power), supplies were brought with difficulty and strikes occurred again.

As an Epilogue: Goodbye to Hollywood...

At the end of this brief inventory of the mechanisms of work, of status and of vocabulary, it is important to note that none of the terms that define the employment of persons 'exactly match the idea of servitude, meaning the possession of the person's body and property, of constraint and degradation, like the Latin or Greek words, *servus, doulos*', concluded Jules Baillet more than a century ago. 'Therefore, what was slavery in Egypt? What is a social state that no word can name?' (Baillet 1907, 6–25).

'An Egyptian code distinguishing the status of persons, and thus between freemen, slaves and bondsmen, has not as yet been discovered', continues Abd el Mohsen Bakir half a century later. 'On the other hand, Pharaonic Egypt was not stationary: consequently, the implications of terms varied from age to age. The difference between the comparatively isolated Egypt of the Old Kingdom and that of later periods with their far-reaching conquests and abundance of wealth, captives and new ideas due to contact with foreign countries, was no doubt instrumental in bringing about these changes' (Bakir El Mohsen 1952).

Another half-century later, Bernadette Menu clearly refused the debate on a nowhere-to-be-found object: 'The existence of a system of forced requisition and **obligatory** work during determined periods of time at the service of the Pharaonic State', 'a system of remunerated drudgery' and that did not abolish the rights of a person, '[applicable] to the whole population and well-attested since the earliest times, makes it pointless to use the institution of slavery' (Menu 2004, 6). Ideologically, the elites could not justify slavery, as it contradicted their principles of seeking prosperity and pushing back chaos for all the country and the ⌗ *rmṯ.w* who lived in it and supported it through their work, even if they were war captives quickly *enrolled* as *bȝkw* or *ḥmw*: 'Slavery does not belong in a society where one does his best, by all means, to not make some people excluded' (Menu 2004, 205).

And as Juan Carlos Moreno-Garcia concludes: the *'logic of the work organisation'*, as well as the forms of its exploitation *'reveal the non-existence of a market of slaves or of a slave economy in Pharaonic Egypt'* (Moreno-Garcia 2008, 131).

BIBLIOGRAPHY

Allam, S., 2010. Les équipes dites meret, ⌗, spécialisées dans le filage-tissage eı Égypte pharaonique. In: B. Menu, ed., *L'organisation du travail en Égypte ancienne et eı Mésopotamie*, Cairo: IFAO, 41–64.

Allen, J. P., 2002. *The Heqanakht Papyri*. The Metropolitan Museum of Art, New York.

Anselin, A., Signes et mots des hiéroglyphes. *Archéo-Nil* 11, 21–43.

Anselin, A., 2012. À propos de l'Etymological Dictionary of Egyptian de Gabor Takacs 2008. Vol. Three, letter m-, Leiden: Brill. *Discussions in Egyptology* 65, 67–72.

Baillet, J., 1907. *Les noms de l'esclave en égyptien ancien*. Recueil de Travaux relatifs à lɛ philologie et à l'archéologie égyptiennes et assyriennes XXVI 1905; XXVII,1906; XIII N.S. 1907.

Cerny, J. A., 1973. *Community of Workmen at Thebes in the Ramesside Period*, Cairo: IFAO.

El Mohsen Bakir, A., 1952. *Slavery in Pharaonic Egypt*, Suppl. ASAE, Cahier no.18.

Erman, A. and Grapow, H., 1927, re-ed 1982. *Wörterbuch der Aegyptischen Sprache*. 13 vols. Berlin: Akademie Verlag.

Exell, K., 2006. *A social and historical interpretation of Ramesside period votive stelae*. Doctoral thesis (published). UK: Durham University.

Gardner, A. H. 1909. *The Admonitions of an Egyptian Sage from a Hieratic Papyrus in Leiden (Pap.Leiden 344 recto)*, Leipzig: Georg Olms Verlag.

Hassan, F., 2007. Droughts, Famines and the Collapse of the Old Kingdom: Re-reading Ipuwer. In: Hawass, Z. and Richards, J., eds., *The Archaeology and the Art of Ancient Egypt. Essays in Honor of David B O'Connor*, Vol I. Cairo: ASAE Cahier no. 36, 357–78.

Kahl, J. et al., 2002,2003,2004. Frühägyptisches Wörterbuch. Erste Lieferung. 3 vols. Wiesbaden: Harrasowitz.

Kanawati, N., 1974. *The Egyptian Administration in the Old Kingdom, Evidence on its Economic Decline*. Doctoral thesis (published). Sydney, Australia: Macquarie University.

Kothay, K. A., 2010. La notion de travail au Moyen-Empire. Implications sociales In: B. Menu, ed., *L'organisation du travail en Égypte ancienne et en Mésopotamie*. Cairo: IFAO, 155–70.

Le Guilloux, P., 2002. *Le Conte du Paysan éloquent. Texte hiéroglyphique, transcription et traduction commentée*. Cahiers de l'Association d'Égyptologie Isis no. 2, Angers.

de Linage, J., 1939. L'acte d'établissement et le contrat de mariage d'un esclave sous Thoutmés III. *Bulletin de l'Institut Français d'Archéologie Orientale* 38, 217–34.

Menu, B., 1998. Les échanges portant sur le travail d'autrui. In: Grimal, N. and Menu, B., eds., *Le commerce en Égypte ancienne*. Cairo: IFAO, 193–206.

Menu, B., 2000. La question de l'esclavage dans l'Égypte pharaonique. *Droit et Cultures* 39/1, 59–79.

Moreno-Garcia, J. C., 1998. La population *mrt* : Une approche du problème de la servitude dans l'Égypte du IIIe millénaire (I). *Journal of Egyptian Archaeology* 84, 71–83.

Moreno-Garcia, J. C., 2008. La dépendance rurale en Égypte ancienne. Compte-rendu du livre de B. Menu, ed., La dépendance rurale dans l'antiquité égyptienne et proche-orientale. *Journal of the Economic and Social History of the Orient* 51, 99–150.

Satzinger, H., 2005. Being Sent to Work: Some More Remarks on an African Etymological Pattern. *Wiener Zeitschrift für die Kunde des Morgenlandes* 93 Band, 319–45.

Takacs, G., 1999,2001,2008. *Etymological Dictionary of Egyptian*. 3 vols. Leiden: Brill.

Takacs, G., 2005. Marginal Notes on 'Working' in Egyptian. *Wiener Zeitschrift für die Kunde des Morgenlandes* 93 Band, 319–45.

Trapani, M., 2004. Un cas d'abus de pouvoir dans l'administration rurale. Le P. Turin 1882 v° In: B. Menu, ed., *L'organisation du travail en Égypte ancienne et en Mésopotamie*, Cairo: IFAO, 211–25.

Valbelle, D., 1998. *Histoire de l'État pharaonique*, Paris: Presses Universitaires de France.

Vychicl, W., 1983. *Dictionnaire étymologique de la langue copte*. Leuven: Peeters.

Slavery and the Slave Trade Within and Across the Red Sea Region

A Preliminary Conceptual Framework

Abdi M. Kusow

BIOGRAPHY

Abdi M. Kusow is Associate Professor of Sociology and African American Studies at Iowa State University. His research has appeared in flagship journals such as *Symbolic Interaction, Ethnic and Racial Studies, Journal of Migration and Ethnic Studies, Journal of International Migration and Integration,* and *Sociology of Race and Ethnicity.* He served as Vice Chair of the Somali Studies International Association from 2007 to 2015.

ABSTRACT

My purpose in this paper is to provide a preliminary conceptual map of the nature of slavery and the slave trade within and across the Red Sea region. This mapping will be articulated by way of what I refer to as the demographic, spatial, gender and racial geography of slavery. The demographic geography captures the size of the slave population absorbed within the Horn of Africa region and those exported across the Red Sea and Indian Ocean. The spatial geography is intended to capture the regional clustering of slavery. The gender and racial geographies capture the ways in which gender and racial identities informed the overall social and economic value of slaves. I specifically argue that understanding the demographic, spatial, gender and racial geographies of slavery is an important analytical tool to capture the nature and dynamics of slavery along the Red Sea region, and particularly to understand who has been enslaved, by whom and how.

Introduction

In reaction to the historically disproportionate focus of slavery scholarship on the Atlantic world, an increasing number of scholars over the past few decades have started to expand the scope of African slavery scholarship to include the slave trade across the Sahara (Wright 2007), the Indian Ocean (Campbell 2004; Gervase and Smith 1989; Jayasuriya and Pankhurst 2003) and the Mediterranean Sea (Hunwick and Troutt Powell 2002). This expansion of scope in slavery scholarship is a welcome contribution, but with very few exceptions (Ewald 1988) has created another blind spot by obscuring an equally important forced migration of African slaves within and across the Red Sea corridor. This lack of scholarship is unsustainable given the fact that slavery in the Red Sea region is arguably one of the oldest, most enduring and most complex systems in the global enslavement of people of African descent. It is arguably one of the oldest because the practice of slavery or unfree labour in the Red Sea region may have existed as far back as the first-dynasty pharaoh in 3000 CE. The Red Sea and the cities on its shores were of strategic importance, and control of these areas was crucial for the Phoenicians, Mycenaeans, Babylonians, Persians, Romans, Turks, and finally, Southern Arabians, each of whom fought bitterly with rival powers to assert control over the region, which was rich in frankincense, myrrh, spices and slaves. The Periplus of the Erythraen Sea, written around the first century CE, discusses the trade in African slaves from the region.

The Red Sea slave trade was one of the most complex, in that, unlike the transatlantic trade, which primarily linked West Africa with the Americas and Europe through the Atlantic, it involved an intricate web of routes and middle passages linking multiple overland and maritime ports and both domestic and external destinations. It involved the movement of slaves from all directions: the Sahara and the Nile Valley, south-western and southern Ethiopia, and the south-eastern Indian Ocean regions of Tanzania and Mozambique to local destinations in Ethiopia, Somalia and Zanzibar. From the Red Sea, slaves were taken to markets in southern Arabia through Sawakin, Tajura, Berbera and Zayla ports; across the Mediterranean to the Persian Gulf region; and to South Asia across the Indian Ocean. More important, the Red Sea slave trade intersected the region's pre-existing and historical commodity trade routes in such a way that the slave trade seamlessly became an integral part of everyday commodity trade.

It was also one of the most enduring in that it lasted much longer than either the Atlantic or Indian Ocean trade systems. Not even the British-led abolitionist initiatives of the nineteenth century could quell the trade, a success the British exhibited in other regions. Slavery in the region remained endemic and persistent, ebbing in one locale while flourishing in another, depending on the nature of global political and economic dynamics. Hence, the size of the slave population arriving in Egypt expanded during the global cotton boom as a result of the American Civil War and declined after the end of the boom in the 1870s. When British blockades dramatically decreased the number of slaves coming from the sea routes originating from Zanzibar and southern Somalia, slave exports increased in the sea ports of Suakin and Massawa to compensate for Arabia's loss of slaves from the Somali and Swahili coasts (Ewald 1988). Even the British navy was unsuccessful in stopping the flow of slaves across the Red Sea because slave traders adopted more ingenious strategies to avoid the British patrol of the major ports of the Red Sea. Slave boats were made indistinguishable from the numerous fishing boats that continuously hovered in the Red Sea from north to south. Boats filled with slaves engaged in evasive tactics and harboured not in the main ports but in isolated spots along the coast (Ewald 1988).

Beyond the tactics of slave traders, however, some European colonial powers' half-hearted commitment to abolition and other imperial motives contributed much to the slow death of slavery and the slave trade in the region (Lovejoy 2000). In the case of southern Somalia, for example, the Italian colony's abolition activities were partly fuelled by their interest in turning freed slaves into plantation indentured servants, which would provide the necessary labour for the Italian colonial dream of creating an industrial agricultural state in southern Somalia. Italy's interest in turning slaves into plantation workers was clear, according to Giotto Dainelli, considering that 'she imports annually from abroad about 150,000,000 lire's' worth of vegetable oils, about 650,000,000 of oil seeds, and about 1,800,000,000 of cotton, all products which can easily be grown in Somalia' (1931, 56). In fact, the Italian colony experimented with using freed slave labour to initiate commercial plantations in southern Somalia several times, once in 1906 along the banks of the Jubba and Shabelle Rivers and once again in 1912–20 at another area of the Jubba River, which failed due to technical and political problems, including World War I. In 1920, under the direction of Luigi di Savoia, the Duke of the Abruzzi, it took a concession for a tract of 25,000 hectares and within five years employed 14,000 freed slave families in a system that was not unlike slavery. The Italian colony created several other plantations that grew sesame, cotton and sunflowers, which collectively increased the annual value of the colonial export from 8,000,000 lire in 1915 to nearly 200,000,000 lire in 1929 (Dainelli 1931), confirming what Paul Lovejoy characterises as Europe's 'reluctant move toward abolition' (2000, 11).

It is, in fact, arguable that the social contexts that led to the formation, development and decline of the Red Sea slave trade were fundamentally different from those that characterised the Atlantic slave trade. Unlike the transatlantic slave trade dominated by Christian communities, the Red Sea slave trade involved interaction and accommodation between Christian and Muslim communities and so reveals the extent to which Muslim and Christian traders and authorities tacitly collaborated on the slave trade in Ethiopia, Sudan and Somalia.

This paper is part of a larger project designed to provide a preliminary conceptual map of the nature of slavery and the slave trade within and across the Red Sea region. This mapping will be articulated in terms of what I refer to as the demographic, spatial and social geography of slavery in the region. The demographic geography captures the size of the slave population absorbed within the region and those exported across the Red Sea. The spatial geography is intended to capture the regional sources and trade networks of slavery, while the social geography captures the sociological aspects of slavery in the region. The demographic, spatial and social geography dimensions should not be understood as methodologically distinct categories, but rather as being interconnected such that the spatial geography informs the sociological aspects of slavery in the region. It also important to note that the spatial geography of the Red Sea is fundamentally linked to the Indian Ocean in a country like Somalia where slavery was linked with both worlds. I specifically argue that the demographic and spatial geographies, or the regional sources of slaves, are important analytical tools for understanding the social geography of slavery, particularly who is enslaved, by whom and how.

The Demographic Geography of Red Sea Slavery

Richard Pankhurst's (1964) question about Ethiopia nearly fifty years ago, 'What is the extent of the slave trade in the nineteenth and twentieth centuries?' remains one of the most difficult questions regarding the slave trade in the entire Red Sea region. The question is complicated by the fact that slavery in the Red Sea region involved multiple sources and markets and oceanic and overland routes as well as clandestine trade and various destinations. Based on testimonials and reports of European travellers, resident missionaries and political consuls, Pankhurst (1964) constructs the first relatively organised data on the size of the slave trade in the region, and concludes that more than 25,000 slaves were exported annually from Red Sea ports, the Sudan frontiers, and, to some extent, the Banadir Coast of southern Somalia along the Indian Ocean. This, according to Pankhurst (1964), translates to about 1,250,000 between 1800 and 1850, or the equivalent of 2,500,000 slaves per century. This number is made more significant given that the population of Ethiopia around the turn of the nineteenth century was not more than 9 million, an indication that a sizeable percentage of the total population of Ethiopia may have been enslaved (Austin 1989).

The second and most important estimate of the slave trade from the region was provided by Ralph Austen (1988) some ten years after that of Pankhurst (1964). Austen organises the data according to the specific ports from which slaves were exported, clustering them into different decades. For example, from 1800 to 1884, some 235,000 slaves were exported from Gulf of Aden ports, with 9,000 and 4,500 in the decades of 1885–90 and 1891–99, respectively. Thus, about 250,000 slaves were exported from the Red Sea during the nineteenth century. Another 111,000 slaves were exported from Massawa, 24,000 from Northern Danakil, and 107,000 from Suakin. Austen concludes that about 492,000 slaves were exported from the

Red Sea during the entire span of the nineteenth century. An important aspect of Austen's estimates is his attempt to correlate the observed data of the sending and receiving ports for selected years. For example, in 1856, ports in western Arabia received 8,659 slaves, when only some 6,000 were exported from Red Sea ports. Austen also provides estimates of the size of the Black resident population in different countries and regions of Arabia and the Persian Gulf, and finds that the size of the Black resident population was much larger than the export estimates. This means that the data gathered from both sending and receiving points do not correlate with the observed resident population in many of the countries and cities of the Arabian Peninsula and the Persian Gulf. In 1831, 50 per cent of the population of Bahrain were slaves or of slave descent, a number much larger than that from the sending and the receiving points. This disjuncture is made more complicated by the observation that the 'Muslim areas in question contained no large-scale plantation systems rivaling those of the New World or even those of Muslims and Europeans in the Western Indian Ocean' (Austen 1988, 39).

Estimates regarding the number of slaves transported from Sudan during the eighteenth and nineteenth centuries are only approximations and rely on the data provided by European travellers of the period. Ritter observes that by 1820 Darfur caravans were filled with slaves numbering in the thousands every year. Burkhardt also notes that more than 5,000 slaves reached the market at Shendi every year and that half this number reached the Red Sea port of Sawakin. Of the remaining half, about 1,500 were transported to Egypt, while the local market absorbed the rest. In Sawakin, the last stop on the eastern frontier of the caravan slave trade route, Burkhardt reports that between 2,000 and 3,000 slaves were transported yearly.

The number of slaves imported into Somalia over the nineteenth century is even more difficult to estimate than for Ethiopia, Sudan or across the Red Sea. Unlike most other slave-importing regions, where historians have attempted to quantify the slave trade by looking at the traces and records both at the exit and destination points, the data for the slave trade in Somalia are primarily based on estimates derived from the size of the runaway slave communities along the Jubba Valley, otherwise known as the Gosha. The most representative comment on slavery in Somalia is that while it is difficult to know the number of slaves imported into Somalia over the second half of the nineteenth century, the remarkable growth of the runaway slave communities in the Goshaland indicates that tens of thousands of slaves may have been imported into southern Somalia. Dundas and Craufurd provide two of the most important estimates of the size of the runaway slave communities in the Goshaland. Craufurd, acting Commissioner and Consul General at Mombasa, proceeding from Kismanyo on 8 June 1895, on his way to Gosha and particularly the Wamo Deshek, provides the following:

On approaching Songoro Mafula's town [Tula], numerous villages and plantations of maize were passed; Tula itself is [a] thriving place, with comfortable bell-
shaped houses divided by a wall into two apartments. Gosha, of which this one of
the principal villages, is a fertile agricultural district extending for about 50 miles
along both banks of [sic] Jub. (1897, 56)

Craufurd estimates the Wamo Deshek population of former or runaway slaves as
25,000 to 30,000. In another trip in the same year, Craufurd visited Aff Madu [Af
Madow] and provides the following description: 'Aff Madu contains about one
hundred villages, with from 15,000 to 20,000 inhabitants, including a considerable
slave population of Gallas, Masai-Kikuyu, and Wakamba' (Craufurd 1897, 57–
58).

Just three years before Craufurd, Commander F. G. Dundas (1893) estimated the
population of the Gosha runaway community as 30,000 to 40,000. It is, in fact,
very likely that Dundas's visit may have coincided with the formation and initial
settlement of the Gosha community because, according to him, 'The clearings in
the forest were still being carried out' (Dundas 1893, 216). In Shonde, the last village he visited, Dundas writes, 'There were only about thirty people in all, and
they had lately arrived from one of the larger villages to establish a settlement and
clear the forest for cultivation' (Dundas 1893, 216).

Another estimation comes from scholars using Cassanelli's (1982) observation
that because land among the agropastoral communities between the Shabelle and
Jubba valleys was collectively owned by the lineage groups, farm size 'rarely ex-
ceeded forty acres; the average was more like five or ten; and therefore, few
landowners had more than ten or fifteen slaves' (Cassanelli 1982, 173). Using the
above comment along with Cerrina-Ferroni's estimate of the 25,000 to 30,000
slaves in southern Somalia out of a population of 300,000 – and her estimate of the
average slaves per household from her fieldwork in the upper Gosha – Besteman
suggests that 3,800 families owned slaves in southern Somalia (Besteman 1999,
56). Using the same assumptions derived from Cassanelli, Martin and Ryan (1988)
construct several deductive assumptions: based on aerial maps taken from the
lower Jubba Valley in the late nineteenth century, roughly 153,600 acres were
under cultivation.

Of this, one-fifth may have been under crop each year; one slave could look
after 1.5 acres per year, requiring roughly 20,500 slaves. The authors further assume a 5 per cent natural decline, which in turn would require a replenishment of
roughly 2,070 slaves per year to reach a population of 35,000 in 1896. The question is: From where did the 2,070 individuals required to build to the above number in 1896 come? The answer, according to the authors, is based on the 3,000
to 4,000 slaves that Sullivan and Ylvisaker reported as being imported to southern

Table 1a
Estimated Slave Population in Southern Somalia, 1800–1900

Region	Total Population	Slave Population	% Slave Population	Source
Banadir	300,000	25,000–30,000	25	Cerrina-Ferroni
Inter-riverine		50,000	16	Cassanelli
Southern Somalia	500,000	100,000	20	Estimate
Lama/Bajun/Banadir		300,000		Martin and Ryan

Table 1b
Gosha Freed/Runaway Slave Population: 1840–1900

Goshaland	Slave Population	Source
	25,000–30,000	Craufurd
	30,000–40,000	Dundas
Avai	2,500–3,000	Cassanelli

Somalia in the 1870s. With a 5 per cent natural decline in mind, the authors con-clude that roughly 300,000 slaves were retained in the Lamu/Bajun/Banadir Coasts. According to Martin and Ryan (1980, 124):

This is over two-thirds of the number believed to have gone to Arabia, Persia, and India from East Africa between 1770 and 1896. It is almost double the number that went from all sources to the Mascarenes. We must therefore view the area of the Bajun and Banadir Coasts as one of the world's major slave markets.

Given the fact that Martin and Ryan compute estimates derived from the entire Lamu area (the Bajun Coast) extending from the Somali border to the Tana River, it is very difficult to know what proportion of the supposedly 300,000 slaves re-tained in the region was actually absorbed into Somalia. Nevertheless, it is clear that southern Somalia absorbed a significant number of slaves, particularly in the last decades of the nineteenth century.

In fact, by the turn of the twentieth century, the three most important port cities along the Banadir Coast had a significant slave population. Nearly one-third of the population in Mogadishu, 33 per cent, was of slave background. About 830 of the 3,000 (about 28 per cent) of the residents in Barava and 14 per cent in Merka were also of slave background. It is apparent from the preceding discussion that the

Table 2
Slave Population in the Three Largest Port Cities of Southern Somalia

Banadir Coastal Cities	Total Population	Slave Population	% Slave Population
Mogadishu	6,700	2,233	33
Barava	3,000	830	28
Merka	5,000	720	14
Total	14,700	3,783	26

Source: Cassanelli, 1988.

Red Sea region must be considered an important slave holding and exporting region of the nineteenth century.

The Spatial Geography of the Red Sea Slave Trade

The majority of enslaved populations within and across the Red Sea region were recruited from three regions: the southern and south-western regions of Ethiopia, the north-western border regions between Ethiopia and Sudan and the south-eastern Indian Ocean regions. Slaves from the southern and south-western regions of Ethiopia primarily came from the Cushitic-speaking Oromo, Sidama and Gurage populations. Slaves from the border regions between Ethiopia and Sudan came from Bantu groups collectively known in Ethiopia and Sudan as Shangalla, and those from the south-eastern Indian Ocean region were primarily taken from Tanzania and Mozambique.

   This regional clustering, or the demographic and spatial geography of the source of slaves in the region, informed the nature and dynamics of slavery and the slave trade in a number of significant ways. First, the regional clustering of the source of slaves correlated slavery with perceived desirability and/or quality by categorising slaves into aesthetically desirable and less desirable groups on the basis of racial characteristics, otherwise known as Red versus Black slaves. 'Red slaves' refers to slaves from ethnic groups perceived to be of lighter complexion and supposedly less African-like, such as the Oromo, Sidama or Gurage from the south-west and southern regions of Ethiopia. 'Black slaves' refers to the so-called negroid ethnic groups, Bertha, Mao, Khoma and the Gumuz; those from along the border regions between Ethiopia and Sudan; or Bantu ethnic groups from the south-eastern Indian Ocean regions of Tanzania and Mozambique (Abir 1968). The distinction between Red and Black slaves was primarily derived from the extent to which the enslaved groups were physically similar to or different from the Hamitic-Cushitic populations of the region and, ultimately, Southern Arabians. Since the Oromo, Sidama and

Gurage ethnic groups from which the Red slaves were taken were not racially different from the Amhara, Tigrinya and Somali ethnic groups in the region and were considered more tolerable in southern Arabia, they were perceived as more desirable. However, since the Black slaves were perceived as racially different, they were seen as less similar and less desirable except as slave labour. In Ethiopia, all non–Hamitic-Cushitic ethnic groups were referred to as Shangilla, meaning slaves. In Sudan, enslaved ethnic groups such as the Bertha and other border groups in the border between and Ethiopia and Sudan are known as (abid), the Arabic word for slave. In Somalia, enslaved groups were referred to as Adoon, meaning slave; Jareer, meaning 'kinky hair'; Gosha, 'people of the forest'; or Shabelle, 'people of Shabelle river', all names indicative of their supposed non-Somali origin.

Consequently, the Red-versus-Black slave dichotomy became a system of slave stratification such that potential slaves were divided into two groups of socially desirable and undesirable slaves, and it imposed a generalised stereotype about which slave group was fit for what occupation and which group brought the highest exchange rate both in the local and foreign destination markets. Richard Burton, who visited Harar in the 1850s, sums up this stereotype by observing, 'If you want a brother (in arms), says the Eastern proverb, buy a Nubian, if you want to be rich, an Abyssinian, if you want an ass, a Swahili (negroid)' (Burton 1966, 193 [footnote]). More specifically, the Red-versus-Black slave dichotomy informed decisions about which slave groups were destined for international markets and which for internal slavery. Red slaves, or slaves from the Hamitic-Cushitic groups, were more expensive and primarily routed to markets in the Middle East and the Persian Gulf. Black slaves were employed in local domestic and rural production.

This distinction between socially desirable versus undesirable slaves became particularly evident in the case of female slaves. In Egypt, Turkey and much of southern Arabia, the demand for concubines created a condition whereby Red slave girls became the most desirable slave companions, particularly after the occupation of Georgia by the Russians in the nineteenth century, which made the enslavement of Circassian female concubines more difficult. According to Abir, 'after the conquest of the Caucasus by the Russians, Ethiopian slave girls took first place in the slave markets of the Muslim world' (1968, 54).

Abyssinian female slaves were desirable, according to Wylde, because they were 'very pretty, have good figures, small hands, and feet, soon became most cleanly in their person and dress, picked up all benefits of civilization, get fairly educated, make good servants, and are faithful and lovable' (Wylde 1882, quoted in Mowafi 1980, 13). In essence, the central comments that informed much of the discussion of the relationship between slavery, the slave trade and gender along the Red Sea region concentrated on the desirability of Red female slaves and were silent on the role of Black female slaves, both in the local and international markets.

Whereas the slaves transported to the New World in the Atlantic from 1663 to 1864 were overwhelmingly male (64.6 per cent), the figures for the Red Sea trade tell a different story. The primary sources – travellers' journals and scholars – almost uniformly agree that 'at least two females arrived for every male' (Mirzai 2002). Indeed, slave women filled a variety of functions in the domestic arena and worked as washerwomen and nursemaids. Many also filled the ranks in the harems of their masters.

From the perspective of Islamic jurisprudence, the purchase of women slaves as concubines was lawful; indeed, this was the most common reason for purchasing female slaves. There is ample evidence to support this view. For instance, the Ummayad caliph Abd-al-Rahman III (r. 912–961) held over 6,000 concubines in the tenth century; and the harem of the Fatamid (909–1171) palace in Cairo housed 12,000 female slaves. Across the Middle East, Persia and Turkey, the ulama (the body of Muslim scholars dedicated among other things to interpreting and applying Shari'a law) accepted that a master could have an unlimited number of concubines, and certainly the owning of female slaves for such purposes became widespread in Arabia and the Persian Gulf (Hodgson 1974, 144). Wealthy families and officials maintained extensive harems with a number of wives and slave women and an equally trusted class of eunuchs and bodyguards who stood watch over them (Levy 1957).

Second, the spatial geography of the source of slaves in the region also correlated slavery with religion such that those who were enslaved were mainly non-Christian and non-Muslim, and those who owned slaves or participated in the trade were either Christian or Muslim. The majority of the population in the southern, south-western and border regions between Ethiopia and Sudan, and those from the south-eastern Indian Ocean, were neither Christian nor Muslim, and, therefore, were targeted for enslavement. Slave diaries collected by Ahmad (1992) suggest that almost all the local merchants and traders along the triangle between Shawa, Harar and the Red Sea coast were primarily Muslim, and those who owned and levied taxes on the slave routes were primarily Christian (Pankhurst 1968, 77–82). Also, according to Ahmad (1996, 548):

> Responsibility for the slave trade from Gumuz country to Dangila and then to Zage did not always lie with Muslim merchants alone. It appears instead Christian priests acted in concert with Muslims of Zage and Dangila to finance much of the internal trade in Gojjam in the early twentieth century.

In other words, both Christians and Muslims in the region participated in a system of division of labour, not only in the slave trade, but in trade generally. This division of labour was informed by two important factors. The first pertains to the social status of the Muslim community in Christian-dominated northern Ethiopia as a minority group. Muslims, as a minority excluded from participating in the political and economic institutions of Ethiopia, had no other means to survive except in the import of trade items from the Arabian peninsula and India and in the export of slaves to southern Arabia. The second factor that facilitated the participation of the Muslim community in the import of foreign commodities and the export of slaves and other Ethiopian products was the religious link they had with southern Arabia. In essence, then, the reason Muslim Ethiopians dominated the slave trade had nothing to do with their religion but rather was that they were excluded from legitimate commerce in Ethiopia and primarily relied on their good commercial contacts with their co-religious community across the Red Sea. Similarly, the reason Christian Ethiopians did not participate in the slave trade had nothing to do with their religion but instead was to do with the fact that they had other economic and political opportunities and did not have any commercial networks across the Red Sea.

Third, the spatial geography of the Red Sea slave trade provided a systematic ideology that offered the necessary justification for the trade. One of the most interesting pieces of evidence of the ideological justification of slavery in Christian Ethiopia is found in a thirteenth-century description of a religious miracle transcribed and copied during the reign of Lebna Dengel (1508–40; Haile 1981). The miracle was witnessed by an Ethiopian slave merchant, who was a God-fearing, devoted Christian.

According to the miracle, one day he bought a slave from a certain slave market, Damot, and was on his way to sell the slave in another, Barara, to make a profit. However, the slave escaped in the market crowd and took off with another man. Grief-stricken, the slave merchant bought a small amount of incense and three candles to give to a church built in the name of Our Lady Mary and sought divine intervention. On his way to the church, he met a woman in the likeness of Our Lady Mary along with two handsome men who asked him where he was coming from. He told the woman about all the grief that had befallen him as a result of losing his slave. After observing the candles and the incense, the lady asked him what he wanted to gain from the offering, and he responded that if Our Lady Mary helped him to secure his slave again, 'I shall please her very much and serve her until I depart from this world' (Haile 1981, 174). She gave him back the candles and the incense, preceded him to the church and disappeared. He then entered the church and gave the candles and the incense to the priest, who in turn prayed with him for the intervention of Our Lady Mary. After he finished his prayer, he found his slave waiting for him in front of the church door; the slave confirmed that a noble-looking lady with two young, handsome men had found him and told him to 'rise up quickly and go to your master, for behold, he is praying and supplicating in my church. She then disappeared from me' (Haile 1981, 175) After realising the divine power of Our Lady Mary, this good man donated his slave to the church in the name of Mary to cut wood and fetch water for the church until his death. The master of the slave thereafter lived celebrating Our Lady Mary and entered the kingdom of heaven by the intercession of Our Lady Mary.

The account of the miracle establishes not only the historical existence of slavery and slave markets within Ethiopia but also that slavery in Ethiopia was geographically and ethnically determined. It shows that slaves in Ethiopia came primarily from the south and that slavery was associated with people of darker complexion more than with the semitised northern and highland populations. Most importantly, the miracle represents a clear indication that, in fact, devoted Christians participated in the slave trade and that religion provided not only an ideological justification but also divine assistance for slave owners to police and recover their slaves when they ran away.

Following Arab influence in northern Sudan in the late 1700s, slave raids became increasingly aggressive along its southern frontier, and slave traders used a number of epithets to label peoples of African descent, including Zanj and Habeshi for the populations of the eastern coast of Africa and the Ethiopians, respectively. These were usually pejorative, with the intention of keeping a distinction between 'Arab' and 'other'. In the same instance, such ideological battles were reproduced within Sudan, perpetuating a series of racial epithets applied to non-Muslim groups in the south. These labels were varied, and included Fertit (for the region below Darfur) and Shankalla (for the area south of Sinnar). Although prohibited according to Islamic law, Muslim individuals were also enslaved, of which there are ample examples (O'Fahey 1985, 85).

The racial epithets used to distinguish non-Muslims were further extended once they were brought into the periphery of the household. For instance, young boys were circumcised and given Arabic names, but, oddly enough, the names were peculiar. Names such as Sabah al Khayr ('Good morning'), Jurab ('Leather bag'), and Ata Minnu ('God's gift') were common. This tacit tactic, adopted partly to distinguish and dehumanise slaves, was a constant reminder that further legitimised the existence and aggressive expansion of the slave trade in eighteenth- to nineteenth-century Sudan. Burkhardt (1829, 98) remarks on this naming distinction between a Muslim and a slave:

> They are seldom honoured [italics added] with a true Muslim name; such as Hassan, Mohammed, Selim, and Mustapha. Most of them bear such names as these: Kheyr el illah [Khayr Allah]; Fadil 'ilah [Fadl Allah]; Fadil Elwasia [Fadl el-Wasi]; Jaber Wadjed [Jabr Wajid]; Om Elkheyr [Umm al-Khayr], and the like.

Table 3
Annual Estimates of Domestic Slave Consumption versus External Trade

	Total Number	*Per cent*
Annual Slave Production	15,000	—
Domestic Slave Consumption	6,500	43
Total Export	7,500	50
Total Unaccounted For	1,000	7
Slaves Retained in Different Locales		
Omotic States (approximate)	1,000	15
Gibe States (approximate)	1,000	15
Shawa	500	8
Gojjam, Wallo, Begemder and Tigre	3,500	54
Harar	500	8
Exit Points of External Slave Trade		
Qallabat	1,600	21
Massawa	1,755	23
Tajura	2,088	28
Zeyla	800	11
Berbera	1,400	19

Source: Fernyhough, Timothy. 1988.

Intersection of Commodity Trade and Slave Trade

The routes used for slavery were the same used for everyday trade in Ethiopia, throughout the region, and across the Red Sea. Therefore, beyond food and water, slavery did not represent extra transportation costs. In fact, it may have even reduced the cost of transporting trade goods from the south to the north and the Red Sea ports because slave labour was used to transport goods. In other words, slaves generated profit both through their labour and through the sale of their bodies. That slaves were used as transport vehicles is corroborated by the diaries of some of the traders between Shawa, Harar and the Somali ports of the Gulf of Aden. One such diary clearly points out that both slaves and camels were used in transporting Amole salt. Even across the Red Sea, slaves were not carried in any specialised or retrofitted dhows; they doubled as part of the trade goods without any extra space or provisions. This was possible because unlike in the transatlantic trade, where specialised ships were used to transport hundreds of slaves at once, the Red Sea dhows carried only several dozen slaves at a time (Abir 1968).

Trade Routes and Domestic Absorption

Another important dimension of Red Sea slavery is the proportion of those absorbed within the region to those exported. One way to explore the intersection between domestic absorption and the size of the external trade is to follow local trade routes and disentangle the size of the exported population from those retained locally. One scholar who attempted that is Timothy Fernyhough, whose local absorption data provides a meaningful framework for studying the intersection between export and local absorption.

Slave traffic across Ethiopia primarily started in the south and proceeded either north or north-east. To the north, slaves passed through Limmu-Enarya to Basso. From Basso, they were taken to Gondor and ultimately to Qallabat, where they were sold in the markets of Sudan and Egypt or to southern Arabia through Massawa. The second, and most important, route took Ethiopian slaves from the south and south-west through Jemma and then to Andodi and Roggi. From there, slaves passed through Harar and were finally exported to southern Arabia and the Persian Gulf by way of Zeyla and Berbera. Others passed through Shawa and Abdel Rassul toward Tajura. However, not all the slaves who passed through these markets were destined for export; a significant percentage was retained at each point of the route.

Following Fernyhough's estimate, between 1830 and 1850, roughly 13,000 to 15,000 slaves were sold in the markets of Kaffa, Kullo, Konta, Kucha, Walamo and Janjera, of which 1,000 were absorbed. From there, an estimated 7,500 were taken to Limmu-Enarya, of which some 500 were absorbed, and about 7,000 passed to Basso, Ifag and Gondor. From Gondor, slaves were sent either to Massawa or Qallabat, where 1,600 were exported to Sudan and another 1,755 to southern Arabia through Massawa. A second slave route took a north-easterly direction, taking 4,500 slaves to Jemma, where roughly 500 were absorbed and the rest continued to Shawa through Andodi and Rogge. From Shawa, slaves were taken to Massawa through Dase or to Abel Rassuel, at which point they were either taken directly to Tajura, or to Zeyla and Berbera through Harar. Harar absorbed about 500 slaves annually as well. Based on the above information, we can generalise that of the 13,000 to 15,000 slaves extracted from southern Ethiopia, roughly equal numbers were absorbed and exported: 43 and 50 per cent, respectively. Of the slaves who were retained, about 30 per cent were absorbed into the Omotic and Gibe states, while more than 60 per cent were retained in Shawa, Gojjam, Wallo, Begemder and Tigre. Another 8 per cent were retained in Harar annually. Of those

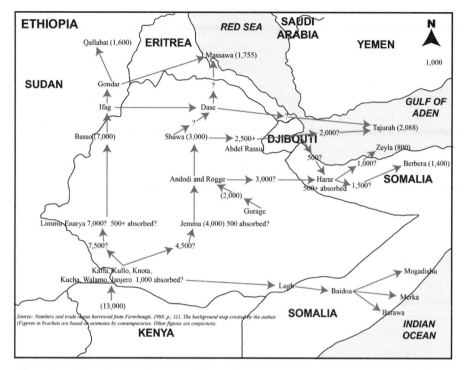

Fig. 1. Tentative estimates of slave traffic and domestic absorption (per annum), 1830–1850.

exported, 21 per cent passed through Qallabat, and roughly 23 per cent passed through Massawa. The rest were exported from the Somali/Djibouti ports of the Gulf of Aden. Of the Gulf of Aden ports, some 11 per cent were exported from Zeyla and another 19 per cent from Berbera. The largest number, however, passed through the port of Djibouti, Tajura, where some 28 per cent were exported from 1830 to 1850. Another source of slaves that is not shown in the figure originated from the north-western borderlands between Ethiopia and the Sudan.

Moreover, understanding the nature of slavery and the slave trade in the Red Sea region will allow us to build on Paul Lovejoy's (2000) articulation of the relationship between slavery as a mode of production and the social formation and transformations that may result from such a mode of production. According to Lovejoy, 'a slave mode of production prevailed whenever slavery was crucial to the productive process in general, and to some sector of the economy, particularly if that sector was tied to the export trade' (Lovejoy 2000, 277).

Lovejoy identifies two important historical and geographical prerequisites for the identification of a particular mode of production as slave mode. First, the identification of a production system as a slave mode requires the availability of an instrument of enslavement institutionalised in the legal, religious and economic structures. Second, for a slave mode of production to be empirically identified, a certain level of hegemonic organisational structure must exist such that 'those who controlled the system collectively benefited from slavery as an institution' (Lovejoy 2000, 278). Based on these prerequisites, Lovejoy suggests that Africa experienced a slave mode of production, which, in turn, contributed to the social, political and economic transformation of many African societies.

Lovejoy's discussion about the nature of the transformation that resulted from the appearance of the slave mode of production in Africa is part of a larger scholarship that has, over the past half century, attempted to wrestle with the question: How did slavery and slave labour contribute to the development of industrial capitalism in Europe, and, by extension, how did slavery transform African societies?

By using the Red Sea slave trade, particularly as it took place in different regions of Ethiopia and Somalia, we hope to suggest that neither the slave mode of production nor the nature of social and economic transformation as a result of slavery can be applied uniformly to the entire region. There is ample evidence that despite extensive participation in the slave trade, some regions within the Red Sea slave sphere did not develop appreciable levels of the slave mode of production, such that one cannot even observe any trace of slavery or the slave trade (Table 1). In the case of Somalia, for example, the Banadir Coast can be characterised as having experienced a slave mode of production, and a significant social and economic transformation occurred. Today, a significant portion of southern Somalia's population is of slave background, distinguishable from the rest of the population. These communities are still stigmatised and discriminated against at all levels of the social, political and economic institutions of the society (Eno 2008).

In the case of the Gulf of Aden ports, Tajura, Zeyla and Berbera, we see a situation where, despite their extensive participation in the Red Sea slave trade, no meaningful trace of a slave mode of production is noticeable historically or contemporaneously. This may have been caused by the prevalence of what I refer to

Table 4
Regional Differences in Slave Mode Production

	Region	*Slave Mode of Production*
Ethiopia	Zage	Yes
	Lasta	No
Somalia	Banadir Coast	Yes
	Gulf of Aden ports	No

here as subsistence slave trade production. By subsistence slave trade production, I mean the existence of large number of itinerant peasant traders in the Red Sea region who bought or sold only a few slaves, and who, as in subsistence production, bought them at a time when much of the profit made was primarily for subsistence consumption. According to Abir (1968, 65):

> One may assume that the gross profit of the slave-merchants of Tajura was about 100 per cent in Tajura and even 200 per cent in Berbera and Arabia. However, the slave merchant spent on average about six months in the process of paying his slaves, waiting for the caravan, travelling to the coast and waiting for the slaves to regain their strength before sending them on to Berbera and Arabia. If one considers all the risks taken by the slave merchant, the expenses on the road and the fact that the average Tajuran could not afford to buy more than a few slaves on each trip, the profits of most Tajuran merchants were small. At most, they might have been sufficient to cover the expenses of his large family. In fact, the accumulation of capital in Tajura was very slow and most of the Tajurans remained poor.

Berbera, one of the principal slave ports of the Gulf of Aden, did not experience a slave mode of production either. Berbera hosted an annual trade fair, which brought trade caravans from all parts of the interior and traders from Arabia, India and the Persian Gulf. The fair, held between October and March, boasted many kinds of commodities, including a significant number of Ethiopian slaves. Lieutenant Cruttenden (1848, 52) writes the following of the fair:

> By the end of March the fair is nearly at a close, and craft of all kinds, deeply laden, and sailing generally in parties of three and four, commence their homeward journey ... and by the first week in April, Berbera is again deserted, nothing being left to mark the site of a town lately containing 20,000 inhabitants, beyond bones of slaughtered camels and sheep ... and in April last year, but a week after the fair had ended, I observed three ostriches quietly walking on the beach.

What is clear from the above statement and many other sources is that the Berbera Fair, which exported a significant number of slaves through the port of Berbera, was primarily a mobile fair and introduced neither a slave mode of production nor any noticeable social transformation. The two contexts in Ethiopia also show a similar pattern. In the Zage region, a coffee plantation with a slave mode of production developed in the first three decades of the twentieth century. However, in the Lasta region, where poor peasants owned the majority of the slaves, no slave mode of production appeared. Supporting this argument empirically will require extensive comparison of regions in both Somalia and Ethiopia.

Conclusions and Future Research Directions

The Red Sea slave trade remains one of the least studied areas of research. While the literature on the transatlantic slave trade is rich, detailed and multidisciplinary, the same cannot be said for that of the Red Sea slave trade, which suffers from a paucity of scholars and a lack of concerted efforts and research interests. This lack of scholarship is unsupportable because, properly studied, the nature of Red Sea slavery and slave trade has the potential to contribute to slavery scholarship in a number of fundamental ways. First, because the social, political and economic contexts that led to the formation, development and decline of the Red Sea slave trade were fundamentally different from those that characterised the Atlantic slave trade, exploring these contexts will advance our understanding of slavery in general. Unlike the transatlantic slave trade, which was dominated by Christian communities, the Red Sea slave trade involved interaction and accommodation between Christian and Muslim communities, and therefore reveals the extent to which Muslim and Christian traders and authorities tacitly collaborated on the slave trade in Ethiopia, Sudan and Somalia. Another important feature of Red Sea slavery is the extent to which slave trade routes were incorporated into existing historical commodity trade routes, which may have lessened the development of social transformation based on the slave mode of production.

Second, exploring Red Sea slavery will further extend our understanding of the intersection between ethnicity and slavery. Unlike in the transatlantic slave trade, Red Sea slavery correlated slavery with ethnic and racial identities and rated perceived desirability and/or quality by categorising slaves into aesthetically desirable and less desirable groups on the basis of racial characteristics, Red versus Black slaves, as discussed above. Consequently, the Red-versus-Black slave dichotomy became a system of slave stratification such that potential slaves were divided into socially desirable and undesirable slaves, and it imposed a generalised stereotype about which slave group was fit for what occupation and which group brought the highest exchange rate both in local and foreign markets.

Third, understanding the nature and dynamics of slavery in the Red Sea region will allow us to build on Lovejoy's seminal 1983 observation that

> slavery as a mode of production in Africa was transformed as a result of its interaction with receiving areas through capitalism, and therefore became a fundamental aspect of social formation of different African societies. (277)

By using Red Sea slavery as a case study, it is possible to extend Lovejoy's Transformations in Slavery concept by examining the extent to which slave modes of production developed along the Red Sea Valley, and if they did, how that affected social formation based on slave modes of production in different regions and coastal areas. More specifically, understanding the nature of Red Sea slavery may give us the opportunity to grapple with the question of why, despite extensive participation in the slave trade, some regions along the Red Sea developed appreciable levels of social formation based on the slave mode of production, while others did not. This question can be explored by comparing the Indian Ocean Banadir Coast of Somalia with the coasts of the Gulf of Aden and the Red Sea, on the one hand, and the highland regions of Ethiopia and the border areas between Ethiopia and Sudan, on the other. In each comparative pair, there is ample evidence that social transformation based on a slave mode of production occurred in some regions and not in others.

However, exploring this scholarly potential will require extensive interdisciplinary oral, archaeological and archival research, the last of which must be conducted at sites of particular importance: National Archives of Sudan (Khartoum), Italian Archives, Addis Ababa University, Ethiopia (Ministry of Baria documents), National Archives of Egypt (Cairo, Egypt) and National Archives of Turkey (Ankara and Istanbul, Turkey). A concerted effort must also be made to collect and assemble oral histories in Sudan, Egypt, Eritrea and Somalia, where populations of ex-slaves continue to live; their narratives are important components of the reconstruction of the Red Sea slave trade. Such an action is but a step in addressing the profound and disturbing silence on the Red Sea slave trade both in academic circles and in the general education system of the countries that exported and imported slaves. Such efforts carry the potential of unearthing a bitter past while paving the way for a discourse that does justice to the millions of victims of the Red Sea slave trade.

Since this work is primarily derived from secondary sources, it is vulnerable to the shortcomings from which all such works may suffer. To comprehend fully the nature of slavery and the slave trade along the Nile Valley and across the Red Sea, we must conduct fundamental research on the different aspects of the slavery in the region. Such research must not only deal with the sources, but also the societies into which these slaves were inserted, the extent to which they assimilated into their host communities, and the kinds of discrimination they faced and continue to face. To do this, we must carefully locate, examine, digitise and record archival records both in the origin and destination points. Travel accounts, literary traditions and oral sources must be translated and analysed. A multi-task and multidisciplinary effort is imperative for the reconstruction and understanding of the history of the Red Sea slave trade.

BIBLIOGRAPHY

Abir, M., 1968. *Ethiopia: The Era of the Princes, Challenges of Islam and Reunification of the Christian Empire, 1769–1855*. New York: Frederick A. Praeger.

Ahmad, A. H., 1996. Priest planters and slaves of Zage (Ethiopia), 1900–1935. *The International Journal of African Historical Studies* 29/3, 543–56.

Austen, R. A., 1979. The Trans-Saharan Slave Trade: A tentative census. In H. A. Gemery and J. S. Hogendorn, eds., *The Uncommon Market: Essays in the Economic History of the Atlantic Slave Trade*. New York: Academic Press, 23–75.

Austen, R. A., 1988. The 19th century Islamic slave trade from East Africa (Swahili and Red Sea coasts): a tentative census. *Slavery and Abolition* 9/3, 33.

Beachey, R. W., 1976. *The Slave Trade of East Africa*. London: Rex Collings.

Besteman, C. L., 1999. *Unraveling Somalia: Race, Class, and the Legacy of Slavery*. Philadelphia: University of Pennsylvania Press.

Burkhardt, J. L., 1829. *Travel in Arabia, comprehending an account of those territories of the Hedjaz which the Mohammedans regard as sacred*. The Association for Promoting the Discovery of the Interior Parts of Africa. London: Henry Colburn.

Burton, R., 1966. *First Footsteps in East Africa*. New York: Frederick A. Praeger.

Campbell, G., ed., 2004. *The Structure of Slavery in Indian Ocean Africa and Asia*. London: Frank Cass.

Cassanelli, L. V., 1982. *The Shaping of Somalia Society: Reconstructing History of a Pastoral People, 1600–1900*. Philadelphia: University of Pennsylvania Press.

Cassanelli, L. V., 1988. The ending of slavery in Italian Somaliland: Liberty and the control of labor, 1890–1935. In: S. Miers and R. Roberts, eds., *The End of Slavery in Africa*. Madison: University of Wisconsin Press, 332–61.

Christopher, W., 1844. Extract from a journey by Lieut. W. Christopher, commanding the H. C. brig of war 'Tigris', on the E. coast of Africa. Dated 8th May, 1943. *Journal of the Royal Geographical Society* 14, 87.

Craufurd, C. H., 1897. Journeys in Gosha and beyond the Deshek Wama (Lake Harding). *The Geographical Journal* 9/1, 56.

Cruttenden, C. J., 1949. Memoir on the Western Edoor tribes, inhabiting the Somali coast of N-E Africa, with the southern branches of the family of Darood, resident on the banks of Webbe Shabeyli, commonly called River Webbe. *Journal of the Royal Geographical Society of London* 19, 49–76.

Dainelli, Giotto, 1931. The agricultural possibilities of Somaliland. *Geographical Review* 21/1, 59–69.

Dundas, F. G., 1893. Expedition up the Jub River through Somali-Land. *East Africa* 1/3, 216.

Eno, O., 2005. The abolition of slavery and the aftermath stigma: The case of the Bantu/ Jareer people on the Banadir Coast of Southern Somalia. In: G. Campbell, ed., *Abolition and Its Aftermath in Indian Ocean Africa and Asia*. London: Routledge, 83–93.

Ewald, J., 1988. The Nile Valley system and the Red Sea slave trade, 1820–1880. *Slavery and Abolition* 9/3, 71–92.

Fernyhough, T., 1988. Slavery and the slave trade in southern Ethiopia in the 19th century. *Slavery and Abolition* 9/3, 103–30.

Gervase, W. and Smith, C., 1989. *The Economics of the Indian Ocean Slave Trade in the Nineteenth Century*. London: Routledge.

Haile, G., 1981. From the markets of Damot to that of Barara. *Paideuma* 27, 173–80.

Hess, R., 1966. *Italian Colonialism in Somalia*. Chicago: The University of Chicago Press.

Hodgson, M. G. S., 1974. *The Venture of Islam: Conscience and History in a World Civilization*. 3 vols. Chicago: University of Chicago Press.

Hunwick, J. and Troutt Powell, E., 2002. *The African Diaspora in the Mediterranean Lands of Islam*. The Princeton Series on the Middle East. Princeton: Markus Wiener.

Jayasuriya, S. D. S. and Pankhurst, R., eds., 2003. *The African Diaspora in the Indian Ocean*. Trenton: Africa World Press.

Kirk, J., 1873. Visit to the coast of Somali-Land. *Proceedings of the Royal Geographical Society of London* 17/5, 340–45.

Levy, R., 1957. *The Social Structure of Islam*. Cambridge: Cambridge University Press.

Lovejoy, P. E., 2000. *Transformations in Slavery: A History of Slavery in Africa*. 2nd ed. Cambridge: Harvard University Press.

Luling, V., 2002. *Somali Sultanate: The Geledi City-State over 150 Years*. London: Haan.

Martin, E. B. and Ryan, T. C., 1977. A quantitative assessment of the Arab slave trade of East Africa: 1770–1896. *Kenya Historical Review* 5/1, 71–91.

Martin, E. B. and Ryan, T. C., 1980. The slave trade of the Bajun and Banadir coasts. *Transafrican Journal of History* 9/1–2, 103–32.

McCann, J., 1988. 'Children of the house': Slavery and its suppression in Lasta, Northern Ethiopia, 1916–1935. In S. Miers and R. Roberts, eds., *The End of Slavery in Africa*. Madison: University of Wisconsin Press, 308–31.

Mirzai, B., 2002. African presence in Iran: Identity and its reconstruction in the 19th and 20th centuries. *Outre-Mers: Revue d'Histoire* 89/336, 234.

Mowafi, R., 1981. *Slavery, Slave Trade, and Abolition Attempts in Egypt and the Sudan, 1820-1882*. Lund: Lund Studies in International History.

O'Fahey, R. S., 1985. Slavery and society in Darfur. In J.R. Willis, ed., *Slaves and Society in Muslim Africa*, v. 2. London: Frank Cass.

Omer, A.H., 2001., Some notes on Harar and the local trade routes: A report on the view of ex-merchants of Shawa (1839–1935). *Annales di Ethiopie* 17, 135–47.

Pankhurst, R., 1964. The Ethiopian slave trade in the nineteenth and early twentieth century: A statistical inquiry. *Journal of Semitic Studies* 9/10, 220–28.

Pankhurst, R., 1968. *Economic History of Ethiopia, 1800–1935*. Addis Ababa: Haile Selassie I University Press.

Pankhurst, R., 1974. Indian trade with Ethiopia, the Gulf of Aden and the Horn of Africa in the nineteenth and early twentieth centuries. *Cahiers d'Etudes Africaneis* 14/55, 453–497.

Wylde, A. B., *'83 to '87 in the Sudan.* 2 vols. London 1888.

Wright, J., 2007. *The Trans-Saharan Slave Trade.* London and New York: Routledge.

Slavery, Ecology and Commerce
A Study of Slave Estates and Trans-Saharan Trade in Katsina Emirate c. 1804–1903

Abubakar Babajo Sani

BIOGRAPHY

Abubakar Babajo Sani, PhD, is a Professor of History in the Department of History, Umaru Musa Yar'adua University, Katsina, Nigeria. Currently, he is also Deputy Vice Chancellor (Administration) at the same university. He studied History at Bayero University, Kano, Nigeria. He taught for several years (1995–2007) at the Nigeria Defence Academy, Kaduna. He is the Editor-in-Chief of *TAGUWA: the Journal of Humanities* of the Faculty of Humanities, Umaru Yar'adua University, Katsina. He was a Post-Doctoral Research Fellow with the Harriet Tubman Institute for Research on the Global Migrations of African People, York University, Toronto, Canada (2011). He is the author of *Trade Diplomacy, Banking and Finance in the Trans-Saharan Trade: An Interpretation of Ahmad Abu al-Ghaith's Ledger, a Trade Consul in Katsina 1824–1870*, published by Pyla-mak, Kaduna, 2012. His main research interest is on aspects of the economic history of Africa, the trans-Saharan slave trade and the economies of the Central Sudan (West Africa).

ABSTRACT

This study answers questions of relative importance in connection to estate slavery, desert-side commerce in Northern Katsina emirate in the nineteenth century. For any meaningful research on aspects of the trans-Saharan slave trade to take place, there must be a review of the interconnection between the plantation economy and societies located on the desert fringes and the desert tribes, especially of Katsina whose location on the desert fringes was of paramount importance. Very little research has been done on these aspects. Within this purview, this research paper explores several plantations or estates established by migrant communities from the desert side whose livelihood depended significantly on the Sahelian region. This dependency resulted in the establishment of slave estates in various districts by desert tribes from North Africa: Teda Daza (Tubu) from Chad; Tuareg from Abzin in several peri-urban districts of Katsina Emirate. These estates were linked in various ways not only as reservoirs of slaves in the trans-Saharan slave trade, but also as grain production centres for the desert side for much of the nineteenth century. This presentation reveals a history of several decades of trans-Saharan slavery and slave trade, economic mingling, migration and cultural miscegenation between the desert side and the Sahelian society.

Introduction

Economic historians and economic anthropologists have long appreciated the role of the areas within the desert fringes in West Africa in their relationship with the desert side. This is because of a very long history of interdependency and, thus, many people have emphasised the need to understand the relationship between desert and savanna. It should be highlighted that Hausaland and Borno were regarded as the granary, as reservoirs of slaves, and as textile-producing centres for the desert people. Since the desert economy could not grow beyond a certain point, the forging of close links between desert and savanna was therefore inevitable. The continued safeguarding of these links hinged on forging strong trade diplomacy between the communities. The desert and savanna were at this level bound together by slavery, migration, estate production of commodities and commerce. For the Tuareg secured a living from the harsh desert environment through specialisation in animal husbandry, trade and transport. Although their mobility and skill in warfare enabled them to dominate the relatively fertile areas of the Sahel, they also relied strongly on estate production of grain and on trade in their relations with both Sahel and savanna. It is along this line that one can understand the importance of peaceful coexistence between the Hausa states, Borno and the Tuaregs, and this apparently was the reason behind the trade and the establishment of safe areas for grain production. For the Tuareg of the Massif, Adar, Azaouak and Damergou, this meant relying on the areas centring on the Hausa states for much of the supply of their food, clothing and other commodities sourced from Hausaland. The Tuareg could live on milk from their animals for extended periods of time, but they required grain to supplement their diet. Millet consumption averaged as much as 150 kg per person per year, a quantity much larger than could be supplied by the scattered and highly unreliable grain production of the 'Air' or desert oases.

Some Remarks on Slavery, Ecology, Desert-side Migration and Commerce

One of the principal north-south corridors of trade and transhumance in the nineteenth century extended from Agadez through Damergou and Damagaram (Zinder), and ended at Katsina and Kano. The Kel-Owi confederation dominated this route, and its members invested considerable capital in trade and in large estates with slaves dedicated to grain production along the corridor (Nicolaisen 1959, 67–131). Sections of the Kel Gress confederation dominated the route that began at Teguidda n'tesemt in the Azaouak, extended south through Adar, and ended in the western Hausa cities, including to as far as Madawa, Tsibiri, Gobir and parts of Katsina along Madarunfa, Kanembakashe, Agge and Maradi. But not all Tuareg in the Air, Azaouak and Adar were as fully or directly involved in the economy of the savanna. The Kel Eferwan and Kel Fadai, for example, seem to have concentrated almost entirely on animal husbandry and had few direct contacts with their sedentary neighbours (Nicolaisen 1959, 67–131). They bought grain and other goods at Agadez and other northern market towns and rarely travelled into the savanna, but their animals were often exported south by livestock dealers from the savanna or Sahel. Such purely nomadic Tuareg, specialising almost entirely in livestock, were less numerous than the Kel Owi and Kel Gress, and they were less wealthy and not as powerful (Baier 1977, 391–411). But even these people had to participate to some extent in the pattern of plantation economy of Hausaland where slaves were extensively used. The Tuareg, particularly the Kel Owi, Kel Gress and their associates, maintained an elaborate commercial infrastructure in the savanna to handle their business, and they invested heavily in real estate, in plantations where slaves were used for grain production and in such other opportunities as presented themselves (Lovejoy 2005, 197–199). The Tuareg invested in farming estates throughout Katsina and Kano emirates and in the Sahel, which supplemented millet obtained from trade and other investments. The sedentary communities provided a safety valve for nomads in times of scarcity.

A consideration of relations between Katsina and Abzin helps us unravel the long historical ties between the two polities. This is necessary especially when we consider that the Abzinawa constitute the largest migrant merchant community in Northern Katsina emirate. Beyond that, they occupied a special position not only in Katsina, where they constituted large commercial communities in Guga gate and Sararin Tsako quarters, but also settled heavily in the peri-urban areas of Northern Katsina. It is important also to mention that, among all the emirates of the Sokoto Caliphate, Katsina was the only place where the Sultan of Agades built a house in the nineteenth century and where he also had a permanent trade consul in the person of Sarkin Turawa (Sani 2004, 195). Foreign commerce, particularly across the Sahara, was in every period in pre-colonial times of great importance to Katsina and Abzin, as well as to North African mercantile communities. Salt was the Saharan product most in demand. The salt in the desert near Ghadames was carried north and was more highly esteemed than that manufactured on the shores of the Mediterranean. Salt from Bilma, in Kawar, was taken south to Borno and Hausaland, perhaps much more to Hausaland because

Borno had alternative sources of supply from Lake Chad (Fisher 1975, 86). Tuaregs of Abzin organised the annual caravans, sometimes with 10,000 camels or more and carrying only salt (Fisher 1975, 86). By the 1760s, Niebuhr learned in North Africa that Hausaland obtained its salt from the city of Abzin, i.e. Agades (Niebuhr 1790, 963–1004).

The North African Arab Slave Estates in the Nineteenth Century

For many centuries North African communities, particularly the rich Ghadames and Tuati mercantile communities in the hinterland of Tripolitania, occupied a predominant position in the trade of the Central Sudan. In the Central Sudan they maintained consulates and slave estates in various commercial cities. The Sultanate of Borno, Katsina, Kano, Katagum and the seat of the Sokoto Caliphate received associated agents in the nineteenth century. Among the consuls and slave estate owners remembered are Bu Kulum, a resident trade consul in Borno; Hajj Muhammad Ben Gumsu, a trade consul sent to Sokoto, the seat of the Caliphate; Hat Salah [or, rather, Hajji Hat Salah] and Hajji Abande, trade consuls sent to Kano city; Ahmad Ben Mas,ud and Ahmad Abu al-Gaith Tuat, [popularly known as al-Hajji Bulgai or Abulgaith] trade consuls sent to Katsina city. In many cities of Hausaland and Borno, the Ghadames, Tuat, Fezzan and Tripolitanian merchants were held in high esteem. In Katsina the ruling classes conferred on these Arabs high prestige. In the nineteenth century, Ahmad Ben Mas'ud was the trade consul in Katsina from c.1794 to 1824, and Sayyid Ahmad Abul Gaith succeeded him as consul from c. 1829 to 1869. They were the Arab leaders who represented the diplomatic and trade interests of the Ghadames, Tuati governments and major capitalists' firms (Sani 2010, 4).

Trade across the Sahara Desert was one of the most important factors that brought together the peoples of Katsina and those of the North African region. Centuries ago, the initial impetus of trade was the carrying of salt from the desert salines, particularly in Bilma, southwards to exchange for millet (Dunbar 1970, 93). Ghadames and Tuat were important cities in North Africa that had been developing since the twelfth century. Ghadames is located 290 miles southwest of Tripoli. The Arabs in Katsina founded four main wards in addition to several slave estates they established outside the city. One prominent slave estate was, for instance, located at Yanrakumma or kwarin rakumma, owned by a Tuati remembered as Ahmad Abul Gaith, along the route from Katsina to Daura. The Arabs also established wards in Katsina, which predate the nineteenth century and are said to be almost as ancient as some of the wards in the heart of the city. They are Yan Siliyu, Al-baba, Tawatinke and Rafindadi. The majority of the occupants of the Yan Siliyu ward originated from the oasis city of Insalah in Southern Algeria. The majority of them were Arabised Berbers (Sani 2010, 4).

Prominent Slave Estates Owned by the Agalawa Immigrants from the Desert Side in Northern Katsina

The Agalawa live in sedentary agricultural communities in rural Northern Katsina emirate; they are only found in the northern parts of the emirate, mainly in the area of Shibdawa in Dan Yusufa district (Sani 2004, 252). They live in the following settlements: Agalawar Gaban Kare, Unguwar Agalawa, Kirya, Mazanya and Yanbaba. These are hamlets that form suburbs around Shibdawa; they are dispersed settlements. None of these hamlets is now on a road or a map. The Agalawa have been devoted to trade, more especially the grain trade, kolanut trade, livestock trade and the trade in horses and donkeys. The Agalawa are great owners of donkeys (Gowers 1921, 21); they purposely used the donkeys in trade as carriers of kolanuts and other merchandise, and they also sold them as merchandise. The Agalawa were mainly settled in the villages mentioned above. There are various perspectives with regards to the historical origin of the Agalawa. (Lovejoy 1980, 75–86; Palmer 1936, 53, 87; Temple and Temple [eds] 1922/1965, 53–66). It is believed in another interpretation of the history of the Agalawa that they descended from a people who once inhabited the extreme southern part of Abzin, before they were pushed down southwards by stronger forces (probably ethnic tensions) by the first quarter of the fifteenth century (Colvin 1971, 212).

The Agalawa Slave-Estate Establishments

As mentioned previously the Agalawa in Katsina had the same ancestral father through Mai Rakumi. The same story was told all over among elders of both the settlements. Alhaji Dagomba lived at Unguwar Agalawa, as a wealthy merchant and estate owner in the twentieth century (Sani 2004, 252). There were other very wealthy merchants at Gabankare, which is the sister Agalawa settlement to Unguwar Agalawa. The following were the most reputable large slave estate owners: Alhaji Babba Mairandi (1850s–1920s), Alhaji Baki (1840s–1900) and Alhaji Haru, (1860s–1930s). They possessed large estates with hundreds of slaves and hundreds of donkeys. They all had very large slave estates where indigo and grain were produced through slave labour (Sani 2004, 252).

The family of Gado was another large merchant family in Agalawar Gaban Kare. Gado, the head of the family, had an estate, which included about seventy slaves and fifty members of his own household. Among these thirty-two were his children, and a great number of them were merchants. Another Agalawa estate establishment was at Yambaba, located to the west of Shibdawa, along the Bindawa road. Mayaki lived in this settlement. He lived from the 1890s to the1950s. He was among the Agalawa who relocated from Gaban Kare and established large slave estates at Yanbaba. Other sister settlements with large slave estates were located at Kirya and Unguwar Agalawa. These settlements emerged first as estates, and then gradually they expanded into big settlements. Mayaki was also an accomplished merchant who participated in the Gonja trade (kola) and the traffic in horses to Ejule, and to Igbo country. The Ejule commerce became his most prominent line of commerce. (Sani 2004, 252). The commerce led Mayaki to rank among the richest in the community of Agalawa merchants in the early twentieth century. Mayaki was said to have been able to take sixty to seventy donkeys and horses in a single caravan trip to Ejule. In addition to this, he also had a lot of camels and large slave estates.

Prominent Tokarawa Slave-Estate Establishments in Northern Katsina c. 1805–1950s

The term Tokarawa is commonly used by a group of merchants in Northern Katsina to identify themselves as a trading group. In addition, most of their settlements are referred to as Tokarci. These included Tokarcin Buyabuki, Tokarcin Salga, Tokarcin Maishudiya and Tokarcin Ajo. All of these settlements are located in Dan Yusufa district in Northern Katsina. Tokarci may be a Hausa corruption of the term Tawarikh or Tamasheik. Tokarawa differ physically from the Agalawa, for the Tokarawa are light in complexion and in fact those who have not intermarried with the Hausa are very light, like the Tuaregs in Abzin. Tokarawa also still maintain large herds of camels, and they maintain their trade link with Abzin. Tokarawa were Tuareg in origin; their original name in Hausaland was Tawarikh. In Benye town, there were immigrants led by a female merchant; she was a wealthy person remembered in Benye oral history as Mairam (c. 1840s) (Sani 2004, 252). The Tokarawa merchants in Tokarcin Buyabuki and Tokarcin Salga in Dan Yusufa district were led by three famous caravan leaders (Madugai), namely, Madugu Bunsuru and his brothers Madugu Salga and Madugu Guga, (Sani 2004, 252).

The other Tokarawa settled in Doro town. They established a suburb in the eastern section of Doro town sometime in the 1840s. This group was led by another caravan leader (Madugu) who is remembered as Falke Audu. This group was also composed of very wealthy merchants, and the suburb they established is called Kauyen Falke (Sani 2004, 252). A number of settlements in Northern Katsina were demographically enlarged in the mid-nineteenth century as a result of a large influx of settlers from the desert side. The growth of Doro town in the 1840s was accelerated by the arrival of the immigrants (Tokarawa) from the desert-side merchants from the desert side. They had a lot of livestock, and they also engaged in long-distance trade. They settled on the eastern side of Doro town where they established a suburb with slave estates called 'Kauyen Falke' (meaning, the merchant village), evidently named after the head of the pioneer merchants to settle in the area. With the arrival of these merchants, Doro became an important centre of trade in the mid-nineteenth century. The merchants were involved in estate grain production, where slaves were used in the cultivation of indigo and tobacco which was exported to the desert side. They also traded locally and to Gonja and Yoruba land, as well as to Ejule and Igbo country (NAK: Kat prof: 1864/Tuareg [Abzinawa] origin of customs of 1926/1927). The extent of the involvement of the immigrant Tokarawa from the desert side in slave estate production was acknowledged in Usman's review on the evolution of Doro town:

> The Fatake [traders] of Doro seem to have become involved in the trade in Bayi, [slaves] which is said to have made the population of Doro very heterogeneous, with people from among the Mandara, Bassa, Angas and Dakarkari retained to work as bayin gandu, [estate slaves] on the estates near the town. Thus Doro became the centre of rather specialized type of trade (Usman 1981, 192–193).

The immigrant merchants from the desert side traversed various places (as mentioned above). The heterogeneous configuration of the town stems from the stereotype of the exchanges. Slave trade was one of the key items in the exchange. This made the population of slaves in the estates very heterogeneous (comprising Mandara, Bassa, Angas and Dakarkari). Essentially, the slaves were employed to cultivate indigo dye stuff (*H. baba*), grain and tobacco; all were exported to the desert side. Other areas with high concentration of wealthy Tokarawa merchants were around Dallaji in Dan Yusufa district. These places included Faru and Kaninkau (Sani 2004, 252). In Jani the Tokarawa are located in places like Adamus (in the eastern section of Jani), Zangon Rimi (located in the western section of Jani) and Kantami. In both Katsina and the peri-urban districts, there were large concentrations of people of Abzin background. In fact, the entire commercial picture of Katsina in the nineteenth century is incomplete without mention of that special Abzin axis. Slaves, kolanuts, salt, livestock, henna, grain and tobacco featured in the Katsina Abzin exchange.

Teda Daza (Tubu) and Tokarawa Slave Estates Established in Jani and Its Suburbs

By the mid-nineteenth century, Jani town was already a walled settlement. The population of the town, however, was akin to that of Doro town, comprising a conglomeration of people of diverse origin. This was due to the settlement in Jani and its suburbs of groups of wealthy and very enterprising merchants from the desert side. In addition to their entrepreneurial activities, they developed elaborate slave estates. The estates founded by these merchants were located in the eastern and north-eastern direction of Jani town. The establishment of the estates was contemporaneous with the arrival of these merchants in the 1840s. In addition to the large slave estates they established, the merchants also engaged in horse breeding, and they also had many camels and cattle. The main attraction of these merchants to Jani was the permanent stream water in the River Jani which had several tributaries that traversed the estates established. Out of the slave estates that were established, the three that were most prominent were Adamus, which is located about two kilometres east of Jani; Zangon Rimi, which was later transformed into an encampment for caravans (it was located to the northeast of Jani); and Kantami estate, which was directly contiguous to Zangon Rimi.

The founders of these slave estates were mainly Tubu and Tokarawa merchants. The Tubu or Teda are a desert tribe; they live in south-central Sahara. Most of them have homes in the Wadis of the Tibesti Mountains, but some groups are settled as far afield as Kufra and the southern Fezzan, on the shores of Lake Chad, and in Darfur bordering Borno. The Tubu or Teda are closely related to the Kanuri; they also have settlements along the lower course of the River Yobe, from where they occasionally pursued their commercial operations as far as the towns of Central Borno and beyond (Benton 1913/1968, 195). According to Fisher:

All trans-Saharan links depended at least on the passive acquiescence and in very many important respects also on the active assistance of the Saharan peoples. Two of these, both nomadic, the Tuareg to the west and Tubu to the east were frequently involved in disturbances towards the south (Fisher 1975, 123).

This is not surprising, considering the control which the two communities had over desert-side traffic, and the important commercial position Katsina occupied in that traffic in the nineteenth century. The two communities struggled for control of the desert salines and trade routes; they also dominated the transport section as principal carrying agents in the desert routes. The arrival of these groups of merchants augmented the commerce of Jani and its suburbs. On their arrival, slave trade became a major business in Jani, supplying outlying areas of Mani, Doro, Mashi and Katsina, the capital of the emirate. Dyeing also became a specialty of the Jani people.

Conclusion

This study depicted several centuries' history of the trans-Saharan slave trade and its attendant impact on the interrelationship between the savanna areas of Northern Katsina emirate and the areas in the desert side. The effect of centuries of interrelationship could also be seen in many aspects of settlements in Northern Katsina. For instance, several places derived their names from these slave estates established by immigrants from the desert side. An example is Tigirmis, which was a slave estate established about seven kilometres east of Katsina town. First, Tigirmis is a Tuareg term (Tamasheik) which means Turban, and clearly indicates that the early settlers were estate slaves of Tuareg aristocracies. The oral history and ethnography of the settlement clearly pointed to this fact.

Overall, the impact of the trans-Saharan slave trade on Katsina Emirate as a gateway of Hausaland desert-side trade was historically similar to that of the Niger Delta area of Nigeria, a gateway of the trans-Atlantic slave trade route. For instance, in his doctoral thesis, published in 1956 (Dike 1956, 30–31), Kenneth O. Dike observed that slavery and the slave trade impacted on the Niger Delta, which culminated in compulsory migration, overpopulation and land hunger in the hinterland and as a part of the trading systems there, leading to the emergence of heterogeneous communities that transcended the old tribal entities. He put a lot of emphasis on the ethnic heterogeneity: 'In the peopling of the Delta no one Nigerian tribe had monopoly, Benis, Ijaws, Sobos, Jekris, Ikois, Ibibio Efik and even the Northern Nigerian tribes were represented' (Dike 1956, 30–31). This is the same as the Katsina community, where Tubu (Teda Daza), Tuaregs, Arabs, Berbers and Kanuri tribes came to establish slave estates and other business in Katsina town and the peri-urban districts. Y.B. Usman, in his doctoral thesis published in 1981, highlighted the implication of centuries of slavery, migration and mingling over the trade relationship between Katsina, the desert side and southern Nigeria, culminating in the heterogeneous configuration in Katsina. He gave the example of Doro, Jani and their suburbs, where Igbos, Igala, Angas, Mandara, Bassa and Dakarkari were found as estate slaves (Usman 1974, 431). Most of these people were brought there as estate slaves by merchants who had established large plantations in the nineteenth century. The merchants traversed various areas in the course of their trade adventures.

BIBLIOGRAPHY

Baier, S., 1980. *An Economic History of Central Niger*. Oxford: Clarendon Press.
Barth, H., 1965. *Travels and Discoveries in North and Central Africa 1849–1855*. London: Frank Cass, vols i, ii, iii.
Benton, P. A., 1913 [reprt. 1968]. *The Sultanate of Bornu*, trans. from the German by Dr A. Schultze. London: Frank Cass.
Boahen, A. A., 1964. *Britain, the Sahara and the Western Sudan, 1788–1861*. Oxford: Clarendon Press.

Bovill, E. W., ed., 1964–1966. *Missions to the Niger: Narratives of travels and discoveries in Northern and Central Africa in the years 1822, 1823, and 1824, by Dixon Denham, Hugh Clapperton and Walter Oudney.* Cambridge: Cambridge University Press, vols ii, iii, iv.

Colvin, L. G., 1971. The Commerce of Hausa Land: 1780–1833. In D. F. McCall and N. R. Bennett, eds., *Aspects of West African Islam.* Boston University Papers on Africa. Boston: African Studies Center, Boston University, vol v.

Dike, O., 1956. *Trade and Politics in the Niger Delta, 1830–1885: An Introduction to the Economic and Political History of Nigeria.* Oxford: Clarendon Press.

Dunbar, R. A., 1970. Datagram (Zinger - Niger) 1812–1902: A History of a Central Satanic Kingdom. PhD thesis. Los Angeles: University of California.

Fisher, H. F., 1975. The Central Sahara and Sudan. In R. Gray, ed., *The Cambridge History of Africa,* Vol. 4: *From c. 1600–c. 1790.* Cambridge: Cambridge University Press.

Gowers, W. F., 1921. *Gazetteer of Kano Province.* London: Waterlow and Sons.

Hallet, R., ed., 1810 [reprt. 1967; facs. edn.]. *Proceedings of the Association for Promoting the Discovery of the Interior Parts of Africa,* London: Dawson and Sons, vols i, ii.

Lovejoy, P. E., 1980. *Caravans of Kola: The Hausa Kola Trade 1700–1900.* Zaria, Nigeria: ABU Press.

Lovejoy, P. E., 1986. *Salt of the Desert Sun: A History of Salt Production and Trade in the Central Sudan.* London: Cambridge University Press.

NAK: Kat Prof: 1864/Tuareg (Abzinawa) Origin of Custom of 1926/1927.

Nicolaisen, J., 1967. *The Ecology and Culture of the Pastoral Tuareg of Air and the Hoggar.* Copenhagen: The National Museum of Denmark.

Palmer, H. R., 1928. *Sudanese Memoirs.* Lagos, Nigeria: Government Printer, vol. ii.

Sani, A. B., 2004. The Mercantile Landscape of Northern Katsina Emirate: 1805–1954. Unpublished PhD thesis. Kano, Nigeria: Bayero University.

Sani, A. B., 2014. *Trade Diplomacy, Banking and Finance in the Trans-Saharan Trade: An interpretation of Ahmad Abu al-Ghaith Tuat businesss ledger, a trade consul in Katsina, c. 1824–1869.* Kaduna, Nigeria: Pyla-mak.

Shenton, R., 1986. *The Development of Capitalism in Northern Nigeria.* Toronto: University of Toronto Press.

Temple, C. L. and Temple, O., eds., 1922 [reprt. 1965]. *Notes of the Tribes, Provinces, Emirates, and States of the Northern Provinces of Nigeria.* 2nd edn. Lagos: CMS Bookshop; London: J. Townsend [reprt. London: Frank Cass].

Usman, Y. B., 1981. *The Transformation of Katsina (1400–1883): The Emergence and Overthrow of the Sarauta System and the Establishment of the Emirate.* Zaria, Nigeria: ABU Press.

Slavery and the Slave Trade in East Africa

Abdulaziz Y. Lodhi

BIOGRAPHY

Dr Abdulaziz Y. Lodhi is Emeritus Professor in the Department of Linguistics & Philology, Uppsala University, Sweden. Since 1973 he has published extensively on Swahili studies and Zanzibar affairs. His most recent publication is *Oriental Loanwords in Swahili* (2015, OUP Nairobi). A new edition of his Swahili dictionary, *Kamusi ya Shule za Msingi*, is forthcoming at OUP Nairobi.

ABSTRACT

Traditionally in tropical/sub-Saharan Africa, numerous societies kept slaves long before regular commercial contact was established with North Africa or coastal East Africa. Many African kingdoms were active participants in slave raiding and slave trading, especially after the arrival of Europeans and the consequent development of the transatlantic slave trade.

Ownership of slaves was an important indicator of power and wealth. Slaves were seldom sold as chattels but could be given away as gifts to others of stature. However, with the discovery of the Americas and the European need for increased cheap labour, Europeans developed the transatlantic slave trade, and African slavery changed character as a result of the escalation of slave raids and the forced diaspora of Africans. Most captives from Africa were transported via Britain to Rio de Janeiro in Brazil, whence they were shipped further to other destinations in the Americas.

Export of slaves from East Africa was mainly to the Middle East, India and some Indian Ocean islands. Female slaves from Asia were brought to East Africa by the Portuguese to work in their fortresses or were sold as concubines. The long process to abolish the slave trade and slavery in East Africa started in 1873 in Zanzibar and ended in Ethiopia in 1942.

Origins of Slavery and Related Practices

The English term 'slave' has its origins in the Latin word 'sclavus', meaning 'captive'. The Romans obtained most of their slaves from Eastern Europe. This trade in humans, mostly females and young boys, continued to an extent well into the ninth century AD, all the way to Muslim Spain.

Slavery can be described simply as the ownership of human beings, the buying and selling of them for the sole purpose of forced and mostly unpaid labour and sexual exploitation. It is an ancient practice that has been found in almost all civilisations in the world. All three Semitic religions – Judaism, Christianity and Islam – recognise slaves as a separate class of people in society. Even the Mayans, Aztecs and other smaller 'nations' kept slaves in the Americas, as did the Sumerians and Babylonians in the Near East, and the Chinese and Japanese in the Far East. Ancient Egyptians and Greeks employed large numbers of slaves, including people of their own nationalities and others such as Jews, Europeans, Nubians and Ethiopians. Many slaves were employed as soldiers, servants, labourers and even civil servants. The Romans captured slaves from what are now Britain, France and Germany. Slave armies were kept by the Egyptians and Ottomans. In the civilisations of the Indus valley and the Indian subcontinent, because of the rigid caste system solidified in their religions, the lower castes and the 'untouchables' provided ample free or cheap labour to the upper castes.

Another very common form of slavery was 'serfdom' – a 'serf' was an unfree person in a condition of almost perpetual servitude, sometimes partial, a condition mostly inherited from his parents, and he was required to render services to a feudal lord. He was commonly attached to the lord's land or household, and though he could not be sold as chattel (movable property), he was transferred with the land from one owner to another, usually together with his family.

In northern Europe (Scandinavia), trälar were a kind of serf, and in Imperial Russia in the first half of the nineteenth century, one-third of the population were serfs, or 'unfree peasants' called 'krepostnoy krestyanin' in Russian, who, like slaves in the Americas, had the status of chattels and could be bought and sold like common goods. They were finally freed in 1861 by Emperor Alexander II. Four years later, in 1865, slavery was abolished completely and legally in the United States of America following the defeat of the Southern States in the American Civil War. However, servitude in various forms, combined with racial discrimination, suppression of human rights and gross exploitation related to slavery, continues to exist to this day in many parts of the world.

Slavery in Africa and the Trade in African Slaves

In tropical/sub-Saharan Africa, there were numerous societies and kingdoms which kept slaves, both belonging to their own tribes and captured from other tribes, long before there was any regular commercial contact established with the Muslims of North Africa and with the Swahili coast of East Africa. Several powerful West African kingdoms, such as those of the Ashanti in Kumasi, Bonny and Dahomey/Benin, were active participants in slave raiding and slave trading, espe-

cially after the arrival of Europeans and the consequent development of the brutal 'triangular' transatlantic slave trade.

Traditionally, most societies in Africa, many with divine kings and strict hierarchical forms of government with local chiefs at village level, kept slaves as body
guards, tax collectors, domestic servants and farm workers. They were an important indicator of power and wealth. They were seldom sold as chattels but could
be given away as gifts to others of stature. However, with the discovery of the
Americas and the European need for increased cheap labour, the character of
African slave ownership changed when Europeans introduced the transatlantic
slave trade and escalated slave raids, the enslavement of Africans and the slaves'
forced migration for use in the Americas. Later, in the early eighteenth century,
the rulers of Dahomey/Benin became major slave traders, raiding neighbouring
tribes and capturing them, providing in some years more than 10,000 slaves to
the Europeans. Some of the captives were themselves former slave traders.

King Tegbesu of Whydah is said to have made about £250,000 selling people
into slavery in 1750. King Gezo of Dahomey during the period 1818–1858 once
said he would do anything the British wanted him to do except give up the very
lucrative slave trade. The Ashanti of modern Ghana had a long tradition of domestic slavery, and gold was their main export commodity until the arrival of Europeans, when slaves displaced gold. The British Colonial Office, however,
tolerated this in spite of the abolitionist movement strongly supported by the
British people and the government.

Leo Africanus, the Moroccan traveller who visited Songhay in 1510 and 1513,
commented with amazement on the great wealth, huge army and large number of
slaves in Gao, the capital of the Songhay empire, which was then at the height of
its power and expansion and trading heavily in slaves – men, women and children.

Most slaves from Africa were transported to Brazil, and from the port of Rio de
Janeiro they were shipped further to other destinations in the Americas.

The East African Slave Trade

Swahili patricians, the ruling class of coastal society of mixed African-Asian origin in the ports and islands of East Africa, comprising sultans, chiefs, government
officials, ship owners and wealthy merchant houses, used non-Muslim slaves as
domestic servants, sailors, coolies and workers on farms and plantations, even in
the interior of modern-day Tanzania around trading centres such as Tabora,
Mwanza on Lake Victoria, and Ujiji and Kigoma on Lake Tanganyika. Swahili
craftsmen, artisans and clerks were free Muslim men or Islamised former slaves.

The divisions between the different social classes were often not very strict because of intermarriage and social mobility. Seyyid Said, Sultan of Oman and Zanz-

ibar, and his relatives and associates, became so rich – thanks to their clove plantations in Zanzibar employing slave labour – that he moved his capital from Muscat in Oman to Zanzibar in 1840, thus becoming the first of twelve Sultans of Zanzibar of Omani origin.

Slavery and slave trading within East Africa were well established on a small scale before the Europeans arrived on the scene. Export of slaves was mostly to the countries of the Middle East, especially to the Persian Gulf region. Africans worked as sailors in Persia, as pearl divers and labourers on date plantations in Oman and the Gulf, as soldiers in the various armies and as workers on the salt pans of Mesopotamia (modern Iraq). Many Africans were domestic slaves, working in wealthy households. Many young women were taken as concubines (i.e. sex slaves). However, the bulk of the slaves in the countries around the Indian Ocean were from South Asia and Southeast Asia, particularly South India, Malaysia, Indonesia and the Philippines. Most were women, many of them brought to East Africa by the Portuguese to work in their fortresses, naval bases and wine-houses or sold as concubines.

After 1729, when the Portuguese were ousted from the Swahili coast by the Omani fleet, Arab, Iranian and Indian settlements increased in East Africa, and the slave trade expanded far into the interior of East and Central Africa and became more organised. There was also an increasing demand for ivory in India, Europe and America, and slaves were needed as porters to carry the ivory from the interior to the coast.

Every year more slaves were required in East Africa, for several reasons:

1. New clove and coconut plantations in Zanzibar and date plantations in Oman needed labour.
2. New farms in the interior of East Africa, established for the production of food crops around inland centres along the caravan routes, needed labour.
3. More slaves were needed as porters to carry trade goods from the coast to the interior, and ivory and other products from the interior to the coast.
4. Brazilian traders, to avoid the British Navy's intercepting their slave ships in West Africa, had started obtaining slaves from the Portuguese in Angola, the Zambezi valley, Mozambique and Tanganyika.
5. The French needed cheap labour on their new sugar and coffee plantations in the Caribbean islands and in the Indian Ocean islands of Mauritius, Seychelles, Reunion, Rodrigues and southern Madagascar. Most of the slaves were taken from the port of Kilwa and had been brought there by the Nyamwezi and the Yao.
6. Many male slaves in Zanzibar and Mombasa would be freed after some years in servitude; older slaves would retire or die; and new ships and businesses, as well as building and construction work, needed new workers.

People of different nationalities – Africans, Arabs, Iranians, Indians and Europeans – were all involved in the trade in slaves from the interior of eastern and central Africa, as well as in transporting ivory, rhinoceros horns, hides, copper and precious stones to the coast. The main suppliers of slaves were these:

1. the Prazeros, descendants of Portuguese fathers and African mothers, operating mostly along the Zambezi River;
2. the Yao of southern Tanganyika and northern Mozambique, working northwest of the Zambezi River;
3. the Makua operating east of the Yao, closer to the coast;
4. the Yeke operating farther north around Lake Tanganyika under the leadership of Chief Msiri of Katanga and the Nyamwezi Chief Mirambo, who established a short-lived trading and raiding kingdom at Urambo during 1860s and 1870s (slaves were brought by them from as far west as southern Angola);
5. the Kamba, Galla/Oromo and the Somali in Kenya;
6. the Christian Amhara and the Oromo, which later systematically raided the Muslim Somali in modern Ethiopia to obtain slaves well into the 1930s.

The most famous trader of all in East Africa during the second half of the 1800s was Tippu Tip (Hamed bin Muhammed Al-Murjebi), a Zanzibari of African-Arab parentage. Tippu traded mostly in ivory, and he owned several hundred slaves, which he used as porters to carry the ivory and also to work as his soldiers, guards and functionaries in the caravans. He later became Governor of the Congo, first under the Sultan of Zanzibar, and later under the King of Belgium.

The Abolition of the Slave Trade and Slavery

Great Britain was the country that profited the most from the trade in African slaves!

Throughout history, slavery (and the accompanying slave trade) has had its opponents; however, the active movement to abolish the slave trade only took off in 1771 when the Non-Conformist activist Granville Sharp brought the case of the escaped African slave James Somerset before Lord Mansfield, Lord Chief Justice of Britain. The fugitive Somerset had been recaptured in England by his American owner, but since a foreigner could not be imprisoned in Britain on the authority of American law, Somerset was set free by Lord Mansfield. But African slaves continued to be brought to and sold in Britain, and British slave ships sailed to the Caribbean as usual with their human cargo from the ports of Liverpool and Bristol where there were busy slave markets visited by planters from the West Indies. In the 1780s, the Quakers (Religious Society of Friends) under Granville Sharp started their long and intensive campaign to abolish slavery and the slave trade. The abolitionists, led by William Wilberforce, tirelessly lobbied public opinion and Parliament in London and also got involved in the question of the Resettlement of Freed Slaves in Africa.

Several factors hastened the international abolition process that brought about the formal end of slavery:

1. Britain's ties with America were weakened when her New England colonies there became free after the American War of Independence in 1776 and the creation of the United States of America.
2. The French Revolution was a period of radical social and political upheaval in France from 1789 to 1799. It profoundly affected both French and modern world history, causing the gradual decline of the power and authority of monarchies and churches, and encouraging the rise of democracy and nationalism, initially in Europe. It brought ideas of universal fraternity, liberty and equality, inspiring those fighting to end slavery. One immediate consequence of this was the successful slave revolt of 1791 in Saint Domingue (with the largest slave population in the Caribbean) that finally abolished slavery and brought independence to Haiti in 1803.
3. The Industrial Revolution in Britain and increasing wealth from her imperial expansion in Asia had brought new demands for efficiency, free trade and free labour in Britain – slavery and slave trading were outdated practices in this new situation.

Although the country that had profited most from the trade in African slaves was Britain, in 1807 the British government declared the buying, selling and transport of slaves illegal – but owning slaves was legal until August 1834 when Parliament passed a bill which gave freedom to all slave children under six in the British West Indies. All other slaves, adults and youth, were classed as apprentices and made to work for six years without pay, though they received food, shelter and clothing. Altogether 40,000 British families, including plantation owners in the New World, were given compensation totalling about £20 million for the loss of slaves. (This sum would amount to several thousand million pounds today.)

The system of apprenticeship was just as cruel and exploitative as slavery, and it was finally abolished in 1838. Many former slaves stayed on the plantations as very low-paid labourers since they could not get other work elsewhere. Those few who managed to leave the plantations in the West Indies were soon replaced by indentured labourers from India.

The abolitionists in Britain now directed their efforts towards ending slavery in America, causing much resentment, especially in the Southern states of the USA.

They also campaigned against slavery in India and East Africa. Concerning East Africa, the missionary explorer Dr David Livingstone proposed the 3 C's (Colonisation, Christianity and Commerce) as the only way of ending slavery and the slave trade. He campaigned for an immediate takeover of the territory where slavery was practised, thus encouraging imperial ambitions in East Africa.

Slavery continued, however, in many parts of the world. It was finally abolished in America after the Civil War, with the defeat of the Southern states in 1865. But the freed slave in the South continued to suffer. All the indignities of segregation and discrimination remained, with inequality in the courts of justice and violent harassment from white Southerners, sometimes resulting in unpunished torture or murder. This continued until very recently, until the rise of the Civil Rights movement of the 1960s, which brought the issue of racism and associated discrimination and segregation forcefully to the attention of authorities and legislators. International opinion was mustered to remove the vestiges of slavery in America. Meanwhile, in many parts of Africa, slavery of the old traditional varieties continued rather undisturbed well into the twentieth century. It was finally outlawed in Nigeria in 1936, and in Ethiopia in 1942.

The Abolition of the Slave Trade and Slavery in East Africa

Since the first anti-slave-trade treaty of 1822 (the Moresby Treaty), international opinion against the East African slave trade had been mounting, and after a long confrontation with the European abolitionists and many threats from the British, Sultan Seyyid Barghash of Zanzibar signed a treaty on 5 June 1873 that made the slave trade finally illegal in his dominions. But the legal status of slavery, which was originally also a common African institution, was not abolished until 1909 in Zanzibar (1904 in British Kenya and 1919 in Tanganyika after Germany lost WWI and Tanganyika became a British trust territory).

Zanzibar became a British protectorate in 1890 after the Heligoland-Zanzibar Treaty between Britain and Germany. The year 1890 was also the year of the signing the Brussels Conference Act (also known as the Slave Trade Treaty) by the Western European countries, which provided for the suppression of the slave trade and the importation of alcohol and firearms into Zanzibar. Alcohol and firearms were exchanged for slaves in the interior of East Africa, and firearms were increasingly being used in the slaving raids both by the local native African peoples of the interior and by the slave traders from the coast.

An international bureau was set up in Zanzibar in the same year to allow the British Navy to enforce the Act.

The 1873 treaty between the British and Zanzibar, and the other treaties which followed it, were not enforced effectively for many reasons. To the benefit of the slave dealers and owners, the British argued for a gradual abolition of slavery out of fear that (as was experienced in the West Indies) mass liberation would lead to lawlessness and the destruction of the highly developed agricultural plantation economy of Zanzibar. After 1890, slaves in Zanzibar could buy their freedom, but few could afford to do so. (Plantation slaves had one to three days a week free to do their own work, cultivating their own plots or working for others to earn cash.) In 1897 the government agreed to pay compensation to slave owners for manumission of male slaves, while concubines were to become legal wives and their children legitimate. But slaves wanting freedom had to apply formally to a court, and since most plantation slaves were illiterate or simply ignorant of the law, only 4,278 slaves were freed. The vagrancy laws (which demanded that every inhabitant of the islands have employment, a home, etc.), intimidation from some slave owners, as well as the wish among many slaves to retain the 'right' to cultivate plots on plantations, also hindered many from becoming free. But the status of slavery was finally abolished in 1909, and compensation for freed slaves could not be paid after 1911. Formally, 17,293 slaves were freed in Zanzibar for a total of £32,502, paid as compensation to the owners. The number of concubines, slave children and aged slaves automatically gaining their freedom must have been several thousand. In place of the closed slave market in Zanzibar Town (Kijiweni/ Stone Town), Bishop Edward Steere built the large Anglican cathedral.

However, a slave could be given freedom at the will of his owner long before the institution of slavery was finally abolished. If a slave had lived and behaved to the satisfaction of the master for a long period, especially if he held an important position in the master's household, the master could write him a document of freedom. The ex/freed slave (mhuru) and the master (bwana/mwinyi) each kept a copy of the document. A master would grant freedom to his slaves when he, the master, had grown old and wanted to thank God and get His reward. Some masters would grant freedom before going on the pilgrimage to Mecca, or when they returned from Mecca.

Slaves were freed in the name of God, since Islam, though it sanctioned slavery, did not present any serious obstacle to its abolition. The Koran, Chapter 24, Verse 32 says: 'As for those of your slaves which wish to buy their liberty, free them if you find in them any promise and bestow on them a part of the riches which God has given you'.

After the slave trade was declared illegal, many slave owners expected the abolition of slavery to follow suit. Shrewd slave owners thus made some slaves buy their freedom from their masters. The price of freedom was usually a large part of the little land the slave had acquired through the kiambo ownership. This kind of 'trade in freedom' developed out of the custom whereby a slave owner wilfully freeing a slave was given a present by the freed slave and his relations if he had any. The present was usually part of the land owned by the slave through his marriage to a free woman. This system increased slightly the plantation owner's arable land, which he customarily could not buy from the Waunguja, the original inhabitants of Unguja/Zanzibar Island.

A slave thus freed was made a 'brother' or a 'son' by the former master, and the ex-slave continued to be attached to the household of his former master. The Certificate of Freedom (Hati ya Uhuru) read as follows:

> I, So-and-So, state that I have granted in writing to So-and-So, freedom before Almighty God, which means he is a free man. No one may interfere in his affairs while I am alive, and even when I am dead there is no way of interfering with him. And whosoever upsets what I have written in this document will be accounted sinful before God for upsetting this document; it is I who have made him a free man. If anyone comes and makes him a slave in spite of my certificate, he will be accounted sinful (Harries 1965, 12).

Originally, the Certificate of Freedom was not required to be endorsed by any official authority; however, some parties involved would have the certificate stamped by the Kadhi (Muslim jurist). After 1873 (when the slave trade was abolished), and especially after 1890 (when Zanzibar came under British protection), the necessary documents were written at a government office and the official stamp put on them. British official policy in Zanzibar was to bring about a gradual abolition of slavery to avoid the situation where the laziest slaves would seek emancipation first and mass liberation would lead to lawlessness and the destruction of the plantation economy.

However, in 1890 the Sultan of Zanzibar was persuaded by the British to declare that slaves could buy their freedom. Since only a few slaves had the cash or the land with which to buy their freedom, the declaration did not help to reduce substantially the number of slaves. The Sultan also decreed that all slaves entering his dominions (Zanzibar, Pemba and Kipini, the part of the Kenyan coast under the flag of Zanzibar) and all slaves born after 1890 were to be freed. All slaves were finally emancipated in Zanzibar and Pemba (excluding the Kenyan coast) in 1897, and the government agreed to pay compensation to the slave owners. Concubines were to become legal wives and their children legitimate.

However, freedom was granted only upon application to the government. Since the government did not have any records on the slaves, and since most of the slaves were illiterate, comparatively few slaves applied for their freedom. Two other factors contributed to the perpetuation of slavery on the plantations despite legal possibilities for a slave to obtain freedom. First, slave owners argued that the compensation paid by the Zanzibar government was too little, hence they did not either inform their slaves, or encourage them, to apply for freedom. Secondly, many plantation owners threatened their slaves that upon becoming free, the ex-slaves would lose their cultivation rights and would not be employed for wages. Many slaves thus remained in slavery until 1909 when Sultan Seyyid Ali bin Hamoud definitively abolished slavery, and compensation for slaves could not be paid after 1911.

Contrary to the horrors associated with the transatlantic slave trade and the brutal punishments inflicted on disobedient or runaway slaves, especially on the plantations in the Americas, domestic slavery in East Africa and in the Indian Ocean world in general is known to have been comparatively benign.

An ex-slave could rise to any position in Swahili society. Of the six successive governors in Zanzibar (the highest official post in Zanzibar) appointed by Sultan Seyyid Said before his moving to Zanzibar in 1839, two were ex-slaves of Ethiopian origin, Khadim Yaqut and Khadim Ambar. This may explain why no mass uprising of slaves occurred in Zanzibar and, contrary to British, Arab and Indian fears, the emancipation of slaves did not result in lawlessness and the disruption of the plantation economy. In fact, during the years following the abolition of slavery, clove and coconut production rose, and the prosperity of Zanzibar did not seriously decline. The economy did decline considerably along the Kenyan coast, through the loss of slaves as a result of abolition and through rebellions led by local rulers in the coastal towns and islands.

Descendants of East African freed slaves in the Middle Eastern countries are greatly assimilated into the society and identify themselves as Arabs. However, in parts of Oman, Saudi Arabia and the Persian Gulf, the khadims (serfs, domestic servants, menial workers, pearl divers) have predominantly African blood.

In the Indian subcontinent, descendants of freed slaves are concentrated in the state of Gujarat, north-west of Bombay, where freed slaves had formed several separate states under British protection, and in Hyderabad and Karnataka. They are known as Sidi/Siddi/Siddhi, speak different Indic languages and follow mostly Islam. In Karnataka and Goa, they are mostly Catholic and Hindu. Some freed Africans were brought back from Arabia and India to East Africa by Christian missions early in the twentieth century.

The Squatter System – From Slavery to Serfdom

A freed/former male slave, mhuru/hadimu (plural wahuru/mahadimu), was made a brother or a son by the former master, and the former female slave, a wife, sister or daughter. Thus, the descendants of freed slaves continued to be attached to the Muslim households of former slave owners, were well integrated in the extended family, and today cannot be distinguished as a separate community, except for those who were converted to Christianity by the European missions. The bondage consisted of obligations during marriage and funerals and the observance of rules of social etiquette. The ex-masters' descendants were obliged to help the ex-slaves' descendants financially at engagements, marriage and funeral ceremonies, just as slave owners were obliged to do during the time of slavery proper. The original owners of the clove plantations known as shamba were in all cases Arabs of Oman and Hadramaut (South Yemen) – either fresh settlers from southern Arabia or members of long-established families of Arab or mixed Arab, African, Iranian, Indian and Indonesian origin in Zanzibar. As agreed between Sultan Seyyid Said and the Shirazi native African ruler Mwinyi Mkuu of Unguja Island, forest lands could be granted to persons of Arab male ancestry who cleared them and planted them mostly with cloves and coconuts using slave labour. The Shirazi native Zanzibaris who were farmers and fishermen entered the plantation economy mostly after the abolition of slavery.

Plantation slaves cultivated food crops among the clove and coconut trees to grow their own food and keep the trees weeded. After the abolition of slavery, the pattern of life on the plantations did not change substantially. Slaves were emancipated, but the plantations in Unguja remained the property of Zanzibaris of Arab and Indian origin and to a certain extent the Shirazi also. Most descendants of the ex-slaves were thus landless farm labourers or urban workers. Some large plantation owners left a few small plantations as 'waqf' (a government trust) for the use of the owners' former slaves. A few were bought by Christian missions to rehabilitate some ex-slaves. The great majority of ex-slaves carried on their old employment or took out plots in the 'no-man's lands' between the Arab plantations and the Shirazi settlements. A very few, who had marriage ties with the Shirazi, settled in the Shirazi villages.

Those who stayed on or moved into the shambas became 'squatters'. The system of squatting had much in common with the institution of slavery on the plantations. Customarily, squatters could build houses on the shamba and plant food crops (including banana plants, which were not considered trees). Squatters were expected to help the owner to pick the cloves at harvest time for a small payment. Squatters did not pay rent, nor did they share their own crops with the owner; and they could not be expelled from the shamba except when there had been a breach of personal relations between owner and squatter. The squatter did not have any economic obligations to the shamba owner. Some owners allowed their squatters to plant fruit trees such as mangoes, limes, lemons, pawpaws, breadfruit, jackfruit and tropical apples. The squatter looked after these plants and picked the fruits. Both the owner and the squatter had an equal share of the produce.

A squatter did not customarily have to ask for permission to settle on a shamba. He was expected to have friendly relations with the owner, the owner's agent or the overseer (who was usually a poor relative of the owner, almost certainly recently arrived from Arabia). A squatter was always welcome as long as there was room for him on the shamba. The area a squatter could cultivate was not limited to any one part of a shamba, or to any one shamba. The rights of a squatter could be inherited by his children and/or relatives if agreed by the owner. Customarily, the owner did not refuse. Squatters, however, could not sell their rights, but could delegate their duties and obligations to their relatives and friends.

Squatters were in fact referred to as 'wasimamizi' (overseers of the plantations), as relations between squatters and owners had been generally good. However, there were times of tension; for example, in the period 1957–63, Arab and Indian landlords had strongly expressed their wish to dispense with the squatter system and replace it with total wage labour to cultivate trees and cash crops such as chillies. This move was contrary to the established rights of the squatters, and it created fears and insecurity among them. The situation was exploited by some feudal supporters of the Zanzibar Nationalist Party, who threatened to expel those squatters who did not join the landlord-dominated ZNP.

The squatter-landlord relationship based on the old slave-master system continued with varying degrees of bondage and attachment for more than half a century until 1964, when the republican revolution changed the social equilibrium.

After abolition, the distinctive system of slavery left its mark on all sorts of activities. Households employed servant boys and girls to a great extent for menial tasks and for shopping and going to the market. This is the case even today, to some extent. Thousands of both urban and rural youths in East Africa are employed as unskilled 'domestic servants' for low wages. Before the revolution in Zanzibar, both the formally organised enterprises of the day and slavery of the past showed traits of an intimate character. Slavery had been considered part and parcel of the feudal and commercial households, and Swahili sailors often spoke of their ship owner's firm and household as their 'mlango' (the door), or extended family.

After the revolution in 1964, all large plantations were nationalised. All squatters, and later interested people from urban areas who had no agrarian background, were given a minimum of three acres each of plantation land. An unspecified number of these were immigrants from East African countries, mostly from Tanganyika (i.e. Tanzania mainland). The surplus plantation lands were turned into state farms or taken over by the new ruling elite.

A social survey of Zanzibar (1962) conducted by the South African professor Edward Baston during 1948–49 gives the following figures for landless adult male Africans of the main island of Unguja, which had been the most involved in plantation slavery and the slave trade:

However, during 1964–65, altogether about 22,000 adults in Zanzibar were given the three-acre plots by the government. In the 1980s the government sold more unoccupied land to citizens and also returned some smaller shambas and houses to their former owners, and speculation in real estate has grown tremendously. The above

Unguja Island	Shirazi/Native	Mainlanders/Non-native
Zanzibar Town	2,220	6,630 (= 8,850)
Rest of Unguja	1,720	8,600 (= 10,320)
Total	3,940	15,230 (= 19,170)

figures of landless Africans in 1948 are close to the number of male slaves freed during abolition – that is, 19,170 landless male Zanzibaris of all origins in contrast to 17,293 male slaves freed by the courts up to 1911 (with some getting compensation several times under different identities in cooperation with the master).

Slavery has not disappeared completely; it exists today in various forms, mainly indoors, behind closed doors, and in remote forests and mining areas in many parts of the world, including Europe, Africa, India and the Middle East.

BIBLIOGRAPHY

Literature on the history and peoples of the Indian Ocean lands is abundant. I have found my data in the following list of references. I have felt it to be inconvenient, unnecessary and, as Prins (1965) states in his Preface, 'impracticable to always quote my sources'. Most paragraphs would have consisted of numerous and redundant footnotes, if I had done so. However, sources have been quoted wherever it has been found meaningful to do so.

Of particular interest to the topic of this paper are the several illuminating works of Professors Edward E. Alpers, Abdul Sheriff, Randolph L. Pouwels, Philippe Beaujard, Thomas Spear and James De V. Allen.

Abu-Lughod, J., 1989. *Before European Hegemony: The World System AD 1250–1350*. New York and Oxford: Oxford University Press.
Abushouk, A. I. and Ibrahim, H. A., eds., 2009. *The Hadhrami Diaspora in Southeast Asia: Identity Maintenance or Assimilation?* Leiden: Brill.
Alpers, Edward E., 1967. *The East African Slave Trade*. Historical Association of Tanzania Paper No. 3., Nairobi: East African Publishing House.
Alpers, Edward E., 1975. *Ivory and Slaves: Changing Patterns of International Trade in East Central Africa to the Later Nineteenth Century*. Berkeley and Los Angeles: University of California Press.
Alpers, Edward E., 2009. *East Africa and the Indian Ocean*. Princeton: Markus Wiener.
Beaujard, Philippe, 2005. The Indian Ocean in Eurasian and African world-systems before the sixteenth century. *Journal of World History* 16/4, 411–65.

Beaujard, Philippe, 2007. East Africa, the Comoros Islands and Madagascar before the sixteenth century: On a neglected part of the World-System. *AZANIA: Journal of the British Institute in Eastern Africa* 42, 15–35.

Benjamin, J., 2006. 'The world and Africa': World-Systems theories and the erasure of East Africa from world history. *World History Bulletin* 22/1, 20–27.

Bose, Sugata, 1996. Culture, Economy and Politics in the Indian Ocean Rim: Theory and History. Unpublished paper. Amsterdam: University of Amsterdam.

Chaudhari, K. N., 1985. *Trade and Civilization in the Indian Ocean: An Economic History from the Rise of Islam to 1750.* Cambridge: Cambridge University Press.

Chaudhari, K. N., 1990. *Asia Before Europe: Economy and Civilization of the Indian Ocean from the Rise of Islam to 1750.* Cambridge: Cambridge University Press.

Chittick, N., 1968. The Coast Before the Arrival of the Portuguese. In: B. A. Ogot and J. A. Kieran, eds., *Zamani: A Survey of East African History.* Nairobi and New York: Humanities Press, 100–118.

Connag, G., 1987. *African Civilization: Pre-colonial Cities and States in Tropical Africa: An archaeological perspective.* Cambridge: Cambridge University Press.

Cooper, Frederick, 1977. *Plantation Slavery on the East Coast of Africa.* New Haven: Yale University Press.

Cooper, Frederick, 1980. *From Slaves to Squatters: Plantation Labour and Agriculture in Zanzibar and Coastal Kenya 1890–1925.* Nairobi: Kenya Literature Bureau.

Coupland, Reginald, 1938. *East Africa and Its Invaders: From the Earliest Times to the Death of Seyyid Said in 1856.* Oxford: Clarendon Press.

Crosby, Alfred W., 2003. *The Columbian Exchange: Biological and Cultural Consequences of 1492.* 30th Anniversary Edition. Westport: Praeger,

Dewar, R. E. and Wright, H. T., 1993. The Culture history of Madagascar. *Journal of World Prehistory* 7/4, 417–66.

Ehret, C., 1988. The East African Interior. In: M. Elfasi and I. Hrbek, eds., *Africa from the 7th to the 11th Century.* UNESCO General History of Africa. London and Paris: UNESCO, v. iii: 615–42.

Freeman-Grenville, G. S. P., 1963. The Coast, 1498–1840. In: R. Oliver and G. Mathew, eds., *History of East Africa.* Oxford: Clarendon Press, v. i: 129–68.

Freeman-Grenville, G. S. P., 1989. The Portuguese on the Swahili coast: Buildings and language. *Studia* [Lisbon: Centro de Estudos de História e Cartigrafia Antiga] 49, 235–54.

Freeman-Grenville, G. S. P., ed., 1966. *The East African Coast: Select Documents from the First to the Earlier Nineteenth Century.* 2nd edn. Oxford: Clarendon Press.

Friedman, J., 2006. From the Local to the Global: Anthropology of World Systems. Paper presented at a Seminar at École des Hautes Études en Sciences Sociales, Paris.

Gray, Sir John, 1962. *A History of Zanzibar (from the Middle Ages to 1856)*. London: Oxford University Press.

Hall, Richard, 1996. *Empires of the Monsoon: A History of the Indian Ocean and Its Invaders*. New York: Harper Collins.

Hamdun, Said and King, Noel, 1975. *Ibn Battuta in Black Africa*. London: Rex Collings.

Hirth, F. and Rockhill W. W., 1911. *Chau-Ju-Kua: his work on the Chinese and Arab trade in the twelfth and thirteenth centuries, entitled Chu-fan-chï*. St Petersburg: Printing Office of the Imperial Academy of Sciences.

Horton, Mark, 1987. The Swahili corridor. *Scientific American* 9, 76–84.

Horton, Mark and Middleton, John, 2000. *The Swahili: The Social Landscape of a Mercantile Society*. Oxford: Blackwell.

Hourani, George, 1951 [rev. edn. 1995]. *Arab Seafaring in the Indian Ocean in Ancient and Early Medieval Times*. Princeton: Princeton University Press.

Huntingfort, G. W. B., trans. and ed. 1980. *The Periplus of the Erythrean Sea*. London: The Hakluyt Society.

Jayaruriya, Shihan de Silva and Pankhurst, Richard, 2003. *The African Diaspora in the Indian Ocean*. Trenton: AFRICA World Press.

Jumbe, Aboud Mwinyi, 1979. *A Short History of Zanzibar*. Zanzibar: State Printing Corporation.

Kirkman, J. S., 1964. *Men and Monuments on the East African Coast*. London: The Lutterworth Press.

Lieberman, V., 2003. *Strange Parallels: Southeast Asia in Global Context, c. 800–1830*. Cambridge: Cambridge University Press.

Lodhi, Abdulaziz Y., 1973. *The Institution of Slavery in Zanzibar and Pemba*. Research Report No. 16. Uppsala: Nordic Africa Institute.

Lodhi, Abdulaziz Y., 1992. African settlements in India. *Nordic Journal of African Studies* [Helsinki] 1/1, 83–86.

Lodhi, Abdulaziz Y., 2008. Linguistic evidence of Bantu origins of the Sidis of India. In: *TADIA: The African Diaspora in Asia: Explorations on a Less Known Fact*. Bangalore: Jana Jagrati Prakashana on behalf the Tadia Society.

Manger, Leif O., 2010. *The Hadrami Diaspora: Community-Building on the Indian Ocean Rim*. New York and Oxford: Berghahn Books.

Manger, Leif O. and Munzoul, A. M. Assal, 2006. *Diasporas within and without Africa: Dynamism, Heterogeneity, Variation*. Uppsala: Nordic Africa Institute.

Manguin, P. Y., 1993. Pre-modern Southeast Asian Shipping in the Indian Ocean: The Maldives Connection. Paper presented at New Directions in Maritime History Conference, International Commission of Maritime History, Australian Association for Maritime History, Fremantle, Australia.

Middleton, John, 1992. *The World of the Swahili: An African Mercantile Civilization*. New Haven and London: Yale University Press.

Masao, F. T. and Mutoro, H. W., 1988. The East African Coast and the Comoro Islands. In: M. Elfasi and I. Hrbek, eds., *Africa from the 7th to the 11th Century.* UNESCO General History of Africa. Paris: UNESCO, v. iii, 568–615.

Morton, Fred, 1990. *Children of Ham: Freed Slaves and Fugitive Slaves on the Kenya Coast 1873 to 1907.* San Francisco and Oxford: Boulder Publications.

Mota, A. and Teixeira D. A., 1978. Some Aspects of Portuguese Colonisation and Sea Trade in West Africa in the 15th and 16th Centuries. The Seventh Annual Hans Wolff Memorial Lecture, 5 March 1976, Bloomington, Indiana.

Ogot, B. A., ed., 1968 [new edn. 1974]. *Zamani: A Survey of East African History.* Nairobi: East African Publishing House.

Oliver, R. and Mathew, G., 1963. *The Oxford History of East Africa.* Oxford: Clarendon Press, v. 1.

Pearson, M. N., 1998. *Port Cities and Intruders: The Swahili Coast, India, and Portugal in The Early Modern Era.* Baltimore: Johns Hopkins University Press.

Pouwel, R. L., 2002. Eastern Africa and the Indian Ocean to 1800: Reviewing relations in historical perspective. *International Journal of African Historical Studies* 35/2–3, 385–425.

Prins, A. H. J., 1967. The Swahili-Speaking Peoples of Zanzibar and the East African Coast. *Ethnographic Survey of Africa.* London: International African Institute.

Ricks, T. M., 1970. Persian Gulf seafaring and East Africa. *International Journal of African Historical Studies* 3, 345–50.

Salim, A. I., 1973. *The Swahili-Speaking Peoples of the Kenya Coast 1895–1945.* Nairobi: East African Educational Publishers.

Sheriff, A. H. M., 1987. *Slaves, Spices and Ivory.* London: James Currey.

Sheriff, A. H. M., 1997a. The Dhow Trade as a Cultural Corridor in the Western Indian Ocean. Paper presented at the Conference on the Northwestern Indian Ocean as a Cultural Corridor, Dept. of Anthropology, Stockholm University, January 1997.

Spear, T., 2000. Early Swahili history reconsidered. In: East Africa, the Comoro Islands and Madagascar before the Sixteenth Century. *The International Journal of African Historical Studies* 33/2, 257–90.

Stone, J. C., 1985. *Africa and the Sea.* Aberdeen: Aberdeen University.

Strandes, Justus, 1973. *The Portuguese Period in East Africa*, ed. by J. S. Kirkman, trans. by J. Wallwork. Nairobi: East African Literature Bureau.

Sutton, J. E. G., 1990. *A Thousand Years of East Africa.* Nairobi: British Institute in Eastern Africa.

Were, Gideon S. and Wilson, Derek A., 1996. *East Africa through a Thousand Years.* London and Nairobi: Evans Brothers.

Wheatley, P., 1975. Analecta Sino-Africana Recensa. In: N. Chittick and R. Rotberg, eds., *East Africa and the Orient.* London and New York: Holmes and Meier, 76–114.

Whitehouse, D., 2001. East Africa and the maritime trade of the Indian Ocean, AD 800–1500. In: B. S. Amoretti, ed., *Islam in East Africa: New Sources*. Rome: Herder, 411–24.

Wilkinson, J. C., 1981. Oman and East Africa: New light on early Kilwan history from the Omani sources, *International Journal of African Historical Studies* 14/2, 272–305.

Wright, H. T., 1984. Early sea-farers of the Comoro Islands: The Dembeni phase of the IXth–Xth centuries AD. *AZANIA: Journal of the British Institute in Eastern Africa* 19, 13–59.

The Trans-American and Caribbean Slave Trade

A Broad Field to Explore

Jesús Guanche

BIOGRAPHY

Jesús Guanche Pérez (jguanche@cubarte.cult.cu): PhD in Historical Sciences with a specialisation in cultural anthropology. Researcher and Professor. He has been visiting professor and lecturer at universities in Africa, America and Europe. Meritorious scholar of the Academia de Ciencias de Cuba and member of the Academia de la Historia de Cuba. He has written several books, among them, *Componentes étnicos de la nación cubana*, Havana, 1996, 2008 and 2013; *Transculturación y africanía*, 2002; *Africanía y etnicidad en Cuba: los componentes étnicos africanos y sus múltiples denominaciones,* 2009 and 2011; *Iconografía de africanos y descendientes en Cuba*, 2010; *Léxico intercultural sobre religiones afroamericanas*, 2011; and *Diccionario etnográfico*. Los pueblos del Caribe insular y México-Centroamérica, vol. I. Los pueblos de Suramérica, vol. II, 2015.

ABSTRACT

Along with the direct trade of enslaved Africans from Africa to the Americas, it is important to acknowledge the constant slave-trade-related transit that took place through the Americas and the Caribbean. What can be identified as the trans-American and Caribbean slave trade is best exemplified by the case of Cuba, which functioned as a centre for the purchase and sale of slaves within the Latin American and Caribbean area. The complexity of the American Mediterranean, from diverse points of view, also has to be assessed in terms of the African legacy and the intercultural contact between the countries that participated as colonial metropolises, not only through direct trade from the African continent, but also through repeated trafficking between the American continent and the islands of the Caribbean Sea, and especially among the islands themselves, where languages, beliefs, traditions and customs, as well as economic, philosophical, and religious conceptions (and many other types of human relationships) were combined and served as the seeds of today's cultural diversity.

Introduction

American and Caribbean national cultures owe a significant part of their historical formation to the settlement of enslaved Africans between the sixteenth and
nineteenth centuries. In the case of Cuba, there has been a constant and multiple
African presence, from the dawn of the colonial era to the accelerated intensification of illegal trafficking during the dusk of Spanish rule on the island. However,
with regards to cultural influences, the wide variety of designations by which more
than a million people were known (i.e. purchased, sold, rented, persecuted) is still
unclear. These peoples were relocated to this part of the Caribbean and had a different identity imposed on them, which almost always resulted in dissociation
from their sense of belonging. And the nature of that identity, in many cases, depended on the place of arrest, slave depot, embarkation site and, sometimes, on the
languages of the African and European traffickers.

The specific issue of the trafficking of enslaved people from Africa to America
has been addressed from different perspectives, depending on the regions
(i.e. Africa, America and Europe), languages and methodological viewpoints. English speakers usually refer to the 'transatlantic slave trade', which carries strong
historical and sociocultural interpretative implications, given the importance and
the relevance of the struggle against racism and racial discrimination and its consequences today. French speakers continue to refer to the 'Traite négrière' (Black
slave trade), which dramatically recalls the lexicon of traffickers regardless of the
seriousness and rigour of the studies carried out. Portuguese-speaking authors, relying on rich documentary sources and oral memory, refer to the 'Comércio Ne-
greiro' (Black trade) to highlight the networks that were established from the
interior of the African continent to the coast.

Yet, on this side of the Atlantic, we must also reflect on and emphasise the trans-
American and Caribbean slave trade (trata transamericana y caribeña), which took
place in parallel to the African slave trade, and which has been referred to with the
most diverse designations encompassing the purchase and sale, capture, and transfer of African slaves and their descendants to slave sorting, reselling and distribution centres, from the south of the United States of America to South America,
with special emphasis on the islands of the Caribbean.

Multiple Ethnic Designations

The African ethnic components in Cuba have had multiple designations, which
were almost always related to the history and vicissitudes of the transatlantic slave
trade, from the early appearance of the 'Berbers' (or Amazighs) in Northern Africa

to the illegal irruption of the Makua in East Africa during the second half of the nineteenth century.

In parallel to the analysis of transatlantic slave trade, the trans-American and Caribbean slave trade must be studied from an intensive and multidirectional perspective as a complex and diverse process. This process is closely related to the colonisation of continental and insular areas and to the socioeconomic growth of the colonies, which depended on military conflicts in European metropolises, the continuous displacement and occupation of the trading outposts on African coasts, the relentless siege by pirates from the seventeenth to the eighteenth centuries, as well as the historic events that marked each part of the Americas and the Caribbean. In Cuba, the names of African slaves and their descendants who came from the Americas and the Caribbean no longer refer to possible ethnonyms or to generic names likely to be identified and classified according to ethnic origin. Any reference to cultural identity is erased and another designation is imposed on them according to the territory from which they came or the language spoken in the reshipment areas. In addition, it is not possible to determine whether the trafficking involved people from the African continent or Creole descendants born in the Americas and the Caribbean.

In Cuba, there are different slave denominations that originate in the territory now known as the United States of America. These names were acquired by slaves in Baltimore, Charleston (Guanche 1998, 50), Florida (de la Fuente 1986, 88, 95), New Orleans (Guanche 1998, 50), Rhode Island (Guanche 1996, 59) and Virginia (Guanche 1996, 59 and 1998, 50), for example. Along with the smuggling of goods and continuous ship trafficking, the presence of a slave workforce was common during the colonial period.

The arrival of one of many ships was announced in the capital with its respective slave cargo, as well as the sale of enslaved individuals:

PAPEL PERIÓDICO DE LA HAVANA,[1] 23 FEBRUARY 1792
Entry of ships: From Providence [Rhode Island] in id Gol el Pescado Dorado, carrying 132 slaves. Captain: Mr. Juan Baseik.

PAPEL PERIÓDICO DE LA HAVANA, 15 FEBRUARY 1811
For sale: creole slave from Florida, approximately 9 years old, very agile, at 300 pesos, available at the headquarters of the military, Sergeant Major of the regiment of Cuba, Joaquín Nezanel will provide information.

(Núñez 1998, 198 and 272)

---

1 T.N.: *Papel Periódico de la Habana* was the first colonial newspaper in Cuba.

We must bear in mind that Americans actively contributed to the slave trade in this area, based on their experience as pirates and smugglers. In this regard, José Luciano Franco underlines:

> The importance of piracy in supporting the trade of the colonies in the North, at least at the end of the seventeenth century, is not generally given enough consideration. English and American pirates armed in the ports of Boston, Newport, Philadelphia and New York and financially supported by respectable merchants, attacked the Spanish fleet in the Caribbean. They then navigated the Red Sea and the Indian Ocean where they boarded ships dedicated to trade with the East Indies and returned to the colonial ports loaded with precious metals, spices and preserves (1976, 3).

> In the first decade of the nineteenth century, between March 1806 and February 1807, thirty American ships entered through the port of Havana, resulting in the sale of five thousand slaves. More details can be found in the records of the National Archives of Cuba (Franco 1976, 13).

During the period of the clandestine slave trade, the Americans reproduced from other places the triangular trade that, in the seventeenth and eighteenth centuries, had filled the coffers of ship owners from Liverpool, Nantes and Bordeaux. In the first half of the nineteenth century, American ships sailed from Philadelphia, New York or Charleston with shipment produced in their home territory. In Havana, they added liquor and tobacco, both very valued on the African coast, where they would then trade both items for slaves. They later sold the slaves at a very good price in Cuba and finally returned back home with substantial profits.

In 1895 Thomas expressed that, 'only in New York, there were eighty-five ships with capacity to carry around thirty to sixty thousand slaves for the slave markets in Cuba. No matter how many slaves were transported, they were sold at the high price of more than a thousand American dollars per head, and even more when the captives knew of agriculture or spoke Spanish' (1998, 764). The business was so profitable that it was preferable to burn the ship after unloading the slave cargo than take the risk of being captured on the way home.

Also, in the opposite direction, the slave trade from Cuba to North America constituted a profitable business for the Cuban 'slave traders' who took advantage of the high prices charged in North America. In Cuba and Brazil, first-quality slaves could cost between 300 and 500 pesos. At the end of the 1819 war, the price for the same type of slave had increased to 900 dollars in Charleston and to 1,100 dollars in New Orleans. After a downturn that lasted more than a decade between 1830 and 1837, prices went up again from 1,000 to 1,200 dollars (Franco cit. Phillips 1976, 7).

With regards to continental America, some denominations found in documentary sources are inaccurate. According to Cremé (1994, 22) and Guanche (1998, 46), some slaves were brought from Costa Firme and, according to de la Fuente (1986, 93), other slaves came from Cuenca.[2] Costa Firme, also known as Province of Tierra Firme, is the old name that the Spanish empire gave to the American continental territory under its rule to differentiate it from the 'islands'. These slaves could be brought from any slave transit and distribution ports. On the Atlantic Coast, slaves could come from the ships that unloaded their cargo in Havana and were then reallocated to Veracruz and Campeche (New Spain); or they could have been unloaded in La Guaira and Cumaná and further reallocated to Cartagena de Indias (New Granada); or they could also have been dropped in Buenos Aires and Montevideo (Rio de la Plata) where they were reshipped to Rio de Janeiro. On the Pacific coast, slaves were disembarked in Acapulco and reallocated to Panama, Lima, El Callao and Valparaiso. Prior to these movements, and in the opposite direction, '[f]rom 1534 onwards, two years before the first foundation of Buenos Aires, the Spanish crown began to grant permits in order to introduce slaves [...] to Rio de la Plata from Africa and Brazil' (Picotti 1998, 37–39).

At the beginning of the nineteenth century slaves of this origin were still sold in Havana:

PAPEL PERIÓDICO DE LA HABANA, 6 JUNE 1802
For sale: mulatto woman from Costa Firme, laundress and cook, healthy, no blemishes, at 500, available at house no. 73 la Merced Street

(Núñez 1998, 248)

Therefore, as highlighted by Cremé (1994, 24) and Guanche (1996, 23; 1998, 46), it is not rare to use designations such as portugués (Portuguese), in plural or singular, to refer to the slaves brought to Cuba from Brazil.

From the second half of the eighteenth century, the slave trade had grown in the Angolan port of Benguela due to the growth of the agriculture sector in the south of Brazil. However, as Thomas points out: 'Many of the slaves in Benguela were shipped to Brazil, but they were often smuggled into Cuba or other ports of the Spanish Empire' (1998, 365).

We must remember that this business intensified during the height of slave trafficking during the years 1850–1860. Until then, slave trade to Brazil had had an advantage due to its proximity to Africa, a calmer sea and less persecution by the

---

2 Due to the characteristics of the source, we consider that it could be a slave from the Ecuadorean city of Cuenca, brought from across the Pacific, from Guayaquil, through maritime trade. Though this was not a common type of trade, the designation is recorded.

English fleet. For these reasons, slaves were always sold cheaper there than in Cuba. Because Brazilian slave ships were designed to make shorter journeys than ships sailing the Caribbean, the first ones that deviated from their original course sailed in appalling conditions, leaving a shocking death toll. Tomas Terry welcomed some of these expeditions, at rock-bottom prices and left the slaves in Juraguá to rehabilitate them and resell them. (Moreno I 1978, 278).[3]

Previously, the press had already reported the entrance of vessels from South America and the immediate sale of slaves:

PAPEL PERIÓDICO DE LA HABANA, 26 JULY 1792
Entry of ships: From Montevideo, Bergantin el Dichoso, carrying 1,706 quintals of jerky, 686 of tallow, 25,053 pesos 7 Spanish dollars and 83 negroes of both sexes, from the coast of Brazil, whose sell would start on July 26TH in the morning. Captain: Mr. Miguel de Costa.

(Núñez 1998, 47)

New denominations appeared such as Honduras (de la Fuente 1986, 88 and 95) and Panamá (de la Fuente 1986, 88 and 95) in Latin America; Campeche (de la Fuente 1986, 93; Ortiz 1987, 45; Ortiz 1991, 94) and Nueva España (de la Fuente 1986, 88 and 95) in Central America; Cartagena de Indias (Cremé 1994, 24 and Guanche 1998, 46) and Santa Marta (Cremé 1994, 24) in Mexico; Caracas (Guanche 1998, 46) in Colombian territory; and Maracaibo o Maracaybo (de la Fuente 1986, 88 and 95; Cremé 1994, 24 and Núñez 1998, 15) in Venezuela. The historical links between Cartagena de Indias and Havana date back to the beginning of the Spanish rule in America, through the fleet of galleons. With regards to African slave trade: 'Cartagena had the painful privilege of becoming the first slave port of Spanish America that back then (1590–1640) received many slaves, mostly of Bantu origin' (del Castillo 1997, 202).[4] Most merchants were Portuguese whose financial resources allowed them to buy positions of regidores (alderman). After the settlement of the Dutch in Curaçao towards 1630 and the English settlement in Jamaica in 1655, slave trafficking to Cuba and Tierra Firme

---

3 The author refers to three expeditions, with a total of 1,595 slaves, and describes his father's experience as an administrator of the *ingenio Juraguá,* along with the evident disproportion of the huge barracks of slaves compared to the tiny hut where slaves were, which helped to 'cover up a reception centre for slaves'.

4 The study on the evolution of trade of enslaved Africans to Veracruz and Cartagena to the island of São Tomé and Príncipe from 1590 to 1640 confirms the predominance of Bantu people captured in the area of Congo and Angola. This study was carried out by Nicolás Ngou-Mwe (2001, 65–83).

increased, through the ports of Riohacha, Santa Marta, Mompós and Cartagena. This trade was welcomed by several governors as a way to counterbalance the monopoly of the fleets. By then, most ships carrying slaves to Cartagena did not come directly from Africa, but from English, Dutch and French colonies in the Caribbean. This profitable business contributed 'also to the illegal introduction of goods on the pretext that they were brought for the use and consumption of the slaves' (ibid., 203).

In 1603, 144 slaves were sent from Cartagena to Havana. During the first half of the seventeenth century, this maritime and commercial trade also thrived in the ports of Santiago de Cuba, Bayamo and Baracoa. This activity continued in a systematic manner since in the 'second half of the eighteenth century, Cartagena slavers were transporting slaves to Havana, the biggest slave market in the Spanish America' (ibid., 204–205).

In 1635, when the Havanan General Díaz-Pimienta commanded the expedition against the pirate base in the island of Santa Catalina, located in the north of Cartagena de Indias, he seized a booty amounting to more than half million pesos, among them '600 negro slaves'[5] that were in their possession as part of the booty.

In the late eighteenth century, the media reported both slave trading and ship entry:

PAPEL PERIÓDICO DE LA HABANA, 16 JUNE 1791
For sale: Ms. Maria de Jesús Arostegui owns a 20-year-old creole negro from Cartagena, and her baby. The slave cooks, sews and does the laundry regularly. She is being sold at 300 pesos.

PAPEL PERIÓDICO DE LA HABANA, 16 SEPTEMBER 1791
Entry of ships: From Cartagena de Indias in 21 Fragata Inglesa el Orange, carrying 187 negroes of both sexes. Captain: Mr. Juan Kyfxin.

(Núñez 1998, 192–193)

Similarly, the historical and commercial ties between Cuba and the Viceroyalty of New Spain, the ports of Campeche and Veracruz in the Yucatan Peninsula and Caracas and Maracaibo in the Viceroyalty of New Granada date back to the colonial era. This is why the previously mentioned slave denominations were common in trade relationships.

During the first quarter of the seventeenth century, slave ships sailing to New Spain made stopovers in Jamaica under the pretext of carrying out some repairs when in reality they were diverting part of the cargo to Cuba in order to avoid taxes.

5 See César García del Pino, 2001, 111.

The royal officials of New Spain lodged a complaint about it, on 27 September 1619, in which they quoted as an example, the case of Tomás Pérez de Mella, who had acquired 97 pieces of frames from an Angolan ship. Slaves that were missing from the cargo were declared dead during the journey.[6]

Slaves from Venezuela and Mexico were announced in the Havanan market:

PAPEL PERIÓDICO DE LA HABANA, 22 JANUARY 1792

Entry of ships: From Matanzas, coming from Guarico in the ship 20 Berg Francés la Descubierta, carrying 123 negroes. Captain: Mr. Joseph Sabianu.

DIARIO DE LA HABANA, 10 NOVEMBER 1810

For sale: Fifteen-year-old girl from Maracaibo, great house servant, cuts and makes tunics, healthy and without blemishes, at 500 pesos, at house no. 87, O-Reylli Street, from Santa Catalina to Monserrate.

DIARIO DEL GOBIERNO DE LA HABANA, 20 AUGUST 1813

For Sale: 10-year-old creole from Campeche, healthy, free of blemishes, at house no. 11, O-Reilly Street, in front of brazo fuerte.

(Núñez 1998, 197 and 287)

The denomination of slaves coming from Puerto Rico (Cremé 1994, 24) and Santo Domingo (Cremé 1994, 24; de la Fuente 1986, 88 and 95; Guanche 1998, 46) can be found in the Spanish-speaking Antilles. The maritime, migratory and commercial traffic between the territories of the Spanish insular colonies in the Caribbean was common in the area. In the mid-eighteenth century, a detailed account of the groups of slaves, which were introduced into the ports of Havana and Santiago de Cuba and came from the new site of Puerto Rico between November 1766 and January 1769,[7] is available. Nineteen ships were connected, which carried a total amount of 4,949 slaves, with an on-board mortality rate of 1.83 per cent (91 slaves). Precisely 64.32 per cent of the slaves that arrived alive were men, and 35.86 per cent were women.

In the case of Santo Domingo, the Letter of Relation written by Diego Velasquez on 1 August 1515, is widely known by historians. In this letter, Velasquez mentions the presence of many 'black slaves' in Santiago de Cuba and requires the officials of Spain to 'send the masters who helped in the works carried out by His Majesty

6 García del Pino, 2001, 63.
7 García-Melis. Op. cit. Document XLV, 257.

along with two pairs of oxen with their respective carts and 12 negroes who know how to carry out construction work'.[8]

The sale of slaves from the neighbouring islands is reported by the media:

DIARIO DE LA HABANA, 20 NOVEMBER 1811
For sale: negro woman from the Dominican Republic, healthy and without blemishes, cook and laundress, at 440 pesos, available at house no. 103, Villegas Street.

DIARIO DEL GOBIERNO DE LA HABANA, 9 FEBRUARY 1814
For sale: two creole negroes from Puerto Rico, one is a carpenter and the other a fieldworker. Both are healthy and with no blemishes: available at house no. 22, San Ignacio Street.

(Núñez 1998, 277 and 290)

The organisation of the smuggling of slaves and goods by Americans in the Spanish Caribbean became more important than piracy in the eighteenth century, and it was practised with impunity due to the venality of Spanish officials. The smuggling was carried out through sloops that were able to disembark in small river basins and that were announced by firing a cannon (Franco 1976, 5). A similar process occurred with the denomination of slaves acquired in the English-speaking Caribbean where references are made to the language, English, to designate 'English people' or 'ingré' (see Cremé 1994, 24; Guanche 1997, 23 and 1998, 46; López 1986a, 49; and Ortiz 1987, 50 and 1990, 241) in the territory of Barbados (de la Fuente 1986, 88, 95), Granada (Guanche 1998, 50) and Jamaica or Jamayca (Cremé 1994, 24; de la Fuente 1986, 88 and 95; Guanche 1996, 59; 1998, 50 and Núñez 1998, 189). The repeated raids carried out by Cuban pirates in Jamaica during the seventeenth century reached such a level that in 1686 the Governor of the neighbouring island, Hender Moleworth, complained to the authorities of Trinidad when he learned that pirates from the Greater Antilles 'were planning an invasion of the north of the island, with the aim of catching some negroes'.[9] This is why historian Ramiro Guerra points out:

At the end of 1687, the English were suffering more damage than the Spanish [...] The marine insurance rate was rising in London and life was getting more expensive in Jamaica [...] Cuban piracy was increasing rapidly. Canoes manned by Spanish and Creoles, negroes and mulattoes, sailed from the river mouth of

8 Pichardo. Op. cit. Document 10, 89.
9 García del Pino, 2001, 200.

the island and from many coves in the coast to attack English merchant ships and make them disembark in the furthest places of the Jamaican coast, with the aim of stealing slaves and livestock.[10]

During the first half of the eighteenth century, the emerging Creole sugar aristocracy felt rejection towards the type of African slave that they were forced to buy from the English, since they were the only providers on the island, because 'the best slaves stayed at Sugar Islands, and Cuba was sent the remains made up by the Congos who were corrupted by all vices, slaves from Calabar, who hung themselves or ran away, the Mandingo and the Bambara' (Moreno cit. Urrutia II 1978, 9). Reports of 1741 on the value of the annual production of the island, the silver entering the island, the slave trade and the price of Cuban sugar set in Cadiz confirm the annual amount for the 300 slaves acquired by English traffickers of the area.

This is shown by the media of that period:

PAPEL PERIÓDICO DE LA HABANA, 12 DECEMBER 1790
For sale: black creole woman from Jamaica, cook and laundress, valued at 280 pesos, with a two-year-old daughter valued at 70 pesos. Available at house no. 223, Paula Casa Street.

PAPEL PERIÓDICO DE LA HABANA, 12 DECEMBER 1790
Entry of ships: From Jamaica in bergantín Inglés el Dorado, carrying 28 negroes of both sexes. Captain: Guillermo Torta.

(Núñez 1998, 189 and 196)

In the French-speaking Caribbean, only the name 'French' appears (Guanche 1998, 46; López 1986a, 49) and 'French Port-au-Prince' (Guanche 1998, 50). However, multiple references are made to slave trade in the French colonies.

The work of the Cuban author José Antonio Saco (1797–1879)[11] provides several examples of intensive exchanges with the Spanish colonies, from the smuggling of 'Indian' slaves between Margarita Island and the mouth of the Orinoco river in Martinique in the late eighteenth century, to the massive exchange of Africans between both parts (Spanish and French) of Hispaniola Island (Santo Domingo and Haiti).

Saint Kitts (or Saint Christopher) is considered to be the first French colony of the New World. In 1635 a French pirate named Pitre 'sold a large cargo of slaves captured from the Spanish in those waters and thanks to whom the island began

---

10 Guerra, 111.
11 *Historia de la esclavitud en las colonias francesas*, Havana, 2002.

to grow' (2002, 146). The French and the Dutch kept introducing slaves in Saint Kitts either directly from Africa or from the ones that were captured from the Spanish on the Brazilian coasts.

Recurring attacks of pirates born or established in Cuba during the seventeenth century also affected the French Antilles. At the beginning of 1685, the Havanan pirate Mateo Guarín (or Marín) owned a galley with which he attacked a plantation in Haiti and captured around forty slaves for a total value of 8,800 pesos, which was declared a 'good catch' in the cities of Baracoa and Port-au-Prince.[12]

Armed conflicts between England and France, and the piracy that was either at their service or at their risk, also contributed to the trafficking of slaves into the area. Saco refers to the following examples:

> Freebooters from the French part of Santo Domingo assaulted Vera Cruz in 1683 and, in addition to the ransom they were paid, took from the city 1,500 negro slaves and free negroes and mulattoes, with whom they returned to Santo Domingo. [In 1694], an expedition made up of three battleships and 20 cargo ships with 1,500 men, departed from Santo Domingo [...], attacked Jamaica, burned down farms, committed other atrocities and finally left with a booty consisting of 3,000 negroes, according to Charlevoix and Raynal, 1,000 negroes according to Bryan Edwards and 1,500 negroes according to Montgomery Martin (2002, 181).

In Cuba, the immigration of thousands of Africans and 'French' Creole descendants during the dramatic events of the Haitian Revolution is well-known. These people were placed in the settlement sites of their respective masters as part of the goods to be transported.

The entry of ships carrying slaves from the neighbouring island is announced by the press:

PAPEL PERIÓDICO DE LA HABANA, 23 FEBRUARY 1792
Entry of ships: From the French Port-au-Prince in Frigate 'la Bezi', carrying 414 negroes: Captain: Mr. Pedro Acuche.

PAPEL PERIÓDICO DE LA HABANA, 24 JUNE 1792
For sale: [...] French negro of around 28 or 30 years old, smart appearance, hairdresser, barber, launderer of silk socks and agile to do all types of household chores but with blemishes, at 300 pesos. Available at San Agustín Street to Santa Clara, house no.36.

(Núñez 1998, 198)

---

12 Véase García del Pino, 2001, 196.

With the French-speaking Caribbean, Cuba also made interesting deals, and offers of slaves illegally smuggled from the French port of Nantes were also becoming interesting. From Santiago de Cuba, in 1825, the firm Dutocq et Cie sent a letter to Mr. Bannaffe and Mr. Laviere who lived in Pointe-à-Pitre, Guadeloupe, which contained the following offer:

> Following the instructions given to us by Mr. Courennneau of Bordeaux, we have the honour to offer our services for this place. As you may know, there is an important advantage in selling ebony in our market [...]. This year, we have received a great number of shipments of this item, from merchants in Nantes. All our sales have been remarkably successful and the longest credits are fourteen months. The last sold cargo is the one from the 'Henriette' from Nantes...
> (Franco 1976, 20–21).

In the Dutch-speaking Caribbean, we can find the following toponyms: Curazao, Curaçao and Curasao (Cremé 1994, 24; Guanche 1998, 50; and Núñez 1998, 188) and the following Spanish linguonyms of 'Dutch': holandés, holandeses, olandés and olandesa (Cremé 1994, 24; Guanche 1998, 46; López 1986a, 49; and Núñez 1998, 125), which reflect the presence of slaves coming from this territory or sold by Dutch traffickers.

The smuggling of goods and slaves from the Dutch territories to Cuba during the seventeenth century is evidenced by the complaint of a 34-piece Dutch ship that was doing business in Bayamo, as well as the illegal disembarkation of slaves through a farmyard in Guanimar, property of Sub-Lieutenant Cristóbal de Poveda, in complicity with his foreman Juan Díaz.[13]

In the late eighteenth century, the press announces:

> PAPEL PERIÓDICO DE LA HABANA, 21 NOVEMBER 1790
> For sale: a negro woman from Curasao, seamstress and laundress, healthy with no blemishes, at 350 pesos. Information available in this printing house.

> PAPEL PERIÓDICO DE LA HABANA, 3 JANUARY 1796
> For sale: Dutch mulatto, around 30 years old, good-looking, hairdresser and barber, healthy with no blemishes, at 350 pesos libres. Available at Obra pía Street, in the bakery close to the missionary school of the RR.PP Capuchins.
>
> (Núñez 1998, 188 and 223)

13 See García de Pino, 2001, 181–82.

Final Considerations

Along with the presence of Africans directly trafficked from the African continent, the continuous trafficking of slaves in the area of the Americas and the Caribbean is very significant. However, we can no longer identify the ethnic composition of the African population. We can only identify the geographical origin and the linguistic reference of the human cargo.

As evidenced by multiple details, this trafficking created a wide network of human interconnections, including cultural, spatial, commercial and political relations, among others, which were initially conditioned by the transatlantic smuggling of African slaves, but did not remain dependent on that. As we have analysed by geographical area and in a chronological manner, the trafficking of slaves inside the Americas and the Caribbean had its own evolutionary process in different periods, from the reallocation of slaves according to provisions set forth by the colonial power, as in the case of Spain and its colonies; to piracy when slave owners were captured as part of the booty; to the purchase of a steady and enduring supply of slaves, as in the case of the markets under the control of Portugal, England and France; to the legal sale and transfer of slaves from different areas and its public announcement in the media at the time; to the tricks to get away with the clandestine trafficking and to avoid systematic persecutions; and, in short, to all the diverse causes that made possible an ebb and flow of intercultural communication that represents another way to assess historical linkages within the area.

The complexity of the American Mediterranean, from diverse points of view, also has to be assessed in terms of the African legacy and the intercultural contact between the countries that participated as colonial metropolises, not only through direct trade from the African continent, but also through repeated trafficking between the American continent and the islands of the Caribbean Sea, and especially among the islands themselves, where languages, beliefs, traditions, and customs, as well as economic, philosophical and religious conceptions (and many other types of human relationships) were mixed and served as the seeds of today's cultural diversity.

BIBLIOGRAPHY

Cremé Ramos, Zoe, 1994. *Pesquisaje sobre la procedencia de los esclavos en la Jurisdicción de Cuba entre 1792–1838*. Havana: Publicigraf.
de la Fuente García, Alejandro, 1986. Denominaciones étnicas de los esclavos introducidos en Cuba. Siglos XVI y XVII. *Anales del Caribe* [Havana] no. 6, 75–96.
del Castillo Mathieu, Nicolás, 1997. Relaciones comerciales y lingüísticas entre Cuba y Cartagena de Indias. *América Negra* [Bogotá: Pontificia Universidad Javeriana] no. 14 (diciembre), 201–209.

Franco, José Luciano, 1976. *Contrabando y trata negrera en el Caribe.* Havana: Editorial de Ciencias Sociales.

García del Pino, César and Melis Cappa, Alicia, 1988. *Documentos para la historia colonial de Cuba.* Havana: Editorial de Ciencias Sociales.

García del Pino, César, 2001. *El corso en Cuba. Siglo XVII.* Havana: Editorial de Ciencias Sociales.

Guerra, Ramiro, 1971. *Manual de historia de Cuba. Desde su descubrimiento hasta 1868.* Havana: Editorial de Ciencias Sociales.

Guanche, Jesús, 1996. *Componentes étnicos de la nación cubana.* Colección La Fuente Viva, no. 3. Havana: Fundación Fernando Ortiz y UNEAC.

Guanche, Jesús, 1998. El Papel Periódico de la Havana y las denominaciones étnicas, geográficas, lingüísticas y raciales de los esclavos africanos y sus descendientes en Cuba durante el siglo XVIII. *Palabras de la Ceiba* [Seville], no. 2.

López Valdés, Rafael, 1986a. Pertenencia étnica de los esclavos de Tiguabos (Guantánamo) entre los años 1789 y 1844. *Revista de la Biblioteca Nacional José Martí* [Havana], año 77, 28/3, 23–63.

López Valdés, Rafael, 1986b. Notas para el estudio etnohistórico de los esclavos lucumí de Cuba. *Anales del Caribe* [Havana], no. 6, 54–74.

Moreno Fraginals, Manuel, 1978. *El ingenio. Complejo económico social cubano del azúcar.* 3 vols. Havana: Editorial de Ciencias Sociales.

Ngou-Mve, Nicolás, 2001. Sao Tomé et la diaspora bantou vers l´Amérique hispanique. In: La traite et l´esclavage dans le monde Lusophone. *Cahiers des Anneaux de la Mémoire* [Nantes], no. 3, 65–83.

Núñez Jiménez, Antonio, 1998. *Los esclavos negros.* Havana: Editorial Letras Cubanas.

Ortiz, Fernando, 1916. [reprt. 1987]. *Los negros esclavos.* Havana: Editorial de Ciencias Sociales.

Ortiz, Fernando, 1991. *Glosario de afronegrismos.* Havana: Editorial de Ciencias Sociales, Havana.

Picotti C., Dina V, 1998. *La presencia africana en nuestra identidad.* Serie antropológica. Buenos Aires: Ediciones del Sol.

Saco, José Antonio, 2002. *Historia de la esclavitud en las colonias francesas.* Havana: Editorial de Ciencias Sociales y Sociedad Económica de Amigos del País.

Thomas, Hugh, 1998. *La trata de esclavos. Historia del tráfico de seres humanos de 1440 a 1880.* Barcelona: Editorial Planeta.

From Freedom to Survival to Dreaming Freedom

The Saga of Afro-Descendants in Latin America and the Caribbean

Quince Duncan

BIOGRAPHY

Writer and human rights activist, Duncan is author and co-author of over fifty books, including historical texts, essays on race relations, educational material and fiction. Educated in Latin American Studies, he has been granted an Honorary Doctorate by St. Olaf College, Northfield, Minnesota, and has won several literary awards. He has lectured in his home country of Costa Rica and in US universities, and has been active in literary and human rights conferences and activities around the world.

Introduction

One of the most common omissions in the field of Africana Studies – the study of those of African and African descent in the Americas – is an overarching view of the resistance of the Black population to slavery and its consequences. Africans and Afro-descendants – men and women – fought on the slave ships, en route to Latin America; they fought on the plantations, whether by passive means or by uprisings; they fled to the woods, where they set up their quilombos, palenques and cumbes, either as a separate group or in alliance with the Indigenous peoples; and they kept the struggle going.

But resistance was not only physical. It was also intellectual. Through petitions, cultural maroonage, alternative religion, music and oral traditions, they forged a world of their own, sometimes mixing with mainstream culture, and in other cases, operating on the verge of the official culture. The outcome has been a sort of 'pan ethnia' stemming from their common cultural origin (at the same time unique and diverse), their internal cultural mixing and their common plight under the yoke of enslavement, racism and racial discrimination, resulting in their being victims of exclusion, invisibility, stigma and even self-rejection.

This essay proposes a brief but global view of their many forms of physical, political, cultural and religious resistance, with the clear objective of continuing to break the silence over the dignified struggle for survival and freedom that Afro-descendants have waged in the Americas. By such means, the final goal is to contribute to the promotion of intercultural and inter-ethnic understanding among the peoples of the world.

The Root of Freedom:
Africa before Transatlantic Slavery

It is now recognised that in central, western and southern Africa, as in Western European countries, there are strong influences from the original civilisations of North Africa. Sufficient evidence is available (Diop 1991) to affirm the presence of cultural elements of Egyptian and Ethiopian civilisations. However, the vast majority of the enslaved persons during transatlantic slavery were brought from the African territory south of the Sahara Desert.

Civilisation did not solely develop in North Africa. Before the transatlantic slave trade, there were well-organised states and consolidated cultures equivalent to or even more advanced than their European counterparts. Learning centres also existed; the one at Timbuktu is an excellent example. Leo Africanus, a Moor born in Granada, Spain, and who travelled extensively throughout Africa, described Timbuktu as a centre with a large quantity of doctors, judges, priests and other cultured men, all kept by the king. This university centre was developed in the context of the tributary kingdoms of Ghana (c. AD 830 to c. 1235), Mali (c. AD 1230 to c. 1600) and Songhai (also spelled Songhay; early fifteenth to the late sixteenth centuries).

From Ghana to Mali and Songhai, these advanced African states of the time, each successively conquering the other and each continuing the cultural achievements of its predecessor, maintained extensive trade with North Africa, and to a lesser degree, with certain European states, such as Spain and Germany.

During the reign of Askia Muhammad, the most extraordinary of its monarchs, Songhai became a model state, with provinces headed by their respective governors and a central government with officers equivalent to our modern government ministries (justice, agriculture and finance, among others); collectors of taxes in each community; inspectors of trade; a standardised system of weights and measures; and a standing army of around 200,000 controlling a territory much larger than the then-existing Holy Roman Empire in Europe.

Unfortunately, Songhai gradually undertook large-scale slave trafficking, producing internal conflicts and continual disputes with its neighbours. These struggles eroded the empire to the point that, in 1589, the Mansur of Morocco crossed the desert leading an army of his own soldiers and European mercenaries, all equipped with firearms, to conquer Songhai. Looted and destroyed, the empire ceased to be a state, and disappeared from the world scene (Shinnie 1970, 70 and 78).

Enslaved Africans were also seized from many other central and south African regions. Two outstanding examples are the Ashanti, a people of Akan culture. They created a political Federation (1701–1896) and succeeded in holding out against the British until the end of the nineteenth century. The other example is the Yoruba – a culture that exercised great influence on the religious thought of Latin America.

The Yoruba states of Ife (eleventh century) and Oyo and Benin (c. 1200) have been frequently compared to the ancient Greek states in terms of their political organisation. Yoruba people maintained their independence to the end of the nineteenth century, when superior military power, economic pressure and a goodly amount of diplomatic manipulations ended up with their becoming British protectorates or colonies.

From a religious point of view, some of the enslaved Africans were Muslims, others Christians (from the Kingdom of Congo), while a third group practised traditional religions.

It is pertinent to highlight the concept of 'ancestral community' among Africans. African cultures nourished the idea of belonging to an ancestral community consisting of the ancestors, the living and the unborn. It was vital to be a part of the collective soul of the tribe, ethnic group or clan, and the worst thing that could happen to a person was to be excluded from this community. Understanding this notion is important to comprehending later attitudes of the Africans en route to the Americas or in the slave mines and on plantations.

African Women in Ancient and Medieval Societies

African women in ancient and medieval societies were much freer than their Western counterparts. While an ancient Greek woman, for example, had to be represented in the judicial system by a man, an Egyptian woman enjoyed a consolidated legal system, including the possibility of representing herself in court. Higher-class women owned and could dispose of their own property. They could buy and sell land and all sorts of goods, servants, slaves, cattle. They could do all of this according to their own free will.

The situation, as a general rule, was the same in the south. Robert Fisher (1998) and María Elisa Velázquez (2006) have written extensively on the matter. Indeed, Muslim travellers such as Ibn Battuta and Leo Africanus, and also Christian missionaries described the extraordinary position of women even under Muslim rule. They were scandalised to see the public role of women; complaints included that they were more respected than men and that some didn't even bother to cover their heads.

According to diverse sources, Kikuyo women were the major food producers and held control over land. Among the Malinke, women were the main support of the family. They cultivated land, inherited and controlled the household economy, paid taxes and exercised very strong influence politically. Egba women were the backbone of the commercial system, with total control over the market in their region.

Some African societies were polygamous. But even in those cases, in general, not only did each wife have her own home, but she also controlled land and cattle, a position that gave her a very ample degree of freedom.

In many of the societies from which people were enslaved, women played vital roles in educating their children and in preserving and transmitting basic knowledge of their common lore.

Another very powerful role played by women in many societies was as spiritual leaders. Even today, this is not a minor role in Africa, where the whole culture is impregnated by religiosity. In fact, in traditional African culture, there is no such thing as a separate secular dimension to life. Every aspect of a person's being, from birth to death, is explained from a religious perspective.

In many African societies, the queen mother held a very superior position, with authority. And even in cases where the ruler was always male, the queen mother played such roles as selecting or sanctioning the successor of the king and fulfilling responsibilities as the voice of women and as the officer entrusted with women's affairs. In some cases, women met in separate assemblies, which had to be consulted on such important matters as going to war.

In Africa there were many queens governing their nations with supreme power – spiritual, economic and military. Nubia was famous for its queens, but this was a common phenomenon in a number of other nations. Queen Nzinga Mbande (1583–1663) of the Mbundu people (southwestern Africa) has been immortalised for her formidable resistance to Portuguese domination.

The Ashanti nation is an outstanding example of women's roles in traditional African societies. Inheritance was matrilineal. The head of each clan and of the Ashanti Federation was always male, but his power was controlled and limited by that of the queen mother, whose privileges included the authority to reprimand the king and to choose his successor from among his nephews – not from his sons. Also, among the Ashanti, children in general were considered a blessing. But a baby girl was double blessing. As a potential mother, she would be able to provide successors for her lineage.

The birth of a boy would be greeted with 'Well, it is OK'; while a baby girl would merit the expression 'We thank God'.

An anecdote told by the Scottish explorer Mungo Park (cited by Northrup, 2002) is illustrative of the audacity of African women. He ran into a town in the interior of Africa, where he was received with surprise and curiosity. After interrogating him, and counting his toes and fingers to make sure he was human, they forced him to unbutton his waistcoat so they could examine his white skin. But much to his disgust, a delegation of royal women visited him a few days later to find out if 'Nazarene' men (Christians) were circumcised as were the Muslims.

As noted by Velázquez, due to the impingements of Muslim faith, as in the case of the great tributary empires (Mali and Songhay), and later Western Christianity under colonial rule, many of these traditional values were lost. But even today in a number of African societies, there remain strong bits and pieces of the past.

Women of African Descent in Latin America

Afro-descendent societies of the Americas were formed over a number of years, on the bases of enslaved Africans and strong racial mixing (*mestizaje*) with the local Indigenous and immigrant European populations. But it is paramount to the understanding of Afro-descendent women's role in the struggle for survival and freedom in Latin America and the Caribbean, to keep in mind the original position. Notably enough, even enslaved women had a higher status in traditional African culture than elsewhere.

Also, it is true, as stated above, that Islamic faith and Christianity changed in diverse ways the status of women in Africa, but many of the enslaved people taken to the Americas still held traditional cultural perspectives, regardless of their allegiance to the 'official' church. It is no surprise that in the caste paintings of New Spain (Mexico), many Black and Afro-mestizo women are depicted in defiant positions in relation to their White husbands.

Rina Cáceres (2000) and María Elisa Velázquez (2006) have written extensively on the role of women in colonial Latin America, the 'esclavas, mulatas and pardas' as they were termed. Slavery was bitter, but it would be a mistake to see the Neo-African and Afro-descendent populations as poor victims. The writings of Cáceres, Velázquez and others render visible the multiple struggles of the Black population in general, underlining specific examples of the role played by Afro-descendent women.

A careful examination of their position over centuries illustrates the fact that, contrary to their Western counterparts, Afro-descendent women were never widely confined to private roles. On the contrary, while restricted in their capacity to exercise power, and although possessing only limited freedom, they were either able to or forced to play their role in public affairs, and as analysed below, were an essential part of the resistance to oppression and of the struggle for freedom.

Enslavement and Resistance:
Men and Women Together

The direct confrontation with the enslaving process to which Africans were submitted started on the Continent. John Newton, an English slave trafficker, documented in 1753 that the Black population probably had the same prejudices against
White men that Whites had against Africans. Fear played an additional role, since
the majority were from the interior and had never seen the sea. According to legend, the sea was the end of the world. Furthermore, Africans were mostly convinced that they were being captured to be eaten (Hart 1984, 67).

In addition to those fears, there were other factors involved, such as religious beliefs. To die far from home would severely jeopardise the possibility of continuing as part of the ancestral community, since it would be difficult for the soul to
maintain contact with the ancestors. For many, death was preferable than being
uprooted and transported across the seas.

Another trafficker involved in the enslavement was Captain Thomas Phillips. In
his journal, he complained about individual resistance. Black people, he said, were
in such horror of leaving their country that they would often jump out of the boat
as they were conducted to the slave ships, and would keep under water, drowning
themselves. This, of course, may seem an extreme act of self-annihilation, but
from the perspective of the captives, it was an act of heroism – the route back to
their ancestral community in Africa. Others, once on the ship, would jump overboard to be devoured by sharks that would follow the vessels during the entire trip
(Hart 1984, 46).

Blake, whose work on slavery was originally published in 1856, cited a pirate to
tell the story of captives on board refusing to eat. 'A man stolen at Galena river [...]
refused to eat, and persisted till dead'. A woman brought on board would neither eat
nor speak. She was submitted to extreme torture for three or four days, at the end of
which she died. Before passing away, she broke her silence to make it clear that
through death she would be able to go back home to her friends (Blake 1969, 132).

These examples explain why controls were very strict on boarding. Thomas
Philips, cited above, wrote in his diary that there were two dangerous moments –
the first, on boarding and as long as the African coast was still in view. The second dangerous moment was on landing – as soon as the ships came near the coast.
For that reason, when at port, the men were kept chained in twos, strictly guarded,
with firearms ready for use. In open sea, the danger receded, since the Africans
were aware of the fact that although they might succeed in freeing themselves,
they did not know how to operate the vessels (Hart 1984, 70–71).

Another form of resistance on the vessels was insurrection. William Snelgrave,
a trafficker who published a book in 1734, said very bluntly that many slave trips

failed due to riots, which in some cases, caused the total loss of the ship and the death of White men; in other cases, it had been absolutely necessary to kill or injure a large number of the enslaved people, with the purpose of preventing total destruction (Hart 1984, 70). Richard Hart, quoting Manis and Cowley, mentioned that there were some fifty-five recorded riots on the slave ships between 1699 and 1865.

In fact, although some controls were lessened during the trips, traffickers were still on the alert, with weapons pointing toward the Africans, fearing that at any moment there could be an uprising.

Resistance continued on arrival. For the enslaved, the arrival in port was a very traumatic experience. Captives that were not directly consigned to a purchaser would have to go by auction, held in a very frightening manner, as a result of which, many Blacks jumped overboard. Western-style auction only confirmed the Africans' impression that the intention of these buyers was to eat them.

Once on the plantations and estates, Africans continued their struggle for freedom. In 1519 in Santo Domingo, Henriques led the first of these revolts, with a contingent of enslaved people brought from Spain and Portugal. By 1522 Cardinal Cisneros complained about what he considered to be 'the Black threat'. But rebellion in the form of open armed confrontation was rare. Africans did not have the arms to launch an open war.

Facing Colonial Strategies

Colonial powers in the Americas practised different strategies to maintain their domination of the population as well as the control and use of the material resources, including wars of extermination. This strategy is clearly observable in North America, where the main objective of the invader was not the control and exploitation of the local labour force but rather land grabbing. For that reason, conflict took the form of military campaigns to exterminate the local population and to replace them with European immigrants. This strategy was not followed by Spain as a consistent policy. It is true that there were cruel practices such as dismemberment and torture, but the majority of victims among Native Americans were not from military confrontations, but rather from the breakdown of the productive cycle and from diseases unknown to the Indigenous people. The Spaniards subjected them to slavery and other forms of servitude with long working days. Nutrition levels fell dramatically, making them even more vulnerable healthwise. Extermination was overwhelmingly the product of extreme exploitation, undernutrition and diseases rather than of open war or military retaliations conducted in response to specific situations. Racial genocide, as an open strategy to replace the local population, was an exception and not the rule in colonial Latin America.

The main objective in colonial Latin America and the Caribbean was the extraction of mineral resources and large-scale produce, a realm of exploitation justified at the time by Friar Juan Ginés de Sepúlveda, a Spanish historian and ecclesiastic. According the Friar, Native Americans were natural slaves. This consideration gave way to racial bias. Spaniards were allotted the mythical right of guardianship: for them, it was a question of a pagan Indigenous population suffering from chronic infantilism and incapable of governing themselves vis-à-vis Christian Spanish masters, civilised, with the obligation to save the Indians' souls.

In light of advanced Amerindian civilisations, such as the Mayan, the Toltec or the Incan, Sepúlveda's doctrine could not withstand close analysis. But this of course was not necessary, since the ideological/religious system of the time, functioning totally on the basis of arbitrary and authoritarian opinions, carefully aligned to justify slavery and colonialism.

In the case of the Black populations, enslavement was the method consistently employed, with support also provided by theology. Pope Nicholas V (1447–1455) decreed perpetual slavery for Black Africans and their descendants. Protestant religious leaders and historians also justified the system. Edward Long, for example, author of *The History of Jamaica,* published in 1774, vindicated the enslavement of Black populations in blatantly racist terms. According to him, the Africans suffered from a lack of intelligence and had no moral system. Invoking Divine Law, Long considered that each member of Creation is properly placed and adapted for certain uses and confined within the bounds set by the Divine Creator. The Black population was not just a different class, they constituted a different species (Long, cited by Hart 1984, 89–90).

It is interesting that while Long articulated his racist myths postulating the chronic mental handicap of Black people, in Africa Emperor Shaka Zulu (1787–1828) created one of the most powerful armies in Africa's history, confronting and defeating the British and the Dutch. By 1824 he had completed his efforts to unify all Zulu clans into a single nation, whose territory was twice the size of Europe. Not only was Shaka a brilliant military man, but also a great statesman. Entirely without European influence, he organised a modern State, with State ministers and regional governors.

Contrary to the alleged lack of morality among Blacks, the ethical discipline in the Zulu regime was high and demanding. For example, the death penalty was applied to any soldier who raped a woman, regardless of his rank. On the contrary, in Long's backyard, the violation of enslaved women was the rule and the rapist enjoyed total impunity.

The need for manpower for the extraction of minerals and large-scale produce gave rise to ethnocide – the systematic destruction of Amerindian and African culture through cultural indoctrination. Although ethnocide does not always have a racial basis, in the context of Latin America, race and ethnicity intersected. This strategy of enculturation implied the loss of the cultural values of Indigenous peoples and peoples of African descent, and it meant the forging at the same time of strong derogative stigmas associated with particular phenotypic characteristics. The final goal of this process of ethnocide, according to the Third Black Code issued by the Spanish Crown, was to try to give the system a legal structure: limited assimilation, that is, the incorporation of the individual into the dominant culture in a subordinated position. Colonial powers thus created the caste system in Latin America and the Caribbean. The word 'caste' was first used to indicate the tribe or place of origin of the Africans. Hence, the terminology 'congo caste' or 'lucumi caste' – and other terms were used to identify African ethnicity and to distinguish Africans from the Black Ladinos Christianised in Spain. But over time, the word 'caste' became associated with the class-race structure of the colonies. Classification of children according to their caste was made at baptism, and registered in birth records.

The objective of this system, therefore, was limited assimilation. It took families six generations of consistent intermarriage with White spouses to 'bleach out'. Whiteness of skin gave status. Different jobs corresponded to each caste-class. As Nina Friedemann points out, the end result was several categories of people who, without being White, aspired to be considered as such, owing to the fact that to a great extent, success was limited or enhanced by caste. (Friedemann 1993, 64). The caste system therefore was not predicated on the absolute exclusion of all non-White people, but proposed the myth of the gradual ascent of families by racial mixing.

To illustrate how vital was the caste system in people's lives, Nina Friedmann cites the case of a Colombian father who sued his own son for offences against the family. In 1787 at Santa Fe de Bogotá, Ignacio Salazar filed a complaint against his son, on the grounds that he did his sisters a great harm by limiting their chances of a good marriage. The afflicted father alleged that his family was composed of honest people, free from any contamination of the Guinea race – meaning African – in spite of which his son married secretly with a 'Mulatto' woman, an act that the father took as a serious affront to his family (Friedemann 1993, 65). In other words, while the system proposed interracial marriages, 'honest high-class White people' such as Salazar's son, were not supposed to wed people from the lower castes.

This bleaching ideology created a lot of problems for the Black communities. Among other consequences, it gave birth to the widespread idea that it was desirable to 'raise' or 'uplift' one's colour. From the point of view of self-esteem, there was much damage done, as it encouraged contempt for intra-cultural heritage. For many, colour became a scourge. The ideal beauty model to emulate was Eurocentric, with no alternative models to European physical traits.

In this matter, there was no total surrender on the part of the Black population. Although not abundant, graphic records of women have survived. In many of these, sophisticated hair styles are observed, for example, hinting that there was strong cultural resistance to phenotypic stereotypes.

Reductions for racist purposes was another of the strategies used. In some cases, ancestral territories claimed by peoples were respected, but areas of confinement were also set up and used to keep populations under control. These confinements were normally to inhospitable terrain, and they gave way to the current stagnation and underdevelopment of these territories. Furthermore, there were many large-scale mobilisations of Indigenous populations from one area to another for military reasons. For example, large numbers of local people were uprooted and taken along to support the Spanish military conquistadores as load bearers and cooks.

'Passive' Resistance and Negotiation of Limited Freedom

Other strategies included different forms of passive resistance and negotiation. There were 'accidental' fires on the plantations, destruction of tools, deliberate release of cattle and feigning of illness. In some cases, negotiation was based on favourable circumstances, as in the case of an enslaved African named Gasparillo who, taking advantage of the fact that he was acquainted with the area by past experience, negotiated his freedom with the Spanish conquistador Alonso Luis Lugo in exchange for serving as a guide (Friedemann 1993, 36).

However, these opportunities for the enslaved to free themselves were the exceptions, not the rule. In Latin America, the legal route was by means of manumission – the purchase of a charter of freedom by the slaves themselves, either directly or through an intermediary. Free relatives would buy and release members of their families by paying the slave owners. In other cases, freedom would come as a gift from the slave master for emotional reasons, such as from White godfathers or fathers, or for women who had breastfed a child of the family, or as a post-mortem concession 'for prolong and faithful' service on the part of the slave (among the diverse reasons for granting manumission).

The option to buy a slave's freedom depended on the possibility of reaching an agreement with the slave masters on price. Some owners even accepted payment in the form of instalments. Some slaves would work with other slave masters or with free Blacks on Sundays and public holidays, thus enabling them to accumulate their own savings. Others reached special agreements with the slave holders, such as in the case of masons or carpenters being hired out to other people. The slaves would then be able to legally keep a part of the revenues or secretly seize a fraction of whatever they earned (de la Guardia 1977).

It must also be noted that there were institutions set up to support special needs of the Black population. These institutions, called 'cofradías' or 'cabildos' and normally associated with the Church, were ruled by free Blacks. Some of these organisations set up programs to fund the liberation of slaves who were kin to their members. Lopez Valdes describes these organisations as ethnically based, set up to provide mutual aid between free Blacks, and sometimes expressing solidarity with Black slaves of the same ethnicity, by raising the money necessary to buy their freedom. The cabildos made possible the continuity of religious practices originating in Africa, as well as dances and music, and language and other cultural expressions (cited by Fleischmann, in *Black America* 6, 1993, 22). Some cofradías were extremely prosperous. For example, Chávez Carvajal documents a sixteenth-century brotherhood operating at the San Francisco Xalpa Church in Michoacán, Mexico, that boasted a membership of twenty families, owned 151 heads of cattle and was able to finance its own hospital. The local priest charged 30 pesos and lunch to officiate their ceremonies (Chávez Carvajal, in Martínez Montiel 1994, 119–120). There were also some individuals who were able to make a fortune for themselves. For example, Miguel Ximénez, an Afro-Mexican, owned 11,000 gold pesos, 200 mules and 13 slaves (Capitaine, in Martínez and Reyes, eds. 1993, 139–140).

The citations above give a clear idea of the organisational capacity of Afro-descendants during colonial rule. Even under cases of extreme oppression, they were able to negotiate the possibility of establishing and operating their own organisations, with highly commendable purposes.

In other cases, freedom was granted to a limited number of slaves as a reward for military service or on the occasion of special feasts. For example, in Puerto Rico slaves were freed after performing heroic acts of war, by informing on betrayals or conspiracies, or to celebrate the birthday of Queen Isabel II.

Another form of successful resistance on the plantations was the preservation and rebuilding of culture. Enslaved Africans came from a region of great wealth in terms of its conception of the world, which was fundamentally religious. Almost all African peoples believed in a Supreme God, which, depending on the ethnic group, took different names – Nyame, Olodumare, etc.

They also recognised an all-prevailing vital force or transcendent intelligence – Ashe, Kra, etc. Another important aspect of their culture was allegiance to the ancestral community – Samamfo, Orishas. These latter entities were living beings, acting in the community as councillors, influencing events directly or acting as intermediaries between the living and the Deity. And in some cultures, there was the figure of the obeahman (power man) or Obayi, which had the special capacity to interfere positively or in a very detrimental way in individuals' lives.

Maroonage (Cimmaronaje)

The ultimate strategy of the Afro-descendants against oppression and racism was maroonage, or 'cimarronaje'. The scheme was simple: slaves would run away from farms to set up a geographic niche, normally in a mountainous area or jungle, sometimes in alliance with Indigenous people. Once organised, they would then start guerrilla warfare with colonial powers. These establishments were termed cumbes, palenques or quilombos.

There are many examples of cimarronaje. As early as 1553 we have the case of Alonso de Illescas, in Ecuador. He had been enslaved in Spain from the age of seven and was brought to the Americas at the age of 25. En route to Lima, with a group of fellow enslaved Africans, he managed to escape from the ship and set up a Maroon community in Esmeraldas, Ecuador. He formed a large-scale alliance with the local Indigenous people, leading a successful war against the Spanish colonial power. The Spaniards sought an agreement, but Illescas would not accept it unless total liberty was given to all enslaved Africans. Since such an agreement was unacceptable to the regime, he continued the struggle until his death in 1585.

Other Maroon movements succeeded in setting up free territories with an autonomous local government which usually abolished slavery. Such were the cases of the settlement established by Benkos Biojo in Colombia, who in 1603 forced the Spanish colonial regime to grant freedom to his Black insurgents and to recognise the area dominated by him as the first free territory in colonial America. A few years later, in 1608, Yanga led an impressive revolt in Mexico. Again, the Crown had to concede, signing a treaty that permitted the foundation of 'San Lorenzo de los Negros', another free territory. In 1713, the Palenque of San Basilio in Colombia achieved its autonomy after fierce battles. In the decade of 1770, Bonnie conducted a broad-based insurrection of 80,000 insurgents in the Guayanas, forcing the Dutch to sign a peace treaty granting autonomy to this group, which then rebuilt its Africanity and lived in freedom (de la Guardia, Friedman, Martinez Montiel, Michele Duchet).

An extraordinary example of maroonage is the case of Queen Nanny of the Maroons (Jamaica). From 1655 to 1740, the Maroons of Jamaica waged a heroic war against the British, led by their leader, Princess Nanny, who had been born around 1686 in Ghana into the Ashanti nation. According to tradition, she was a member of a royal family. As a child, she was captured and enslaved, sold along with other members of her family and sent to Jamaica. She worked on a sugar cane plantation in the Saint Thomas Parish, under very harsh conditions. Growing up, she became associated with the Maroon movement and ran away with her brothers Cudjoe, Quao and Johnny, integrating into the Blue Mountain group. Nanny gradually became a leader of her runaway slave community, along with her brothers, setting up villages throughout the region.

By 1720, Nanny, her husband Adou and her brother Quao controlled an area in the Blue Mountains which they named Nanny Town. The British tried again and again to capture the town, but all efforts failed. Indeed, during her thirty-year reign, the Maroons burned down many plantations, seizing weapons and food and rescuing more than 800 slaves who were then absorbed into their ranks.

In addition to her military skills, Nanny proved to be a brilliant community organiser. Her older brothers and many of the runaway slaves helped to organise the Maroon territory under traditional Ashanti expertise. They were very good at raising cattle and growing crops. Nanny also possessed ample knowledge of herbal and other traditional healing methods, which allowed her to be recognised as the physical and spiritual healer of her community.

Queen Nanny was assassinated by a mercenary slave in 1733, but the Maroons continued their struggle until they obtained British colonial government recognition by means of a treaty in 1739. The five Maroon towns were recognised as a self-governing, non-slave territory.

Maroon States

One of the most interesting cases for its extension in time is that of the Garífuna people. In 1635, following the tactic of seeking refuge among the Indigenous people, Blacks who were being transported in two Spanish ships that had been shipwrecked managed to escape (after killing their captors) and make their way to the island of St. Vincent, where they took refuge among the Carib Indians, with whom they ended up creating a successful alliance. Before the end of the seventeenth century, they became the dominant group on the island. In 1719, after defeating an invasion of 500 British soldiers, St. Vincent became a prosperous state. In 1795, the Garífuna fought alongside the French revolutionaries but lost the war, and in 1797 were exiled by the British who were fed up with their indomitable spirit. The British exiled 5000 of them to the island of Roatan, Honduras, where they were left to their fate (Andrade Coelho 1995). The Garífuna then spread from Honduras to Guatemala, Belize and Nicaragua.

But the most outstanding Maroon state was the Quilombo dos Palmares, established by King Ganga Zumba in Brazil in 1670. Ganga Zumba created the Republic of Palmares, the first modern independent state in the Americas (United States declared independence on 4 July 1776). Again, this was not a 'free territory'. It was a major state the size of Portugal. The government was well organised, with ministries, governors and an effective control of commerce and security.

Their warriors were experts in capoeira, an African martial arts form enhanced in Brazil. Around 1678, the Portuguese proposed an agreement to recognise Palmares as a free territory. King Ganga Zumba was inclined to accept the proposal, but there was resistance on the part of other leaders. Shortly after, Zumbi, a young and well-educated leader, assumed total control and refused to accept any agreement that would not include total freedom for all slaves in Brazil. Palmares resisted the recurrent attacks on the part of the Portuguese, but was finally defeated by the Portuguese army in 1694, after 67 years of independence. Zumbi escaped but was captured the following year and beheaded.

Wars of Independence

The Haitian Revolution should be viewed as the continuation of the struggle of the Africans and their descendants to obtain the abolishment of slavery and the possibility of controlling their own destiny. Uprisings occurred in the context of the French Revolution, and at first, it was more a movement of the higher classes – children and grandchildren of resident French men – imbued with libertarian ideas. But gradually the Black majority, many of whom were recently enslaved Africans brought from regions where there were armed conflicts, and who were therefore experienced warriors, also revolted under the leadership of François Dominique Toussaint-Louverture.

As an illustration of how connected these movements were, in a speech in 1799, Toussaint declared challengingly: 'Isn't General Hedouville aware of the fact that in the mountains of Jamaica there are Blacks that have forced the British to sign agreements with them? Well, I am Black like them, and I know how to wage war' (cited by Hart 1984, 135).

The main legacy of the Haitian Revolution was the destruction of two of the main racist myths: the alleged absolute superiority of Europeans, reflected in the Europhilia of the ruling classes in Latin America, and alleged inferiority of the Afro-descendants, reflected in Endophobia, as they saw in Haiti the recovery of pride and identity. The myth of European superiority was seriously damaged from several points of view. However, military defeat was the most devastating. Toussaint faced and defeated the three major European powers of the time: the Spanish and British empires and the France of Napoleon. This outcome had a big impact in Latin America; Haiti demonstrated that the colonial powers were not invincible.

This daring action was never forgiven by the colonial powers. The Haitian nation had to suffer from isolation, blockades, occupations and neo-colonialism, apart from its internal residual problems resulting from the caste-class system imposed by the French. However, the Haitian Revolution shattered forever the myth of the racial inferiority of Africans and their descendants. In addition, Haiti was the first Western nation to prohibit the slave trade and to abolish slavery. And while not putting an end to the colonial system, Haiti became for many years the beacon of freedom and independence for colonised peoples of the world.

Indigenous Uprising and Creole Wars of Independence

The most notable precursor of Latin-American independence was Tupac Amaru II (1780), a Peruvian Amerindian chief and a direct descendant of the royal family of the ancient Incan Empire. Tupac married an Afro-descendent woman named Micaela Bastidas Puyucawa. His insurrection succeeded in liberating much of the Viceroyalty of Peru. This was one of the greatest efforts to achieve independence. Again, the objective was not to set up a free territory, but to re-establish the Incan Empire.

After prolonged battles, the Spaniards reconquered the Viceroyalty. They captured the leaders, inflicting extremely cruel torture on them, followed by execution (1781). Beyond doubt, the cruelty applied by the Spanish colonial government gives a clear idea of how shaken the Empire was by this uprising, and of the degree of concern regarding its possible consequences. The Spaniards went on to search out and kill all members of the royal family, so that there would be no future descendants to claim the former Incan Empire.

But although this first large-scale rebellion was defeated, it raised consciousness throughout the region. During his short-term rule, Tupac Amaru II released all the slaves and, by means of his wife Micaela, dignified the status of women – Indigenous, Afro-descendent and Mestizo, once again underscoring female involvement in the public sphere.

Continental Uprisings

In the second half of the eighteenth century, and leading into the nineteenth, a series of uprisings against the colonial governments broke out all over Latin America. These actions were led by Indigenous people, Afro-descendants and Creoles. The struggle was no longer limited by ethnic boundaries, but included all elements of the population. People of African origin continued to lead or participate in major uprisings. In New Spain (Mexico), by joining the revolutionary movement of priest Miguel Hidalgo, his former teacher, Afro-descendant José María Morelos took an important part in the movement between 1810 and 1815. In addition to initial success in the military leadership, Morelos succeeded in mobilising large sectors of the population in favour of independence. One of the major decisions taken was specifically the abolition of the caste system and slavery. Again, in this case, the Spaniards were able to defeat the movement, executing both Hidalgo and Morelos. But the ideals of freedom and independence had spread throughout the Viceroyalty, and others would continue the struggle.

At the beginning of the nineteenth century, the struggles for independence were widespread, with the decisive participation of the Criollos – sons of Iberian Peninsula families born in America. The ruling class was divided between patriots and royalists at the beginning of the wars and later between internal factions. The majority claimed freedom. In Chile, Bernardo O'Higgins led the fight for independence. In Venezuela, Francisco de Miranda and Simon Bolívar declared its independence in 1811 and, although this first republic was suppressed militarily by the Spaniards, forcing Bolívar to pursue exile in Jamaica, the movement was far from ending. Bolivar was re-armed by Haiti and returned to the continent in 1822, this time releasing New Granada and proclaiming the Republic of Greater Colombia, composed of Venezuela, New Granada and Ecuador.

The conflict intensified in the region of La Plata, with an external factor that encouraged patriotism – the occupation of Buenos Aires by the British (1806–1807). Once the British were expelled, the patriots took on a new perspective and actively demanded independence from Spain. In these struggles, José de San Martin played a critical role through his decisive participation in the independence of Argentina, Chile and Peru. The thrust for independence also affected Central America, where, following the example of Mexico, the locals claimed independence in 1821.

Spain managed to conserve the Caribbean colonies of Puerto Rico and Cuba until well into the nineteenth century, but was not exempt from conflicts. In Cuba, for example, open war was waged for independence and the abolition of slavery. Starting in 1868, Carlos Manuel de Céspedes started a ten-year war. At the end, the Spaniards suppressed the movement. However, in the context of the Spanish-American war (USA), Spain lost these remaining American colonies. In the case of Cuba, as a result of the combination of the struggles of Cuban patriots and the advancement of the American army, the royal troops surrendered in 1898. Throughout Latin America, Afro-descendants fought actively in the wars of independence. This part of the struggle has not been sufficiently documented. There is an enormous debt of the official historiography in this field. But it is beyond discussion that Afro-descendants participated in the process, including the enormous contribution made by Haitians who welcomed and re-armed Simón Bolivar after his first attempt was defeated.

Toward the end of the eighteenth century the caste system was very limiting. The Spanish Crown decided to give the Mestizo population access to certain posts in the public administration (Caracas, 1795). The White Creole sector reacted with outrage at what they considered an affront to their inherited rights, and requested that the law be obeyed but not enforced.

Afro-Descendent Women in the Wars of Independence

There are notable examples of the active participation of Afro-descendant women in the wars. Many contributed arms-in-hand to the liberation of their respective peoples. Micaela Bastides, for example, participated in the war alongside her husband Tupac Amaru II, forming part of the Council of Five responsible for processing the captured Spanish authorities. She became famous by her proclamations and for the way in which she would lead the troops into battle. Her importance cannot be minimised, since she was on the front lines. Author Sara Beatriz Guardia, stresses the point that Micaela had a leading role in the revolutionary army. In a letter addressed to her husband, she reprimands him for not marching immediately on Cuzco, a fact which ultimately precipitated defeat (Letter from Micaela Bastidas to Tupac Amaru, 6 December 1780, cited in Guardia 2002, 115)

Another brilliant example is the Afro-Venezuelan Juana Ramirez (1790–1856). She was called Juana la Avanzadora for her willingness to always march into battle. She is most honoured for the battle fought in May 1813 against the realistic force. It was a fierce battle that lasted all day, ending in favour of the freedom fighters, owing to the decisive intervention of Juana's female battalion. Another extraordinary example was that of María Remedios del Valle, an Afro-Argentine heroine. First, she fought as part of the Andalusian Battalion that defended Buenos Aires against the British invasion. Over a thousand people of African heritage, including slaves, helped forge the memorable triumph over the invading army (Yao 2009, 74)

María Remedios del Valle was incorporated into the regular army in July 1810 to fight for freedom, along with her husband and children, all of which she lost during the war. At first, General Manual Belgrano took a machista stand, refusing to accept women. But owing to her tenacity, Maria finally convinced the general and ended up being appointed captain. Her active participation in the war and her tender care for the wounded explains why the troops spontaneously gave her the title 'Mother of the Nation'. She survived the war, but although there was an agreement to recognise her contribution and give her a pension, the agreement was never executed, and like many others who fought for independence, María Remedios died in poverty and oblivion.

A third case among thousands of women who committed themselves to the fight for independence was Mariana Grajales Coello, daughter of free pardos (1815–1893). Mother of the Maceo brothers, she was an active contributor to the so-called Ten Years' War for Cuban independence. During the war she lost her husband and most of their children, fighting for political freedom and the abolition of slavery. Mariana was an active participant, an inspiration for the soldiers and a nurse to the rebel forces. At the beginning of the war, the freedom fighters gathered at the Maceo's hacienda. Mariana took a crucifix and spoke to them with great mystic power, commanding them to go down on their knees and swear in the name of Christ 'that was the first liberal who came into the world' that they would free the homeland or die in the effort.

The rebel troops were defeated at the end, and Mariana had to accept exile in Jamaica, where she continued to encourage the continuation of the struggle for independence. The goal was achieved but Mariana did not live to see it, since she died in 1893 in Kingston.

From Colonialism to Exclusion

Taking into account the active participation of Afro-descendants in the independence process, one would expect that they would not only achieve freedom, but would also have the opportunity to fully integrate into the new society. However, very soon it became clear that that would not happen. On the contrary, in the building of the new nations, the leaders opted to create 'White nations', under the assumption that civilisation and progress were only possible among the White population.

Doctrinarian Racism

Factual doctrinarian racism began to develop when Pope Nicholas V (1447–1455), in the wake of the exploration of the African coastline on the part of the Portuguese, published his guideline recommending perpetual slavery for Africans, and later, when Fray Juan Ginés de Sepúlveda, proposed the so-called 'fair titles' to legalise conquest.

Not all Christian theologians shared the Friars' point of view. There were indeed divergent voices, such as that of Fray Antonio de Montesinos, who condemned the practice of enslavement of Indigenous people with great rigour. From his viewpoint, the 'Indians' were rational beings and deserved to be treated as such. In 1510 he proclaimed himself a voice in the desert and insisted that the Spanish oppressors were living in sin. 'You are in mortal sin and in sin you live and die, because of the cruelty and tyranny that you apply to these innocent people', he denounced. But the words of Montesinos fell on barren ground. The conquest and domination of native peoples advanced rapidly, and in Europe, intellectuals began, for the first time in human history, the systematic development of the doctrine of racial superiority that gradually became a fundamental aspect of Western culture as we understand it today. Racist rationalisation and indoctrination were designed to attenuate the historical responsibility of colonialism.

Carl Linnaeus (1758), the well-known naturalist, launched the rationale of racism in his treatise *Systema Naturae*, in which he classified humanity into four groups, attributing to each distinctive characteristics. According to him, *Homo Americanus* (Native Americans) are choleric, eager, lazy and bound by custom; *Homo Asiaticus* (Asians) are melancholic, avaricious, severe and governed by opinion; *Homo Afer* (Black Africans) are phlegmatic, negligent and governed by the arbitrary and, of course, *Homo Europaeus* (White) are intelligent, inventive and governed by laws. This, of course, postulated the superiority of the White race. Linnaeus never made a field trip to see prima facie the races that he was classifying. His work was done from the desktop. But immediately after, a number of followers continued in his path. Count Buffon (1774) postulated that the original colour of human beings was white and that in contact with the tropics they underwent degeneration, turning black and losing mental faculties. He was the first in the field of academia to apply the word 'race' to human groups. By 1810, the racist theory had achieved total respectability in Europe, to the point that a scientific specialty was opened at the University of Göttingen under Professor Barthold Niebuhr, who considered 'race' to be one of the most important elements of history.

In the nefarious 1815 Congress of Vienna, the European powers partitioned Africa by means of a treaty. Immediately, two theses were presented: that of Marx and Engels (1848, 1867) that explains human progress through the struggle of the classes, and that of Arthur Count Gobineau who, in his 'Essay on the Inequality of the Human Races' (1853), postulated that the struggle among races was unavoidable. For Gobineau, class and race were indistinguishable.

Social Darwinism, attributed to English philosopher Herbert Spencer (1820–1903), gained momentum. Interpreting the theories of Charles Darwin and developing Gobineau's postulates, intellectuals adhered to the idea that the struggle between the White race and the other races was unavoidable, the former being Christian and civilised, they alleged, and the latter, savage or barbaric with severe mental handicaps, including chronic and incurable infantilism. Efforts to substantiate scientifically the idea of White superiority and African inferiority led to such novelties as the theory of the 'facial angle' suggested by the Dutch anatomist Pieter Camper (1722–1789). Facial angles of Africans were measured and compared with those of Europeans to 'scientifically demonstrate' differences with regard to intellectual capacity. In that context, there is also the Theory of Eugenics, proposed by the British explorer and scientist, Sir Francis Galton (1822–1911), cousin of Charles Darwin. Galton suggested the use of artificial selection to improve race. His idea was to promote the 'desirable traits' and to eliminate the undesirable, using genetics. His theory was widely welcomed in Europe and in the United States.

In Latin America, social Darwinism took on Eurocentric, ethnophobic and endophobic viewpoints. Eurocentrism was expressed as a cult to Europe. The term

Europhilia is applicable – with the Creole and Mestizo populations of Latin America and the Caribbean self-defining themselves as 'White' and adhering to an idealised image of European culture.

The mixed population of Latin America fought for its political and economic independence and finally freed itself. However, once this objective was achieved, this group assumed the identity of the conqueror, idealising France and, to a lesser degree, adopting the idea of Spain or Portugal as the Mother Country. Bypassing phenotype, the vast majority of the Mestizos, including many Afro-Mestizos, were redefined as White.

Latin American poet Ventura García Calderón praised Paris as follows: 'In the example of your civilized parks that obey an occult geometry, I long to purify every morning my barbaric soul' *(Cantilenas 17*, cited in Schwartz 1999, 15). And the Central American poet Rubén Darío claimed that Paris receives and embellishes everything with the magic influence of a secret empire' ('Pilgrimages', cited in Schwartz 1999, 11).

The second characteristic of Latin American social Darwinism is ethnophobia. The Latin American elite, desiring to end every memory of castes, but at the same time embracing social Darwinism, advanced the idea that ethnic diversity was backward and a serious threat to national unity. Fear and rejection of diversity became a part of Latin American culture. Juan Bautista Alberdi, one of the principal theorists of the construction phase of the national states in the region, stated that in 'America anything that is not European is barbarian'. He placed himself immediately in the civilised sector, adding that there is no other division than this: the Indigenous peoples which he labelled 'savage' and the European, 'those of us born in America, who speaks Spanish and believes in Jesus Christ' (Anglarill 1994). In another of his writings, Alberdi insisted that 'To populate is to civilize' providing that you populate with civilised people, that is, with inhabitants of civilised Europe. (Alberdi 1928; quoted by Graciela Sapriza).

A quote from the Chilean newspaper *El Mercurio* clearly summarises the Latin American thinking of the time: 'There are Indigenous Americans, African Americans and European Americans. It was the latter who civilized America. The Indians and the Africans always rejected it and by their barbaric instincts hindered the efforts of the white race to impose it. *(El Mercurio,* 7.8.1863; cited by Fernández Retamar, in *Casa de las Américas,* no. 102, p. 44). In direct allusion to people of African descent, psychiatrist José Ingenieros wrote that 'Men of colored race must not be considered our equals, either politically nor legally; they are inept for the exercise of civil functions and should not legally be considered as persons' ('Las razas inferiores', 1906).

The third racist element, endophobia, is a logical consequence of the other two. It is the rejection and even hatred of the inherited culture and the justification of negative national trends on racial basis. Sociologist and journalist Laureano Ballenilla Lanz (1870–1936) justified local caudillos (political dictators) as necessary and natural to control 'the barbaric illiterate masses' of Latin America. According to him, his countrymen were 'human herd in natural state, plainsmen, Blacks and Mestizos' (*Cesarismo Democratico,* cited in Devés Valdez 2000, 69). Psychologist Carlos Bunge, for his part, went so far as to consider that race mixing in Latin America produced Mestizo individuals with a 'certain lack of psychological harmony, relative sterility and absence of morality' (*Nuestra América,* cited in Devés Valdez 2000, 71). By the same token, psychiatrist José Ingenieros hoped that by means of the introduction of the civilised European population, a new Euro-Argentine race would surge, cultured, industrious and democratic. This new civilisation would of course be founded on the extermination of the colonial race –gaucho, illiterate and anarchic.

The founders of these national states and their followers all over Latin America were well convinced of the inferiority of the Black race and therefore agreed with the idea of their own racial superiority. According to Francisco Cruz, Director of Statistics of Honduras, Blacks had smaller skulls than other races, a fact that made them more exposed to idiotism than madness (Francisco Cruz, 1820–1895, cited in Devés Valdez 2000).

In the context of these national states, Afro-descendants actively took part in the effort to set up the new social order. In many instances, traditional ties with one party or another was the rule, usually owing to the stand taken by those parties in relation to the rights of the Black populations. Such were the cases of the Partido Liberal in Colombia, which favoured the abolition of slavery; the support given by Afro-Argentines to General Juan Manuel de Rosas, who, notwithstanding his slavist past, supported the Black communities and their culture and recurred to a series of manipulations to keep power with their support; and in recent years, the support of the Afro-Caribbean population of Limón, Costa Rica, for the Liberation Party because its founder, José Figueres Ferrer, abolished at the end of the 1940s laws that had discriminated against them.

Independence then, did not lead to the expected freedom and equality. The 'raise your colour' ideology inherited from the colonial caste-class system unrelentingly held sway at the time. The Mestizo elite and the White minority continued enforcing their adopted Eurocentric identity – Europhilia, ethnophobia and endophobia included. Fair-skinned Mestizos were incorporated into the White elite. Traditional Indigenous civilisations were idealised as showcase in an effort to equate ancient Greco-Roman civilisation. But the descendants of the Aztecs, Maya, Toltec and Incas were marginalised, excluded from power and economic structures.

Afro-descendant communities were also excluded and rendered invisible. Elite Afro-descendants were assimilated under the continuing 'bleaching' ideology inherited from colonial days. Racial mixing intensified, as the elite continued to claim a place in the international White community – a seat that was constantly denied, as observable in the following citation of William Walker, a US filibuster that invaded Central America in 1856 with the intention of setting up a slave state throughout the region. According to Walker, Central Americans constituted a 'a mixed and degenerated race, disguised as White'. He went so far as to affirm that stable relations between the 'pure and White' superior American race and the mixed Indo-Spanish inferior race, as it existed in Mexico and Central America, were impossible (quoted by Leopoldo Zea, *Journal Universum*, año 12, 1997).

Throughout the region, limited democracies were established, followed by dictatorships supported by the US government. In Argentina, the Black population sided with one of the factions in conflict, the one led by President Rosas, a move that triggered retaliation on the part of Rosas' opposition. In Cuba, Juan Francisco Manzano, the first published Afro-Latino writer, participated in the struggle for abolition. Falsely accused by the colonial Cuban government (Cuba was under Spanish rule until 1902), he barely escaped death and had to give up writing. Afro-Mestizos were actively involved in these political disputes, and some had access to power. In Colombia, Costa Rica and Honduras, for example, there were Afro-Mestizo presidents, but by then, ethnic allegiance had been severed. Historians and ideologists had carefully proceeded to 'bleach out' these Afro-descendants, through colour-blinding or through the use of euphemisms. Ethnic differences were considered contrary to national unity. Afro-descendants who did not become part of the elite or of the minority that refused to accept the situation were rendered invisible.

After independence, Afro-descendants in Brazil, Uruguay and Cuba, reflecting that they had been betrayed by their criollos counterparts – with whom they had waged war against the Spanish colonial power – set up political entities to enhance their struggle against continuing oppression. The most outstanding cases were the Partido Independiente de Color (PIC) in Cuba and A Frente Negra Brasileira (FBN) in Brazil. These efforts were rapidly suppressed by the system.

The PIC was founded by Afro-Cuban leader Evaristo Estenoz to facilitate participation in the electoral process and was well received by the masses. Resenting its rapid growth, the Cuban bipartisan system accused the group of racism and, alleging constitutional violations, went on to outlaw the PIC in 1910. When the party held a public event to protest against illegality, carrying arms – they were mainly freedom fighters that had taken part in the War of Independence – the government took advantage of the situation. President José Miguel Gómez ordered a military intervention that annihilated the party members. It is estimated that more than 3000 PIC militants were killed.

A Frente Negra Brasileira (FBN) was established in 1931 by a group of Afro-Brazilians. The objective of the FBN was to create awareness among the Black population, and to boost and highlight their intellectual, artistic, professional and physical capacities. To that end, the Frente would develop programs to grant economic, social and legal protection, as well as defence, to 'la Gente Negra' – the Black population. The FBN was well received and supported by the urban Black populations of southern Brazil, but in 1936 Getulio Vargas, the incoming dictator, banned all political parties.

The third case was that of Partido Auténtico Negro in Uruguay (PAN) founded in 1936 by Elmo Cabral, Ventura Barrios, Pilar Barrios and Salvador Betervide. PAN centred its effort on denouncing occupational discrimination and trying to unite the Black population and lower-class Uruguayans on common interests. Unfortunately, PAN was dissolved in 1944 as a result of internal disputes.

The Lull

The second quarter of the twentieth century can be considered a lull, as far as civil rights of the Black population are concerned. Rampant dictatorships throughout the region left no space for particular agendas. Politically, any who dared question these authoritarian regimes found their lives at stake. The only option was to join civil wars or guerrilla warfare against the government. Externally, strong racist ideologies such as the Jim Crow system in the US, Nazism and fascism in Europe, surging apartheid in South Africa, the two world wars, the advancement of communism and the resulting cold war, all conspired against any particular effort on the part of the Black and Indigenous populations to further their specific agendas. But it was during this period that the Black populations of the world began to consider their struggle a global issue.

In the first quarter of the twentieth century, Trinitarian Henry Sylvester Williams, a brilliant intellectual, convened the first Pan-African Conference. Thirty delegates from the US, Canada, Ethiopia, Liberia, Sierra Leone, Côte d'Ivoire and the English Caribbean took part in the conference held in London (1900). The final Declaration, entitled 'Message to the Nations of the World, was written by W. E. B. Dubois, among the most outstanding of African-American scholars. Addressing the audience at Westminster Hall, Dubois stated prophetically, 'The problem of the twentieth century is the problem of the color line' (25 July 1900).

In 1920, in a grand convention held at Madison Square Garden in New York by the United Negro Improvement Association, 25,000 delegates, recognising Marcus Garvey as 'Provisional President' of Africa, approved the 'Declaration of the Rights of the Negro Peoples of the World'. Marcus Garvey was descended from a Jamaican Maroon family. He had travelled extensively through Latin America and the Caribbean, some thirty-eight US states, Canada and Europe. He worked for the railway company in the province of Limón, Costa Rica; in that country he also published an alternative newspaper, and later went on to do the same in Panama.

Garvey's movement was different from all previous efforts – it was a movement of the Black masses, with a universal view and in direct defiance of colonial powers the world over. The UNIA soon set up chapters all over the Caribbean and in several Latin American countries, as well as in the United States. Black institutions were organised, and ships were acquired through the generous and sustained support of members. The movement gradually became a serious threat to the British and United States governments.

Garvey's ideas were rejected by the Black elite. The UNIA was seriously infiltrated, subjected to sabotage and its leader accused of fraud, and there was even an attempt to put an end to Garvey's life. Incarcerated in the US and finally expelled, Garvey died in London in 1940.

Although the ultimate goal of the UNIA – the creation of a free superpower in Africa – was not achieved, Garvey's ideas had strong influence on the African diaspora. African students (members of WASO, a student organisation sponsored by Garvey) later became freedom fighters in Africa, and several of them became the first heads of independent African states, as the process began and developed from 1958 onwards. Among the members of WASO were Harry Thuki of Kenya, Kwame Nkruma of Ghana, Azikiwe of Nigeria, and several of the founding members of the African National Council – Nelson Mandela's organisation. Garvey also influenced some of the most prominent leaders of the US civil rights movement, through family links or through his writings and example. Among those were Martin Luther King and Malcom X. Stokely Carmichael even adopted Garvey's 'Black Power' motto: the Black man has the right to free himself by any means he esteems necessary.

Garvey's movement enhanced universal consciousness on the part of Afro-descendants. The idea that rights were not to be asked for, but rather to be seized, changed the viewpoint of the struggle. He convinced the masses that Africans and Afro-descendants were all part of the Black race – a once-mighty race that had been conquered and deprived of its heritage, but a race that potentially had the power to rise again to rule itself.

The UNIA and the successive Pan-African conferences opened the door to new perspectives. In the 1930s the Négritude movement was launched in France. This movement stemmed from L'Étudiant Noir, a student organisation established in the Barrio Latino of Paris. Among the founders were Leopold Senghor, who later became President of Senegal; Aimé Césaire, in later years governor of Martinique; León Damas from Guyana; Paulette Nadal from Martinique; and Alioune Diop from Senegal. The ties between Africans and Afro-descendants were very quickly re-established and valued anew. Négritude was the effort of diasporan intellectuals to take a fresh look at their African cultural heritage. It had significant influence in the field of art, poetry and music. Aimé Césaire, years later, claimed that Négritude was a sudden awaking of consciousness, the rejection of a negative self-image and a direct confrontation of the Eurocentric view of history, according to which civilisation was the sole product of Europe.

The Italian invasion of Ethiopia (1935), then the only surviving free state in Africa, and the confrontation of Joe Louis, the African-American boxer, with Max Schmeling, the German boxer considered by the Nazis a clear example of the superior Aryan race, contributed to the forging of a new 'pan ethnic' spirit among Afro-descendants. Louis lost the first fight in the 12th round, but won the second in the 1st round. In addition, Afro-Latino and Afro-Caribbean soldiers, returning home after taking part in the world wars, had a lot to say about Africans and other Afro-descendent soldiers that they encountered.

Although the Afro-descendent organisations were for the most part dormant, halfway into the twentieth century the struggle against exclusion and oblivion was moving from the local to the universal. Black people began to acquire a new awareness of their numbers and potential.

New Perspectives

The end of WWII put an end to the lull. After WWII, the Charter of the United Nations was adopted in 1948, followed by the Declaration of Human Rights. The idea that the basic confrontation would be between the White race and others had been shattered by the intra-White wars. The ultra-superior Aryan race had been defeated – losing many a battle to supposedly inferior African and Afro-descendent fighters. Black resistance was rekindled and decolonisation begun with Libya in 1951. Egypt nationalised the Suez Canal and waged a successful war against France and England. In 1957 came the independence of Ghana under President Kwame Nkruma and the well-publicised independence war in Congo, including the assassination of leader Patrice Lumumba in 1961, and the independence of Jamaica in 1962, and Barbados in 1966. All of these events served to shift the sense of belonging and dignity among Afro-descendants.

In addition, the civil rights movement in the US gained momentum, serving as inspiration to the Black Latino and Caribbean populations. Martin Luther King and Rosa Parks' non-violent movement, as well as the belligerent strategies of Malcom X, Stokely Carmichael and Angela Davis all became well known, and African-American leaders were admired.

During the 1950s and 1960s, new organisations emerged in Colombia, Costa Rica, Honduras, Panama, Nicaragua, and other Latin American countries, and some survived in spite of being blatantly ignored and submitted to extremely hostile conditions. From the social Darwinist viewpoint, racial and ethnic assertions were considered a threat to national unity and offensive to the individual.

In this period, socialist and communist movements advanced in the world. Many Black leaders were inclined to incorporate their struggle into the revolutionary movements. But there was a problem that for many years seemed insurmountable: the idea that the basic struggle in society was a class struggle, and that once the class system was resolved, racial differences would vanish. All references to race were considered reactionary, and for that reason were seen to have no place in socialism. Ethno-racial approaches to society were therefore strongly rejected and combated by revolutionary leaders. In fact, it took the Cuban revolutionaries many years to finally admit that doctrinarian racism was embedded into Western culture, and that the idea that it would disappear automatically under socialism was naïve.

In Nicaragua, this lack of understanding led to armed confrontation with the Sandinista Party. After a series of dogmatic decisions on the part of the government, including the forceful displacement of Afro-Indigenous populations from their traditional lands, efforts to ignore or suppress cultural differences, and expressions of overt racism on the part of some government officers and party members, many 'costeños' (Caribbean Mestizo, Afro and Indigenous people and communities) joined the counter-revolution. Fortunately enough, these painful confrontations ended with the Nicaraguan State reforming its constitution, recognising itself as a multicultural state. Autonomous status was granted to the Caribbean region.

The International Perspective; Zapata Olivella

In 1977 Manuel Zapata Olivella convened the First Congress of the Black Cultures of the Americas. The conference, held in Cali, Colombia, was a turning point for the resistance and continuing struggle. The lull was over, but Black consciousness was still internally oriented and infused with admiration for the US civil rights movement.

This posed a problem, since there was a strong anti-American feeling in large sectors of the population. And at the same time, both authoritarian and democratic governments, although supported largely by the US, insisted that racial inequality was a North American problem, and that no such thing existed in Latin America. The Cali Congress, followed by several others, served to create an Afro Pan-American world view. Afro-Latinos suddenly became aware of the fact that they were not a regional minority. New ties began to be established with the Caribbean and with African Americans. Afro-descendants began a sustained trend to recover their history, to defend specific elements of their culture and to claim the right to be different.

Symposiums and conferences were held in Costa Rica (1978), Panama (1980) and in other countries to emphasise Black Culture and the Black presence in the Americas. In 1980 the churches began a process of incorporating Afro-descendant culture into their agendas and liturgy. The Catholic Church held a number of pastoral consultations in South America: in Buenaventura, Colombia, in 1980; in Esmeraldas, Ecuador, in 1983: and in Portobelo, Panamá, in 1984. The Protestant sector followed the same path. In 1981 the Programme to Combat Racism, established by the World Council of Churches, asked member churches in its Zimbabwe meeting to look into the situation of Black minorities in Latin America.

In the secular field, a great step forward was taken at the Third Congress on Black Cultures of the Americas, held in San Pablo, Brazil. Although the issue of women had been part of the discussion at the First Congress, the specificity of the matter was not emphasised until 1982. Women delegates insisted that it was time to recognise their role in the transmission of ancestral culture and values, and their contribution to the economic development of Latin American societies (Palenque, año 8, no. 3). Furthermore, the conference highlighted the internal conflict with machismo and other patriarchal ideologies, as well as the fact that women were restricted to menial positions in the movement and denied leadership roles. With the Third Conference, women's issues became a permanent part of the Black agenda in the region (Palenque, año 8, no. 3, 9).

In Alajuela, Costa Rica, the Third Consultation of Social Scientists and Theologians, held in 1983, prioritised the discussion of racial problems. The idea gained ground that the reduction of social conflict to a simple class struggle was erroneous. Race and gender were emphasised as inseparable parts of the social dynamic. Raúl Vidales incorporated the concept of ethnic insurgence; the role of ethnia and race in the building of the Latin American nations was introduced by Quince Duncan; and the issue of equality and gender from a Biblical perspective was the core of Elsa Tamez' contribution. (Vidales and Rivera Pagán, eds., 1983).

In an effort to have a broader discussion on the struggles of the Black population and on the concept of race as the main problem facing Black Latinos specifically, a Consultation on Black Culture and Theology was held in Nueva Iguaçu, Río de Janeiro, Brazil in 1984. Afro-descendant leaders, including Manuel Zapata Olivella (Colombia), Nicomedes Santa Cruz (Peru), Quince Duncan (Costa Rica), Laennec Hourbon (Haiti) and Maria Lourdes Sequeira (Brazil), among others, discussed with Third World theologians the importance of religiosity in Black communities, as well as the centrality of racism in the struggle for equality. Attendees included members of Christian churches and representatives of traditional afro religions (Duncan, 1986). In the following year –1985 – the Latin American Episcopal Conference called on religious leaders to accompany Afro-descendants assuming their social situation, their cultural values and the affirmation of their identity. The most important part of the declaration was the affirmation that the Church must avoid the idea that to be Christian, people of African origin should have to become culturally White (Palenque, año 6, no. 1, 2).

As a direct result of the Colombian Peace Process conducted under President Virgilio Barco, a series of 'Concertation Boards' was created. The Afro-Colombian populations were able to have a voice in the negotiations and managed to incorporate some of their objectives. The Asociación Campesina Integral del Atrato, an Afro-Colombian organisation, succeeded in mobilising in their favour an impressive panel of national and international specialists on ethnic rights, and led an exceptional struggle to regain control over their ancestral lands. By 1991 the process had advanced to the point that the Colombian constitution was reformed. Article 7 of the new constitution recognises multiculturalism and orders the State to protect the ethnic and cultural diversity of the Colombian nation.

Following this constitutional directive, a very important law was approved in 1993, the Ley 70, that set up the framework for the protection of the culture, dignity and equality of Afro-Colombians, as well as the protection of their ancestral territories.

In spite of these important judicial conquests, Afro-Colombians have suffered from the violence inflicted by warring parties in the guerrilla war. Paramilitary forces put a lot of pressure on ancestral territories, forcing population displacement. But even in the midst of the conflict, Afro-Colombians have been able to achieve important steps on the road to equality.

The largest and most significant cultural event of the 1980s was the Florida International University conference convened by Carlos Moore and others (1987). Delegates from all over the world attended. The papers read and the conferences delivered had a wide audience that ran into the thousands. This 'Negritude, Ethnicity and Black Cultures of the Americas' conference had an active participation of world leaders and young Black Latin American intellectuals. Among those delivering papers were the founders of the Négritude movement, Aimé Césaire and Leopold Senghor; Maya Angelou, the outstanding African-American poet; Manuel Zapata Olivella, through whose initiative the Congress on Afro Cultures was held; Roy Guevara Arzú, a Garífuna intellectual; Bassette Cayasso, from the Nicaraguan Misquitto; and Quince Duncan, Afro Costa Rican writer.

In 1992, the Red de Mujeres Afrolatinoamericanas, Afrocaribeñas (Afro Latino and Afro Caribbean Women's Network) was organised in the Dominican Republic, its goals being to combat racism, sexism and poverty and also to promote the empowerment of Black women. The Red de Mujeres has been able to integrate more than 200 organisations throughout the region and has fought vigorously for the inclusion of Afro-descendant culture and issues in the public agenda.

Preparation for the UNESCO 'World Conference against Racism, Racial Discrimination, Xenophobia and Related Intolerance,' which was to be held in Durban, South Africa, injected new life into the international arena. The regional preparatory conference was held in Santiago, Chile, in 2000. This was a dual event – a civil organisation conference followed by an official government meeting. As a direct result of these preparatory events, conducted by Afroamerica XXI and the Red de Alianza Estratégica Afro Latinoamericana y Caribeña, attendance and participation of Black delegates from all over the continent was impressive.

At the Santiago conference, the name 'Afro-descendants' in reference to people of African descent was proposed and adopted for the first time, at the initiative of Sueli Carneiro, a Brazilian social scientist. The word was important, as it came from inside the Black community. It was also a means of getting rid of the colonial term 'negro' with its negative connotations. And more significant was the fact that the Black delegates present represented organisations from all over the Americas. The name, along with the proposals adopted in the Santiago Conference, was taken to the Durban conference and was incorporated into the United Nations nomenclature.

After Durban, many Latin American governments made changes to their constitutions to recognise multiculturalism. A number of laws have been issued, granting representation in government structures, and many government officers have been appointed. Ironically, these appointments, politically oriented, have in some cases added strain to the struggle. For the first time, such divisive terms as 'Afro derecha' have been used by militant Blacks still caught up in the myth that the race problem is the direct result of class division. Notwithstanding, it is interesting that although there has been division over the years, the struggle for freedom has continued.

Residual and Institutional Racism

At present, the practice of racism in the region can be considered to be residual. Residual racism is present when you have a situation in which there is no strict stratification on an ethno-racial basis, but the concepts that came into being during a period of doctrinarian racism are still used. Before, they were integral parts of so-called scientific racism, designed to uphold racial domination. At present, these concepts have no standing since the objective structures that explained their genesis are no longer in place. Overt doctrinarian racism is to a certain degree 'a thing of the past', but institutional racism continues to be an integral part of everyday life, firmly rooted in traditions and customs, keeping in place discriminatory practices against Indigenous and Afro-descendant people, submitting them to exclusion, invisibility, stigmas and territorial aggression.

Local organisations such as ODECO in Honduras; Asociación Proyecto Caribe in Costa Rica; ONEGUA in Guatemala; Mundo Afro in Uruguay; GELEDES, Instituto de la Mujer Negra (Brazil); Movimiento Cimarrón in Colombia; Confederación Nacional de Organizaciones Campesinas Indígenas y Negras del Ecuador (FENOCIN); Oro Negro in Chile; Coordinadora Nacional de Organizaciones Negras in Panama; and the newly formed ODECA in Mexico, as well as international organisations such as the Black Central American Organization (ONECA), and the Red de Mujeres Latinoamericanas and others, continue the struggle. Among the reiterated objectives is the idea that diversity should be viewed as an asset. Afro-descendants and Indigenous peoples should be accepted fully as inseparable parts of the national states. Self-identity is pursued as a desirable goal. Demands on the educational system for a balanced and unbiased approach to history are front and centre. Intercultural competence and empowerment are considered necessary to solve the problems of poverty. A conference of Afro-descendant youth, held at Cali Colombia (13 to 17 March 2007), highlighted the fact that, considering the distribution of the national wealth, Latin America is one of the most inequitable regions of the world. The youth conference demanded programs to enhance inclusion and combat racism, xenophobia and other forms of social discrimination.

In the same vein, the Black Pastoral movement of the Latin American Council of Churches (CLAI), as a result of their regional meeting in Managua, Nicaragua, from 22 to 25 June 2011, demanded that the churches, universities, institutes, seminars and Sunday schools revise the curricula to include Afro-descendant issues and culture as part of their standard programs. A transversal approach should be assumed.

The Second Festival Oaxaca Negra, held in Oaxaca, Mexico, in 2011, while celebrating the capacity of the Indo-Afro-Mestizo population to resist oppression and outlining its social and cultural productivity, also demanded in the Declaration a rightful recognition of their role as carriers and creators of new forms of civilisation and of hope for the building of a new world.

The Red de Mujeres Afrolatinoamericanas, Afrocaribeñas y de la Diáspora, issued a defiant declaration in Brasilia in July 2010. This Declaration, in addition to enumerating the present-day issues confronting Afro-descendants, is in itself a plan of action. The Red continued to propose the consolidation of a broad-based women's movement into one that would incorporate ethnicity, race and gender, pointing out the discrimination and other violations of human rights to which the Black population has been subjected over time. The Red then went on to call for pressure on governments and other institutions. A comprehensive solution is imperative.

BIBLIOGRAPHY

Academy of Sciences of the USSR, 1983. Moscow: Soviet Ethnographic Research.

Acosta Saignes, Miguel, 1978. *Vida de los esclavos negros en Venezuela.* Havana: Casa de las Américas.

Acosta, María Luisa, 1996. *Los derechos de las comunidades y pueblos indígenas de la Costa Atlántica.* Nicaragua: Agencia Canadiense para el Desarrollo Internacional.

Africamérica. Revista de la Fundación [Venezuela: Fundación Afroamérica], 6 (julio 99–julio 2000).

Aguado Odina, Teresa. 2007. *Racismo qué es y como se afronta.* Madrid: Pearson Education S.A.

Aguirre Beltrán, Gonzalo. 1972. *El Negro en México.* Fond de Cultura Económico.

Alberdi, J. B., 1928. *Las bases y puntos de partida para la organización política de la República Argentina. La cultura Argentina.* Buenos Aires. Cited by historian Graciela Sapriza)

Álvarez D'Armas, Arturo, 1981. *Apuntes sobre el estudio de la toponimia africana en Venezuela.* Venezuela: UNERG.

Andrade Coelho, Ruy Galvao de, 1995. *Los Negros Caribes de Honduras.* Honduras: Editorial Guaymuras.

Anglaril, Nilda Beatriz, 1994. El estudio de la población de origen africano en la Argentina. Ponencia. Ier Coloquio Internacional de Estudios Afro-Iberoamericanos, Alcalá de Henares.

Araujo, Nara, ed., 1983. *Viajeras al Caribe.* Havana: Casa de las Américas.

Arocha Rodríguez, Jaime, 1994. Cultura Afrocolombiana. Entorno Derecho Territoriales. Ponencia. Ier Coloquio Internacional de Estudios Afroiberoamericanos, Alcalá de Henares.

Banco Mundial, 2000. *La raza y la pobreza: Consulta interagencias sobre afrolatinoamericanos.* Documento de Trabajo No. 9 de LCR en Desarrollo Sostenible. Washington: Banco Mundial.

Barnet, Miguel, 1976. *Biografía de un Cimarrón.* 4th edn. México: Siglo XXI.

Benítez, José A., 1977. *Las Antillas : colonización, azúcar e imperialismo.* Havana: Casa de las Américas.

Bermingham-Pokorny, Elba, 1994. La frontera del color en las literaturas y culturas de las Américas del Siglo XX. Ponencia. Ier Coloquio Internacional de Estudios Afro-iberoamericanos, Alcalá de Henares.

Bilbao, Ion et al., 1979. *Darien: indios, negros y latinos.* Panamá: Centro de Capacitación Social.

Blake, W. O., 1860. *The History of Slavery and the Slave Trade.* Columbus, Ohio: H. Miller.

Boletín de Estudios de la Diaspora Africana [Washington] 1/1 (Oct 1984).

Bourgois, Philippe. 1994. *Banano, Etnia y Lucha Social en Centro América.* San José: DEI.

Bryce-Laporte, Roy and Mortimer, Delores M., 1981. *Female Immigrants to the United States: Caribbean, Latin American and African Experiences.* Washington: Smithsonian.

Burgos Cantor, Roberto, ed., 2010. *Rutas de Libertad, 500 Años de Travesía.* Bogotá: Ministerio de Cultura.

Cáceres, Rina, compiler, 2001. *Rutas de la Esclavitud en Africa y América Latina.* San José: Editorial de la Universidad de Costa Rica, 2001.

Cáceres, Rina, 2000. *Negros, mulatos, esclavos y libertos en la Costa Rica del siglo XVII.* Mexico: Instituto Panamericano de Geografía e Historia.

Campbell Barr, Epsy, ed., 1998. *Justicia y Discriminación.* San José: Comisión Nacional para el Mejoramiento de la Administración de Justicia.

Cangabo Kagabo, Massimango, 1994. La nueva inmigración africana en México. Ponencia. Ier Coloquio Internacional de Estudios Afro-iberoamericanos, Alcalá de Henares.

Caramagnani, Marcello; Hernández Chavez, Alicia; Romano, Ruggiero, coords., 1999. *Para una Historia de América. Los Nudos (1).* México: Fondo de Cultura Económica,.

Caramagnani, Marcello; Alicia Hernández Chavez; Ruggiero Romano coords., 1999. *Para una Historia de América. Los Nudos (2).* México: Fondo de Cultura Económica.

Caramagnani, Marcello, Alicia Hernández Chavez y Ruggiero Romano coords., 1999. *Para una Historia de América. Las Estructuras.* México: Fondo de Cultura Económica.

Casey Gaspar, Jeffrey, 1979. *Limón 1880–1940. Un estudio de la industria bananera en Costa Rica.* San José: Editorial Costa Rica.

Castro, Carlos D., 1972. Notas para una sociología del negro antillano. *Revista de la Lotería Panameña* 202, septiembre.

CCHR, 2006. *La psiquiatría, una industria de la muerte.* Video.

Centro de Estudios del Caribe, 1981. *Anales del Caribe,* no.1. Havana: Casa de las Américas.

Charles, Gerard Pierre, 1978. *Haití: la crisis ininterrumpida, 1930–1975.* Havana: Cuadernos Casa, no.19.

Cimarronas [San José: Red de Mujeres Afro Latinoamericanas y Afro Caribeñas]. 1999 (no. 6, abril), 2000 (no. 8, mayo).

Coll Gallabert, Jorge, 1980. *Haití: apuntes sobre su historia y cultura.* Santo Domingo: Instituto Nacional de Pastoral.

Coordinadora Nacional de Organizaciones Negras de Honduras, 1997. *Plan Nacional de Desarrollo de las Comunidades Afrohondureñas.* Roatán, Honduras.

Dallas, R. C., 1980. *Historia de los cimarrones.* Havana: Casa de las Américas.

De la Guardia, Roberto, 1981. *Las tres oleadas de población sobre el Istmo de Panamá: tres historias.* Panamá: Academia Panameña de Historia.

De la Guardia, Roberto, 1977. *Los negros del Istmo de Panamá.* Panamá: Instituto Nacional de Cultura.

Declaración de Líderes Afrolatinoamericanos y caribeños. 2000. San José: Instituto Interamericano de Derechos Humanos.

Devés Valdés, Eduardo, 2000. *Del Ariel de Rodó a la CEPAL.* Buenos Aires: Editorial Biblos.

Diez Castillo, Luis A., 1981. *Los cimarrones y los negros antillanos en Panamá.* Panamá.

Diop, Cheikh Anta. 1991. *Civilization or Barbarism.* New York: Lawrence Hill Books.

Drimmer, Melvin, ed., 1969. *Black History.* New York: Anchor Books.

Duncan Quince, 1994. In: Luz María Montiel, et al., *Presencia Negra en América Central.* México: Consejo Nacional para la Cultura y las Artes.

Duncan, Quince and Carlos Meléndez, 1974. *El Negro en Costa Rica.* 2nd edn. San José: Editorial Costa Rica.

Duncan, Quince and Powell, Lorein. Dos estudios sobre el racismo. *Cuadernos de Temas de Nuestro América.* IDELA, Universidad Nacional de Costa Rica.

Duncan, Quince and Powell, Lorein. 1988. *Teoría y Práctica del Racismo.* San José: Dei.

Duncan, Quince, 1986. 'Apuntes para una teoría general del racismo' and 'Racismo, Iglesia y Teología'. In: Duncan, et al. *Cultura Negra y Teología.* San José: Dei.

Duncan, Quince, 1983. 'Idénticos o diversos'. Factores de etnia, raza y nación en la construcción del pueblo latinoamericano. In: Vidales, Raúl and Luis Rivera Pagán, eds., *La esperanza en el presente de América Latina.* San José: Dei.

Duncan, Quince, 2001. *Contra el Silencio.* San José: Euned.

El Mercurio, 7.8.1863. Cited by Fernández Retamar, in *Casa de las Amèricas,* no. 102, p.44

Fisher, Robert, 1998. *West African Religious Traditions.* New York: Obis Books.

Fortune, Armando. 1970. Los negros cimarrones en Tierra Firme y su lucha por la libertad. *Revista de la Lotería Nacional,* no. 171 (feb.)

Friedemann, Nina S. 1994. Africanía y Religión en Colombia: Cosmovisiones e Imaginarios. Ponencia. Ier Coloquio Internacional de Estudios Afroiberoamericanos. Alcalá de Henares.

Friedmann, Nina S., 1993. Expedición humana a la zaga de la América oculta. *América Negra* [Bogotá], no. 6.

Friedmann, Nina S., 1993. *La Saga del Negro.* Bogotá: Instituto de Genética Humana.

Goldstein, Rhoda L., ed., 1971. *Black Life and Culture in the United States.* New York: Apollo.

Guardia, Sara Beatriz, 2002. *Mujeres Peruanas, Al Otro Lado de la Historia.* Lima, Perú: Librería Editorial 'Minerva' Miraflores.

Gudmundson, Lowell. 1984. Black into white in nineteenth-century Spanish America: Afro-American assimilation in Argentina and Costa Rica. *Slavery and Abolition* 5/1, 34–49.

Hamilton, Ruth Simms and Powell-Bernard, Lorein. 1990. African identity lost or de-nied: The case of La Mansión, *Costa Rica* [Michigan: Mayo] 2/1.

Hamilton, Ruth Simms, 1988. Creating a Paradigm and Research Agenda for Comparative Studies of the Worldwide Dispersion of African Peoples: Proceedings of the African Advisory Committee of the African Diaspora Research Project, Nov. 9–11, Michigan.

Hart, Richard, 1984. *Esclavos que abolieron la esclavitud*. Havana: Casa de las Américas.

IIDH et al, eds., 2006. *Compilación de observaciones finales del Comité para la Eliminación de la Discriminación Racial, sobre paises de América Latina y el Caribe (1970–2006)*. Santiago de Chile: Alfabeta Artes Gráficas.

Inter-American Development Bank, 2000. Political Feasibility Assessment: Country Potential for New Research on Race in Latin America. Executive summary. Encuentro Internacional, Todos Contamos, Colombia.

Landers, Jane G. and Robinson, Barry M., eds., 2006. *Slave, Subject and Subversives*. Albuquerque, NM: University of New Mexico Press.

Lang, Berel, ed., 2000. *Race and Racism in Theory and Practice*. Lanham, Maryland: Rowman and Littlefield Publishers.

Llarch, Joan, 1970. *Martín Luther King. Una vida por la paz*. Barcelona: Editorial Juventud.

Lucena Salmoral, Manuel, 1996. *Los Códigos negros de la América Española*. España: UNESCO, Universidad de Alcalá.

Luepke, Rolf, 1978. Racism in West-German Protestant Religious Instruction Textbooks. Potencies: First Workshop on Racism in Children's School Textbooks. Federal Republic of Germany.

Martín, Tony, 1983. *The Pan African Connection*. Massachusetts: The Majority Press.

Martínez Montiel, Luz and Juan Carlos Reyes G., eds., 1993. *Memoria del III Encuentro Nacional de Afromexicanistas*. Gobierno del Estado de Colina.

Martínez Montiel, Luz, 1994. *Presencia Africana en México*. Mexico: Consejo Nacional para la Cultura y las Artes.

Maya Restrepo, Adriana, 1992. Las Brujas de Zaragoza: Resistencia y cimarronaje en las minas de Antioquia, Colombia, 1619–1622. *América Negra* 4 (dic.), 85–99.

Medina, João and Henriques, Isabel Castro, 1996. *A Rota dos Escravos*. Lisbon: Cegia.

Moore, Carlos; Sanders, Tanya R.; Moore, Shawna, eds., 1995. *African Presence in the Americas*. New Jersey: Africa World Press.

Moreno Fraginals, Manuel, 1997. *Africa en América Latina*. Mexico, Siglo XXI.

Morrish, Ivor, 1982. *Obeah, Christ and Rastaman*. Cambridge, UK: James Clarke.

Mosquera Rosero-Labbé, Claudia; Laó-Montes, Agustín and Rodríguez Garavito, César, eds., 2010. *Debates sobre Ciudadanía y Políticas Raciales en las Américas Negras*. Bogotá: Universidad del Valle.

Nederveen Pieterse, Jan, 1992. *White on Black*. New Haven: Yale University Press.

Ngou-Mve, Nicolás, 1996. *El cimarronaje como forma de expresión del África Bantú en la América Colonial. El ejemplo de Yanga en México*. Libreville: Anales de l'Université Omar Bongo.

Northrup, David, 2002. *Africa's Discovery of Europe*. New York: Oxford University Press.

Obenga, Théophile and Souindoula, Simäo, eds., 1991. *Racines Bantú*. París: Sepia.

ONECA, 2000. *Declaración de la cumbre continental de los pueblos afroamericanos frente al desarrollo económico, político y social y contra el racismo y la discriminación*. La Ceiba, Honduras: ONECA.

Palenque. *Boletín informativo del Centro Cultural Afro-ecuatoriano*. año 5, no. 3; año 6, no. 1; año 6, no.2; año 7, no. 4; año 8, no. 2; año 8, no. 3.

Rojas, Axel, 2008. *Aportes para Maestros*. Colombia: Universidad del Cauca.

Schwartz, Marcy, 1999. *Writing Paris*. Albany, NY: New York State University Press.

Seligson, Mitchell Allan, 1980. *El campesino y el capitalismo agrario de Costa Rica*. San José: Editorial Costa Rica.

Stein, Stanley J. and Stein, Barbara H., 1973. *La Herencia Colonial de América Latina*. Mexico, Siglo XXI.

Stewart, Watt, 1967. *Keith y Costa Rica*. San José: Editorial Costa Rica.

Thomas-Hope, Elizabeth M. Hopes and reality in West Indian migration to Britain. In: *Oral History*.

Thomas-Hope, Elizabeth, 1978. The Response to West Indian Migration Settlement in Panama, Costa Rica and Cuba. (Consulted the draft.) See also: Caribbean Social Relations monograph series [UK: University of Liverpool], no. 8.

Thomas-Hope, Elizabeth M., 1978. *The Establishment of a migration tradition: British West Indian movements to the Hispanic Caribbean in the century after emancipation*. In Colin G. Clarke, ed., *Caribbean Social Relations*. Liverpool: Centre for Latin American Relations. Monograph Studies no. 8, 66–81.

Thornton, John, 1998. *African and Africans in the Making of the Atlantic World, 1400–1800*. 2nd. ed. Cambridge and New York: Cambridge University Press.

UNAM, Centro de Estudios Latinoamericanos. *El Caribe Contemporáneo* [México], no. 2. (marzo-junio).

Van den Berghe, Pierre L., 1967. *Race and Racism. A comparative perspective*. New York: John Wiley and Sons, Inc.

Van Dijk, Teun A., 2003. *Racismo y Discurso de las Élites*. Barcelona: Editorial Gedisa.

Van Sertima, Ivan, 2000. *The Golden Age of the Moor*. London: Transaction Publishers.

Velásquez, María Elisa and Correa, Ethel, comps., 1993. *Poblaciones y culturas de origen africano en México*. Mexico, INAH.

Velásquez, María Elisa, 1994. Mujeres Afromexicanas en la Nueva España. Ponencia. IV Encuentro de Afromexicanistas. México.

Velázquez, María Elisa, 2006. *Mujeres de Origen Africano en la Capital Novo Hispana, Siglos XVII and XVIII*. México: INAH.

Vicariato Apostólica de Esmeraldas y Centro Cultural Afroecuatoriano. 2009. *Enciclopedia del Saber Afroecuatoriano*. Quito: Gráficas Iberia.

Williams, Eric, 1970. *From Columbus to Castro: The History of the Caribbean*. New York: Vintage.

Wilson, Carlos Guillermo, 1994. El legado de plácido. Ponencia. Ier Coloquio Internacional de Estudios Afro-iberoamericanos. Alcalá de Henares.

World Council of Churches, 1982. Geneva: P.C.R. Information, no. 15.

Yao, Jean-Arsène, 2009. *Los Afroargentinos*. Madrid: Editorial Mundo Negro.

Zenón Cruz, Isabelo, 1974. *Narciso Descubre su Trasero*. Puerto Rico: Editorial Furidi.

The Haitian Revolution and the Rights Secured by the Descendants of the Victims of the Slave Trade, Slavery and the Colonial System in the Caribbean-Americas

Oruno D. Lara

A speech given by the author for the Working Group of Experts on People of African Descent for the United Nations Human Rights Committee in Geneva on 29 September 2003, during its 60th session, for the Commemoration of the Bicentennial of the Republic of Haiti (1804–2004).

BIOGRAPHY

Oruno D. Lara (Guadeloupe) is a historian and founding director of the 'Centre de recherches Caraïbes-Amériques' (CERCAM), Centre for Research for the Caribbean-Americas, founded in 1982 at the University Paris X. He collaborated on the implementation of various projects devised by UNESCO's Division for Intercultural Dialogue. He is the author of numerous books on the history of the Caribbean-Americas and on the resistance to human trafficking and slavery (translated into English and Spanish). Recently published: *Space and History in the Caribbean*, Princeton, 2005; *La Liberté assassinée. Guadeloupe, Martinique, Guyane et La Réunion, 1848–1856*, Paris, 2005; *Guadeloupe. Le Dossier Sénécal* (*Guadeloupe: The Sénécal File*), Paris, 2012; *Révolutions caraïbes : Les premières lueurs, 1759–1770* (*Caribbean Revolutions: The First Glimmers*, 1759–1770), Paris, 2015; *Abolition de l'esclavage, 1848–1852* (*Abolition of Slavery*, 1848–1852), Paris, 2016. He is currently preparing *Une Histoire des Caraïbes* (*A History of the Caribbean*).

ABSTRACT

The Haitian Revolution between 1791 and 1804 instituted a triple process of destruction: i.e. of the slave trade, of slavery, and of the colonial system. Three potent issues pervade the nineteenth century that set the Caribbean ablaze. The governments of the colonies of the Caribbean and South and North America enforced measures in the hope of limiting the 'contagion of insurrection'. Nevertheless, revolts struck Jamaica, Cuba, Guadeloupe, Martinique, Curaçao, Puerto Rico, Venezuela, Colombia, Brazil, the Guianas, the states of Louisiana and Virginia. Haiti, in particular, provided support to Bolivar in his battle against the Spanish Empire and offered protection to the captives of the intercepted slave ships. Slave uprisings were inspired through the nineteenth century by this former French colony that had gained its independence in 1804.

It is a history that is not well known that is presented today to the United Nations Human Rights Committee and the Working Group of Experts on People of African Descent: a history that has demanded scientific research, attention to conceptual detail and critical methodology. To begin with, I would like to reflect with you on some fine methodological points concerning the terminology used in the American Caribbean and when speaking of their past colonisation, human trafficking and slavery. This history is paved with concepts of different origins, particularly engendered by the colonial systems and their pro-slavery foundations.

Concepts and Methods: The Meaning of Words

The historian who works on this region of the world, the Caribbean-Americas, is confronted with the common use of racist terminology inherited from the colonial period colonisation (Lara 1992, vol. I, 17–20; id. 1998, 8–10). Analysis of this terminology, and more generally a critical analysis of the conceptual field, would require a scientific debate among experts.

Among the concepts stemming from the colonial period, we can consider 'colonisation', which translated into [American] English is 'colonization', and which doesn't have the same meaning in 1816 in the United States of America in the expression American Colonization Society, where 'colonization' means deportation. How could we translate 'colon' (a colonist, settler) in English, the way it is used in French or in Spanish for example? I personally have adopted the concept 'système colonial', or colonial system, rather than colonization to define a process of colonial construction that did not start, as we only too often believe, with the Conquest, the extermination of the indigenous population, the pillaging, the expropriations of land, but rather appeared with the creation of large capitalist commercial companies (the West Indische Compagnie in 1621,The Dutch West India Company, the British West Indian Company and the French West India Company, etc.), and the organisation of the colonial administration, slavery and the slave system (Code Noir in 1685 for France, Codigo Negro for Spain, Codes and Slave Laws for the British and different rules and regulations for the other colonial maritime powers, Portugal, the Dutch Republic, Denmark and Sweden).

Other concepts included in this terminology inherited from the colonial past continue to convey racism – for example, the French terminology and classification created by the plantation owners of Saint-Domingue, and codified by the Creole magistrate Médéric Louis Élie Moreau de Saint-Méry in his famous publication *Description topographique, physique, civile, politique et historique de la partie française de l'Isle Saint-Domingue* (Philadelphie, 1796): métis, sang-mêlé, mulâtre, mamelouc, griffe, sacatra, quarteron and marabous. We inherited the English classification as well, used in the colonial colonies and the United States: sambos, mulattos, quadroons, mustees, musteefeenas, quintroons et octoroons. The Spanish and Portuguese colonists have left us a series of terms of miscegenation (Schmidt 2003): mestizo, castizo, mulato (from mulo, the mule); in the Kingdom of New Spain: morisco, albino, lobo, zambaigo, cambujo, albarazado, barcino, coyote, chamisa; in Peru: cholo, chino, pardo et zambo (the last two terms are also used in Venezuela). In all the Spanish colonies, the words indio and turco were used to define the Syro-Lebanese.

Several concepts were handed down by the colonial system and the slave system and even the slave trade. I will mention 'habitation' (that means 'plantation', estate in English), 'grand'case' (the house of the slave master, 'casa grande', which means big house). How could we translate 'senzala', the Portuguese word for the Negro quarters? The word 'Nègre' (Negro) itself, commonly used in the colonial and slave-trade period, cannot be translated into English simply by 'black', for Nègre is a historical concept with a precise meaning. The word 'Nègre' can be found as a founding principle of the African slave trade. The Nègre is the individual who has been put by force on a slave-trading ship and who will spend the Middle Passage in the ship's hold as an African captive. Upon arrival in the Caribbean, he/she will be sold to become a 'Negro slave' in the towns, in the mines or on the plantations. It is during the slave trade that a split emerges between the Africans, who remain on the continent, and the Nègres, who are captured and enslaved, victims of the many traumas suffered on the voyage and then by the colonial system. Other concepts deserve critical thought as well, such as the term 'colons békés', in English 'buckras'; the word 'créole' that sometimes contains odd restrictions, applying only to whites, while in general it means born and raised in the colonies. Thus, there are white Creoles and Negro Creoles.

Certain concepts go back to Columbus and the beginning of the colonization, Indian or Amerindian, West Indies, the Antilles (the Greater and Lesser Antilles, so dear to French colonial geographers), the word 'métropole' (and metropolitan) derived from the French slave ports which refer to mainland France, the 'Hexagon' and its inhabitants. In French, the words 'Antilles' and 'Antillais' allude to a dotting of islands which some authors mockingly call the 'confetti of the Empire', 'France's danseuses' or 'scattered islands'. In French, 'Antilles' automatically means Guadeloupe and Martinique, exclusively. This chaplet of islands results from the very perception that France has of this Caribbean ensemble, the Caraïbes and the taking of a portion of this territory and having it belong to France. In this talk, I would like to clarify the close ties binding the African slave trade, slavery and the colonial system. The slave trade cannot be seen as a deportation towards America or a simple transfer of population, as it is too often referred to. It is a dramatic journey by land (by caravan in Africa), then by sea, the supplying of a decisive workforce for slavery. We have privileged the study of the slave trade over the study of slavery and the colonial system. Well, if slavery is closely associated with the slave trade, slavery was the fundamental economic basis of the colonial system. In order to illustrate this essential point, it would suffice to imagine the voyages of the African slave-trade ships to the Caribbean as if they were trains during the Second World War, transporting prisoners towards the Nazi concentration camps. To consider these slave ships as cargo of captive Africans would be analogous to simply seeing the sinister trains and their unfortunate passengers. The captive Africans who became slaves were subjected to the rigours of slavery in ways that can be compared to treatment in the Nazi concentration camps, as Stanley Elkins (Elkins 1959, 103–115) and the major Negro poet Aimé Césaire (Césaire 1948, 1–28; Lara 1998, 13–14, 36) have rightly pointed out.

Several terms need clarification: one is 'indigène' (translated in English by 'native'), laid claim to today by populations that have abusively inherited terms such as Indians or Amerindians or Bush Negroes from Guyana, and who wish to be called something different. Consider the example of the Black Carib, deported by the British in 1797 to the island of Roatán and who became the Garífuna community. (Speaking of these terms, Carib, Galibi and Garífuna are all identical.)

Fortunately, this geo-historical region benefits – since the creation in 1994 of the Association of Caribbean States – from the Anglo-Saxon concept, The Caribbean; El Caribe, in Spanish; and les Caraïbes, in French (Lara 1997). Caraïbe is used in French as an adjective as well (Caribbean), but Karib (Carib) refers to the indigenous population, insular or continental, and Cariban to the contemporary inhabitants of the Caribbean centred on the Mediterranean Caribbean. To be more precise, we can speak of the following concepts: Eastern Caribbean, Western Caribbean, and Northern and Southern Caribbean.

Let us end with a few other concepts to keep in mind, such as 'cimarron', which produced marron and maroon, and that claims an autochthonous origin (having originated in the island of Ayti [Haiti]). Also, the Spanish words 'hacendado' and 'ingenio', which are difficult to translate, and 'créolisation'. The latter term is used by historians to characterise one of the seven dimensions associated with the Caribans today: the native dimension, the African dimension, the European dimension, the Middle-Eastern dimension (Syria, Lebanon), the Asian dimension (India, Indonesia, Malaysia, China, Japan) the Jewish dimension, and the endogenous (or Creole) dimension.

The concepts Latin America (Amérique Latine, born in Paris in 1860 during the Mexican adventure of Napoleon III), Central America, Centroamérica, Hispanoamerica or Iberoamerica, and Lusoamerica are more difficult to handle. The term Centroamérica or Amérique centrale (Central America) is replaced today by Western Caribbean (Caraïbes occidentales in French).

The concept of Latin America – Amérique Latine in French – so common in Western Europe, and in America obviously, deserves to be criticised. I don't use it in my writing and I suggest in passing that countries like China, India, Pakistan, Thailand, Vietnam, Japan, Russia, Algeria, Egypt, Iran, Romania, Sri Lanka and Syria could contribute a fundamental critical appraisal of it. The concept in Paris in 1860 aimed to promote a Latinity that would emerge under the pressure of the French military in Mexico. Napoleon III, like his uncle Napoleon Bonaparte, dreamt of fashioning himself, through the use of military force, an American Catholic kingdom that would face up to the United States. The French project failed and after the French intervention from 1861 to 1867, the concept America Latina was adopted and used by the Creole Hispanic-American oligarchy at the end of the nineteenth century. Indeed, the concept, associated with the dominance exerted by the Creoles, excludes 50 million native inhabitants from Mexico to Chile, the Garífunas, millions of English-speaking Blacks/Negros from the Caribbean who don't have anything Latin about them, and all the Negros from the Caribbean, of which I am one, who classify themselves as People of African Descent (Arencibia-Huidobro 1978).

Finally, the last two concepts, African Diaspora and People of African Descent, have precise, scientific meanings. Used in French they can cause confusion. The French anthropologists in the circle of Yves Coppens, a professor at the Collège de France, have for years published works and produced films for television proving the African origin of all human beings as belonging to the *Homo sapiens sapiens*. The Japanese television channel NHK and its scientific programmes on quality popular science equally contend this origin. For these French anthropologists and their English, North American and African colleagues, this concept People of African Descent is a tautology, a Genesis axiom. The African Diaspora suffers the same review; it covers the dispersion from Africa of the *Homo sapiens sapiens* who appeared approximately 200,000 years ago. I believe that if we apply it exclusively to the victims of the slave trade, slavery and the colonial system and their descendants we are restraining, limiting and dwarfing a powerful concept.

Moreover, it is understood that in this talk I use Saint-Domingue for the period between 1791 and December 1803, and Haiti for the period starting on 1 January 1804.

Revolutions

Three revolutions illuminate the end of the eighteenth century, in the United States, in France and in Haiti. We often speak of the first two, but rarely of the third.

The first two of the above mentioned (the American and the French Revolutions) are associated with the Declaration of the Rights of Man (and of the Citizen): 'Men are born free and remain free and equal in rights'. In the United States, the Declaration of Independence adopted by the Second Continental Congress (Philadelphia, 4 July 1776), states that 'all men [...] are endowed [...] with certain unalienable Rights, that among these are Life, Liberty and the Pursuit of Happiness'. The Constitution of 1787 (the Bill of Rights) was ratified in 1791. Therein, slaves were considered to be worth three-fifths of a white person. The abolition of the slave trade was not to come for twenty more years. Finally, as we well know, illegal slave trading and slavery were perpetuated until 1865.

During the French Revolution, the Declaration of the Rights of Man and of the Citizen was passed on the 26 August 1789. A Declaration of the Rights of Man and of the Citizen was then adopted by the Assembly on 24 June 1793 (recognising the right of insurrection), but did not come into effect the way the Constitution did. Finally, the Declaration of the Rights of Man and of the Citizen was adopted on the 5th Fructidor, year III. But slavery lasted until 1848 with a short ephemeral interlude of the abolition of slavery – but not of the African slave trade – between 1794 and 1802. Then, Napoleon Bonaparte ordered the reinstatement of slavery in the French colonies. The Haitian Revolution, on the other hand, did not proclaim any declaration, but rather applied itself to providing its core desire of liberty to all men who were bonded to the rigours of slavery and colonial oppression. Let us note that a detachment of men from Saint-Domingue/Haiti participated in the War for Independence in the United States (in the Battle of Yorktown, 19 October 1781). The majority of the men stayed for a long period of time in the United States before being sent back to Haiti. Christophe Rigaud was one of them, as were other Negros, from Guadeloupe and Martinique.

The Deployment of the Haitian Revolution in the Caribbean

During the years 1791–1804, a short reminder concerning the Haitian Revolution as it intrinsically played out on an island where two colonies coexisted (Saint-Domingue and Santo Domingo, the Spanish colony) is necessary.

The Revolutionary Rupture, 1791–1804

In the French colony of Saint-Domingue, the uprising of the Negro slaves in August 1791, at first confined to the 'Plaine du Nord' (North Plain) engendered a general insurrection that led to the war of independence. On 29 August 1793, the French 'Commissaire' Sonthonax decided to abolish slavery, a tactical measure to defuse the 'bomb' that the general slave insurrection had become, having gained the whole colony; a measure that also allowed him to recruit soldiers to fight the English and the Spanish who had invaded the French colony. On 4 February, the 'Convention' confirmed and generalised the abolition of slavery in the French colonies. This decree affected only Guadeloupe and Guyana. Martinique was occupied by the British; Bourbon Island (now Reunion Island), refused to apply the law. Toussaint Louverture promulgated his constitution on 8 April 1801, and began to shatter the colonial system. In 1802, Napoleon Bonaparte reinstated slavery in the French colonies and dispatched two military expeditions to the Caribbean. The first went to Saint-Domingue, led by Leclerc and later Rochambeau, the second to Guadeloupe led by General Richepanse. In Saint-Domingue, the colonial war took place in the period 1802–1803. Toussaint Louverture was arrested in June 1802 and deported and imprisoned in the Fort de Joux in the Jura mountains until his death on 7 April 1803. The war continued in Saint-Domingue up to the defeat of the French troops in October-November 1803 and the capitulation of Rochambeau. Haiti proclaimed its independence on the 1 January 1804 under the presidency of Jean-Jacques Dessalines.

The insurrection of 1791 inaugurated a triple process of destruction: the destruction of slavery; the destruction of the slave trade; and the destruction of the colonial system. Three strong currents, intimately connected, that run through the nineteenth century. Now is the moment to underline a frequent mistake which privileges the abolition of the slave trade over the other two aforementioned processes.

Migrations and Slave Uprisings, 1791–1804

Between 1791 and 1804, Haiti is the revolutionary centre where these three processes take place and break out to ignite the Caribbean-Americas. The propagation of the revolution occurred as a result of several vectors; the distress voiced by the colonists in 1791 towards Spain and Britain; and the emigration of the colonists and plantation owners, sometimes with their slaves, who sought refuge in the United States (Louisiana, New Orleans, Florida, Georgia, Virginia and New England, Baltimore, Philadelphia and New York), in the Spanish colonies (Cuba,

Puerto Rico, Central America [Western Caribbean zone], Venezuela and New Spain), in the British islands (Jamaica and Trinidad), and in the Dutch colonies (Curaçao and Surinam). The vectors of the revolutionary propaganda are the Negro slaves themselves and the freed Negros who sought asylum abroad; they organise the teaching, communicate through the press, open Masonic lodges and divulge the rights of man founded on liberty.

The Spanish government recommended prudence to its colonial administrators. The minister Floridablanca requested the observance of a strict neutrality from the viceroys of Mexico and Santa Fé, and from the governors of Cuba, Puerto Rico, Santo Domingo, Trinidad and Cartagena. Nevertheless, he recommended that the white colonists be assisted with goods, arms and ammunition according to local availability, to cope with the Negros, the criminals and the pirates. He stated it was necessary to stop 'the contagion of insurrection so it would not affect the Spanish Possessions'.

The amplification of the revolutionary process born in Saint-Domingue forced the Spanish to intercede in the conflict. The Royal ordinances on 17 April and 23 April 1792 promulgated in Madrid forced governor Garcia to organise the defence of Santo Domingo. After the death of Louis XVI on 21 January 1793, England and Spain went to war with France. The Spanish-American troops coming from Santo Domingo entered the western part of the French colony. Their regiments came from Venezuela (1,000 men approximately), from the Cantabria regiment, (Puerto Rico), and regiments from Caracas, Maracaibo, Mexico, Puebla and Cuba (from Havana, and others). The Spanish-American military troops remained on the island until 1799. The English troops landed in the south.

As of 1791, the French colonists sought refuge in the Spanish part of Santo Domingo until the Treaty of Basel in 1795 when Toussaint Louverture occupied it. At this point, some colonists travelled to Cuba while others stayed and settled in the old Spanish territories. They were driven out by General Barquier in 1809 when he capitulated. The Spanish administration had had to negotiate with the English naval forces for the evacuation of the colony of Santo Domingo and for its protection against the corsairs and the pirates in January–February 1801.[1] The plantation owners of Santo Domingo, who at first also sought asylum in Jamaica, settled permanently in Cuba between 1803 and 1809. The arrival of several hundred colonists led to changes in the way things were conducted on the plantations and for the slaves of this large island. The 'Cabildo', the town council of Havana, on 16 December 1796 expressed its worries concerning the plots and conspiracies of the French and the people of colour who arrived from many different places; and of the slaves that came from Saint-Domingue,[2] who all arrived in Cuba. This Negro immigration provoked deep

---

1 'La Relación del General Kerverseau', *Clio,* July 1948, 91–98. Documentos sobre la evacuación de la Isla de Santo Domingo, *Boletin del Archivo Nacional,* Cuba, 1949, 178–81.

repercussions. It brought about the multiplication and strengthening of the palenques of Negro cimarron, principally in the 'Oriente', the eastern part of the island, in the copper mining regions of 'Santiago del Prado del Cobre'. The authorities in Madrid demanded that the governor Luis de las Casa take appropriate measures to destroy the palenques.[3] After the Treaty of Basel (1795), the freed and former slaves from the French part of Saint-Domingue, who sided with the Spanish camp and had fought at their side, were evacuated to Cuba. In 1795, the authorities in Cuba decided to divide them up and send them to different Spanish territories in the Caribbean in an effort to neutralise them. Jean-François and Biassou were taken to Trujillo (Honduras) with their families. They participated in the defence of the city, which was attacked by the English in 1797. These exiles, called 'negros republicanos', Black republicans, who had received land and tools settled in Nicaragua in 1804, throughout San Vincente de Comayagua, Leon, San Salvador, Granada, Sonsonate, San Miguel Realejo and Castillo de San Juan.[4] In the commerce raiding which took place between 1795 and 1815, refugees from Saint-Domingue became corsairs with home ports in Havana, Santiago de Cuba, and Barracoa, on the southern tip of the island. This privateering was centred on Saint-Domingue and Cuba. Some French colonists and their families procured the financial means to establish themselves on coffee plantations in Cuba or sugar plantations in Louisiana.

Slave uprisings were numerous between 1792 and 1793 on the sugar plantations close to Havana and Puerto Principe and Trinidad. They were easily quelled, but in 1795 the revolt led by Nicolas Morales, a free Negro, which had started in Bayamo, spread very quickly to the eastern part of the island. The Negros joined forces with whites and demanded equality, the abolition of taxes and the distribution of land.[5] A rebellion broke out in 1796 on a sugar plantation, Boca Niguia. These resistance movements that advocated freedom, initiated by the freed Blacks of the cities and spread mostly by the slaves working on the sugar plantations, were appeals that were easily halted and severely reprimanded by the Spanish army. The leaders were ruthlessly hanged.[6]

2 Proceedings of the Havana Cabildo, *Boletin del Archivo Nacional*, 1949, 158–60. Testimonios del Cabildo celebrado por el Ayuntamiento de la Ciudad de La Habana en 16 de diciembre 1796 et Bando del Gobernador de Santiago de Cuba para se presenta todos los extranjeros y nacionales…, 1799.

3 Real Orden signed at Aranjuez on 21 March, addressed to Captain General D. Luis de las Casas, J. L. Franco, *La presencia negra en el Nuevo Mundo*, 99.

4 J. Houdaille, 'Les Français et les Afrancesados en Amérique Centrale, 1700–1810', in *Revista de Historia de America*, n° 44, Dec. 1957, 305–30.

5 S. Aguirre, *Lecciones de Historia de Cuba. Primero Cuaderno*, Havana, 1960, 85–86. In *Journal of Negro History*, vol. XIV, January 1929, 96.

6 In *Journal of Negro History*, vol. XIV, January 1929, 96.

Santiago de Cuba became the point of reference of the French slavers in their last efforts to stop the revolutionary process.[7] Many planters left Saint-Domingue between 1791 and 1806, taking with them when possible their slaves and their fortunes. Some headed to the United States or England. Others preferred to stay in the Caribbean, in Jamaica, Cuba, Trinidad, Mexico or Louisiana. The church members were also forced to emigrate. They took refuge in the United States.[8] Two thousand Dominicans travelled to Venezuela and sought asylum there after the reunification of the island (Saint-Domingue) by Toussaint Louverture in 1801.

The decree passed by the Convention in 1793 opened the doors of Saint-Domingue, especially the Cape, to open trade with the United States. The duties paid for the goods imported from the US were aligned with the taxes the French ships paid. Salem and other ports of New England recovered the activities they formerly had with the Leeward Islands. Toussaint Louverture sustained cordial relations with John Adams, Washington's vice president, then president of the United States from 1797 to 1801. His relations with Jefferson, third president of the US (1801–1809), were rather cold because of Jefferson's Francophilia, which led him to take sides with Napoleon Bonaparte.[9]

When the war intensified in 1802–1803 and the strength of the Negro revolutionaries increased, the colonists fled in great numbers. The defeat of Rochambeau (who succeeded Leclerc) provoked a general panic. The plantation owners fled to Cuba, either as a definite sanctuary or just as a temporary step before settling in Jamaica or the Unites States (Louisiana, Florida, New England). Georges Nugent, the governor of Jamaica, complained to his minister in March 1803 of the arrival in Kingston of these French immigrants, slaves from Saint-Domingue, 'of the worst possible kind', who constituted a grave threat to the colonial society of the island. The majority of the 20,000 white refugees from Saint-Domingue, along with their slaves, settled in the American South and devoted themselves to wholesale and retail commerce and the teaching of French, dancing, music and fencing. The colonists opened cabarets, restaurants, gambling houses, show houses and boutiques, and also rented out slaves. The establishment of schools and colleges and Masonic lodges, and the production of artistic events (theatre and concerts)

7 J. L. Franco, *Historia de la Revolución de Haïti,* Academia de Ciencias de Cuba, Havana, 1966, 222.

8 M. E. McIntosh and B.C. Weber (eds), *Une correspondance familiale au temps des troubles de Saint-Domingue (1791-1796): Lettres du marquis et de la marquise de Rouvray à leur fille,* Paris, 1959, 31–33.

9 Jefferson's international Policy should also be emphasised, which leads him to adopt a very tough attitude towards Santo Domingo and Haiti. See Joseph J. Ellis, *American Sphinx: The Character of Thomas Jefferson,* New York, Vintage Books, 1998.

played an important cultural role not to be underestimated in North American so-ciety. The presence of the hundreds of Negros from Saint-Domingue who arrived in North America only increased the fears of the Southern plantation owners. Ne-gros were blamed for any unrest or stirrings on the plantations. The treatment of slave owners became rougher in the US, while numerous revolts and uprisings undermined slavery, which nevertheless survived until 1865.

From the beginning of the insurrection in 1791, the colonists in Saint-Domingue looked for ways to get rid of the Negro rebel freedom fighters, who had been im-prisoned, by selling them abroad. In October 1791, the 'deportation of the slaves that took arms with the freed slaves', who were called 'Suisses', the Swiss, was planned. It was decided that they be sent along with ploughing tools to Guatemala, on the Mosquito Coast. They were embarked on 2 November on a ship called the *Emmanuel* from Nantes. The *Philippine*, a frigate, escorted them; four 'commis-saires' (superintendents) were put in charge. After having vainly tried to sell the Black 'Swiss' in the depths of the Gulf of Mexico', Captain Colimin, of the *Em-manuel*, threw them overboard close to Jamaica, which caused an angry outcry from the English authorities.[10]

From this time on, and all during the wars up to 1803, the plantation owners and the French officers struggled to sell or abandon slaves from Saint-Domingue or Guadeloupe on the continent. A consular agent beginning in 1800, then a 'com-missaire' (superintendent) of the Spanish Emperor, Victor Hugues, signalled the arrival of the *Nathalie* and the *Rhinoceros*, sent from Le Cap by General Leclerc and carrying deported Negros (army staff of Toussaint Louverture) in his letters to the minister, dated 10 August and 1 November 1802. The 'commissaire' in-sisted on the grave danger they represented for the tranquillity of the status quo in Guyana.[11]

Slave Uprisings in the Foreign Colonies

Through analysis, the agents that spread the revolution can be discerned: the distressed appeals of the colonists, the agents and spies who gathered infor-mation, the wars, the migrations of the colonists with their slaves, the selling of Negro rebels on the coast of the continent or in Guyana, the activities of the Freemasons, the press and the intensification of piracy were innumerable. The multiplication of corsairs with the help of Toussaint Louverture, Dessalines

---

10 Thomas Madiou, *Histoire d'Haïti, Volume 1, 1492-1799*, Port-au-Prince, 1989, 109–110.

11 Anom, *Archives nationales d'outre-mer,* Aix-en-Provence, France, Guyane C14 (80), ff. 94 and 144.

and then Boyer, are revealed as agents of propagation capable of provoking important uprisings (for example, in Venezuela) in the colonial system and era of slavery.

The slave uprisings succeeded one another in the Caribbean, influenced by the Haitian Revolution. A process of liberation was associated with the ideas of liberty and equality leading to the path of independence. In Jamaica, the Second Maroon War took place from July 1795 to March 1796; the governor Alexander Balcarres, successor to de Sir Adam Williamson, had to confront the resistance of the enslaved Negros and the freedmen. In a letter dated 30 May, the Duke of Portland, also 'secrétaire d'État' of the Colonies, related an attempt to burn down Kingston, and complained of the French emigrants residing on the island: 'Agents, particularly mulattos and Blacks from Saint-Domingue, are infiltrating the interior of the island', he wrote. Let us not forget that the French in question are Negros from Haiti.[12]

The Jamaican Maroons sent an ultimatum to the British colonial administration for the island to be evacuated. The governor Balcarres proclaimed martial law on 8 August and called up the militia. The Maroons attacked the English lines and defeated the troops and the militias on 12 August. They withdrew to the Cockpits region, an almost inaccessible hideaway. Another British force was ambushed on 12 September and was annihilated. The insurrection took place when the majority of the regular troops were busy in Saint-Domingue. The slave owners, terrified by the possibility of a union between the Negro rebels of Saint-Domingue and the Maroons, set out to organise a ferocious repression. They welcomed more than 1,500 soldiers who joined the thousands composing the militias. Two Maroon leaders remain famous: James Palmer and Léonard Parkinson. Finally, the English started the deportation of 568 Maroons who left on 6 June 1796 for Nova Scotia. A slave rebellion subsequently broke out in 1798 in Jamaica, led by the Negro Cuffy, of Akan origin.

In the Dutch colonies, the 1795 uprising in Curaçao was also influenced by the Haitian Revolution, and severely repressed by the colonial authorities. All the rebel leaders were killed. The colony of Demerara-Essequibo (capital: Stabroek, Georgetown) suffered French and English attacks from 1794 to 1795. Negro cimarrons and Negro slaves joined forces in the countryside to gain their freedom; the rebels cried out revolutionary slogans: 'liberty' and 'freedom'. Troops were sent from Berbice and from Surinam. The captured Negros were instantly shot. The Netherlands finally ceded Demerara, Essequibo and Berbice

---

12 PRO, Public Record Office, London, Colonial Office C.O. 137/95, Balcarres to Portland, 30 May 1795.

to the English in August 1814; that was to become British Guyana on 4 March 1831. The Second Carib war against the English (with hotbeds in Saint-Vincent and in Granada), took place from 1797 to 1802, with the help of Negros from Saint-Domingue and Guadeloupe. The English decided in 1798 to deport 5,000 Black Caribs to the island of Roatán, in the bay of Honduras. They are the origin of the Garífuna community that lives in Belize, Guatemala, Honduras and Nicaragua today. Chieftains of the Black Caribs obtained authorisation to seek asylum in French Guiana under the rule of Governor Victor Hugues.

From 1795 to 1800, slave insurrections sapped the Spanish and Portuguese possessions in Centroamérica, Nueva Granada and the Guyanas, and Brazil, all the way to Rio de la Plata and Uruguay, and mostly in Venezuela (Coro, Cumana, Carupano, Cariaco, Rio Caribe, Maracaibo) and Cartagena, in Colombia. The region of Coro was rattled on 10 May 1795, by a rebellion counting 300 Negros and pardos, led by two freedmen José Léonardo Chirino and Josef Caridad Gonzales (Lara 1992). Many 'haciendas' were pillaged, and the white owners who attempted to defend themselves were killed. The rebels spread out into the city of Coro and proclaimed their rights openly:

- the application of 'la loi des Français', the French law, for the establishment of a democratic republic;
- the freedom of the slaves and the abolition of slavery;
- the suppression of mandatory tributes paid by the Indians (demora) and taxes such as the 'alcabala';
- the elimination of the white aristocracy.

Badly prepared and badly armed, without any contacts abroad, this first seditious movement was rapidly quelled by the local authorities and many rebels were shot. Many Negros who participated in this uprising, led by the 'zambo' Chirino, were refugees from Curaçao, which had close ties to the Negros from Haiti. The insurgent Negros from Coro also had ties to the 'French' corsairs who were often on the coasts (La Vela, Maracaibo and Puerto Cabello) and disseminated insurrectional ideals in the province of Venezuela. We have the testimony of Justicia Mayor, the lieutenant-colonel Andrès Boggiero, regarding the popularity enjoyed by the Haitian Revolution among the Black masses in Coro. In his 'Comunicación' dated 24 February 1801 he states 'Don Ariola, from these parts, who runs with the freedmen and the slaves from the Serrania, mountains of Coro, has made public the noteworthy news of the taking of the island Española de Santo Domingo, by the Negro Tusen, where they are manifesting great joy and celebrations, chanting the refrain ¡anda, fiate de tison! (Go on, trust a charred log), which is followed by the chant: 'that is so you can see (him)...'.[13]

Another fostering conspiracy in 1794 called for 'liberty and equality' for all. It was led by Manuel Gual and José Maria España, two 'hacendados', land owners, and resistance fighters, who fought for 'slavery to be immediately abolished, as contrary to humanity'. A third partisan, Juan Bautista Picornell, who sought asylum with these friends at La Guaira, wished to proclaim the independence of Venezuela, 'on the foundations of a federal republic...'. Betrayed, the federal conspiracy was dismantled in July 1797. España and Gual were judged and condemned. España was quartered on the Plaza Mayor of Caracas on 8 May 1799, while Gual was able to escape and took refuge in Port of Spain, Trinidad. Picornell, at first imprisoned then set free, died in Cuba, in the small town of San Fernando de Nuevitas, in September 1825. In Guadeloupe in 1797, Juan Picornell published a translation of the Declaration of the Rights of Man and of the Citizen.

An uprising of slaves from the French islands and of several bossals was aborted in Cartagena in April 1799. The plan had been to occupy the fortress of San Felipe de Barajas and the fort of Cerro de la Popa. The Black rebels only succeeded in burning one hacienda. They planned a vast insurrection for 2 May with the connivance of the volunteer local pardos, led by their chief Manuel Iturien. Negros of Haitian origin also elaborated a plan to take the port of Maracaibo on 17 May 1799.

Slave rebellions flared on the plantations in Louisiana with the help of freedmen in 1794–1795. These revolts were harshly quelled by the governor D. Luis Baron de Carondelet (1748–1807). He demonstrated implacable, unremitting cruelty, ordering the hanging on the quays of New Orleans of 25 Negro rebels, and the deportation to Havana of '37 individuals, whites and of colour, implicated in the uprising conspiracy of this province'.[14]

Haitian influence reached as far as Brazil and Uruguay where slaves revolted and concentrated on the island of Rio Yi, proclaiming a republic under the auspices of the Ley de los Franceses, the Law of the French, and the goals of the French Revolution, with the cries of Liberty, Equality and Fraternity.[15] In Brazil, the con-

13 Archivo General de la Nación, Caracas, tome XCV, f. 217. Original version : 'Ha dado parte don Ariaola, de este vecindario, que corre entre los libres y esclavos de la Serrania (de Coro) muy valida la noticia de la toma de la Isla Española de Santo Domingo por el Negro Tusen y que manifiestan gran regocijo y alegria con ella, usando del estribillo de ¡anda, fiate de tison ! respondiendo el a quien se lo dicen : eso es para que lo vean...'

14 *Boletin del Archivo Nacional,* Habana, a.XI, 1941, 59.

15 E. F. S. de Studer, *La trata de negros en el Rio de la Plata durante el siglo XVIII,* Universidad Nacional de Buenos Aires, 1958; L. Machado Ribas, *Movimientos revolucionarios en las colonias espanolas de America,* Edit. Claridad, Buenos Aires, 1940.

spiracy of the Tailors, also called the Inconfidência da Bahia, took place in Salvador de Bahia in 1798, rooted in the formation of a Masonic lodge in 1797. The lodge had its headquarters in the suburban districts. The conspiracy counted about 600 'members'. With handwritten placards they announced an upcoming uprising and displayed them in public places and on church walls. Recruited among the Black population, this movement counted a majority of soldiers and tailors (*alfaiates*), freed pardos and Black slaves. The rebellion conspiracy set for 28 August failed because of a betrayal. The inquiry revealed at least 31 people had participated in the conspiracy.

The majority of the accused were members of the humblest social groups, including slaves. The 'French ideas' they proclaimed, somewhat imprecisely, invoked the notions of liberty, equality and fraternity and alluded to democracy, to a republic and to a confederation. The plotters planned to sack the city, pillage and redistribute the seized goods and objects. They had planned to open the monasteries and the prison doors, to liberate the prisoners, to abolish all the customary prejudice concerning colour and to open the free port of Bahia to all ships, of all nationalities. The governor was to be forced to agree to the plan under threat of being killed by the rebels if he disagreed.[16]

At the end of the inquiry, the Prince Régent D. João, in a letter dated 14 December 1798 (Carta do Governador) ordained that the accused be judged by the Relação de Bahia, the court of appeals of Bahia. The lawyer José Barbosa de Oliveira was appointed to the defence. The judgement ended with the sentences pronounced on 7 November 1799. The four principals accused were condemned to be hanged (*enforcados*) and quartered (*esquartegados*). The following day, on 8 November, the two military men Luis Gonzaga das Virgens and Lucas Dantas, and the two tailors João De Deus and Manuel Faustino, were executed, and parts of their bodies were put on display in several different localities.

Fighting the Slave Trade

Great Britain inaugurated in 1806 and 1807 its crusade to end the slave trade. The Royal Act of 23 May 1806 put an end to any British subject undertaking a slave-trade expedition, then the Act of 25 March 1807, that came into force on the following first of May, outlawed the African slave trade everywhere on the coast or

---

16 *Inconfidência da Bahia em 1798. Devassas e sequestros (La conspiration de Bahia de 1798).* Offical investigation report and documents seized. The texts of the seditious documents were published by Brás do Amaral, annexed to his study: 'A Conspiraçao republicana da Bahia de 1798', *Revista do Instituto Historico, Geografico e Etnografico Brasileiro,* Rio de Janeiro, 99, 344.

territories of Africa. England then sought to convince the United States, France, Portugal, Spain, the Netherlands, Sweden and Denmark. In 1810, Britain had successfully convinced Denmark and Sweden, but had failed to impose abolitionism on the other slave-trading powers. Yet, Great Britain was able to count on Haiti as a staunch ally. Haiti, as we well know, had begun its crusade to abolish the slave trade with Toussaint Louverture.

Haiti alone fought the slave trade for a decade, from 1798 to 1807. After Dessalines' death in 1806, three Haitian presidents, Henri Christophe, Alexandre Pétion and Jean-Pierre Boyer, took radical measures to enforce abolition. On 2 February 1811, the brigantine Santa Ana (Capitan José Maria Peoly), which had cast off from the coasts of Africa and headed for Cuba with a cargo full of slaves, was intercepted by a Haitian war ship and taken to Gonaïves; here the Haitian authorities set the 205 African captives free and returned the ship to a Cuban port.

At the beginning of October 1817, a Portuguese schooner, the Maria-José, coming from Sierra Leone on its way to Havana, made a stopover at the Cap in order to escape the pursuit of a Royal Navy cruiser. The port officials went on board and discovered 145 African captives crammed in the hold, in a pitiful state. The ship, a known slave-trading ship, did not receive permission from the Haitian authorities to set sail again. Swiftly, the Haitian authorities decided to free the slaves. An article in the *Gazette du Cap* recounts: 'The Haitians hastened to remove their irons, while telling them they were free and had arrived among brothers and compatriots. It is impossible to describe the joy felt by these miserable freed captives; they fell to their knees to thank their brothers and their liberators as they shed tears. The Haitians, touched by this moving scene, cried as well. Only the slaver tormentors watched the scene, impassive, with regret at having lost their prey'. The freed passengers were taken to Acul du Limbé where they were treated. The schooner, the Maria-José, fell under the jurisdiction of the Court of the Admiralty of Le Cap, and after examining the case, it ordered the liberation of the captives after the following sentence was pronounced:

Considering that the Portuguese schooner, the Maria-José and its crew entered the port of this capital in order to avoid being captured by an English war ship pursuing them, seeking refuge and accomplices to continue their illicit, atrocious, and criminal traffic, Considering that according to the schooner's documents it has been discovered and recognized that it is the same schooner previously called the Rodeur, a French buccaneer that sailed from Cayenne, engaged in the slave trade in the name of Elisa Field, citizen of the United states of America, that was captured by the colonial brig of Her Majesty the Queen of England, the Prince-Régent, taken to Sierra Leone, seized and sentenced there, subsequently resold to Elisa Field for the sum of 375 pounds sterling, thereupon the schooner charged its cargo of 145 victims in Bonavista, Cabo Verde, under the orders of João Antonio Coelho, resident of this same locality, for their sale thereafter in Havana, Cuba.

Given that the shameful and barbaric slave trade has been abolished by most of the law-abiding world powers, declared contrary to the laws of morality, justice and humanity,

Given that the world powers above mentioned, solely driven by the principles of humanity and justice that they profess, abolished the slave trade in common accord, the government of His Haitian Majesty, is particularly interested and forced to condemn it and to engage all its efforts in stopping the shameful slave trade, within all its power to do so. The court, according to the conclusions of Maître René Bernadin Bayron, Crown prosecutor,

Commands that the 145 Africans, men, women, and children shall be immediately released and freed from their bonds, that they will be forthwith disembarked on the lands of His Majesty to be in full possession of their natural, sacred and imprescriptible rights, and are subject to the advantages of the laws, statutes and constitutions that the Crown grants to all those who live on its territory.

Commands that the aforementioned schooner Maria-José, as it stands with its apparel, gear, and equipment is, and will remain seized and confiscated for having engaged in an illicit and criminal traffic forbidden by civilized nations, a trade banned and forbidden by the aforementioned laws, statures and constitutions of the Crown, regarding the schooner and all contingent on it, it will be sold at auction to the highest bidder, and the funds from the sale will be available for the subsistence of the unfortunate Africans who were uprooted from their land of birth, by perfidy, deception and violence.

Commands the João Feliciano and his entire crew will leave the Kingdom shortly to go where well they please on the first vessel that sails abroad, that the present sentence will be delivered in due form, issued for all legal intents and purposes, condemning them one and all for acting collectively, they are ordered to pay the costs and expenses of the legal proceedings, the court commands and orders, etc. (*Gazette du Cap*, October–November 1817).

In December 1819, the Haitian war corvette, the *Wilberforce*, seized the *Yuyu ou Dos unidos*, a Spanish slave-trading brigantine, with a home port in Cadix, and escorted it to Port-au-Prince where the hundreds of captives it carried, destined for slavery in Cuba, were freed. The 25 March and the 4 September, the Spanish authorities of Madrid and of Havana demanded from President Boyer, in vain, the restitution of the freed captives.

After the surrender of Cartagena in 1815, the corsairs established new hideouts in Port-au-Prince, Cayes in Haiti and on the island Margarita. The captured ships were taken to Juan Griego on the island of Margarita (then under Bolivar's power), to Jacmel in Haiti, or to Saint-Barthelemy, a Swedish island at the time (the

Swedish government supported the raids). Pirates overran the islands; Haitian war vessels unrelentingly chased the Spanish pirates of Santiago de Cuba and Barbacoa or those of Trinidad. These pirates captured young Black men in order to sell them as slaves to the Cuban plantation owners. The Haitian raids originated in Port-au-Prince, or in Cayes or Jacmel, and were considered an instrument of war at sea for a country that incessantly and energetically fought against the slave trade that plagued the Caribbean.

Campaigns to End the Slave Trade

Dessalines, Christophe, Pétion and Boyer were totally committed to abolishing the slave trade that afflicted the Caribbean. Representatives or emissaries were dispatched to foreign colonies in order to foment insurrections. In order to stave off these agents, Spain and France respectively organised a network of spies to monitor Haitian operations. Between 1815 and 1848, the governors of Guadeloupe and Martinique extended their activities to finance spies on the islands of Saint-Eustache (Dutch at the time), and the Danish Virgin Islands.

As for the Spanish, their spy network was controlled by the brigadier Escudero, governor of Santiago de Cuba. In the documents *Informes*, 1816, addressed in particular to the 'Pacifier', D. Pablo Morillo and other Spanish administrators in the Caribbean, Escudero publicly condemned the activities of Bolivar, and rebuked the collaboration of Haiti and Jamaica with the Venezuelan revolutionaries. Escudero did not stop at only informing the Spanish authorities, he addressed the French military authorities asking for their aid in destroying the revolutionary hotbeds in Venezuela and Mexico.

Haitian emissaries contributed to inciting revolts in the French colonies – in Guadeloupe in 1818; in Martinique in 1822, 1831 and 1833 (Insurrection of Grande Anse) – and played an important role in the progression of the process of destroying slavery in these two colonies. In Guadeloupe in 1818, a 'campaign of rumours' spoke of the landing of English and French troops led by Lord Cochrane and Christophe at Pointe-à-Pitre and Le Moule (letter dated 17 July 1818, from the governor of Guadeloupe, Baron Vatable, to the minister). In February 1831, a conspiracy took form in Pointe-à-Pitre (Guadeloupe) with the announcement made by a freed Negro called Gusman, known as Occoli, enslaved anew in 1802, of the imminent arrival of a force 3,000 men strong from Haiti. In Martinique in August–December 1833, the insurgents and Black militias invoked the Haitian example to foment insurrection in Grande Anse. The same phenomenon was taking place in 1808, in English Guyana, in the slave rebellion in Demerara, 1823 (Moore 1971; Viotti da Costa 1994; St Pierre 1999) and in other insurrections that erupted in Puerto Rico in 1812 (Rio Piedras), 1821 (Bayamo), 1822 (Guayama, Naguabo),

1826 (Ponce), 1828 (Guayama), 1832 (Vega Baja), 1833 and 1839 (Ponce), 1840 (Guayanilla and Vega Baja), 1841 (Ponce), 1843 (Toa Baja) and 1848 (Ponce, Vega Baja). The insurrection of 1831–1832 in Jamaica must also be mentioned.

In the United States, the arrival of Haitians led the authorities to reinforce the social control of the slave system which in turn led to many slave uprisings, in particular in Louisiana: 1804 (Nouvelle-Orleans [New Orleans]), 1805 (two uprisings), 1811 (500 Blacks march on New Orleans). The conspiracy in New Orleans that counted Blacks and whites, on 13 August 1812, was mercilessly repressed by Governor Claiborne. Their leader Joseph Wood was condemned and executed on 13 September 1813. Let us mention the insurrections of 1829, 1835, 1837, 1840, 1841, 1842, 1856, and those in Florida (Talbot Island, 1820) and Jacksonville (1856). Toussaint Louverture inspired the heroic resistance of men like Denmark Vesey (1822), Gabriel Prosser and Nat Turner (Virginia, 1831).

The colonists who fled to Cuba (suspected of Bonapartist leanings) were driven from the island by the Franco-Spanish War and arrived in New Orleans, Louisiana. The Normand, James Pitot (1766–1831) arrived in Louisiana at this time, and became mayor of the city of New Orleans. A decree issued by the Captain General of Cuba, Salvador Del Muro Y Salazar, Marquis de Someruelos, installed on 12 March 1809 'juntas de vigilancia' groups of vigilantes with the purpose of identifying and expelling the French and not-naturalised Spanish, and to 'keep the Negroes under control and at work'. A violent anti-French campaign gained strength from March 18 to 26, with cries of 'Death to the French!', in Matanzas, Port-au-Prince, and Santiago de Cuba (Maso 1976). In Cuba from 1810 to 1812, the conspiracy of José Antonio Aponte in Havana was modelled on Haiti. The conspiracy started with the arrival of a ship from the Western Caribbean (Centroamérica) that arrived in Santo Domingo. On board was the brigadier Gil Narciso and several officers who had participated in the war against the French in the colony of Saint-Domingue, under the orders of Commander Jean-François and of Biassou. Wary of the effect these Black military men could have on the population of Afro-Cubans, the Captain General had them disembark, and housed them in the barracks of Casa Blanca, Barrio, on the outskirts of Havana. Three men, José Antonio Aponte, Juan Barbier and Salvador Ternero were nevertheless able to meet with them several times. These meetings were crucial in determining the tactics of the armed rebellion. The three leaders gained access to detailed information regarding the sequence of events unfolding in the Haitian Revolution. Bound by a secret oath (Abakua rite), Brigadier Narciso agreed to become the leader of the rebellion once they had obtained all the arms they had planned to lay their hands on. The Havana conspirators divulged their plans to the abolitionists and to the Negro freedmen, even to slaves in other countries – North America, Jamaica, Santo Domingo, 'Terre Ferme', on the continent, all the way to Brazil in secret correspondence, inciting these to revolt as well.

In Cuba, Aponte set out to educate the masses though political conscientisation in the backlands of the island. He used a portrait of the King Henri Christophe, which the monarch had sent him, making it understood that Christophe had promised to supply them with arms and ammunition. Barbier took the name of Jean-François in honour of the famous Haitian general who had led the general insurrection of 1791. The revolt planned for 15 March 1812, was to follow a detailed plan including the burning of sugar plantations and industrial facilities in the provinces of Havana and Matanzas, the surprise capture of the Castillo de Atarés and of the Cuartel de Dragones (barracks), from which the insurgents would open fire with guns and cannons. Aponte's other lieutenants Hilario Herrera, known as El Inglés, Salvador Ternero, Juan Barbier and five other leaders (Clemente Chacon, Juan Bautista Lisundia, Estanislao Aguilar, Francisco Javier Pacheco and José del Carmen Penalver) were charged with attacking other cities after having created the uprisings in the immediate areas. Herrera, El Inglés, was in charge of prompting the men on the haciendas and the sugar mills of Port-au-Prince (Camagüey et Bayamo) to rise up, and then to seize these two cities.

Three conspirators, Cristobal de Sola and Pablo and José Benito Valdés, had the opportunity on several occasions of talking to Luis, Captain General Someruelos' Black coachman, concerning the rumours pertaining to the suppression of slavery. Aponte, with the help of Javier Pacheco, drew up a proclamation alerting the population to the toppling of the tyranny. In a circular he urged the white traders and shopkeepers in Havana to meet and discuss the possibility of 'toppling the column', proclaiming a victorious rebellion in the phrase 'Que en la Iglesia se cantaría la gloria antes del Sábado Santo'. ('The church would sing in glory before Holy Saturday'). The proclamation displayed on the wall of the Palacio de los Capitanes Generales, and the circular delivered by a man of trust to the Catalan trader D. Pablo Serra – who feared for his life, and brought the circular directly to Captain General Someruelos – and other careless moves among the conspirators, such as Sola and Valdés mentioning the rebellion to the governor's coachman, resulted in arrests. On 9 March 1812 Cristobal de Sola was arrested and imprisoned. Shortly thereafter, Pablo et José Benito Valdés, joined him in prison. On 15 March 1812, Juan Barbier, Juan Bautista Lisunda and Francisco Javier Pacheco commenced the revolt and undertook the burning of the sugar mill, Peñas Altas, in Guanabo (Province of La Havana).

Because of several betrayals, orders were given to arrest José Antonio Aponte, Salvador Ternero, Clemente Chacon and Juan de Dios Mesa. During the inquiry they were joined by other defendants, such as Juan Barbier, Juan Bautista Lisunda, Estanislao Aguilar, the slaves working on the sugar mills of Peñas Altas, Trinidad, El Rosario and Santa Ana, the rebel insurgents who lived in the villages of Alquizas and Santo Antonio de los Baños. Ignacio Rendó, licensee, and the lawyer Don Sebastián Fernandez de Velazco were appointed to conduct the inquiry. José Antonio Aponte, and his principal lieutenants and partisan followers, freed and enslaved, were sentenced to death and then executed by hanging. Aponte's head was showcased; the Grand Masonic Lodge of Cuba was built and stands in that very same place today. The executions continued inexorably over the following months. We should mention the decisive role played in this conspiracy by women residing at San Juan de los Remedios or in Bayamo. In Remedios, Maria Merced Llanes and Maria del Buen Viaje Orihuela; in Bayamo, Caridad Hechavarria, Dolores Figueredo, Juana Villegas, María Josefa de la Asuncion Naranjo, Josefa Muñoz, Maria Candelaria Borrero and Maria Dolores San Diego.

In 1823, the 'Conspiración de los Soles y Rayos de Bolivar' broke out, which appears as a precursory project for Cuba's independence. The conspiracy counted among its participatants the Colombian José Fernandez Madrid; the Cuban José Francisco Lemus, who served in the Colombian army, and the Haitian Sévère Courtois, officer of the Colombian marine. In August 1812, Santo Domingo experienced an uprising similar to Aponte's, fomented by Blacks Pedro de Seda, José Leocadio and Pedro Henriquez. The objective was to attack the haciendas, burn the fields and free the slaves.

Colonists who fled from Guadeloupe, Haiti, Martinique and the United States sought asylum in Puerto Rico between 1803 and 1815. They proceeded to be naturalised in 1815 and 1816, choosing the benefits of the Spanish slave system.[17] On this island, after the revolt of Aguadilla in January 1795, the governor Ramon de Castro struggled to diminish the revolutionary influence spreading from Saint-Domingue with rallying cries such as 'Vive la liberté !'[18] ('Live Freedom!'). Once Haiti had gained its independence, Dessalines, head of the government, sent emissaries to Puerto Rico to incite the slaves to rebel. One of these emissaries, Chanlatte, arrived on the island in 1805. In a circular dated 30 November, the Puerto Rican authorities described him as aged 18 to 20 years old, of normal stature, with frizzy hair, and able to speak French, English and Spanish, and demanded he be arrested before he could 'spread the damned seeds on an island that enjoys perfect tranquillity...' (Diaz Soler 1970, 210).

Toribio Montes, the governor, took measures to forbid entry to the island of 'any man of colour arriving from Saint-Domingue.[19]' The secret agents passed through Saint-Thomas and successfully entered Puerto Rico where they fomented

---

17 E. C. de Loubriel, *Catalogo de Extranjeros residentes en Puerto Rico en el Siglo XIX*, Ediciones de la Universidad de Puerto Rico, Rio Piedras, 1962.

18 Archivo General de Indias, Ultramar, Legajo 6375, Letter from Ramon de Castro to the king, 22 January 1795.

19 Archivo General de Indias, Estado 86, Documento 26, 1806, Diaz Soler, 1970, 210.

slave rebellions in 1821, 1822 and 1825. In 1827, the Spanish colonial authorities heard of a revolutionary Haitian conspiracy to free the islands of Cuba and Puerto Rico. Haitian agents on these islands spread propaganda among the slaves to incite them to break free from their chains.[20] Governor La Torre produced a circular stating that any slave involved in a conspiracy would be brought before the military courts, which punished the convicted harshly. The circular stayed in effect until February 1833. Santiago De Mendez Vigo, the governor, was seen forced to quell the insurrection of Toa Baja, 26 and 27 March 1843, symbol of the obduracy and resolution of Black Puerto Ricans to defeat the slave system and to claim their liberty.

Insurrections Against the Colonial System

Francisco de Miranda, with the financial help of some of his friends in the United States, was able to buy a 180-tonnage ship there, the *Leander*, and *Bacchus* and *Bee*, two small schooners. Along with 200 volunteers and arms and ammunition, he sailed for Haiti, leaving New York on 2 February 1806, arriving at Jacmel on 17 February. Miranda asked Dessalines for assistance, and he charged two generals, Ambroise (military commander of Jacmel) and Pétion to give Miranda arms, ammunition and recruits. Haitian soldiers and sailors volunteered to accompany the expedition that left Jacmel on the 28th and arrived, on 2 April in Aruba where Miranda imposed intensive military training on them.

At this time a spy network working from Cuba was designed for the surveillance of the revolutionary forerunners. In March and April 1806, the spy Joseph Covachich (from the Croatian Kovachich), pretending he was Venetian, determined he would follow Francisco de Miranda and inform the Spanish authorities of his expedition to the coasts of Venezuela. The activities of this spy are known to us through the correspondence of the consul in New York, Thomas Stoughton, with the Marquis de Casa Irujo, Spanish ambassador to Philadelphia, and the latter's correspondence with D. Manuel De Guevara Vasconcelos, Venezuelan Captain General, and also through Covachich's own journal.[21]

Henry, a Jamaican merchant who had the good fortune of knowing two Haitians, Sabourin and Inginac, from Pétion's staff, persuaded Bolivar to travel to Haiti to seek the help of President Pétion. Bolivar left Jamaica on 19 December 1815 and

---

20 *Boletin del Archivo Nacional*, vol. XLVI, 1947, Havana, 1948, 160–61.

21 *Boletin del Archivo Nacional,* n° 149, Caracas, t. 28, March–April 1942, 1–37. Covachich and the disposition of King Carlos IV signed at San Lorenzo on 10 October 1806, by which he conceded to Covachich the designation of Honorary War Commissioner of his Armies.

sent a letter to President Pétion to request a meeting. He arrived at Cayes at the end of December and was welcomed by the authorities of the city and General Ignace Marion, military commander. He met with Venezuelan refugees who had been brought to the island by Luis Brion.

Belonging to a rich Dutch-Jewish family from Curaçao, Brion was born on this island on 6 July 1782. He was educated, and later entered the military, in the Netherlands. A fervent supporter of Bolivar, he offered his services in 1811 at Cartagena, and was named commander of the ships of the United Provinces of Granada. He went to Haiti in November, 1815, and sent the buccaneer ship *La Popa* to Bolivar, then in Jamaica. After the naval battle of Frailes, where he was wounded on 2 May 1816, Bolivar appointed him Admiral of the Republic by decree.

President Pétion met with Bolivar on 2 January 1816. Bolivar expounded his battle plans and asked Pétion for help in many areas. Pétion gave him the necessary support for commencing the battle. He only attached one condition to this aid: 'the generalised freedom of all the slaves in the province of Venezuela and all those they were able to assemble under the flag of independence'.[22] Bolivar promised to satisfy the president. He received money, men, ships, arms and munitions, as well as a printing press. He wrote to Pétion on 8 February to thank him for his crucial help:

I am overwhelmed by the weight of your good deeds. Our affairs are practically fixed ... I await only your last favours [...]. Through Monsieur Inginac, your honourable secretary, I dare make some new requests. In my proclamation to the inhabitants of Venezuela, and in the decrees that I must deliver for the freedom of the slaves, I do not know if it would be permissible to mention my heart-felt feelings towards Your Excellency, to leave for posterity an irrevocable monument to your philanthropy. I do not know, I say, if I should name you as the author of our liberty [...]. I beg Your Excellence to let his wishes be known to me.[23]

But the invasion of the mainland that had begun in May–August failed. Bolivar returned to Jacmel on 4 September. He received renewed aid from President Pétion and stayed for more than three months in Haiti. On 18–19 September 1816, a Mexican flotilla arrived at Port-au-Prince, including the *Calédonien* and the brig *Calypso*, commanded by General Francisco Javier Mina. He had coura-

---

22 Archivo Nacional de Cuba: Asuntos politicos, legajo 123, n° 2 et legajo 124, n° 35. Cf. Ardouin, Beaubrun, *Études sur l'histoire d'Haïti*, Paris, 1856 et 1858, volume 8, p. 182; P. Verna, R. Sutherland, *Un amigo de Bolivar en Haïti*, Fundación Boulton, Caracas, 1966.
23 Idem.

geously fought the French on the peninsula in 1808–1814 and had decided to continue fighting in Mexico in 1816 side by side with the insurrectionists. The Mexican revolutionaries arriving from the United States solicited the support and assistance of the Haitian government for the liberation of their country. They received arms and the authorisation to recruit Haitian sailors and soldiers.

Bolivar mentioned in his letter to Pétion on 9 October 1816, the need for Venezuela to be in solidarity with Haiti: 'I ardently desire that Venezuela become free in order to establish more regular relations with the valiant Haitians, and to be able to show the fraternal feelings the Venezuelan people have for them, mine in particular'. He set off from Jacmel on 26 December 1816 on the *Diane* heading to Venezuela. After Pétion's death on 29 March 1816, the Venezuelan authorities solicited help from the King Henri Christophe. The Republic of Colombia, through its general commercial agent, Juan Bernardo Elbers, contacted President Boyer in September 1820. He delivered a letter from Bolivar, asking for arms and ammunition. Boyer answered this request favourably, providing Bolivar with 1,000 guns fitted with bayonets and 16,000 pounds of lead shot.

But in 1819, the Angostura Congress marked the beginning of a process that signified a reconstruction of the slave system in Venezuela. According to various witnesses, in 1827 Bolivar agreed with the Creole authorities not to press forward on the subject of abolition. He had two obsessions: the slave revolts that had taken place in Venezuela in 1824–1827, and those that had occurred in Quito in 1825–1826. Incidentally, he feared what he called the pardocracia. He maintained many times to his friends that a Negro revolt 'was a thousand times worse than a Spanish invasion'.[24]

In 1826, Bolivar did not invite Haiti to the Panama Congress. How can we be surprised? Haiti was out of place in this learned assembly of slave states: the United States and Venezuela (where abolition did not take place until 1854). Slavery was abolished in Mexico in 1829, in Colombia in 1851, in Argentina in 1853 and in the United States in 1865.

Migrations of Negro Slaves and Negro Free Men to Haiti: 1804–1865

During this period, Haiti became a sanctuary of freedom for the oppressed Negros of the Caribbean. Emigration of Negro slaves from the French colonies towards Haiti began between 1804 and 1848. From 1848 until the end of the century, many Negros from Guadeloupe, in particular, left the archipelago to arrive in Haiti. This is how the historian, Joseph Saint-Rémy (known as 'Saint-Rémy des Cayes',

---

24 Letters from Bolivar to Paez, 26 November 1827 and to Mendez 7 May 1828, in Lecuna, V., *Cartas del Libertador,* vol. 7, pp. 87 and 257.

born in Basse-Terre, Guadeloupe, in 1818), arrived in Haiti with his parents. They settled in Les Cayes. Parallel to the abolition of slavery in the French colonies (decree dated 27 April 1848), there was a reinforcement of the colonial system. Without its slave system foundation, French colonisation turned under pressure (police, army, navy, church and education) towards the assimilation professed since 1795 by the conventional Boissy d'Anglas (Schmidt 1994–1999; id. 2000).

In Guadeloupe, between 1848 and 1851, Léonard Sénécal, a Black man, and his friends (Babeau, Bigue, Alonzo) attempted to destroy the French colonial system. The Haitian Revolution was their model, and they advocated for the independence of Guadeloupe. They succeeded in creating two handwritten newspapers, in Creole, that they distributed in the countryside, making sure they were read out loud by special messengers. The repression was atrocious. The archipelago, governed by Fiéron, an infantry colonel, proclaimed a state of siege. Sénécal and his friends were judged and sentenced. The Black Sixième was executed with an axe in Pointe-à-Pitre. Léonard Sénécal was sentenced to hard labour for some 10 years before he was able to leave and take refuge in Haiti (Fisher-Blanchet 1981; Lara 2012).

Recent research has revealed the constant vigilance of the colonial authorities over Guadeloupe and of Martinique, starting in 1820 and more noticeably from 1848 onward, as they were dreading the eventual meddling of Haitian government agents in the newly freed populations. The governors were given the order to close the ports to all ships coming from Haiti. This measure relied on the 1825 and then 1838 Convention, which established the terms between France and its former colony. The French government also made reference to the troubles in 1849 on the neighbouring island of Saint Lucia, where the name of the Haitian president Soulouque became a rallying cry.[25]

The United States

How could the emigration of the freed Black men be brought about? This was the concern of many American presidents from Thomas Jefferson to Abraham Lincoln. A solution rapidly appeared between 1801 and 1862: to encourage the departure of these groups towards Haiti. Thomas Jefferson left his thoughts on the subject in his *Notes on the State of Virginia*.[26] A plan to return to Africa is at the heart of the American Colonization Society, which was founded in 1816, and of

25 Service Historique de la Marine, Paris, Correspondence of the Minister of Marine and Colonies to the Commander of the Naval Station of the Antilles and the Gulf of Mexico.
26 Paris, 1785, London, 1787, and Philadelphia, 1788.

Liberia. Thousands of freed Negros living in the United States were transported by this society to Liberia from 1817 to 1890.

Moreover, the Haitian heads of state, Jean-Jacques Dessalines, Henri Christophe and Alexandre Pétion promoted the emigration of Blacks and Indians from the United States to Haiti. In the 1816 Constitution, an article of law (art. 44) envisaged the emigration of these citizens from the continent. Articles 2 and 3 of the Constitution stated that the slaves who escaped successfully from other colonies and took refuge in Haiti would be eligible to become free citizens.

The Republic of Buenos Aires (Argentina), and Colombia, on 19 June 1822, were recognised by the United States, followed by Chile and Mexico, but not Haiti. In 1825, more than 20,000 Negros from the United States had emigrated to Haiti. President Adams, in his message to Congress on 6 December 1825, tried to justify this refusal by the Federal State in these terms: 'We have found new reasons not to recognize the Republic of Haiti in the recent events, when this people accepted from France nominal sovereignty, granted by a foreign king, with conditions suitable to a vassal colony, where independence is but an empty notion'.

In spite of the protests by the Haitian authorities, the United States continued to ignore Haiti as an independent state, yet sent commercial agents to Port-au-Prince and Les Cayes. The Federal State only recognised Haiti in 1862.

In his autobiography, William Edward Burghard Dubois (1868–1963) mentions his grandfather, John, who lived in Haiti from 1821 to 1830. He was between 18 and 27 at the time. He married a Haitian woman belonging to the family of Elie Dubois, a famous Haitian educator. In 1830, he hastily left his wife and his son, Alfred, born in 1825. Alfred is the father of W. E. B. Dubois. John, the latter's grandfather, returned to Haiti in 1861 for a short period. He returned to the US with his son Alfred.

The pastor James Theodore Holly (1829–1911), born in Washington of free parents, became the person in charge of those willing to settle in Haiti. He went there in 1855 to see what opportunities were offered to the Blacks coming from the Unites States. He negotiated with the Haitian government, which in 1858 made an official invitation to Blacks. President Fabre-Geffrard (1859–1867) further confirmed this official encouragement in October 1860 by granting guarantees to the immigrants. In spite of the opposition shown by Frederick Douglass – a bitter adversary of the emigration of his compatriots – many convoys of emigrants left the United States. Holly left Philadelphia with a group of 2,000 people and chose to settle permanently in Haiti. He organised the Anglican church there and became the first bishop of the Orthodox Apostolic Church of Haiti. He wrote an article in 1859 on Christianism in Haiti in the *Anglo-African Magazine* (Lara 2000, 76). The migratory movement continued at the beginning of the American Civil War with its highest point in 1862.

Allow me before concluding, to evoke a personal memory. Oruno Lara, my grand-father, along with his brother H.-Adolphe Lara, fervent admirers of Haiti, heard about the newspaper *Le Nouvelliste de Port-au-Prince* (1873). In 1909, H.-Adolphe created his own newspaper which he called *Le Nouvelliste de la Guadeloupe*.

After having analysed the three destructive processes that span the nineteenth century after the Haitian Revolution, slave trading, slavery and the colonial sys-tem, we will logically finish our trip in Africa.

At the end of the nineteenth century, three men had a deep-seated intention to fight the colonisation that was tearing Africa, and its population, to pieces. They evoked Pan-Africanism for the first time. It is interesting to observe that the term Pan-African appeared at that time, in the Caribbean, around 1897 to 1899. Two of the three men mentioned above are Haitian, the other from Trinidad. The Haitians are marine Lieutenant Benito Sylvain, born in 1868, who was a guest of the Ethiopian court of Négus Menelik II in 1897, and Anténor Firmin (1850–1911), a diplomat, a statesman and author of a book entitled *De l'égalité des races humaines* (Paris 1885), a book that he wrote to oppose the racist theories of Gob-ineau. Candidate to the presidency in 1902, Firmin believed that the organisation of the state of Haiti 'should contribute to the rehabilitation of Africa'.

Between 1875 and 1898, Anténor Firmin elaborated a project known as Con-fédération caraïbe, a Caribbean Confederation, which would encompass Cuba, Haiti, the Dominican Republic, Jamaica and Puerto Rico. The third man is the lawyer Henry Sylvester Williams (1869–1911), who founded the Association Africaine in 1897.

These three men organised the Pan-African Conference held in London in July 1900. That year was a good choice, given the universal World Fair in Paris that was attracting visitors from all over the world. More importantly, the meeting in Paris of people from the Caribbean, the United States, Brazil and Africa engen-dered common rallying projects. Many of these travellers, particularly the English-speaking ones, had to pass by London, or an English port.

W. E. B. Dubois – Haitian by his father and grandmother – embarked on the trip, leaving New York for Paris, where he was charged with supervising the part of the exhibition dedicated to the Blacks in the Unites States. He participated in the con-ference and was assigned to write the General Report. The London Pan-African Conference, in 1900, launched Pan-Africanism. After the London conference, five other famous Pan-African congresses took place in the twentieth century; these, as you know, led to the establishment of the Organisation of African Unity, OAU, in 1963.

The Haitian Revolution resulted in a fracture between France and its Caribbean colonies. Haiti was thus able to rid itself of the three plagues that had tormented her since the seventeenth century: slave trading, the slave system and the colonial system. The first Haitian leaders – Toussaint Louverture, Dessalines, Christophe, Pétion and Boyer – fought tenaciously to gain independence and to defend it. They actively contributed to making the rights of men and women – captured and imprisoned, indentured and held on plantations in the Caribbean – heard and respected. The abolition of the slave trade led to the end of slavery – the last country to have abolished slavery was Brazil in 1888 – but the colonial system has endured until the twenty-first century.

Some of the colonies in the Caribbean suffered the hardships of the colonial system more severely than others. In 1848 in the French colonies, for example – Guadeloupe, Guyana and Martinique – the colonial system evolved towards the assimilation of the populations, with the corollary of 'forgetting the past'. This breakdown of colonised populations, which ruptured their connection to their historical experience, has led to behaviours denounced by Franz Fanon and Aimé Césaire, who spoke about 'larbinisme intégral', or 'comprehensive minionism'.

For the aforementioned colonies, as for their brothers in the Caribbean territories that became independent, the Haitian Revolution remains a model. It showed the way, the only path possible that the victims of the three nefarious processes must undertake.

The Caribbean territories, which particularly suffered the effects of the slave trade, the slave system and the colonial system, gained the right to live free and independently as well as the right to shape a democratic society. They need the support of the United Nations in undertaking the construction of a democratic society. The Haitian Revolution, which started in 1791–1804, continues to spread in front of our eyes, in the battles against ignorance, illiteracy, racism and social discrimination, and in how it still speaks for the independence of people and nations.

BIBLIOGRAPHY

Arencibia-Huidobro, Y., 1978. Amérique Latine et Caraïbes. *Cultures* 5/3, 151–81, UNESCO.

Césaire, A., 1948. Introduction. *Esclavage et colonisation*. Paris: Presses Universitaires de France.

Diaz Soler, L. M., 1970. *Historia de la esclavitud negra en Puerto Rico*. Puerto Rico: Editorial Universitaria.

Elkins, S., 1959. *Slavery: A Problem in American Institutional and Intellectual Life*. Chicago: University of Chicago Press.

Fisher-Blanchet I., 1981. L'affaire Sénécal en Guadeloupe, 1848–1851. In: *Cimarrons*. Institut de recherche historique. Guadeloupe and Paris: Éditions Jean-Michel Place.

Lara, O. D., 1986, reed. 1997. *Les Caraïbes*. Paris: Presses Universitaires de France.

Lara, O. D., 1992. *Caraïbes en construction : espace, colonisation, résistance*. 2 vols. Paris: CERCAM, Centre de recherches Caraïbes-Amériques.

Lara, O. D., 1998. *De l'Oubli à l'Histoire. Espace et identité caraïbes*. Guadeloupe, Guyane, Haïti, Martinique, Paris: Maisonneuve et Larose.

Lara, O. D., 2000. *Breve Historia del Caribe*. Caracas: Academia Nacional de la Historia.

Lara, O. D., 2000. *La naissance du Panafricanisme. Les origines caraïbes, américaines et africaines du mouvement au XIXe siècle*. Paris: Maisonneuve et Larose.

Lara, O. D., 2002. *Caraïbes entre liberté et indépendance. Réflexions critiques autour d'un Bicentenaire, 1802–2002*. Paris: L'Harmattan.

Lara, O. D., 2005. *La colonisation aussi est un crime. De la destruction du système esclavagiste à la reconstruction coloniale*. Paris: L'Harmattan.

Lara, O. D., 2005. *La liberté assassinée. Guadeloupe, Martinique, Guyane, La Réunion, 1848–1856*. Paris: L'Harmattan.

Lara, O. D., 2006. *Space and History in the Caribbean*. Princeton, NJ: Markus Wiener.

Lara, O. D., 2012. *Guadeloupe. Le Dossier Sénécal. Voyage aux sources de notre indépendance, avec trois escales : Martinique, Guyane, Haïti*. Paris: Editions du CERCAM, Centre de Recherches Caraïbes-Amériques.

Lara, O. D., 2015. *Révolutions caraïbes. Les premières lueurs, 1759–1770*. Paris: L'Harmattan.

Maso, C. C., 1976. *Historia de Cuba*. 1st edn. Miami: Ediciones Universal, 125–26.

Moore, R., 1971. *Slave Rebellions in Guyana*, Mimeo, Univ. of Guyana.

Schmidt, N., 2000. *Abolitionnistes de l'esclavage et réformateurs des colonies. Analyse et Documents*. Paris: Karthala.

Schmidt, N., 2003. *Histoire du métissage*. Paris: Editions de La Martinière.

Schmidt, N., 1994, reed. 1999. *Victor Schoelcher*. Paris: Fayard.

St-Pierre, M., 1999. *Anatomy of Resistance: Anti-colonialism in Guyana 1823–1966*. Warwick University, Caribbean Studies. London: Macmillan Education.

Viotti da Costa, E., 1994. *Crowns of Glory, Tears of Blood: The Demerara Slave Rebellion of 1823*. New York: Oxford University Press

Cultural Resistance to Slavery
The Creation of Maroon Culture

Doudou Diene

BIOGRAPHY

Currently president of the International Coalition of Sites of Conscience. Member of the Scientific Committee and initiator (in 1994) of the UNESCO Slave Route Project. Former director of the UNESCO Division of Intercultural and Interreligious Dialogue (Silk Routes, Slave Route, the Route of Faith, Al Andalus Route). Former UN Special Rapporteur on the Contemporary Forms of Racism. Former UN Independent Expert on the Human Rights Situation in Côte D'Ivoire. Former member of the UN Human Rights Council Independent Fact-Finding Commission in Gaza. Former head of the UN Fact-Finding Team in Togo.

Introduction

According to French historian Jean-Michel Devaux, the history of the transatlantic slave trade is 'the greatest tragedy in human history because of its scale and duration' and is a story of lasting resistance. Cultural resistance, which is less known than physical resistance, has become an intense force among enslaved people because it signals resilience and daily ingenuity. The force of it has permitted enslaved people to stand tall and recapture the humanity that was denied to them due to the ideology that legitimised slavery, that is, racism. Their every spiritual and cultural expression has given meaning and substance to the ongoing battle against dehumanisation, violence and the total absence of human rights, through a subtle strategy of subverting the slavery order. This cultural and spiritual resistance has given rise to a profound and enduring cultural dynamic among societies of the Western hemisphere.

It is of historical importance to address the link between memory and human rights. In the battle for human rights, the intellectual front has been neglected for too long; yet, it is on this front that ongoing resistance to all forms of oppression, domination, human rights violations and discrimination is created. The accent has been placed on the political front, which is crucial, as well as on the judicial one. But we forget that every form of oppression, human rights violation and discrimination is primarily a mental construct. This is how it starts. Elie Wiesel once said 'the executioner always kills twice, the second time through silence'. What Wiesel meant was that the executioner who oppressed and exterminated people did so not only physically, but also by wiping them from memory. Silence is a major ideological weapon in this regard. At the root of all systems of oppression and domination is silence, 'the zombification of memory': the tactic is an old one, trying to make victims forget the circumstances and even the reality of their pain, oppression and domination.

But what is the mechanism of this weapon of silence? I will attempt to address it before delving into the theme of cultural resistance. It works by erasing or ma-nipulating memory. This mechanism is first and foremost based on a crucial point: the mental construct of silence and the forgetting of oppression, extermination and even genocide.

This mental construct always begins with the depiction of the dehumanisation of the victims, be they Jew, Black, colonised, Arab, or, nowadays, Muslim. Sec-ondly, it is important to remember that this construct has a long history, meaning that oppression did not come out of nowhere but can be dated and is long-lasting. Indeed, this intellectual dehumanisation – the mask of and justification for the domination that is trivialised and inscribed into our thinking through education and into our collective consciousness through culture – operates through social, economic and political invisibility, and through the silence of the collective mem-ory, of the national narrative and, therefore, of national history.

This process illustrates the rhetorical figures of the 4Ms of colonisation: the military, missionary, merchant and memorialist (chronicler). The military always comes first, to subject bodies to non-resistance and to acceptance of domination. The missionary is next, to transform hearts and souls with talks about a common humanity and faith in one God, and with the destruction of the victims' heritage, whose spiritual and cultural expressions are cast aside as fetishes. Then, there is the merchant who imposes new cultural values and practices involved with eating, dress style, housing and aesthetics. This is the one who insists on eating with forks rather than gourds, on wearing a shirt and tie rather than a boubou, etc. And, lastly, the chroniclers are those who provide input into the memory, who get to decide what actions and facts of the previous 3Ms to keep for future reference. They do this through the natural and human 'sciences', historical writings and the trans-mission of knowledge through education, literature and information. These peo-ple are the historians, anthropologists, ethnologists (all three disciplines are the intellectual daughters of the colonial enterprise) and media professionals (former newscasters and modern journalists).

The chronicler is the principal player in silencing oppression and in imposing domination, and in invisibilising victims. His/her main objective is to have victims forget they are victims, through forgetfulness brought on by historical silence or by educationally induced ignorance. The chronicler gives meaning and substance to the proclamation that colonisation is necessary to civilise people and that resistance, as a means of subversion and disorder, is to be prevented at all cost. All these figures (the 4Ms) make up the ontological structure of domination through a complementarity organised by political power. Several issues are important to them. Identity is a priority issue. It is by reconstructing the identity of the victims that the latter become invisible. This process is a process of 'zombification' whereby the victim is stripped of any human reference, cut off from all spiritual and cultural roots, and is literally 'reconstructed' from the interior, in such a way that he/she accepts, recognises and is satisfied with his/her new identity. Memory is the preferred domain of this identity reconstruction. The historian of the new dominant power is the sworn manager of memory. He/she is the one who gives credence to the process of civilisation, who transforms the slave ship into an instrument of discovery and commerce.

The chronicler is also the one who gives a new identity to locations, by transforming the slave marketplace into a 'commercial centre'; the holding areas for the captives and slaves in transit into 'forts for defence and protection'; and slave cemeteries, especially mass graves, into anonymous and faceless plots that are quickly covered over by administrative and commercial buildings. The anthropologist takes part in the exercise by redefining the history of the dominated people into 'myths', gods into 'fetishes', spirituality into 'magic beliefs', and languages into 'dialects'.

The preferred vehicles for this 'remaking' are education (primarily), especially the writing and teaching of history, and the designation of emblematic figures to venerate and commemorative events and dates to celebrate. History is the principal area of concoction: it is the pot in which humanity and facts are re-cooked. Look at all the history books of imperial powers, and you will see that these history books are constructions built by silence and reconstruction. And all the great dramas of history, such as slavery, colonisation, the holocaust, mass exterminations and genocides have always been rewritten and revised.

In this construction of silence and victim invisibility, the issue of integration is indicative of a dynamic continuity. The dominant discourse, at least here in Europe, is what I call 'integration-negation' or striptease integration, whereby foreigners and ethnic, cultural and religious minorities are literally asked to arrive naked at Europe's borders, to rid themselves of all cultural, religious and, if possible, ethnic specificity or uniqueness.

In France, for instance, only after becoming oblivious to what he/she used to be would a migrant or foreigner become worthy of putting on the mantle of the Republic, a guarantee of eternal happiness and equality for him/her. As if the Republic were an ahistorical and eternal entity, innocent by its very nature of any attempt to dominate, exterminate or discriminate, like the colonisation for which it provided the institutional framework.

This talk of integration is not new. It is simply a continuation of the historical discourse that has legitimised slavery and colonisation, meaning the negation of humanity and of the civilisation of dominated people, basically non-Europeans. Because when immigrants, asylum seekers or foreigners are asked to strip themselves of their culture at the border, we deny the fact that they may be bringing something, culture or religion or, ultimately, civilisation that could add, contribute and enrich the host society. Hence, this renewed discourse on integration is the reformulation of the old mental construct whereby silence and invisibility served as ideological pillars for all dominations and exterminations.

This ideological continuity surfaced during the November 2005 French uprisings in the suburbs. Those events were the obvious expression of the economic and social marginalisation and discrimination experienced by entire communities that were largely from former colonies. Their principal demands were about ending the discrimination and inequality that prevail in the Republic. However, the intellectual, political and media elite made it out to be an ethnic and community problem, and a refusal to accept the Republic's 'values'. The concept of 'communitarianism', which was concocted by the elites in this context, is literally obscene as it relies on the fundamental assumption of a double voluntary closure in ethnicity and in the suburb. This version of events, in fact, is a denial of the historical process of rejection, and of social and spatial marginalisation on the outskirts of large Western metropolises, as well as employment and housing discrimination experienced by people who are in a constant battle against relegation and marginalisation. These populations, seeking permanent integration, are systematically enclosed in their ethnicity and religion. This process confirms Elie Wiesel's reflection on the executioner who kills twice: marginalised, and socially and geographically discriminated against, these populations that have become security risks are accused of 'communitarianism' and of retreating into ghettos from which they are prevented from leaving.

The same ethnic and 'communitarianist' reading into these events is reproduced through reductionist analyses, such as the one by Mme Carrère D'Encausse, Permanent Secretary of the Académie Française – the highest intellectual institution in this country – who blamed these uprisings on 'polygamy'. Indeed, the word 'polygamy' hints at an African cultural practice, which according to the colonial anthropology construct reflects the compulsive sexual behaviour of people who cannot control their procreative habits. It also connotes large families and 'wild children', who are supposedly the ones behind the violence and disorder in the 'no rights zones' that those suburbs have become.

In a similar vein, Alain Finkelkraut, a respected member of the intellectual elite and current member of the Académie Française, has not only attributed the uprisings to a form of cultural resistance against the values of the Republic, but has also philosophised loudly about how all of Europe was ridiculing the all-Black composition of the French national football team, which was not 'blue, white, "Beur"[1] but black, black, black'.[2] Similarly, Georges Frêche, socialist president of the Conseil Général du Languedoc-Roussillon, publicly expressed his "embarrassment" at the number of Black players on the French national football team.[3]

It should be noted that these interpretations, which were magnified by the media and politicians and which revolved around the defence of national identity, surfaced at a time when the youth of the suburbs were starting to express claims beyond discrimination issues that had to do with the need for a pluralistic national identity and the recognition of certain historical events, like slavery and colonisation, in the national memory, meaning in the writing and teaching of national history.

Similar resistance from the elite to an emerging pluralistic national memory was yet again expressed when intellectuals and historians opposed the adoption of 'memorial laws', such as the one proposed by Christiane Taubira (who was the Guyana parliamentarian at the time and later became Minister of Justice) that declares the transatlantic slave trade as a 'crime against humanity'. Given the silence by the large majority of historians on this tragedy and victim invisibility, this law also provides for the teaching of transatlantic slave trade at school.

Two 'lock-concepts' that aim to perpetuate the invisibility of victims and their historical silencing are being used to prevent multiculturalism in Western societies: 'communitarianism' and 'memory competition'. And finally, in a similar line, the other expression of this silence and invisibility is what we are experiencing now, namely the political, legal and judicial harassment against the visibility of religious, ethnic and cultural minorities, particularly in their external expressions: places of worship and cultural practices, religious symbols and style of clothing.

Cultural Resistance to the Transatlantic Slave Trade: Memory and Human Rights

The history of slavery is one of enduring resistance from the beginning of the triangular trade until the abolition of slavery. Perhaps the most profound and most radical resistance was cultural resistance. Throughout this era, slaves understood

---

1 'Beur' is a colloquial term to designate French-born people whose parents are immigrants from North Africa.

2 Cf. L'Obs, Paris, 24 novembre 2005, 'Finkelkraut, les "noirs" et les "arabes"'.

3 Cf. L'Obs, Paris, 13 septembre 2007, 'Harkis qualifiés de "sous-hommes" : Georges Frêche relaxé'.

quickly that, in a way, slaveholders had put themselves in a vulnerable situation in the long term. This vulnerability was the result of two factors. The first factor: the contempt of slaveholders for the slaves' culture, which was the basis of the system, prevented them from really understanding and assessing the true potential for the African cultural resistance. Moreover, slaveholders were only interested in the physical body of the slave that they turned into docile and obedient work tools. This was the first of two factors that led to the development of what I call the maroon culture.

The second factor was the subversion and the permanent inventiveness of the slaves to re-interpret, recover and transform all the practices, habits and cultural beliefs that slaveholders tried to impose on them. It is in this spiritual and religious domain, the most fertile field of this life force, that the maroon culture found its most enduring expression.

The history of resistance, and especially this prodigious intelligence and the ethics of the 'maroon' culture resistance, allows the descendants of slaves to regain the dignity and humanity that were denied to them, by becoming aware of the fact that they are descendants of men and women who stood firm, awake and in solidarity during the long dark night of the completely arbitrary system of slavery.

The transatlantic slave trade was described by French historian Jean-Michel Devaux as 'the greatest tragedy in human history because of its scale and duration' (*La France au temps des négriers*, Éditions France-Empire), a tragedy that, thanks to Christiane Taubira, was declared a crime against humanity by the French legislature, as well as by the September 2001 World Conference against Racism in Durban. But the recognition of this crime is paradoxical given its invisibility in humankind's historical memory and its persisting impunity.

The slave trade is perhaps the historical fact that was subject to the most historical revisionism. This historical silencing is all the more astonishing when we know that the transatlantic slave trade, which followed the trans-Saharan slave trade, was legalised by the Codes Noirs, organised by States, and legitimised by the intellectual construct of anti-Black racism, and that it lasted for around four hundred years. The designation of slaves as 'commodities' by the French Code Noir was accompanied by the 'scientific' construct of the cultural and ethnic inferiority of the Black 'race' on the part of naturalists, intellectuals and philosophers, particularly from the period of the European 'Enlightenment'.

The dominant religious and political powers of the time endorsed this construct through the injunction made to the slaveholders to, not free the slaves, but evangelise them, so that they would realise that obeying their master was a Christian virtue, which would eventually lead them to heaven. The ultimate weapon to make this a lasting and significant construct was the memory work, systematic in its duration, and based on three objectives: to convince slaves of their 'inborn' inferiority and make them accept their situation, to erase the violence and the tragedy of slavery from memory and emphasise the primary responsibility of the African powers, and to underscore the civilisation work and the economic benefits of the triangular trade. The historic omission of the slaves' permanent resistance is central to this reconstruction, as it confirms the image of natural and consenting victims. Cultural resistance is the form of resistance that was the most radically silenced.

Indeed, while that resistance eventually eradicated the ontological, intellectual and moral basis of the slavery system, the history of this resistance, by which slaves, in their long dark night of slavery, were able to recapture their denied humanity, has not yet been written. Yet, by its resilience, inventiveness and its human and ethical dimension, this cultural resistance represents a major milestone in the historical construction of today's human rights movement.

At the root of the cultural resistance is the slaves' initial observation of the slaveholders' blindness to their racial prejudices, as in all forms of racism. Slaves, who were depicted as 'ethnically and culturally inferior' were simply seen by slaveholders as instruments of work, devoid of any feeling, imagination or human vision. In order to survive, slaves who constantly observed their master quickly learned to use this ignorance and blindness as weapons. As a result, they sought refuge in their inner life, their gods, myths, and rituals that slaveholders could not see, and hence could not control or monitor. So they progressively developed a strategy of cultural recovery from, and subversion and transformation of, all the manifestations of servitude that slaveholders wanted to impose on them.

Many examples demonstrate this cultural resistance intelligence, at spiritual and religious levels. Slaves subverted their cosmos and spiritual lives and integrated Christ and the Virgin Mary, the new religious figures imposed on them by their masters. They did this by giving them a new identity and a status equivalent to African divinities and spiritual figures such as the Orishas. This process was a form of resistance, as well as an expression of the most profound African spirituality of the sacred unity of all.

It resulted in the creation of a dynamic and syncretic spirituality such as the Candomblé and Santeria religions. In Brazil, slaves circumvented the ban on weapons by inventing the Capoiera, a combination of dance and martial arts, of which slave owners only saw the aesthetic dimension. Carnivals and festivals were used by slaves, behind a veil of festivity, as special collective gatherings to bring together slaves that were otherwise dispersed. These were opportunities for sharing information, sending messages, organising uprisings and performing theatre plays that derided the slavery system by featuring comical and caricatural characters, masking the subtler work of identification and memorisation achieved through these plays. Last but not least, carnivals and festivals also served for preserving the vitality and the cultural, artistic and spiritual creativity of the slaves' cultural identity.

The Saint Domingue uprising of August 1791, which deeply shook the slavery system and its legitimacy and gave rise to the first Black republic, namely Haiti, was organised and carried out on the basis of the invisible 'poteau-mitan'[4] of the cultural and spiritual resistance, particularly the Voodoo. But it is mainly at the ethical level, where human values were denied to them, that slaves regained their humanity. Solidarity, equality, dignity, justice, compassion, collaboration, family life as a source of healing and humanity, and the central role of women as resistors, guardians and life givers, are only a few of the values that, profoundly and in the last analysis, made up the vital force needed to survive slavery during the four hundred years of complete oppression and lack of rights. The closely linked values of aesthetics and ethics were the main drivers of this resistance. The history of this cultural and ethical resistance, which is the basis of modern human rights due to its historical depth, resilience, ability to transform the victims into central actors able to seek freedom, and its universal dimension, is yet to be written on a global scale. It is a fine example of the fact that the fight for human rights is primarily a fight to keep memory alive.

---

4 In the Antilles, the 'Poteau-mitan' refers to the central pillar in Voodoo temples.

In Slavery and Freedom
Domestic Service in the Caribbean

Michele A. Johnson

BIOGRAPHY

Michele A. Johnson, York University, johnsonm@yorku.ca
Johnson's research interests include gender relations; race, racism and raciali-
sation; labour and migration; and domestic slavery and domestic service in
Jamaica, the Caribbean and Canada. Her publications include articles, book
chapters and *Neither Led nor Driven: Contesting British Cultural Imperialism in Jamaica, 1865–1920* (2004) and *'They do as they please': The Jamaican Struggle for Cultural Freedom after Morant Bay* (2011), both coauthored
with Brian L. Moore.

ABSTRACT

This paper follows the domestic service sector in the Caribbean, from the period of European colonisation and enslavement of Africans through emancipation to the free societies of the late twentieth century. It argues that the
deployment of workers was by no means arbitrary, and instead reflected the
influence of ideologies of race/colour, status/class and gender as they were articulated in the region. During the period of slavery, significant proportions of
bondswomen and some men were required to labour for the personal and domestic comfort of their enslavers while in 'freedom'; the sector often existed
outside of modern labour laws and operated as a large residual occupational
sector for poor women, most of whom were of African descent. Triply demoted by the hierarchies of race/colour, status/class and gender, the majority
of domestic workers continued to work in a sector which might have been devalued, but which offered a livelihood for themselves and their families.

At the end of the fifteenth century, Caribbean societies, which had been
originally settled by aboriginal peoples including the Ciboneys, Tainos and
Kalinagos, were irrevocably changed by the arrival of Europeans in the region. As European colonisers endeavoured to extract wealth from the
Caribbean, the harsh labour regimens, diseases and warfare which they visited upon the aboriginal residents resulted in their demographic collapse
(Rouse 1992; Boucher 1992). In response and also as a means of addressing
the problems of poverty in Europe, poor Europeans were impressed or re-

cruited as indentured labourers in the region (Beckles 1985; Beckles 1989a; Beckles 2000a; see Johnson & Watson 1997).[1]

With the expansion of plantation-based commercial agriculture and a growing need for workers, indentured servants made way for millions of enslaved Africans and their descendants whose labours would benefit the individuals, companies and nation-states involved in the European colonial enterprise in the Caribbean (Curtin 1969; Dunn 1972; Inikori 1976; Lovejoy 1982; Palmer 1997; Klein 1999).

In Slavery ...

The economic revolution that resulted from the commercial production of tropical staples was accompanied by enormous demographic, socio-political and cultural changes, primary among which was the escalation of the enslavement of millions of Africans and their descendants. According to available data, between 1700 and 1870 the Caribbean received just over four million ethnically and culturally diverse enslaved Africans who toiled in brutal and exploitative conditions (www.slavevoyages.org; Dunn 1987; Moitt 2001; Knight 1970; Knight 2000).[2] While the majority of enslaved persons worked for the direct generation of profits for the colonising and imperial forces, a significant proportion also laboured as domestic workers. According to Bernard Moitt, in Guadeloupe up to 15 per cent of the enslaved workforce served as domestic workers, while B. W. Higman estimates about 10 per cent of the enslaved population in the British colonies worked as 'house servants, washerwomen, cooks, chamber maids, nursery maids, scullions, butlers, valets, waiting boys, grooms and hostlers' in 1834 (Moitt 2000; Higman 1983, 49). As varied as their tasks were, it is important to note that the enslaved persons, as well as a small number of free persons (discussed below), who were required to labour as domestic servants, operated within ideologies and

1 The indentured European labour force included convicts whose punishment was 'transportation', as well as vagrants and other 'undesirables'. While the indentured population was dominated by men, there were poor women who worked in the fields or as domestic servants in harsh frontier conditions (see Beckles 1985).

2 According to Richard Dunn, enslaved Africans were assigned to one of eight broad categories of workers: drivers (*commandeurs* in the French colonies), craft workers, stock-keepers and transport workers, field workers, domestics, marginal workers (grass cutters and hog herders among others), watchmen and nurses (*infirmières*) and nonworkers. The majority of enslaved workers were field hands (*nègres* or *négresses de place*), who were divided into three gangs of workers – the first/great gang (*grand atelier*) of stronger workers to perform the heaviest labour, the second gang of ailing, pregnant or weaker persons and the third gang, primarily children (who started between five and seven) in training (Dunn 1987, 795–822).

intersections of gender, race/colour and class/status that dominated Caribbean slave societies.

While the enslaved population in the Caribbean shared the horrors of the vile system of labour, slavery was not gender-blind. In keeping with prevailing gender ideologies which promoted patriarchal domination and male elevation, when positions offered relative authority (slave drivers) or autonomy (looking after livestock), or where they required training and skill (sugar boilers or carpenters), they were usually assigned to enslaved males. Comparatively, despite the construction of ideologies of 'true' womanhood which determined ideal women's piousness, obedience, chastity and frailty, these ideas were not extended to enslaved female workers who comprised 30 to 40 per cent of the labour force in the region; instead, most enslaved women were concentrated in arduous agricultural labour (Welter 1966; Roberts 2002; Guy 2002; Dunn 1987; Moitt 2001; Bush 1990; Mathurin Mair 2000). At the same time, some of the expectations associated with archetypical femininity – especially tasks associated with domesticity – were assigned to enslaved women who were required to labour for the domestic and personal comfort of their enslavers. As a result, then, of the curious and uneven application of gender ideologies, according to Higman, domestic work 'involved a much larger proportion of the female slave population than of the male' (Higman 1983, 49). Enslaved women worked in the domestic sphere, often under the supervision of other (free) women, who benefited enormously from their labour (Beckles 1999; Bush 1981).

As was the case with the smaller number of enslaved male domestic workers (discussed below), there existed a hierarchy among enslaved female workers. Those who were utilised as housekeepers were often in charge of other domestic staff and sometimes worked as ladies' maids. According to contemporary observers like Mrs. Carmichael, John Stewart, Maria Nugent and Elizabeth Fenwick, the enslaved female domestic staff also often included waiting maids, chambermaids, general cleaners and laundresses, many of whom completed their tasks at streams, rivers or common water sources (Carmichael 1833; Stewart 1808; Stewart 1823; Nugent 2002; Wedd 1927; see Buckridge 1999; Moitt 2001; Beckles 1999; Beckles 1989b). Symbolic of the experiences of domestic workers in the period, laundresses in urban areas not only worked hard but, according to Félix Matos-Rodríquez, were vulnerable to verbal, physical or sexual attacks in the public spaces in which they worked (Matos-Rodríquez 1995). The gendered perception of a great deal of the labour associated with domestic service was further emphasised when enslaved women were required to perform child care, including wet nursing. While enslaved women's nursing of the infants of slaveholders was an accepted part of slave society, for some contemporaries like Edward Long, the practice was believed to be a dangerous one, since it both exposed the children of the enslaving classes to danger and undermined the full and authentic claims of ideal motherhood among enslaving women (Long 1774, vol. 2). For enslaved women who were required to nurture the children of their enslavers (who were also their future 'owners'), there was sometimes the development of what Carmichael referred to as 'unnatural' bonds between the enslaved and 'young miss or master', which she and others found to be disturbing (Carmichael 1833, vol. 1, 121). As a result, nursemaids were closely watched and punished harshly for (real and imagined) violations. And they were not alone.

While they worked outside of the harsh conditions of field labour, enslaved female domestic workers were usually under intense surveillance and frequently chastised for supposed incompetence and/or defiant attitudes. Their vulnerability to punishment was often increased by refusals to perform sexual labour by predatory males who demanded access to their bodies as part of their 'domestic duties', while 'compliance' could generate hostility from mistresses whose husbands were involved, even though the extant structures of racial and gender oppression could hardly have resulted in any other outcome. According to contemporaries, at times, mistresses vented their frustration on enslaved female domestics for a range of 'breaches' within the domestic space. Mary Prince's recollection of 'the smart of the rope, the cart-whip, and the cow skin' applied to her naked body by her 'savage' mistress's 'own cruel hand' provides a window into the world of enslaved women's lives and labours (Prince 2000, 170; see Hall 1999; Bush 1990; Beckles 2000b; Turner 1999). While it might be suggested that these moments emanated from an intrinsic penchant for cruelty among enslaving women, Brereton argues that intragender confrontation and violence took place within a larger context of gendered powerlessness among women in the male enterprise of Caribbean colonialism (Brereton 2001).

In the gendered world of domestic work where female workers were dominant, although they were not in the majority, some enslaved men were also deployed. As enslaved persons who would have experienced a subjugated masculinity in keeping with reconstituted gender ideologies (which obtained in Caribbean slave society), enslaved male servants were either utilised as 'outside servants' (coachmen), or placed in charge of directing a domestic staff (butlers), or in skilled positions (chefs) or in positions of trust (valets) (Beckles 2004; Carmichael 1833, vol. 1; Wedd 1927; Moitt 2000). Despite its perverse application, the fact that male privilege obtained among enslaved servants was reflective of white patriarchal authority, conscious as they were that any moment of male elevation, no matter how marginalised, would redound to their ultimate benefit. Still, while enslaved male servants tended to be elevated above their female counterparts, unless they were children, elders or men who were otherwise deemed to be unthreatening, enslaved male domestic servants were usually restricted from providing personal service to colonising women. In the racialised and racist slave societies of the Caribbean, most enslaved males were stereotypically marked as (innate) potential sources of unrestrained and uncontrollable sexuality and constructed as representing a danger to colonising women who, along with their male 'protectors', took precautions and treated (perceived) violations with the greatest severity.

If domestic service was proscribed by reconstituted ideologies of gender, it was no less marked by the ideologies of race/colour which defined Caribbean race-based slave society. By the middle of the seventeenth century, an individual's 'race' was a major determinant of his/her civil status: whiteness indicated 'freedom' and, unless otherwise established, non-whiteness was assumed to indicate bondage. However, this was not always the case: across the region, there emerged groups of 'coloured' (mixed race) persons who were almost always the products of sexual relations between white males, many of whom were quite debauched, and enslaved/free, black/coloured women. While the Euro-gender order usually determined and confirmed paternal pre-eminence, in Caribbean slave society, children's statuses were linked to their mothers, lest their fathers' free status remove these coloured issue from the enslaved labour force. While some coloureds were born free (see below) due to their mothers' previous attainment of freedom, and some were freed after birth, many were enslaved, sometimes by those to whom they were related, including their fathers.

In racist societies such as these, where socio-economic, legal and political power resided with European colonisers, the closer one was to the phenotypically desirable state of 'whiteness', the more elevated one's social status was assumed to be. This was no less the case among the enslaved: those who were coloured were usually ascribed higher status and relieved of heavy, low-ranking labour in the fields: coloured males tended to be assigned to skilled or domestic occupations while their female counterparts were often assigned to domestic service. So frequently was this the case that in Jamaica, Higman calculates that, by 1834, when enslaved coloured persons constituted 10 per cent of the total slave population, 'at least 60 per cent of the slave domestics in Jamaica were coloured' (Higman 1983, 126). While it is important to note that not every coloured slave performed domestic service and that not every enslaved domestic was coloured, there was enough of a correlation between 'colouredness' and domestic slavery for contemporaries to comment on the supposed link between race/colour and occupation (Carmichael 1833, vol. 1; Stewart 1808; Stewart 1823).

Whilst a large proportion of those who laboured as enslaved domestic workers performed their duties within the agricultural concerns that dominated the Caribbean, there was also a significant concentration of domestic workers in the urban areas which dotted the region. According to Higman, 'some 8 per cent of West Indian slaves in the British Caribbean lived in settlements called "towns" by

some contemporaries' and importantly, '[m]ost urban slaves worked as domestics' (Higman 1984, 39; see Welch 1995). Despite their numbers, enslaved urban-
based domestic workers were usually part of smaller contingents of slaves than
their rural counterparts: for example, according to Higman, 90 per cent of the slave
owners in Kingston possessed between one and ten slaves in 1820 (Higman 1984).
Urban-based slaves also increasingly lived in slaveyards which were quite separate from their enslavers' homes, and many were employed on the self-hire system.
Here, too, enslaved coloured female domestic workers were dominant; according
to Mathurin Mair, they performed a wide variety of personal services 'such as
laundering, sewing or hawking, domestic work in private homes, in lodging houses
and in taverns' (Mathurin Mair 2006, 270–71). As was the case in the rural context, in urban areas, when enslaved women were hired out as domestic workers,
there tended to be an understanding that their male employers included access to
their bodies as part of 'the job'; in other cases, enslaved women were directly pros-
tituted for 'paid pleasure'. Along with private arrangements, in the taverns, bars
and inns in the main towns and cities across the region, there was a flourishing
business where enslaved prostitutes earned substantial incomes for their owners,
who included men and a significant number of white, free coloured/black women
(Beckles 1999; Beckles 2000c).

Because domestic slavery has been portrayed as involving occupations of relative status and privilege within Caribbean slave society, and because some domestic workers had familial connections to the enslaving groups in the society,
enslaved domestics have often been assumed to have had little participation in the
ethos of resistance which characterised slave society. However, the stereotype of
the passive domestic, characterised by attitudes of subservience, can readily be
challenged; domestics may have been required to adapt to the culture of their enslavers, but they often found means of maintaining their personal and cultural ve-
racity and to resist their circumstances. Time and again, members of the
slaveholding class complained of the confrontations that they had with recalci-
trant, defiant and even violent enslaved domestics (Carmichael 1833, vol. 1; Hall
1999; Burnard 2004; Lewis 1969; see Bush 1987). In many enslaving households,
there was a general concern and in some cases a quiet dread, since, according to
Mathurin Mair, all were aware that enslaved domestic workers were 'often well
placed to do mischief in the white household' (Mathurin Mair 2006, 243; Mathurin Mair 1995). With enough frequency to cause alarm, according to Moitt, some
domestic servants were 'engaged in poisoning as a form of resistance', whether on
their own behalf or on behalf of the wider enslaved community (Moitt 1996, 250;
Moitt 2000). The idea, then, that enslavers existed in a state that might conform
with what literary scholar Kenneth Ramchand labelled 'terrified consciousness'
was not at all far-fetched (Ramchand 1970, 224–25).

If domestic service in the Caribbean during the period of slavery was charac-terised by gendered and racialised considerations, the status/class of individuals also played a role in their placement within the sector. While there is no argument that the vast majority of persons who performed domestic service were enslaved, there were free persons – Europeans (including those who had completed their indentured contracts), persons of colour born of a free mother or those who had purchased their freedom – who worked in domestic service, sometimes in com-petition with the enslaved, above whom they were usually placed (Beckles 1985; Beckles 1989a). Those who were white men or women in service were usually in-stalled in higher-status occupations (housekeepers or butlers), and although they represented a disruption of the expected intersections of class/status, race and gen-der in Caribbean slave society, they could expect not to answer to those who were their 'racial inferiors'. Instead, where they were employed, they often directed the labour of other domestic workers (who might be free or enslaved). They could also be recruited as 'elite' personal servants (ladies' maids, valets, governesses and nursemaids) or even as skilled specialists (cooks/chefs) (Nugent 2002). While they were relatively few in number, the presence of (highly ranked) free white domestics in some elite households in the period implies that any automatic as-sociation between domestic work and enslaved labour during the period of slav-ery be viewed with caution.

In addition to free white servants who were placed into elite positions, free coloured and black male and female domestic workers were also active in the sec-tor. If proximity to whiteness elevated the status of enslaved servants, when the benefits of 'colour' intersected with freedom, the status of free coloureds was even further inflated. At the other end of the spectrum, in keeping with the racialised ranking that pervaded the societies, it was in the least attractive positions (such as laundresses or 'yard boys') that free blacks congregated; they sometimes worked for multiple households and were often recruited to perform heavy, menial, dirty work (see Higman 1983; Klooster 1994; Cuales 1998; Carmichael 1833 vol. 1; Matos-Rodríquez 1995). Indeed, in many ways, since they tended to work in the lowest-ranked positions and to be paid less than their coloured counterparts, free black domestic workers often lived in circumstances not far removed from some of their enslaved colleagues, except in the important area of legal status.

As was the case with enslaved workers, free domestic workers, and especially those who were coloured and black women and whose duties brought them into greatest proximity with their male employers, the possibility that the services that they were expected to offer would include sexual and emotional labour was quite high. In some cases, domestic workers were able to leverage these demands as well as the personal relationships that sometimes developed in their execution of domestic service into material benefits and even to gain their freedom, sometimes becoming (unofficial) partners of colonising men and the mothers of their children, whether or not they were married (Beckles 2000b; Stewart 1808; Stewart 1823).

In Caribbean slave society, the provision of the domestic labour deemed necessary for personal, familial and social maintenance was largely answered by the application of the un/holy triad of 'class/status-race/colour-gender'. Thus, domestic labour, perceived as outside of the profit-driven agendas of the colonisers yet required for the colonisers' comfort, and perceived also as worthless and yet essential, fell to those whose relative lack of socio-economic status placed them in positions where they could be hired or utilised as servants. In these Caribbean slave societies, while there were small numbers of white servants and a significant cohort of free coloured/black servants, it was not surprising that the majority of those who performed heavily gendered domestic labour were enslaved coloured/black women. Low-status and enslaved, non-white in racist societies where Euro-colonisers held socio-economic and political power, relegated to the sphere of domesticity where the oppression of women was a largely uncontested tenet of patriarchy, the majority of domestic workers in the Caribbean during the period of slavery were multiply oppressed. The echoes of their subjugated condition, where they were required to perform personal service and where their subservience was demanded, would carry beyond the period, into the 'free' societies that would emerge after emancipation.

… and in Freedom

With the abolition of slavery in the Caribbean (over a period ranging from 1794 in Haiti to 1886 in Cuba) the question of how the economies and societies of the region would survive without access to unpaid labour became an enormous preoccupation among the imperial and colonial powers (Knight 1997; Fick 1991; Scott 1984). As a lack of investment, poor agricultural techniques, depleted soils and decreased access to protected European markets coincided with the requirement to remunerate the labour forces, in Caribbean colonies such as Jamaica there was a crisis in the sugar industry and a general decline in economic prospects. In response, many in the planter, merchant and professional classes abandoned estates, businesses and territories, resulting in a decline in the number of potential employers of domestic service.[3] At the same time, although

---

3 The general economic crisis of the 1830s and 1840s was worsened after 1854 when the Sugar Duties Act, which equalised sugar duties, led to the erosion of a protected market for sugar in Britain and severe economic difficulties for sugar producers and those associated with the sector. As a result, whereas one-fifth of the 670 sugar estates had resident proprietors

among workers, as Senior points out, 'the options open to both men and women were: to continue to labour on the plantations for wages; to establish themselves as peasant proprietors; to combine wage labour with own-account work; or to hire themselves out in the towns, mainly in domestic service', as Brereton argues, women and their families decided if and when to withdraw women's labour as it suited their family's needs (Senior 1991, 107; Brereton 2005; Colón & Reddock 2004; Higman 1983). These family strategies also affected domestic service.

In the case of Jamaica, though as Higman argues, 'the post-emancipation abandonment of estates was more important than the contraction of domestic staffs in reducing demand,' the overall result was a decline in the domestic service sector well into the 1880s when the trend was reversed and the sector entered an upward trajectory (Higman 1983, 117). This was linked to the growth of the middle classes, including local teachers, clergymen and civil servants, whose demands for domestic workers led to an expansion of the sector (Higman 1983; Reddock 1994). Indeed, in Jamaica, by 1921 the number of persons employed as domestics surpassed the number employed as servants immediately after emancipation (Higman 1983). For many in the new middle classes, domestic servants were symbols of their status and their ability to employ others to perform unappreciated and undervalued work while maintaining the appearance of domestic order, cleanliness, comfort and respectability.

In the early twentieth century, according to the available data, though there was a decline in the number of persons working as seamstresses/dressmakers, given the increasing popularity of 'ready-to-wear' clothes and the increase in washerwomen /laundresses as commercial laundries multiplied, the overall growth in the domestic service sector continued into the 1960s (Higman 1983; Reddock 1994). With limited educational and occupational opportunities, according to Reddock, 'for many women, [domestic service] remained a kind of residual category within which they could find work when there were no other options' (Reddock 1994, 81). Up to and beyond the middle of the twentieth century, so important was the sector in the Caribbean that it greatly influenced the migratory flow to urban centres where employers tended to congregate, as well as intra-regional migration to places like Trinidad and Tobago and Aruba, not to mention emigration to larger countries with high demands for domestic workers, such as the United States and Canada (Higman 1983; Peake 1993; Reddock 1994; Aymer 1997; Cohen 1987; Bakan & Stasiulis 1997; Silvera 1989).

---

in 1832, one-half of the 224 sugar estates did so in the 1880s. With the dominant sector in decline and the traditional employers of domestic service affected, the domestic service sector was also affected (Higman 1983, 117 and 121).

While the numbers of persons hired as domestic servants expanded in many Caribbean territories well into the 1960s, so that the sector became the largest employer of women in urban areas and was second only to agriculture in the economies of the region, there was another noticeable trend: many of the newer middle-class (or upper lower-class) employers of domestic labour were not wealthy enough to hire specialist domestic staffs and tended, rather, to hire solitary general domestic workers (Higman 1983; Brereton 2001; Reddock 1994). As these workers, the vast majority of whom were women, assumed many of the gendered responsibilities associated with domesticity (including childcare), they made it possible for increasing numbers of middle-class women to enter the workforce. That they did so often at the expense of their own households and children, who were sometimes sent to live with relatives, was among the many difficulties facing domestic workers in the region (Reddock 1994; Johnson 2015). The conditions under which many domestic service workers performed their duties were less than ideal. In the immediate post-slavery period, in several colonies, the employing classes and the colonial powers (where the latter were usually a subset of the former) moved to reinstate and re-inscribe old hierarchical labour relations. In British colonies like Jamaica, for instance, the authorities instituted a Masters and Servants law by which domestics could be tried, convicted, fined or imprisoned for breaking their service contracts and for acts of 'misconduct, miscarriage, misdemeanour, or ill-behaviour' (Masters and Servants Law 1842). Limited in their options, and concentrated in a sector that, by and large, remained unprotected by labour laws that had emerged in the wake of regional labour uprisings in the 1930s, tens of thousands of persons who laboured as domestic servants continued to work without set hours, time off, minimum wages or workmen's compensation and, as Mohammed points out, with 'no protection against sickness, maternity and old age disabilities' (Mohammed 1986, 43; Reddock 1994). Further, said Mohammed, since 'the value of household work and related activities' were not included in the Gross National Product and National Income accounts of the region, the contributions of these workers were devalued and ignored (Mohammed 1986; Senior 1991). In her view, in Caribbean society, domestic service has been assigned 'a negative, and often demeaning, status in the hierarchy of work roles.'

The domestic worker, therefore, automatically fills a low-status position in society as determined by the definitions of social class which rely on occupational classification. Of even greater concern is the fact that domestic labour includes some of the most repetitive, tedious, unfulfilling and unrewarding tasks; that it is normally carried out in isolation from other workers; and that women compose the large majority of domestic workers. These workers are among the most exploited on the labour market today (Mohammed 1986, 41).

Together, these circumstances often resulted in the workers' existence in conditions of poverty, which was in some cases quite appalling. According to Hugette Dagenais, in Guadeloupe, during the 1980s, the women who spend their working days cleaning other people's homes are themselves badly housed: in 1982 over 40 per cent of them lived in one or two rooms, 44 per cent lived in housing without running water and approximately one-third were without electricity; they have few household appliances to help accomplish their own domestic chores and if they themselves are household heads the situation is even worse. Present-day Guadeloupe is organised in such a way that domestic work is relegated to a particular group of women – the most economically and socially disadvantaged (Dagenais 1993, 96).

These sentiments were echoed across the region and corroborated Mohammed's argument that, by the later twentieth century, while attempts were made to organise the workers and some legislation was in place, 'the situation of domestic workers appear[ed] to be grim in the Caribbean' (Mohammed 1986, 45). The fact that domestic service in the Caribbean was historically and customarily linked to centuries of servitude did not enhance its profile, nor did the fact that it was increasingly identified with triply demoted poor, black women, many of whom were of rural origin and did not have access to a great deal of education (Johnson 2002; Shepherd 1999; Colón & Reddock 2004; Senior 1991). Although the domestic service sector in the post-slavery period came also to include, among others, formerly indentured servants who entered the region primarily from Africa, China and India between 1834 and 1917 and their descendants, domestic service in the Caribbean was marked by its historical links to bondage and servitude in the region (Reddock 1993; Shepherd 1995; Moore 1993; Moore 1987; Schuler 1980; Renard 1993; Laurence 1994; Look-Lai 1993; Turner 1993).[4] Further, as had been the case during slavery, the fact that domestic service was envisioned as 'women's work' did not help its status in what continued to be largely patriarchal and sexist societies (Moore & Johnson 2004; Moore and Johnson 2011; Johnson 2002; Johnson 2007; Johnson 1996; Johnson 1993; Reddock 1994; N'Zengou-Tayo 1998; Dagenais 1993). Under- and devalued as workers, those whose employment was tied to domesticity and the deployment of 'female skills' constantly found themselves at the bottom of the racist, classist and gendered hierarchies that marked (and mark) the Caribbean.

While there is little doubt that the historical tentacles which connected domestic slavery to domestic service in the 'modern' Caribbean affected the perception of those who laboured in the sector, and while many of the women who worked

---

4 Between 1834 and 1917, the Caribbean received more than 800,000 immigrants from Europe, Madeira, Africa, Java, China and India who were recruited through restrictive contracts of indenture, primarily to work in commercial agricultural concerns.

as servants were extremely vulnerable, this did not necessarily mean that they displayed the subservience that many employers expected or even required. As had their foremothers (and forefathers), some domestic servants resisted their relegation to lower status: they made it clear that although they may have offered personal service, this ought not to result in automatic displays of servitude. Among other things, domestic workers and their employers struggled over wages, hours, tasks, and residence, as well as modes of dress and address. Against a background of high unemployment rates, long-standing cultural practices and severely skewed legal guidelines, domestic workers negotiated and contested their circumstances as best they could, while operating within a largely undervalued and unregulated sector and confronting the often debilitating dynamics of class, race and gender in the Caribbean (Johnson 2007). That poor, black/coloured women were often recruited by more affluent women to assist them with, or, sometimes to assume entire responsibility for, the domestic chores that were ascribed to wives/mates and mothers due to the combined expectations of sex and gender, seemed only to confirm the power of the race/colour, class/status and gender hierarchies of the region. Still, in spite of the multiple status demotions which placed (and place) the majority of domestic workers at the base of every sort of hierarchy and the socioeconomic context in their societies – demotions which are less than encouraging – persons who labour in the domestic service sector continue to do their utmost to improve their conditions. As they continue to provide for their families and insist on the maintenance of their dignity in often trying circumstances, their struggles are sometimes nothing short of remarkable.

BIBLIOGRAPHY

Aymer, P. L., 1997. *Uprooted Women: Migrant Domestics in the Caribbean.* Westport, CT: Praeger.

Bakan, A. B. and D. Stasiulis, eds., 1997. *Not One of the Family: Foreign Domestic Workers in Canada.* Toronto: University of Toronto Press.

Beckles, H. McD., 1985. Plantation production and proto-white slavery: White indentured servants and the colonization of the English West Indies. *Americas*, 41: 21–45.

Beckles, H. McD., 1989a. *White Servitude and Black Slavery in Barbados, 1627–1715.* Knoxville: University of Tennessee Press.

Beckles, H. McD., 1989b. *Natural Rebels: A Social History of Enslaved Black Women in Barbados.* New Brunswick, NJ: Rutgers University Press.

Beckles, H. McD., 1999. *Centering Woman: Gender Discourses in Caribbean Slave Society.* Kingston: Ian Randle; Princeton: Markus Wiener; Oxford: James Currey.

Beckles, H. McD., 2000a. A 'Riotous and Unruly Lot': Irish Indentured Servants and Freemen in the English West Indies, 1644–1713. In: V. Shepherd and H. McD. Beckles, eds., *Caribbean Slavery in the Atlantic World: A Student Reader*. Kingston: Ian Randle; Princeton: Markus Wiener; Oxford: James Currey, 226–38.

Beckles, H. McD. Beckles, 2000b. White Women and Slavery in the Caribbean. In: V. Shepherd and H. McD. Beckles, eds., *Caribbean Slavery in the Atlantic World: A Student Reader*. Kingston: Ian Randle; Princeton: Markus Wiener; Oxford: James Currey, 659–69.

Beckles, H. McD., 2000c. Property Rights in Pleasure: The Marketing of Enslaved Women's Sexuality. In: V. Shepherd and H. McD. Beckles, eds., *Caribbean Slavery in the Atlantic World: A Student Reader*. Kingston: Ian Randle; Princeton: Markus Wiener; Oxford: James Currey, 692–701.

Beckles, H. McD., 2004. Black Masculinity in Caribbean Slavery. In: R. Reddock, ed., *Interrogating Caribbean Masculinities: Theoretical and Empirical Analyses*. Kingston: University of the West Indies Press, 225–43.

Boucher, P., 1992. *Cannibal Encounters: Europeans and the Island Caribs, 1492–1763*. Baltimore: Johns Hopkins University Press.

Brereton, B., 2001. Gendered Testimony: Autobiographies, Diaries and Letters by Women as Sources for Caribbean History. In: B. L. Moore, B. W. Higman, C. Campbell and P. Bryan, eds., *Slavery, Freedom and Gender: The Dynamics of Caribbean Society*. Barbados: University of the West Indies Press, 232–53.

Brereton, B., 2005. Family Strategies, Gender, and the Shift to Wage Labour in the British Caribbean. In: P. Scully and D. Paton, eds., *Gender and Slave Emancipation in the Atlantic World*. Durham, NC: Duke University Press, 143–61.

Buckridge, S. O., 1999. The 'Colour and fabric' of Jamaican slave women's dress. *Journal of Caribbean History* 33/1–2, 84–124.

Burnard, T., 2004. *Mastery, Tyranny, & Desire: Thomas Thistlewood and His Slaves in the Anglo-Jamaican World*. Barbados: University of the West Indies Press.

Bush, B., 1981. White 'ladies', coloured 'favourites' and black 'wenches': some considerations on sex, race and class factors in social relations in white Creole society in the British Caribbean. *Slavery and Abolition* 2/3, 245–62.

Bush, B., 1987. Towards Emancipation: Slave Women and Resistance to Coercive Labour Regimes in the British West Indian Colonies, 1790–1838. In: Dr Richardson, ed., *Abolition and its Aftermath: The Historical Context, 1790–1916*. London: Routledge, 27–54.

Bush, B., 1990. *Slave Women in Caribbean Society, 1650–1838*. Kingston: Ian Randle; Bloomington: Indiana University Press; Oxford: James Currey.

Carmichael, Mrs., 1833. *Domestic Manners and Social Condition of the White, Coloured, and Negro Population of the West Indies*. London: Whittaker, Treacher, and Co.; New York: Negro Universities, Press, 1969, 1 & 2.

Cohen, S., 1987. 'Just a Little Respect': West Indian Domestic Workers in New York City. In: E. Chaney and M. Garcia Castro, eds., *Muchachas No More: Household Workers in Latin America and the Caribbean*. Philadelphia: Temple University, 171–94.

Colón, A. and Reddock, R., 2004. The Changing Status of Women in the Contemporary Caribbean. In: B. Brereton, ed. *General History of the Caribbean.* Vol. V: *The Caribbean in the Twentieth Century.* Paris: UNESCO; London: Macmillan Caribbean, 465–505.

Cuales, S. M., 1998. In search of our memory: gender in the Netherland Antilles. *Feminist Review* 59, 86–100.

Curtin, P. D., 1969. *The Atlantic Slave Trade: A Census.* Madison, Wisconsin: University of Wisconsin Press.

Dagenais, H., 1993. Women in Guadeloupe: The Paradoxes of Reality. In: J. H. Momsen, ed., *Women & Change in the Caribbean: A Pan-Caribbean Perspective.* Kingston: Ian Randle; Bloomington: Indiana University Press; London: James Currey, 83–108.

Dunn, R. S., 1972. *Sugar and Slaves: The Rise of the Planter Class in the English West Indies, 1624-1713.* Chapel Hill: University of North Carolina Press.

Dunn, R. S., 1987. 'Dreadful idlers' in the cane fields: The slave labor pattern on a Jamaican sugar estate, 1762–1831. *Journal of Interdisciplinary History* 17/4, 795–822.

Fick, C., 1991.The Saint Domingue slave insurrection of 1791: A socio-political and cultural analysis. *Journal of Caribbean History* 25/1–2, 1–40

Guy, D. J., 2002. True womanhood in Latin America. *Journal of Women's History* 14/1, 170–75.

Hall, D., 1999, *In Miserable Slavery: Thomas Thistlewood in Jamaica, 1750–1786.* Kingston: University of the West Indies Press.

Higman, B. W., 1983. Domestic Service in Jamaica, Since 1750. In: B. W. Higman, ed., *Trade, Government and Society in Caribbean History, 1700–1920: Essays Presented to Douglas Hall.* Kingston: Heinemann Educational Books Caribbean, 117–38.

Higman, B. W., 1984. Urban Slavery in the British Caribbean. In: E. Thomas-Hope, ed., *Perspectives on Caribbean Regional Identity.* Centre for Latin American Studies, University of Liverpool: Monograph Series, 11, 39–56.

Inikori, J. E., 1976. Measuring the Atlantic Slave trade: An assessment of Curtin and Anstey. *Journal of African History* 17/2, 197–223.

Johnson, M. A., 1993. Intimate enmity: control of women in domestic service in Jamaica, 1920–1970. *The Jamaican Historical Review* 18, 55–65.

Johnson, M. A., 1996. Decent and fair: Aspects of domestic service in Jamaica, 1920–1970. *Journal of Caribbean History* 30/1–2, 83–106.

Johnson, M. A., 2002. Young Woman from the Country: A Profile of Domestic Service in Jamaica, 1920–1970. In: V. Shepherd, ed., *Working Slavery, Pricing Freedom: The Caribbean and the Atlantic World since the 17th Century.* Kingston: Ian Randle Press, 396–415.

Johnson, M. A., 2007. 'Problematic bodies': Negotiations and terminations in domestic service in Jamaica, 1920–1970. *Left History.* Special Issue: *Domestic Service* 12/2, 84–112.

Johnson, M. A., 2015. 'Ah look afta de chile like is mine': Discourses of Mothering in Jamaican Domestic Service, 1920–1970. In: V. Haskins and C. Lowrie, eds., *Colo-*

nization and Domestic Service: Historical and Contemporary Perspectives. New York: Routledge, 79–96.

Johnson, H. and Watson, K., eds., 1997. *The White Minority in the Caribbean.* Kingston: Ian Randle; Oxford: James Currey; Princeton, NJ: Markus Wiener.

Klein, H. S., 1999. *The Atlantic Slave Trade.* Cambridge: Cambridge University Press.

Klooster, W., 1994. Subordinate but proud: Curaçao's free blacks and mulattoes in the eighteenth century. *New West Indian Guide Nieuwe West-Indische Gids* 68/3–4, 283–300.

Knight, F. W., 1970. *Slave Society in Cuba during the Nineteenth Century.* Madison: University of Wisconsin Press.

Knight, F. W., 1997. The Disintegration of the Caribbean Slave Systems, 1772–1886. In: F.W. Knight, ed., *General History of the Caribbean: The Slave Societies of the Caribbean.* London: UNESCO Publishing/Macmillan Education, vol. 3, 322–345.

Knight, F. W., 2000. Slavery in a Plantation Society. In: V. Shepherd and H. McD. Beckles, eds., *Caribbean Slavery in the Atlantic World: A Student Reader.* Kingston: Ian Randle; Princeton: Markus Wiener; Oxford: James Currey, 398–412.

Laurence, K. O., 1994. *A Question of Labour.* Kingston: Ian Randle.

Lewis, M. G., 1834 [reprt.1969]. *Journal of a West India Proprietor Kept During a Residence in the Island of Jamaica.* New York: Negro Universities Press.

Long, E., 1774. *The History of Jamaica, or General Survey of the Ancient and Modern State of that Island: With Reflections on its Situations, Settlements, Inhabitants, Climate, Products, Commerce, Laws and Government.* 3 vols. London: T. Lowndes.

Look-Lai, W., 1993. *Indentured Labour, Caribbean Sugar: Chinese and Indian Migrants to the British West Indies, 1838–1918.* Baltimore: Johns Hopkins University Press.

Lovejoy, P. E., 1982. The Volume of the Atlantic slave trade: A synthesis. *Journal of African History* 23/4, 473–501.

Mathurin Mair, L., 1995. *The Rebel Woman in the British West Indies during Slavery.* Kingston: Institute of Jamaica Publications.

Mathurin Mair, L., 2000. Women Field Workers in Jamaica during Slavery. In: V. Shepherd and H. McD. Beckles, eds., *Caribbean Slavery in the Atlantic World: A Student Reader.* Kingston: Ian Randle; Princeton: Markus Wiener; Oxford: James Currey, 390–97.

Mathurin Mair, L., 2006. *A Historical Study of Women in Jamaica, 1655–1844.* Jamaica: University of the West Indies Press.

Matos-Rodríquez, F. V., 1995. Street Vendors, Pedlars, Shop-Owners and Domestics: Some Aspects of Women's Economic Roles in Nineteenth-Century San Juan, Puerto Rico, 1820–1870. In: V. Shepherd, B. Brereton and B. Bailey, eds., *Engendering History: Caribbean Women in Historical Perspective.* New York: St. Martin's, 176–93.

Mohammed, P., 1986. Domestic Workers. In: P. Ellis, ed., *Women of the Caribbean*. Kingston: Kingston Publishers, 41–46.

Moitt, B., 1996. Slave Women and Resistance in the French Caribbean. In: D. B. Gaspar and D. Clark Hine, eds., *More Than Chattel: Black Women and the Slavery in the Americas*. Bloomington: Indiana University Press, 239–58.

Moitt, B., 2000. Women, Work and Resistance in the French Caribbean during Slavery, 1700–1848. In: V. Shepherd and H. McD. Beckles, eds., *Caribbean Slavery in the Atlantic World: A Student Reader*. Kingston: Ian Randle; Princeton: Markus Wiener; Oxford: James Currey; 1017–29.

Moitt, B., 2001. *Women and Slavery in the French Antilles, 1635–1848*. Bloomington: Indiana University Press.

Moore, B. L., 1987. *Race, Power and Social Segmentation in Colonial Society: Guyana after Slavery*. New York: Gordon and Breach.

Moore, B. L., 1993. The Social Impact of Portuguese Immigration into British Guiana after Emancipation. In: H. Beckles and V. Shepherd, eds., *Caribbean Freedom: Economy and Society from Emancipation to the Present*. Princeton: Markus Wiener; London: James Currey; Kingston: Ian Randle, 152–60.

Moore, B. L. and Johnson, M. A., 2004. *Neither Led nor Driven: Contesting British Cultural Imperial in Jamaica 1865–1920*. Kingston: University of the West Indies Press.

Moore, B. L. and Johnson, M. A., 2011. *'They do as they please': The Jamaican Struggle for Cultural Freedom after Morant Bay*. Kingston: University of the West Indies Press.

N'zengou-Tayo, M-J., 1999. 'Fanm se poto mitan': Haitian woman, the pillar of society. *Feminist Review* 59/1, 118–42.

Palmer, C.A., 1997. The Slave Trade, African Slavers and the Demography of the Caribbean to 1750. In: F.W. Knight, ed., *General History of the Caribbean: The Slave Societies of the Caribbean*. London: UNESCO Publishing/Macmillan Education, vol. 3, 9–44.

Peake, L., 1993. The Development & Role of Women's Political Organizations in Guyana. In: J. H. Momsen, ed., *Women & Change in the Caribbean: A Pan-Caribbean Perspective*. Kingston: Ian Randle; Bloomington: Indianapolis University Press; London: James Currey.

Prince, M., 1831. History of Mary Prince, A West Indian Slave, Related by Herself. London and Edinburgh. Reprinted In: V. Shepherd and H. McD. Beckles, eds., *Caribbean Slavery in the Atlantic World: A Student Reader*. Kingston: Ian Randle; Princeton: Markus Wiener; Oxford: James Currey, 843–57.

Ramchand, K., 1970. *The West Indian Novel and its Background*. London: Faber and Faber.

Reddock, R., 1993. Indian Women and Indentureship in Trinidad and Tobago 1845–1917: Freedom Denied. In: H. McD. Beckles and V. Shepherd, eds., *Caribbean Freedom: Economy and Society from Emancipation to the Present*. Princeton: Markus

Wiener; London: James Currey; Kingston: Ian Randle, 225–37.

Reddock, R., 1994. *Women, Labour and Politics in Trinidad and Tobago: A History.* Kingston: Ian Randle.

Renard, R., 1993. Immigration and Indentureship in the French West Indies, 1848–1870. In: H. McD. Beckles and V. Shepherd, eds., *Caribbean Freedom: Economy and Society from Emancipation to the Present.* Princeton: Markus Wiener; London: James Currey; Kingston: Ian Randle, 161–67.

Rouse, I., 1992. *The Tainos: Rise and Decline of the People who Greeted Columbus.* New Haven: Yale University Press.

Schuler, M., 1980. *Alas, Alas Kongo: A Social History of Indentured African Immigration into Jamaica, 1841–1865.* Baltimore: Johns Hopkins University Press.

Scott, R.J., 1984. Explaining abolition: Contradiction, adaptation, and challenge in Cuban slave society, 1860–1886. *Comparative Studies in Society and History* 26/1, 83–111.

Senior, O., 1991. *Working Miracles: Women's Lives in the English-speaking Caribbean.* Cave Hill, Barbados: Institute of Social and Economic Research, University of the West Indies; London: James Currey; Bloomington: Indiana University Press.

Shepherd, V. A., 1995. Gender, Migration and Settlement: The Indentureship and Post-indentureship Experience of Indian Females in Jamaica 1845–1943. In: V. Shepherd, B. Brereton and B. Bailey, eds., *Engendering History: Caribbean Women in Historical Perspective.* New York: St. Martin's, 233–57.

Shepherd, V., 1999. *Women in Caribbean History.* Kingston: Ian Randle.

Silvera, M., 1989. *Silenced: Talks with working class Caribbean women about their lives and struggles as Domestic Workers in Canada.* Toronto: Sister Vision.

Stewart, J., 1808. *An Account of Jamaica, And its Inhabitants. By a Gentleman long resident in the West Indies.* London.

Stewart, J., 1823. *A view of the past and present State of the island of Jamaica: with remarks on the moral and physical condition of the laves, and on the abolition of slavery in the colonies.* Edinburgh.

Turner, M., 1993. Chinese Contract Labour in Cuba, 1847–1874. In: H. Beckles and V. Shepherd, eds., *Caribbean Freedom: Economy and Society from Emancipation to the Present.* Princeton: Markus Wiener; London: James Currey; Kingston: Ian Randle, 132–40.

Turner, M., 1999. The 11 o'clock flog: Women, work and labour law in the British Caribbean. *Slavery and Abolition*, 20/1, 38–58.

Wedd, A. F., ed., 1927. *The Fate of the Fenwicks: Letters to Mary Hays, 1798–1828.* London: Methuen.

Welch, P. L. V., 1995. The Slave family in the urban context: Views from Bridgetown, Barbados, 1780-1816. *Journal of Caribbean History* 29/1, 11–24.

Welter, B., 1966. The Cult of true womanhood, 1820–1860. *American Quarterly* 18,

151–74.

Wright, P., ed., 2002. *Lady Nugent's Journal of Her Residence in Jamaica from 1801 to 1805*. Barbados: University of the West Indies Press.

Voyages: The Trans-Atlantic Slave Trade Database (http://www.slavevoyages.org/) Laws of Jamaica, An Act to enlarge the powers of Justices in determining Complaints between Masters and Servants, and between Masters, Artificers, and others, 1842 (Law 5 Victoria, C.43), also called the Masters and Servants Law, 1842.

Suriname Maroons
A History of Intrusions into their Territories

Alex van Stipriaan

BIOGRAPHY

Alex van Stipriaan Luïscius is Professor of Caribbean History at the Erasmus University of Rotterdam, the Netherlands. Since the 1980s he has been working particularly on slavery and its aftermath in Suriname, as well as on heritage in the Dutch Caribbean islands. He has also published on diverse aspects of Afro-cultures, Caribbean art, Maroons, the search for African roots, and on traces and legacies of slavery in the Netherlands. He has also curated museum exhibitions on, among other topics, slavery, Maroons and race relations.

ABSTRACT

Maroonage has been an important aspect of the history of slavery in Suriname. Maroons liberated themselves and conquered a more or less autonomous place beyond the borders of colonial society. At the same time, they remained dependent on that society for their subsistence. This made them enter the colonial money economy, although they stayed in relative isolation. When it turned out that their territories held enormously rich natural resources, a process of intrusion was started by colonial society to appropriate these riches. This has not stopped in postcolonial times. As a result, Maroons have found themselves constantly split between wanting to earn money to buy goods and prosperity, while in doing so, contributing to the destruction of the lifestyle they created during and after slavery.

From the very first moment that Africans were forcibly brought to the Americas, they made successful attempts to escape slavery and start a new life far from colonial centres. This process did not stop until the last days before the abolition of slavery. In Suriname, the process began with the first English plantations that were built there from 1650 and continued, increasingly, after the takeover by the Dutch in 1667 until the Emancipation on 1 July 1863.

Essentially, there were two types of maroonage: so-called *petit marronage* (small-scale maroonage) and *grand marronage* (large-scale maroonage). The first refers to the individuals and small groups who absconded from the yoke of slavery without the direct intention of settling deep into the interior of the colony. This was often a temporary action, sometimes even a form of strike (van Stipriaan 1995), which often ended in a forced or voluntary return to the plantation or the slave master. It could be an impulsive, desperation action, but also a well-thought-out plan. Sometimes the refugees stayed away for only a few days; in other cases they stayed at the edges of the colonised area for years. Despite the fact that the flight was temporary, the *petit marronage* made clear that the power of the enslaver was limited and that it would never succeed in enslaving the Africans completely. The colonial authorities and the slave owners considered the *petit marronage* as a kind of business risk. Admittedly, it was difficult and it cost money, but up until the nineteenth century, it was hardly considered a threat. That changed when it gradually became clear that *petit marronage* was undermining the system from the inside out and had become an effective strike weapon of what in the meantime was actually becoming an enslaved (proto-) peasantry (see van Stipriaan 1995).

Grand marronage was the process whereby groups of refugees gathered in the unexplored, non-colonised forests of the interior of the colony to set up independent communities and to attack the colony from there. These actions focused on the liberation of – sometimes literally – brothers and sisters who still lived in slavery, and also on obtaining people and means to maintain the group, varying from tools, seeds and weapons to women.

It is truly remarkable that the Maroons undertook so many actions against the colonisers, because these actions always provoked a military response and resulted in long-term pursuit campaigns aimed at their extermination. The Maroons thus led a fairly hunted existence. In addition, they had to survive in an environment that was initially unknown to them, against which they had to protect themselves, although they were sometimes helped by the original inhabitants of the territory, the Indigenous, or Native Surinamese. This double threat to Maroons obviously stimulated strong forms of social organisation, kinship and religious systems, which developed from a very early stage.

Colonial society experienced *grand marronage* as very threatening. It was a daily challenge to the slave system on which the entire colonial existence was based, and the costs in money and human lives were huge. Moreover, for the enslaved the mere existence of Maroon villages formed living proof that there was an alternative to slavery, however slight this might be. Because of the locations of the Maroons in swampy or densely wooded areas, and also because of the wooden palisades – protective walls and pitfalls behind which they were entrenched – it was difficult for the colonial armies to pursue and fight the Maroons. And this was complicated even more by their inability to deal with the guerrilla tactics used by the Maroons.

Initially, it was predominantly men who fled slavery. Women had less opportunity to escape because of the care they had to provide for the children and usually also for the elderly. Men often did not always live with them and were more mobile. Therefore, there was always a great shortage of women among the Maroons, especially during their formation period. Obviously, for the survival of the group, women were of vital importance, which is why obtaining women was often part of the raids Maroons undertook on the slave plantations. Often, women did not want to join the Maroons and only went with them involuntarily. Maroon existence was hard and difficult and their future very uncertain. It often happened that women with their children eventually returned to the plantations they had come from. Emotionally, this must have been extremely difficult; because of their children and relatives, they exchanged the relative freedom of Maroon life for the non-freedom of slavery (van Stipriaan 1992). Price (2003) points out that the chronic female shortage regularly led to mutual conflicts, too. Also, raids for women were sometimes undertaken among the Indigenous people, which led to tensions in the free territories of the interior. Indigenous people were of great significance for the Maroons virtually everywhere. They were the original inhabitants of their settlements and knew them very well. The Maroons could learn from them, and they could trade with them and maintain other forms of exchange. At the same time, the Indigenous people were sometimes competitors or even enemies, because they served as guides for the colonial armies. This combination of cooperation and suspicion led to an often ambiguous relationship between Maroons and Indigenous people.

This ambiguity can also be found in the mutual relationships between and within the Maroon communities (Price 2003). Disagreement about women was often the breeding ground for this; adultery with someone else's wife was one of the most serious offences. With respect to newcomers – who could be traitors – a great suspicion also often applied. Long waiting times and even forms of imprisonment often preceded admission to the Maroon community.

Between 1650 and 1750, many smaller groups eventually formed a few larger Maroon peoples. The most important ones were and still are, the N'dyuka or Okanisi in the southeast and a later split off the Paramaka or Paamaka in the east; the Boni or Aluku also in the east (now mainly in French Guiana) and the Saramaka or Saamaka and Matawai and Kwinti in Central Suriname. At one point the Maroons had become such a major threat to the slave colony that the colonial authorities thought it was more sensible to make peace with most of them in exchange for peace and the delivery of new refugees. The Maroons were thus definitively recognised in their freedom, had the promise that they would no longer be attacked in their territories and received a sort of tribute payment in the form of an annual cargo supply. Of course, delivery of new Maroons as well as the tribute payments often led to conflicts. However, when finally, the Aluku, with whom no peace treaty had been settled, retreated to neighbouring French

Guiana around 1780, the Maroon wars were over. Incidentally, these peace agreements were not unique to Suriname. Other slave colonies sooner or later made peace with Maroon groups as well, such as Brazil, Colombia, Ecuador, Cuba, Hispaniola (Haiti and the Dominican Republic), Mexico and Jamaica (Price 2003, 609). The phenomenon was taken over and replicated as a useful means of dealing with Maroons and vice versa. For example, the Surinamese peace treaties of 1760 (N'dyuka) and 1762 (Saamaka and Matawai) were based on those of Jamaica from 1739 and 1740, and both parties concerned used this method. In the prelude to the Surinamese peace treaties, it turned out that a Maroon negotiator named Boston even appeared to have possession of the text of the Jamaican peace agreements (Dragtenstein 2002).

In many slave colonies, after the peace treaties the Maroon communities disappeared and gradually merged into the colony. None of the Maroon communities remained entirely independent of colonial economies. Trade (exchange) took place everywhere, legally or illegally, since the Maroons could not produce some products themselves, such as gunpowder, rifles, iron tools and other necessities. This also applied to the Surinamese Maroons; however, they belong to the few who maintained contact with the colonial society, but at the same time managed to continue to live their autonomous existence outside colonial territory. That autonomous space, however, turned out to become increasingly threatened when it became clear how rich their territory actually was.

From the peace treaties of the mid-eighteenth century and the withdrawal of the Boni/Aluku in French Guiana a few decades later until the end of the nineteenth century, this autonomous Maroon territory in Surinamese interior lands was largely 'terra incognita' for the colonial society in the northern coastal strip; there weren't even maps of it. The only interest that the colony in the region showed was in logging, which was provided by the Maroons. For them this meant an important source of income, with which they could purchase goods in the colony that they themselves did not produce. Thus, despite their relative isolation, they were part of the colonial money economy at an early stage, long before the abolition of slavery. At that time, their number was estimated to be around five thousand.[1]

An example is the Groot-Marseille sugar plantation along the Cottica River. The plantation bookkeeping shows that in the 1820s the N'dyuka traded a large amount of processed wood each year for an average of 2,200 litres of dram, a rough type of rum, plus an average amount of 850 guilders. Together this amounted to approximately 1,150 guilders, as much as the annual salary of the director of this plantation.[2] With the money earned, consumer goods were purchased, such as weapons, pots

1 Cf. National Archives Netherlands, Ministry of Colonies, A796.
2 Philadelphia, James Ford Bell Library, arch. B1482.

and textiles. It must have been a strange situation when the acting Maroons came to trade with the plantations where the working population still lived in slavery. Even after the abolition of slavery in 1863, logging remained important and the Maroons almost got a monopoly in this field. However, when the colonial authorities started to realise how dependent the colonial economy had become on the Maroons in this respect and how much money they could earn with it themselves, they intervened. 'The sooner the entire property disappears and is taken up among the ordinary residents of the colony, the better [...]' and '[...] those gentlemen have already played the boss in our upper rivers for too long', stated some senior officials in 1904 (quoted in Scholtens 1994, 58). As a result, logging was released for anyone who wanted to do it, and by 1920 half of this activity was in the hands of private companies. Increasingly larger concessions were issued by the authorities, which was not in keeping with the autonomy of the Maroon habitats and thus often led to major conflicts. Therefore, the colonial Maroon supervisor at that time said, 'The only means of preventing such instances of legal uncertainty seems to me to gradually deprive the Bushnegroes of the right to cut wood wherever they want. Incidentally, it is also generally desirable to bring these Bushnegroes gradually more directly under the authority of the [colonial] Board' (quoted in Scholtens 1994, 181). When, as a consequence of this new policy the Saamaka granman (supreme Maroon authority) Dyankuso was summoned to the city against his will in 1924, he sighed: 'We have come here to listen to the laws that the whites make for us, about us, without us' (cited in Scholtens 1994, 83).

Increasing Intrusions

It was clear to the colonial government that the interior part of the country had much more potential than previously thought. Between 1855 and 1890, at least ten cartographic and geological expeditions took place and another seven between 1901 and 1911. Many of the old Surinamese collections in European museums nowadays consist of objects collected during all these expeditions. However, apart from this exotic interest in Maroon culture, colonial entrepreneurs and authorities felt like the Maroons were an obstacle to colonial progress. But at the same time, they could not possibly do without their cooperation. Maroons were at home in the interior. It had been their territory for a long time; to those from the colony it still was unknown and almost 'foreign' jungle territory. Generally, Maroons did not greatly like these strange, prying eyes. Although it generated revenue, many expeditions and commercial enterprises were thwarted because their territorial rights were violated and they knew that ultimately these activities would maybe not be in their best interest. The observations of expedition leaders are telling in this respect. Although they praise the capabilities of Maroons as jungle guides and boatmen, they mainly portray them as lazy and unreliable; the N'dyuka granman Alabi was, for example, described as 'hateful of Europeans and a schemer' (Wentholt 2003, 151).

In some places Maroons managed to keep out the intruders for a long time. For example, a colonial official reported that specific areas had been declared by the N'dyuka as no-go areas for outsiders, 'on the pretext that their Gods forbade it', he stated. They refused to allow gold diggers and others access to the area, or, elsewhere, they – 'as rightful owners of the lands' – demanded tax from the yields of these outsiders (Van Lier 1919, 19; Scholtens 1994, 91). Nevertheless, the colonial government had already issued between 700,000 and 1,000,000 acres of land – to gold concessions – along the Upper Suriname, the Saramacca, the Marowijne and the Lawa rivers, all areas inhabited by Maroons. The 5,000 to 10,000 people working on the concessions in the forests were predominantly outsiders; still, the gold sector and the balata (natural rubber) sector became the big money-makers for Maroons. With their knowledge of the interior of Suriname, they made themselves indispensable as boatmen, guides, cargo carriers and unskilled labourers. The peak of this new wealth was reached between 1900 and 1925. Obviously, colonial Surinamese and foreign gold, balata and timber companies made the real money, but Maroons also managed to get their piece of the pie. When, for example, the Balata Company was shut down in 1931 because of severe foreign competition, about one-third of the more than 1,000 redundant workers were Maroon. At that time about 20,000 Maroons lived in Suriname, almost without exception in their traditional territories (Scholtens 1994, 89–94).

The most important sector for the Maroons was cargo shipping with their long canoes. The highlight of that activity coincided, obviously, with that of the gold and balata production between 1880 and 1930. These activities mainly took place in East Suriname and neighbouring French Guiana, meaning that especially the N'dyuka and the Paamaka were active in these sectors. Yet, large groups of Saamaka, Matawai and Aluku participated too, sometimes causing mutual tension (Scholtens 1994, 81). However, every Maroon involved in cargo shipping earned quite a bit of money, which made the intrusion of the money economy into Maroon societies deeper and deeper. Estimates of the annual number of cargo-shipping runs range from 1,000 to 2,500, with at least two or three Maroons being involved in each trip. This means that many hundreds of Maroon households – and probably more, because many men had several women – benefited from cargo. On average, a bagasiman (cargo boatman) earned around four guilders per day, though a substantial proportion of that went to the Maroon boat owner. An indentured labourer on a plantation, however, received on average about sixty to eighty cents a day, which the bagasiman considered a tip, at most. In the period 1880–1920, their average annual income was around 2,500 guilders, in those days a capital (Scholtens 1994, 62; Thoden van Velzen 2003, 25).

Maroons actually had a monopoly position in cargo shipping, a situation which the colonial government looked on with dismay. They tried to gain control by introducing all kinds of new rules and pass systems. In 1921, a large strike broke out among the boatmen when gold and balata production declined and freight rates dropped, while at the same time the prices of goods in the stores increased. Moreover, most of the bagasiman were illiterate and were often deceived by the weight of the freight shipped by their clients. Eventually the colonial Maroon supervisor broke the strike by manipulating the political and religious affairs of the N'dyuka and humiliating their granman. The sociocultural damage he caused was still felt four decades later when an anthropologist was hit 'by the sharpness of the feelings about the strike, the aversion felt for Maroon supervising official Van Lier and the tensions that still existed between some of the descendants' (Thoden van Velzen 2003, 48).

An even larger effect than the intrusions of the gold, balata and logging enterprises came from the rise of a new industry: bauxite mining and refining, which began to boom from the 1940s onward. In particular, the construction of the reservoir in Central Suriname for the benefit of that new industry had a lasting impact. During the 1920s, when gold and balata production were beginning to decline, the American multinational Alcoa started winning bauxite in Suriname, the raw material for aluminium, and was later joined by the Dutch multinational company, Billiton. Soon bauxite became the largest production and export sector of the country, which was further stimulated by the Second World War's enormous demand for aluminium for military aircraft production. Moengo became the bauxite company town of Suriname, in the middle of the Maroon area, but Maroons were not allowed to settle there and only entered with a day pass.

As bauxite production increased, energy requirements also grew exponentially. In 1958 a large infrastructure project was started in order to build a dam in the Suriname River and thereby generate hydroelectric energy. The Maroons, however, were not consulted and many of them did not understand what was going on until the very end. Quite a few even worked as labourers on the construction of the dam. In just a few years, nearly 1,600 square kilometres were flooded and five to six thousand Maroons had to leave their original habitat. The grounds of their ancestors, the holy places of the spirits, the villages, their livelihood, everything drowned. A large number of the expelled Maroons ended up in soulless transmigration villages closer to the city, which today still offer a desolate sight. Others settled south of the reservoir. The promised financial and material compensation was very disappointing and not paid at all or only partially paid (see Landveld 2009). The facilities also lagged behind what had been promised, and prosperity (including electricity) at the time never reached the Maroons further to the south. Moreover, the situation widened the gap more than ever between Maroons in the interior and the townspeople. Their complaints and protests were seen in the city as an obstacle to progress, including by descendants of those who had once come to Suriname enslaved like them. Statements could be heard to the effect that they should be happy 'now that instead of palm leaves they have a house with a roof over their head', and 'let the government send them back to Africa, there they will learn what suffering is' (Landveld 2009, 7).

The Maroons involved, including those in majority Saamaka and also some N'dyuka, felt abandoned. They were almost literally uprooted and experienced the reservoir as the umpteenth attack on their existence, which was characterised by a long history of contempt for their rights by 'the city'. In the meantime, the city of Paramaribo was no longer a colonial Dutch capital, but had become in 1975 the centre of the independent Republic of Suriname. To Maroons this hardly made a difference. Or actually it did, for the worse. In 1986 a civil war broke out between the army of the then-military coup leader (and currently democratically elected president) Bouterse, and a rebel group led by the Maroon, Brunswijk, Bouterse's former bodyguard. Many Maroons died, the population of the village of Moiwana was massacred, and tens of thousands of Maroons fled from their homesteads, many of them to refugee camps in neighbouring French Guiana. Most have to this day never returned to their original villages. Meanwhile, the two rivals built up great interests in the once-again-flourishing gold sector, and both have been convicted in absentia in the Netherlands for large-scale drug trafficking via the Surinamese interior. This new gold sector is now the biggest ecological threat for the Maroons. Large areas are deforested, huge amounts of mercury are ending up in the environment, and cyanide is leaking from industrial waste tanks. In addition, a whole new population group has been added to the inhabitants of the interior, namely several tens of thousands of Brazilian gold diggers. The Central Bank of Suriname calculated in 2014 that about a third of the total workforce in Suriname is employed in the gold sector – not counting thousands of illegal immigrants – including a very large number of Maroons.[3] The latter group are in a complicated paradoxical situation. On the one hand, gold mining offers perspectives on prosperity much larger and more within reach than ever before. On the other hand, gold is structurally undermining and poisoning the world they have built up on their own since the days of slavery.

In Conclusion

Maroons are considered by most Surinamese to be the heroes of resistance against slavery. They even managed to force the colonial authorities into peace, including

3 [https://www.cbvs.sr/images/content/governors/2014/LeadingSectorsofSurinameDecem ber2014.pdf] (accessed 10-08-2017)

tribute payment and recognition of their more or less autonomous residential areas. Since then they have been able to build up their societies and culture in relative peace. However, they remained dependent on the colonial economy for specific utensils and consumer goods. After the abolition of slavery in 1863, when it be-came increasingly clear how rich the area is that the Maroons lived in, a relent-less process was initiated by the colonial society and its postcolonial successor to invade and exploit that area. To this end, Maroons were indispensable as guides and transporters, but otherwise they were mainly considered an obstacle in the way. Traditional rights turned out to be worth nothing. Descendants of those with whom they had previously lived in slavery, but who had gone into maroonage, had begun to look down on them after Emancipation and even support the intruders of Maroon territory. Eventually they even became part of the postcolonial gov-ernments from whom Maroons could expect as little as from the colonial gov-ernments before. Traditional rights were not respected at all, mineral and other resources were taken away from them, and their environment deteriorated quickly. As a result, they have taken up arms again, but this time juridically. Twice they presented their case to the Inter-American Court of Human Rights, and twice, in 2005 and 2007, the court ruled in their favour. However, this so-called land rights issue has still not been settled definitively. Meanwhile, Maroons increasingly leave their original habitat, and half of them now live in and around the city of Paramaribo, mostly in second-rate neigbourhoods.[4] There is, however, one im-portant difference than before: Maroons have gathered in two – opposing – Ma-roon political parties, which are represented in parliament and are on and off part of government coalitions. They are now intruding into the territory of the intrud-ers. It remains to be seen, however, whether this will lead to a stronger and more respected position, or to their gradual incorporation in the Suriname nation state.

BIBLIOGRAPHY

Dragtenstein, Frank, 2002. 'De ondraaglijke stoutheid der wegloopers'; Marronage en koloniaal beleid in Suriname, 1667-1768. Utrecht: Culturele Antropologie Univer-siteit Utrecht.

Landveld, Erney R.A.O., 2009. Alles is voor eeuwig weg; de transmigratie van Marrons in historisch perspectief. Paramaribo: Bureau Conos.

Lie, Willem F. van, 1919. Iets over de Boschnegers in de Boven-Marowijne. Paramaribo: Van Ommeren.

4 Half of the estimated 118.000 Maroons in Suriname now live in and around Paramaribo; between 2004 and 2012, their share in the urban population went up from 10 to 16 per cent [file:///C:/Users/gebruiker/Downloads/presentatie-districts-resultaten-vol1-070314.pdf] (ac-cessed 10-08-2017)

Price, Richard, 2003. Maroons and their communities. In: Gad Heuman and James Walvin, eds., *The Slavery Reader*. London: Routledge, 608–25.

Scholtens, Ben, 1994. *Bosnegers en overheid in Suriname. De ontwikkeling van de politieke verhouding 1651-1992*. Paramaribo: Afd. Cultuurstudies/Minov.

Stipriaan, Alex van, 1992, Het dilemma van plantageslaven: weglopen of blijven? *Oso, Tijdschrift voor Surinaamse Taalkunde, Letterkunde, Cultuur en Geschiedenis* 11/2, 122–41.

Stipriaan, Alex van, 1996. Suriname and the abolition of slavery. In: G. Oostindie, ed., *Fifty Years Later: Antislavery, Capitalism and Modernity in the Dutch Orbit*. Pittsburgh, PA: University of Pittsburgh Press, 117–42.

Wentholt, Arnold, ed., 2003. *In kaart gebracht met kapmes en kompas. Met het KNAG op expeditie tussen 1873 en 1960*. Heerlen/Utrecht: ABP/KNAG.

Africans and Afro-Descendants in Mexico and Central America

Overview and Challenges for Studies of their Past and Present

María Elisa Velázquez

BIOGRAPHY

María Elisa Velázquez Gutiérrez is a sociologist, anthropologist, researcher and professor. Her works concern the history and culture of Mexican people of African Descent. M. E. Velázquez has been president of the International Scientific Committee of the UNESCO Project 'The Slave Route: Resistance, Liberty, Heritage'. She is Director of the Ethnology and Anthropology Department of the Instituto Nacional de Antropología e Historia, INAH, UNAM, Mexico, Professor of Museums and Art Studies at the Universidad Iberoamericana, Mexico City, and a member of the International Fund for the Promotion of Culture, UNESCO.

Among her numerous publications: *Juan Correa, mulato libre, maestro pintor* (1998), *Mujeres de origen africano en la capital novohispana, siglos XVII y XVIII* (2006), *La huella negra en Guanajuato. Retratos de afrodescendientes de los siglos XIX y XX* (2007) and *Afrodescendientes en México, una historia de silencio y discriminación* (2012).

ABSTRACT

The economic, social and cultural contribution made by the thousands of Africans who arrived in Mexico and Central America – first during the colonial period, having been forcibly transported against their will, and later during the nineteenth and twentieth centuries as workers in some Central American countries – has long been recognised by academics and civil organisations. Pioneering studies began appearing from the mid-twentieth century. Then, from the 1990s, for a different set of social, political and economic reasons,[1]

---

1 Each country had a particular set of circumstances which has inspired the labours of investigators and social organisations interested in the area. Without doubt, these have been influenced by Indigenous movements, by the worsening economic conditions suffered by the majority of these communities in our countries, and by the development of academic ideas around cultural diversity and around combating racism and discrimination.

important social movements and teams of investigators began to raise awareness and reclaim the experiences, struggles and contributions of the women, men and children of African origin who helped form our societies.

The aim of this article is to offer a general overview of the historical and anthropological studies made in this area in Mexico and the countries of Central America, and to highlight advances made and areas for future investigation. A general description will be given of the sources used for the investigation of slavery, and of the contribution and participation of Africans and people of African descent in their societies. This paper will fundamentally be concerned with the viceroyalty and with reflections on the concepts and terms debated. The study also aims to make known some of the investigation, education and dissemination of information that has taken place in our countries, and to propose areas to be promoted and supported to ensure that the groups' contributions, past and present, are recognised and valued, and, above all, that the communities enjoy all of the rights owed to them by their nations.

Before beginning, it is important to emphasise the necessity of continuing to investigate the characteristics of slavery, and in particular the damage caused by the transatlantic business of trafficking people from Africa. First, as is well known, slavery as a form of subjugation transgressing basic human rights is, sadly, not confined to the past; various societies continue to exhibit relations based upon slavery and subjugation, especially towards women and children. Moreover, the investigation of slavery and an awareness of the devastation it causes, together with the recognition of the contribution made by the millions of enslaved people of the world in building our societies, is an essential contribution to mutual understanding and peaceful coexistence between cultures, and to combating prejudice, discrimination and racism. Today, people of African descent in Mexico, principally those who inhabit the regions of the Costa Chica de Oaxaca y Guerrero; the Garífunas of Honduras, Guatemala, Nicaragua and Belize, and the people of African descent in Costa Rica and Panama, among other places, are fighting for recognition not only of their history, but of their communities as distinct entities with their own cultures resulting from slavery, the colonial period and the associated historical processes. Slavery and its consequences, then, are not just problematical affairs of the past, but part of the present.

The State of the Question

Despite the historiography of Mexico and Central American countries having made significant contributions to the field in question, the theme continues to have a low academic profile and is frequently perceived to be of minor importance. It is telling that, for instance, in official histories the theme still lacks a place of importance, as was the case in recent editions of general history books of Mexico, particularly in relation to the colonial period.[2] Moreover, the role of slavery, the experiences and contributions of African slaves, together with the lives of their descendants, did not occupy an important place in the recent bicentenary independence celebrations held for Mexico and the Central American countries.

However, Mexico and the majority of Central American countries do have a track record of significant investigation into the theme. While some periods, situations, processes and events have been more thoroughly investigated in some countries than in others, overall the nature of slavery during the colonial period – and the related processes of resistance movements, ways to obtain liberty, economic and social mobility, and the experiences of free people of African descent – has had an important place in studies in the majority of countries.[3] In the countries of Central America, studies have been made about groups of people of African descent, such as the creoles and the Garífunas, giving emphasis to the historical processes and the political and social movements that have characterised them.

2 A series of books was published about daily life in Mexico in the colonial period, coordinated by the historian Pilar Gonzalbo. Whilst various aspects are covered, none of the volumes considers the experiences of Africans. See: Pilar Gonzalbo (ed.), *Historia de la vida cotidiana en México*, México, Fondo de Cultura Económica/El Colegio de México, 2005. (3 vols.)

3 An extensive bibliography of publications about Mexico exists. Some of the most pioneering and representative works are: Gonzalo Aguirre Beltrán, *La población negra en México*, México, Fondo de Cultura Económica, 1946; Luz María Martínez Montiel (coord.), *La presencia africana en México*, México, Conaculta, 1994; Adriana Naveda, *Esclavos negros en las haciendas azucareras de Córdoba, Veracruz. 1690-1830*, Xalapa, 1987; María Elisa Velázquez, *Mujeres de origen africano en la capital novohispana, siglos XVII y XVIII*, Colección Africanía 1, México, INAH-UNAM, 2006. There are also key works covering Central American countries, among which are: Carlos Meléndez and Quince Duncan, *El negro en Costa Rica, San José,* Editorial Costa Rica, 1974; Rina Cáceres, *Negros, mulatos y libertos en la Costa Rica del siglo XVII*, San José, Instituto Panamericano de Geografía e Historia, 2000; Lowell Gudmundson, *Mestizaje y población de procedencia africana en la Costa Rica colonial*, San José, UNA, 1981; Paul Lokken, 'Presencia africana en siete comunidades salvadoreñas 1671-1711: Evidencia del Archivo Eclesiástico Guatemalteco', in *Repositorio Organo de divulgación del Archivo General de la Nación*, El Salvador, III Epoca, no. 2; Lowell Gudmunson and Justin Wolfe (eds.) *Between Race and Place: Blacks and Blackness in Central America*, Durham, Duke University Press, 2010; Beatriz Palomo, 'Perfil de la población Africana en el reino de Guatemala 1723-1773', in Rina Cáceres, *Rutas de la esclavitud en África y América Latina*, San José, Editorial Universidad de Costa Rica y Asociación Pro-historia Centroamericana, 2001; Rafael Leiva Vivas, *Tráfico de esclavos negros en Honduras*, Tegucigalpa, Editorial Guaymuras, 1982; Germán Romero Vargas, *Las sociedades del Atlántico en Nicaragua en los siglos XVII y XVIII*, Managua, Fondo de Promoción Cultural, Banic, 1995; Roberto de la Guardia, *Los negros del Istmo de Panamá*, Panamá, Instituto Nacional de Cultura, 1977.

Moreover, a lot has been written about the workers of African descent who arrived in the nineteenth and twentieth centuries, diversifying the cultural composition of the group in the Central American region. Written testament to the importance of people of African descent in the history of El Salvador since colonial times has been found, despite the fact that until a few years ago, it was considered that the group had played no part in the country's history. In July 2011, the Salvadoran Academy of History (Academia de Historia de El Salvador) organised the first round table of studies about the theme in the country.[4]

In Mexico, historiographic revisions and extensively detailed bibliographies of areas investigated, methodologies employed and characteristics of sources have been made. Amongst these, mention should be made of the works of Emma Pérez and Gabriel Moedano, Juan Manuel de la Serna, Odile Hoffmann, María Elisa Velázquez and Ben Vinson II.[5] In Central America, key studies and comprehensive historiographic revisions have been produced by historians such as Lowell Gudmundson, Rina Cáceres, Paul Lokken and Dario Euraque, among others.[6] Re-

---

4   The round table is organised as part of a series of conferences entitled, *Diálogos sobre el Bicentenario.* Among the very few historians who have explored the theme are Pedro Antonio Escalante, who published an article entitled 'Presencia negra en El Salvador' in 1998, and Carlos Loucel, who has begun archival research on the theme.

5   See, among others: Emma Pérez and Gabriel Moedano, *Aportaciones a la investigación de archivos del México colonial y a la bibliohemerografía afromexicanista,* México, INAH, 1992; Juan Manuel de la Serna, 'La esclavitud africana en la Nueva España. Un balance historiográfico comparativo', in Juan Manuel de la Serna, (coord.), *Iglesia y sociedad en América Latina colonial. Interpretaciones y proposiciones,* México, UNAM, 1998; María Elisa Velázquez and Ethel Correa (compilers), *Poblaciones y culturas de origen africano en México,* México, Colección Africanía 1, INAH, 2005; Cristina Díaz, *Queridato, matrifocalidad y crianza entre los afromestizos de la Costa Chica, México, Conaculta,* 2003; Odile Hoffmann, 'Negros y afromestizos en México: viejas y nuevas lecturas de un mundo olvidado', *Revista Mexicana de Sociología,* 2006, num.68/1, 103–135; Ben Vinson III and Bobby Vaugh, *Afroméxico. El pulso de la población negra en México: una historia recordada, olvidada y vuelta a recordar,* México, CIDE-Fondo de Cultura Económica, 2004; María Elisa Velázquez and Odile Hoffmann, 'Investigaciones sobre africanos y afrodescendientes en México: acuerdos y consideraciones desde la historia y la antropología', in *Diario de Campo, Boletín de Investigadores del INAH,* México, núm.91, marzo-abril, 2007.

6   Rina Cáceres, *Negros, mulatos, esclavos y libertos en la Costa Rica del siglo XVII,* op. cit.; Paul Lokken, 'From Black to Ladino: People of African Descent, Mestizaje and Racial Hierarchy in Rural Colonial Guatemala, 1600-1730' doctoral thesis, University of Florida, 2000; Lowell Gudmundson and Justin Wolfe (eds), *Between Race and Place: Blacks and Blackness in Central America,* Durham, Duke University Press, 2009, and Dario Euraque, *Conversaciones históricas con el mestizaje y su identidad nacional en Honduras,* San Pedro Sula, Honduras, Centro Editorial, 2004.

cently, a very comprehensive article on the theme[7] was published by Lowell Gudmundson, and as part of the outcomes of the International AFRODESC and EURESCL project, a workbook was produced under the stewardship of Carlos Agudelo and Nahayeilli Juárez, containing a bibliographic compilation and a selection of texts about the populations of African descent in Central America.[8]

Thanks to these studies, made over the course of almost 60 years and beginning with the pioneering works of Gonzalo Aguirre Beltrán for Mexico[9] and of Carlos Meléndez and Quince Duncan for Costa Rica,[10] we know, for example, that around 250,000 Africans of both sexes were forcibly brought to Mexico during the viceroy period, principally between 1580 and 1650. It has been shown that a large number of them came from west, central and south Africa, the major regions of Senegambia, Guinea, Congo, Angola and Mozambique, and that they performed a range of activities throughout the territory of New Spain, which at that time encompassed an important part of Central America.

Research based upon documentary sources, such as contracts of purchase and sale, denouncements to the Inquisition, wills, appraisals, marriage certificates, letters of freedom and contracts stating that Africans and those of African descent were not comprised of homogeneous groups, reveals that the majority of these people arrived as slaves. However, many managed to acquire their freedom and obtain better living conditions for themselves and their dependents. Research reveals them to have been working on farms, in refineries, mines and workshops, in guilds, as members of militias, as architects, painters and famous singers, and leading resistance movements like that of Yanga in Veracruz, which culminated in the granting of freedom to the 'cimarrones', and in the recognition of San Lorenzo de los Negros as a free town in 1609.

Research has also revealed the experiences of women. They are shown as heads of family, fighting for their and their children's rights and heading movements

---

7 Lowell Gudmundson, 'De categorías suprimidas y clasificaciones anacrónicas: fuentes y estrategias recientes para el estudio de la historia afrocentroamericana', in María Elisa Velázquez (coord.), *Debates históricos contemporáneos: africanos y afrodescendientes en México y Centroamérica,* México, Colección Africanía 7, INAH/CEMCA/UNAMCIALC/IRD, 2011.
    8 Carlos Agudelo and Nahayeilli Juárez (coord.), *Poblaciones negras en América Central. Compilación bibliográfica y selección de texto,* Guatemala, Proyectos Internacionales AFRODESC y EURESCL, Cuaderno de Trabajo no. 10, mayo 2011. Available for consultation at: http://www.ird.fr/afrodesc/
    9 Gonzalo Aguirre Beltrán, (1946) *La población negra en México,* op.cit.,
    10 Carlos Meléndez and Quince Duncan, *El negro en Costa Rica,* Editorial Costa Rica, ECR, San José, 1989.

seeking justice and better living conditions, as in Omoa, Honduras[11] in the eighteenth century, and in innumerable activities related, mainly, to domestic service.[12] From monographs and studies in rural and urban zones, the differences between plantation and domestic slavery have been documented, giving new perspectives on contemporary family, social and cultural relationships.

Other research has focused on themes such as the slave trade, work and the colonial economy, and resistance movements: not only 'cimarronaje', the attitude of resistance, and the mutinies, but also on the cultural practices and actions that were shown in response to domination and subjugation in daily life. Furthermore, some studies have been made of the situation of people of African descent in the nineteenth century, and their role in insurgent movements and the formation of the nation-state.

Studies have been carried out into the migrations of people of African descent to Central America, which initially established communities and villages with the Indigenous people of the region, before arriving in Jamaica and other regions of the Antilles, especially Belize, Costa Rica, Nicaragua and Panama. These have revealed the working conditions and the socioeconomic difficulties faced by these workers inserted into these new societies. A number of studies have documented the characteristics of what scholars have termed 'creole' communities found around the Panama Canal and along the length of the Caribbean coastline, in the north of Belize, in Costa Rica, Nicaragua, Honduras and Guatemala. Notable works in the fields of anthropology, linguistics and ethnomusicology have also been produced, giving insights into aspects of life such as the creole languages used by groups of people of African descent (among them, the Garífunas, also known as 'caribes negros', who live on the Isthmus' Caribbean coast), aspects of traditional medicine, the singularities of musical expression, and the social and political demands of the groups' movements.[13]

Regarding the situation of communities of the Costa Chica de Oaxaca and Guerrero in Mexico, studies have explored themes related to identity, history and demonstrations of cultural expression, together with the characteristics of social movements asserting the recognition of groups as black peoples or peoples of

---

11   Rina Cáceres, 'Omoa: cruce de identidades', Yaxkin, Honduras, vol. XXIV, núm.1. 2008.

12   See, among others: María Elisa Velázquez, *Mujeres de origen africano en la capital novohispana, siglos XVII y XVIII,* Colección Africanía 1, México, Instituto Nacional de Antropología e Historia/Universidad Nacional Autónoma de México, 2006.

13   Francisco Lizcano, 'La población negra en el istmo centroamericano', in *Presencia africana en Centroamérica,* México, Conaculta, 1993; Joseph Palacio, 'The multifaceted Garifuna: juggling cultural spaces in the 21st century', in Joseph Palacio (ed.), *The Garifuna, A nation across borders: Essays in Social Anthropology,* Belize, Editorial Cubola, 2005.

African descent. It is important to note that the difficulties resulting from racism, economic exclusion and social integration have also attracted the attention of many writers, social scientists and leaders of social organisations. Countries such as Panama, Belize, Costa Rica and Honduras have an important track record in this area,[14] while Mexico has hardly started working on the recognition of these communities, the discrimination suffered or the development of favourable strategies in public policies.[15]

Significant Historiographical Debates and New Themes of Investigation

Studies have demonstrated that context and location in each period determined the social and cultural situations in which Africans and their descendants lived during the colonial period and the nineteenth and twentieth centuries. Moreover, studies – particularly the historical investigations in Mexico and the countries of Central America, such as Costa Rica and Honduras – have underscored the importance of distinguishing the singularities pertaining to the different periods of the viceroy and the characteristics of the documentary sources. For instance, at the beginning of the sixteenth century, what have been called 'socio-racial' relations (if these, indeed, existed) did not play the determining role which they would later

14 Quince Duncan, *Contra el silencio. Afrodescendientes y racismo en el Caribe Continental Hispánico*, San José, EUNED, 2001; Diana Senior Angulo, 'Pluralidad de los afrocaribeño en Costa Rica: aproximación a la naturaleza de sus organizaciones sociales' in Victorien Lavou Zoungbo y Marlène Marty (eds.) *Imaginaire racial et projections identitaires*, Perpignan, Presses Universitaries de Perpignan; Alfonso Arrivillaga y Alfredo Gómez, 'Antecedentes históricos, movilizaciones sociales y reivindicaciones étnicas en la costa atlántica de Guatemala', in *Estudios Sociales Centroamericanos*, San José, Costa Rica, 1988; Nancy Martínez, 'La historia como discurso de identidad, la dominación y el arte de la resistencia entre los garífunas de Guatemala', in *Revista Pueblos y Fronteras*, vol.5, núm.8.; Mark Anderson, *Black and Indigenous: Garifuna activism and consumer culture in Honduras*, Minneapolis, University of Minnesota Press, 2001; Gurdian Galio, Charles Hale and Edmund T. Gordon, 'Derechos, recursos y memoria social de lucha: reflexiones sobre un estudio acerca de los derechos territoriales de las comunidades indígenas y negras en la Costa Caribe de Nicaragua', in *Revista del Caribe Nicaragüense*, Wani, núm. 29; George Priestley and Alberto Barrow, 'El movimiento negro en Panamá: una interpretación histórica y política', in Odile Hoffmann (coord.) *Política e identidad. Afrodescendientes en México y América Central*, Colección Africanía 4, México, INAH/UNAM/CEMCA/IRD, 2010.

15 In March 2011, a year-long consultation of communities of African descent began, organised by the Comisión Nacional de Desarrollo Indígena. The consultation aimed to identify communities so as to establish public policies and affirmative action promoting their recognition and full integration in society.

assume, when skin colour, physical features and economic status became closely linked, imposing barriers and strictly codified power relations. These temporal distinctions allow us to outline other possible cultural configurations which, though they did not come to fruition due to the racist model of the eighteenth and nineteenth centuries, sowed the seeds of other realities, such as that of a specific mix which will be considered later in this article.

On another note, the studies in Mexico and the countries of Central America have underscored the heterogeneous, diverse character of Africans and their descendants in the society of New Spain, and have documented the complex set of relations with other cultural groups. Sometimes these were marked by alliance and solidarity, and at other times by rivalry and antagonism. In the case of the Central American countries, studies have been made of the African colonial presence, the subsequent migrations and the resulting set of specific social dynamics.

In studies made to date, it is possible to distinguish different academic trends resulting from the influences of economic, regional, demographic, social and cultural historiography, the fruits of debates, and years of research and reflection in the field. The importance of including an anthropological and cultural-historical focus in analysis has been demonstrated, as has that of gender perspectives. The importance of contributions from other sources, such as artistic expressions, oral tradition and literary works, has also been underscored.

Recent works have brought interesting new perspectives to historical analysis. The substantial data revealed by research into the confraternities of 'negros y morenos' in the viceroy period has opened up new spaces of reflection, amongst which are, for instance, the ties of identity between cultural groups, the participation of women and servants, and the problems of power and alliances.[16]

Another important theme is that of enslaved, and free, children of African origin. Studies of infancy can reveal information about family dynamics, the conditions and character of child labour, both enslaved and free, and other domestic communities.[17] Pictorial sources of analysis have also been systematically used, representing an important resource for historical periods for which there is an absence of documentary information, such as the nineteenth century. In addition, studies have been made of electoral lists and population censuses of people of African descent. In spite of the limitations and inaccuracies of these sources, in-

---

16 Nicole Von Germeten, *Black Blood Brothers. Confraternities and Social Mobility for Afro-Mexicans,* University Press Florida, 2006.

17 The historian Cristina Masferrer has been the first to explore the childhood of slaves in Mexico City, see: *Familia, niñez e identidad social entre los esclavos de origen africano de la ciudad de México en la primera mitad del siglo XVII,* degree dissertation, México, Escuela Nacional de Antropología e Historia, México, 2009.

formation can be gleaned as to the social composition and demography of this population in Mexico and the countries of Central America in the viceroy period and nineteenth century.

There has been an increase in the anthropological, ethnographic and sociological studies of the characteristics, situations and problems of the communities in Mexico and the countries of Central America. As has been mentioned in the case of Mexico, various studies have been made about the Costa Chica de Guerrero and Oaxaca relating to kinship networks, social organisation, and cultural and musical expression. Important works have also explored identity problems, migration and childhood in this region.[18] However, there is a lack of more comprehensive ethnographic studies analysing the material conditions in the zone, the relationships with other groups, particularly with Indigenous populations, and social and cultural forms that characterise communities, such as traditional medicine, the role of women, and the problems of racism and discrimination. Moreover, there is a need for research into communities of people of African descent such as the Mascogos in Coahuila and other populations in states such as Morelos, Guanajuato, Michoacán, Tabasco and Campeche.

As has been mentioned, significant studies have been made of the populations in Central American countries. For example, recent years have seen research into the situation of women in communities in Nicaragua which have highlighted their importance in the economy, their situational vulnerability and the problems they face as heads of family. Countries such as Panama, Costa Rica and Honduras also have a significant track record of studies denouncing the racism and discrimination suffered by those of African descent. Nevertheless, there is a need for studies and research into characteristics and problems more specific to the regions with populations of African descent in other countries such as Mexico and Guatemala. In this way, strategies and public policies can be developed to combat racism and discrimination and to promote comprehensive social inclusion.

Characteristics of Research Sources

For research into the slave trade, slavery, and the general role played by Africans and their descendants in Mexico and the countries of Central America, the basic resources used are testimonies of the colonial period found in various archives. However, some of these are in states of disorganisation and deterioration, and many regions do not have such documentary archives at all. It is, therefore, es-

---

18 Citlali Quecha, *Cuando los hijos se van,* México, Universidad Nacional Autónoma de México, doctoral thesis, 2011.

sential that governments, educational and cultural institutions are made fully aware of the importance of the conservation of these testimonials.

The sources for particular periods of the viceroy differ according to time and region; that is, the sources for the sixteenth, seventeenth and eighteenth centuries have different characteristics and, as will be discussed, differ in context and function. Sources from this period are found in various public and private archives, of which the principal ones will now be discussed.

In Mexico, a great part of the country's administrative and historical documentation is held in the national archives (El Archivo General de la Nación). This contains a section specialising in the viceregal period, with testimonies from what was then the viceroyalty of New Spain. As such, it holds documents for consultation pertaining to various Central American countries, and given such valuable coverage, it is worth detailing the nature of the documentation. Areas include marriages, the Inquisition, general records, lands, national assets, edicts, local regulations, taxes, the historical archive of public finance, royal decrees and civil and Jesuit sources, all of which provide valuable research material. For instance, the marriages section furnishes information relating to the characteristics of documents requesting marital unions taking place in Mexico City's Sagrario Metropolitano and in the parishes of Santa Catalina Mártir and Santa Veracruz, mainly in the seventeenth and eighteenth centuries. These register information relating to ages, origins, legal and civil statuses and occupations. The section relating to the Inquisition contains valuable information relating to the personal lives of a large percentage of Africans and people of African descent, not only of those who were denounced, but also of those who acted as witnesses at trials. In addition to details of origin, legal and civil status, and, in some cases, even physical and emotional description, these documents reflect the social and moral dynamism of New Spain's society. As such, they represent an invaluable resource in understanding the role of Africans and their descendants, both free and enslaved, in social and gender relations. Similarly, these sources offer information about the groups' trades, the treatment received from owners, and how they were perceived by other members of viceregal society, both in terms of solidarity and of antagonism.

For its part, the section dealing with national assets contains an important number of documents relating to a variety of areas. Some of these are legal claims and cases dealing with the sale of slaves, endowments and lawsuits connected with inheritance; others are official denouncements of couples living in common-law marriages, and there are also valuable testamentary references. Many of these reflect the daily life, legal and economic, of the group in religious institutions within the context of slavery and its social dimensions. Other sections, such as edicts, local regulations, general records and royal decrees provide information about various pieces of legislation pertaining to the issuing of licences, the payment of taxes, the regulation of labour, and the social behaviour of Africans in New Spain.

Almost all Central American countries have national, state and municipal archives in which administrative and legal information pertaining to each entity or region tends to be found. State and municipal archives house municipal record books which include material relating to the life of trade guilds, such as contributions, duties, tariffs, prices, public services, licences, regulations, ordinances and fiestas.

Notary archives are a valuable resource for information and data about the characteristics of slavery, containing documents such as forms, deeds, wills, deeds of sale of enslaved people, deeds of sale of furniture, and mortgage and loan testimonials, together with proxy statements. Parochial and convent archives are not only a source of information about the institutional life of the church, but can include information about social and cultural life, as well as genealogical and demographic data.

There are also archives and reserved resources relating to historical, social and economic aspects of the theme housed in universities and other public and private institutions. Sources of valuable information are to be found in archives such as those of the Indias in Seville, which now has a catalogue on its web page; in other departments in Spain, England, Paris, and Germany; and in the various private archives and collections of documentary sources held by institutions in the United States.

All of these archives – some catalogued in databases, others in lists, some ordered, others neglected and in disarray – contain an immense variety of documents of different types. Among the great many sources for the viceroy are found chronicles, geographic writings, visits, correspondence, edicts, ordinances, acts, complaints, wills, bills of sale, donations, various types of lawsuits, censuses, electoral lists and even Christmas carols and prohibited dances and songs.

Images, such as paintings and photographs, have also become a valuable source of investigation. It is important to note that the use of such sources requires the application of a rigorous methodology that takes into account factors such as the contexts in which the images were produced, and the identities and purposes of their producers. Social reality may be mirrored in the paintings of the time, but rather than being completely faithful to the moment, the images recreate the ideas of New Spanish society, its values and ideals. In researching the nineteenth century, documentary sources exhibit a diverse set of characteristics. For instance, in countries such as Mexico, the references to castes and qualities disappear, posing problems for researchers wanting to identify people of African descent. However, other sources, such as travellers' chronicles, magazines, newspapers, gazettes and certain censuses, which in spite of restrictions, continued to use racial denominations, offer important information. Central American studies have made significant advances in relation to these periods in which the identification of people of

African descent is problematic, and for the end of the nineteenth and the beginning of the twentieth century, photographs are an invaluable source of identification. Lowell Gudmundson sets out three strategies which have served as a guide in this: first, advantage should be taken of the few cases in which census officials continued to use racial categories; secondly, in-depth studies of villages which are evidently of an African or Afro-descendent character should be undertaken; and, finally, critical rearticulation of genealogical studies and of nationalistic heroic images should be made.[19] Archival sources related to migration can also help in reconstructing the characteristics of the populations of African descent in Mexico and the Central American countries in this period. Moreover, the relevance of ethno-historical studies which allow an approximation of history from an anthropological perspective needs to be considered.

Although I will not go into detail on the characteristics of the ethnographical and sociological data which has been sourced for the investigation of contemporary communities of African descent, it is important to note certain peculiarities of investigative work and the characteristics of the data that may be recorded. In addition to monographs and regional histories, it is important to record the life stories and other information, carefully registering ethnographic information about social organisation, economy, ritual life, traditional medicine, family and kinship networks, and cultural expressions, among other themes. These investigations are the base on which the cultural patrimony of the communities of people of African descent and their historical memory is built.

Concepts and Terms

There is a significant track record of research which has analysed and reflected upon the use of certain denominations, concepts and terms in the studies of Africans and their descendants in Mexico and the countries of Central America. Perhaps the biggest debates have been (1) those surrounding themes such as the denominations used to identify people of African descent; (2) the use of certain concepts to refer to the historical process related to slavery and the transatlantic slave trade; and (3) the interpretation of social organisation in the colonial period related to the process of coexistence and exchange, known in our countries as *mestizajes*.

---

19 Lowell Gudmundson, 'De categorías suprimidas y clasificaciones anacrónicas: fuentes y estrategias recientes para el estudio de la historia afrocentroamericana', in María Elisa Velázquez (coord.), *Debates históricos contemporáneos: africanos y afrodescendientes en México y Centroamérica,* Colección Africanía 7, México, INAH/CEMCA/UNAMCIALC/IRD, 2011.

The conquest and colonisation of territories in Asia, Africa and America converted groups from different cultures into subjects classified into a single category. In Mexico, the Nahuas, Ñañus and Mayas were at first indiscriminately referred to as 'indios' (Indians), and the same happened with regard to other cultures in Central and South America. Moreover, Mandingos, Wolofs, Berbers, Fangs and Bantus, together with the peoples of the Orient and the Indian Ocean with features of African origin, were classified as 'negros' (blacks) and, in some cases, as 'chinos' (Chinese). Gradually, missionaries and thinkers concerned with gaining knowledge of the new lands and their inhabitants began to study and differentiate amongst the peoples who formed these categories.

The prevailing terms used in today's historic studies are those of 'negros', 'mulatos', 'pardos', and at times 'chinos' to refer to the population of African and Oriental origin. In my view, these terms are problematic, making research into the presence, origin and singularity of the individuals comprising the populations of our societies difficult. Moreover, their use poses problems for the analysis and the comprehension of different cultural phenomena that took place during the period. Whether we agree with this view or not, it seems important to define and create concepts that help us to understand the historical subjects which we are studying, and the processes in which they were immersed. Terms such as 'negritud' (blackness), 'tercera raíz' (third race) and 'culturas negras' (black cultures) also appear to me to be ambiguous concepts, which if they were representative in some periods, do not always help in the understanding of what is revealed by data and new research. For example, it makes little sense to speak of 'tercera raíz' in ports such as Veracruz or Acapulco in Mexico, which were basically founded and constructed by Africans.

Terms such as 'calidad' (quality), 'raza' (race), 'nación' (nation) and 'mestizaje' (mixing) have also attracted controversy and analysis. I will give a summary outline of, in my judgement, the most significant reflections. Firstly, we will consider the role and significance of denominations and categories that were used at the time. 'Nation' was synonymous with cultural origin, as shown in dictionaries of the period, or with place of birth of the inhabitants of a province.[20] For this reason, in many documentary sources, references to slaves as being of the 'nación Congo' or 'nación Angola' can be observed. Moreover, the term 'casta' (caste) was closely linked to the idea of mestizaje, and was frequently used in the plural to refer to the different ancestries in New Spain, principally of 'mulatos', 'morenos' and 'pardos', 'mestizos', 'lobos', 'coyotes' and 'zambos', depending on the region. Interestingly,

---

20 *Diccionario de Cobarrubias* (1610), *Tesoro de la Lengua Castellana o Española,* Madrid, Ediciones Turner (facsimile) and *Diccionario de Autoridades* (1737), Real Academia Española (facsimile).

in the *Diccionario Cobarrubias* (1610), 'caste' alludes to the state, 'of noble and pure lineage' and 'who is of a good line and descent'; that is, it was in no sense, at least formally, a derogatory term. At a later date, in the *Diccionario de Autoridades* (1737), the term also means, 'generation and lineage from known parents' 'to make caste, procreate and have children', which reminds us of the purpose and intention behind the famous pictorial works known as 'cuadros de castas o de mestizajes'. As can be seen, then, the use of this category in New Spain was distinct from its use in other cultures, such as India, where there was strict separation between groups in areas such as the law, work, residence and family.

The category of 'raza' (race), which although used less frequently in New Spain from the sixteenth century, had a very different meaning to that which it would assume in the mid-eighteenth century. Before then, it had connotations of lineage, origin and nation. The seventeenth-century dictionary makes no mention of the term, while that of the first half of the eighteenth century refers to it as being like a caste, quality of origin or lineage. As has been seen, it acquires new connotations from the pseudoscientific discourse of the eighteenth and nineteenth centuries, when it is used with high frequency.

Authors such as Banton and Mörner have placed emphasis on the different senses of the term between the fifteenth and seventeenth centuries. For instance, according to Mörner, prior to the sixteenth century differences in the value-ranking of races was unremarkable.[21] However, some historians, mainly from the USA, have stated that the presence of racism in New Spain dates from the Spanish Conquest. For example, it is said that racism was expressed through the formulation of what was known as 'limpieza de sangre' (blood purity), whose use was to show viceregal and metropolitan authorities that aspirants for 'honourable' posts did not have any Jewish or Muslim ancestors. However, this norm had more to do with religious-political affairs inherited from the Reconquista of Spain, which had just finished circa 1492. Also, as Mörner shows, paganism gave a useful excuse to justify conquest and enslavement. Whilst true that the formulation was used with the mulatos, there were also 'illegal' ways to 'whiten', or 'correct' ancestors.[22]

Finally, there is the term 'calidad' (quality), which has received the attention of a number of historians specialising in the colonial period. The term seems very

21 Magnus Mörner, *La macla de razas en la historia de América Latina*, Buenos Aires, Paidós, 1969.
22 This happened in the case of the father of the famous baroque painter, Juan Correa, whose application for the position and title of 'barber-surgeon' was objected to on the grounds that he had 'the colour of mulattos'. Seemingly, the objection had no consequences as the doctor continued in his role. María Elisa Velázquez, *Juan Correa, mulato libre, maestro de pintor*, México, Conaculta, 1998.

appropriate for understanding the complexities of identification and denomination. The term was used at the time as a concept to encompass considerations of race, money, occupation, and individual and family respectability.[23] As Pilar Gonzalbo and Robert McCaa have emphasised, the term marked the importance of the family situation, social recognition, the category assigned to one's profession or occupation, and personal prestige, all crucial elements in the understanding of social distinctions.

In summary, these variables help to explain that the way people were rated, at least until the mid-eighteenth century, seemed to be based more upon economic position and social recognition than on an open form of discrimination or segregation based on skin colour. While it is true that slavery represented a servile and denigrating condition and was associated with the African population, it did not constitute, at least in these centuries, an insurmountable barrier to coexistence, exchange and certain economic opportunities. It cannot be denied that racial distinctions had a place in the society of New Spain, but they were much more complex and a lot less rigid than in other societies and at later times.

The definition of the concept of mestizaje has also been a source of controversy in Mexico and in the countries of Central America. On one hand, as a cultural process, that is to say as an exchange between different groups and as a creator of complex forms of coexistence and re-creation, mestizaje has characterised our societies. However, it is also true that it has served as an ideology, at least since the colonial period, but in a more determined way in the nineteenth and twentieth centuries, to deny the participation of groups, such as those of African origin, in the construction of the nation-states. The ideology of mestizaje aggrandised the union of the Spanish and the Indigenous peoples, 'españoles e indígenas', as homogenous cultures, denying and belittling the economic, social and cultural contributions of other groups, amongst which are found Africans and people of African descent. In this sense, I consider it important to distinguish between mestizaje as a cultural-historical process and its ideological use as a national, political and intellectual project developed, mainly, in the nineteenth century.

What Remains To Be Investigated

In spite of the advances made, much remains to be done. First, new archives need to be discovered and explored, including resources in regions that have not yet been studied, such as those in the north of Mexico. There is still a need for fur-

---

23 Pilar Gonzalbo, *Familia y orden colonial,* op. cit., 13 and 14; Robert McCaa, 'Calidad, clase y matrimonio en el México colonial: el caso de Parral, 1788-1790', in Pilar Gonzalbo (comp.), *Historia de la familia,* México, Instituto Mora/UAM, 1993.

ther investigation of zones basic to the understanding of the African presence in Mexico, such as, for example, the Costa Chica de Guerrero and Oaxaca. Although we have made a start there, we still lack a well-documented history of Africans and their descendants in the zone; for instance, the past of Africans in the port of Acapulco, in the Costa Grande de Guerrero and on the road which ran to Mexico City, known as 'de China' (from China) remains to be investigated. For anthropologists, interested in understanding the cultural processes of these communities, key pieces of the puzzle remain to be found.

Research is needed into the contexts and historical processes in Guatemala, Nicaragua and El Salvador. While advances have been made, data is needed to explain the invisibility of the economic, social and cultural participation of Africans and those of African descent in societies such as in El Salvador, for instance. Moreover, there is a need for studies into the use of terms such as 'ladino' in the different contexts of Central America, and a need to identify electoral lists and censuses offering more exact demographic data.

In spite of the limitations of resources, it is important to make use of more creative criteria in studying historical periods such as those of the nineteenth century. The study of artistic resources, chronicles and censuses has shown that it is possible to identify and investigate groups of African descent. Moreover, reflection is needed on the ideology of liberalism: the political changes which influenced its nature, its taking of mestizaje as a symbol of nationalism and the effects of this on groups of African descent.

As has been mentioned, while research has begun to identify the African regions and cultures of origin, much remains to be done in this area. More needs to be known about the characteristics of these cultures: social and family relationships, their worldviews, their religions and customs. How can the practices of African origin be differentiated and analysed, if the cultures have not been studied? Colin Palmer highlighted some years ago the need to understand the complexity of history and of African cultures in order to assess the extent to which this background informed the way in which lives were organised and led in New Spain.[24] Moreover, other regions of origin, which have not received due attention, need to be identified, such as West Africa (via the South Sea route across the Pacific). This will allow for the richness of cultural exchanges, the historical processes of mestizaje, and the constitution of the enforced, or free (yet, marked by power relations) global traffic in people, to be understood. This circuit was the first expression of a globalisation which today has reached previ-

---

24 Colin Palmer, 'México y la diáspora africana: algunas consideraciones metodológicas', in María Elisa Velázquez (comp.), *Poblaciones y culturas de origen africano en México*, Colección Africanía 1, México, INAH, 2005.

ously unseen intensities and proportions, and is now analysed under the concept of diaspora.

Although dialogue between historians and anthropologists has taken place for years, there is a need to increase the amount of shared reflection on the data and forms of interpretation. Likewise, it important that dialogue and reflection is enriched by other disciplines, by investigators from Central and South America, and by investigators who have undertaken studies of other cultural groups who can bring their own experiences and focus. As has been shown, each context determines and limits the potential for comparison, while at the time widening and informing it with similarities, contradictions and differences. Comparison allows for the points of divergence and convergence to be ordered in time and space, and in the process, shows which factors of the dynamic are individual or shared.

While our work in this area has been published and disseminated, and degree and postgraduate theses have been written with the aim of innovating and exploring little-known situations, much still remains to be done. For instance, it is of interest that few studies result in doctoral theses. In any case, there is a need to generate a greater number of publications, creating mechanisms for their dissemination and making them accessible to wider society.

Finally, there is a need for studies to be undertaken of the problem of racism, both historic and contemporary, in countries such as Mexico and Guatemala. Whilst this has been studied in relation to Indigenous populations, there have been very few studies focused on people of African descent in these regions. This calls for spaces where research experiences from Mexico and the countries of Central America can be shared. Surveys on discrimination, amongst which is that carried out by Conapred in Mexico, show that there is a need for information and reflection on the group's role in the formation of Mexico.[25] Moreover, there is a need to promote investigations into records of historic sites into slavery and resistance, into the process of obtaining freedom, and, in general, into the cultural patrimony of people of African descent in Mexico and the countries of Central America. Among the many tools by which these initiatives may be carried out are web pages, books, national and international recognition, and catalogues of archives.

In summary, while there has been a significant increase in investigations of the field in Mexico and the countries of Central America, new studies are necessary. These need to be based on in-depth study of documentary sources drawn from the analysis of new archives, themes and periods. Moreover, ethnological and sociological investigations of communities of people of African descent in countries such as Mexico should be promoted, alongside diagnostic studies that make

25 *Encuesta de discriminación 2010*, Conapred, México.

known the material conditions of these populations, their cultural patrimony and the problems experienced.

Academic Spaces and Civil Organisations

The last decade has seen growth and diversification in the academic spaces dedicated to the study of enslaved people of African origin in Mexico and the countries of Central America. For example, in the 1990s the Nuestra Tercera Raíz programme was created in Mexico in the Dirección General de Culturas Populares del Consejo Nacional para la Cultura y las Artes. This involved national and international meetings and the production of valuable publications on the area, amongst which was a compilation of articles on Central America. Some years after this, in 1997, the standing seminar Poblaciones de origen africano en México, attached to the Dirección de Etnología y Antropología Social del Instituto Nacional de Antropología e Historia, was set up. Over the first thirteen years of its operation, it held working sessions for the presentation of projects and research results on the theme, together with international congresses, conferences, courses and exhibitions. It has produced various publications, including the Africanías series, which numbers six volumes to date. From 2008, the seminary joined the international project of investigation AFRODESC, which includes researchers from a range of institutions in France, Colombia and Mexico. Alongside this project, exchanges have taken place with academics from Senegal, the United States and the Caribbean. Among the most notable results of the project, which came to an end in December 2011, was the international congress, Diáspora, nación y diferencia: Poblaciones de origen africano en México y Central America, held in the port of Veracruz with 150 speakers. There was also the publication of four volumes of articles by Mexican, French, US, Costa Rican, Honduran, Nicaraguan, and Belizean investigators on different historical and contemporary themes of Africans and people of African descent in Mexico and in the countries of Central America.[26]

A number of investigators have paid attention to the training of students interested in the field. In Mexico, the Escuela Nacional de Antropología e Historia has

---

26 Odile Hoffman (coord.), *Política e identidad. Afrodescendientes en México y América Central,* Colección Africanía 4, México, INAH/CEMCA/UNAM/IRD/AFRODESC, 2011. Elisabeth Cunin (coord.), *Mestizaje, diferencia y nación. Lo 'negro' en Amèrica Central y el Caribe,* Colección Africanía 5, México, INAH/CEMCA/IRD/UNAM, 2011. Juan Manuel de la Serna (coord.) *De la abolición y la libertad. Africanos y afrodescendientes en México e Iberoamérica,* Colección Africanía 6, México, INAH/CEMCA/UNAM/IRD/ AFRODESC, 2011; María Elisa Velázquez, (coord.), *Debates históricos contemporáneos. Africanos y afrodescendientes en México y Centroamérica,* Colección Africanía 7, México, INAH/CEMCA/UNAM/IRD/AFRODESC, 2011.

a line of investigation in the History and Ethno-history postgraduate programme, and also some material in its first-degree course, while in Costa Rica, training material is available for those specialising in the field in human resources. However, there is still a need for more educational space for the field, in particular with regard to the history of African countries, so as to facilitate the understanding of the numerous processes and factors related to the continent.

Similarly, institutions such as the Universidad Nacional Autónoma de México, through its Programa México Nacional Multicultural, and the Centro de Investigaciones de América Latina y el Caribe, have undertaken a number of academic activities and been involved in the wider dissemination of the theme, supporting civil organisations in the Costa Chica in the organisation of forums and meetings. Furthermore, the Centro de Investigaciones Sociales de Antropología Social and universities such as those of Guanajuato, Veracruz, Estado de Mexico, Yucatán and Guerrero, among others, have developed important projects related to the field. Civil associations, organisations concerned with human rights and women's networks have worked, above all, in the countries of Central America, to support the investigation into, reflection on, and dissemination of the history of Africans as well as investigation into the problems faced by today's communities of people of African descent.[27]

Museums, Educations, Dissemination and Government Action

Advances in the study of slavery, the slave trade and the contributions of millions of Africans to the formation of Mexican and Central American societies have begun to reach the domains of education. However, much remains to be done to raise awareness of the importance of this group in both the past and the present of Mexican and Central American societies. At the time of writing, there are no museums dedicated to the theme.

Temporary exhibitions on the slave trade, slavery and the contribution of people of African descent in the formation of our societies, featuring visual material, have taken place in some countries, with others featuring travelling collections from various Mexican states and the United States. In addition, in Mexico in 1995

27 There are various organisations in different countries, among others: in Panama, la Coordinadora Nacional de Organizaciones Negras Panameñas, composed of social and cultural groups, societies, civic associations, and community organisations; in Mexico, *movimientos* mainly exist in the communities of African descent in the Costa Chica de Oaxaca y Guerrero, such as México Negro, A.C., Africa A.C., Epoca, Ecosta, among others; in Honduras la Organización de Desarrollo Etnico Comunitario Afrodescendiente A.C., in Costa Rica the Centro de Mujeres Afrocostarricenses, and in Nicaragua la Red de Mujeres Afrocaribeñas, Afrolatinoamericanas y de la Diáspora, among many others.

the Museo de las Culturas Afromestizas was inaugurated in Cuajinicuilapa, Guerrero, in the Costa Chica region, supported by the Dirección de Culturas Populares del Consejo Nacional para la Cultura y las Artes, the municipal government and the communities. Nevertheless, without permanent funding or the support of the present government authorities, the museum faces a number of economic difficulties. On a different note, various photographic exhibitions have been held featuring the population of people of African descent in Mexico in Mexico City, Acapulco, Veracruz, Guanajuato and other places. Most recently, and perhaps with the greatest social impact, was that of *Abriendo los Ojos* (Opening Eyes), held in August 2011 on one of Mexico City's main streets – Reforma in the Bosque de Chapultepec city park, marking the International Year for People of African Descent. The exhibition consisted of the work of three artists and featured thirty huge photographs of people of African descent in communities in Oaxaca, Guerrero and Veracruz.[28]

To make known the characteristics of the slave trade, and the experiences of enslaved people and their contribution to the formation of Mexican society, as well as to the countries of Central America, it is necessary for museums of history, anthropology, ethnography and popular culture to cover the theme of slavery, popular resistance movements, and in general the importance of Africans and people of African descent and their economic, social and cultural contributions. It is also necessary to consider the creation of permanent museums to explain and make known the history of the thousands of Africans and their descendants in our societies through collections of objects, visual information, videos and other museum initiatives.

Education is, without doubt, a central theme in the construction of democratic societies which respect diversity and cultural differences. Costa Rica and Honduras have made important efforts to equip teachers with the skills they need and to disseminate books about the history and rights of people of African descent, through a project driven by the historian Rina Cáceres.[29] In Central America an assessment of the field's situation in the curriculum of education programmes has been made, the findings of which revealed that while some countries have made

---

28 *Abriendo los Ojos. Exposición fotográfica temporal de Paulina García Hubard, Franck Courtel y Manuel García,* Texts by Marcia Zepeda y María Elisa Velázquez, Ciudad de México, Gobierno de la Ciudad de México, Consejo Nacional para Prevenir la Discriminación, Instituto Nacional de Antropología e Historia, Fondo Cultural Banamex, Kodak, agosto-noviembre, 2011.

29 Rina Cáceres, (ed.), *Del olvido a la memoria: africanos y afromestizos en la historia colonial de Centroamérica,* San José, UNESCO, 2008, tomo 1; *Del olvido a la memoria: esclavitud, resistencia y cultura,* San José, 2008, tomo 2: *Del olvido a la memoria: África en tiempos de la esclavitud,* San José, UNESCO, 2008, tomo 3.

efforts to give this history a higher profile, much remains to be done. In Mexico, the historical role of Africans and of people of African descent is only addressed in a very general way in the third-grade primary book, which contains erroneous information. Mexican society has completely ignored the history of Africans in the country, along with the existence and situation of communities of African descent today. It is, therefore, unsurprising that racism continues to manifest itself within the family, the school, the workplace and the mass media.

Thanks, among other things, to the proclamation of 2011 as the International Year for People of African Descent, the concerns expressed by academics and civil organisations have begun to be listened to. Some governmental institutions have shown an interest in learning about this area and supporting investigations, diagnostic studies, forums, and consultations to produce constitutional reforms which recognise the populations of people of African descent, and to develop public policies to improve living standards among the group. Organisations in Costa Rica, Panama, Honduras, Nicaragua and Guatemala have worked systematically to raise awareness of the characteristics of the group and of the various economic problems, discrimination and racism that many of them suffer. In Ceiba, Honduras, almost eight hundred people participated in the Cumbre de Afrodescendientes (The Summit of People of African Descent).

On a different note, for the past few years Conapred in Mexico has carried out investigations, assessments, diagnostics and initiatives concerning the problem of racism and discrimination suffered by the populations of people of African descent. September 2011 saw the presentation of a guide, the *Guía para la acción pública para población afrodescendiente en Mexico*, as part of the Foro sobre Discriminación y Racismo a 10 años de la Reunión de Durban, to be circulated through government departments and available free to the general public.[30] Also in Mexico, the state government of Oaxaca, which in 1985 recognised the population of people of African descent in the constitution, opened a department dedicated to this group as part of the Secretaría de Asuntos Indígenas. Rina Cáceres and Quince Duncan have run training workshops and courses for teachers in Costa Rica, Honduras and El Salvador with the aim of raising awareness of the history of Africans and of people of African descent among children and young people at different stages of education.

In summary, in recent years the investigation and dissemination of the theme has advanced significantly. However, much remains to be done to ensure that the history of Africans and of people of African descent in Mexico and the countries of Central America occupies its rightful place, and that not only those of African

---

30 *Guía para la Acción Pública. Población Afrodescendiente en México*, México, Consejo Nacional para Prevenir la Discriminación, 2011.

descent, but the communities and societies of our countries, feel pride in their African and Afro-descendent past.

BIBLIOGRAPHY

Agudelo, Carlos and Juárez, Nahayeilli, coord., *Poblaciones negras en América Central. Compilación bibliográfica y selección de texto*. Guatemala: Proyectos Internacionales AFRODESC y EURESCL, Cuaderno de Trabajo no. 10, mayo, 2011. http://www.ird.fr/afrodesc/

Aguirre Beltrán, Gonzalo, *La población negra en México*. México: Fondo de Cultura Económica, 1946.

Anderson, Mark, *Black and Indigenous: Garifuna Activism and Consumer Culture in Honduras*. Minneapolis: University of Minnesota Press, 2001.

Arrivillaga, Alfonso and Gómez, Alfredo, Antecedentes históricos, movilizaciones sociales y reivindicaciones étnicas en la costa atlántica de Guatemala. *Estudios Sociales Centroamericanos*. San José: Costa Rica, núm. 48, septiembre-diciembre, 1988.

Cáceres, Rina, *Negros, mulatos y libertos en la Costa Rica del siglo XVII*. San José: Instituto Panamericano de Geografía e Historia, 2000.

Cáceres, Rina. Omoa: cruce de identidades. *Yaxkin*, Honduras, vol. XXIV, núm.1. 2008.

Cáceres, Rina, ed., *Del olvido a la memoria: africanos y afromestizos en la historia colonial de Centroamérica*. San José: UNESCO, 2008, t. 1.

Cáceres, Rina, ed., *Del olvido a la memoria: esclavitud, resistencia y cultura*. San José: 2008, t. 2.

Cáceres, Rina, ed., *Del olvido a la memoria: África en tiempos de la esclavitud*. San José: UNESCO, 2008, t. 3.

Cunin, Elisabeth, coord., *Mestizaje, diferencia y nación. Lo "negro" en América Central y el Caribe*. México: INAH/CEMCA/UNAM/IRD, 2011.

Díaz, Cristina, *Queridato, matrifocalidad y crianza entre los afromestizos de la Costa Chica*. México: Conaculta, 2003.

Diccionario de Cobarrubias (1610). *Tesoro de la Lengua Castellana o Española*. Madrid: Ediciones Turner (facs. edn.).

Diccionario de Autoridades (1737). Real Academia Española (facs. edn.).

Duncan, Quince, *Contra el silencio. Afrodescendientes y racismo en el Caribe Continental Hispánico*. San José: EUNED, 2001.

Escalante, Pedro Antonio, *Presencia negra en el Salvador*. El Salvador: Academia Salvadoreña de Historia, 1998.

Euraque, Dario, *Conversaciones históricas con el mestizaje y su identidad nacional en Honduras*. San Pedro Sula, Honduras: Centro Editorial, 2004.

Galio, Gurdian; Hale, Charles; and Gordon, Edmund T. Derechos, recursos y memoria social de lucha: reflexiones sobre un estudio acerca de los derechos territoriales de las comunidades indígenas y negras en la Costa Caribe de Nicaragua. *Revista del Caribe Nicaragüense*, Wani, núm. 29.

Gonzalbo, Pilar, dir., *Historia de la vida cotidiana en México*. México: Fondo de Cultura Económica/El Colegio de México, 2005, 3 vols.

Gonzalbo, Pilar, *Familia y orden colonial*, op.cit., pp. 13–14; Robert McCaa, Calidad, clase y matrimonio en el México colonial: el caso de Parral, 1788-1790. In: Pilar Gonzalbo, comp., *Historia de la familia*. México: Instituto Mora/UAM, 1993.

Guardia de la, Roberto, *Los negros del Istmo de Panamá*. Panamá: Instituto Nacional de Cultura, 1977.

Gudmundson, Lowell, *Mestizaje y población de procedencia africana en la Costa Rica colonial*. San José: UNA, 1981.

Gudmundson, Lowell and Wolfe, Justin, eds., *Between Race and Place: Blacks and Blackness in Central America*. Durham, NC: Duke University Press, 2010.

Gudmundson, Lowell, De categorías suprimidas y clasificaciones anacrónicas: fuentes y estrategias recientes para el estudio de la historia afrocentroamericana. In: María Elisa Velázquez, coord., *Debates históricos contemporáneos: africanos y afrodescendientes en México y Centroamérica*. Colección Africanía 7, México: INAH/CEMCA/UNAM-CIALC/IRD, 2011.

Guía para la Acción Pública. Población Afrodescendiente en México. México: Consejo Nacional para Prevenir la Discriminación, 2011.

Hoffmann, Odile, coord., *Política e Identidad. Afrodescendientes en América Central*. México: INAH/UNAM/CEMCA/IRD, 2010.

Hoffmann, Odile, Negros y afromestizos en México: viejas y nuevas lecturas de un mundo olvidado. *Revista Mexicana de Sociología*, num. 68/1, 2006.

Leiva Vivas, Rafael, *Tráfico de esclavos negros en Honduras*. Tegucigalpa: Editorial Guaymuras, 1982.

Lizcano, Francisco, La población negra en el istmo centroamericano. *Presencia africana en Centroamérica*. México: Conaculta, 1993.

Lokken, Paul, Presencia africana en siete comunidades salvadoreñas 1671-1711: Evidencia del Archivo Eclesiástico Guatemalteco. *Repositorio Organo de divulgación del Archivo General de la Nación* (El Salvador), III Epoca, no. 2, 2006.

Lokken, Paul, From Black to Ladino: People of African Descent, Mestizaje and Racial Hierarchy in Rural Colonial Guatemala, 1600-1730. Doctoral thesis. University of Florida, 2000.

Martínez Montiel, Luz María, coord., *La presencia africana en México*. México: Consejo Nacional para la Cultura y las Artes, 1994.

Martínez, Nancy, La historia como discurso de identidad, la dominación y el arte de la resistencia entre los garífunas de Guatemala. *Revista Pueblos y Fronteras*, vol. 5, núm. 8, 2009.

Masferrer, Cristina, Familia, niñez e identidad social entre los esclavos de origen africano de la ciudad de México en la primera mitad del siglo XVII. Degree thesis. México: Escuela Nacional de Antropología e Historia, México, 2009.

Meléndez, Carlos and Duncan, Quince, *El negro en Costa Rica*. San José: Editorial Costa Rica, 1974.

Mörner, Magnus, *La macla de razas en la historia de América Latina*. Buenos Aires: Paidós, 1969.

Naveda, Adriana, *Esclavos negros en las haciendas azucareras de Córdoba, Veracruz. 1690-1830*. Xalapa, 1987.

Palacio, Joseph, The multifaceted Garifuna: juggling cultural spaces in the 21st century. In: Joseph Palacio, ed., *The Garifuna, A Nation across Borders: Essays in Social Anthropology*. Belice: Editorial Cubola, 2005.

Palmer, Colin, México y la diáspora africana: algunas consideraciones metodológicas. In: María Elisa Velázquez and Ethel Correa, *Poblaciones y culturas de origen africano en México*. Colección Africanía 1, México: INAH, 2005.

Palomo, Beatriz, Perfil de la población Africana en el reino de Guatemala 1723-1773. In: Rina Cáceres, *Rutas de la esclavitud en África y América Latina*. San José: Editorial Universidad de Costa Rica y Asociación Pro-historia Centroamericana, 2001.

Pérez, Emma and Moedano, Gabriel, *Aportaciones a la investigación de archivos del México colonial y a la bibliohemerografía afromexicanista*. México: INAH, 1992.

Priestley, Georges and Barrow, Alberto, El movimiento negro en Panamá: una interpretación histórica y política. In Odile Hoffmann, coord., *Política e identidad. Afrodescendientes en México y América Central*. México: INAH/UNAM/CEMCA/IRD, 2010. (Serie Africanía no. 5)

Quecha, Citlali, Cuando los hijos se van. Doctoral thesis. México: Universidad Nacional Autónoma de México, 2011.

Romero Vargas, Germán, *Las sociedades del Atlántico en Nicaragua en los siglos XVII y XVIII*. Managua: Fondo de Promoción Cultural, Banic, 1995.

Senior Angulo, Diana, Pluralidad de los afrocaribeño en Costa Rica: aproximación a la naturaleza de sus organizaciones sociales. In: Victorien Lavou Zoungbo and Marlène Marty, eds., *Imaginaire racial et projections identitaires*. Perpignan: Presses Universitaires de Perpignan, 2009.

Serna, Juan Manuel de la, La esclavitud africana en la Nueva España. Un balance historiográfico comparativo. In: Juan Manuel de la Serna, coord., *Iglesia y sociedad en América Latina colonial. Interpretaciones y proposiciones*. México: UNAM, 1998.

Serna, Juan Manuel de la, coord., *De la abolición y la libertad. Africanos y afrodescendientes en México e Iberoamérica*. Colección Africanía 6, México: INAH/CEMCA/UNAM/IRD/ AFRODESC, 2011.)

Velázquez, María Elisa, *Juan Correa, mulato libre, maestro de pintor*. México: Conaculta, 1998.

Velázquez, María Elisa, *Mujeres de origen africano en la capital novohispana, siglos XVII y XVIII*. Colección Africanía 1, México: INAH-UNAM, 2006.

Velázquez, María Elisa and Correa, Ethel, comp., *Poblaciones y culturas de origen africano en México*. Colección Africanía 1, México: INAH, 2005.

Velázquez, María Elisa and Hoffman, Odile, Investigaciones sobre africanos y afrodescendientes en México: acuerdos y consideraciones desde la historia y la antropología. In: *Diario de Campo, Boletín de Investigadores del INAH*, México, núm.91, marzo-abril, 2007.

Velázquez, María Elisa, coord., *Debates históricos contemporáneos. Africanos y afrodescendientes en México y Centroamérica*. Colección Africanía 7, México: INAH/CEMCA/UNAM/IRD/AFRODESC, 2011.

Vinson III, Ben and Vaugh, Bobby, *Afroméxico. El pulso de la población negra en México: una historia recordada, olvidada y vuelta a recordar*. México: CIDEFondo de Cultura Económica, 2004.

Von Germeten, Nicole, *Black Blood Brothers. Confraternities and Social Mobility for Afro-Mexicans*. Gainesville, FL: University Press Florida, 2006.

'The African Diaspora in Frontier Lands'

The Case of Spanish Central America during the Colonial Period

Rina Cáceres

BIOGRAPHY

Rina Cáceres is Coordinator for the Chair in African and Caribbean Studies and Professor of History at the Universidad de Costa Rica. She is also a representative to the National Commission of University Rectors (CONARE), a member of the Commission for African-Descendant Studies in the Ministry of Education, Government of Costa Rica, and a member of the International Scientific Committee of the UNESCO Slave Route Project. Her publications include *Negros, mulatos, esclavos y libertos en la Costa Rica del siglo XVII* (México IPGH, 2000); *Rutas de la esclavitud en África y América Latina* (San José: Universidad de Costa Rica Editorial, 2001); *Haití, Revolución y emancipación* (edited with Paul Lovejoy; San José: Universidad de Costa Rica Editorial, 2008); and *Del Olvido a la Memoria: Historia de la población afrodescendiente en Costa Rica* (San José: UNESCO-UCR, 2008–2010, 5 vols.). She is a recipient of the Ricardo Caillet-Bois Award for History, bestowed by the Pan-American Institute for Geography and History, OEA, and she has also received the Costa Rica National Aquileo Echeverría History Award.

ABSTRACT

This article analyses the presence of an Afro-descendent population in Central America during the colonial period before c. 1820. This aspect of the history of people of African descent is rarely discussed in textbooks. The study aims to document the presence of African descendants and explores the connections between Africa and the Caribbean ports. It also demonstrates how enslaved Africans employed different strategies to gain their freedom, as well as how the freed Afrodescendent population established their identities during the colonial period.

Introduction

The African diaspora experience in the central region of the Americas dates to the invasion by the Spanish in the sixteenth century. From that point onwards, Central America was divided into three administrative regions: (1) the Kingdom of Guatemala (including the area from modern day Chiapas in Mexico to Costa Rica); (2) the Lands of Belize, Río Tinto, and la Mosquitia along the Caribbean coast, which was under the influence of the British Crown from the late seventeenth century through the eighteenth century, despite constant disputes with the Spanish government; and (3) Panama, which was part of the Viceroyalty of Peru and later Nueva Granada (Colombia). The geographical position of Panama linked the Caribbean with the Pacific coast throughout the period in a permanent relationship that actually dated to precolonial times.

Various indigenous populations lived in this region, but they were displaced, annihilated or marginalised by the Spanish colonial structure. The military occupation led to the death of perhaps two hundred thousand people, a rapid drop in population as seen in the following graph. The high death rate was not only due to war but also, and more importantly, to the spread of disease, total social dislocation and famine. Africans and Afro-descendants were present in the region, initially coming from the Iberian Peninsula but also from Africa, from the time the indigenous population began to decline.

The African Diaspora during the Colonial Period

Africans and Afro-descendent people arrived in multiple waves throughout the sixteenth, seventeenth and eighteenth centuries. Most of their descendants became part of the cultural and social landscape which characterises the region today. Many of those who arrived in the region were free men, but others were enslaved and brought through a network of slavery which extended from the ports of Jamaica, Veracruz and Cartagena. Others were brought directly from Africa. This enslaved population was employed to work in the mines of Panama, Honduras and Nicaragua; on the sugar plantations in San Jerónima (Verapaz), Palencia (Amatitlan) and la Hacienda del Convento Viejo in Guatemala; and on cacao plantations in Costa Rica. Some were also enlisted in the military, such as those at Omoa in Honduras.[1]

Anti-slavery resistance also characterised the colonial period for both the indigenous population that was subjected to enslavement and the African population.

---

1 Murdo McLeod, *A Socioeconomic History of Hispanic Central America, 1520-1720 (Historia socioeconómica de la América central española, 1520–1720*; Guatemala: Piedra Santa, 1980); Lowell Gudmundson, The Afro-Guatemalans at the end of the colonial period: The Dominican homes of Amatitlán and San Gerónimo (Los afroguatemaltecos a fines de la colonia: las haciendas dominicas de Amatitlán y de San Gerónimo), presented at the conference, *La Ruta del Esclavo en Hispanoaméria*, San José, 1999); and Beatriz Palomo de Levin, The Black Population in Guatemala (La población negra en Guatemala), in Rina Cáceres, *Slave Routes in Africa and Latin America (Rutas de la esclavitud en Africa y América Latina)*, San José: University of Costa Rica Editorial, 2001.

Table I
Indigenous population in Central America, 1519–1821

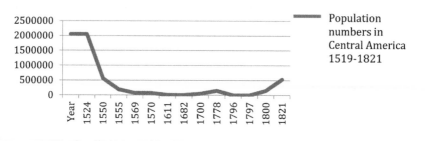

Source: Data taken from the 'Spanish Conquest of Central America' by Wendy Kramer, George Lovell and Christopher Lutz, in *A General History of Central America*, vol II, (Madrid: FLACSO, 1993), 80–81.

From 1520 to 1540, there were various indigenous rebellions in Guatemala, Honduras, Nicaragua, Nicoya and Costa Rica. A few decades later, enslaved Africans staged a rebellion in San Pedro, Honduras. Groups of fugitives who were escaping slavery were found along the Pacific coast and in San Antonio Suchitepéquez, Guatemala. In Sonsonate, El Salvador, a community of fugitives was engaged in trade. There were also individual acts of resistance to slavery, examples of which can be seen in the lists of those incarcerated in the Santiago de Guatemala prison, in the kingdom's capital, according to which 50 per cent of the inmates were fugitive slaves.[2] By the middle of the sixteenth century, as early as the 1530s and 1540s, Panama also experienced anti-slavery resistance.

African Resistance to Slavery in the Sixteenth Century

Panama played an important geopolitical role during the colonial period because of its connections with Jamaica and Cartagena. It was the link between the Caribbean and the Pacific, and thereby provided access to the Viceroyalty of Peru

---

2 Paul Lokken, From the 'Kingdoms of Angola' to Santiago de Guatemala: The Portuguese Asientos and Spanish Central America, 1595–1640, in *Hispanic American Historical Review* 93/2 (2013); Genesis of an Afro-Indigenous community: the San Diego de la Gomera Villa in the seventeenth century, in *Mesoamérica* 50 (2008); A Maroon moment: rebel slaves in early seventeenth-century Guatemala, in *Slavery and Abolition* 25/3 (2004); Marriage as slave emancipation in seventeenth-century rural Guatemala, in *The Americas* 58/2 (2001); and Angolans in Amatitlán: sugar, African migrants, and gente Ladina in colonial Guatemala, in Lowell Gudmundson and Justin Wolfe (eds.), *Blacks and Blackness in Central America: Between Race and Place* (Durham, NC: Duke University Press, 2010).

and its important silver mines. Panama City (Ciudad de Panamá), located on the Pacific coast, has a substantial number of Africans and Afro-descendants whose numbers continued to increase throughout the sixteenth and seventeenth centuries. Africans worked in a wide range of activities besides mining, including pearl diving and farming, and they worked also in mills, hospitals, convents, households, construction, stone masonry and on the boats transporting goods across the isthmus and onto Peru.[3] Many lived in shacks on the outskirts of the city and had to journey to their various jobs on a daily basis.

The extent of repression that was inflicted on the Afro-descendent population became increasingly violent in response to anti-slavery resistance. The population experienced persecution, was exposed to the lashes of whips, was imprisoned, was sent into exile, and was even subjected to physical mutilation. Despite these measures, it was evident that the authorities were unable to maintain firm control over their territory. During the 1540s, Africans stood up to their political captors. They attacked warehouses on the road between Nombre de Dios on the Caribbean and Ciudad de Panamá on the Pacific. Under the direction of Felipillo, they established a Maroon community thirty leagues from the Ciudad de Panamá. Ten years later, some 800 Africans of various origins who had run away from slavery were living to the east of the Camino Real, alongside the indigenous population. On the Caribbean coast, other fugitives were successful in asserting their autonomy as well.

Of all the rebels, Bayano was perhaps the most influential. In the middle of the sixteenth century, he was able to mobilise more than 1,200 enslaved males and females, according to reports by the authorities, and found a community on the upper part of a steep hillside surrounded by deep precipices. Two villages were built by 1580, one in Portobelo and the other in Cerro de Cabra. One of Bayano's communities was led by Anton Congo, and the Portobelo community was led by Luis Mozambique; their names indicated where they had come from in Africa.[4] Although Spanish authorities tried to suppress the anti-slavery rebels, it was evident that they were not successful. According to Castilleros, their failure to achieve

---

3 María del Carmen Mena García, *La sociedad de Panamá en el siglo XVI* (Sevilla: Diputación provincial, 1984), 391.

4 Mena, *La sociedad de Panamá en el siglo XVI,* 413–41, 414 and 415, and AGI Justicia 378/8. Panamá 1552 y AGI Patronato 193/31, in Carol F. Jopling (ed.), *Indians and Blacks in Panama in the Sixteenth and Seventeenth Centuries (Indios y negros en Panamá en los siglos XVI y XVII;* Guatemala: Cirma, 1994); Patricia Lund Drolet, *The Congo Ritual in the Northeast of Panama (El ritual Congo del noroeste de Panamá;* Panamá: Instituto Nacional de Cultura, Colección El Hombre y su Cultura, 2008). For a history of Panama, see Alfredo Castillero-Calvo, *Historia General de Panamá* (Panamá: Comité Nacional del Centenario, 2004).

military victory forced them to recognise that the rebels were no longer enslaved and were now free.

In 1579, a peace treaty was signed which recognised Luis Mozambique as governor of the village, which would later become Santiago del Principe. In exchange, the Africans stopped their anti-slavery protests, pledged allegiance to the Spanish authorities and agreed to settle in specific designated areas. Don Luis Mozambique, as he was called in the reports of the period, was chosen as official leader of the Portobelo community, where 'peoples of different nations' lived. In the same year, a similar treaty was concluded with the Cerro de Cabra community. Over time, Bayano's community was the largest and home to many scattered populations, each protected by hills and located close to routes which gave them access to food and weapons. The authorities agreed to give these communities land and freedom cards (for their members and their descendants), as well as livestock and grain to sow. In exchange, they asked for collaboration in military defence against the invading English.

Origins, Networks and Connections

But who were the Africans who rose up against slavery in the Panama isthmus? Their surnames provide us with a clue as to their origins. Examples of these include Domingo Congo, Antón Mandinga, Juan Jolofo, Vicente Sape, Gaspar Bran, Juan Luzumi, Antón Tigre and Antón Mandinga. If the surnames refer to their ethnic origins, it seems likely that these were multi-ethnic communities.[5]

A list of the many nations involved in anti-slavery resistance is documented for a meeting in Portobello reported by the Spanish authorities. Most of the participants' surnames suggest origins in West Africa, such as Biafara, Bañol, Zape, Bioho (Bijago) and Bran. Others came from west central Africa, such as Congo, Casanga and Yalango. A minority came from southeast Africa, particularly from Mozambique. Those present included Catalina Bran, Gaspar Bran, Baltasar Bran, Antón Bañol, Juan Biafara, Catalina Biafara, Miguel Biafara and Baltasar Bioho (Bijago), whose names all suggest the Upper Guinea coast, while Cristóbal Sape, Ana Sape, Don Pedro Sape, Marcos Sape and Francisco Sape came from the interior of the Sierra Leone River, while Ana Zelopfa (Wolof), Marcos Mandinga and Pedro Mandinga were probably Muslims from the interior of Senegambia. Similarly, Francisco de Terranova and Leonor Terranova appear to have come from the Bight of Benin, while Antón Congo, Mateo Congo, Pedro Congo, Diego

---

5 AGI Panamá 234/1/5, in Carol F. Jopling (ed.), *Indians and Blacks in Panama in the 16th and 17th Centuries* (*Indios y negros en Panamá en los siglos XVI y XVII*; Guatemala: Cirma, 1994).

TABLE II
Origins of those present at the Portobello meeting in the sixteenth century

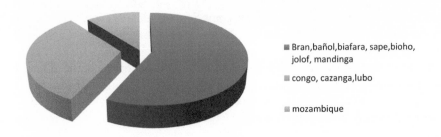

■ Bran,bañol,biafara, sape,bioho, jolof, mandinga

■ congo, cazanga,lubo

■ mozambique

Source: AGI Patronato 234/1/3, ff., 62–67.

Congo, Sebastian Congo, María Conga, Juan Congo, Francisco Lubo (Luba), Gaspar Cazanga and Rodrigo de Tierra de São Tomé most likely came from west central Africa. Finally, Luis Sebastián and Pedro Mozambique apparently came from south-eastern Africa.

According to Vila Vilar, there were three main African ports responsible for sending enslaved Africans to the greater Caribbean region, including the mainland, in the sixteenth century.[6] These were Santiago in Cape Verde, São Tomé in the Gulf of Guinea, and San Pablo de Loanda (Luanda) in Angola. These ports were fed by routes and sub-routes connecting the interior of Africa. Bissau on the Upper Guinea coast, for example, was particularly important, as demonstrated by Walter Rodney who has emphasised 'the almost exclusive relations between Upper Guinea and the middle of the Americas'.[7] The Africans followed several different routes in an intricate network that linked the transatlantic slave trade with Central America. Panama and Cartagena were ports on the route to the Pacific shores of Central America and were involved in the transfer of gold and silver from Peru to Spain and imports from Spain.

Some traders travelled directly from Africa in the sixteenth century, such as Manuel de Carballo, who landed in Panama in the 1590s and set himself up as a slave trader. Others made use of slave licences (asientos), such as Francisco de Barrionuevo, who in 1534 was granted a licence to transport forty enslaved men and thirty women; and Brother Tomás de Berlanga, who in 1540 was granted a li-

6 Enriqueta Vila Vilar, *Hispanic America and the Slave Trade* (*Hispanoamérica y el comercio de esclavos*; Seville: Escuela de Estudios Hispano-Americanos, 1977).

7 Walter Rodney, Upper Guinea and the significance of the origins of Africans enslaved in the New World, *Journal of Negro History* 54/4 (1969), 329.

cence to bring over four and then twenty enslaved captives from Spain, Portugal, Cape Verde and Guinea to help build Panama's cathedral.[8]

A small number of merchants controlled the largest shipments of enslaved Africans. In 1589, Pedro de Feire, Ambrosio de Taide, Diego Enríquez and Simón Ferreira de Malaca were granted a contract for the Cape Verde islands that lasted six years. In 1582, the São Tomé contract was assigned to Juan Bautista Rovelasca, while in 1595, Baltasar and Hector Rodríguez de Chaves secured the contract. The contract for the Kingdom of Kongo was awarded to Pedro de Sevilla and Antonio Méndez de Lamego from 1587 to 1593, then to Gómex Reinel and Juan Rodríguez Coutiño, the governor of Angola, from 1593 to 1603. Rodríguez Coutiño, who initially lived in Panama as a livestock farmer, secured the asiento in 1602, along with his brother, Manuel de Souza Coutiño, who would later become known as Louis de Sousa, a Dominican monk in Cartagena. Tomás de Fonseca was also sent to live there by Gómez Reinel and was similarly given a position in Río Hacha and Nombre de Dios.[9] These men were part of a complex network of civil servants and employees in key positions in a vast commercial network.

The Cape Verde islands played an especially important role in the Atlantic slave trade in the first century of the trade.[10] In 1468, a military governor appointed by the Portuguese Crown occupied the island of Santiago, and from there facilitated trade with the Senegambia coast, the Sierra Leone River and the many rivers that connected this area of the Upper Guinea coast to the interior of the continent. The Portuguese were interested in products from the region that would fetch a high price on the Mediterranean market, such as gold, spices and ivory. Santiago and Fuego – the two largest islands in the archipelago – produced cereals, fruit, vegetables, cotton, indigo, livestock (goats, cattle, horses) and salt, which were sent to regional markets on the mainland.[11]

Between 1513 and 1516, around three thousand enslaved Africans who had been brought from the mainland passed through the islands of Santiago.[12] According to Brasio, a large number of these captives ended up in the Antilles and

---

8 Mena, *La sociedad de Panamá en el siglo XVI*, 88.

9 Vila Vilar, *Hispanoamérica y el comercio de esclavos*, 29, 70–107.

10 Father Sandoval confirmed that many of the slaves arriving in Cartagena and other Central American and Antilles ports originally came from Cape Verde, the Guinean rivers, rivers in Santo Domingo, and Cacheu. See Alonso De Sandoval, *A Treatise on Slavery* (*Un tratado sobre la esclavitud*; Madrid: Alianza Universidad, 1987).

11 Antonio Carreira, *Cabo Verde, formação e extinção de uma sociedade escravocrata (1460–1878*; Lisboa: Centro de Estudos da Guinea Portuguesa, 1972), 24 and 32.

12 Carreira, *Cabo Verde*, 50.

Central America, while a small number were sent to Cadiz and Seville. Teixeira de Motta suggests that the Antilles was the principal destination for these enslaved Africans, whose numbers increased steadily until the second half of the sixteenth century.[13] Some of the enslaved were subsequently transported to Panama, where they were transferred via smaller ships to Peru – the main silver market. From there they were dispersed from Ecuador to Chile. Others went from Cartagena and Panama to various places in Central America, notably to Costa Rica and Nicaragua. The towns along the coast and across the isthmus were therefore the homes of small communities of African descendants and transit points for the enslaved African immigrants who were being moved to their final destinations. The living conditions in these places were atrocious. The Africans were treated with unrestrained violence. In Panama, they were placed in barracks where they could spend weeks before being loaded onto another ship and sent to a new destination. Some of the enslaved tried to escape from their captors, but it was difficult to do so.

Mobility Strategies

Over time, the social map of the Central America region was redrawn. By the seventeenth century, it was clear that alongside the enslaved African population, an Afro-descendent community of freedmen emerged that began to move around the region, working as farmers, traders and producers, and even managing to enter professional associations and guilds and join the militias. These people gained their freedom in a variety of ways. Sometimes they rebelled and escaped from slavery, establishing communities of fugitives, and other times individuals were able to buy their freedom. People began moving around in groups, which reflected an ever-growing population. By the middle of the seventeenth century, there were large communities of black and mulatto freedmen in Guatemala, Honduras, Nicaragua, Costa Rica and Panama. They were scattered around urban areas and worked on the land. Many of these people had been born free and had never been enslaved.

The Spanish colonial system divided the population into two republics, one for the indigenous population and other for the Spanish people. This division roughly divided the population, shaped its workforce, regulated taxation and determined access to land. The Spanish corporate system assigned specific and separated residential areas to both groups. The mixed-race population, and those of African descent, whether free or enslaved, were legally and socially part of the Spanish settlement. The range of activities that the Afro-descendent people were employed in was relatively extensive. In some urban areas, free people who were classified as mulatto worked as artisans, including tailors, blacksmiths, carpenters, weavers, shoemakers

13 Cited in Carreira, ibid., 127.

and merchants, while others were employed in the service sector. In rural areas in Costa Rica, such as in the Matina valley near the Caribbean, they worked on farms and on cacao plantations, and were active in the local trade network. Many free people of African origin settled outside the parishes of the urban areas. But there was concern over the proximity of some African-descent people living alongside the indigenous population, and the government attempted to keep them separate. The arguments in favour of segregation focused on the alleged 'bad customs, laziness, excesses and vices' that the African-descendent population was accused of spreading to the indigenous population. The authorities blamed those of mixed background of African descent for violence, drunkenness and vagrancy. The Guatemalan tribunal, for example, as in the rest of Hispanic America, enforced regulations that prevented people of African backgrounds from living alongside the indigenous people.[14]

But there were other reasons, including fear of a possible alliance with Protestant corsairs. The Maroon communities and Indians had been relatively quiet throughout the first century of colonial occupation, but in the seventeenth century, colonial authorities became concerned with pirates who, it was thought, would exacerbate the problems arising from the proximity of fugitive slaves to indigenous communities. It was thought that privateers might establish alliances with fugitive communities and the indigenous people against Spanish authority, as indicated in the following comments by the authorities, who thought that pirates were undermining the loyalty of the Indians, 'telling them about Lutheranism and about the existence of another monarch more powerful than that of Castile and other things in this tone, that it would be better for the Indians not to know them, nor to understand them for now'.[15]

In fact, the perceived danger was not just a threat to social behaviour. Rather, there were economic reasons for such concern. The expanding trade in cacao was being diverted, which led to a decline in revenue for the Spanish Crown. The indigenous people, who had been required to pay a proportion of their crop to the Crown in lieu of a tithe, found ways of selling their harvest to interlopers and hence avoid the tax. They claimed that they were producing less when in fact they had found alternative markets, often selling to middlemen of African descent. Consequently, colonial authorities introduced various methods to separate the

14 Richard Konetzke, *Colección de documentos para la historia de la formación social hispanoamericana* (Madrid: Consejo Superior de Investigaciones Científicas, 1953–1958), 585, 728. De ahora en adelante CDHFSH.

15 CDHFSH, *Real Disposición* (1681), 728; and Magnus Mörner, *La Corona española y los foráneos en los pueblos de indios de América* (Estocolmo: Instituto Estudios de Iberoamérica, 1970), 99.

mixed-race African[16] population from indigenous producers, prohibiting their entrance to the plantations following the harvest and compelling those of African descent to relocate to populated areas that were under Spanish control.

Hence in 1628, a law was passed banning blacks and mixed-raced individuals from residing among the indigenous population. The punishment for disobeying the law was 'one hundred lashes and four years of exile'. The law also stated that no indigenous person could buy, receive in exchange for payment or keep African slaves, and if discovered, the government could confiscate the Africans. The tithe paid by the indigenous population also declined because the mixed-race population that included people of African descent was able to acquire land in their towns. In some areas, the Crown's income was reduced to one quarter of what it had been at its peak. To counteract this development, the Crown intensified its determination to require separate residential areas, although this policy was widely debated. In Peru, for example, Captain Andrés de Deza argued that it was impossible because they had obtained the land by purchase or dowry from the same Indians and because free Afro-descendants already owned haciendas there. They held property, cattle, orchards and plantations, which they could not be expected to abandon by moving to the Spanish towns, and they were involved in trade that was not centred on these towns. Furthermore, some of the Afro-descendants had become relatively wealthy and provided substantial contributions to the military defence of the Crown, much of which was at their own cost. Some individuals acquired such titles as captain and lieutenant, and they had the right to bear arms.

The attempts to control the residential area of mixed-race population went hand in hand with efforts to raise taxes. As early as 1572, the Guatemalan tribunal stipulated that the mixed offspring of blacks and indigenous persons had to pay tax, which began to be enforced a year later. Even more categorical was the Royal Decree of 1574, which required wealthy black and mulatto freemen to pay taxes 'as was thought to be customary in their lands back in Africa'.[17]

At the same time, people of African descent were joining the militias that had begun to be organised in the second half of the sixteenth century. Military service was one of the few methods whereby mulatto, black, and mixed-race freemen could climb the social ladder. The security of the internal and external borders was of vital importance to the Spanish colonial government, and recruitment was therefore essential. Several mixed-raced militias were established. In the city of Guatemala alone, there were militia companies made up of mixed-race freemen. Some of their members even held positions of authority. One such example was

---

16 CDHFSH, *Ordenanzas* (1628), 321.
17 CDHFSH, *Real Cédula* (1574), 308, 467, 470, 482.

Felipe de Fuentes, a lieutenant who was promoted to captain and later sergeant major.[18]

The influence of these militias developed early in Panama's history. In 1560, they were mobilised to suppress an uprising in Veragua. They also took part in the fight against fugitive slaves. By 1625, the Company of Free Morenos of Panama, initially led by Spaniards, was now under the command of mixed-race Africans. By the end of the century, this unit was active in crushing an indigenous uprising, which had the support of the British on the Caribbean coast. One of its officers, a mulatto, was made governor of Chagres as a reward.[19] In Nicaragua they were incorporated into the militias of towns and cities of the Pacific coast from the second half of the seventeenth century. In 1685, there were militias in León, Granada, Managua, Masaya and Nandaime, all made up of people of Afro-mestizos people. They were employed as keepers of the peace.[20]

This emergence of militias of mixed background was the result of a long process of negotiation. The men enlisted were able to be exonerated from the payment of taxes and receive advance payment for rendering their services. They were granted three advance payments and the exoneration of the nabor tax during the time they were in service. Nonetheless, members of the militia in Realejo in Nicaragua complained about low wages and failure to receive their monthly payments. In the case of Costa Rica, from the mid-seventeenth century, members of black and mulatto militias were promoted to positions of rank, including captain and commissioner, as was the case for Diego de Zúñiga in the capital, Cartago, and Lucas de Contreras in Esparza, who were also exonerated.

The Afro-Descendant Settlements

Resettlement was crucial to the Spanish process of colonisation, and large programmes of resettlement were established to forcibly resettle individuals and communities, most notably the indigenous communities but also the black and mixed-race populations who were moved into more concentrated areas, separate from the indigenous population (or at least such was the intention). In the seventeenth century, many villages were created to concentrate Afro-descendants. Villa

18 Lutz, *Historia sociodemográfica de Guatemala 1541-1773* (Guatemala: CIRMA, 1982), 263.

19 Alfredo Castilleros, Los negros y mulatos libres en la historia social panameña, in *Lotería* (julio 1989), 30, 31.

20 German Romero, La población de origen africano en Nicaragua, in *Presencia africana en Centroamérica* (México: Consejo Nacional para la Cultura y las Artes, 1993), 164, 165, 166.

de la Gomera was established in Guatemala; and El Realejo and San Felipe de Austria in León, Santa María del Haro in Nueva Segovia, and Abierto in Grana, all in Nicaragua. In El Salvador and Costa Rica, the villages of San Vicente and La Puebla de los Pardos were founded, respectively.

In Cartago, the colonial capital of Costa Rica, the authorities also tried to concentrate the Afro population. Little by little they were confined to the eastern part, where in 1635 or 1638 an image of the Virgin of the Angels appeared. Three years later, the brotherhood of the Virgin of the Angels was established. And they took its name in her honour. The brotherhood and local chapel were extremely poor in the seventeenth century, but they were in the hands of the Afro-descendants who lived with a certain amount of independence, as guaranteed by the Orders of 1676, which granted them rights equal to those of the Spanish.[21] In 1676, at a city council meeting in Cartago, the Afro-descendants in the neighbouring Puebla de Nuestra Señora de los Angeles planned to continue expanding its territory, laying out streets and claiming the right to appoint their own authorities,[22] as well as eliminating the payments for the land. However, the resettlement process was slow, partly due to the constant abuses committed by the authorities. In 1707, Captain Blas de Ancheta complained to the tribunals that, faced with the threats of servitude, the men in his militia, their wives and sons were leaving the village. They moved to other areas, including the city of Esparza, at the time on the border with Nicaragua, where the shadow of slavery, illegal on all counts, could not reach them.

At the beginning of the eighteenth century, Puebla de Nuestra Señora de los Angeles had fifty-five houses and one church. The inhabitants were mostly militiamen who worked on the cacao plantations in the valley of Matina, inland from the Caribbean, as well as in domestic services and local artisan workshops. By this time, the brotherhood of the Virgin had become one of the wealthiest in the area and owned a substantial number of ranches. Because of its control of capital, the brotherhood became an important lender. Three Spaniards and three mixed-race men were charged with organising annual festivities in honour of the Virgin. By 1798, the town had 231 houses.

In the city council meeting in Cartago in 1818, the topics of exemption from taxes and rights over land were revisited. As a result of considerable economic pressure, the council decided to review the agreements of the seventeenth century because 'many whites, under the pretext that the land is for everyone, occupy large areas of pastures and fenced land without paying for use of the public land as oth-

---

21 Victor Manuel Sanabria, *Documenta Historica Beatae Mariae Virgins Angelorum* (San José: Imprenta Atenea, 1945), 140 and 207.
22 ANCR C1109, 1676. Y CC736 f35.

ers do'.[23] The community imposed sanctions to prevent such abuse. Rights to land continued to preoccupy the mixed-race African population in Costa Rica. In 1824, two years after independence from Spain, the Virgin of the Angels was declared patron saint of Costa Rica. Coincidentally, the Federal Republic of Central America Constitutional Assembly abolished slavery in Central America in the same year as one of the first moves taken by the newly independent nations.

Conclusion

At the end of the eighteenth century, the diversity of the African-descendent population in Central America was enriched by the arrival of other Afro-descendants such as the Garifuna people from the island of San Vincent as well as the Afro-Caribbeans from Haiti who had fought under the banner of the Spanish Crown during the anti-slavery rebellions and who were forced into exile, some to Florida, others to Cadiz and the rest to Central America.[24]

Central America has a black and mulatto population that is not a socially homogenous group. The historical record demonstrates a complex evolution and transformation that involved distinct social groups, with different origins, languages, changing legal status and divergent political agendas. Nonetheless, during the colonial period, the African population, despite its ethnic, linguistic and religious diversity, was unified by a common experience in its fight against slavery. Most important, in the area controlled by Spain, the free descendants became Hispanicised over time and consequently integrated into the colonial social structure, while on the Caribbean coast, the British influence would persist with the English language and religion to this day. As other Africans arrived, cultural differences increased despite the common roots in the African past.

During the nineteenth century, this impulse stopped, paradoxically, following the independence of the various countries of Central America. With the formation of nation-states, societies were defined as white or at best mestizos, with only one language and one religion, some societies with a glorious indigenous past, but most with a single historical experience inspired by the Spanish epic tradition that denied the presence of Africans and Afro-descendants. Blacks were categorised, as was the case with other cultural groups, as 'races of inferior status', an ideo-

23 ANCR, CC1329 y C1056, fl.
24 See Carlos Esteban Deive, *Las emigraciones dominicanas a Cuba* (Santo Domingo: Fundacion Cultural Moninicana, 1989); and Jane Landers, Rebellion and Royalism in Spanish Florida, in David Barry Gaspar and David Patrick Geggus (eds.), *A Turbulent Time, The French Revolution and the Greater Caribbean* (Bloomington: Indiana University Press, 1997).

logical position that extended across Latin America and indeed North America as well. Restrictive migration policies were developed against those whose origins lay in Africa, China and the Ottoman Empire.

In this context, another wave of the African diaspora swept across Central America after 1870 from the Caribbean islands, mostly from Jamaica. This migration was stimulated by the building of railways, the construction of the Panama Canal and the establishment of banana plantations. These immigrants arriving in Costa Rica questioned the official narrative of whiteness, opening new ways of understanding the multiculturalism that characterises Central American societies. While this chapter in the history of the cultural and demographic complexity of Central America is essential in understanding contemporary society, it must be remembered that the earlier phase of social and cultural transformation was built on an equally profound multiculturalism that was connected to both the difficult survival of the indigenous population and the often involuntary inclusion of an African population that slowly but irreversibly shaped the cultural landscape of the region.

Afro-Descendants
and the Founding Story of the Nation
Monuments and Commemorative Dates

Ana Frega

BIOGRAPHY

Ana Frega has been Professor of History at the Instituto de Profesores Arti-gas and then at the Facultad de Humanidades y Ciencias de la Educacion, University of the Republic, Montevideo, Uruguay. She is also professor at the Universidade Federal de Santa Maria, Brazil. She was a member of the Inter-national Scientific Committee of the UNESCO Project 'The Slave Route: Resistance, Freedom, Heritage' from 2011 to 2015. Among her latest publica-tions: *Cuartel general y villa de la Purificación. Enfoque histórico,* co-authored with Ariadna Islas, Daniele Bonfanti and Magdalena Broquetas, 2004; 'Guerras de independencia y conflictos sociales en la formación del Estado Oriental del Uruguay, 1810-1830', in *Dimensión Antropológica,* N° 35, México, Instituto Nacional de Antropología e Historia, 2005; 'El asalto de la memoria. Experiencias sobre su abordaje histórico'. Clío y asociados. *La Historia enseñada,* Santa Fe, Argentina, 2008; *Los orientales en armas. Estudios sobre la experiencia militar en la revolución artiguista,* Udelar, CSIC, Montevideo, 2015; *Uruguay. Revolución, independencia y construcción del Estado, 1808-1880,* Planeta, Fundación Mapfre, Montevideo, 2016.

ABSTRACT

In the context of the bicentenary of emancipation in Uruguay, this article dis-cusses the progression and regression in the social acknowledgement of Afro-descendants' participation in the emancipation process. The study takes as a starting point the centennial of the independence of Uruguay (1925–1930), and from there on analyses the search for a 'black hero' and its meanings, and for a date to commemorate the contribution of the people of African descent to the construction of Uruguay (and, thus, to a common heritage). A central theme is the significance of three public monuments erected in Montevideo. The sculpture of a water bearer, entitled 'El aguatero' and unveiled for the centenary to pay 'tribute to the black race', unintentionally reproduced the historical place attributed to people of African descent and the stereotype that associated them with servility. The monument to 'Ansina', a former slave and 'assistant and faithful companion' of José Artigas, unveiled in 1943, provides the black community with a figure representing their place in the emancipation process. And lastly, the town square 'Plaza Senzala-Caserío de los Negros', inaugurated in 2006, is presented as a place for remembrance, resistance and the struggle against discrimination, reflecting the strengthening of Afro-descendant associations and of public awareness of forms of discrimination in Uruguayan society.

Introduction

Bicentenary celebrations of Uruguayan emancipation have given new impetus to reflections on the diversity of the social and cultural components that form the identities of the Uruguayan people, at a time when the Afro-descendant community is organising and rallying for the promotion of legislative policies – which are still inadequate – to combat discrimination and promote the recognition of socio-cultural diversity.

The introduction of the 'ethnicity-race' variable in statistical surveys has allowed an approximate calculation of the percentage of the population that acknowledges having African or black ancestry. Data from the 2006 Extended National Household Survey (Encuesta Nacional de Hogares Ampliada – ENHA) estimate that figure to be 9.1 per cent of the total population of Uruguay. While the survey question focused more on the self-identification of cultural roots than on racial discrimination, the results concerning the living conditions of Afro-descendants compared to white people are striking. The poverty rate for people of African descent (50 per cent) is double that of the white population (24 per cent). Furthermore, Afro-descendants have higher rates of unemployment, lower wages, fewer years of education and worse health conditions.[1]

These major disparities are not simply attributable to the impediments of slavery, but nonetheless, the historic 'place' attributed to people of African descent, even today, and the persistence of associated stereotypes alluding to their servile condition, licentious behaviour or laziness has a clear influence on their position in society.[2] As we have said before, there has been an extreme case of silencing the past with regard to communities of Afro-descendants in Uruguay. An elitist view of 'national history' has biased education concerning the nature of their forced arrival as slaves in the country, their forms of resistance, their cultural ex-

---

1   Bucheli; Cabella (2010).
2   Islas; Frega (2007), 383.

Mural at the headquarters of the Afro-Uruguayan social and cultural association 'Asociación Cultural y Social Uruguay Negro' (ACSUN) in Montevideo, dated 10 August 1991. The artist encapsulates the journey of the African diaspora in Uruguay: their native land, arrival as slaves, participation in the independence wars, productive activities, education, and football and cultural expressions, such as the organisations they named 'salas de nación' (nation halls) and the 'candombe' tradition.

Afro-Uruguay. Ruben Galloza (1926–2002).

pressions, their participation in the local economy and society, and their involvement in the independence revolution and in building the Eastern Republic of Uruguay. Furthermore, the continuance of various forms of racial segregation and discrimination until now have been silenced.[3] The first step in reversing this situation is to raise awareness of the existence of this discrimination. In order to fight against racism, xenophobia and discrimination, the Honorary Commission was created (Law No. 17.817, of 6 September 2004) and tasked with planning action in this sphere. By the same token, Law No. 18.059 of 20 November 2006 declared 3 December of each year 'National Day of Candombe, Afro-Uruguayan Cultural and Racial Equity'. Article 2 of Law No. 18.059 states that the celebration 'will be the framework for the appreciation and dissemination of the cultural expression called "candombe" and the contribution of Afro-descendants to building the nation and shaping the cultural identity of the Oriental Republic of Uruguay'.[4] It should be noted that candombe is a traditional cultural expression that includes drumming, dancing and singing, and that since 2009 it has been inscribed on the Representative List of the Intangible Cultural Heritage of Humanity (UNESCO).[5] In 2007, the Commission for the National Cultural Heritage (Comisión del Patrimonio Cultural de la Nación – CPCN) devoted Heritage Day to the recognition and dissemination of 'Afro-Uruguayan Cultures' and declared the 'Caserio de los Negros' – the place where victims of the River Plate slave trade were quarantined in the Bay of Montevideo – a historic national monument.

In this connection, the article explores some aspects of the presence of Afro-descendants in the social memory of Uruguayans. The first part examines the centenary of Uruguay's independence (1925–1930), where the prevailing discourse posited the existence of a European-style homogeneous society. The second part looks into one of the rallying points of the Afro-descendants' rights movement: the contribution of the 'black race' (using the expression as an identity reference) to the emancipation of Uruguay. Lastly, the article reviews the primary stakeholders in the complex process of finding a commemorative date for people of African descent in Uruguay. As an epilogue, some lines of action are proposed for the

---

3   Frega (2011), 389.

4   The complete texts of the laws are available online in Spanish:
http://www.parlamento.gub.uy

5   The element inscribed is 'The Candombe and its socio-cultural space: a community practice'. In 2010 an advisory group was formed by traditional knowledge holders of the candombe and Uruguayan culture specialists, which operates under the auspices of the Committee for the National Cultural Heritage tasked with contributing to the development of a plan to safeguard and disseminate this heritage.

'Memory sites of slavery in Uruguay' project, which is being developed under the UNESCO Slave Route Project in Argentina, Paraguay and Uruguay. The central theme is the erection of three public monuments. The etymology of the word 'monument', as pointed out by the French historian Jacques Le Goff, is intertwined with remembrance – 'remind', 'enlighten', 'instruct' – with the purpose of perpetuating the memory.

Afro-Descendants during the Centenary of Uruguay's Independence

The festive atmosphere of the centenary was tainted by views, both inside and outside its borders, portraying Uruguay as a country where 'almost all the inhabitants are white', without 'the disturbing problems of Indians or Negros that were such a great cause for concern to the American nations in general'.[6]

This concept of a young country with advanced social legislation and opportunities for progress was presented as the result of the large influx of European immigrants. Protests, in any case, were linked more with the 'dangerous' elements of this immigration – anarchists and socialists – and with the development of urban culture to the detriment of the rural roots – nativism – of identity.[7] School textbooks 'taught' students that the Uruguayan population was 'Caucasian', and the educational authorities boasted that '[o]ur country offers the special case of a cosmopolitanism formed in exceptional conditions', in which '[a]ll white-race countries have contributed to our formation and perfection'.[8]

In the deluxe edition of *El Libro del Centenario del Uruguay, 1825-1925* (The Book of Uruguay's Centenary, 1825–1925), which is very large and lavishly illustrated, the composition of Uruguay's population is defined in these terms: 'Uruguay's population is white, entirely of European origin' (…) 'The indigenous race no longer exists' (…) 'The small proportion of Ethiopian origin (…) brought from the African continent to establish slavery in this country is considerably diminished, to the point of comprising an insignificant proportion of the population'.[9] The book itself nonetheless contains photographs showing the presence of Afro-descendants in the countryside and the city.

6 Nin and Silva (1930), 10
7 Islas; Frega (2007), 360–61.
8 Report by Abel J. Perez in the Report on Primary Education in the early twentieth century (Memoria de Instrucción Primaria), cit. in Leone (2000), 202–203.
9 Prepared by Perfecto López Campaña and Raúl Castells Carafí, published in Montevideo by Agencia Publicidad Capurro & Cía. in (1925), 43.

The caption reads:
'Troop of native horses held in a makeshift corral and ready to be saddled',
with no mention of the worker in the foreground.
El Libro del Centenario, 69.

The caption reads: 'The grinding and
canning of meat in one of the largest meat-
packing depots in Montevideo'.
El Libro del Centenario, 131.

Infantry Sergeant.
Photograph c. 1897.
National Image Archives-SODRE.

Washerwomen in 1900. Photograph. Municipal Museum and Archives.

Street Sweeper. Montevideo Town Hall Photography Centre (CMDF)

Coach driver. Empty can collection cart (CMDF)

Other photographic evidence documents the presence of Afro-descendants employed as washerwomen, street sweepers, soldiers and coachmen, and, except for the technological advances, resembles lithographs of local customs from the first half of the nineteenth century.

In the mid-1920s, Lino Suárez Peña, an Afro-Uruguayan, spoke out against this concealment of the Afro-descendant population and tried, in his own way, to write a history of the presence of black people in the country from the beginning of slavery to its abolition, including their cultural contributions and main achievements, requesting that the public education authority ensure that 'all these things

The Water Bearer. José Belloni (1882–1965)

Located in Plaza Viera (Avenida Rivera y Francisco.
Muñoz), Montevideo. Photograph: Ana Frega.

be included in national history, since the present emerges from the past, like a tree emerging from the womb of the Earth'.[10]

The centenary celebrations in 1930 included the creation and installation in public spaces of a series of works by Uruguayan sculptors symbolising the 'agents contributing to the construction of our nation'.[11] Thus, along with the 'immigrant', 'stevedore', 'urban worker', 'owner' and 'farmer', the 'water bearer' (*El aguatero*) became part of Montevideo's landscape.[12]

The outstanding Uruguayan sculptor José Belloni was awarded the commission for the sculpture, which was originally named *The Black Water Carrier* (*El negro aguador*). Inaugurated in May 1932, its pedestal bore the inscription: 'The water bearer. Tribute to the Black Race. Centennial Commission, 1930'.[13] The burden of slavery was revealed in this representation that, while seeking to achieve the op-

10 Manuscript dated 1924, cit. in Chagas (2007), 9.

11 *El Día* Sunday supplement, Montevideo, 5 March 1933, cit. in Antola; Ponte (2000), 224.

12 Eastern Republic of Uruguay. National Centennial Commission. 1830–1930, Memoria de los trabajos realizados (Report on the work carried out), Montevideo, Impresora Uruguaya, S.F., 28–29.

13 Located in Plaza Viera, Avenida Rivera y Francisco. Muñoz, Montevideo.

posite, reproduced the historic place attributed to black people and the stereotype linking them to servility.[14]

This is the type of image used in school textbooks or newspaper articles to illustrate the place attributed to Afro-descendants in society. In spite of their longstanding presence in the Republic's frontline army, when it came to choosing a motif to remember the 'contribution' of black people to the 'Nation', their participation in the struggle for independence was not used. This differs from the monument to the 'gaucho' (cowboy), inaugurated in 1927, upon which the inscription reads 'To the first workers and forgers of national independence', or even to the Charrúa people (indigenous Uruguayans), to whom the Centennial Commission dedicated a monument entitled 'The Last of the Charrúa', recalling the transfer to France in 1833 of two chiefs, a shaman and a woman, to be 'exhibited'. The set of sculptures, by Edmundo Prati, Gervasio Furest Muñoz and Enrique Lussich, was inaugurated in 1938. The socially accepted traits of this ethnic group included its indomitable and brave character, reflected in positive expressions such as 'garra charrúa' (Charrúan tenacity). School textbooks of the period, such as the *Historia del Uruguay* (*History of Uruguay*) by Arturo Carbonell and Debali (first edition published in 1927) reflected these changes with regard to gauchos and indigenous peoples, by noting their participation in the wars of independence alongside General José Artigas.[15]

The Demand for a Black Hero

In the mid-1920s, people started demanding the black community's right to take its place in national history, fuelling a movement to pay tribute to Ansina, a companion of José Artigas during the last 30 years of his life, which he spent in Paraguay. Little was known about the life of the revolutionary leader in that country. An article published in the Montevideo newspaper *El Constitucional* in 1846, which recounted a visit made by José María Artigas to his father, referred to 'an old man named Lenzina who had accompanied him into exile'.[16] In 1860, the newspaper's editor, Isidoro de María, published a biography written by José María Artigas in which, as far as we know, Ansina was mentioned for the first time: 'Ansina, his old comrade from emigration, who was four years older than

---

14 Antola and Ponte (2000), 225, questions Belloni's work, arguing that it does not represent a water carrier but an excrement collector, who fulfilled that function in houses without latrines.

15 See Leone (2000), 176–77.

16 *El Constitucional* newspaper, Montevideo, 1 July 1846, p. 2 (Emigration of General Artigas to Paraguay. His life and situation), cit. in Ardao; Capillas de Castellanos (1958), 3.

Sergeant Manuel Antonio Ledesma.
According to Mario Petillo (1956, 9), the photograph was taken by Maximo Fleurquin in Paraguay.

the General, stayed by his former leader's side and took care of his daily needs'.[17]

In the early twentieth century, campaigning led to the inclusion of Ansina's name in Montevideo's directory of names.[18] It was during those years that there was a mix-up between Sergeant Manuel Antonio Ledesma, the 'last Artiguist soldier' – whose identity had been documented in the 1880s at the time of the preparation of General Maximo Tajes' trip to Paraguay – and Artigas' 'faithful companion and assistant' Ansina. Despite doubts arising from the weakness of the evidence,[19] reports submitted by the Ansina Committee of Guarambaré (the town where Ledesma lived out his last years) and the steps taken by Augustín Carrón, Uruguayan consul in Paraguay, were considered valid. The authorities then began the process of repatriating the mortal remains of Sergeant Ledesma, which had been exhumed in February 1925 and placed in the church of Guarambaré. The repatriation was completed in October 1938.[20]

17 De María (1860), 34.
18 See Rodriguez (2006), 94–95, which states that the initiative was presented in 1917 by Marcelino Bottaro. For Bottaro's participation, see also Victor Pereyra Perez, 'Let's fight', in *Ansina*, Year IV, no. 4, Montevideo, 18 May 1942 (n.p.).
19 See Ferreiro (1927).
20 Petillo (1956), 27–28 and 51–52.

It is interesting to highlight the mobilisation of the black community in these instances. Between 1939 and 1942, the magazine *Ansina* was published once a year by the Committee for the Tribute to Manuel Antonio Ledesma (Ansina). On 18 May 1939 – a national holiday commemorating the anniversary of the Battle of Las Piedras, an important victory won by José Artigas in 1811 against the pro-Spanish forces – a vigil was kept at the foot of the monument to Artigas in Plaza Independencia over 'the remains of the man who had been his loyal assistant, Don Manuel Antonio Ledesma'. Subsequently, the urn 'alongside the ashes of the Father of the Nation' was moved.[21]

The Uruguay Patriotic Association and a group of Afro-descendent organisations, forming the Committee for the Tribute to Manuel Antonio Ledesma, chaired by Juan C. Arizmendi, had called for that recognition. The press reflected the significant popular support given to the ceremonies. As a personality, he symbolised a model of the integration of Afro-descendants into Uruguayan society. He was illuminated by his 'proximity' to Artigas – 'dark made light', in the words of the writer and poet Juan Zorrilla de San Martín – representing 'the prototype of loyalty', according to Member of Parliament Julio V. Iturbide, author of the bill introduced to enable his remains to be placed in the National Pantheon, and he was 'our gaucho', to quote Mario Petillo, Inspector of Primary Education of the Army, linking him with the popular sectors of the Banda Oriental campaign.[22]

In subsequent years, the Committee focused on campaigning for the erection of a monument to Manuel Antonio Ledesma, Ansina. According to Ildefonso Pereda Valdés, 'all the bronze wasted on poorly representing Negroes should be melted down and cast into a future statue that sums up the highest qualities of black people; and nobody could better embody them than the soldier Ansina'.[23] Sculpted by José Belloni, the monument was inaugurated on 18 May 1943.[24] The seated figure was reproduced from a photograph of an elderly Ledesma, taken around 1884 in Paraguay. The sculptor replaced the walking stick held in his right hand with a tacuara (an improvised lance used by gaucho militias consisting of a knife blade tied to a type of bamboo reed). The monument is backed with a grey granite stele depicting in bas-relief the figure of Artigas in the Citadel of Montevideo,

21 National Register of Laws of the Oriental Republic of Uruguay. 1939, Montevideo,Imprenta Nacional, 1940, Law No. 9814 of 24 March 1939 (pp. 264–65), and Law No. 9822 of 12 May 1939 (p. 386).

22 See Ansina, Year 1, No. 1, Montevideo, 18 May 1939 (n.p.). The editor was I. Casas Pereyra and the editorial secretary was Washington Viera.

23 Pereda Valdés (1941), 116.

24 Located at the junction of Avenida 8 de Octubre and Avenida Italia in Montevideo, Uruguay.

based on the oil painting by Juan Manuel Blanes. The inscription carved on the base of the granite stele reads: 'Together in exile. Together in eternity. Together in their homeland for the glory of a grateful nation'. The researcher Alejandro Gortázar, analysing the symbolism of the sculpture – and particularly the significance of Artigas standing and Ansina sitting – questions 'how much of this imagined relationship between master and slave, present in slave-based societies, is in this representation'.[25]

In the early 1950s, coinciding with the commemoration of the centenary of the death of Artigas, the debate on Ansina's identity was reopened. According to Daniel Hammerly Dupuy, Ansina's real name was Joaquin Lenzina, a minstrel and poet who witnessed and narrated the 'Epic of Artigas'.[26]

In addition to 'faithful assistant' were other attributes that Ledesma did not have. The Artiguist soldier Sergeant Manuel Antonio Ledesma lost the aura and the glory gained through 'proximity to the hero' Artigas and recovered his role as a member of the Oriental troops. This entailed, among other changes, the removal of his name from the monument to Ansina and the relocation of his mortal remains. After a complex journey, the urn containing his remains was laid to rest on 14 May 2011, in front of the Bicentennial Pavilion, located in the Canelones Department at the site commemorating the Battle of Las Piedras (18 May 1811).[27]

Daniel Hammerly Dupuy and his son Victor Hammerly Peverini included in their work 'Artigas in American Poetry' a collection of poems that they tried to prove were written by Ansina. Based on the information in one of the compositions entitled 'A Century of Memories', Daniel Hammerly sketched out a biography of Joaquin Lenzina.[28]

Among other information, it says that Ansina was born the son of enslaved African parents in Montevideo, in 1760.

He travelled around the countryside where he learned to play the guitar and improvise songs as a payador (a gaucho troubadour) and was enslaved in Brazil until General Artigas set him free. From that moment onwards, Ansina remained by Artigas' side through the revolution and 30 years of exile in Paraguay, where he reportedly died in 1860. The chapter title 'Ansina: Faithful payador of Artigas' illustrates the main characteristic attributed to him.

What interests us here is not the controversy that erupted over the authenticity of the verses and the autobiographical information contained in them – the originals

---

25 Gortázar (2003), 236–38.
26 Hammerly Dupuy (1951). Published previously in *El País* newspaper on 29 September 1950.
27 http://archivo.presidencia.gub.uy/sci/noticias/2011/05/2011051407.htm
28 Hammerly; Hammerly (1951), Vol. I, 23–34.

LEFT *Ansina.* José Belloni (1882–1965). Unveiled on 18 May 1943. The inscription carved on the granite stele reads: 'Together in exile. Together in eternity. Together in their homeland for the glory of a grateful nation'. It is located at the junction of Avenida 8 de Octubre and Avenida Italia in Montevideo. Photograph: Ana Frega.

RIGHT *Artigas at the Citadel.* Juan Manuel Blanes (1830–1901)

were reportedly copied by Daniel Hammerly in 1928 in Asunción and were then lost – but the transmutation of Ansina's subordinate role, 'illuminated' by his proximity to Artigas, into a 'black hero' of the Artiguist movement. After the restoration of democracy in 1985, there was a growing interest in recognising the indigenous and African roots of Uruguayan identity and in promoting Latin American integration. However, given the persistence of paternalistic attitudes and the absence of a satisfactory response from academic studies and circles to this social demand, reports and articles with varying methodological rigour were disseminated. In some cases, the fragmentation of the past and memory were hypothesised, developing a new kind of 'mythical discourse'.[29] In other words, they maintained the story of a nation based on 'founding heroes', tributary of the conception of history as an element of social integration and affirmation of the State units they constituted, quite unconcerned about the study of social processes in all its complexity.

29 Teresa Porzecanski (1992), 49–61.

As of the 1990s, the figure of Ansina took on a new dimension. In 1996, the collection of poems by Joaquín Lenzina published by Daniel and Víctor Hammerly in 1951 was republished in Uruguay. Under the title *Ansina me llaman y Ansina yo soy* (*Ansina they call me and Ansina I am*), the interdisciplinary team 'Recovering the Memory of Ansina' sought to show that he was a man 'who had survived, over time, in our memories, and we no longer had an excuse to forget him'.[30] The subsequent developments of some of the team members reinforced the tendency to suspect all historiographical production, considering the very methods of historical documentation and analysis insufficient to find the conclusions sought after. Hammerly Dupuy's 'faithful payador of Artigas' was now the 'outstanding fighter and African Oriental sage', 'leader of the Afro-American libertarian movements'.[31]

It is clear that this is far removed from the scientific criterion that states that historians 'cannot invent the facts', as emphasised by Eric Hobsbawm when commenting on the danger of some views of history that blur the borders between reality and fiction.[32] Along somewhat different lines – reacting equally against 'those who insist on maintaining the traditional status quo' and the 'fanciful eulogies, harmful inventors of a black leader practically superior to Artigas' – another team member has resumed work on the historical figures of Joaquin Lenzina and Manuel Antonio Ledesma alongside an Afro-descendant named Montevideo or Martinez and who was also linked to Artigas in Paraguay, in an attempt to weave a story of their lives from eyewitness accounts and memories that have been maintained/recreated up to the present.[33]

From our perspective, consideration of the role of Afro-descendants in the construction of the nation should not continue to reproduce the traditional interpretative model that perceived the wars of independence as 'national enterprises', approaching them from only one angle, which excludes the study of the process in its ethnic and cultural diversity. The vision of the past that has omitted – and continues to omit – the participation of Afro-descendants in the historical narrative of the construction of the nation cannot be challenged by following the same linear scheme and merely 'adding' other people or social groups.

Hailing José Artigas as a national hero has led to distorting or silencing the task of addressing the various contradictions contained in this historical process. The

---

30   Interdisciplinary team 'Recovering the Memory of Ansina' (Rescate de la memoria de Ansina) (1996), 12. Team members were, in alphabetical order: Danilo Antón, Nelson Caula, Isabel Izquierdo and Armando Miraldi.

31   Abella (1999). See electronic version online at: http://www.chasque.net/vecinet/ abella00.htm. Consultation: 20-10-2009.

32   Hobsbawm (1998).

33   Caula (2004), 213–78.

'cult' has ended in 'betrayal', according to Uruguayan historian José Pedro Barrán in a thought-provoking article on the participation of the popular sectors of society in the formulation of measures taken by the revolutionary government.[34] A renewed study of the independence process cannot cover up what survives of the slave system, or condemn other ways of obtaining the freedom of slaves that did not involve enlistment in the patriotic forces. Several proclamations during that period presented the revolution as the 'cry of the people of the Americas for their freedom'. However, the meaning of the concept varied according to the interests and position of the person stating it, and in Spanish American revolutions, in general, it was particularly restrictive with regard to the institution of slavery. Although at this stage some tendencies that came from colonial times were gaining ground – such as a slave's right to buy his or her freedom (and his or her family's freedom), or to request a 'sales slip' in the event of abuse – obtaining freedom was a complex process of individual and collective experiences disallowing a univocal reading and involving a variety of responses and reactions. As we have noted elsewhere, the institutional breakdown led to a rise in fugitive slaves and the conscription of free and enslaved Afro-descendants, and it even promoted the issuance of provisions for the gradual abolition of slavery. Institutional measures either joined – complementing and putting on pressure – or opposed the various paths of resistance taken by the enslaved population.

There was evidence of tension between the contradictory 'rights' covering the various groups leading the revolution. On the one hand was the individual right to freedom, favouring abolitionist measures; on the other was the individual right to property, protecting slave owners who supported the cause; and, lastly, there was the right that, in most cases, prevailed over the other two: the governments' right to conscript armies for the 'defence of the Nation', which supported the compulsory drafting of slaves under a promise of granting their freedom, in battalions of 'pardos' and 'morenos' (terms meaning brown- or dark-skinned, used in Colonial Spanish America to classify racially mixed individuals).

Paths of Freedom in Revolutionary Times[35]

The revolutionary rupture shook the entire social order in the River Plate. Broad slogans – often referring to the fight for freedom, recognition of customary rights, aspirations to a 'fairer' world or the return to a primitive equality – rallied occupiers of land with no title, farm labourers, free individuals and fugitive slaves,

---

34 José Pedro Barrán, 'Artigas: del culto a la traición' (Artigas: from cult to betrayal), in *Brecha*, Montevideo, 20 June 1986, 11.

35 This section largely summarises the article of the same name listed in the bibliography.

Scene from '*Exodus of the Oriental People*', Guillermo Rodriguez (1889–1959). Painted circa 1923. National History Museum of Montevideo.

The painting refers to events that took place in late 1811, when more than 4,400 people joined the troops of the Banda Oriental army in order to escape subjugation by Spanish rule. The census of families conducted before they crossed the Uruguay River recorded around 500 men and women slaves.

among others, who had the chance to realise their aspirations by joining José Artigas. In the Oriental Province, because the free Afro-descendants were recognised as 'unfortunates', they were first in line to receive farm lots and cattle confiscated from 'bad Europeans and worse Americans'.[36]

Some of the various paths taken by slaves to obtain their freedom are given below. They seek to give a rough idea of the ideological perception of men and

36 Article 6 of the Provisional Regulations of the Oriental Province to promote its campaign and the safety of its landowners (Reglamento Provisorio de la Provincia Oriental para el fomento de su campaña y seguridad de sus hacendados), General Headquarters, 10 September 1815. In: CNAA (1987), Vol. XXI, 93–98.

women slaves during the revolution. They also show the disparity between the revolution's proclamations and the continued conditions of subjugation and exploitation, as well as the sacrifice and submission of the slaves who hoped to improve their individual or collective condition, laying bare the hitherto anonymous 'heroes' and 'heroines', and giving a good indication, without idealisation, of the participation of Afro-descendants in the independence process.

One of the first consequences of the revolutionary outbreak was the flight of slaves. In November 1811, the head of the naval base in Montevideo reported to the Spanish authorities that there had been insurgents numbering 'over 1,000 men and women slaves'.[37] Interestingly, although both sides promised to grant freedom to male slaves who enlisted, some women slaves reinterpreted these promises in their own favour and demanded the benefits promised to those who escaped from their pro-Spanish owners. After the defeat of the Spanish in June 1814, owners and slaves appeared before the courts to assert their rights.

One such case was that of Ana, slave of Doña Manuela Antonia Cuba, who had managed to cross over to the besieging army, where she married a moreno from the battalion of the emancipated.[38] When the City of Montevideo was surrendered to the Directorate of the United Provinces, in July 1814 Doña Manuela demanded that her slave be returned to her, arguing that 'she had spent her lifetime trying to escape'. The revolutionary authorities decided to declare her free, making use of their right to seize 'enemy property' in 'open warfare'. Another example was that of María del Pilar, slave of Doña Rosa Fernández. Although she had obtained her 'civil liberty' in 1814 from the Directorate, following the victory of the Artiguist troops and the leadership change in 1815, she had to face a new demand from her former owner, who alleged that her escape had not occurred during wartime.[39] As the court ruled in favour of her owner, María del Pilar had to appeal, providing as evidence a slip of paper signed by General José Artigas, Citizen and Chief of the Oriental troops, dated December 1813, during the war. Thanks to this document, the Montevideo town council registered Maria del Pilar's 'carta de libertad' (a document issued once a slave was emancipated) in the official records (Libro de Protocolos). In both cases, the owners had accused their slaves of seeking to escape at every possible opportunity and had made a clear case for 'order'

---

37 CNAA (1953), Vol. IV, 369–75. A census of Montevideo corresponding to 1810, although with imperfections in the recording of information, showed that of the 11,554 inhabitants, 4,210 were Afro-descendants (3,646 slaves and 564 free men and women). General National Archive (Archivo General de la Nación – AGN), Book No. 249.

38 AGN, Government and Treasury Notary Holding (Fondo Escribanía de Gobierno y Hacienda) (EGH), Box 108, exp.25.

39 AGN, EGH, Box 111, Report No. 50.

and their individual right to property. They had also sought to take advantage of the fact that different governments coexisted and overlapped in the Banda Oriental. Legal rulings, at the same time, did not question the institution of slavery and resorted to rules that, according to the law of nature and nations, regulated war between nations. In April 1812, the tendency towards the gradual abolition of slavery was shown in the River Plate by a decree that banned the slave trade and by the newly founded General Constituent Assembly's resolution, which provided that from 31 January 1813, nobody would be born a slave in the United Provinces.[40] Unlike in the old colonial capital, where the children of slaves were registered as free, in the Oriental Province it appears that compliance with the provision had to be obtained in court. One slave owner even called for relations to be broken off between the United Provinces and the Federal League in order to insist that this rule did not apply in the Banda Oriental. In the case in question, the document submitted by the applicant stated: 'Don José Artigas, who was in charge of this Province, never refused this favour, before ensuring that it was granted'.[41]

An interesting case – revealing the chasm between proclaimed freedom and continued slavery practices – is that of Gregoria Fruanes, a 'parda and native of Montevideo' who appeared before the Artiguist authorities in 1815 to defend the rights of her son.[42] She was protesting against her owner, Don Juan Méndez Caldeyra, for having included in her sale price the value of her two-year-old son, born free in the City of Montevideo, 'in the happy time of a liberal system and of freedom, so similar to the general cry of America and of the same nature'. Gregoria's argument referred to the contradiction between the words and the deeds of Méndez Caldeyra. She denounced the ingratitude of her owner after 'seven years of service, of having fed him and looked after his children [...] and rendered other services forced [on her] by the circumstances and misery of slavery (which are better kept buried in silence)'. She also questioned the fact that her owner 'only looked after his own interests and his actions did not match his words on patriotism and integrity'. And if those political and humanitarian arguments were not enough, she added that previous buying and selling transactions did not include the payment of municipal tax, which, according to a provision from colonial times, would entitle her to her freedom. Juan Méndez Caldeyra had been with the moderate wing of the revolution in various capacities: supplier of troops; town coun-

40 Frega; Borucki; Chagas; Stalla (2004), 117–18.
41 AGN, Court Records, Box 18, Maldonado and its jurisdiction, Record No. 29 'Don Vicente Ramos claiming the baby of a black woman slave that he owned'.
42 AGN, EGH, Box 112, Record No. 55, fs.1–2. The note is signed 'at the request of the petitioner' by José Ma. Storache. The proceedings were interrupted when she caught sight of her owner.

cillor while the city was governed by Buenos Aires; in charge of collecting donations for the uniforms of the Regimiento de Dragones de la Libertad (Regiment
of Dragoons of Freedom); and Captain of the Compañía Cívica de Cazadores
(Civic Company of Hunters) in 1815. He was also a major slave owner, and this
was not the first time that he had been faced with claims brought against him by
his slaves. The proceedings focused on the question of the scope of the 'liberal
system and of freedom' proclaimed by the revolution. It is clear that Méndez
Caldeyra – like many of those supporting independence from Spain – wanted the
revolution to bring about the replacement of the authorities without the adoption
of other measures that could call into question their social position or property
rights.

In November 1820, when the Oriental Province was already under Luso-Brazil-
ian control, Don Vicente Ramos, inhabitant and judge of the town of San Salvador, appeared before the authorities of Colonia claiming ownership of a 'little
black girl' who was the daughter of his former maid Cristina. He argued on his
own behalf that 'in the Banda Oriental there had been no such order of freedom
for any newly born black child'. The document presented by his slave Cristina, on
the contrary, maintained that 'Don José Artigas, who was in charge of this
Province, never refused this favour', and had officially informed 'all the clergy of
the Banda Oriental on the method to be observed when registering freedmen and
women in the Parish Church'. It also mentioned the existence of previous cases
with favourable rulings in that very court, which also confirmed the need to appeal to courts to enforce this provision.

A review of the court records shows the persistence of pro-slavery ideas in society at that time. In addition to claims for the restitution of slaves or the implementation of mechanisms to avoid conscription, they continued to refer to slaves
as 'objects'. 'Owners have property rights over their slaves as for other objects that
belong to them', said a resident of Maldonado in June 1820, appealing against a
judgement that ordered him to give a sale slip to a slave who had been mistreated.
In his opinion, '[a]ll owners are authorised to punish servants who go astray without it resulting in sufficient reason for dispossession'.[43]

The Artiguist government did not shirk from using slaves to reinforce its
troops, and the conscription of morenos and pardos – whether slaves or free – was
one of the first steps taken in 1815. Their preferred use was to increase the artillery corps, where, in addition to purely military functions, they had to haul
weapons, dig ditches, build sheds and carry out other heavy work. When determining remuneration for the troops in the garrison of Montevideo, the ruling
town council ordered that the soldiers of the regiments of morenos and pardos re-

43 AGN, AGA, Libro 291, fs.76–86.

ceive three pesos per month, in contrast to the six pesos that was paid in the other regiments.[44]

The enlistment of Afro-descendants in the army affected individual interests and, unless they were 'enemies of the system', owners successfully managed in many cases to have their slaves returned or instead received payment for their loss. In April 1816, the town council of Montevideo ordered the arrest of the 'multitude' of slaves who had chosen to flee to the countryside, taking advantage of the 'confusion' created by the revolution, and warned those who harboured slaves that they would be punished with the obligation to pay owners for 'all the time the slaves were hidden in their homes'.[45] The fact that several mayors and commanders answered that there was nobody in that situation in their region, or only sent one or two people at most, could be interpreted either as an acceptance of the runaways' right to freedom or as an expression of the labour needs in the area.

In 1816, the Portuguese invasion forced the Artiguist government to give less consideration to the needs of 'the property-owning classes'. The Delegate of Artigas in Montevideo, Miguel Barreyro, ordered the formation of a new battalion of morenos. Anticipating complaints, he said: 'Negroes will serve as militia, so their owners may be sure to recuperate them having learned discipline, order and absolute obedience'.[46] In one week he had recruited 390 slaves and in the muster roll of January 1817 (immediately before the abandonment of Montevideo by the Oriental troops), the combined total of new slaves and old companies of free pardos and morenos came to 555 soldiers, 72 corporals, 14 drums and whistles and 39 sergeants.[47] Although it was not specified that integration in the battalion as militia established the possibility of attaining freedom, that was how it was understood by the slave owners who branded the move as 'despotic', having their slaves taken away from them 'without even receiving any documentation'.[48]

The slaves viewed enlistment in the patriotic lines as a transitional stage. Just as they had fled from the homes of their owners, they could desert the regiments and gain their freedom sooner. The experience of colonial times was not far behind, where a multi-ethnic rural open space fuelled the thoughts of the runaway slaves, and even fuelled the bid to form a rural settlement known as a 'palenque' or 'quilombo', as had emerged from the 'mass' escape attempt of 1803. This was the case, for ex-

---

44 CNAA, (1991), Vol. XXIV, 272–73. In 1816 there was a general cut in wages to three pesos for soldiers of veteran troops, and two pesos and a half for 'pardos' and 'morenos', equivalent to the wages of the Civic Cavalry Regiment. (ibid., 417–18.)

45 CNAA (1993), Vol. XXVII, 88, 139, 169, 198 and 290.

46 CNAA (1998), Vol. XXXI, 199–200.

47 AGN, AGA, Book 894, fs.13–24, 53 y 61–64.

48 Ardao (1954), 83.

ample, for Antonio Rodriguez, a moreno who presented himself to the town council of Montevideo in April 1816 requesting his freedom – he was imprisoned in the Citadel – in exchange for enlisting 'in the artillery militia' where 'as a free moreno [...] I will be as helpful as I can be to the Nation'.[49] According to his statement, he had served in Regiment No. 10 after the Directorate's troops seized the City of Montevideo.[50] He did not hesitate to report that afterwards he had deserted – it must be remembered that the Oriental troops led by José Artigas were at war with the Directorate of the United Provinces – and had made a living by hiring himself out for rural tasks. His former owner had sent him to prison when he refused to continue to give him 'all or part of his labour'. In his argument, Antonio stated:

> Your Excellency, I became free when I enrolled in the army and the abovementioned Lord ceased to be my owner the moment I surrendered. Why, therefore, against all justice, does he wish to enslave me again? When the Nation freed me and endowed me with my rights. Were the abovementioned Lord an American, or had he lavished his attention on this government out of commitment to the System, I would not argue and would submit to his authority; however, Sir, he is a European and an enemy of the country in which I live.

In this petition, the appropriation of the revolutionary message – the restoration of rights and the struggle for freedom – and the contrast between 'Europeans' (Spanish) and Americans is remarkable.

In early 1817, the Portuguese, led by Carlos Federico Lecor, Baron of the Laguna, entered Montevideo. They were supported by the Spanish-Uruguayan elites of the Banda Oriental and the Directorate of the United Provinces of the River Plate. For those who remained opposed to the return of Spanish rule, but did not desire the 'social revolution' presented by Artiguism either, both the United Provinces and Portugal offered an alternative. The insubordination of the Regiment of Freedmen was a successful operation for the Portuguese, since out of the nearly 700 men who made up the army corps of pardos and morenos, more than 400 arrived in Montevideo under the protection of the edict delivered on 9 June 1817, offering favourable conditions for all commanders, officers and individuals who agreed to lay down their weapons. Any armed slaves who passed into the Portuguese army or any of the points occupied by its detachments, would, without exception, 'gain their freedom that day'.[51] According to Lecor's report to his

49 AGN, EGH, Caja 113, file 35.
50 Enrolment in Infantry Regiment No. 10 was mixed, with approximately 75 per cent 'moreno', 8 per cent 'pardo' and 17 per cent white. Andrews (1990), 144.
51 Blanco Acevedo (1950), 205.

government, in late September negotiations on the conditions of transfer of the troops to Buenos Aires were under way with officials. The Portuguese leader was confident, moreover, that the Directorate could not take full advantage of the force either, since it was likely that 'most Negroes would not want to embark'.[52]

The account of the Spanish colonel Juan Jacinto de Vargas, the ambassador in Río de Janeiro, provides indications about the individual and collective behaviour of black people in that instance. By the agreement signed on 29 September 1817, soldiers who crossed into Portuguese lines were billeted in the outskirts of Montevideo and then ferried to the ships that would take them to Buenos Aires. According to Vargas,

> on behalf of all, or most, representations had been made to him [Lecor] stating [that] they were not going to Buenos Aires voluntarily, but had been forced by their officers, and that they wanted to stay in Montevideo. Owing to this and to the fact that a number of them had jumped in the water, they were disembarked after two or three days on board and were billeted, albeit without weapons, in the City.[53]

Bauzá protested in vain against the 'obvious enticement' to desertion of the freed troops and the support they received from sailors of the Portuguese fleet. Lecor's responses, although with the purpose of conserving in Montevideo this potential fighting force, alluded to the rights of soldiers to decide their fate. He defended the right of asylum for individuals of all classes – 'If the freedmen take refuge under the Portuguese flag, neither can I deny them its protection nor am I obliged to use force to send them to Buenos Aires' – and emphasised the slaves' desire for freedom:

> Everyone knows and is witness to the efforts of the free, to come to enjoy their freedom, [...]. Your Lordship is mistaken in his assumption that the behaviour of Negroes is the result of enticement, when the hope for freedom is a very powerful incentive [...] needing no influence from feeble hints dropped by sailors.[54]

Just as the Portuguese sought to gain the Afro-descendant soldiers who had served in the Oriental regiments, the Artiguists appealed to all those who had deserted the battalions of the United Provinces. In early 1817 the Commander-in-Chief of the Oriental troops sent word to the Governor of Santa Fe, Mariano Vera, ordering the transfer to headquarters of 'all Freedmen' from the Buenos Aires

---

52 CNAA (2000), Vol. XXXII, 242–44.
53 National Historical Archives, Madrid (AHN-M), State, Record 3791, Box 1.
54 AGN, Historical Museum and Archive Holding, Box 12.

troops who 'are loose in this town' because 'this regiment and the Blandengues regiment are being formed'.[55]

A battalion of some two hundred black soldiers maintained the struggle against the Portuguese under the command of Colonel José María Gorgonio Aguiar. This commander, of aristocratic origin, was part of the core of officers who promoted and defended the radical phase of the revolution. After the military defeats on the Uruguay River coast in 1818, Aguiar was sent with his troops to the region of Maldonado. His mission was to 'contain the arbitrariness of the peasants' who collaborated with the Portuguese.[56] In December 1819, he took his battalion of black soldiers to the Portuguese border; in 1820 they joined the last Artiguist forces fighting against Francisco Ramirez and, finally, in September 1820, they entered Paraguay. According to reports later gathered by Héctor Francisco Découd, some of the soldiers had reportedly been installed in Laurelty, a town about two leagues from Asunción, where they were given farming tools.[57] In the reports concerning the situation of Manuel Antonio Ledesma, they had reportedly been moved to different places, including Guarambaré, giving rise to the Artigas-Cué community.[58] Interestingly, until recently, their descendants were regarded almost as the 'only' black people of Paraguay, ignoring the significant presence of slave labour that had characterised the Jesuit settlements.[59]

In late 1820, the French naturalist Auguste de Saint-Hilaire toured part of the eastern territory after the defeat of Artigas. Among the accounts in his diary he noted that the soldiers who were remarked upon for their courage were always slaves, 'because they fought for their own freedom'. Others, however, said that the social order was being 'undermined' by the slaves' enrolment in the army. In the words of a farm owner in the area, 'often a black man, a mulatto or an Indian proclaimed himself an officer and went with his band to rob the ranchers' and yet, 'he had to say that he was satisfied'.[60]

The participation of slaves in the armies, where they learned organisation for collective action and occupied positions of strength, increased the slave owners' needs to implement control mechanisms. Afro-descendants without owners or employers were considered dangerous and had to be persecuted. An example of this is the action taken against a moreno 'named Juan Antonio' who 'served the

55 CNAA (2003), Vol. XXXIV, 25.
56 CNAA (2006), Vol. XXVI, 59–60.
57 Découd (1930), 13–14.
58 Caula (2004).
59 Report by Ignacio Telesca for the project 'Sites of memory of slavery in Argentina, Paraguay and Uruguay', unpublished.
60 Saint-Hilaire (2005), 79.

Nation with [Gorgonio] Aguiar' and said that he had been 'a slave to an officer of the Portuguese troops, who had stayed behind when they entered these lands for the first time'. In February 1821, he was sent by the mayor of San Carlos to the town council of Maldonado, saying that he had been held prisoner for nine days for having insulted 'a neighbour in the middle of the night and in a state of inebriation'. The official statement added that other measures should be taken, 'on the grounds that this moreno wandering the countryside could not be very useful to the local community'.[61] Although it was accepted that after joining the army, morenos and pardos could gain their freedom, it was felt that, like Indians, gauchos and 'freedmen', they should be 'disciplined'. Ethnic prejudice was combined with the fear of social 'disorder'.

The ruling on the moreno Antonio Rodriguez was far from being upheld. The 'Nation' had not effectively freed him. The only full defence of Afro-descendants' interests would arise from their own strategies. Military conscription had opened roads to freedom, but not exclusively from the promises made at the time of enrolment. It gave them organisational experience, generated solidarity and provided conditions for negotiation that they did not have previously. The study of these particular processes is a necessary dimension for understanding the complexity of the role of the popular sectors in the revolution and in the constitution of the Oriental State of Uruguay.

What Should Be Commemorated?

On 12 December 1942, at the request of the National Committee for the Centenary of the Abolition of Slavery, commemorations were held to pay tribute to outstanding figures of the black community. However, there were notable differences of opinion within the protest movement in those years. The articles in the pages of the journal *Ansina* reflected that diversity. Aguedo Suárez Peña stressed that Uruguayan democracy promoted 'solidarity among all its components, without paying attention to racial differences'. In contrast, Omar Olivera denounced the 'democratic formulas, often debased by despotic political manoeuvring' and called for a 'new social order based on the legitimate rights of everyone, without distinction of caste or race'.[62] As noted by the American historian George Reid Andrews, some centres and associations of the Afro-descendant community – such as the Uruguay Social and Cultural Association (ACSU) founded in 1941 – represented 'an ambitious upwardly mobile stratum of Afro-Uruguayan society that sought the full benefits of membership in the

---

61   AGN, AGA, Book 291, f. 313.
62   See Ansina, Year II, No. 2, Montevideo, 18-5-1940 (n.p.).

[...] "middle class"'.[63] The date chosen was politically controversial. During the Great War, a regional and international conflict that took place between 1838 and 1852, the government associated with the Colorado Party passed the afore-mentioned Law of 1842. This government was not recognised as legitimate by the White Party, which in the context of the war, besieged Montevideo in early 1843 and set up a parallel government that passed a law abolishing slavery on 28 October 1846.[64]

In the 1960s, celebrations were held for the 150th anniversary of the Oriental Revolution and 200th anniversary of the birth of José Artigas. The commemorations were an opportunity for various Afro-descendant associations to present to the authorities the need to choose a date to remember the 'black race'. In 1964, the year of the bicentenary of the birth of Artigas, the Rosa Negra Cultural Centre proposed holding 'Loyalty Day' on 12 December – for the abolition of slavery adopted in 1842 – honouring Ansina. The proposal was not approved.[65] The initiative combined a vague reference to the existence of slavery in Uruguay – by choosing one of the dates of its abolition – with the recovery of the 'black hero', highlighting his attachment to the 'Father of the Nation'.

In 1975, sesquicentennial of the historical events of 1825 and designated by the civil-military dictatorship as the 'Year of Orientality', a new initiative to recognise the participation of the black community in the Uruguayan independence process was proposed. The National Committee for Tribute to Black Heroes, located in the premises of the Uruguay Social and Cultural Association (ACSU), proposed 7 September – recalling that on that day in 1825, the House of Representatives had determined that nobody would be born a slave in the Oriental Province – as a date 'to remember the various components of our race who actively participated in the struggle for independence'. In response to that notice, the Commission of the Sesquicentennial of the Historical Events of 1825 decided to take up the previous proposal to designate 12 December as 'Loyalty Day'.[66] While they did not agree on the event that they should commemorate, they did share the idea of highlighting loyalty as a virtue. The tribute to Ansina was based on his loyalty to Artigas, and it was extended to those who joined the patriot armies. At no point was it suggested that these battalions of pardos and morenos may have only

---

63 Andrews (2010), 106.

64 For the characteristics and application of both laws, see Borucki; Chagas; Stalla (2004).

65 It was referred to as a precedent in 1975. See Uruguay, Council of State, Council of State Proceedings, Session of Tuesday 8 June 1982, Official Journal No. 21.291, 201–203.

66 Uruguay, Council of State, Council of State Proceedings, Session of Tuesday 8 June 1982, Official Journal No. 21.291, 201–203. Statement by Councillor Antonio Gabito Barrios.

fought for their own interests, which were perhaps removed from political independence and closer to the resistance against slavery and the quest for freedom.

In March 1982, a new proposal was submitted to the Council of State to declare 12 December as 'Loyalty Day' as a matter of civic commemoration and tribute to Ansina. In his explanatory statement, Councillor Fernando Assunçao said that the date on which slavery had been abolished was 'ideal so as to rejoice in those sentiments and honour Ansina, faithful black servant of General Artigas, and with him the memory of all the other coloured people who had served the nation in the independence movement'.[67] During the debate, however, the meaning of the commemoration was changed, removing any reference to slavery, the 'black race' or the existence of racial discrimination in Uruguay. On 14 June 1982, Decree-Law No. 15290 was passed, declaring '5 September as 'Artiguist Loyalty Day' as a matter of civic commemoration and tribute to Ansina, faithful servant and companion of General Artigas from his youth to his death'.[68] The Rapporteur, Marcial Bugallo, said that it did not matter whether it was Ledesma or Lencina, the tribute was 'to a loyal and faithful servant of our great leader' and, through him, to all men of 'dark skin and clear spirit' who had fought for the ideals of the nation. Councillor Wilson Craviotto said that he would have preferred 5 September (1820), the date that Artigas entered Paraguay, because the commemoration was not simply about loyalty, but Artiguist loyalty, and 'because in order to achieve the racial equality so long sought after, proclaimed and put into effect in our country, tribute should not be made to one particular race'. Councillor Jorge Amondarain went further to say that the social treatment and rights of the 'black race' did not differ from those of 'white citizens'. On the contrary, in Uruguay 'we are rightfully proud that black citizens are present in all levels of our society, without the slightest hint of possible differences'.[69] Without wishing to contradict the councillors of the civil-military dictatorship, it should be noted that an Executive Decree of 1978, which empowered the municipal government to judge the quality of 'ruinous farms' and to evict the occupants by use of police force, led to the first evictions of iconic sites of the Afro-descendant community and Uruguayan society overall, such as the Conventillo 'Medio Mundo' (a large house where rooms were rented to various families) in the Barrio Sur district of Montevideo and the 'Barrio Reus

67   Uruguay, Council of State, Council of State Proceedings, Official Journal No. 21.220, Session of Tuesday 30 March 1982, 67.

68   Electronic Spanish version of the Draft Law available at the following link: http://www.parlamento.gub.uy/leyes/AccesoTextoLey.asp?Ley=15290&Anchor See: 18-10-2009.

69   Uruguay, Council of State, Council of State Acts, Official Journal No. 21.291, Session of Tuesday 8 June 1982, 197–99. The bill was passed unanimously at the session.

al Sur' (Ansina) housing complex in the Palermo district, in order to demolish them.[70]

The restoration of democracy in 1985 gave new impetus to the Afro-descendant movement in Uruguay. New partnerships were formed – in 1988, Organizaciones Mundo Afro began to act, for example, calling for the recognition of Afro-descendants' contribution to the social and cultural development of Uruguay, and the adoption of affirmative measures that would contribute effectively to improving the living conditions of the Afro-descendant community in the country.

Two decades passed before a date was adopted to commemorate the Afro-Uruguayan cultural heritage and to rally against discrimination. The initiative came from Edgardo Ortuño of the Broad Front party, who was a member of parliament at that time. The day of remembrance he proposed was the date of an act of resistance by the Afro-descendant community during the civil-military dictatorship: the last call of candombe drums in the Conventillo 'Medio Mundo' on 3 December 1978. In the explanatory statement he said: 'What happened that day was a spontaneous act and farewell tribute to one of the inspirational birthplaces of candombe, in commitment to its legacy and charged with the rejection of and resistance to an arbitrary racism of those who maintained that "Negros" and their drums impoverished the city'.[71] In this way, the perspective of the commemoration changed. Instead of action 'from above', with laws partially advancing the struggle for freedom, the date chosen to 'remember together' commemorated action 'from below', where the protagonists were in the Afro-descendant community, claiming their cultural roots and their rights.

Epilogue

As part of the second stage of the Slave Route Project, a workshop took place on 'Sites of Memory of the Slave Route in Argentina, Paraguay and Uruguay' sponsored by UNESCO's Culture Sector and Office in Montevideo. The objectives included: (a) furthering knowledge about trafficking conditions and slavery in the region; (b) encouraging research on the cultures, languages, music, dress and rituals of the enslaved populations, in order to rebuild ties with their origins; (c) raising the visibility of their forms of resistance and their preservation of their cultural values; (d) appreciating the contribution of the African diaspora in the construction of the national history and traditions; (e) exposing the consequences of slavery today, and (f) promoting equitable and democratic

---

70 Alfaro (2008), 79.

71 Uruguay. Journal of the House of Representatives, No. 3369, 47th session, 10 October 2006, 8.

Lágrima Rios, stage name of Lida Melba Benavidez (1924–2006), singer and activist for the rights of the Afro-descendant community in Conventillo 'Medio Mundo'. CMDF.

Conventillo 'Medio Mundo', 1954. Photo: Ferruccio Musitelli.

social structures that respect diversity. The short- and medium-term objectives combine research, education and outreach, focusing on the definition of 'sites of memory' conceived as places from which to break the silence and treat the issue of slavery objectively.[72]

One of the 'sites of memory' proposed by Uruguay is the 'Caserío de los Negros' or 'Caserío de Filipinas', located on the coast of Montevideo, on the left bank of the Miguelete River. Historically it was the site where, from the late eighteenth century and at the peak of the slave trade, slaves shipped to the River Plate were disembarked and kept in a compound, first by the Royal Company of the Philippines (1787–1789) and then by private dealers, until the large-scale slave trade ended in 1812 with the independence revolution. Montevideo was the main slave port for this part of America, receiving slaves from the six African regions of embarkation involved in the transatlantic trade (Southeast Africa, West Central Africa, the Bight of Biafra, the Bight of Benin, the Gold Coast, and West Guinea) and from Brazil. The aim was to re-embark them and ship them to Buenos Aires, Chile, Upper Peru and Lima.[73] During the revolutionary period, the buildings were designed to accommodate troops or prisoners and there were even plans to locate a leper colony there. Over time, the facilities were dismantled and the site was divided up and passed into private hands. The site nevertheless kept its name for several decades.

---

72 See Slave Route Project (Uruguay) working document. Summary of the task force meetings. Uruguayan National Commission for UNESCO, 2009, mimeo.

73 Borucki; Chagas; Stalla (2010).

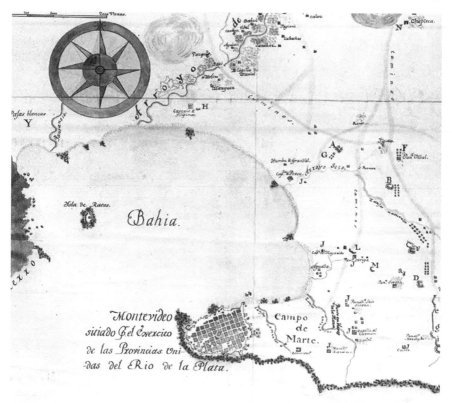

Montevideo besieged by the Army of the United Provinces of the River Plate. Map made by Father Bartolomé Muñoz in 1813. To the north, in the vicinity of the mouth of the Miguelete River [on the map, to the right of the compass rose], is the Caserio de Filipinas. Muñoz wrote in his journal: 'I was afraid to look out at the bay from the Caserio de Filipinas because they warned me that from the City they had seen me with glasses, and I wanted them to forget even my name'. During the revolution the 'Caserio' was used for military purposes. National Image Archives-SODRE

Seventy years have passed since Ildefonso Pereda Valdés, one of the pioneers of research on the African roots of Uruguayan culture, first promoted awareness about this place, outlining the possible location.[74] Further historical and archaeological research is necessary to find out the exact location of the Caserío de los Negros facilities, Montevideo's role in the River Plate slave trade, the connec-

---

74 Pereda Valdés (1941), 33, locates the 'Caserío de los Negros' on República Francesa street and Rambla Sudamérica, in the Capurro district of Montevideo.

Caserío de los Negros.

Memorial monolith in the public space of the same name, located in the Capurro neighbourhood, Senzala Square, south of the intersection of the streets Solis Grande and Coraceros.

Photograph by Ana Frega.

tions between Brazil and Buenos Aires and other regions of the present States of Argentina, Bolivia and Peru, as well as the various shipping activities to and from the 'Caserío' associated with the site where slaves were disembarked, maintained, supervised, buried and auctioned, among other things. In recent years there has been some progress, but this is not sufficient. One site – located on the grounds of the distillery of the State-owned company that produces petroleum, alcoholic beverages and Portland cement, 'ANCAP', was declared a national historic landmark in 2007. At another, in the school 'Escuela No. 47 Capurro' and its park, a pilot project is being developed linking the public school with the University of the Republic for research contributing 'to the recognition of the impact of cultural diversity and minorities in the historical development of Uruguayan society'.[75] Likewise, on 15 May 2006, following action by several Afro-descendant associations and similar groups, the Municipality of Montevideo designated the 'Caserío de los Negros' an open space located in the neighbourhood of the two aforementioned sites, and inaugurated it on 2 December 2006, on the eve of the first National Day of Candombe, Afro-Uruguayan Cultural and Racial Equity.

75 ANEP. Council of Early and Primary Education. Official Letter No. 145 of 18 August 2009.

Much remains to be done. This is what the French historian Jacques Revel called 'a duty to history'. Memory demands an evocation, which often pertains to objects rather than relationships. It is not a place to come to but one from which to depart in an eventful journey that leads to giving meaning to those objects and revealing their meanings. One of the historian's tasks, indeed, is to explore those relationships, inviting reflection on a time and place and on an understanding of memory that must be studied.

BIBLIOGRAPHY

Abella, Gonzalo, 1999. *Artigas. El resplandor desconocido*. Montevideo: Ediciones Betum San.

Achugar, Hugo; Caetano, Gerardo, comp., 1992. *Identidad uruguaya: ¿mito, crisis o afirmación?* Montevideo: Trilce.

Alfaro, Milita, 2008. *Medio mundo, sur, conventillo y después*. Montevideo: Medio&Medio.

Andrews, George Reid, 1980. *The Afro-Argentines of Buenos Aires 1800–1900*. Wisconsin: University of Wisconsin Press.

Andrews, George Reid, 2010. *Blackness in the White Nation: A History of Afro-Uruguay, 1830–2010*. Chapel Hill, NC: University of North Carolina Press.

Ántola, Susana; Ponte, Cecilia, 2000. La nación en bronce, mármol y hormigón armado. In: Caetano, Gerardo (dir.), *Los uruguayos del Centenario. Nación, ciudadanía, religión y educación (1910–1930)*. Montevideo: Taurus, 219–243.

Ardao, María Julia, 1954. *Apuntaciones históricas sobre la Revolución Oriental (1811-1851) por Carlos Anaya*. Montevideo: Imprenta Nacional.

Ardao, María Julia; Capillas de Castellanos, Aurora, 1958. *Bibliografía de Artigas*. Montevideo: Comisión Nacional Archivo Artigas, vol. II.

Blanco Acevedo, Pablo, 1950. *El federalismo de Artigas y la independencia nacional*, 2nd ed. Montevideo, s.e.

Borucki, Alex; Chagas, Karla; Stalla, Natalia, 2009. *Esclavitud y trabajo. Un estudio sobre los afrodescendientes en la frontera uruguaya, 1835-1855*. Montevideo: Mastergraf. [1st ed. 2004].

Borucki, Alex; Chagas, Karla; Stalla, Natalia, 2010. Sitios de memoria de la Ruta del Esclavo en Uruguay. Informe final. Montevidéo: Comisión del Patrimonio Cultural de la Nación, mimeo.

Bucheli, Marisa; Cabella, Wanda, 2010. El perfil demográfico y socioeconómico de la población uruguaya según su ascendencia racial. In: *Notas de población*, No 91, ECLAC, 161–200.

Caula, Nelson, 2004. *Artigas Ñemoñaré*. Montevideo: Rosebud, vol. 2.

Chagas, Karla, 2007. La lucha por sus derechos y contra la discriminación. In: *Culturas afrouruguayas*. Montevideo: Comisión del Patrimonio Cultural de la Nación, 9–10. (Brochure published for Heritage Day, 6–7 October 2007)

[CNAA] Comisión Nacional Archivo Artigas, Archivo Artigas, Montevideo, Monteverde, (1953) Vol. IV; (1987) Vol. XXI; (1993) Vol. XXVII; Montevideo, Imprimex, (1998) Vol. XXXI; Montevideo, Iconoprint, (2000) Vol. XXXII; 2003), Vol. XXXIV; Montevideo, Tarma, (2006) Vol. XXXVI.

De María, Isidoro, 1860. *Vida del Brigadier General D. Jose Jervacio Artigas, fundador de la nacionalidad oriental*. Gualeguaychú: De María y Hermano.

Découd, H. F., 1930. *El campamento de Laurelty*. Montevideo: El Siglo Ilustrado.

Ferreiro, Felipe [1927]. Documentos oficiales. Informe del Dr ... sobre el Memorandum relativo a los antecedentes y gestiones para la comprobación y exhumación de los restos del Sargento Manuel Antonio Ledesma (a) Ansina, asistente y fiel compañero del General José Gervasio Artigas en su voluntario exilio. Con algunos apuntes de referencias respecto de sus últimos años en Guarambaré (Paraguay). In: *Revista del Instituto Histórico y Geográfico del Uruguay* [Montevideo], 5/2 (agosto), 731–52.

Frega, Ana, 2000. Caminos de libertad en tiempos de revolución. Los esclavos en la Provincia Oriental artiguista, 1815-1820. In: *História Unisinos* [San Leopoldo: Universidade do Vale do Río dos Sinos] 4/2 (julio–diciembre), 29–57.

Frega, Ana, 2010. La patria me hizo libre. Aproximación a la condición de los esclavos durante las guerras de independencia en la Banda Oriental. In: Mallo, Silvia C.; Telesca, Ignacio, ed., *'Negros de la Patria': Los afrodescendientes en las luchas por la independencia en el antiguo Virreinato del Río de la Plata*. Buenos Aires: SB, 171–86.

Frega, Ana, 2011. Sitios de memoria de la esclavitud en el Uruguay. In: Marisa Pineau, ed., *La Ruta del Esclavo en el Río de la Plata: Aportes para el diálogo intercultural*. Caseros: EDUNTREF, 389–98.

Frega, Ana; Borucki, Alex; Chagas, Karla; Stalla, Natalia, 2004. Esclavitud y abolición en el Río de la Plata en tiempos de revolución y república. In: *Memoria del Simposio La Ruta del esclavo en el Río de la Plata: su historia y sus consecuencias*. Montevideo: UNESCO, 115–47.

Frega, Ana; Chagas, Karla; Montaño, Oscar; Stalla, Natalia, 2008. Breve historia de los afrodescendientes en el Uruguay. In: Scuro, Lucía, coord., *Población afrodescendiente y desigualdades étnico-raciales en Uruguay*. Montevideo: UNDP, 93–102.

Gortázar, Alejandro, 2003. Del aullido a la escritura. In: Achugar, Hugo, comp., *Derechos de memoria. Nación e independencia en América Latina*. Montevideo: FHCE, 189–263.

Hammerly Dupuy, Daniel, 1951. Rasgos biográficos de Artigas en el Paraguay. In: Narancio, Edmundo, dir., Artigas, Montevideo, *El País* newspaper, 285–98.

Hammerly Dupuy, Daniel; Hammerly Peverini, Víctor, 1951. *Artigas en la poesía de América*. 2 vols. Buenos Aires: Noel.

Hobsbawm, Eric, 1998. *On History*. New York: The New Press Interdisciplinary Team 'Recovering the Memory of Ansina' (1996): Ansina me llaman y Ansina yo soy. Montevideo: Rosebud.

Islas, Ariadna; Frega, Ana, 2007. Identidades uruguayas: del mito de la sociedad homogénea al reconocimiento de la pluralidad. in AA. VV., *Historia del Uruguay en el siglo XX (1890–2004)*. Montevideo: Ediciones de la Banda Oriental, 359–91.

Leone, Verónica, 2000. Manuales escolares e imaginario social en el Uruguay del Centenario. In: Caetano, Gerardo, dir., *Los uruguayos del Centenario...* op. cit., 139–215.

Montaño, Óscar, 1997. *Umkhonto: Historia del aporte negro-africano en la formación del Uruguay*. Montevideo: Rosebud.

Nin Y Silva, Celedonio, 1930. *La República Oriental del Uruguay en su primer centenario, 1830–1930*. Montevideo: Sureda.

Pereda Valdés, Ildefonso, 1941. *Negros esclavos y negros libres. Esquema de una sociedad esclavista y aporte del negro en nuestra formación nacional*. Montevideo: s.e.

Pereda Valdés, Ildefonso, 1964. *El negro en la epopeya artiguista*. Montevideo: Barreiro y Ramos.

Petillo, Mario, 1956. *El último soldado artiguista Manuel Antonio Ledesma (Ansina)*. Montevideo: Centro Militar. [1st ed. 1936].

Porzecanski, Teresa, 1992. Uruguay a fines del siglo XX: mitologías de ausencia y de presencia. In: Achugar; *Caetano*, op. cit., 49–61.

República Oriental del Uruguay. Comisión Nacional de Centenario. 1830-1930, *Memoria de los trabajos realizados*. Montevideo: Impresora Uruguaya, s.f.

Revel, Jacques, 2005. *Un momento historiográfico: Trece ensayos de historia social*. Buenos Aires: Manantial.

Rodríguez, Romero, 2006. *Mbundo Malungo a Mundele*. Montevideo: Ediciones Rosebud.

Saint-Hilaire, Auguste de, 2005. *Al sur del Brasil, al norte del Río de la Plata*. Montevideo: UdelaR/AUGM. [1st ed. in French, 1887]

Slavery in Mauritius

Between History and Memory

Vijaya Teelock and Jayshree Mungur-Medhi

BIOGRAPHIES

Vijaya Teelock teaches Mauritian and Indian Ocean history at the University of Mauritius. Her research interests include eighteenth- and nineteenth-century Mauritian slavery and the situation of descendants of the enslaved and indentured in Mauritius.

Jayshree Mungur-Medhi is an archaeologist and expert in heritage management. She has undertaken several archaeological and heritage projects and worked on the nomination dossiers of Aapravasi Ghat, Le Morne, and Rani ki Vav (World Heritage Properties [(WHP]) and on the listing of International Cultural Heritage (ICH) elements on UNESCO's lists.

ABSTRACT

In this paper, the authors trace the evolution of the study of Mauritian slavery over the past thirty years and the circumstances that have favoured or hindered the emergence of a local historiography of slavery and the preservation of sites associated with slavery.

The study of the history of slavery in Mauritius is only some thirty years old, begun when taboos about speaking openly about the history of slavery began to be broken. Although poets and writers had written about Mauritian African origins in their works previously, none had openly broached the subject of slavery. Today, few can deny that huge advances have been made since then. Apart from a wealth of history books, research on heritage sites related to slavery has led to their becoming national and international heritage sites. A public holiday was declared for 1 February of every year to commemorate the abolition of slavery. State institutions have been created to research and promote the study of history and the memory of slavery. A Truth and Justice Commission was established in 2009 to study the consequences of slavery. Its report was published in 2011.

There has, however, been a counter-reaction to this, which deserves to be studied further. While research on slavery and discussing slavery-related issues in open forums has brought about a certain confidence and pride among descendants of enslaved persons, one is also facing, in Mauritius today, a 'revisionist' trend by those who wish to reduce the visibility of the history of slavery in public spaces, in institutions and in education. This shows us more than ever that the battle to ensure that the history of slavery is not forgotten in Mauritius is a continuous one and must never cease. This chapter will examine the history of the emergence of a Mauritian historiography of slavery and the debates surrounding the preservation of slave heritage sites.

The years 1985 and 2015 represent two seminal years in the study of the history and memory of slavery, because in these two years, two very different types of conferences on slavery were held in Mauritius. These conferences and the period in between represent the journey that Mauritius has travelled in its conceptualisation and writing of the history of slavery and how Mauritians choose to remember and study it.

The very first international conference on slavery was held in 1985 in Mauritius at the Mahatma Gandhi Institute (MGI), an educational and research institution. It was conducted using a 'traditional' conference format. The year 2015 witnessed another international seminar on slavery, using a very different approach. Unlike the 1985 conference, people from all walks of life were brought together to listen to one another and to discuss the history of slavery and its consequences. Scholars of slavery and members of the public were encouraged to interact and to engage in joint reflection on the history of slavery. According to most observers and participants, it was a unique event.

In terms of the profile of attendees, the content and format of research papers, and the type and quality of interaction, the two conferences could not have been further apart. Without the 1985 conference, however, the stimulus for further research would have been far less. Comparison of the two is important as it helps us to understand the evolution of Mauritian society over three decades and the very important advances made in our understanding not only of the history of slavery but of how, in a post-slavery society, one can approach and conceptualise the history of slavery in ways that are quite different from how the history of slavery is seen and studied in countries that have engaged in and benefited from colonial slave trade and slavery. In other words, the history of slavery seen from the colonised or the enslaved countries' view requires a different conceptual and methodological approach.

The 1985 conference represented a 'watershed' moment and took some courage on the part of those who decided on this conference. The local context of research in the 1980s needs to be understood: slavery was a taboo subject, not to be talked about openly for fear of offending the Franco-Mauritian elite. In the early 1980s, the pioneers of this move to break the taboo on slavery included historians and intellectuals such as Jocelyn Chan Low, Sadasivam Reddi, Sateean and Peerthum, Muslim Jumeer, the Michel brothers, and countless artists and literary figures (the list is too long to name each individually). They popularised Mauritian history, wrote 'history from below', and introduced non-European heroes in Mauritian history; this, in order to create a better self-image for the population of Asian and African ancestry. This post-independence movement represented the attempt to democratise the writing of Mauritian history and the entrance of 'non-elite' groups into the scholarly world.

Nevertheless, despite this, in the 1980s the history of slavery was still marginalised in Mauritian historiography. Apart from the compilation of conference papers undertaken by the MGI,[1] activities and research on slavery were not publicly funded. Historians of slavery in Mauritius published in newspapers such as *5-plus* and *Le Militant*.

At that time, it was not easy to break the 'deafening silence' or 'l'histoire du silence'[2] concerning slavery in Mauritius. Attempts to undertake fieldwork on local history were met with many refusals on the part of descendants of slaves to speak about their lives and those of their grandparents. Many expressed fear that the 'burzwa'[3] would get angry. Overseas scholars, however, maintained a steady flow of research and publications. The contrast was great, as many researchers suffered from the insularity of Mauritius at this time, and the lack of interaction with outside scholars and the lack of access to books and other resources led to methodological and conceptual weaknesses in their works. Favoured themes were related to the resistance demonstrated by slaves and – in particular, maroonage.

In addition to these scholarly beginnings in Mauritius, there were also intellectuals, activists and priests attempting to promote some kind of recognition of the population descended from slavery. The Michel brothers attempted to raise 'black consciousness' and highlighted the acute problems faced by descendants of slaves.[4] At that time, the term 'Creole' to describe the population of African or slave ancestry was not used much and was even frowned upon. Gaëtan Benoit spoke of 'Afro-Mauritians' in his book (also published by the MGI).[5]

By this time, the African Cultural Centre (now the Nelson Mandela Centre for African Culture [NMCAC]) funded by the government, had opened in a modest building in Bell Village, a suburb of Port Louis, the capital, and begun the publication and collection of various aspects of African and Creole culture under the direction of Colette Le Chartier, at that time in charge of the library and docu-

---

1 U. Bissoondoyal and S. B. C. Servansing, (eds.), *Slavery in South West Indian Ocean* (Moka, 1989).

2 Gerbeau Hubert, *Les Esclaves Noirs. Pour une histoire du silence* (Paris, 1970).

3 From the French 'bourgeois'. In the Mauritian context, their employer.

4 See L. Sylvio Michel, *L'Organisation fraternelle: noir sur blanc* (Port Louis: Swan Printing, 1998).

5 Gaëtan Benoit, *The Afro-Mauritians: An essay* (Moka: MGI Press, 1985).

mentation.[6] Literary output began to increase and was focused on contemporary themes.

The 1990s were very rich in the production of publications on slavery, beginning with Karl Noel's *L'esclavage à l'ile de France*,[7] which was based on his 1958 PhD thesis. His main thesis was that slavery in Mauritius was 'mild' compared to Caribbean slavery. He used as evidence the many laws enacted to 'protect' slaves. However, the fact that these laws were enacted to protect property that included slaves seemed immaterial. The rich archival material of the Mauritius National Archives do not seem to have been used much. Bitter Sugar[8] focused on slavery and sugar expansion in the nineteenth century and attempted to counter the thesis of the 'mildness' of Mauritian slavery by showing how under sugar expansion, slavery was anything but mild, even with British attempts at amelioration. In those years, the author was repeatedly told that 'nobody will ever publish this in Mauritius'. The MGI, however, which must be given full credit, was brave enough to publish, and the book was launched by no less a figure than the prime minister in 1998. Maroonage continued to be the favourite topic of Mauritian scholars: Jocelyn Chan Low published a series of articles, 'Récits de Marrons', in 1996 in the *5-Plus* newspaper, while Amédée Nagapen published *Le marronage à l'Isle de France-Ile Maurice*. Overseas, Anthony Barker published *Slavery and Anti-Slavery in Mauritius, 1820–1835*, and Richard Allen published his PhD as 'Slaves, Freedmen and Indentured Laborers in Colonial Mauritius', in which land ownership by ex-slaves, termed the 'petit morcellement', was brought into the limelight.[9]

The mid 1990s were interesting years as far as analysis of contemporary Mauritian society was concerned. The sense of 'Creoleness' sought for by the Michel brothers began to surface publicly. The term 'malaise creole' coined by Roger Cerveaux became the hot topic of the day, and scholars inside and outside Mauritius analysed its causes and possible remedies. The history of slavery was rewritten and reconceptualised to explain this malaise and the history of the Creole community. The exclusion of Creoles of African origin, particularly from many public institutions, and the continuation of discrimination against people of African origin were intensely debated (and continue to be) up to today.

In 1996, the African Cultural Centre embarked on a project entitled 'Origins of Slaves through a Study of Their Demographic and Spatial Movements 1815–1971', funded by the Mauritius Research Council (MRC). The aim was to at-

6 Marcel Didier, *Pages Africaines* (Bell Village: ACC, 1987).

7 Karl Noel, *L'esclavage à l'ile de France. Editions Two Cities* (Paris, 1991).

8 Vijaya Teelock, *Bitter Sugar: Sugar and Slavery in 19th Century Mauritius* (Moka: MGI, 1998).

9 Richard B. Allen, *Slaves, Freedmen and Indentured Laborers in Colonial Mauritius* (Cambridge: Cambridge University Press, 1999).

tempt to locate the geographic and cultural origins of Mauritian slaves through a study of registration returns, through historical research in Mozambique and Madagascar, and through attempting to retrace the family histories of descendants of ex-slaves. The project lasted about five years and resulted in several important outcomes: the first, related to the psychological impact on the descendants, who for years had been told that, as they had lost their original names and identities, their history could not be told. To counter this belief, data from three slave registration returns, those of 1823, 1826, and 1835, were collected and digitised. The registration returns showed that there was continuity in the names and that, for the slavery period at least, it was possible to reconstruct slaves' family histories. Five families were identified to form part of this team for family history research, and their histories all yielded different results. The most successful family histories compiled were those of the families of Joyce Fortune, Auguste Merite, and Nicole Papeche. Historically speaking, it represented a breakthrough because no one had thought it possible that a descendant in the later twentieth century could trace his or her ancestry as far back as 1826.

The research also showed how, although there had been intermarriage with other communities over the years, the same names were transmitted from generation to generation, making it easy to trace ancestry all the way back to 1826. The results of these findings were publicised in 1999 during an exhibition, and a publication emerged some years later, including a moving chapter by Joyce Fortune on her personal experience while tracing her family history.[10]

As stated earlier, many descendants had kept their original slave names, which allowed the Centre and the families concerned to compile their family histories. However, for many families, the search for family in the immediate post-emancipation period is the most challenging part, as there was much internal migration within Mauritius, and it is indeed painstaking work to keep track of the movements of families at this time. Detailed archival searches are required, but it is not an impossible task.

During the course of the Origins Project, the slave registration returns unintentionally attracted attention from non-governmental organisations (NGOs) and soon became a focal point for demands by some political parties, such as that of Sylvio Michel, in their long-standing claim for reparations and compensation. By demonstrating that the slave registration returns had been successful in helping descendants trace their slave ancestry, the politicians argued that as it was now possible to identify slave descendants by name, there was no longer any barrier to giving compensation. The staff of the Centre became inundated with requests for searches, and it became an activity that fully absorbed the working days of the

10 Vijaya Teelock and Edward Alpers (eds.), *History Memory Identity* (NMCAC, 2000).

staff of the Centre for several years. The Origins Project was continued by the Centre at its own cost long after the MRC funding had run out.

The impact of this project is still being felt. The Truth and Justice Commission recommended that a Genealogy Institute be created to facilitate family history research, a recommendation that still awaits materialisation. It is also important to tap archival sources on the French period in France, Portugal, Mozambique and India. However, it is unfortunate that sufficient funding has not yet been received to continue the compilation of demographic information about slaves.

Furthermore, the project showed the necessity of including oral history in historical research in Mauritius. It is a sad fact that there were many illiterate Mauritians who did not realise the importance of the documents in their possession. Today, their memories can supplement our knowledge of Mauritian history.

In addition to this, compiling the family history of descendants of slaves is particularly revealing for Mauritian history as there is a huge gap in our understanding of what happened to the ex-slaves after abolition. Family histories are today slowly allowing us to piece together the history and movements of ex-slaves in post-emancipation Mauritius.

Two further conferences were held, one in 1998 at the Municipality of Port Louis driven by Jocelyn Chan Low,[11] and one in 1999 at the MGI to commemorate the 160th Anniversary of the End of Apprenticeship. They were similar in that both tried to understand the experiences of the ex-slave population and their descendants after the abolition of slavery, as up to then, historical studies had focused on the period of slavery. The views expressed in these conferences were very varied. In contrast to the 1985 conference, which consisted only of academic papers read and discussed among scholars, the wave of memorialisation activities and dynamic leadership within the Creole population led to the 1998 and 1999 conferences being forums for active and creative discussion complementing the academic papers.

The riots of 1999 which occurred following the death of the well-known Mauritian singer Kaya (of African descent) added fuel to the heated debates. The division between the academic interests of overseas scholars and local events was intensely felt. The 1999 conference at the MGI also raised one important issue – that of land ownership and the dispossession of ex-slaves and their descendants. Papers by Joyce Fortune and Allan Charlot highlighted the numerous examples of land ownership by ex-slaves and their subsequent dispossession.

The twenty-first century brought new avenues of research for the study of history. Oral history and archaeology became increasingly used. The Maroon Slave Archaeological Investigation,[12] commissioned by the National Heritage Fund in

11 J. C. Cangy, J. Chan Low, and M. Paroomal (dir.), *L'esclavage et ses séquelles, mémoire et vécu d'hier et d'aujourd'hui* (University of Mauritius, 2002).

12 University of Mauritius 2002–2003. MSAIP Final Report.

the year 2002–2003 and undertaken by a team from University of Mauritius, opened up new avenues for research on slavery. Several sites, including caves and rock shelters used as refuges by runaway slaves, were surveyed, and three of them were extensively studied with excavations. It added a new paradigm to the concept of the enslaved, from that of 'victim' to 'hero' of resistance. No one could claim from then on that there was no tangible heritage emanating from the enslaved.

The discovery of caves and overhangs on Le Morne gave further impetus to the consideration of this mountain as a symbol of resistance and fight for freedom. With the Government of Mauritius wishing to inscribe Le Morne Brabant Mountain as a Maroon site on the World Heritage Site list, a large number of works relating to maroonage and other forms of resistance were published and republished.[13] New projects exploring the different facets of Le Morne's rich history were undertaken, such as an Archaeological Survey of the Slave Cemetery and another at a camp settled by descendants at Makak.[14]

In 2006, the official annual commemoration of the abolition of slavery in Mauritius, held since 1985 in another location, was shifted to Le Morne, which by now had become an iconic site in the eyes of the world. The commemoration did not consist solely of a mere official ceremony, but became an occasion to bring the masses together, an opportunity not missed by political leaders. The site became more than a symbol of resistance or commemoration of the abolition of slavery, but also a symbol for people of African descent in Mauritius. In order to remind Mauritians that enslaved persons were not only brought from Africa, a Slave Route park was inaugurated, containing sculptures representing the different regions and countries from which persons had been enslaved and brought to Mauritius.

Creole intellectuals focused their studies on contemporary Creole identity, on exclusion, on citizenship and on the role of the Church in slavery and on Creoles' present status. They initiated a campaign to have the Creole language accepted at the national level. As far as historical research was concerned, Pier Larson came out with a ground-breaking study of the Malagasy origins of Mauritian slaves. Richard Allen added to the debate regarding how many slaves had been brought into the Mascarenes after the legal abolition of the slave trade by suggesting that the number was not as high as estimated by Larson. Scholars in Mauritius became involved in memorialisation activities.

In 2008, UNESCO funded an Inventory of Slave Sites for Mauritius, and a multidisciplinary team[15] at the University of Mauritius listed some eighty sites relat-

---

13 Vijaya Teelock (ed.), *Maroonage and the Maroon Heritage in Mauritius* (Réduit: University of Mauritius Press, 2005).

14 J. Mungur-Medhi, *Archaeological Survey of Macaque* (LMCL, 2007 and 2017).

15 UNESCO/University of Mauritius, *Inventory of Slave Sites in the Republic of Mauritius*, 2008.

ing to slavery. New geographical areas were explored: the slave histories of the outer islands of Rodrigues, Chagos, and Agalega were begun. Joel Edouard was the first Rodriguan to write on Rodriguan slavery. New avenues in the study of the slave trade were explored by Richard Allen, regarding trade in children and in Indian slaves to Mauritius. Pritilah Rosunee examined female manumission in the Revolutionary period. Megan Vaughan brought out the first postmodernist history of slavery in Mauritius under French rule using court records.

Between 2009 and 2011, the research undertaken by the Truth and Justice Commission was possibly the most massive research undertaking to date, employing over fifty researchers and research assistants for two years. Some pioneering research work was achieved by those researchers but little of that research has been disseminated or has found its way into history textbooks for schools. Excavation of the Old Cemetery, also known as Slave Cemetery at Le Morne, was another added dimension to research on slavery. This was the first time that a cemetery composed of people of African and Malagasy descent had been found. Osteological analysis of eleven of the skeletons confirmed the poor state of health of this population and the fact that they had started hard physical labour at a very young age.

Oral history, oral tradition, ethnography, archaeology and the study of all non-textual forms of information have been shown to be necessary parts of any historical methodology of slavery, complementing and sometimes supplanting archival research. The wish of Hubert Gerbeau in the 1970s that scholars use non-textual methodologies to study the history of slavery and of descendants is only today beginning to emerge in Mauritius. Many scholars are producing pioneering work, and this will no doubt continue to lead us to a better understanding of contemporary manifestations of the slave legacy.

Heritage has become another site of contestation and of 'cultural competition', where parallel and often conflicting histories, based on ethno-religious background, regularly occur. The attempt to 'insert' slavery into Mauritian historiography or Mauritian heritage has not been without opposition. An examination of the National Heritage list reveals that until the listing of Le Morne as a National Heritage site, most sites listed 'belonged' to the Franco-Mauritian and British elites and consisted mainly of tombs and monuments. Indeed, until 2000, only monuments were considered heritage.[16]

Among the many examples of 'contested' heritage is that relating to the presence of the statue of Adrien d'Epinay, a nineteenth-century public figure known for his active pro-slavery stance. An attempt to place a plaque next to the statue portraying an alternative version of the history of d'Epinay ended by its being removed by the National Heritage Fund on the grounds that it was 'defacing' a national her-

16 Ancient Monument Act of 1985.

itage monument. There was no questioning in this institution whether the statue of a public figure such as d'Epinay's should have remained.

Despite Le Morne Cultural Landscape being a World Heritage Site and Mauritius being the first country to introduce a site with a strong symbol of resistance to slavery to the list, within Mauritius, only five National Heritage sites relate to slavery: the Monument Commemorating the 141st Anniversary of the Abolition of Slavery in Mauritius, located in Port Louis and listed in 1978; a slave cemetery at Pamplemousses, listed in 1999; the Monument des Esclaves in Mahébourg in 2005 (though unveiled in 1985); Le Morne Brabant, listed in 2006; and the Old Cemetery at Le Morne, listed in 2016.

The case of the Bassin des Esclaves demonstrates the continued unwillingness of elites to list sites relating to slavery and has led to some strange twists of historical interpretation. Alain Mathieu, president of the Société de l'Histoire de l'Ile Maurice chose to write in a Catholic newspaper in response to another newspaper article on the listing of the Bassin as a National Heritage site. He stated that there had been an erroneous interpretation of sources and that there had never been a water structure for slaves in the centre of the village – thus, demands for the structure to be listed could not be entertained.[17] Up to the time of writing, the Bassin is still not National Heritage.

On the positive side, growing consciousness among the Mauritian public about the preservation of peoples' heritage and identity, combined with pioneering research, is slowly taking over this fear of elites and leading to increased demands for the heritage dating from the period of slavery to be recognised. While no further listing as National Heritage has occurred despite the voluminous existing research on heritage sites, further listings on the Intangible Heritage list have taken place: the Mauritian and Rodriguan traditional music and dance, the Sega Tipik (2016) and Sega Tambour (2017), both emanating from slavery, are now on UNESCO's List of Intangible Cultural Heritage. There is an increasing number of potential sites awaiting listing as National Heritage. The project of establishing an Intercontinental Slavery Museum, a strong recommendation of the Truth and Justice Commission and seen as a reparatory measure for descendants of the enslaved, will hopefully soon materialise. These events have had an important psychological impact on slave descendants and on the Mauritian population in general. It has given a certain pride to the descendants, who are no longer ashamed to claim their slave ancestry.

---

17 Iain Mathieu, 'Nous voudrions attirer l'attention', *La Vie Catholique*.

BIBLIOGRAPHY

Allen, R. B., 2006. Carrying Away the Unfortunate: The Exportation of Slaves from India during the Late Eighteenth Century. In: Jacques Weber, ed., *Le monde créole: Peuplement, sociétés et condition humaine, XVIIe-XXe siècles*. Paris: Les Indes savantes, 285–98l.

Allen, R. B., 2001. A traffic repugnant to humanity: children, the Mascarene slave trade, and British abolitionism. *Slavery and Abolition* 27, 219–36.

Allen, R. B., 1983. Licentious and unbridled proceedings: the illegal slave trade to Mauritius and the Seychelles during the early nineteenth century. *Journal of African History* 42, 91–116.

Appleby, J., Seetah, T. K., Calaon, D., Čaval, S., Pluskowski, A., Lafleur, J.-F., Janoo, A., and Teelock, V. 2012/2014. The Non-adult cohort from Le Morne Cemetery, Mauritius: a snapshot of early life and death after abolition. *International Journal of Osteoarchaeology* (22 June): DOI: 10.1002/oa.2259.

Asgarally, Issa, 1989. Les revoltes d'esclaves dans les Mascareignes ou 'l'histoire du silence', in U. Bissoondoyal and S. B. C. Servansing, eds., *Slavery in South West Indian Ocean*. Moka, Mauritius: Mahatma Gandhi Institute Press, 176–88.

Boswell, R., 2006. *Le Malaise Créole: Ethnic Identity in Mauritius*. New York and Oxford: Berghahn Books.

Boswell, R., 2005. *Slavery, Blackness and Hybridity: Mauritius and the Malaise Creole*. London: Kegan Paul International.

Boswell, R. and Chan Low, Jocelyn, 2001. Entre malaise et rédemption : L'Eglise Catholique à l'île Maurice à l'aube du 21ème siécle. *Revue Historique des Mascareignes*, Vol 4.

Boswell, R. and Chan Low, Jocelyn, 2000. In the politics of the rainbow: Creoles and civil society in Mauritius. *Journal of Contemporary African Studies* 18, 277–94.

Chan Low, Jocelyn, 1996. Récits de marrons. *Hebdomadaire 5-Plus*, 31/03/96 – 22/09/96.

Chan Low, Jocelyn, 1998. Esclaves, Exclus et Citoyens. Colloque sur L'Esclavage. Mun. of Port Louis/University of Mauritius, September.

Edouard, Joel, 2005. A History of Slavery during the French period in Rodrigues. BA dissertation. Moka: University of Mauritius.

Gerbeau, Hubert, 1978. Des minorités mal-connues : Esclaves indiens et malais des Mascareignes. *Migrations, minorités et échanges en océan indien, XIXe-XXe siècle*, IHPOM Etudes et Documents No. 11 Aix-en-Provence, 160–242.

Harmon, Jimmy, 2017. *Heritage Language & Identity Construction: A Study of Kreol. Morisien La Tour Koenig*. Pointe aux Sables, Mauritius: NMCAC.

Larson, P. M., 2000. *History and Memory in the Age of Enslavement: Becoming Merina in Highland Madagascar, 1770–1822*. Portsmouth, NH: Heinemann.

MGI Conference 1999: Post-emancipation Mauritius 1839–1911. Includes papers by: Chan Low, Jocelyn, 'Roots, Rasta and Riots'; Fortune, Joyce, 'Possession and Dispossession – Case Studies of Afro-Mauritian Land Ownership in the 19th Century' (1999); Charlot, J. M., 'The New Race Order: The Case of Camp Marcelin'; Gayan, Soorya, and Gopauloo, Nagamah, 'Socio-Economic and Cultural Interaction between Ex-Apprentices and Indentured Labourers 1835–1851 Century'.

Mungur-Medhi, Jayshree, 2007, 2017. Archaeological Survey of Macaque. Commissioned by Le Morne Heritage Trust Fund.

Nagapen, Amédée, 1999. *Le marronage à l'Isle de France-Ile Maurice: Rêve ou riposte de l'esclave?* Port Louis: Centre Culturel Africain.

Rosunee, Pritilah, Manumissions in the Revolutionary Period 1794–1803. MA dissertation. Cape Town: University of Cape Town.

Vaughan, Megan, 2005. *Creating the Creole Island: Slavery in Eighteenth-Century Mauritius*. Durham, NC: Duke University Press.

African Roots of South Asians

Shihan de Silva Jayasuriya

BIOGRAPHY

Dr Shihan de Silva Jayasuriya, Senior Fellow, Institute of Commonwealth Studies, School of Advanced Study, University of London. (email: shihan.desilva@sas.ac.uk). His main research interests include Indian Ocean African migration and slavery; cultural memory; language maintenance and loss; and Afro-diasporic music. Recent publications include *African Migrants in Asia: Cultural Effects of Forced Migration* (New Jersey: Markus Wiener, 2008) and *The African Diaspora in Asian Trade Routes and Cultural Memories* (Lampeter, Wales, UK: Edwin Mellen Press, 2010).

ABSTRACT

This paper explores the historical links between Africa and South Asia, with particular reference to South Asians with African ancestry. The number of South Asians in this category is small in comparison to the total populations of these countries, but the numbers are significant and cannot be ignored. How do these communities fit in with the local societies? What has been their role? Issues of identity and belonging will be considered with specific reference to cultural loss and maintenance through language and music.

Introduction

My interest in South Asian communities with African ancestry began when I encountered the Afro-Sri Lankan community in Sirambiyadiya, a small village a few miles inland from Puttalam on the north-western coast. Puttalam is an important port city, and Ibn Batuta, the fourteenth century Moroccan traveller, entered the island from this point.

My research on the current status of Indo-Portuguese, a Creole language, which should have died out with the end of Portuguese rule in 1658, led me to this community. In this small Afro-Sri Lankan community, Indo-Portuguese (Sri Lanka Portuguese) still survives in the lyrics of their songs called manhas (de Silva Jayasuriya 2014a, 2014b). How had this lingua franca survived among people with

African ancestry? And what were the mechanisms which ensured that survival? (de Silva Jayasuriya 2012a, 2012b).

Most Sri Lankans are not aware of this small African community, though its grand matriarch, Ana Miselyia, and others were portrayed on Sri Lankan television in a documentary during the 1970s and there have been subsequent programmes in recent years. I learnt about their past from their own accounts of their history. Various oral histories had been handed down to them. They told me that their ancestors were brought from Mozambique, Madagascar, Goa and Portugal as slaves and soldiers by the Europeans who dominated the island for almost half a millennium. But there are more subtle and far-reaching reasons which have a bearing on their current position. To understand this we have to move beyond the shores of Sri Lanka.

Historian Joseph Harris (1996) reminds us that free and forced movement of Africans were simultaneous processes. But movement of Africans to South Asia was fuelled by the slave trade. Between AD 900 and AD 1900, an estimated 12.5 million Africans were moved across the Sahara, the Red Sea and the Indian Ocean to unfamiliar lands where they were re-rooted (Lovejoy 2000; Roberts 2006). The number of Africans involved is not different to that of the transatlantic slave trade which was concentrated over a few hundred years. But easterly movement was spread over a longer period of time and spanned a wider geographical area.

Movement of Africans eastwards covers a wider economic and social range of activities than Atlantic slavery. It has deeper roots and is complicated by European intervention in Indian Ocean trade. It is complemented by the parallel process of free labour movement and by the rise of slaves, however few, occupying administrative, military, religious and political roles. But this model does not help us account for the legacy and significance of slavery as the migrants lwere assimilated into new societies. The otherwise silent African presence is alive in music and dance.

How do we approach the study of slavery in the East? Does this process help us understand the fate and status of those of African descent in contemporary Asian societies? Is it important to recognise the African presence in South Asia?

The Indian Ocean slave trade involving concubines, eunuchs, soldiers and servants was not confined to a plantation economy. It was also complicated by European commercial expansion and by the free moment of African seafarers, sailors and merchants, which ran alongside and parallel to the slave trade. The trade in humans moved millions of Africans both overland and across the world's giant waterways. But we must not forget that free movement of African seafarers, sailors and merchants to Asia did not stop whilst the slave trade was continuing.

Asians are becoming more interested in their past as their countries are becoming economically powerful. But the historical picture is untidy and patchy, and there are gaps in our knowledge which we cannot fill. The long duration of easterly movement inevitably led to several streams of migration involving various points of origin and destination.

Why were Africans moved over vast distances, across land and sea, to South Asia? Their presence has left little trace in historical documents. But Africans are conspicuous in some of the roles that they performed, even whether anonymously as soldiers, jockeys, musicians, entertainers, sailors, servants, palace guards, body-guards or cooks.

Migration of Africans to Asia has been a continuous process over the centuries. But why is this not widely known? The obvious reason is that slaves are marginal people. Although Afro-Asians live in urban areas, they are lost in the diversity of South Asia's cosmopolitan cities. They are often taken for African tourists until they begin to speak in the local Asian language!

Compared to the population of 1.2 billion in contemporary India, the estimated 60,000 Sidis may seem small. The statistics that we have are patchy and represent 25,000 Sidis each in the states of Gujarat and Karnataka, about 10,000 in Andhra Pradesh, and smaller numbers in other states such as Maharashtra, Uttar Pradesh and Madhya Pradesh (de Silva Jayasuriya 2012c, 2015).

Identifying Africans poses a challenge to scholars (de Silva Jayasuriya 2006). Terms such as 'Africa' and 'Africans' are problematic. Those whom we call Africans today were associated with the area that they originated from, for ex-ample, Zanj or al Habashat, and were called Zanzibaris or Habshis. At other times, their religious affiliation gave them an ethnic label. Cafre (non-believers) became an ethnonym for Africans, a name which Arabs called non-Muslims. Another Ara-bic word, Sidi or Shidee, has become the most commonly used ethnonym in the subcontinent. But Africans are also known by other terms such as Makranis (in Pakistan), Chaush (in Andhra Pradesh) and Baburu (in the Maldives) in South Asia, which associate them with a geographical location or a role they played.

Africans in the Military

From various travel accounts, we get an insight about the occupational role Africans have played. When Ibn Batuta sailed down the south-west coast of India in the early fourteenth century, his ship had 'fifty Abyssinian men-at-arms'. They were the guarantors of safety in the Indian Ocean, and if there was one Abyssin-ian on a ship, it was avoided by Indian pirates and idolaters (Gibb 1929/1986, 229–230). In Calicut (South India), Batuta noted that the owner of the Chinese junk that he embarked on also had Abyssinian guards – carrying javelins, swords, drums, trumpets and bugles – who stood with their lances on both sides of the door.

Africans were prominent in several parts of India. Ibn Batuta, referred to the governor of Alahapur, Badr, an Abyssinian and a former slave of the Rajah of

Dholpur (Baptiste, McLeod & Robbins 2006, 127). About a hundred years later, the ruler of Bengal, Sultan Rukn al-Din Barbak Shah (1460–1481), had 8,000 African slaves, some of whom he elevated to higher ranks. When Barbak Shah's grandson, Sikander II, was deposed in 1481, after ruling for only a few months, his successor, Jalal-ud-din Fath Shah (1481–1486), attempted to control the power of the Habshis. In 1486, however, under the leadership of the chief eunuch, Sultan Shahzada, the Habshis conspired and murdered Fath Shah, and gained the throne of Bengal (Pankhurst 2003). But this was not a united Habshi rule. Indil Khan, a Habshi commander-in-chief, avenged his master's death by murdering Shahzada. Indil Khan then ascended the throne as Saif-ud-Firuz, mainly due to pressure exerted by Jalal-ud-din's widow and the courtiers of Gaur (the capital of Bengal).

Off the west coast of India near Mumbai, the island of Janjira was a trading post for Africans long before it became their power base from the early seventeenth century. From 1618, for three and a half centuries, Janjira was a princely state ruled by Africans. Its geographical boundaries extended to the western coast of India and were not confined to the island. From 1791, Africans also ruled another state, Sachin, which is in today's Gujarat (McLeod 2006). A year after India's independence, in 1948, both these states together with other princely states became part of the Indian Union. But ex-royal Africans still live in India and are well respected locally.

Elite military slavery, though not unique to Africans or South Asia, paved the way for some slaves to reach high positions and wield much power. Faaeza Jasdanwalla, a granddaughter of the last Nawab of Janjira, discusses the process by which the Sidi Sardars (African Chiefs) appointed a new leader based on a system of merit, aptitude and capability, and were not constrained by social rank and hereditary links (de Silva Jayasuriya 2011a). But as Faaeza Jasdanwalla (2011, 56) emphasises, this democratic system which enabled a high degree of social mobility was replaced by hereditary succession a century before India regained her independence.

A few Sidis have been able to reach the echelons of power and engage with India's elite. The best-known is Malik Ambar, a freeborn Ethiopian, sold to slavery by his parents. As an elite military slave, Ambar was purchased by the Peshwa (prime minister) of Ahmednagar, Cengiz Khan, himself a Habshi and a former elite slave (Sakar 1955, 6). Through military and strategic capabilities, Ambar himself became the Peshwar of Ahmednagar and held on to that office for more than a quarter of a century (1600–1626) until his death. He appointed sultans of his choice, from the Nizam Shahi dynasty, who were merely figureheads. Ambar built waterways, mosques, palaces, tombs and schools. His tomb in Ahmedabad (in today's state of Maharashtra) is testimony to the respect that he commanded.

But not all African soldiers were elite slaves. Many South Asian rulers engaged African soldiers in their armies. In Andhra Pradesh, Sidis from the disbanded African Cavalry Guard of the Nizam of Hyderabad, are nostalgic for their lost past; Indians respected them when they accompanied the Nizam on his parades. But a year after India's independence, when the princely states were absorbed into the new India, these Sidis (also called Chaush) lost their important role. Impoverished, they now live in an area called AC (African Cavalry) guards (Minda 2007).

The story is similarly bleak in Uttar Pradesh, where descendants of the Nawab of Oudh's African Bodyguard and Cavalry Guards live on the poverty line. During the Indian Mutiny in 1857, ancestors of these Sidis fought bravely and loyally for the Nawab (Llewellyn-Jones 2011). Perhaps somewhat surprisingly, the Nawab had a female bodyguard and the British were not aware that they were fighting women soldiers until their dead bodies were found in the Sikander Bagh in Lucknow, the site of a fierce battle between Indians and the British which marked the turning point of British presence in the subcontinent.

It is clear that Islamic rulers valued African military skills. Whilst this demand was supplied from Ethiopia, Tanzania and Zanzibar, for example, another network operated with different sources of supply. Expansion of European commerce, international trade and territorial gain was an impetus for African movement to South Asia.

The need to defend territories from invading forces also was a contributing factor. Intra-Asian activities in the Indian Ocean were interrupted from the sixteenth century on by Europeans, who were establishing themselves at various coastal entrepôts. The Portuguese, who had begun exercising political and economic control over parts of India, particularly on the Konkan coast, transported East African slaves to India from about 1530 to 1740. Sayf al-Mulk Miftah, the governor of Daman during the Portuguese occupation in 1530, was a Habshi chief whose force included 4,000 Habshis. In the 1730s, Indian Gujarati merchants on Mozambique Island owned a small number of slaves, and a few were shipped to the Portuguese enclaves of Diu and Daman (Machado 2004).

Cultural Survivals

Whilst we are not able to paint a comprehensive picture of African migration eastwards due to its antiquity and the lack of historical records, from travel accounts we get an idea of the tasks that Africans performed and the languages they spoke. From the ethnographic writings of Sir Richard Burton (1992) in the Sindh, we get an idea of how and why incoming Africans tried to maintain their own language. Migrants were not necessarily a homogeneous group even if they originated from a single point in Africa. A lingua franca, such as KiSwahili or

Indo-Portuguese, would have served as the bridging tongue (de Silva Jayasuriya 2011b).

Shidees born locally attempted to speak to the incoming slaves in an African language, which he did not identify or name. I was able to find KiSwahili equivalents to most of these words (de Silva Jayasuriya 2008). Perhaps this is not surprising, given that KiSwahili was a lingua franca in eastern Africa. KiSwahili would have served as a bridging tongue among a heterogeneous pool of African slaves. Once Africans became acculturated or assimilated, they spoke the local Asian language. Nowadays, Shidees speak Sindhi or Urdu, the local languages that they use on a daily basis. Similarly, in India, Sidis speak Gujarati, Marathi, Kannada, Konkani, Telugu, Hindi and Urdu. Changes in trading patterns affect the dynamics of language.

In the process of resettling and adapting to a new homeland, Africans have lost most of their traditions and customs. But music is the most vibrant cultural survival among the diaspora. Songs also encapsulate memories of lost homelands. Indo-Portuguese songs of Diu, for example, refer to the Mozambican territory – Inhambane, Sofala, Sena, Macua – and indicate from where Africans originated (Cardoso 2010, 107).

Similarly, in Sri Lanka, a genre of song called 'manha' differentiates those of African descent from other ethnic groups. Indo-Portuguese lyrics of manhas remind us how African migrants themselves were transformed in the process of resettling. Today, Indo-Portuguese is an endangered language, and the lyrics of manhas encapsulate the vestiges of a once widely spoken creolised form of Portuguese.

Muslim Sidis consider themselves talented singers, since Bilal, a freed African slave, had been selected by Prophet Muhammed to be the first reciter of azan (the call to prayer). Some Sidis have found a role as spiritual healers (Basu 2003). Shrines of African Sufi saints are frequented by Hindus, Christians, Zoroastrians and Muslims alike. Devotees are not concerned with the ethnicity of the Saints or the spirit mediums through whom they simply expect to fulfil their desires or cure their illnesses. As Beheroze Shroff (2007, 305) points out, Sidis who work as caretakers of shrines in Mumbai are accorded dignity and status by the Muslim, Hindu and Zoroastrian communities.

Their sacred music revolves around their ancestral saint, Bava Gor, believed to have been an Abyssinian, who came to India several centuries ago around the thirteenth century. Whilst maintaining their traditional role as fakirs (religious mendicants), Sidi Goma, a group of Sidis from Gujarat, have brought their music and dance to the world stage (Catlin-Jairazhabhoy 2006). Their performance, called goma (a Swahili word ngoma, which means 'drum' and also 'dance') or dhamal (in Gujarati), has been performed for audiences in Europe, America, Africa and

Asia. Public performances have become an arena for embodying identity through music and dance (Catlin-Jairazabhoy 2006, 19).

With their bodies painted and dressed in animal skins and peacock headgear, the Sidi Goma perform a sacred traditional dance to the rhythm of the dhamal (small drum), madido (big drum), mugarman (footed drum), mai mishra (coconut rattle), nafir (conch trumpet), malunga (braced musical bow) and other musical instruments. Urs (the death of a Muslim saint), celebrated over several days, provide an occasion for dhamal, off the stage. In the noble courts, Sidi servants danced ngoma to the rhythms of drums, rattles and shells on special occasions, such as birthdays and weddings, to entertain the guests.

A significant number of Pakistanis are of African descent. Given the strategic importance of the Makran coast in Balochistan, which was on the trade route to and from Africa, Arabia, Central Asia and South Asia, it is not surprising that African slaves also travelled on this route. As early as the third century, Omani Arabs settled on the Makran coast, becoming important slave dealers and middlemen, and feeding the South Asian demand. Toponyms, such as Mombasa Street and Sheedi Village Road in Karachi, consolidate the African connection with Pakistan (Badalkhan 2006).

In northern Karachi, Fatima Bhutto (2010) describes the shrine that the Shidees protect and serve. Ancestors of the Shidees settled down on the coast of Balochistan and the shores of the Sindh from the early seventh century onwards. Their roots are believed to go back to Ethiopia, Tanzania, Kenya and Zanzibar. An annual event celebrated by the small Shidees, devotees of the Sufi saint Baba Mango Pir, attracts other ethnic groups. Girls offer specially prepared food to the crocodiles in the pond outside the shrine (http://karachi.g2gm.com/crocodiles-festival.htm). Lyrics of the songs that accompany the drumbeats are, according to the Shidees, a mixture of Swahili and Baluchi.

Musical traditions of the Shidees are closely related to maritime activities and seafaring. Makran-Baloch maritime contacts with the eastern and north-eastern African coasts lasted until the first half of the twentieth century. Sailors learnt Swahili songs when they were stationed in Zanzibar and other East African ports. Elderly Shidee sailors recall how sailors from all parts of the Indian Ocean joined the drumming and dancing sessions when they were stationed in African coastal towns (Badalkhan 2006).

Musical traditions reveal the extent of acculturation and sociocultural transformation that was inevitable in the process of displacement, adaptation and resettlement. In Oman, Dieter Christensen, an ethnomusicologist, refers to the descendants of slaves who perform Lewa and play the musundu (African-type drums). The lyrics of their songs are in Swahili and Arabic, and they refer to East Africa and seafaring. According to Sabir Badalkhan, a Pakistani folklorist, the difference between the traditions in Oman and Makran is that the dance in Oman leads to a trance, and in Makran it is simply a festive and merrymaking dance, which does not end in a trance.

In Andhra Pradesh (South India) the drum bands of the Sidis are hired to play music and to dance in 'African ways' on special occasions such as weddings. These musicians are called Daff Parties due to the instrument central to their perform- ance. The daff (daf) is a round single-headed frame drum associated with Islamic culture used in folk music, art music, dance music and Sufi rituals. In Africa, the daff is also played by the Swahili and Swahili/Nguja people, in Dar-es-Salaam and Tabora, Tanzania. The daff reveals the Chaush's link with Muslim culture, and their African roots (de Silva Jayasuriya 2006, XIJ).

Whilst Afro-Asians have not been able to maintain many aspects of their cultural traditions, it is quite striking that they have been able to hold on to forms of music and dance which have also encapsulated vestiges of their languages. The rhythm- driven music of the Roman Catholic Afro-Sri Lankan community in Sirambiyadiya and their songs, called manhas, reverberate in my mind. Language change is in- evitable, but music is more robust and the lyrics are preserving the vestiges of Indo-Portuguese, an endangered language. In the Indian Ocean, music is a recep- tacle of the cultural memories of Afro-Asians, in addition to being a vehicle for ex- pressing identity and resistance. But music is also intertwined with religion. Moreover, it is a form of entertainment. Above all, music is a site of tension be- tween integration and assimilation, and rings out the sounds of identity.

Call and response, asymmetric rhythms and polyrhythms characterise this music, which begins slowly, gathers momentum and increases in intensity and then ends abruptly. A combination of ad hoc instruments and Sri Lankan drums is played.

The melody and rhythm of their music and dance movements mark Afro-Asians out from the other ethnic groups. An upbeat triplet, a rhythmic figure found in East African, Ethiopian and Swahili coast music, is produced with a glass bottle and metal spoon. Metal vessels and objects beaten with wooden sticks provide a metallic sound at different pitches. Two coconut halves and a wooden chair pro- vide an accompaniment to the music. Two types of drums – a rabāna and a dhōlak – are played. The rabāna is a round flat frame drum which is also played by other ethnic groups: Sinhalese, Malays and Burghers (people of European descent). The large double-headed drum called a dhōlak is played by Sri Lankan Buddhists and Hindus. Various substances are used in percussion instruments – skin, wood and metal – providing different voices. Everyone participates in the performance. Those not playing an instrument clap and mark time on the beat. The music is in 6/8 time (six quaver beats to a bar). Singing stops at the utterance of machete, a signal indicating that only the music should go on. The machete is a small four- stringed instrument of the guitar family and is better known as cavaquinho but is not played now by this community. The melodies, rhythms and instruments indicate the changes that have affected the Afro-Sri Lankans. A few years ago, Ana Miseliya, the grand matriarch of this community, predicted that it is only through music and dance that their descendants would be identifiable in the future as their physiognomic features are diluted by out-marriage. In-marriage is rare.

Whilst the Afro-Sri Lankans trace their presence to the colonial era when the Portuguese, Dutch and British successively dominated parts or the whole of the island from the sixteenth to the mid-twentieth centuries in the nearby Maldives, Baburu Lava, now a popular form of music, is a reminder of the Maldives' African connection. Africans were brought to these islands as slaves on Arab dhows until about the mid-nineteenth century. In 1834, two British naval lieutenants who visited Male, reported that 'From the information we were able to collect – it appears that Muscat vessels do not often visit this place: when they do, they generally bring a cargo of slaves. Five years ago, one came and sold about twenty-five lads, at an average price of about 80 rupees each' (Forbes & Ali 1980, 19). Secondly, sultans returning from the Hajj brought back slaves who were freed on conversion. Freed slaves were absorbed into the Maldivian population which was historically accustomed to migrant settlers. Africans intermarried with the indigenous Maldivians. Most Africans worked as raveris, or coconut plantation keepers, which suggests that there may have been a shortage of labour.

The sound of African drums is believed to have been introduced to the Maldives by African settlers and slaves. As drums are considered to be the quintessential African instrument, this is perhaps not surprising. Bodu Beru (which means 'large drum' in Divēhi, the Indic language of the Maldivians) is a genre of music that is associated with the Africans who came to the Maldives. Bodu Beru is played by the descendants of Sangoaru who live in the Island of Feridu in Ari Atoll. (For administrative convenience, the islands are grouped into Atolls.) It is also played in other islands in Ari Atoll and in Felidhoo Island which is in Vaavu Atoll. The drummers traditionally wore a loincloth. Maldivians cannot understand the lyrics of the authentic songs, Babaru Lava ('African songs'), that accompanied the original Bodu Beru. The words of these songs might be in an African language such as Swahili, but further research is necessary in order to validate this hypothesis. Nowadays the lyrics of the songs are in Divēhi or Arabic. Spontaneous dancing by men crouched low is spurred by the rhythms of the drums. Shoulder-shaking and head-shaking prevail. Men engage in duels akin to wrestling, which end in head-butting and cackling.

Bodu Beru is now commercialised and adapted for tourists. Nowadays, a typical Bodu Beru group has three drummers, a lead singer and a chorus of ten to fifteen men. Most songs begin slowly and increase in tempo. A few men from the group break into unchoreographed dancing, flinging their arms and legs, and swaying to the beat as the music reaches a crescendo. Bodu Beru, the most popular form of music in the Maldives, is popular among both young and old, females and males alike. The themes of Babaru Lava vary from love to religion, riches to poverty, from enjoyment to courage or praise of the Sultan. Babaru nisun ('African dance') is performed to the beat of the Bodu Beru and the singing of lava. The dancers sway from side to side, and the Divēhis (meaning 'the islanders' and a name for the Maldivians), who are of non-African origin, blacken themselves to perform the dance. The drums are two-and-a-half feet long and are made out of breadfruit or coconut wood with a goatskin membrane on each end.

The legends and historical facts of African movement to South Asia indicate that the ancestors of today's Afro-Asians were soldiers, traders, slaves or mendicants. Change is inevitable, and over the centuries some Afro-Asians have assimilated. Acculturation is faster with religious conversions.

Africans had a high profile in India from the fourteenth to the twentieth centuries. But today most Sidis live on the margins. Many have been affected by the political dynamics which their employees or owners felt. In Saurashtra (Gujarat state) and Yellapur (Karnataka state), however, Sidis have been accorded Scheduled Tribe status. This status enables them to benefit from the Indian government's affirmative action schemes available to those recognised as socially and economically marginalised. Other Sidis now deliberate as to why they have not been accorded this status.

In Lucknow (Uttar Pradesh), where the number of Sidis is small, they are considered an Other Backward Class (Llewellyn-Jones 2011). Sidis generally consider themselves a jāti or jamāt (caste). Basu (1993) states that the Sidis in Gujarat are mainly descendants of slaves who were without caste, affiliation, ancestry or family, but were integrated into a caste of black people by mediation of fakirs. Their role of fakirs is based on their bond to the shrine of Bava Gor. Fictive kinship ties provided the Sidis with a social identity, which was needed for establishing marital relations. Runaway and freed slaves who went to Bava Gor's Shrine (dargah) in Gujarat felt the need to recreate a community based on their African roots.

With improved communication networks, Afro-Asians are becoming more aware of their ethnic origins and cultural roots. Sidis have their own youth organisations such as Ratanpur Yuvak, Mandal, Vadava Sidi Yuvak Mandal, and Sidi Rastriya Yuvak Mandal. There are also several Sidi societies and groups in India today – Sidi Development Society and Sidi Sanskriti Kala Mandd in Yellapur, the Sidi Goma Al-Mumbrik Charitable Trust and Sidi Goma Group in Gujarat, and the Arabi Daff Party in Andhra Pradesh – all of which help to consolidate an identity based on a shared ethnic origin and common cultural heritage.

Concluding Remarks

Waves of African migrations, over land and across the oceans, were propelled by commercial and socio-religious factors. Africans experienced different religious practices and were converted to Islam or Christianity. They could not maintain African dialects and learnt the local Asian language or a lingua franca (a second or third language which enables people who do not speak one another's mother tongue to communicate).

Though not all Afro-Asians are descendants of forced migrants, enslaved Africans were not able to carry their tangible belongings with them. Music may have consoled the forced migrants and helped them to recreate an imagined homeland. Music may also have been a way of keeping in touch with their homelands, to which they could not return.

Some forms of Afro-Asian music are linked to socio-religious activities, while others have become forms of entertainment. They are vehicles for Afro-Asians to express their identity, and a reservoir of their cultural memory. Afro-Asian music has survived long-distance migration, the slave trade, colonisation, post-independent rule and indigenisation.

Social mobility, out-marriage and religious conversion were also catalysts in the process of assimilation which made Africans invisible in South Asia. Yet, there are a significant number of South Asians who identify themselves with Africa. Their physiognomy may not always fit into a stereotypical African phenotype; out-marriage and acculturation have contributed to a wider range of features and the loss or dilution of African physiognomy and characteristics. Identity is a complex issue – dynamic and multi-faceted.

Afro-Asians are small powerless minorities today or have assimilated with the other ethnic groups in Asia. Afro-Asian culture has not been adequately represented. Music nevertheless empowers Afro-Asians, giving them a voice. It rings out their identity and brings their roots to the fore. When all other cultural elements have been transformed, forced African migrants continue to cling to their music and dance forms. Their history is embodied in the dance movements and the sound of their music.

BIBLIOGRAPHY

Badalkhan, S., 2006. On the Presence of African Musical Culture in Coastal Balochistan. In: H. Basu, ed., *Journeys and Dwellings: Indian Ocean Themes in South Asia*. New Delhi: Orient Longman.
Baloch, A. A., n.d. Manghopir's Crocodiles Festival.
http://karachi.g2gm.com/crocodiles-festival.htm.

Baptiste, F. A., Mcleod, J. and Robbins, K. X., 2006. Africans in Medieval North India, Bengal and Gujarat. In: K. X. Robbins and J. McLeod, eds., *African Elites in India*. Ahmedabad: Mapin.

Basu, H., 2003. Slave, Soldier, Trader, Faqir: Fragments of African Histories in Western India (Gujarat). In: S. de Silva Jayasuriya and R. Pankhurst, eds., *The African Diaspora in the Indian Ocean*. New Jersey: Africa World Press, 223–50.

Bhutto, F., 2010. Mangho Pir. *Granta* 112, 227–41.

Burton, Sir R., 1851 [reprt. 1992]. *Sindh, and the races that inhabit the valley of the Indus: with notices of the topography and history of the province*. New Delhi: Asian Educational Services.

Cardoso, H., 2010. The African slave population of Portuguese India. *Journal of Pidgin and Creole Languages* 25/1, 95–119.

Catlin-Jairazhabhoy, A., 2006. From Sufi shrines to the world stage: Sidi African Indian music intervention and the quest for 'authenticity'. *Musiké* 2, 1–24.

Collins, R., 2006, The African slave trade to Asia and the Indian Ocean islands. *African and Asian Studies* 5/3–4, 325–46.

De Silva Jayasuriya, S., 2006a. Identifying Africans in Asia: What's in a Name? *African and Asian Studies* 5/3–4, 275–303.

De Silva Jayasuriya, S., 2006b. Mapping Afro-Asian musical traditions. *Musiké* 2: VIJ-XXIV.

De Silva Jayasuriya, S., 2008. *African Migrants in Asia: Cultural Effects of Forced Migration*. Princeton, NJ: Markus Wiener.

De Silva Jayasuriya, S., 2010. *The African Diaspora in Asian Trade Routes and Cultural Memories*. Lampeter, Wales, UK: Edwin Mellen Press.

De Silva Jayasuriya, S., 2011a. African migration: Understanding trends and traditions. (Introduction). *African and Asian Studies* 10, 7–13.

De Silva Jayasuriya, S., 2011b. Language Maintenance and Loss among Afro-Asians in South Asia. In: K Ihemere, ed., *Language Contact and Language Shift: Grammatical and Sociolinguistic Perspectives*. Munich: LINCOM Studies in Language Typology, 179–94.

De Silva Jayasuriya, S., 2012a. *Manha, Kaffrinha and Baila: Postcolonial Identities and Innovations*. Awaaz, Nairobi.

De Silva Jayasuriya, S., 2012b. Musing on Kaffrinha and Baila. *Ceylankan Australia* 60, Vol. XV (November): 24–28.

De Silva Jayasuriya, S., 2012c. India's hidden African communities. *Global* 12, October.

De Silva Jayasuriya, S., 2014a. A South Asian community of African descent. *SAARC Culture* 5, 46–73.

De Silva Jayasuriya, S., 2014b. Linguistic influences on Portuguese burghers and Afro-Sri Lankans. *Ceylankan Australia* (August).

De Silva Jayasuriya, S., 2015. Indians of African descent: Emerging roles and new identities. *Journal of African Diaspora Archaeology & Heritage* [Leeds: Maney Publishing], 1–18.

Forbes, A. and Ali, F., 1980. The Maldive Islands and their historical links with the coast of Eastern Africa. *Kenya Past and Present* 12/1, 15–20.

Gibb, H.A.R., tr., 1929. [reprt. 1986]. *Ibn Battúta: Travels in Asia and Africa*. London: Routledge.

Harris, J., 1996. African diaspora studies: Some international dimensions. *A Journal of Opinion* 24/2, 6–8.

Jasdanwalla, F., 2011. African settlers on the west coast of India: The Sidi elite of Janjira. *African and Asian Studies* 10/1, 41–58.

Llewellyn-Jones, R., 2011. The colonial response to African slaves in British India: Two contrasting cases. *African and Asian Studies* 10/1, 59–70.

Lovejoy, P., 2000. *Transformations in Slavery: A History of Slavery in Africa*. New York: Cambridge University Press.

Machado, P., 2004. A Forgotten Corner of the Western Gujkarati Merchants, Portuguese India and the Mozambique Slave Trade c.1730–1830. In: G Campbell, ed., *The Structure of Slavery in Indian Ocean Africa and Asia*. London: Routledge.

McLeod, J., 2006. The Nawabs of Sachin. In: *African Elites in India*, K. X. Robbins and J. McLeod, eds. Ahmedabad: Mapin.

Minda, A., 2007. Dynamics of ethnic identity among the Siddis of Hyderabad. *African and Asian Studies* 6/3, 321–45.

Pankhurst, R., 2003. The Ethiopian Diaspora to India: The role of Habshis and Sidis from medieval times to the end of the eighteenth century. In: S. de Silva Jayasuriya and R. Pankhurst, eds., *The African Diaspora in the Indian Ocean*. New Jersey: Africa World Press, 189–222.

Sakar, J., 1955. *House of Shivaji. Studies and Documents on Maratha History, Royal Period*. 3rd edn. Calcutta.

Shroff, B., 2007. Sidis in Mumbai: negotiating identities between Mumbai and Gujarat. *African and Asian Studies* 6, 305–19.

Abolishing Slavery
A History and a Process As Yet Incomplete

Nelly Schmidt

BIOGRAPHY

Nelly Schmidt is research director at the CNRS (French National Centre for Scientific Research), Paris IV-Sorbonne University. She has recently chaired the International Scientific Committee of UNESCO's Slave Route Project: Resistance, Liberty, Heritage. Her publications include *Victor Schœlcher* (1994), *Abolitionnistes de l'esclavage et réformateurs des colonies* (2000), *Histoire du métissage* (2003), *L'abolition de l'esclavage. Cinq siècles de combats, XVIe-XXe siècles* (2005), and *La France a-t-elle aboli l'esclavage?* (2009) and *Lettres sur l'esclavage et l'abolition dans les colonies françaises, 1840-1850* (2015). She also mounted the virtual exhibition *Les abolitions de l'esclavage* for the French National Archives: lesabolitions.culture.fr, 2014. Her latest book is *Esclavage et liberté aux Caraïbes. Une plantation de Guadeloupe au XIXe siècle*, 2019.

ABSTRACT

The abolition of slavery, the arguments to which it gave rise in the eighteenth and nineteenth centuries, and the pledges it stimulated require a multifaceted rereading and analysis over a long period of time, highlighting the strengths and weaknesses of the means of action used by the protagonists. A host of questions arise in the face of a historiography which was undoubtedly too quick to regard the abolitionist currents – and their mentors – as well known and requiring no critical perspective. The international declarations and pledges instigated by instances of servitude in our day, which are of unprecedented scope, draw heavily on the arguments and strategies of past experience extending over several centuries. In the light of the past/present analysis, the process still seems far from complete.

'Either these abolitionists do not understand the full meaning of the word they are using or they have fairly powerful reasons for taking a serene view of the continued commission of a crime, or else they do not see what their personal obligations are in this matter [...] What I fear most is not opposition to my ideas but indifference and inaction.' (Guillaume de Felice, *Émancipation immédiate et complète des esclaves, Appel aux abolitionistes* [Immediate and Complete Emancipation of Slaves, An Appeal to the Abolitionists], 1846.)

A study of the anti-slavery pledges in Europe, and more particularly in France, from the late eighteenth century to the mid-nineteenth century still raises many questions. If we are to review sources already considered, we need to cast a critical eye over the arguments used, the strategies for fighting servitude and the colonial policies adopted at the time of abolition. The processes for outlawing slavery set in motion at the end of the eighteenth century at the time of the slave rebellion in the French colony of Saint-Domingue, their origin, and the procedures adopted seem to be increasingly well known. They nevertheless still constitute a very extensive field of research.

In the same period, the anti-slavery positions adopted by philosophers, politicians, religious figures, jurists and western travellers – on both sides of the Atlantic – took no account of the two centuries of resistance to slavery already experienced by the captives deported from Africa to the Caribbean and the Americas. That ignorance, that act of oblivion, was not picked up either by the abolitionists themselves, prolific though they were, or by the historians who succeeded them. An international comparison of the anti-slavery movements, evaluating their influence on each other and their strategies, does, however, make it possible to analyse the abolition procedures set in motion by governments in Europe and in the Americas. Many questions arise when our analysis of the arguments and the strategies envisaged to combat contemporary servitude, also known as modern slavery, inevitably leads us to refer to eighteenth and nineteenth century texts, while taking care to avoid conflations or anachronisms. Many questions remain unanswered, thus constantly opening up new perspectives for researching and interpreting sources (Schmidt 2000, 2005, 2010, 2014). Here these considerations will be applied to the early periods of doubt and disapproval regarding the slave system in the eighteenth century, the century of abolition and of the slave revolt in Saint-Domingue in 1791 that led to the first general emancipation decided on by the Revolutionary Convention in Paris in 1794, and then throughout the nineteenth century.

French Abolitionism: Strengths and Weaknesses

The arguments of the European anti-slavery campaigners in the eighteenth and nineteenth centuries – for the purposes of this text more particularly the French campaigners – call for multiple reinterpretations and an analysis of their arguments over a long period of time, thus pointing up the strengths and weaknesses of their pledges and the means of action they used.

From the tragic to the illusory...?

'The words slave and rights contradict each other and are mutually exclusive.'
J. J. Rousseau, 1762

Let us begin with a comment on the innumerable sources available to those re-searching colonial issues, and more particularly slavery, in the late eighteenth cen-tury and during the French Revolution. The documents from colonial and government authorities are generally well preserved. The debates of assemblies and the proceedings of the many commissions at which maritime and colonial in-terests were discussed are available (*La Révolution française,* 1968; Dorigny, Gainot 1998). There are, however, yawning gaps. Take for instance the archives of the plantations – accounts, work records, slave registers – or the papers of the planters who experienced the events directly.

Some observers dismissed the passing of the decree abolishing slavery by the Convention on 16 Pluviôse year II (4 February 1794) as a 'farce', or as a 'derisory and tragic illusion' (Sala-Molins 1987, 1992; Wanquet 1998). It is in light of these contradictions and of the bold leaps of thought made by the philosophers of the eighteenth century that we can assess what that period achieved. Eigh-teenth-century thinkers assumed a foundational role in the criticism of the sys-tem of the slave trade/slavery, although some of them did not challenge the racist theories that were used to justify the system. We shall therefore measure the ex-tent and duration of their influence, in France and abroad, on the condemnation of trafficking and slavery. We shall also examine the murky areas, the paradox-ical blindness shown by the men of the Enlightenment in the face of the suffer-ing that the status of servitude inflicted on a proportion of their contemporaries. At a time when economists in Europe were developing theories on the produc-tivity of labour that lasted to the mid-nineteenth century and an anti-slavery movement was being developed on grounds of morality, religion and humanism, there was a genuine lack of understanding of the extent of the colonial slave sys-tem that had developed in the Caribbean and the Americas and that had brought a peak of prosperity.

Another question that arises is why it took so long for the first opinions un-favourable to the slave trade and slavery to be published in the West. Jean Bodin, in Chapter 5 of Book 1 of the *Six Livres de la République* published in 1576 (Paris, Jacques Du Puys), had deemed freedom to be a supreme natural good: 'the father could sell, barter, exchange or even take the life of his children: but he could not deprive them of their freedom, [...] so the good and generous heart will always prefer to die in dignity than to serve in indignity as a slave'. He then went on to demonstrate the vanity of the 'natural' quality of slavery: 'I agree that servitude is natural where the strong, brutal, rich and ignorant obey the wise, prudent, and humble, poor though they may be. But no one would deny that to subject wise men to fools, the well informed to the ignorant, saints to sinners is against nature'. Bodin then set out several arguments undermining the notion that slaves were well treated by certain masters and questioning all the alleged justifications of servitude in Antiquity and in the Middle Ages.

Yet it is scarcely surprising that the positions on the trade in humans and slavery expressed in France in the first half of the eighteenth century are contradictory when we take account of the fragmentary nature of the information about colonial regimes available to the people of the time and also of the ambiguities of the period's attitude to natural law, 'climate destiny' and servitude. While many inadequacies on these issues were identified in Diderot et D'Alembert's *Encyclopédie ou Dictionnaire raisonné des sciences, des arts et des métiers* (Encyclopaedia, or Systematic Dictionary of the Sciences, Arts, and Crafts) (Ehrard, in *Les abolitions* 1995), it was in that publication that Chevalier Louis de Jaucourt penned the clearest and firmest condemnation of slavery as a state of war declared by the purchaser against the slave and then by the person sold against his owner. Yet the Encyclopaedia also sets out one of the arguments that was to be used for over a century by those in favour of maintaining the slave trade and slavery, i.e. that it saved those deported to the Caribbean and the Americas from the still more horrible fate that awaited them as slaves in Africa.

There is no space in this paper to carry out an exhaustive analysis of the questions posed by the Encyclopaedia and the various writings of the period relating to slavery. Research on these issues is still in progress. The objective is to open up a sphere of doubt, to make the extent of the contradictions inherent in the political and economic reflections of the eighteenth century even more obvious. To elucidate the point, the idea is to contrast the extreme development of the transatlantic slave trade and colonial production in the Caribbean at the end of the eighteenth century against Jean-Jacques Rousseau's statement, a total condemnation if ever there was one, both of the Code noir and of slavery itself. The statement is just one sentence, taken from his book, *Du contrat social, ou Principes du droit politique* (The Social Contract or Principles of Political Right), published in 1762: 'The words slave and rights contradict each other, and are mutually exclusive' (*The Social Contract,* translated by G. D. H. Cole, London and Toronto: J. M. Dent and Sons, 1923, 'Slavery', Book I, Ch. 4).

The writers of the Enlightenment called on their contemporaries to criticise the institutions of their time, but did they devote the same conviction and the same ardour to criticising the laws and practices of servitude? Did they help inform their contemporaries of what was happening in the colonies? In colonial matters, despite declarations that seemed to say the opposite, did they not simply bow to the pre-eminence of local customs that shaped the law, endowing the planters and their assemblies with powers that those writers would have categorically denied for mainland France, branding them as retrograde and contrary to the universal rights of equality for all? Montesquieu, for example, recommended respect for customs and traditions as the expression of local necessities specific to each region of a country. In the case of the colonies, he did not express any doubts about that principle.

Should some of those writings be interpreted with as much perspicacity as indulgence, as is normal practice? One of the first texts to cast doubt upon the system, as celebrated as it is ambiguous, was *L'Esprit des lois* (The Spirit of the Laws) by Montesquieu (Ehrard, article cited in *Les abolitions* 1995). But might we not cast doubt upon the irony detected in the chapter of that book entitled 'On the Slavery of Negroes'? Are we to consistently understand that Montesquieu thought the opposite when he wrote in Book 21 that 'most of the peoples on the coasts of Africa are savages or barbarians', are 'without industry' and 'have no arts'? However subtle and ironic these considerations on the slave trade and slavery may be, are they not in reality quite superficial when set against the fundamental principle expressed at the same time by economist Jean-François Melon de Pradou – 'The colonies are necessary for the nation, and slaves are necessary for the colonies' – in his *Essai politique sur le commerce* (Political Essay on Trade [1734]) and often accepted by the very same authors who denounced slavery and the cruelty it involved?

What use was made of the argument that slavery was 'natural' by virtue of being almost universal and longstanding in human history? Since natural 'legitimacy' and the mechanism of power were analysed in detail, how was it possible to justify slavery on the grounds that it had been legalised by various governments across the planet? After Jean Bodin, Pierre Jurieu, in his *Lettres pastorales adressées aux Fidèles de France qui gémissent sous la captivité de Babylon* (1686–1689) (Pastoral Letters, Directed to the Protestants in France Groaning under the Babylonish Tyranny) argued that: 'There is no relationship in the world which is not based on a mutual pact, be it explicit or tacit, except for slavery as practised among pagans which gave a master the power of life and death over his slave with no requirement of evidence or investigation. That right was false, tyrannical, entirely usurped and contrary to all the rights of nature' (16th letter). Leaving aside the discussions on the 'natural' character of slavery, it was widely accepted throughout the eighteenth century that servitude was 'useful' when it was not the result of an injustice. Thus, reduction to servitude as a result of a war or legal conviction regarded as just could not be considered contrary to the law.

Centuries of resistance

How did the social and political theorists and particularly the abolitionists see the problem of social exclusion – what we would now call the social death of the slave, as Orlando Patterson (1982) and Oruno D. Lara (1992, vol. I) have argued? Were they once again content with the response by Montesquieu who considered that whether it was dangerous to possess and possibly even arm slaves depended on the type of government: 'It is less dangerous to arm slaves in a monarchy than in republics', for the simple reason that in a monarchy the nobility governed, regulated servility, and knew how to resist slave revolts? Montesquieu did, of course, see despotism as the most dangerous system of government by virtue of its extremist character and also the system least able to counter any slave revolt.

How was news of the many slave rebellions, or the constant threat of such rebellions, perceived during the Enlightenment? Once again, did everyone assume, as Montesquieu did, that '[m]en grow accustomed to anything, even to servitude, provided that the master is not harsher than the servitude' (*Spirit of the Laws*, Book 15, Ch. 16)? Were the very frequent manifestations of resistance in the Caribbean colonies in the eighteenth century regarded simply as a matter of the right balance between servitude and good governance of slaves and a careful balance between masters, colonial authorities and slaves?

To what extent were the colonial debates at the end of the eighteenth century influenced by the myriad instances of resistance over the seventeenth, eighteenth and nineteenth centuries (see the chronologies of slave rebellions in the Caribbean, sixth to nineteenth century, Lara 1992, 1997; Schmidt 2005; Heuman 1986, Aptheker 1993; and more particularly the slave rebellion in Saint-Domingue in 1791)? At the time, what actual repercussions did events in Paris have for debates taking place within the colonies? The analysis so far published points up the need for further analysis. Additional work may throw further light on these questions in the colonies at the end of the eighteenth century and in the first decade of the nineteenth century, moving beyond the conflict aspects or even the purely maritime and military aspects. Both for the Caribbean colonies and for the Mascarene colonies in the Indian Ocean, a study of the documents makes it essential to take account of the internal evidence of deep discontent by colonial planters in the middle of the eighteenth century and their aspiration to autonomy in relation to decisions coming from Versailles and later Paris. The French Revolution accentuated the spirit of insurrection in the colonies already fostered by local internal movements of revolt or secession, independently of European events (Wanquet 1998; Lara 1992, 2002; *Les abolitions,* 1995; *Rétablissement de l'esclavage,* 2003). Both responses were closely linked to the high level of social tension perpetuated in the colonies by slave rebellions that had been a feature of their history since the beginning of colonisation.

Recent studies have demonstrated that the revolutionary process began in Saint-Domingue and other French colonies and in all the territories in the Caribbean as early as the 1760s, particularly after the Seven Years' War which ended in 1763. Oruno D. Lara recently published a synopsis demonstrating the decisive influence and scope of those 'first sparks' of revolution (Lara 2015). Saint-Domingue, Jamaica, the provinces of Berbice and Surinam (Dutch Guyana) experienced uprisings involving several thousand slaves which provoked unprecedented measures of repression. Nor were the colonists far behind. In Saint-Domingue, as in Louisiana, demands for commercial and political autonomy grew ever more strident. In 1768–1769, Whites and freed slaves came together to start an insurrection in the west and the south of the Saint-Domingue colony, bringing their slaves with them. From then on, the great settler families no longer hesitated to confront the colonial State. A similar process developed in the colonies in the Indian Ocean.

Beyond the reach of the law:
On the frontiers of 'colonial government'

In the eighteenth century there was little analysis of the quite specific form of government necessitated by the possession of colonial territories which were subject to central administration but whose geographical remoteness gave them a kind of implicit autonomy accepted on both sides. Was the principle of moderation in the exercise of government, defended by Montesquieu and by many others at the time, compatible with the possession and management of colonies with slaves in which the slave system could be maintained and protected against the constant resistance of the slaves only by coercive legislation and the continuous use of violence? Montesquieu wrote: 'I say, and it seems to me that I have written this work only to prove it: the spirit of moderation should be that of the legislator; the political good, like the moral good, is always found between two limits' (*Spirit of the Laws,* Book 29). But had those limits not already been overstepped in the slave-holding colonies in the Caribbean and in the Indian Ocean? Had Nicolas de Caritat, marquis of Condorcet, alias Joachim Schwartz, not gone beyond them when, in his *Réflexions sur l'esclavage des Nègres* (Reflections on Negro Slavery) in 1781, he stated that, in the case of African slaves, 'whatever the cause which made them incapable of being men, what the legislator owes them is not so much to give them their rights as to ensure their welfare' (Ch. 8, 'Examination of the reasons which may prevent the legislatures of States in which black slavery is tolerated from adopting a law of general enfranchisement in order to fulfil the duty of justice whereby they are obliged to give them their freedom', Neufchatel, Société typographique)?

Did Montesquieu himself not overstep the limits when, in the very book in which he set out his substantive arguments against slavery, *The Spirit of the Laws,* he stated that '[t]here are climates in which the physical aspect has such strength that morality can do practically nothing. Leave a man with a woman; a temptation is a fall, attack is sure, resistance null. In these countries there must be bolted doors instead of precepts' (*The Spirit of the Laws,* Book 16, Ch. 8). His consideration of the kingdoms of Guinea prompted him to say that '[i]t seems that in these countries, the two sexes lose everything, including the laws proper to them' (*The Spirit of the Laws,* Book 16, Ch. 10).

Should the Enlightenment's silence on the Codes noirs be attributed to the fact that, in the eyes of the observers of the time, those texts were deemed to regulate the relationships between slaves and their owners? Did not Western thinking in this instance very quickly prove astonishingly limited? Montesquieu did not indeed systematically condemn slavery but recommended that it be used sparingly in carefully calculated numbers. Taking the view that '[n]othing brings the condition of the beasts closer than always to see freemen and not to be one', he considered that '[s]uch people are the natural enemies of society, and it would be dangerous for them to be numerous' (*The Spirit of the Laws,* Book 15, Ch. 13). 'Most of the peoples on the coasts of Africa are savages or barbarians [...]. They are without industry, they have no arts; they have precious metals in abundance which they take immediately from the hand of nature. Therefore, all peoples with a police are in a position to trade advantageously with them; they can make them have a high regard for things of no value and receive a very high price for them' (*The Spirit of the Laws,* Book 21). He went on to approve and legitimise the right of masters to have jurisdiction over their slaves: 'When the law permits the master to take the life of his slave, it is a right he should exercise as a judge and not as a master; the law must order formalities, which remove the suspicion of a violent action' (*The Spirit of the Laws,* Book 15 , Ch. 17).

That justification was accompanied by many expressions of pity regarding the barbaric treatment suffered by slaves, but there was no consideration of the legitimacy of such treatment. The regulations on slavery, and, by extension, slavery itself, were thus regarded as justifiable, so that the system was in the end regarded as in compliance with the limits accepted as to what lay beyond the law.

The eighteenth century: A treasure trove of arguments

Despite all the prevarications in legal considerations of slavery, a study of the eighteenth-century texts on servitude in the colonial context reveals a succession of statements against slavery and its human consequences. Reactions to the slave trade/slavery system produced a treasure trove of anti-slavery arguments which is now being mined, very often in ignorance of the origins of those arguments. Both the slave trade and slavery were defined as crimes – either implicitly or openly and directly – by Clarkson, Wilberforce, Condorcet and Abbé Grégoire, and then by Victor Schœlcher who stated in the first report submitted to the Provisional Government by the commission he chaired that the 1848 abolition decree would put an end to 'a crime against humanity' in the French colonies. The publications by French – and more generally European – economists, political thinkers, religious figures, jurists and philosophers who approached the subject in the eighteenth century still provide a matrix in our day, a reservoir of ideas and arguments against all forms of servitude. Their pledges did not lead to immediate practical results, but the founding arguments were put in place for the next two centuries. The intellectual foundation for the later anti-slavery campaign had thus been established and solidly substantiated, even though that was not the objective of some of those Enlightenment philosophers who had expressed their views on slavery. Montesquieu in *The Spirit of the Laws* therefore found himself, in spite of himself, at the head of an anti-slavery body of opinion that outstripped him. That gave his detractors free rein to denounce his purely theoretical condemnation of slavery which produced no practical effects – or even to accuse him of indifference to the sufferings inflicted by the system of slavery – and to tax him with condescension because he acknowledged slavery as a necessary evil in certain parts of the world. None of these writers went to the Caribbean or the Americas to observe the situation of slave populations and gauge the interests at stake in the debate that was beginning the possibility of putting an end to the system of slave labour. Their knowledge of slavery came from the regulations governing it, from the orders issued by the central power and from travellers' tales. Except in rare cases, they were not direct witnesses to what they were denouncing on the basis of moral principles rather than of anything they had seen. That did not prevent their writings from becoming longstanding references in a public debate which grew more intense from 1755–1770 onwards.

Their aspiration to universalism, their affirmation that rights were by nature equal for all, their rejection of the living conditions and the injustices imposed on certain categories of people have inspired, sometimes word for word, the great international human rights texts of the twentieth and twenty-first centuries. Likewise, human trafficking and servitude in the twentieth and twenty-first centuries are generating the same firm condemnations in principle and the same ambiguities and surprising silences. Indeed, those silences and the impunity and freedom enjoyed by the trafficking and servitude networks could well be seen as being in line with the principle of utility so often invoked in the eighteenth century.

A Long Century of Abolitions

Following a period of slave liberation that began with the rebellion in Saint-Domingue/Haiti in 1791 and spread to Guadeloupe and French Guyana in 1794, the military expeditions Napoleon Bonaparte sent to Guadeloupe and Saint-Domingue in 1802 led to a colonial war in both those colonies. The French mission was to restore colonial order and slavery but resulted in the defeat of French troops in Saint-Domingue in 1803; yet slavery was restored in Guadeloupe in July 1802 and in Guyana in 1803. The colony of Saint-Domingue declared its independence on 1 January 1804 and recovered its Karib name of Ayti (Haiti). The process had begun. The Haitian Revolution was to have a decisive influence on the movement to abolish slavery throughout the Caribbean and the Americas that lasted over a century.

Many different approaches were employed during the nineteenth century to put an end to slavery. At a quick glance, we see that there was immediate emancipation in Haiti in 1793, then in the French and Danish colonies in 1848; progressive or gradual emancipation in the British colonies (1833–1838) (Richardson 1986), in the Dutch colonies (1863), and in some Spanish colonies following the adoption of the Moret law providing for progressive emancipation in Puerto Rico in 1873 and in Cuba in 1886 (Scott 1985); emancipation in conflict situations in all the Spanish colonies in South America, in Cuba during the Ten-Year War (1868–1878) and in the United States during the Civil War, also known in France as the War of Secession (1863–1865) (Lara 1992, vol. 2; Schmidt 2005, 2014; Aptheker 1989). Finally, the Lei Áurea (Golden Law) of 13 May 1888 confirmed the suppression of slavery in Brazil, the last abolition in the Americas.

Everywhere central governments sought to protect the interests of colonial planters, particularly in the British and French colonies where they received compensation in proportion to the number of slaves they owned. The slaves themselves received no compensation whatsoever. Everywhere, too, the proclamation of freedom was followed, if not accompanied, by a period of social control and by discrimination, in practice a reinforcement of colonial supervision intended to compensate for the disappearance of the slavery regulations.

A Note on method and historiography

From the beginning of the nineteenth century and particularly from 1848 onwards, a series of historical myths profoundly influenced the writing of the history of the French colonies in the Caribbean and the way in which it was passed on and celebrated. In the twentieth century, several commemorative events enshrined manipulations of the past, some designed to meet paradoxical economic and commercial needs and others dictated by the desire for a large-scale colonial display. High points were the celebration of the 'Tercentenary' of those colonies in 1935 and the cente-nary of the abolition of slavery in 1948. They confirmed certain standards, products of that quite specific record of French colonial action in the Americas. In 1998, the 150th anniversary of abolition saw the rise of awareness of the yawning gaps left in our knowledge of that history. There then began a phase of increasing awareness of the trade in human beings from Africa, slavery, the resistance the slaves provoked and the acts of abolition. Transmission began through the schools and the media, and a commemorative policy came into being, confirmed to an extent by the passing of the law declaring the slave trade and slavery to be crimes against humanity.

Since then, the historians, who had begun to exploit new sources and raise new questions in the 1960s, have nevertheless not yet succeeded in bridging the chasm between the outcome of their investigations and the various means for dissemi-nating knowledge. A long period of transition and discussion has opened up and it is often ambiguous and contradictory. Debates have taken place, which have led to some clarification of the facts themselves: the events of 1848, the events marking the end of slavery, the policy of the time which was to consign the past to oblivion, the functions attributed to the historical myths created, the com-memorations and the educational approach enshrining them. Moreover, at the in-ternational level there have been few studies of the interactions among the great anti-slavery movements. That history is still most often approached from a na-tional standpoint, despite the fact that all abolitionist approaches influenced each other. For instance, the British influence on other abolitionist movements from the end of the eighteenth century right through the nineteenth century has been un-derestimated, not only as a point of reference in terms of the arguments put for-ward and the methods used, but also as a perennial source of reliable information on the persistence of slavery in the world (Green 1976; Schmidt 1995, 2000).

And hardly any attention is paid in the French context to the role played in the processes of abolishing servitude by the captives, by the slaves and by their re-sistance. Very few of the abolitionists recognised the impact of slave rebellions and the constant social tension in the colonies on the abolition decisions. Yet throughout the eighteenth and nineteenth centuries all the colonies in the Caribbean and the Americas experienced frequent revolts and threats of revolt by slaves, so that there were constant social fears (Hart 1980–1985).

Resistance and survival

In addition to the forms of resistance we are familiar with – resistance at work-places, flight from the plantations (marronage), suicide as a way of escaping slav-ery, collective resistance, rebellions – there was a system of survival through the establishment of parallel or underground social relationships. From the eighteenth century onwards a network of social relations developed, linking different planta-tions, different districts of the colonies and sometimes different colonies.

In addition, 'societies', also known as 'associations' or 'convoys' of slaves, came into existence and met at such occasions as funerals and festivals. That was one of the aspects of a culture of resistance which was, for the slaves, a factor in their day-to-day survival. Such groups used various insignia for identification, rib-bons of different colours, hats, particular musical instruments. They are well doc-umented in several colonies – British, Spanish and Brazilian – but evidence of their existence in the French colonies is extremely rare (Schmidt 2009). A few re-ports from prosecutors and governors do mention them. The colonial authorities chose to permit such groups to exist in order to prevent them from becoming com-pletely clandestine and therefore out of reach of all control and police surveillance.

When we see, for instance, that in the immediate aftermath of the abolition of slavery in Guadeloupe, the first independence movement to appear on the island since 1848 – the one led by Léonard Sénécal – was closely linked to such 'asso-ciations' of slaves, it becomes clear that there was opposition of which the colo-nial authorities were particularly mistrustful; yet colonial authorities, on their own admission, were unable to ban them or even to restrict their influence over the population (Lara 2012).

Dealing with the 'dialectic of oppression'

Observers of the colonial system rarely described the ill-treatment and punish-ment of slaves of which they had become aware, or which they had themselves wit-nessed in the slave colonies. Some did, however, describe the consequences of such treatment, both physical and moral. Victor Schœlcher reported the 'moral terror' prevalent on the plantations of Guadeloupe and Martinique. Ecclesiastics, magistrates, navy officers and law enforcement officers were not deterred by fear of being disowned by their superiors if they gave public testimony on what they had observed during their years of service in the colonies. The writings of Abbé Dugoujon, Gendarme Joseph France and Magistrates Xavier Tanc, Adolphe Jus-ton and Jean-Baptiste Rouvellat de Cussac constitute a veritable corpus of horror (Schmidt 2000). Schœlcher says that on his first tour of the Caribbean, described in his article 'Des Noirs' ('On Blacks') published in the *Revue de Paris* in 1830, he encountered 'dry-eyed' slaves with 'faces impassive', and he was struck by the 'expression on their infernally satyrlike features in the midst of the most atrocious pain' (vol. XX, 73–74). A 'dialectic of oppression', the term used by Oruno D. Lara in *Caraïbes en construction : esclavage, colonisation, résistance* (The Caribbean in Construction: Slavery, Colonisation, Resistance), had come into being between masters and slaves (Lara 1992, 278 et seq).

Revolts and threats of rebellion were particularly frequent in Guadeloupe and in Martinique in the first half of the nineteenth century, following the restoration of slavery. Plantation masters, managers and commanders were on trial for 'illegal ill-treatment' of slaves – something that had hardly ever happened previously – but they were most often acquitted or had their cases dismissed. Whipping, the commonest punishment applied in all circumstances, was ubiquitous. In 1786 an order was issued to restrict whipping administered on the order of the master in the French colonies to fifty strokes, and an order issued on 4 June 1846 on the 'discipline regime for slaves' and the 'policing and disciplining rights of masters over their slaves' limited whipping to fifteen strokes. The latter text provided that only men could be whipped and that whipping had to be carried out in the presence of the other slaves. In the eighteenth and nineteenth centuries planters exercised absolute power. They had practically no accountability to the public authorities on the manner in which they dispensed justice on their estates. They exercised power of a quite specific kind, intended not to curb offences or apply punishment for them, but to spread terror by making an example of those punished.

The French National Archives have an abundance of files for the 1830–1848 period in the French colonies on 'illegal abuse of slaves' and 'barbaric and inhuman treatment' – the expression comes from the Code noir (Black Code) of 1685, article 24. Specially mandated prosecutors in Guadeloupe and Martinique drafted relatively detailed reports on these abuses. After his *Des colonies françaises. Abolition immédiate de l'esclavage* (The French Colonies: Immediate Abolition of Slavery), Schœlcher published two volumes of *Histoire de l'esclavage pendant les deux dernières années* (History of Slavery over the Past Two Years), an analysis of cases of ill-treatment of which a magistrate, Hardouin, regularly sent him the records.

Some Aspects of Abolitionist Activity in France in the Nineteenth Century

Plans for emancipation prepared by the abolitionists multiplied from the 1820s onwards, after two decades of almost total silence following the restoration of servitude in 1802. Until the 1840s, all the abolitionists proposed gradual or progressive suppression of slavery over the long term, while guaranteeing the protection of public order and the interests of the planters. Between 1835 and 1845 the British intervened more and more frequently in the development of abolitionist thinking in France. Members of the British and Foreign Anti-Slavery Society set themselves the objective of becoming the voice of [their] brother slaves suffering throughout the whole world (Blackburn 1988; Schmidt 2000). The society disseminated brochures translated into French in favour of immediate emancipation without a period of apprenticeship, such as the one signed by George William Alexander and John Scoble, *Liberté immédiate et absolue ou esclavage* (Immediate and Absolute Freedom or Slavery), in 1844. The Society also provided financial support for the publication of other works in France (such as the *Appel aux abolitionnistes* [Appeal to the Abolitionists] by Guillaume de Felice in 1846), the Netherlands and Germany.

Yet the French abolitionist movement relied essentially on individual actions intended for the parliamentary world, and on a review, *L'Abolitioniste français,* which was little read outside interested circles in the colonies and the navy. Petitions gathered relatively few signatures – a few thousand for those most widely disseminated – falling way below the level of mobilisation achieved in Great Britain. When the Société française pour l'abolition de l'esclavage (French Society for the Abolition of Slavery) launched a similar campaign, it addressed the general councils, some political figures, the chambers of commerce, and a few newspapers which devoted only a few lines to it, but no full-scale public campaign was organised.

Most of the abolitionists never went to the colonies and had no knowledge of the social realities as they existed between masters and slaves. From 1842 onwards, the principle of 'full and immediate' emancipation became a more frequent feature of French demands. The failure of apprenticeship in the British colonies, a system ended prematurely in 1838, acted as a spur to the idea of abolition without transition. But the French Society for the Abolition of Slavery only came out in favour of immediate emancipation at a very late stage, through Schœlcher, who was the author of the petition to that effect which the society addressed to parliament in 1847.

Until then, the question of the abolition of slavery, when raised in parliament, annually faced the issue of the compensation demanded by the planters, by all the chambers of commerce in the colonies and in the great Atlantic and Mediterranean ports, and indeed by nearly all the abolitionists themselves, particularly Schœlcher, whose voice was one of those most widely listened to. None of the abolitionists launched a proper adversarial attack on the pro-slavery economic argument. Nobody engaged in any forward thinking on the colonial economies and their viability. That demonstrates the weakness of the arguments they used to counter the economic costs alleged in every debate. None of the anti-slavery speeches and none of the anti-slavery writings provided any figures or any systematic statistical demonstration. The economic considerations put by the abolitionists were most often no more than half-measures, unfinished, their consequences remaining vague and unevaluated. When abolitionists addressed the question of commercial, maritime, real estate and financial interests, they were primarily concerned with protecting the interests at stake and making that very clear. Schœlcher did, of course, prepare comparative tables of economies with and without slavery, but the overall argument remained very theoretical. Proposing to abolish servitude, in the eyes of those sensitive to colonial issues, meant putting France's diplomatic and commercial position at risk in the face of British competition.

It should be noted that no nineteenth century abolitionist questioned the very principle of colonial expansion and of reducing the population of the territories occupied to the status of colonised peoples. Yet there was no lack of information. Figures and evaluations, arguments and projects were published on all sides. As for those social reformers sometimes labelled utopian, they said relatively little about slavery and colonisation, taking the view that clever associative organisation would, there as elsewhere, put an end to inequalities and that the colonisation of new land and new peoples would bring social progress. Some even considered the situation of the people of the colonies of little concern at a time when there was so much to be done, both as a priority and in more considered fashion, for the British and French proletariat whose numbers were increasing by the day.

In summary, the types of abolition proposed would, in the eyes of its advocates, guarantee respect for private property, the production, export and pricing of sugar, and the interests of the merchant navy, and would attract new investors to the colonies: that was the abolitionists' economic platform. That was an attitude that indirectly served the interests of planters and ship-owners, leaving the issue to drag on endlessly from one parliamentary session to another.

Moreover, some anti-slavery campaigners showed sensitivity to the prejudices harboured by the planters and their delegates against the slaves. Many of them even took the view that the slaves were hardly capable of measuring the price of their freedom and would continue to work after emancipation.

When Abolitionists Took History into Their Own Hands

'What country have I come to live in?'
Xavier Tanc, magistrate in Guadeloupe, 1832

In France, many of the partisans of abolition stepped forward to give their contemporaries more accurate descriptions of servitude, to demonstrate some of the realities of slavery and to put their personal careers on the line. And that was undoubtedly one of the strengths of a movement that was otherwise rather disparate. Their direct testimonies, though few, were pertinent and they gradually built up a corpus reflecting the background to their commitment.

For instance, Cyrille Bissette from Martinique published articles in the *Revue des Colonies* describing life on the plantations, the punishments inflicted on slaves and the lives of the Maroons in Guadeloupe and Martinique and, above all, in

1835 he took the pioneering step of submitting a proposal to the government for a law on the immediate abolition of slavery. Each of his contributions was accompanied by small prints representing the scenes he described. As he explained to Guillaume de Felice in a letter dated 31 December 1847, he had chosen to 're-produce a table of slavery in pictures', thus hoping to have people 'read and understand' the cause of the abolitionists (Schmidt 2000, 781–84). He was, in fact, adopting the same strategy as Auguste de Staël, who in 1825 had bought all the models of slave irons and fetters he could find in the shops in the port of Nantes and exhibited them for the Society for Christian Morality's Committee for the Abolition of the Slave Trade and Slavery.

Magistrates and religious figures saw their careers or missions interrupted – as they were sent home from the colonies by the governors then in office – after they denounced the slave system they had seen in operation. One gendarmerie lieutenant posted to Martinique, Joseph France, published a summary of the reports he had received about ill-treatment inflicted on slaves and about abuses of authority and acts of cruelty by some plantation masters. In *La vérité et les faits ou l'esclavage à nu* (The Truth and the Facts or Slavery Laid Bare), he wanted to 'pay [his] dues to truth and to humanity'. Xavier Tanc, who came from the Hautes-Alpes, was removed from his post in 1834 for having denounced some of the practices of his fellow magistrates in the colonies. As a justice of the peace at Capesterre in Guadeloupe in 1830, he noted his observations and in 1832 published *De l'esclavage aux colonies françaises et spécialement à la Guadeloupe* (Slavery in the French Colonies and particularly in Guadeloupe). 'What country have I come to live in?' he asked in the face of the 'general despotism' he witnessed on his arrival. He had 'sworn not to confine [his] compassion to sterile tears, but to raise a courageous voice against tyranny, so ill-adapted to the laws of a free people claiming to be the protector of the oppressed'.

It was to the Minister for the Marine and the Colonies that Adolphe Juston addressed his *Lettre d'un magistrat de la Guadeloupe, pour rendre compte de sa conduite et pouvant servir de mémoire à consulter* (Letter from a magistrate in Guadeloupe giving an account of his conduct and designed to be a memorandum for consultation) (Paris, Imprimerie de Dezauche) in 1832. Jean-Baptiste Rouvellat de Cussac, who had been a magistrate in Guadeloupe and Martinique since 1829, was also recalled to France for insubordination to local rules. In *Situation des esclaves dans les colonies françaises* (Situation of the slaves in the French colonies), he stated that the abolitionists had so far 'achieved nothing', that 'we have been on the road for over fifty years, and it would seem that we are still at the starting line'. His objective was to 'show how necessary it is to change a social situation in our colonies which now brings shame on a nation whose gentle mores and whose enlightenment have for so long placed it at the head of European civilisation'. He also declared that he owed his contemporaries 'truth and justice' since 'much care is being taken in our Antilles to ensure that everything done in relation to slaves remains unknown in France and to consign appalling deeds to the deepest oblivion'. He was also one of the rare witnesses to have direct contact with the slaves themselves.

The French government used every means to impede the abolitionist movement. For instance, in the summer of 1835 the Ministry of the Marine prepared an 'emancipation plan to meet the questions which the Chambers might put to the government'. On the grounds that slaves should not be 'prematurely granted freedom' which they were not ready to receive, Saint-Hilaire, director of the Colonies, demanded that the plan not be communicated to the planters' delegates whose systematic hostility he feared. He recommended 'absolute silence' on the 'gradual emancipation plan' which would free all children who were aged twelve on 1 January 1838 and those born after that date. Another delaying tactic by the government was the decision to ban the World Anti-Slavery Convention which was to be held in Paris in 1842, for fear of anti-slavery street disturbances in the city during the meeting.

Abbé Dugoujon, curate at Sainte-Anne in Guadeloupe in 1840–1841, was sent back to France by the governor at the request of the planters in his parish because of his disapproval of the treatment of their slaves. In 1845 he published *Lettres sur l'esclavage dans les colonies françaises* (Letters on Slavery in the French Colonies) which, in the eyes of the authorities, placed him among the most intransigent abolitionists (Schmidt 2015). Schœlcher published books and articles almost without interruption between 1842 and 1847, following the observations he made in 1840–1841 during a mission to the Caribbean with an eye to abolition. The notes he brought back enabled him to publish *Des colonies françaises : Abolition immédiate de l'esclavage* (The French Colonies: Immediate Abolition of Slavery) and then *Colonies étrangères et Haïti* (Foreign Colonies and Haiti) in 1842, works in which he described the continued existence of slavery in French possessions. He also proposed a social and economic development policy without slavery and he produced a comparison of the slave system and a free labour system to demonstrate the advantages of the latter. His *Histoire de l'esclavage pendant les deux dernières années* (History of Slavery over the Past Two Years), published in 1847, comprised two hefty volumes detailing the most recent legal cases relating to illegal punishments inflicted on slaves. At the same time, Schœlcher published substantive articles in various magazines and contributed the colonial column to the Paris newspaper *La Réforme* (Schmidt 2016).

While the slaves, despite their many revolts or attempted revolts, despite their trials as a result of acts of resistance and refusal to submit to the slave system, were reduced to silence in the sources, the abolitionists set out their own history and a typology of their options and also developed a discourse with its own specific vocabulary. They wrote and disseminated their interventions, their works and their articles. Their discourse was closely linked to the myth that had gradually grown up around abolitionism, a myth which anticipated what was to happen after emancipation.

The slaves remained the silent partners in that history. There is no slave testimony in existence for the French colonies, either during slavery or at the time of abolition or afterwards. That leaves a major documentary lacuna.

Moreover, the monumental corpus of documents from Western abolitionists also has gaps and inaccuracies: gaps relating to the abolitionists' reactions to the commitments of the slaves themselves, and relating to the abolitionists' response – or lack of response – to the incessant calls to action represented by the slaves' acts of resistance which were no less intense in the nineteenth century than in earlier periods. What use did the abolitionists make of the concrete testimonies available to them on the realities of the slave system and the survival strategies gradually developed by the slaves? In the same vein, what doubts did they express about the information available to them in Europe?

Pastor Guillaume de Felice, in the 'Appeal' he made 'to the abolitionists' in 1846 with financial help from British anti-slavery campaigners, irrefutably condemned them:

Either these abolitionists do not understand the full meaning of the word they are using or they have fairly powerful reasons for taking a serene view of the continued commission of a crime, or else they do not see what their personal obligations are in this matter.

Reaffirming the urgency of 'establishing that colonial slavery is totally criminal', he concluded: 'What I fear most is not opposition to my ideas but indifference and inaction', and he called on abolitionists to communicate with each other, to exchange proposals, and to overcome their political divides and their personal pride.

Yet in December 1846 the working-class paper *L'Atelier* reported that:

Far away from us, in the colonies, that prime territory for crime and suffering, atrocious things are happening that we would know nothing about if it were not for the vigilant and devoted men who make it their special duty to miss no opportunity to plead the cause of the blacks who, as we know, are subject to the most severe oppression in our colonies.

1848 – A New Colonial Policy

The decrees signed by the provisional government in Paris in April 1848 to accompany abolition introduced rights and freedom of assembly and expression, freedom of the press, universal suffrage for men in the election of representatives of the colonies to the National Assembly, freedom to work, access to education for all and protection of the weakest. Yet they also laid the groundwork for a negation of those freedoms in that they contained all the necessary legal means to control, regulate and reduce to nothing the access of the 'newly free' to these new rights (Lara 2005). Victor Schœlcher, as chairman and rapporteur to the Provisional Government on the proceedings of the Commission on Abolition, took inspiration from the work of the French Revolution in colonial matters, from the 1833 British Abolition Act and from the proceedings of the French colonial commissions from 1838 to 1843, ranging from the commission which considered Hyppolite Passy's plan for progressive abolition to the commission headed by Duke Victor de Broglie between 1840 and 1843. In the First report from the Commission on Emancipation to the Minister for the Marine and the Colonies published in the *Moniteur universel* on 3 May 1848, Schœlcher told the government that the commission had undertaken 'a great act of reparation of a crime against humanity' to be 'accomplished in the manner most beneficial to those who had been its victims' while forestalling 'any pernicious influence [that might] jeopardise the outcome', that is to say, interfere with public order, work and production (Schmidt 1994; id. 1998).

In May 1848, the serious incidents which took place at Prêcheur and Saint-Pierre in Martinique and the many gatherings of slaves and threats of rebellion in Guadeloupe following a long period of social tension led to the proclamation of freedom in Martinique on 23 May and in Guadeloupe on 27 May, even before the decree from Paris reached those colonies. A decree and a set of implementing decrees were promulgated in Guyana on 10 August 1848, in Senegal on 23 August 1848, in Réunion on 20 December 1848 and in Nossi Bé on 16 January 1849. In the first weeks following those proclamations of abolition, a series of measures was adopted to restrict the freedoms announced and to restore tight social control.

In *La liberté assassinée. Guadeloupe, Martinique, Guyane, La Réunion, 1848-1856* (Freedom Assassinated: Guadeloupe, Martinique, Guyane, La Réunion, 1848–1856), Oruno D. Lara reproduced all the documents showing how this policy of emancipation was conducted through control and strict economic, social and political supervision of the population (Lara 2005). Between 1848 and 1857, former slaves known as the 'newly freed' had become potential wage-earning workers, ready to occupy posts in the early sugar production units and later in the central sugar factories. They were to enrol their children in the schools to be opened in each town but would have to pay higher taxes if they wished their children to attend school after the age of 10. Their wages were to allow them to save in the savings banks. But nowhere was the wage system immediate and regular.

Instead, unemployment and underemployment became a long-term occurrence. The social protection measures intended to provide for abandoned children, the sick and the old remained an illusion. The planters who had owned slaves received compensation. The slaves, by contrast, received no financial compensation and no land, contrary to the wishes expressed by Victor Schœlcher as chairman of the Commission on Abolition but rejected by the government (O. D. Lara and I. Lara, 2010 and 2011).

In the weeks after they came into force in the colonies, the rights and freedoms proclaimed were gradually reduced. The effervescence sparked by the grant of freedom of association, freedom of expression and press freedom, shortly after the legislation was voted through in August 1848, and a proliferation of political clubs run by the Masonic lodges and of press outlets prompted the commissioners of the Republic to issue orders to restrict them or even to dissolve them. Two types of response were considered to the problem of the labour force, regarded by the planters as insufficient and too expensive following abolition: one was to use contract workers brought in from abroad – India, Africa, China, Japan – or to transfer 'men of colour' or 'mulattoes' considered as 'dangerous' to public order or 'useless' in the work reorganisation process to Algeria. The latter proposal – dispatching 'colonial battalions' to Algeria to maintain order – was the subject of a mission to Guadeloupe and Martinique by Emile Thomas, Louis Blanc's collaborator in the Labour Commission and co-author of the long report emerging from it, *Rapport à M. le Ministre de la Marine et des Colonies sur l'organisation du travail libre aux Antilles françaises et sur les améliorations à apporter aux institutions coloniales, 15 avril 1849* (Report to Minister on the organisation of free labour in the French Antilles and the improvements to be made to colonial institutions, 15 April 1849). As from 1852, agreements were concluded with the British government to recruit tens of thousands of underpaid contract workers from India, China and Africa, 'immigrants' who experienced living conditions that some contemporaries, including Schœlcher, compared to 'a second slavery'. Moreover, an anonymous memoir from the Ministry of the Marine and the Colonies published in the 1850 *Colonial Review* proposed 'deporting' those categories of the population of the French colonies in the Caribbean most likely to disturb order and work. In 1856–1857, an order on 'policing labour' made it compulsory for anyone travelling from one commune to another to carry a work pass and an 'internal passport', failing which they would be punished as vagabonds. In 1872, in *L'arrêté Gueydon à la Martinique, l'arrêté Husson à la Guadeloupe (*Paris, Le Chevalier), Schœlcher described all those measures as 'attacks on individual freedom'.

It was also through an effective policy of intimidation of the population and of consigning the past to oblivion that the colonial authorities concealed from the collective memory for over a century the most resounding political trial to take place in the Caribbean in the nineteenth century, that of Guadeloupean independence campaigner Marie-Léonard Sénécal and his companions. Sénécal was accused of attempting to do the same in Guadeloupe following abolition in 1848 as had been done in Saint-Domingue. He was sentenced to imprisonment in a penal colony in 1851, and leaflets were published at government expense containing the record of the discussions and the sentences designed to be exemplary, with a view to putting an end to any notion of 'separatism' (Fisher-Blanchet 1981; Lara 2012).

Memory Channelled

Colonialism is particularly revealing as regards what is left unsaid and the gaps which still exist when colonisation and servitude are looked at from a historical standpoint. There are so many received ideas, not only in education but also in the media and even in some research circles. The recent conflations which happened in France in connection with the 'memorial' laws exposed the yawning chasm that still exists between research and the channels for making the wider public aware of the past.

One of the effects of the silencing of the past that took place after the abolition of slavery in 1848 can be seen in the reactions of surprise, even denial, when a history of oppression was relegated to such a minor role, often sugar-coated and sometimes falsified, in the promotion of national commemoration. It is still a laborious task to lift the veil on what was really at stake in colonisation and slavery. Have the policy of burying the past implemented in 1848 and the control of memories thus achieved their objectives?

The colonial context, whatever the standpoint, generated specific phenomena of supervision and channelling of history and its transmission. Perhaps it should be remembered that when historians delve into that world of misery and inconsistency that was the slave trade and slavery in the Caribbean and the Americas from the sixteenth to the nineteenth century, they very quickly become aware that none of the normal rules and criteria of historical reconstruction operate; none of them are applicable to a historical process never encountered before. No comparison to other systems of enclosure and exploitation of forced labour is operable.

The channelling of memory has called for quite specific means of transmission, via carefully constructed myths designed to be impervious both to the reality of what happened and to the passage of time. Many of the myths constructed in the immediate aftermath of abolition in 1848 are still with us. Historians and citizens are still trying to understand the 1848 revolutions, to decipher the symbols and ambiguities that the period of the abolition of slavery brought to light and provoked. Historians are once again called upon to cast a critical eye over what actually happened and the myths created. New issues have come to light, requiring further diversification of the sources.

But not all of the many questions posed by the sequels to slave trading, the slave system and the forms of social control that followed its abolition have been answered. The troubles that occurred in Guadeloupe, in Martinique, in Guyana and in Réunion at the beginning of 2009 proved how topical the problems which arose in 1848 still are, and they surprised and bewildered observers and politicians.

Past/Present

Since the end of the nineteenth century, systems for trafficking in human beings and putting them into servitude have multiplied, despite a constant international proclamation that they are illegal. Of course, any attempt to create a parallel between those constantly expanding phenomena in the twentieth and twenty-first centuries and the realities of slave trading and slavery in earlier centuries most often leads to anachronisms and regrettable conflations. However, the comparison between past and present takes on quite a different significance when applied to the campaigns against such trafficking and such processes of enslavement. In our day, the relative ineffectiveness of attempts to ban trafficking of humans and 'modern' slavery lead us to look to the past, particularly the eighteenth and nineteenth centuries when lines of argument developed which, then as now, had to face economic and social forces and particularly relentless prejudices. Since the end of the nineteenth century, international bodies, national governments, and nongovernmental organisations have been endeavouring to widen the definition of servitude in order to identify it and denounce it more effectively.

It is particularly revealing to reread the texts and recommendations issued since the 1890 General Conference in Brussels on slave trading and slavery in Africa and the Address to Queen Victoria issued by the Delegates at the Pan-African Conference held in London in 1900. The records of cases of servitude published by Anti-Slavery International (which succeeded the British and Foreign Anti-Slavery Society in 1909) and by the International Labour Office (ILO) founded in 1919, the League of Nations Slavery Convention adopted in 1926, the Forced Labour Convention adopted by the ILO in 1930, and the Conventions on the Abolition of Slavery, the Slave Trade, and Institutions and Practices Similar to Slavery adopted by the United Nations in 1949 and 1956 profoundly altered the 'definition' of slavery, extending it to many forms of submission and subordination of human beings, both physical and moral. When the United Nations established a Working Group on Contemporary Forms of Slavery under the auspices of the Office of the High Commissioner for Human Rights in 1974, it opened the way for a proliferation of sentinels identifying instances of servitude at all levels. The International

Convention on the Rights of the Child adopted by the United Nations General Assembly in 1989 and implemented by UNICEF since 1990, was followed in 2002 by ILO Convention 182 concerning the Prohibition and Immediate Action for the Elimination of the Worst Forms of Child Labour. Through its Charter of Fundamental Rights in 2000, the European Union initiated a campaign against slavery, forced labour and trafficking in human beings. In 2001 the World Conference against Racism, Racial Discrimination, Xenophobia and Related Intolerance held in Durban classified the slave trade and slavery as crimes against humanity, as did the French Parliament; Senegal did likewise in 2010 (Quirk 2008, 2011, 2015; Schmidt 2005; id., Open Democracy 2015).

The anti-slavery discourse in the twentieth and twenty-first centuries faithfully reflects the arguments put forth in the eighteenth and nineteenth centuries. The historical link is indeed logical over the long term, but it is also a formidable admission of weakness. How long will the campaign against modern slavery be content to rely on a brilliant list of arguments inherited from previous centuries in the face of worldwide economic, social, financial and political systems that seem more powerful than ever?

BIBLIOGRAPHY

Aptheker, H., 1989. *Abolitionism: A Revolutionary Movement*. London: Twayne Publ.

Aptheker, H., 1993. *American Negro Slave Revolts*. 6th edn. New York: International Publishers.

Blackburn, R., 1988. *The Overthrow of Colonial Slavery, 1776–1848*. London: Verso.

Dorigny, M., ed., 1995. *Les abolitions de l'esclavage, de L.F. Sonthonax à V. Schœlcher, 1793, 1794, 1848*. Paris: Presses Universitaires de Vincennes, Éditions de l'UNESCO.

Dorigny, M., Gainot, B., eds., 1998. *La Société des Amis des Noirs, 1788-1799. Contribution à l'histoire de l'abolition de l'esclavage*. Paris: Éditions de l'UNESCO.

Fisher-Blanchet, I., 1981. L'affaire Sénécal en Guadeloupe, 1848-1851. In: *Cimarrons*. Institut de recherche historique. Guadeloupe and Paris: Éditions Jean-Michel Place.

Green, W. A., 1976. *British Slave Emancipation: The Sugar Colonies and the Great Experiment, 1830–1865*. Oxford: Clarendon.

Hart, R., 1980–1985. *Slaves Who Abolished Slavery*, 2 vols., I – *Blacks in Bondage*, II – *Blacks in Rebellion*. Mona, Jamaica: Institute of Social and Economic Research, University of the West Indies.

Heuman, G., ed., 1986, *Out of the House of Bondage: Runaways, Resistance and Marronage in Africa and the New World*. London: Frank Cass.

Lara, O. D., 1992. *Caraïbes en construction : esclavage, colonisation, résistance*. 2 vols. Paris: Editions du CERCAM, Centre de recherches Caraïbes-Amériques.

Lara, O. D., 1997. Luttes et résistances. In *Diogène*. Special Issue: *Routes et traces des esclaves*. Paris: UNESCO.

Lara, O. D., 2002. *Caraïbes entre liberté et indépendance. Réflexions critiques autour d'un Bicentenaire, 1802-2002.* Paris: L'Harmattan.

Lara, O. D., 2005. *La liberté assassinée. Guadeloupe, Martinique, Guyane, La Réunion, 1848–1856.* Paris: L'Harmattan.

Lara, O. D. and Lara, I., 2010. *Propriétaires d'esclaves de la Guadeloupe, 1848.* Paris, CERCAM: L'Harmattan.

Lara, O. D. and Fisher-Blanchet, I., 2011. *Propriétaires d'esclaves en 1848. Martinique, Guyane, Saint-Barthélemy, Sénégal.* Paris: L'Harmattan.

Lara, O. D., 2012. *Guadeloupe. Le Dossier Sénécal. Voyage aux sources de notre indépendance. Avec trois escales : Martinique, Guyane, Haïti.* Paris: Éditions du CERCAM, Centre de recherches Caraïbes-Amériques.

Lara, O. D., 2015. *Révolutions caraïbes. Les premières lueurs, 1759-1770.* Paris: L'Harmattan.

La Révolution Française et l'abolition de l'esclavage. 12 vols. 1968. Paris: Éditions d'histoire sociale.

Patterson, O., 1982. *Slavery and Social Death: A Comparative Study.* Cambridge: Harvard University Press.

Quirk, J., 2008. *Unfinished Business: A Comparative Survey of Historical and Contemporary Slavery.* University of Hull's Wilberforce Institute for the Study of Slavery and Emancipation (WISE), and UNESCO.

Quirk, J., 2011. *The Anti-Slavery Project: From the Slave Trade to Human Trafficking.* Pennsylvania Studies in Human Rights. Philadelphia: University of Pennsylvania Press.

Quirk, J., 2015, ed., *Open Democracy, Beyond Trafficking and Slavery.* Rétablissement de l'esclavage dans les colonies françaises, 1802. Ruptures et continuités de la politique coloniale française (1800-1830). Aux origines d'Haïti, 2003, Actes de colloque. Paris: Maisonneuve et Larose.

Richardson, D., ed., 1985. *Abolition and Its Aftermath: The Historical Context, 1790–1916.* London: Frank Cass.

Sala-Molins, L., 1987. *Le Code noir ou le calvaire de Canaan.* Paris: Presses universitaires de France.

Sala-Molins, L., 1992. *Les Misères des Lumières : sous la raison, l'outrage.* Paris: Robert Laffont.

Scott, R., 1985. *Slave Emancipation in Cuba: The Transition to Free Labour, 1860–1899.* Princeton, NJ: Princeton University Press.

Schmidt, N., 1994. [reprt. 1999]. *Victor Schœlcher.* Paris: Fayard.

Schmidt, N., 1995. *L'engrenage de la liberté. Caraïbes-XIXe siècle.* Publications de l'Université de Provence, Aix-en-Provence.

Schmidt, N., 1998. 1848 et les colonies : perspectives françaises, perspectives internationales. In: *Cent Cinquantenaire de la Révolution de 1848.* International Conference held by the Société d'Histoire de la Révolution de 1848 et des révolutions du XIXe siècle, Assemblée nationale. Paris: Créaphis.

Schmidt, N., 2000, *Abolitionnistes de l'esclavage et réformateurs des colonies. Analyse et documents, 1820-1851.* Paris: Karthala.

Schmidt, N., 2005. *L'abolition de l'esclavage. Cinq siècles de combats, XVIe-XXe siècles.* Paris: Fayard.

Schmidt, N., 2009. *La France a-t-elle aboli l'esclavage ? Guadeloupe, Martinique, Guyane, 1830-1935.* Paris: Perrin.

Schmidt, N., 2010. *Slave Routes: A Global Vision* (fact sheets, international bibliography, DVD). Paris: UNESCO, Slave Route Project.

Schmidt, N., 2014. *Les abolitions de l'esclavage. Exposition virtuelle* (textes, documents et images). Archives nationales d'outre-mer, Archives de France, abolitions.culture.gouv.fr.

Schmidt, N., 2015. *Abbé Dugoujon, Lettres sur l'esclavage et l'abolition dans les colonies françaises, 1840–1850.* Paris: L'Harmattan.

Schmidt, N., 2015. Different Times, Same Weaknesses: Abolitionism Past and Present. In: J. Quirk, ed., *Open Democracy, Beyond Trafficking and Slavery.*

Schmidt, N., 2017. *Textes inédits de Victor Schœlcher.* Paris: L'Harmattan.

Wanquet, C., 1998. *La France et la première abolition de l'esclavage, 1794-1802: le cas des colonies orientales, Ile de France (Maurice) et La Réunion.* Paris: Karthala.

African Contributions
to Science, Technology and Development

Paul E. Lovejoy

BIOGRAPHY

Paul E. Lovejoy is Distinguished Research Professor, York University, Toronto, Canada Research Chair in African Diaspora History, Fellow of the Royal Society of Canada, Former Director of the Harriet Tubman Institute for Research on the Global Migrations of African Peoples and General Editor of The Harriet Tubman Series on the African Diaspora, Africa World Press, Trenton, NJ. He has been a member of the International Scientific Committee of the UNESCO Project 'The Slave Route: Resistance, Freedom, Heritage.' Among his recent books and essays are *Slavery, Abolition and the Transition to Colonialism in Sierra Leone* (co-ed. with S. Schwarz, Trenton, NJ, Africa World Press, 2014); *The Transatlantic Slave Trade and Slavery: New Directions in Teaching and Learning* (co-ed. with Benjamin Bowser, ibid., 2013); *Crossing Memories: Slavery and African Diaspora* (co-ed. with A. L. Araujo and M. Pinho Cândido, ibid., The Harriet Tubman Series on the African Diaspora, 2011); *Slavery, Islam and Diaspora* (ibid., 2009); *Haiti – Revolución y emancipación* (co-ed. with Rina Caceres, San José, Editorial Universidad de Costa Rica, 2008); *Pawnship, Slavery and Colonialism in Africa* (co-ed. with Toyin Falola, New Brunswick: Africa World Press, 2002); *Trans-Atlantic Dimensions of Ethnicity in the African Diaspora* (co-ed. with D. Trotman, London, Continuum, Black Atlantic Press, 2002); *The Biography of Mahommah Gardo Baquaqua: His Passage from Slavery to Freedom in Africa and America* (Markus Wiener Publishers, Princeton, 2001, reed. 2007); *Slaves and Slave Holders on the Gold Coast: Towards an Understanding of Social Bondage in West Africa* (P. Schglettwein Publ., Basel, Switzerland, 2000); *Identity in the Shadow of Slavery* (Black Atlantic Series, Cassell Academic, London, 2000).

ABSTRACT

Scientific discovery and the application of technology to the natural environment have been essential to the history of Africa and in the development of the African diaspora throughout the world, and especially in the Americas. When Africans migrated, whether under conditions of slavery or as voluntary travellers, they took with them knowledge of agricultural techniques and skills in exploiting the natural environment that were necessary for development. As people have done elsewhere in the world as well, Africans depended for their survival upon the ability to adapt successfully to specific ecological settings and to apply acquired knowledge in a manner that increased production and otherwise enhanced the quality of life.

Introduction[1]

The African contribution to science and technology can be appreciated with respect to the impact on the development of the Americas, which suffered severe population destruction through disease and European conquest after 1492. Spain, Portugal and then other western European countries took advantage of military superiority and the demographic catastrophe in the Americas to confiscate vast tracts of land, which only needed labour, and transferred technology for its development. European empires generated enormous wealth, which depended upon access to virtually free and very fertile land, as well as labour and technology that largely came from Africa. Through the exploitation of labour, huge profits were amassed because workers were not paid and the technology of tropical production was confiscated. It is crucial to note that none of the major plantation crops in the Americas and only a few of the foodstuffs consumed by people in the Americas came from western Europe; virtually all of the newly introduced crops originally came from Africa and were grown there before their introduction to the Americas. Sugar cane was first grown in the Mediterranean and in southern Morocco before spreading to offshore islands in the Atlantic and only then to the Americas. Cotton was grown and made into textiles in the western Sudan and in the interior of the Bight of Benin for centuries before being introduced to the Americas, along with weaving, indigo dyeing and the decorative arts associated with textiles. Rice, indigenous to West Africa, was introduced into the sea islands of South Carolina and Georgia, as well as into the Mississippi valley, Maranhão in north-eastern Brazil, and elsewhere, while numerous foodstuffs and stimulants were transferred from Africa as well. As Judith A. Carney and Richard Nicholas Rosomoff have proven, Africans established 'botanical gardens of the dispossessed', in which they cultivated many familiar foods, including millet, sorghum, coffee, okra, watermelon and the 'Asian' long bean, for example, all of which were native to Africa. Archaeological records, oral histories and even documentary

1 I wish to thank Leidy Alpizar, Vanessa Oliveira and Feisal Farah for their assistance with this project, which received support from the Canada Research Chair in African Diaspora History and the Harriet Tubman Institute for Research on Africa and its Diasporas, York University, Canada.

evidence of European slave owners and merchants demonstrate that Africans in diaspora planted many of the same crops that were grown in Africa for their own subsistence, and in the course of doing so, African farms and gardens became the incubators of African survival in the Americas and Africanised the ways of nourishing the plantation societies that benefited Europe.

The transfer of knowledge has sometimes been called the 'Columbian' exchange to emphasise the transfer of disease and botanical knowledge across the Atlantic, as if the ships that followed Christopher Columbus transferred knowledge through European mediation, when in fact the ships moved people who had the experience that developed the Americas. Knowledge was transferred to the Americas in various ways; people took ideas with them in their heads, from their own training and through efforts at copying what they observed and then experimenting subsequently. The reference to this exchange as 'Columbian' privileges European agency, when we know that the exchange of knowledge and the transfer of technology were a much more complicated process. The exchange focused on what was known in Amerindia and Africa, and also indeed in Asia, and included knowledge from the Islamic sciences as well. We now know that indigenous understanding of botany and zoology was crucial in the evolution of modern science. Similarly, the application of technology to develop such commercial products as Coca-Cola, Worcestershire sauce and soap derived from palm-oil relied on African plants that first came to the notice of Europe and the Americas through the migration of people on slave ships.

While it may have been possible that these crops and skills would have reached the Americas anyway, the fact is that the transfer of technology and the accumulation of scientific knowledge underlying that technology were done under conditions of slavery. Why it was necessary to use slave labour to generate development is still not entirely clear, since all these commodities can be produced without the coercion of slavery. Nonetheless, the fact remains that the technology and science of Africa were harnessed to the benefit of humanity largely because the countries of western Europe and their various colonies exploited Africans to realise profits from this cultural exchange. Hence it was not Africans and their descendants who benefited, but those who exploited them, despite the contributions of Africans and their involvement in technology transfer and development. Hence crops that were often grown under conditions of family and communal labour in Africa were grown under conditions of slavery in the Americas. Slavery was not the innovation, since slavery also existed in Africa. Rather, the forced extraction of profits arising from the transfer of technology under conditions of slavery crossing the Atlantic was the innovation. Indeed, many of the same crops, such as rice and cotton, were produced under conditions of slavery in Africa, including being grown on plantations in which scores and hundreds of individuals produced crops under conditions that were remarkably similar to the plantations of the Americas. But these agricultural estates and the use of slave labour in Africa did not generate the levels of wealth that resulted in the military and political domination that western European countries achieved over land in the Americas and the enforced labour of Africans who were bought or captured in Africa to work that land. European control of shipping across the Atlantic enabled this exploitation. European elites produced crops in the Americas under conditions of slavery on land that was confiscated at no cost other than the cost of European wars among the countries trying to maximise their wealth. Moreover, the wealth that was derived benefited a relatively small class of individuals from western Europe, their governments and their churches, and only indirectly the bulk of the European population. Some scholars have referred to these two layers of appropriation (the theft of land and enslavement of labour) as a product of entrepreneurship, but this conceptualisation neutralises what later generations would consider crimes against humanity and injustice to indigenous communities who lost their land.

An examination of African contributions to science and technology is hampered by the problem arising from racialised views of history and the relegation of Africa to an 'underdeveloped' or 'undeveloped' stereotype. It might seem that the political history of the post-colonial era in Africa has been unstable, with corresponding economic stagnation and poverty. Hence there is the image that Africa is the poor cousin of the global community, backward, suffering and incapable of intellectual contributions that might contribute to development. Despite this image, the fact is that Africans and the descendants of Africans are gainfully employed as doctors, scientists, engineers and professors in Europe, North America, Latin America and the Caribbean, as well as in continental Africa, which demonstrates the fallacy of these stereotypes and should lead to questions about the important contributions of Africans to development.

The legacy of slavery, both in the Americas and Africa, is seen as undermining and limiting African contributions to development, especially in the diaspora of enslaved Africans in the Americas and the Islamic world. Slavery suggests to many people a victimisation that impeded, if not prevented, the conveyance of knowledge, whether to the Americas or to the Islamic world. The image of African 'slaves' as savage, barbaric, primitive and tribal only reinforces the stereotype that Africa had nothing to offer in terms of scientific knowledge or practical technology. If Africans were involved in development, this stereotype holds, it was only through the forceful application of their brute labour. A more unbiased view of past achievements would establish that the crop development and related technologies largely originated in Africa, not Europe, and the European contribution to development was the forceful transfer of skills and knowledge from Africa across the Atlantic and the accumulation of capital through appropriation.

There are many problems with the stereotypes of African underachievement that have to be addressed. First, it is not true that Africa was a continent of little achievement. We can re-examine the contributions in various areas, especially agriculture, mining and pharmacology that will demonstrate that contributions in these areas alone have been important. Moreover, it is argued here, we must overcome narrow conceptions of science and technology that undermine our understanding of development – how things happen and what it has taken in terms of human intellect to achieve practical goals and improve standards of life. A review of African contributions to science, technology and development asks the crucial question: why was slavery necessary in the 'development' of the Americas? Wasn't it possible to have achieved similar or even better results without slavery? Why has it been popular to conceive of development as a product of science and technology, as if slavery has not existed? Would not the scientific and technological development of the modern world have been greater without slavery? These questions frame this discussion of African involvement in development and challenge the stereotype that Africans have made only marginal, if any, contributions to modern science and technology. Rather, it can be shown that slavery stripped Africa of more than just people who might have helped in the development of Africa, since the forced migration also confiscated technological knowledge that was based on previous experience and training that was transformed in the Americas and had a ripple effect in enabling the development of Europe.

Slavery was particularly inefficient in allocating skilled people to where their skills were needed most, but this was the way technology was transferred for purposes of development to benefit the few. The fact that slaves were not paid meant the cost of their labour was the purchase price and the investment in subsistence beyond what the slaves themselves could sustain in their own gardens. While technical skills and scientific knowledge were transferred, slavery nonetheless involved a form of exploitation that required unskilled, brute labour that minimised technology and was exposed to even less science. How is it, one might ask, that one of the ancestors of the modern scientific world is slavery, whose legacy is the under-appreciation of the knowledge of Africans?

The failure to recognise African contributions to science and technology demonstrates that conceptions of scientific knowledge have been racialised, as if knowledge and discovery bear some correlation with the colour of skin. The classification of nature and the exploration of the environment for practical application are universal, whether in the Arctic or the tropics and whether in Africa, Asia or Europe. The development of the modern disciplines of botany, zoology, pharmacology and medicine has occurred because of classification, comparative methodologies that emphasise the discipline of observation, and experimentation

Kofar Mata Dyeing Centre, P. Lovejoy

that attempts to verify results. To some extent what is often considered to be modern science has developed in isolation from bodies of knowledge that were developed in non-western locations, such as China, the Islamic world, the indigenous Amerindian populations of the Americas and Africa. Modern science to some extent has been based on a racialised premise: if it is not 'discovered' in a European or North American laboratory, there has been no discovery and it is not science. It is only recently, that 'scientists' have increasingly turned to bodies of knowledge that derive from alternative systems of classification and analysis.

A botanical vocabulary in Yoruba, based on scientific knowledge collected from specialists in Bahia by Pierre Verger, not in Nigeria, is over 700 pages. If the knowledge of botany in Nigeria were added to this compendium, the encyclopaedia would be more extensive. This scientific knowledge has considerable pharmacological significance. Similarly, the chemical composition of the numerous salts of the central Sahara and the Lake Chad basin was generally understood in terms of the applications in pharmacology, cuisine, tanning, textile dyeing and veterinary care. The distinctions between sulphates, carbonates and chlorides was recognised, and to some extent efforts were made to isolate these various salts in a manner that reveals a level of scientific enquiry that was certainly transferrable to the Americas. Both Yoruba botany and the scientific knowledge underlying salt production demonstrate a sophistication that was transferred within West Africa and could have been transferred to the Americas and the African diaspora there.

A distinction clearly has to be made between the ability to transfer knowledge and whether or not the knowledge that arose from discovery in Africa was actually transferred. Besides its brutality and arbitrariness, slavery was not an efficient method of transferring actual knowledge that could be applied, although in the cases of rice cultivation, tending livestock and growing cotton and indigo, it is more likely that there was direct transfer. Individuals who were enslaved in Africa were not enslaved because of their skills or knowledge, but rather for political, opportunistic and occasionally religious and legal reasons. There was no thought about reallocating knowledge or harnessing brain power for purposes of technology and development. That was not the purpose of slavery, but individuals who were enslaved had skills and specialised knowledge that could be and often were transferred.

To a great extent, therefore, the actual transfer of scientific and technological knowledge was coincidental, not intentional. While the enforced migration of Africans to the Americas was based solely on the desire for raw labour, not specific skills, the fact that some individuals were literate, or had been blacksmiths, or knew how to grow rice or tend cattle led to benefit that almost entirely accrued to slave owners. The movement of enslaved Africans within the Islamic world also was not focused on skills or knowledge, for instance, in the market for eunuchs, the demand for concubines, or recruitment for military service. Eunuchs and concubines might well find themselves close to those in power and therefore could acquire knowledge and even affect decisions relating to development, and slave soldiers could even seize power. However, their background knowledge of science and technology was not essential and often was unimportant. Hence, slavery almost always intercepted the transfer of knowledge and undermined the maximisation of technology. It is ironic, therefore, that the 'European' and 'western' worlds have often received credit for the advancement of science and the application of technology for development. Yet if one looks in the laboratories and colleges of the world today, there is no racialised environment. It is as if the world is finally catching up with the realisation that science and technology arise from the collective knowledge of the human experience. The fact that laboratories and universities today are staffed by individuals from all parts of the world has implications for evaluating the African contribution to science and technology in the past. In doing this evaluation, it is important to recognise that one of the consequences of slavery has been that African contributions to science and technology have not been recognised. This denial of contribution and the misappropriation of the knowledge of Africans are further reasons why slavery should be considered a crime against humanity. The type of development that occurred in the colonial context with slavery, dominated by European and American regimes, was distorted in several important ways, including who benefited from the application of technology and who has received credit for scientific discovery. The failure to recognise African contributions therefore explicates the extent of the criminality.

African contributions to science, technology and development began with the dawn of civilisation and the domestication of agriculture, which introduced crops that have long continued to be important in food production. This innovation alone shaped the history of humanity, as the underlying technologies of production were applied in new settings throughout the world, and included specialisation in livestock production. Without the agricultural skills that pervaded the African continent, there would have been little point in relying on African labour for the development of the Americas. Considering that many crops were indigenous to Africa or relied on technologies originating in Africa, it is essential to appreciate the history of agricultural change in Africa and how the transfer of knowledge from Africa paralleled continued improvements in agriculture through applied technologies in Africa, as elsewhere in the world. Africa imported new crops, such as tobacco, cassava and maize from the Americas, and new strains of crops, such as Asian rice, bananas and plantains, which increased production and improved outputs. Similarly, an examination of craft production and mining demonstrates African contributions in textile and leather manufacturing, salt and mineral production and industrial development. Also, Africans made important contributions in architecture, such as in mosque construction and in the churches of Coptic Ethiopia.

Once the African contributions to science and technology are examined, it is possible to counter the ignorance and racialised interpretations that have been extended to people of Africa and the African diaspora today. The contributions of African peoples through innovation in science and technology have helped shape the modern world. In Africa these achievements related to environment and society, and the desire to overcome the limitations of ecologies and maximise the ability to exploit natural resources for human needs and wants. In the African diaspora, some of these achievements were forcibly transferred across the Atlantic through the deployment of labour and the use of talents and knowledge of enslaved Africans when convenient. Basically, however, people were enslaved for their labour only and in consequence were deprived of their dignity through a denial of intellectual achievement.

Although racial stereotypes and xenophobia that dismiss or minimise the extent of African contributions are often asserted, the historical record demonstrates achievement – as in other parts of the world. People have often adjusted to their environment, seeking ways to improve output, increase production and raise living standards. Technology has usually been harnessed in accordance with the extent of local skills and knowledge. The African continent was not isolated from other parts of the world, and the movement of people and ideas was crucial not only to the development of Africa but also to wherever Africans were found in diaspora. The purpose of this essay is to provide examples of African achievements and thus a factual basis to counter racial and ethnic stereotypes and otherwise disseminate new knowledge about African enterprise to a global audience. An understanding of the African contributions to science, technology and development accounts for the enterprise and activities of Africans in diaspora.

The Dawn of Civilisation

African contributions to the ancient world are well known. The pyramids of Egypt attest to the skills of engineering and architecture. Classical Egypt crossed all the frontiers of north-eastern Africa and south-western Asia. The populations of this area were mixed. Those who built the pyramids included Africans from the middle and upper Nile River Valley, as well as people from the Mediterranean and elsewhere. The science behind the technology was not racialised but crossed many cultures. Similarly, the Nok culture, of what is now central Nigeria, displays an antiquity in art forms that reveal a knowledge of metallurgy, terra cotta, and stone sculpture that has similarities to other parts of the world but that was independently developed. It is important to recognise that technological and scientific breakthroughs occurred separately in many parts of the world. The spread of iron technology is a case in point. Africans could transfer the skills of blacksmithing to the Americas because these skills were ancient in Africa, as they were in Europe. If anything, some African skills were not transferred into diaspora, such as the ability to work in other metals, including bronze and silver, although the skills were known. Generally, there was no need for these skills in plantation America, while there was a need for the ability to work in iron. These examples of technological knowledge that was common in Africa but was not transferred into diaspora indicate that some skills were lost, retarding development. Such inefficiency underlying slavery as a system could undermine the transfer of skills.

The construction of ancient monuments, palaces and temples in the Nile Valley demonstrates an architectural tradition that was continued in the construction of mosques in West Africa and along the East African coast, as well as with the churches in Ethiopia. The knowledge of mathematics and engineering is ancient and was closely tied to the availability of building materials. In the Americas, architectural contributions can be seen in the construction of forts and churches, especially in Cuba and mainland Latin America, where Africans and people of African descent were involved in both construction and maintenance. Many of the palaces, mosques, temples, churches, and fortifications have been designated

UNESCO Heritage sites from medieval times onward. The ancient pyramids of the Nile Valley demonstrate that the issue of what was 'African' and what was not is a question of definition. Certainly, the pyramids are unique and as much a part of the history of African contributions to technology and development as they are of the Mediterranean. The ruins of Zimbabwe, the Ethiopian Coptic churches, the Islamic architecture of the East African coast highlight such achievements. The spread of adobe mosque and palace construction associated with the tradition of al-Sahili establishes links across the Sahara. In addition, African skills in architecture and construction spread to the diaspora. Some of the cathedrals of Hispanic America, dating from the sixteenth to the eighteenth centuries, as well as fortifications, were built by architects who were of African descent. Similarly, Africans, many from what is now Ghana, constructed the buildings in the colonial towns of Newport, Rhode Island, Kingston, Jamaica and elsewhere.

The Domestication of Agriculture

It is clear that African contributions to agriculture have underpinned the development of the African continent and, to a great extent, the Americas as well. This can be seen with respect to several agricultural innovations, including the domestication of millet (including bulrush millet and sorghum), rice, yams, kola and coffee. The base line for understanding the contribution of Africans to agricultural development, both in Africa and then elsewhere in the world, is the emergence of civilisations that are reflected in the sculpture of the Nok complex in Nigeria and the enclosures of Zimbabwe in southern Africa. Agriculture, including animal husbandry, evolved independently in Africa, which in a real sense was not only the origin of all people but also the cradle of food production, crop specialisation and experimentation in systems of agriculture and transhumance livestock management. These great advances in the technology of production demonstrate Africa's contribution in the evolution of the ancient world into the modern world. A focus on technological and agricultural innovation establishes that skills acquired in Africa could be transferred to the Americas and therefore could affect development. One of the questions to be asked, therefore, is what was the nature of African knowledge of agriculture, and to what extent was this knowledge transferred and furthered in the Americas under slavery? It is contended here that extensive knowledge was transferred, especially with respect to certain crops, such as rice, indigo and cotton, whether or not there was any intention on the part of slave owners in the Americas to harness that expertise. Rather, it seems, Africans were foremost seen as brute workers with no transferable skills or any previous knowledge that might prove useful. Any benefits arising from the transfer of knowledge for purposes of development was purely coincidental and has been seldom recognised.

Agriculture developed independently in different parts of Africa, as well as in several parts of the world. In West Africa and Ethiopia, at least, various crops are known to be indigenous, including rice and millet, and in forested tropics, yams and other roots and tree crops, including the oil palm. The various millets were particularly important and have formed a staple of food production in many parts of Africa to this day. Production techniques show great variation from swidden ('slash and burn') systems to methods of intercropping. Similarly, the domestication of the yam has enabled demographic expansion of people into forested regions of Africa. In the Americas, the cultivation of root crops in plantation settings was often done on the side, not as part of the workload for the slave owners but for the subsistence strategies of the African population. In times of food shortages or natural disasters such as hurricanes, survival depended upon access to root crops. Agricultural innovation does not just involve the domestication of new crops but also the adoption and adaptation of imported species of foodstuffs, including bananas, maize and manioc, and their significance in expanding agricultural production and achieving sustainability in population growth. Similarly, farmers inevitably experimented with different strategies of agricultural cultivation, from swidden systems to irrigation, and from the propagation of tree and root crops to that of grains, fruit, vegetables, condiments and spices.

An examination of rice cultivation demonstrates how African technology was transferred to the Americas and how knowledge that derived from Africa was exploited through slavery. Rice was domesticated in the savanna region of West Africa and along the upper Guinea coast very early, well before contact with the Americas, and spread from there to South Carolina, Louisiana, the Amazon region of Brazil and elsewhere. An examination of the different techniques of production and how these were adapted in the Americas demonstrates the important role of Africans in the development of the Americas. The Bambara, Fula, Mandinke and Songhay had long relied on growing rice along the Niger River, while Serer, Mende, Temne, Kissi, Papel and Baga utilised their own special techniques of rice production from Senegal to the Ivory Coast. There are extensive scholarly studies of rice-producing societies on the upper Guinea coast, including the Doala, Bran and others.

Of the more than twenty species of rice found on the planet, only two were domesticated, one in Asia (*Oryza sativa*) and the other in West Africa (*Oryza glaberrima*). The latter has erect, compact flower clusters and red grains, and was grown as early as 1500 BC along the Casamance River in Senegambia and in the inland delta where the Niger River flows northeast towards Timbuktu. It is believed that *O. glaberrima* was originally domesticated in the freshwater wetlands of the inland delta of the middle Niger River in Mali some two thousand years ago. Genetic diversity also suggests two secondary centres of African rice innovation and development: north and south of the Gambia River and the Guinean highlands between Sierra Leone, Guinea Conakry and Liberia. There are important differences between African and Asian rice. African rice is better adapted to soil nutrient conditions, such as acidity, salinity, excessive flooding, iron toxicity and phosphorus deficiency. It grows quickly, which makes glaberrima more competitive with weeds in its early growth cycle than sativa. But under optimum soil and water conditions, the Asian species typically provides higher yields. One factor limiting the extension of glaberrima cultivation over a broad area of the world is the notorious difficulty of milling African rice for consumption. The indigestible husks of African rice must be removed through a processing method that keeps the grains whole; the African mortar and pestle (Portuguese: pilao) serve this purpose of milling.

Although some studies attribute the early presence of rice in West Africa to Portuguese navigators who brought it from Asia to the upper Guinea coast, the species of rice reported by early European accounts was *Oryza glaberrima*. However, rather than introducing rice, Portuguese caravels depended upon the purchase of locally produced foodstuffs, especially rice, that were marketed in Africa and that fed the people on Atlantic ships. Europeans referred to the coast where rice was grown as the Rice Coast, as distinct from the Grain Coast, where millet and sorghum could be purchased. By the sixteenth and seventeenth centuries, West Africans were selling rice to slave traders to provision their ships, including food for the Africans who were being taken to the Americas. Much later, the adaptable Asian species, *O. sativa*, which has leaning clusters and white grains, and has a greater yield, was introduced into the western Sudan and the upper Guinea coast. The Asian species and hybrids tended to replace the indigenous species. However, the successful introduction of Asian varieties occurred because a system of irrigated rice culture and methods to mill the rice already existed.

The region where rice was grown in West Africa is divided into a northern and southern portion, depending upon the amount of rainfall. Because of this factor, two distinctive land-use systems for rice cultivation developed over the centuries. In the northern zone, in areas that receive less than 35 inches (89 cm) of annual precipitation, rice cultivation unfolds on wetlands in conjunction with cattle grazing. To the south, in areas receiving more than about 35 inches (89 cm) of rain, animals figure less centrally as land use shifts from an agro-pastoral eco-setting to a mostly agricultural system. Three principal water regimes influence West African rice planting: rainfall, groundwater and tides. The resultant rice systems are respectively known as upland, inland swamp and tidal production.

The upland system, which may actually be only a hundred feet above sea level, where rainfall reaches at least 1,000 mm, is characterised by clearing forest for the planting of well-drained soils. Seed is planted in furrows, either by broadcasting or by dropping rice grains into a hole made by puncturing the soil with a special hoe. Then the shallow hole is covered with the heel of the foot. Because the upland rice system is regulated by the length of the wet season, West African farmers usually plant seed varieties of short duration, grown over a three- to four-month period. Generally, upland rice cultivation occurs under favourable climatic, soil and land-use systems in Sierra Leone and Liberia.

The second principal rice system encountered along a West African landscape gradient is cultivation in inland swamps, where groundwater reaches the root zone for most of the growing period. The broad range of inland swamps sown with rice reflects a sophisticated knowledge of soils and their moisture-retention properties, as well as methods to facilitate water impoundment for supplemental irrigation. As Judith A. Carney observes, planting rice in inland swamps requires careful observance of topography and water flow. Farmers often construct bunds, small earthen embankments, around plots to form a reservoir for capturing rainfall or stream runoff. The practice keeps soils saturated through dry cycles of short duration during the cropping season. If excess flooding threatens the rice crop, the plot can be quickly drained by puncturing the bund. Farmers sometimes improve drainage and aeration in inland swamp plots by ridging the soil. Rice grains are sown directly atop the ridges, or seedlings are transplanted – the latter method often being favoured when water-logging poses a risk to seedling development.

Tidal rice cultivation occurs in three distinct floodplain environments: along freshwater rivers, seasonally saline rivers and coastal estuaries with permanent marine water influence. Mangrove rice is the highest-yielding crop in the West African rice region, characterised by farming in saline estuaries. From Cape Verde to Sierra Leone, the topography determines the development of mangrove technology in rice cultivation. In the estuaries of numerous silt-laden rivers, mangrove roots clutch the earth and hold the alluvium, producing the rich soil ideally suited to rice culture. Farmers clear the mangrove swamp of underbrush and construct a dike to keep out the salt water of the Atlantic Ocean. A levee is closed with sluice gates of wood at high tide and opened again at low tide so that the saline soil may be washed by fresh waters of rain and rivers. The field is subdivided by canals and causeways that aid irrigation. By repeated drainage over a long period of time that may take years, the rice fields are cleaned of the alluvium of salt. Farmers, using a log shovel, construct ridges to keep out the sea. Meanwhile, women, using small hoes, prepare other fields on higher ground and sow rice seeds to be later transplanted to the fields. After the harvest, the manure of cattle provides further nourishment throughout the entire trypanosome-free zone of the rice region. Rice farmers south of the trypanosome belt do not have these advantages: in the absence of cattle they rely on other techniques to maintain soil fertility, such as rotating fields with nitrogen-fixing legumes and intercropping plants that add crucial nutrients to the soil.

The labour of women proved crucial to the rice-cropping system in West Africa in ways that were not the case with other cereals such as sorghum and millet. Their activities included selecting the seeds, hoeing and harvesting the rice, milling, and transporting rice in baskets, as well as processing, cooking, and selling rice in markets. The role of female labour varied in relationship to the significance of rice in the farming system, with male participation in cultivation being greater in places where rice was the dietary staple. When rice was a secondary crop in the regional food system, the crop was often farmed solely by women.

One of the chief contributions of enslaved Africans to the Americas was the transmission of the West African rice-knowledge systems – land-use principles, the advantages of gendered division of labour and processing techniques. In at least two important areas of New World slavery, South Carolina and the eastern Amazon in Brazil, European planters drew on African expertise in rice farming to develop plantations based on the crop. In both landscapes, the techniques of rice cultivation were very close to those practised in West Africa. Since many enslaved Africans were experienced rice producers, British colonists in South Carolina were able to cultivate the crop successfully. The development of rice as a cash crop for export to Europe coincided with the arrival in considerable numbers of Africans who had knowledge of rice cultivation. English colonists were fully aware of African knowledge of rice cultivation. Hence, many of the practices of early production in South Carolina paralleled those in Africa, which demonstrates that enslaved Africans were active rather than passive participants in the founding of South Carolina.

Africans played an important role in the development of the commercial rice industry in colonial South Carolina and Georgia. Enslaved labourers on South Carolina rice plantations were skilled. Africans planted rice in the spring by pressing a hole with the heel and covering the seeds with the foot; the motion used was similar to that employed in West Africa. In summer, Carolina blacks moved through the rice fields in a row, hoeing in unison to work songs that followed the pattern of cultivation in West Africa, and not one that was imposed by Europeans. In October when the threshed grain was 'fanned' in the wind, the wide, flat winnowing baskets were made by black hands after an African design. Also, the process of removing rice kernels from their husks was made with the use of the mortar-and-pestle technique from Africa. Based on this technological evidence and the presence of enslaved Africans from the upper Guinea coast and the rice-producing interior, it is clear that African technology and knowledge of rice production was transferred to the Americas.

Throughout the eighteenth century, planters placed a positive value on slaves brought from rice-growing regions, which is revealed in newspaper advertisements by South Carolina planters searching for runaway slaves. Colonists preferred captives from the Rice Coast, despite the predominance of Congo-Angola slaves. Merchants in Charleston and Savannah maintained a close relationship with the owners of Bunce Island in the Sierra Leone River, whose captives often were destined for rice plantations in South Carolina and Georgia. Planters using enslaved Africans subsequently transmitted rice-growing technology to Texas, Louisiana and Brazil. Maranhão began to export rice in the late 1760s and remained the principal source of exports from this part of Brazil into the nineteenth century. Between 1760 and 1810, two out of every three Africans who arrived in the rice-growing region of Maranhão came from the upper Guinea coast; indeed, almost all embarked at Cacheu and Bissau. Elsewhere in Brazil, there were virtually no Africans from the upper Guinea coast and the rice-producing regions of West Africa. Rice cultivation in north-eastern Brazil depended upon a predominance of Africans from rice-producing regions of West Africa.

Stimulants

Africa was the origin of three important pharmacological substances known as alkaloids (coffee, kola, khat). The principal characteristic of these agricultural commodities is that they have pharmacological properties that stimulate the brain and the central nervous system. Like other alkaloids (tea, cacao, betel, coca, tobacco, opium, etc.), they have virtually no food value but rather provide the sensation of reducing hunger and fatigue. The active ingredients in the various alkaloids vary, with caffeine (kola, coffee) and theobromine (tea, kola) being two of the most important. Moreover, all alkaloids are addictive to varying degrees, with nicotine (tobacco) being the most addictive. The extent to which alkaloids lose their properties after harvest determines the distribution of these commodities, which have often been considered luxury goods, depending on how perishable they were. How alkaloids are activated varies as well; some have to be taken as a beverage (coffee, tea), while others are smoked (tobacco) or eaten (kola, and to some extent, tobacco). Several alkaloids are indigenous to Africa, including kola, coffee and khat, a stimulant developed in Ethiopia, but which has not spread extensively beyond northeast Africa because it cannot be transported easily and loses its properties once dried. Here the focus is on kola and coffee because of the implications of these two commodities for the transfer of knowledge from Africa to the rest of the world and, hence, for their ability to influence the spread of science and determine particular kinds of development.

Coffee was developed as a consumable drink in Ethiopia and subsequently spread to Arabia and from there throughout the world. Coffee contains several compounds, particularly caffeine, but also theophylline and theobromine, each of which has different biochemical effects on the human body. The major compound in coffee is caffeine, which is a mild stimulant that can enhance alertness, concentration, and mental and physical performance. Because caffeine influences the central nervous system in a number of ways and because a small number of people may be particularly sensitive to these effects, individuals sometimes have bad reactions to coffee consumption. Despite this caveat, coffee became one of the most important consumables in the world. Coffee can be transported easily once the beans have been roasted.

The coffee plant is a woody perennial evergreen dicotyledon that belongs to the Rubiaceae family. The plant can grow to a relatively large height, but when pruned, it more accurately resembles a bush. It has a main vertical trunk (orthotropic) and primary, secondary and tertiary horizontal branches (plagiotropic). Other members of the family include gardenias and plants which yield quinine and other useful substances, but coffee is by far the most important member of the family economically. There are several different coffee species, but the two main species that have been cultivated are *Coffea arabica*, or Arabica, and *Coffea canephora*, or Robusta. Arabica coffee is indigenous to the highlands of Ethiopia, while Robusta is indigenous to the forests of West and Central Africa. The origins of coffee consumption can be traced to Ethiopia, specifically to the forests of the Kaffa region, where the plant grew wild. The region of Kaffa gave coffee its name, although in Amharic 'bun' or 'buna' is the word for coffee. *C. arabica* is also found in the Harar region. The popular theory about the origin of coffee in Kaffa attributes the discovery to a sheep herder known as Kaldi, who noticed that his sheep became hyperactive after eating the red 'cherries' of the coffee plant. Kaldi is credited with trying the beans himself, whereupon he discovered the effects of caffeine, the active ingredient in coffee. Whether or not this legend has any historical accuracy, the story emphasises the act of observation and discovery. Certainly, coffee has been consumed in Ethiopia for a very long time. Among the Galla, coffee beans were ground and mixed with animal fat. The mixture was often consumed on long hunting and military expeditions. These 'energy bars' are still consumed in Kaffa and Sidamo today. In Ethiopia, coffee has always been regarded as a medicine, a food and a beverage. Sometimes, coffee was eaten with grain, and coffee cherries can be mixed with butter, pepper and other spices as a snack. As a food, the coffee cherries had to be fresh, which limited their area of consumption, but the roasted beans can be preserved for a long time without losing their stimulating properties. As a drink, fresh coffee cherries can be boiled to produce a greenish liquid that is known as 'white coffee.' While consumed locally in Ethiopia, the far more popular method of preparing coffee starts with roasting the coffee, grinding it and then brewing it with water.

Kola nut production, particularly *Cola nitida*, is indigenous to western Africa, where the nuts were consumed as a stimulant because of their caffeine content.

Table 1
Caffeine and Theobromine in Mild Stimulants (per cent)

Stimulant	Caffeine	Theobromine
Kola	1.0–4.0	0.02–0.09
Coffee	0.7–3.0	None
Tea	1.0–4.7	Traces
Cocoa	0.07–0.36	0.8–4.0

The nuts were later used in the development of cola drinks, which were first popularised in the United States and Europe in the 1880s and 1890s. This section examines the pharmacology of kola as a medicine, stimulant and item of consumption. Although the nuts provided the inspiration for 'kola' drinks, kola nut consumption has been largely confined to West Africa for reasons relating to the nature of the commodity. Only *C. nitida* can be transported relatively easily and stored for many months. Unless handled with care, the nuts perish quickly and lose their properties. Other varieties of kola do not last very long once they reach maturity; the other main variety, *C. acuminata*, is only consumed locally to any significant extent.

Kola nuts, which are eaten because they contain caffeine, theobromine and kolatin, have long been a popular stimulant in many parts of West Africa. Like other mild stimulants, including coffee, tea and cocoa, kola nuts are moderately addictive. Of the two most common varieties, *C. nitida* contains from 1.0 to 4.0 per cent caffeine by weight, as well as traces of theobromine, while *C. acuminata* has from 1.5 to 3.6 per cent caffeine and from 0.02 to 0.09 per cent theobromine. Both caffeine and theobromine are alkaloids which stimulate the nervous system and the skeletal muscles. Both varieties contain small amounts of kolatin, a glucoside heart stimulant, and tannin. In combination, these properties make kola as effective as other mild stimulants, including coffee, tea and cocoa (Table 1). Although kola nuts were not reduced to a drink in West Africa, the nuts have sometimes been compared with coffee, even being called the 'coffee of the Sudan'.

Kola is indigenous to the West African forest, but is found as far east as Gabon and the Congo River basin. Of its more than forty varieties, four – *C. nitida*, *C. acuminata*, *C. verticillata* and *C. anomala* – are the most common of the edible species, and have been important in the commerce of West Africa, even if only locally in the case of the more perishable varieties. These four types are similar in their chemical composition and use. They contain, together with other compounds, large amounts of caffeine, and smaller quantities of theobromine, kolatin, and glucose. All these are stimulants: caffeine affects the central nervous system, theobromine activates the skeletal muscles, kolatin acts on the heart, and glucose provides energy to the body as a whole. Because of these properties, kola had various medicinal uses, which demonstrates that there was knowledge of the pharmacologic importance of kola, particularly *C. nitida*, as a medicine and stimulant. When chewed – and it appears that kola was not cooked or made into drinks anywhere in Africa – the nuts have an effect similar to that of coffee, tea or cocoa, and consequently kola, being an excellent refreshment, can be used to relieve hunger, thirst and fatigue, lending itself well to social situations.

The fruit of the kola grows in pods that contain from three to twelve nuts. *C. nitida* nuts are divided into two cotyledons and can be easily separated at the time of consumption, while *C. acuminata* has from two to five cotyledons. Each nut is about the size of a chestnut, approximately one to two inches (2.5 to 5 cm) in diameter. The nuts spoil easily and must be kept damp and protected from the air. The care of *C. nitida* nuts involves constant inspection to remove insect-infested nuts, mouldy nuts and others that have been spoiled or which have withered. To protect the nuts in transit and during storage, they were and still are wrapped in leaves.

Red, white or shades in between, the *C. nitida* nuts in particular were valued because they cleansed the mouth, provided a spurt of energy and were credited with numerous medicinal and other properties. Kola is also mildly addictive, which was an important, if not always recognised, reason why thousands of common folk chewed it at naming ceremonies, weddings and other occasions, although it constituted a luxury. For the wealthy, kola nuts were a necessary sign of their hospitality and affluence. Other varieties of kola, less widely distributed and less prestigious, had similar physiological effects.

The taste for kola is acquired because the nuts are bitter. Consumption of only a small piece of the nut affects the body, and hence consumers often break a nut into pieces and share the pieces; as a result, there are terms for the size of a piece. Once a nut is broken open, moreover, it quickly oxidises, turning dark red and then black as it dries, and losing virtually all of its effect. Because nuts were shared, the social dimension of consumption was important. The taste of the nut lingers for some time after chewing and has the effect of making water taste sweet and refreshing, no matter how tainted the water might be from natron or other common minerals found in well water. When consumed in sufficient quantities, kola stains the teeth and lips slightly red, which was considered pleasing and a sign of good health, if not prosperity.

Kola has had a ready market almost everywhere in West Africa for many centuries, at least one thousand years, particularly in the savanna, where demand was high in the absence of tea, coffee or other consumables that stimulated the central nervous system and brain. Their consumption tended to increase with the spread of Islam and its prohibitions on alcoholic beverages and with the absence of tea, coffee and cocoa, which have similar effects on the body. People consumed kola in forest areas, where alcohol was also drunk, and there kola was often associated with rituals and ceremonies.

The kola-producing zone of West Africa was divided into two parts, one in the forests to the west of the Volta River, where *C. nitida* was grown, and the other to the east of the Volta River, where *C. acuminata, C. verticillata* and *C. anomala* were common and where there was no *C. nitida*. This division is significant because *C. nitida* was by far the most important variety in terms of trade between forest and savanna, and because its zone of cultivation was geographically separated from that of the other varieties. There does not appear to be any difference in the techniques of cultivation that would account for this. The explanation as to why one variety assumed such importance commercially while the others did not also remains unclear; one can only note that a market had to be developed, since taste for the nuts is acquired, and that, whatever the reasons, demand for the other varieties has always remained small by comparison. An important factor probably was the relative ease of preserving *C. nitida* nuts, in comparison with other varieties, as long as the nuts are inspected carefully and regularly.

Although kola was indigenous to the whole forest region of West Africa, only certain areas have been important historically in the production of *C. nitida*. Kola trees can grow in the forest region south of approximately 10° N latitude, but the main area for *C. nitida*, which is the variety discussed here unless otherwise indicated, has been between 60° and 80° N, from the Volta to the rivers of the Upper Guinea coast. Before the last decade of the nineteenth century, the production of *C. nitida* was confined to the forests west of the Volta River, except for a very limited output in Nupe, near the confluence of the Niger and Benue rivers, which was a late introduction dating probably to the sixteenth century and involving careful management. This variety of kola was in particular demand among Muslims, and since areas of production were far away, it had to be transported considerable distances in order to reach the most eastern markets in the central Bilad el-Sudan. *C. acuminata* was the primary variety grown in Yorubaland, the Igbo country, and areas further east; some was sold outside the forest zone, but it figured more prominently in local trade. *C. verticillata* also was grown in the forests of Yorubaland, and perhaps further east too; some was exported north into the savanna, where it was known to Hausa consumers as hannunruwa; it was also used in Borno, although demand there appears to have been far less than for *C. nitida*. *C. verticillata* was considered slimy, and women used it as much for cosmetic purposes as for its caffeine. *C. anomala* was grown only in Bamenda, in Cameroon, and was exported north, at least by the middle of the nineteenth century, and unlike *C. verticillata*, it was an acceptable substitute for *C. nitida* in the markets of the savanna. The production area was limited, however, and possibly little *C. anomala* was cultivated before the expansion of Hausa trade into southern Fombina (Adamawa) in the nineteenth century.

Proximity to the savanna was significant in determining potential output, the most productive region beginning from 125 to 150 kilometres inland and ending approximately 300 kilometres from the coast. This belt was subdivided into four parts. The first area was the coast between the Scarcies and Nunez rivers in Sierra Leone and Guinea, where the Temne and Bullom collected kola for export inland from the coast and through the Futa Jallon highland. The second area, really an extension of the first, was inland further east astride the present Sierra Leone Liberia Guinea boundary near the source of the Niger River: a variety of people exported kola from this zone, including, from east to west, the Dan, Gerze (Kpelle), Toma, Kissi, and Kono. Kola was also cultivated north of this broad belt, but then only in small groves near villages where conditions were favourable; usually these nuts were smaller, and were consumed locally. Trees had to be tended carefully, and their presence in Futa Jallon, Kuranko country, and even near Kankan indicates their commercial importance. The third area, which was further east, straddled the Bandama River, including the Guro country, but also the Bete area to a lesser extent. This area supplied the Worudugu region to the north. Finally, the Akan forests were the principal source in the Volta River basin.

In the nineteenth century kola was found in Asante, from Mampong in the east through Tekyiman and the Tano River valley, and it also grew in the Ano region along the Comoé River, 200 to 300 kilometres from the coast. This region not only supplied areas to the north but also to the north-east as far as Lake Chad. In many places, *C. nitida* trees were planted, as probably had been the case for centuries. Cultivation was common among the Temne, Baga, Kissi, Toma, Gerze, Dan, Mano, Ge, Guro and Gan and perhaps in Asante. Groves of thirty to sixty trees were common near Ge villages, while the Kissi planted trees in the forests by their villages. Among the Gerze and Toma, groves were located along the Diani River, in Kabaradougou and in Simandougou. In the Ano region, which supplied Kong and areas further north, kola was planted in groves of 250 to 300 trees. Trees were elsewhere planted in smaller numbers. The Guro planted individual trees when girls were aged six or seven in preparation for puberty rites, but there were no plantations. The Mano planted a tree or two on gravesites, this sometimes resulting in the formation of small groves.

Even when trees were wild, they were often claimed and marked. The Toma, Gerze and their neighbours, after clearing the land around newly discovered trees, used bundles of straw, old machete handles with small stones tied to them, pieces of calabash stuffed with bombax 'cotton,' and other devices to establish a claim. In Gerze country, abandoned villages were visible because of the number of kola trees at their locations. The Guro practised their cultivation differently: except for a few trees, most nuts were gathered in forests, where access was a lineage right. In the area between Kumase and Nkoranza in Asante, kola trees were so thick in the 1980s that they formed a gigantic kola forest. While some of these trees may have been planted, in most cases underbrush was simply cleared away to protect seedlings, which must have been a regular practice for a long time. As with the Guro, the gathering of kola seems to have been possible for any member of a lineage, which maintained collective rights to the trees.

It is difficult to know how long there has been an active trade in kola and therefore a concern with kola cultivation. Customs associated with planting trees on gravesites and with the preliminary stage in puberty rites are very old. The question is how old and how significant such practices have been in spreading *C. nitida*. One text from the sixteenth century indeed states that 'plantations of kola' existed then, but this being the only reference, it remains theoretically possible that, as the market for kola developed, commercialisation at first only involved nuts tapped from trees in their natural state. Nonetheless, *C. nitida* spread throughout the area from the Scarcies and Nunez rivers eastward to the Volta. As a result of the movement of villages, the opening of new lands and local trade, kola trees were planted and those found in the wild were protected and cleared of brush.

Linguistic data indicate that the likely origin of *C. nitida* cultivation was in the Guinea–Liberia–Sierra Leone border area. Although there is no evidence for ascertaining a date of initial development, 'kola' is common to languages that are classified as West Atlantic, as distinct from Mande languages and other languages in West Africa. Kola was certainly traded to the savanna by the thirteenth century, and possibly much earlier. Moreover, Mande-speaking groups moved into the kola forests in the sixteenth century, which resulted in the expansion of kola production for commercial purposes. Kola production in the Akan forests, which developed later than in areas to the west, was important by the fifteenth and perhaps the fourteenth century. This corroborates the thesis that kola cultivation was initiated well before this time in the original area of production. Furthermore, evidence of kola imports into the region that is now Northern Nigeria demonstrates that demand was quite large in the savanna by the fifteenth century, since this area was at a considerable distance from areas of production. Finally, information on trade along the upper Guinea coast gives some indication of the scale of production at the time when the movement of Mande groups into the forest initiated major changes in the original production zone. The coastal trade must have represented only a fraction of the interior trade, but it was, nonetheless, on the order of several hundred tons per year for a relatively restricted geographical area of consumption in the savanna. It seems likely that other parts of West Africa of comparable population density imported at least as much by the same time. The total trade, therefore, probably involved the distribution of thousands of tons of kola annually by the late sixteenth century. Although kola consumption, especially for pharmaceutical reasons, spread from West Africa to North Africa and elsewhere in the Muslim world, it never really spread to any significant degree to the Americas, although some kola was found in Nueva Granada, now Colombia, in the eighteenth century, and in Bahia in the nineteenth century. The impact of kola on global consumption patterns did not develop until the late nineteenth century, with the development of kola tonics. Nonetheless, the innovation relating to kola consumption was clearly based on discoveries in West Africa and reveals the importance of technological change in Africa. The distinct taste of kola provided the inspiration for numerous cola drinks. Such wondrous potions as kola wine, kola cocoa and kola chocolate were experimented with in Great Britain in the 1890s, although only Wellcome's 'Forced March Tabloid' was a preparation that retained the original taste of the bitter nut. Otherwise, sugar and other sweeteners were added to neutralise the natural bitterness of the nuts. Of course, in carbonated form, Pepsi-Cola (known simply as Pepsi, now) and Coca-Cola are currently the most popular, but there are many other brands throughout the world. These carbonated beverages today usually do not have any kola in them but rely on artificial chemicals and ingredients that are usually kept secret. Their consumption has virtually no impact on kola production and the drinks are not bitter, as the nuts that have been traditionally chewed in West Africa are. The consumption of the nuts continues on a massive scale in West Africa, despite the presence of kola drinks as well.

Manufacturing and Industry

An examination of the technological development of particular manufacturing items includes a number of items. This section focuses on the early spread of cotton cultivation, drawing especially on the work of Colleen Kriger. Since at least 1,000 CE, and probably much earlier, there was also local production of raffia cloth and the use of skins and leather for clothing. The most significant development, however, was the spread of cotton textile manufacture, which was based on indigenous innovation. This can be seen clearly with indigo dyeing, including the development of dye pits using locally produced cement. It should be noted that the production of indigo for industrial purposes spread to the Americas via the African diaspora. Similarly, cotton production spread to the Americas, and expanded especially in the United States in the nineteenth century, although not using the variety of cotton that was grown in West Africa.

Cotton had been cultivated, harvested, cleaned, spun into thread and woven into cloth for centuries in West Africa, long before direct trade with Europeans. Cotton was being grown in the region of Senegambia and probably across the whole of the savanna by AD 1000 at least. Consumer markets for certain types of textiles were already in place when Portuguese mariners began exploring the African coastline in the fifteenth century. Early centres of textile production arose in at least two areas of the West African interior. A western centre was located around the upper Niger, Gambia and Senegal watersheds, and in contiguous areas on the desert edge. An eastern centre was located around Lake Chad, and the area of the early Hausa kingdoms.

Cloth is made from fibres, but not all fibres are spun into thread, and not all threads are woven into textiles. In many parts of Africa's rainforest, for example fibres from young leaves of the raphia palm (*Raphia viniferera*) were selected and carefully processed (but not spun) and woven into textiles that served many uses, including circulation as a currency. Then there is bark cloth, a category of nonwoven fabrics that can be very sturdy or thin and delicate. Such cloths were made in West and Central Africa by carefully removing sections of the inner bark of certain selected trees and then pounding the material with a mallet to make them wider, softer and more flexible. In other cases, various types of fibre were spun and then twisted together into heavier threads or cordage that would then be knotted, twined or plaited by hand into clothing and other useful articles. The direction in which the fibres are spun is another important feature of thread and involves turning the spindle on which the thread is wound in one direction or the other, clockwise or counterclockwise. The spinning direction can be clearly seen in the thread itself. In one direction there is an 'S' while in the other direction the pattern forms a 'Z'.

Weaving is a particular process by which two independent sets of threads are interlaced together using a loom. The threads that are lengthwise, or warp, are held under tension in the loom, and the threads that are across the loom, or weft, are passed between sets of raised and lowered warp threads. The weft is then beaten into place so that it intersects each warp thread at a right angle. This process is then reversed so that the orientation of the warp threads is the opposite – the threads that had been raised are now lowered, and the ones that have been lowered are now raised. Each weft thread is passed back through the opening in the threads and beaten against the previous weft. A firmly bound edge is maintained on each side of warp by passing the weft thread back and forth, forming a self-edge, or selvedge. All textile fabrics are produced on a loom that requires such weaving.

As Kriger has demonstrated, weaving is a craft based on calculation and counting. In order to set up a loom, the weaver must estimate how much thread is needed for the warp, which depends on the type of thread, its thickness or fineness, and the intended dimensions and density of the fabric. Then the warp threads have to be measured out to the correct length, placed in sequential order, and arranged on the loom. How the warps are arranged and manipulated creates different types of fabric structures. The most common, elementary textile structure is a plain weave, with single alternating warp threads raised or lowered and single weft threads passed through and beaten in. Using pairs of thread rather than single threads, often of different colours, for the warp and weft creates a basket weave. Other types of structures are made by changing the proportion of warps to wefts. When there are many more warp than weft threads per square inch, the wefts can hardly be seen in the fabric and hence create a warp-face weave. When there are more weft than warp threads per square inch, the weave is weft-faced. Tapestries are weft-face textiles, their imagery made with different colours of weft threads completely covering the warps.

Weavers working with vertical looms have employed a variety of fibres either gathered in the wild or cultivated, and processed locally or imported from elsewhere, and some of them were spun into thread and others not. The earliest forest textiles were most likely woven of unspun fibres, such as young palm leaflets, which required soaking, beating and combing before being dressed and woven on the loom. Of the various palm trees that have been used to make textiles in Africa, the most important ones in the lower Niger region were several species of Raphia vinifera, which was valuable also as a source of palm wine. There is no evidence that raphia palms were deliberately cultivated for the specific purpose of producing textiles on a large scale in West Africa; rather, they were a by-product of the production of palms for wine tapping. In parts of Central Africa, however, raphia fibre was a principal reason why palms were grown, and unlike tapping trees for their wine, which killed the trees, the production of raphia fibre did not endanger the life of the trees.

Even after the introduction and spread of cotton textiles, raphia cloth continued to be made, even in competition with textile imports from overseas, which suggests that consumers in Central Africa, at least, continued to prefer it for certain purposes and considered it necessary for special ceremonial occasions. Even in West Africa, cloths woven entirely of raphia fibre were deemed significant enough in Yorubaland to be designated by their own specific vernacular name, odun, meaning a grass cloth made from bamboo fibres, and odon or odun, meaning a cloth of palm leaf fibres.

Textile manufacture in the savanna regions, particularly in the Sokoto Caliphate in the nineteenth century, was impressive not only because of the quantity of cloth produced but especially because of its recognisably superior quality. The specialised yarns and densely woven cloth were famous throughout West Africa and the Sahara and certainly higher in quality than the tellem cloths, and equal or finer than the best of the Indian cottons that were traded before industrialised cotton manufacture in Europe and North America became common. Furthermore, it appears that the finest cloth was selected to make garments and wrappers strictly for Muslim consumers, both male and female. For these consumers, dress was an indicator of character, taste, acumen and worldly achievement. Prominent Muslim men wore tailored clothing – as long as it was made of acceptable fabrics and in an appropriate style – as an outward sign of their inner qualities and public position. In the Sokoto Caliphate, sak'i cloth in particular was reserved for the tailored robes and trousers that were most esteemed, the cloth destined to be embellished with embroidered imagery.

Indigo has played an important role in local, regional and international economic histories. Indigo is native to tropical areas of south Asia, the Americas and Africa. Various parts of the plant yield medicines and dyestuff that came to be highly valued in the ancient Mediterranean world and were imported by the Greeks and Romans by at least the last centuries BC. *Indigofera tinctoria* was native to eastern and southern Africa, though it has been widely cultivated in West Africa as well, and it was vigorously promoted in Nigeria after 1905 as a richer source of dye than *I. tinctoria*. Another species, from a different genus, *Lonchocarpus cyanescens*, has been harvested in the wild and also cultivated by farmers in the rainforest and the moister savanna areas of much of West Africa. Its presumed antiquity and ubiquity in Yorubaland have earned for it the alternative vernacular term 'Yoruba wild indigo'. Another Indigora species, *I. suffruticosa*, was originally native to tropical America and the West Indies before being introduced into certain parts of Africa through the transatlantic trade. It has been an important dyestuff of international commerce.

The making of indigo-dyed cloth has a long history in the lower Niger region, as reflected in the making of adire eleko. This adire eleko tradition owes much to the Atlantic trade, which brought new patterns, techniques and materials that transformed the way dyed wrappers were made and how they looked. A number of discoveries were made about particular varieties of indigo that could be used as a dye. The efficacy of indigo as a colouring agent varies with the species, growing conditions and timing of harvest, and the resulting differences can be easily recognised in textile products by an experienced and discerning customer. Dyers were conscious of these differences in visual qualities and could achieve deeper shades of blue and even black.

The efficacy of the indigo dye also varied according to the composition of the dye vat and the particular qualities of other ingredients. Additional substances are key to generating a deep blue colour and making sure the colour adheres well to the fibre of the cloth. Much of the dyeing process involves preliminary treatment of the fibre with a mordant to fix the colour, but indigo dyeing is based on an entirely different set of chemical principles and procedures than other dyes. The process has two separate stages. Indigo is insoluble in water; hence it must first undergo reduction to dissolve it, a procedure that also changes the dye bath into a clear liquid called 'indigo white'. Fabric dipped into this bath and taken out again has a yellowish colour that soon changes to green and then to blue. The second stage, the oxidation of the dye, completes the dyeing process. Creating a strong indigo blue was not a simple or easy task, especially when using natural ingredients with all their attendant irregularities and impurities. African dyers, many of them women in the forested areas and men in the savanna, discovered various ways of creating effective solutions for reducing indigo. Furthermore, West African dyers used particular kinds of salts, often sulphates, for making an alkaline vat.

West Africa's consumers, including urban elites and political leaders, were Muslims, especially after the eleventh century. As a result, tailored garments were the preferred clothing for prominent men, and cotton wrappers and head scarves became the clothing of women. Garments of all sorts, especially shirts, robes, pants, veils and turbans made their way across the Sahara into markets along the sub-Saharan sahel and savanna belt. These imports in turn inspired textile manufacturing in West Africa. Woollen cloth was also imported from the Maghreb and was especially associated with Berbers. Similar sturdy woollen blankets and other textiles were also produced south of the Sahara, often from camel hair as well as sheep's wool. Silks were the most exotic and luxurious of the imports, and local silks were also harvested.

Salt Production and Pharmacology

An examination of salt production and pharmacology in the central Sudan of West Africa demonstrates the impact of technological developments in West Africa. As the chemistry of the various salts that were exploited suggests, there was considerable knowledge of NaCl (sodium chloride), sodium sulphates, potassium chlorides and sulphates. Different types of salt, including natron, trona, vegetable salts and sea salt, had significance as medicines, for culinary purposes, for the tanning of leather, and in other ways.

This section discusses salt production and pharmacology, including the chemistry and uses of various salts. The types of salt ranged from pure NaCl (sodium chloride), to sodium sulphates, potassium chlorides and sulphates, natron, trona, vegetable salts, and sea salt. The different salts were used for cooking, as medicines, for tanning leather, to fix dyes in textile production, as well as mixed with tobacco for chewing or snuff. It should be noted that tobacco was grown in West Africa, after being introduced across the Atlantic from the Americas. Because of Muslim prohibitions on smoking, tobacco was more often chewed or taken up the nose, which also released the nicotine, the active ingredient and also an alkaloid with stimulating effects similar to coffee and kola.

Salt was scarce in Africa before the twentieth century. Salt was found in scattered deposits, mostly in the Sahara and in the desert area near the Red Sea but was also released through brine springs in widely scattered locations. Salt was also extracted from sea water through evaporation. The residue in pots that had boiled dry was also used as a salt substitute in areas deficient in salt. In many places, salt earth was scraped from the ground after rain water had evaporated, and in places where there was considerable natural evaporation, the deposits of salt could be used as salt licks for animals and the salt earth could be marketed for animals.

The most sophisticated production of salt developed in the central Sudan, and particularly in the area dominated by the state of Borno, and its predecessor, Kanem, in the basin of Lake Chad. Borno, a Muslim country since at least the eleventh century, controlled the oases of Fachi and Kawar, on the caravan route to North Africa and crucial not only for trans-Saharan trade but also as the sites of major salt deposits. The types of salt from these sites included red natron (Dirkou), white natron (Djado, Sequidine), kantu salt (Bilma, Fachi) and small quantities of purer, higher-priced salt (beza, bilma). These sources are the best known of the production sites in the southern Sahara and the region of Lake Chad. Their position on the route to North Africa meant that medieval Arabic writers were familiar with their locations, although there is no mention of salt production, except for alum. Because of the importance of Kawar in trans-Saharan communication, they have loomed large in Borno history. It seems likely that the salt resources were exploited from an early date. Because Borno had firm control of Kawar and Fachi in the sixteenth century, at least, the state dominated the trade with North Africa and hence benefited from the salt industry of the desert. The northern side of the Komodugu Yo in effect consisted of a broad belt, which stretched from the Sosebaki states in the west to the shores of Lake Chad. The region subdivided into Muniyo, Mangari, Kadzell, and the islands and eastern shore of the lake. Only the lake itself was not under the political control of Borno, but even so, the state was able to influence trade across the lake and hence salt distribution. The types of salt included several kinds of natron, baboul or kige, which was derived from the ashes of bushes, and many varieties of manda, which was a mixture of natron and sodium chloride, and from the eastern shores of Lake Chad, ungurnu, or trona.

Borno salts consist of sodium chloride, sodium sulphate, sodium carbonate, potassium chloride, calcium carbonate, sodium phosphate, potassium sulphate and calcium sulphate in various concentrations. Those referred to as natron (kanwa) have low concentrations of sodium chloride (less than 4 per cent) and are high in sodium carbonate (20–75 per cent) but can include high concentrations of sodium sulphate and/or calcium carbonate. Mangari salt has even a greater variation in composition but generally has a higher concentration of sodium chloride (12–68 per cent), usually with significant amounts of sodium carbonate (many samples range from 11 to 31 per cent, but some are as low as 0.18 percent) and sodium sulphate (15–56 per cent). Small amounts (less than 5 per cent) of potassium chloride are often found in these samples and occasionally traces of other salts (sodium phosphate and potassium sulphate) are present. Baboul or kige salt contains virtually no sodium carbonate or sodium sulphate and consists primarily of sodium chloride and potassium chloride, with smaller amounts of calcium carbonate, potassium sulphate and calcium sulphate. Gwangwarasa is different from the other types of natron in that it consists almost completely of sodium sulphate, and hence cannot be consumed by humans. The greatest variation in chemical composition is found in the natron and salt from the regions of Muniyo, Mangari and Kadzell. Geological conditions differed greatly throughout this wide area, so that the output from different places was unique. Indeed, the salt and natron of Mangari and Muniyo can be thought of as falling on a continuum based on the amount of sodium chloride present. The desert sites were fewer, and while variations existed among locations, there were in effect only five or six types, compared to the hundred or more found in the sahel.

Borno salt was used for a variety of industrial purposes. By far the greatest industrial use was as a salt and medicine for livestock. White natron in powdered form (gari) was used for this purpose the sannana. Natron was used as a mordant in dyeing textiles, although this function was replaced to a great extent in the Hausa centres of the nineteenth century by using the residue from dye pits. In earlier times, however, when the Borno textile industry was more important, its use may have been greater. White natron was also used in making soap and it was mixed with ink. Gwangwarasa, found in only a few locations in Mangari, was used in tanning hides and skins. Since the leather industry was second only to textile production in the central Sudan, the demand for gwangwarasa was very great.

The medicinal uses of the different salts were numerous: ungurnu, or trona, from the eastern shores of Lake Chad, white natron from Mangari and Kawar, and red natron from Mangari and Kawar contained high concentrations of sodium carbonates and hence were excellent for stomach ailments. Local medicinal knowledge credited the different types of natron with specific properties: some were milder and better for children and elders, while others were useful in pregnancy. Because Mangari salt was so similar to natron, it, too, could be used as medicine. In addition, natron and varieties of Mangari salt were used in various mixtures to treat dandruff, problems related to pregnancy, eye disorders and infertility; they were also used as an ingredient in curative potions and mixtures.

Culinary uses were equally specialised. Specific recipes required their own salt or natron. The standard Hausa millet porridge, for example, could be made with various grades of white natron, ungurnu, red natron or Mangari salt; each recipe had a different name. Special meals were prepared for new mothers, in which the hooves of cattle were cooked in brine made from Mangari salt. Most salts could be used as substitutes, and consumption depended to a great extent on price and availability. Nonetheless, it is clear that market demand influenced output. Since the tastes of the various salts differed, it is in culinary uses especially that Borno salts faced competition from other sources. While Mangari salt was in great demand in rural Kano and Zaria, baboul was seldom exported that far west. Its consumption was confined largely to Borno, which suggests that production was never great enough to satisfy western demand. Similarly, the highest quality Kawar salt, beza, never filled the demand, and, consequently, good quality salt from Teguidda and other desert locations farther west was found in the central Sudan markets. Salt from the Benue River valley, especially from Awe and probably Keana and other sites, was also shipped north, since it was relatively pure in sodium chloride when compared with the Borno types. Salt and natron were also mixed with tobacco, which was commonly chewed or taken as snuff. Salt, whether from Kawar, Mangari or Lake Chad, was used widely for this purpose as far west and south as Asante, the Yoruba states, and elsewhere. Ungurnu from Lake Chad was especially popular in Asante, but white natron from Muniyo was also common. Any salt could be added to bring out a pungent taste in the tobacco, and preference appears to have varied with the consumer and availability.

Salt production in Muniyo and Mangari was far more scattered than the desert industry. First, natron was processed throughout Muniyo and Mangari, sometimes at large sites, sometimes simply by scraping natron from the ground wherever it appeared. Second, manda salt was made at perhaps one hundred sites from western Muniyo to an area that was only a few kilometres from Birni Gazargamu. This salt required filtering devices and furnaces, and hence production centres gained a degree of permanence. Some sites were quite large, but there were also many small ones. Third, baboul salt, which also needed filters and ovens, was even more dispersed; there were no large sites. Salt camps consisted of only one or two furnaces, and workers shifted location from year to year. Their camps were found primarily in Kadzell, but some were located in northern and eastern Mangari, again within a few kilometres of Birni Gazargamu. There were also sites south of the Komodugu Yo along the western shore of Lake Chad.

The production of natron in Muniyo and Mangari differed from the manufacture of manda. No furnaces were used and no filtering was necessary. The natron was simply scraped from the ground or from the edges of the ponds and lakes that filled the many depressions between the sand dunes of the countryside. Red natron was only worked in bogs, because the crystals, which formed in a completely dry bed, were too difficult to extract. Red natron was found at Yamia, Saouarni, between Guidjigaoua and Adebour, and at other places. White natron was best mined in completely dry conditions, if loose, producing the impure variety (gari), which was packaged in mats. Pieces of white natron came primarily from the edges of retreating lakes and ponds. Because of the impurities in the natron, 'white' natron (Hausa: farar kanwa) was in fact classified into three types: white, grey and black. Finally, gwangwarasa, used in tanning, was only found at a few sites, and was worked in the same fashion as white natron. The production of manda involved boiling filtered brine in ovens, which contained from forty to one hundred and seventy small pots. The product, often referred to as cones of salt, weighed three to six kilograms and varied greatly in purity and chemical composition. The techniques of manufacture were the same, however, and the organisation and number of workers at each furnace appear to have been very similar, at least for the first few decades of the twentieth century when information is available on production. Work units consisted of ten to twenty people, mostly men, who carried brine, scraped salt earth for the filters, made the filters and furnaces, fetched firewood and packaged the finished salt cones for transport. A headman was in charge of the furnace and other workers (kandine) made the moulds for the salt boiling, while male and female workers (bagazao) did the rest. At Ari Koumbomiram, a major location near Cheri, for example, there were ten furnaces in operation in the early 1940s, and these were organised into work units of approximately ten people each. At one furnace there were five kandine, including the furnace master, and five bagazao. This unit included eight men and two women, who were the wives of the furnace master and one of the workers. The salt season lasted from five to eight months, depending upon the year and the site. In a seven-month season, a work unit could stage twenty-seven boilings, which produced fifty cones each time, for a total of 1,350 to 1,400 cones.

Production of salt in Kadzell involved a different process than in Mangari and Muniyo. The salt, baboul or kige, was made primarily from the ashes of a bush, *Salvadora persica* (Kanuri: babul, kaligu; Arabic: arak, siwark). The bush grew throughout Kadzell, eastern Mangari, the area south of the Komodugu Yo near Lake Chad and also to the east of the lake. Other plants were also burned to produce salt, including three varieties of grass (Kanuri: pagam, kalaslim and kanido), which were found near Lake Chad, and the bush, *Capparis aphylla* (Kanuri: tundub), which was found as far south of the Komodugu Yo as Kukawa. The equipment used in making baboul was similar to that used in Mangari and Muniyo, but first the bushes and clumps of grass were burned, and the ashes placed in a filter similar to the ones used in the production of manda. The brine was then boiled in ovens or in single pots over a fire.

The salt to the east of Lake Chad, ungurnu, was relatively pure trona, which was found in the valleys east of the lake. Although these areas of production were not part of Borno in the nineteenth century, much of the production was exported across the lake to Borno, while the rest passed through tributary states to the south of the lake. The Yedina, who lived on the islands and manned large fleets of canoes, controlled much of this production and transported the ungurnu across Lake Chad. While the Yedina never submitted to the Borno government, commercial relations were so important that an informal dependency was in fact established. Without the Borno commercial infrastructure and its connections with the wider central Sudan market, there would have been no commercial outlet.

The processing of ungurnu was simple. Since the lake was subject to constant evaporation, the salt (trona) was forced to the surface on the neighbouring valleys to the east and north-east of the lake in the region known as Foli, and all that was required was to break the deposited trona into chunks for transport to Borno. The Yedina appear to have used slaves for this task. Sometimes, they travelled east of the lake, particularly to the region of Kelbouram in Kanem, where deposits were to be found at Kelbouram, Betra, Liga, Tergouna, and Anjia. The ungurnu was cut into flat cone-shaped blocks weighing about thirteen kilograms each. This type of salt was distributed widely in West Africa because of its medicinal importance and because people who liked to chew tobacco or take tobacco as snuff liked to add it for purposes of increasing the pungency of the nicotine effect.

Conclusion:
African Contributions to Science and Technology

This exploration of technological innovation demonstrates the dimensions of African contributions to scientific discovery, although full historical analysis must await further research. The extensive writings of West African scholars at Timbuktu and other places in the sahel and savanna undoubtedly contain important information on past discoveries, especially in mathematics. Moreover, the achievements of the Dogon in astronomy, and the contributions to navigation in the Indian Ocean and Red Sea, as well as in the Atlantic, are further examples of exploration. Hence, the properties of salt, iron, copper, tin and gold are only some examples of scientific knowledge well understood in Africa, long before any direct trade with Europe.

It has been argued by some that the transfer of rice technology to the Americas had little if anything to do with African production of rice or with knowledge of the organisation of labour required to produce rice in varying ecological and environmental conditions. In fact, rice production in West Africa was extensively developed. In some places, production techniques were based on a gendered division of labour, while along the Gambia River and elsewhere plantations using slave labour were common. The technology employed to create conditions for maximum rice production involved extensive experimentation in drainage, construction of polders, and methods of desalination and irrigation that were extended and amplified in the Americas. Even the initial variety of rice cultivated in the Americas was the black rice of West Africa.

Some would discount the importance of these contributions to the introduction and development of rice cultivation in the Americas, laying emphasis instead on European entrepreneurship and the investment of capital. These claims ignore certain key historical facts. First, rice was not grown in Europe, and as with all other crops that were exploited using slave labour, there was no knowledge of the crop in scientific, military or entrepreneurial circles until after the introduction of slave labour in the Americas. Second, rice was purchased early in the coastal trade with West Africa, first by the Portuguese and later, by other European countries as they entered the trade of the Atlantic world. Rice was bought to feed the enslaved on board ships because it could be stored easily and because many Africans were accustomed to rice as a mainstay of their diet. Third, Europeans did indeed bring innovation and entrepreneurship to the Atlantic world. The principal innovations were naval technology that permitted control of the Atlantic and ultimately global sea lanes, which meant the ability to transport goods and people and otherwise reorganise the intercontinental division of labour and the factors of production.

Entrepreneurship, however, was confined to two forms of theft: first, the use of slave labour to intensify production, and second, the arbitrary confiscation of land in the Americas that had previously belonged to other people. In both cases, appropriation was achieved through various forms of theft that prompted wars among European nations over control of the spoils. The same observation also applies to the confiscation of technology for producing rice and other crops. The resulting profits were based on the transfer of technology, and, admittedly, its further enhancement, as well as on labour that was subjected to slavery and exploited to the advantage of individuals who today would be charged with crimes against humanity. Not only was labour not paid and land taken without payment, but those who benefited most paid no taxes either. Some scholars have argued that this larceny represented an expression of agency on the part of enterprising people, but for those who were enslaved and those who lost not only their resources but often their lives, slavery and the exploitation that benefited British, French, Dutch, Spanish, Portuguese and other Europeans, and their descendants in the Americas, inflicted lost income, denied investment opportunities, undermined dignity and plagiarised legitimate claims to technological innovation.

The failure to recognise African contributions to science and technology and the transfer of expertise to the Americas minimises the role of enslaved Africans in the development of the Americas, despite the often-inefficient use of the skills and talents of these same individuals. Africans and their descendants were primarily responsible for the production of staple export crops and the mining of gold and silver. They also had to feed themselves, a task which to a great extent relied on food crops and recipes brought from Africa. African labour was important in maritime commerce and in the activities of port towns throughout the Atlantic world as well. Even where technology was known in Europe, such as blacksmithing, many smiths in the Americas were from Africa, whence they brought their own technological expertise and skill in metallurgy. Excellence in European technology was largely confined to weaponry and naval wares. Otherwise, whether in textile and leather production, or agriculture and mining, there was little technological contribution from Europe that superseded that brought from Africa, at least before the nineteenth century. Was it necessary, therefore, to secure the development of the Americas through the confiscation of land, the appropriation of labour and technology through slavery, and the use of military and naval superiority to subjugate people? Whether it was or not, we can conclude that the concentration of wealth involved excessive violence and that the gains from exploiting tropical production were based on enslaved labour, mostly from Africa but also involving Amerindians. The profits that were generated were instrumental in the emergence of banking, insurance, joint stock companies and other capitalist institutions that were located in the financial centres of Europe and the Americas. This concentration of wealth was based on the appropriation of technological advances, whatever their origins, in the interests of entrepreneurs who found ways to reap undue profits through activities that relied on theft and slavery.

BIBLIOGRAPHY

Bocoum, Hamady, ed. *The Origins of Iron Metallurgy in Africa: New Light on its Antiquuity, West and Central Africa.* Paris: UNESCO, 2004.

Carney, Judith Ann. *Black Rice: The African origins of rice cultivation in the Americas.* Cambridge: Harvard University Press, 2001.

Carney, Judith Ann. 'With grains in her hair': Rice in colonial Brazil. *Slavery and Abolition* 25/1 (2004), 1–27.

Carney, Judith Ann. Landscapes of technology transfer: Rice cultivation and African continuities. *Technology and Culture* 37/1 (1996), 5–35.

Carney, Judith Ann and Rosomoff, Richard Nicholas. *In the Shadow of Slavery: Africa's Botanical Legacy in the Atlantic World.* Berkeley and Los Angeles: University of California Press, 2010.

Crosby, Alfred. *The Columbian Exchange: Biological and Cultural Consequences of 1492.* Westport, CN: Greenwood, 1972.

Eltis, David; Morgan, Philip and Richardson, David. Agency and diaspora in Atlantic history and Reassessing the African contribution to rice cultivation in the Americas. *American Historical Review* 112/5 (2007), 1329–58.

Fields-Black, Edda L. *Deep Roots: Rice Farmers in West Africa and the African Diaspora*. Bloomington: Indiana University Press, 2008.

Goodman, Jordan; Lovejoy, Paul E. and Sherratt, Andrew, eds. *Consuming Habits: Drugs in History and Anthropology*. 2nd ed. London: Routledge, 2008.

Gomez, Michael A. *Exchanging Our Country Marks: The Transformation of African Identities in the Colonial and Antebellum South*. Chapel Hill: University of North Carolina Press, 1998.

Hall, Gwendolyn Midlo. *Slavery and African Ethnicities in the Americas: Restoring the Links*. Chapel Hill: University of North Carolina Press, 2005.

Kriger, Colleen E. *Cloth in West Africa History*. Lanham, MD: Altamira Press, 2006.

Kriger, Colleen E. Guinea Cloth: Production and Consumption of Cotton Textiles in West Africa before and during the Atlantic Slave Trade. In: Giorgio Riello and Prasannah Parthasarathi, eds., *The Spinning World a Global History of Cotton Textiles, 1200–1850*. New York: Oxford University Press, 2009.

Lovejoy, Paul E. Kola in the history of West Africa, *Cahiers d'études africaines*, 20/1–2 (1980), 173–75.

Lovejoy, Paul E., The 'Coffee' of the Sudan: Consumption of Kola Nuts in the Sokoto Caliphate in the Nineteenth Century. In: Goodman, Lovejoy, and Sherratt, *Consuming Habits*, 98–120.

Lovejoy, Paul E. *Salt of the Desert Sun: A History of Salt Production and Trade in the Central Sudan*. Cambridge: Cambridge University Press, 1986.

Pollitzer, William S. *The Gullah People and Their African Heritage*. Athens, GA: University of Georgia Press, 1999.

Stemler, A. B. L., Harlan, J. R., and Dewet, J. M. J. Caudatum sorghums and speakers of Chari-Nile languages in Africa. *Journal of African History* 16 (1975), 161–83.

Thornton, John. Precolonial Africa industry and the Atlantic trade, 1500–1800. *African Economic History* 19 (1990), 1–19.

The Memory of Slavery
and the Representation of Self
in the Construction of the Social Identity
of the Agudàs in Benin

Milton Guran

BIOGRAPHY

Milton Guran, anthropologist and photographer, Ph.D in Anthropology from l'École des Hautes Études en Sciences Sociales (EHESS, Paris) and senior associate researcher at the Laboratory of Oral History and Image (LABHOI) at Fluminense Federal University (Niterói, State of Rio de Janeiro, Brazil). Since 2013, he has been the coordinator of the working group proposing the candidature of the Archaeological Site of Valongo Wharf as a World Heritage Site. A specialist in the African diaspora, he has published *Agoudas : les Brésiliens du Bénin* (Paris: La dispute, 2010) and held several photographic and historical exhibitions in Latin America, Europe and Africa.

ABSTRACT

The central argument of this text is the exemplary way in which enslaved Africans in Brazil who returned to West Africa used their own experience of slavery as raw material to socially align themselves with the Brazilian slave traders established in that region, and, thus, to construct for themselves a new social identity that allowed them to play a role in social and economic life as first-class citizens in the society that had rejected them. These are the Agudás or 'Brasileiros', present in Benin, where the phenomenon is numerically and politically more expressive, and in Nigeria and Togo.

The text values the use of photography as a methodological resource to describe more efficiently the process of construction and reproduction of the Agudá social identity in Benin.

This text presents and summarises the research carried out during my doctoral thesis,[1] which has been unfolding and growing richer to this day. At the time, I

---

1 Held at the École des Hautes Études in Social Sciences between 1992 and 1996, under the guidance of M. Jean-Pierre Olivier de Sardan. See Guran (1996).

was in the position of being the first Brazilian researcher to develop a lengthy study in Benin. It is worth mentioning that this research took place at a time of great visibility for Brazil, due to its four football (soccer) championship wins in 1994. The media force of this sports event and the popularity of football among Africans made Brazil effectively present in everyday life in the country. 'Africa cheered for Brazil, we won!' was the enthusiastic exclamation of people as soon as they knew my nationality. The Agudás themselves, known as 'brésiliens', took the opportunity to publicly and proudly display their origins, especially in Porto Novo. In this city, the Agudás celebrated the conquest of the World Cup with a street carnival where there was no lack of Brazilian flags, 'to show that we are Brazilians,' said Jean Amaral, from one of the most traditional Agudá families in the city, and president of the Association des Resortissants Brésiliens – Bourian.[2]

In this extremely favourable context, I was able to establish fraternal and even intimate relationships that introduced me to the everyday life of the 'Brazilians' as someone from the family. Thus, I was able to acquire a wide range of information from various social levels and representing the most varied positions within the proposed study. I came to many of my interlocutors thanks to the surnames inscribed on the doors of their houses, a situation in which my own maternal surname, Monteiro, well known to the Agudás, helped me a lot. In addition, several people spontaneously came forward to 'defend their origins', which is a sign of the weight that this issue of ethnic identity has on social life in present-day Benin. Finally, during the research period for the thesis, I had the opportunity to participate in two major instances of the expression of the Agudá identity: the celebrations of the Catholic feast of Our Lord of Good Ends (Nosso Senhor do Bonfim), which in 1995 and 1996 still preserved their traditional form in Porto Novo; and the process of choice and enthronement, after twenty-six years of vacancy, of Chachá VIII, successor to the famous Don Francisco Féliz de Souza. These situations of identity in action have marked my research significantly, since they represent real moments that synthesised the social process of representation, construction and public reaffirmation of an ethnic identity. In this work, I gathered my expertise as anthropological photographer, consolidated during field experience documenting indigenous communities in Brazil (1978–1991), with the goal of understanding the cultural practices and representations of an ethnic group whose references to Brazil were very evident. From this investment resulted the refinement of a methodology, which had been some-

2 Interview with Jean Amaral, Porto Novo, 13 January 1995.

what overlooked by the anthropology of the time, in which photography is put at the service of an anthropological understanding of the visible world, carried out through a discourse constructed by the articulation between text and image.[3] Thus, I was able to identify in the cultural universe of the Agudá community, through scenes, the important traits of a cultural performance that triggers the memory and the tradition of belonging to an ancestral Brazil, as a way of constructing an identity of their own.[4]

This text is another investment in this exercise of reflecting on the relationship between Africa and Brazil, and so I propose a script that begins with the meaning of words and arrives at the meaning of images and memory in the construction of the social identity of the Agudás.

The Meanings of Words and Behaviours

Once in Cotonou, on learning that I was Brazilian, a Beninese said to me 'So you are not a foreigner, you are an Agudá, like our relatives from Uidá'. In fact, in the languages of the Gulf of Benin, all those with a surname of Portuguese origin are designated as Agudás. In French, the Agudás are called and call themselves simply 'brésiliens', between quotation marks when in writing.[5] In present-day Togo, the word Agudá also means the members of the Syrian, Lebanese and Indian colonies; while in Nigeria in the last century the name applied to all Catholics, regardless of origin (Cunha, M., 1985, 189).

The word 'agudá' probably originates from the transformation of the word 'ajuda' (help), a word widely known in the region for being present in the name

---

3 On the use of photography as a research tool in the social sciences, see Guran (1996 and 1998).

4 The process of building the Agudá social identity in Benin is analysed by me more completely in Guran (1996, 2000, 2010, 2014.) On the Agudás, see also Almeida Prado (1954), Braga (1968 and 1970), Castillo (1990), Castro (1965), Costa e Silva (1989 and 1994), Cunha (1985), Freyre (1990, 1st ed., 1962), Lewicki (1967), Lima (2013), Krasnowolski (1997), Rodrigues (1962), Rossi (1965), Soumonni (2001), Turner (1975) and Verger (1953, 1968 and 1992), Yai, (1997).

5 Since the 1980s, some Beninese social scientists have begun to use the expression Afro-brésiliens to designate Agudás. I prefer, however, to use the already consecrated expression – 'Brazilians' – not to be confused with the adjective for African diaspora culture in the Americas, and, above all, because 'Brazilians' is the term used by all the populations involved, which represents in itself an important factor of affirmation of a social identity.

of the Portuguese fortress of the city of Uidá, the Fort of São João Batista da Ajuda, currently the Historical Museum of Uidá.[6]

Agudás have diverse origins and are currently found in all social classes, being mostly Catholics or Muslims. Most of them, undoubtedly, are descendants of former slaves returned from Brazil,[7] to whom are added a considerable number of descendants of Brazilian or Portuguese merchants or slave traders established on that coast, those whose ancestors never had any connection with Brazil, although they were socially or economically linked to the Brazilians established on the Coast, and were then absorbed by their cultural dynamics. They are descendants of the slaves of these returnees or of the slave traders, or even simply foreign whites of other origins who have united socially with the Agudás. Among the most notorious cases of this occurrence is that of the descendants of François Nicolas Olivier de Montaguère, a Frenchman who settled in Uidá around 1623 (Hazoumé 1937, 31), whose surname changed from Olivier to Oliveira at the height of the influence of the Agudás in the region, when the family was an ally of Chachá I. Later, with the establishment of French colonial domination, a part of the family returned to the original surname.

It is worth remembering that the presence of Brazilians – or of Portuguese who transited through Brazil – was so important in that region that the Portuguese language played the role of a lingua franca. The Catholic Mission of Lyon, which founded the first school in the region, taught its classes in Portuguese, since the Agudás practically constituted the totality of its clientele. Incidentally, it is quite symptomatic that the capital of Benin even maintains a name of Portuguese origin, Porto Novo, designated by the slave trader Eucharistis Campos in 1745, to the detriment of its two traditional names, Hoagbonou and Ajacê, as the Yorubas called it, In the city (Guran 2010, 2000, 1996).

Also very significant is the role played by the slave trader Don Francisco Félix De Souza, who became 'blood brother' of King Ghezo, and who, with the king's accession to the throne, took on the functions of viceroy of Dahomey, with the title of Chachá. It was of great political importance, overlapping even with the yovogan, the minister of the king in charge of the white foreigners, including act-

---

6   Paul Hazoumé (1937, 35) presents the word *agouda* as a transformation of the word *fom* or *huéda* (original language of the city of Uidá) *agouram,* which referred to the Europeans as 'vain and indolent'. This version, however, does not seem compatible with other available historical data and is not taken up by any other author, for which reason I preferred to consider the current explanation to the present day (see Braga, J. S., 1968).

7   The return of former slaves to this region of Africa gained importance, especially because of the deportations that followed the Malcolm Revolt of 1835. In this regard, see Reis (1987).

ing as a kind of guarantor of the Agudás; and of great economic importance, since he held the monopoly on the slave trade in the name of the king of Dahomey. Don Francisco created a dynasty in Uidá, and although his eighth successor does not have political powers anymore, he still has considerable prestige (Costa e Silva 2004; Guran 1996, 2000, 2010; Law 2004).

Brazilian traffickers and former returnees have settled in various parts of the Slave Coast, but it is in Benin, the reference country of this study, that Brazilian culture has established its strongest roots. To this day, we can still find obvious elements of this culture preserved in surnames, buildings (the oldest in the country), typical foods, festivities and even a lighter skin tone among the Agudás.

However, at first glance, other elements may be less evident or even invisible, despite their importance. Such is the case in the manner of introducing or dressing oneself, of receiving visitors, of behaving at table or even in the nature of domestic organisation and of children's education, to cite just a few examples.

In fact, the first Brazilians, whether merchants, slave traders or even former slaves, considered themselves all great masters and lived effectively as such, within the local setting. These former slaves had actually undergone a process of urban socialisation as domestic servants, appointed as foremen or managers of small businesses or in other functions (as slaves of gain, for example) similar to those of their masters in their daily lives. Their cultural reference therefore lies between their masters and not only in the most popular layers, and it is this behaviour of the Bahian elites that they will seek to reproduce in Africa, hence to be commonly referred to as 'those who have white manners'.

The construction of this new social identity, which allowed the insertion of this group of returnees into that African society in transformation in the second half of the nineteenth century and the beginning of the twentieth century, was a reaction to at least two socially adverse situations: the indelible stigma of slavery and the cultural shock between the conditions of life they had enjoyed in Brazil, despite the vicissitudes of slavery, and the way of being of Africans, embodied in the opposition between the notions of 'civilisation / modernity' and 'primitivism / savagery'. This equation emerges from the fact that, for the natives at the time of the return and until the present day, the 'Brazilians' were and still are considered 'slaves' or, at best, 'imported people'; while for the 'Brazilians,' the autochthonous are in turn always treated as 'savages'. All the Agudás interviewed, without exception, affirmed they have been treated as slaves and as 'imported people' by the other Africans, who consider themselves 'from the country'. The latter defend themselves by saying they are merely reacting to the label 'savages' given to them by the Agudás. This confrontation occurs mainly in school, at work and in the market, where, naturally, competitive situations exist.

'Relations (between raptor peoples and battered peoples) remain based on non-recognition of exoticism and perpetuate an irreducible otherness', explains C. Meillassoux (1986, 74). Thus, 'this relation of alterity', he adds, 'is in fact the ideological explanation of a dominator-dominated relation that sets the free citizens of slavery societies against all the battered populations, beaten in the past, in the present and in the future'. It is precisely this relationship between dominator and dominated that the old slaves will subvert through the construction of a new identity – without, however, being able to completely erase the relations of alterity, or otherness, that are just irreducible.

Memory and Social Identity

A social identity is always built in relation to the other, and from this difference (Poutignat & Streiff-Fenart 1995, 41). As Manuela Carneiro da Cunha (1985a, 206) emphasises, '[...] what has been gained by studies on ethnicity has been the precise notion that identity is constructed situationally and by contrast; that is, it constitutes a political response to a given conjuncture, an articulated response with the other identities involved, with which it forms a system'.

In this process of valuing differences, how the returnees – whether of Yoruba, Fon, Mahi, Mina or other origin – differed from other Africans was precisely through the experience of having been slaves in Brazil, which translated into the fact that they spoke Portuguese, had 'white manners' and called themselves mostly Catholics, or Muslims. It was from the memory of this life experience acquired in Brazil, common to all of them, that these returned former slaves were able to assimilate themselves to the Agudás – as the Brazilians or Portuguese established in that region were already known – and thus share the same place in local society (Guran 2007 and 2002). This allowed them, above all, to overcome the stigma of slavery and to insert themselves in the economy alongside those who gave orders, and not simply as a labour force. At a time when the confrontation between traditional culture and expanding capitalism became clearer in the region, as the slave trade was in its final days and a new form of wealth production was imposed, these returnees trained to dominate the basic codes of Western culture, to take on the role of masters and to propel the economy alongside Brazilian merchants and slave traders.

The union between these two groups – one composed of Brazilian and Portuguese merchants and slave traders, and the other of former slave returnees – is unique in bringing together executioners and their victims, so to speak, and has fashioned the profile the Agudá community has today. In it we find, simultaneously, the pride of the slave owners – a condition many of them actually acquired, if not before, then at least after their arrival back in Africa – and the popular habits of slaves acquired in Brazil.

The idea that there is an Agudá collective memory concerning a common cultural heritage to be preserved remains present at various levels in both the discourse and the daily life of the 'Brazilians'. To the memory of the time spent in Brazil, so dear to the former slave returnees (and which, incidentally, served as raw material in the bricolage of the new social identity) is added the memory of the very construction of this identity.[8]

Affirmations such as 'we have done everything in this country' and 'we are very proud of our ancestors' invariably appear in the speeches of the Agudá when it comes to emphasising an ethnic belonging. Thus, they highlight the fact they have an important past with achievements to honour, which is a differentiating factor for them and allows them to establish an ethnic border with other social groups. This past is common to the descendants of slave traders, the former returned slaves and their former slaves in the country: 'The sheet that long wrapped the soap soaps like soap...' is often said in Benin.

There is, then, the memory of the achievements and, by its side, that of a different way of being which complements the first memory and currently reinforces the cultural border between the Agudás and the rest of the population. This different way of being does not mean having 'white manners', exactly, as was the case at the time of the return. Since colonisation vulgarised white manners throughout the country, the Agudás claim a peculiarity of their own, that of having a 'Brazilian white manner'.[9] They affirm this particularity in their way of introducing themselves, in their greetings, by their cuisine, by their condition as first Catholics, by the Portuguese pronunciation of their names, and by the use of some Portuguese words and expressions in their conversations amongst themselves. These words and expressions are known to practically all Agudás, including the young.

Mr Bruno Rodriguez, from the town of Bohicon, when asked what characterises the Agudás in the present day,[10] replied that they had among themselves a 'way of doing' things differently, a common memory composed of recollections shared by all Agudás. A carpenter by profession, he was at age 70 perhaps the greatest connoisseur in the region of the folk tradition of the Burrinha spectacle, and the last specialist in the manufacture of the puppets for the show. 'We have memories

---

8 Field survey in Benin and Togo carried out from 1994 to the present.

9 This logic is sometimes taken to extremes. I have found among the descendants of traffickers, countless people who consider themselves Brazilian citizens, and who hope to see this condition recognised one day by the Brazilian government, or who consider themselves to be white people who have black skin, since their ancestors were forced to marry black women.

10 Interview with Bruno Rodrigues, 14 February 1996, in Bohicon.

that are only ours,' he tells me, 'stories of the past and also ways of speaking and greeting each other...'. I interrupt him, speaking in Portuguese: 'How are you?' And he responds at once (in Brazilian Portuguese): 'Well, thanks'.

The Most Visible Face of Acute Identity

The representation of the self is one of the most evident aspects of the construction of an identity.[11] Given that this process of constructing the new social identity has become perennial, we can follow the still visible traces until the present day. The portraits of the founders and other ancestors of the Agudá families of all origins, exhibited inside homes according to the custom of the country, always show masters dressed in the European style. What seems to be aimed at in these images is that the masters were already 'evolved', to use a term employed by themselves, before French colonisation spread 'white manners' among the majority of the population.

It should be pointed out that photographic practice in postcolonial societies is part of a two-pronged type of representation that relates, on the one hand, to the traditions of valorisation of the ancestors characteristic of this world dominated by the colonisation process and, on the other hand, to the incorporation through photography of a modernity instituted by this same process. The result of this is the production of this material medium – the photographs – which can be framed in two ways. The first is related to the photograph's condition as object that sustains a public and private identity, present in the different types of documents used for the social control of subjects in a modernized institutional order, as well as in the photographs of familiar life that are used to compose the record of a personal memory in which the past tense – associated with belonging to a common trajectory of the group – is updated in the present at every moment the photograph is seen. The second framework, of an invisible nature, includes the speeches and images that inform the photographer's eye and, at the same time, shape the capacity of potential spectators to understand it. In this invisible order are included other photographs, visual texts and verbal discourses – ethnological, touristic, bureaucratic and missionary – that guide the eye and teach the viewer how to see.[12]

In this sense, a kind of background is created in the photographic mise-en-scène, in which what is proper to colonially dominated societies and defines them in their specificity intends to represent what is seen as typical, or even exotic, in relation to the experiments of Western modernity. Thus, as Appadurai (2004) states:

---

11 Cf. Bourdieu (1965) and Goffman (1973).

12   On the role of postcolonial photography cf. Appadurai (2004); Pinney & Peterson (2005); On the material dimension of photographs, cf. Edwards & Hart (2009).

'In postcolonial societies, photography backdrops tell us about ways in which the medium of photography (and not just the subject of the photograph and the photographer) is itself contained, contextualised and sometimes contested. This is because photography is a particularly powerful way in which visual modernity enters societies dominated by other forms of visual representation. Because of its affinity with its susceptibility to mechanical reproduction, its relative technical accessibility and its susceptibility to mechanical reproduction, photography invites indigenous participation and enters everyday life more fully than many other visual practices'.

As such, in order to better evaluate the processes of self-representation, focused as an instrument of construction and affirmation of a new postcolonial identity, we can examine the family portraits exhibited in the parlour of Mr. Eustache Prudêncio, in Cotonou (the images referred to are available at http://www.afroasia.ufba .br/pdf/afroasia_n28_p45.pdf, pp.55, 56 and 57).[13] Mr. Prudêncio, a poet recognised and honoured in France and in Benin, former minister, retired ambassador, officer of the French Legion of Honour and Order of Dahomey, knight of the National Order of Benin, whose mother comes from the De Souza family, is certainly one of the most eminent personalities in Benin. His name is pronounced Prudêncio, in the best Portuguese accent, and not with the tonic accent on the final 'o', where the French place it.[14] His grandfather's father, of Yoruba origin, would have been, according to him, a collaborator of the famous viceroy of Uidá, Don Francisco Félix de Souza, more precisely his bokonon, the one who practises the Fá.[15] The Brazilian slave trader would have taken him to Bahia, where he would have been baptised under the name of Prudêncio. As is quite common among the Agudás, their first name would then have been turned into a surname. The Prudêncio family always lived alongside the De Souza concession in Uidá. Therefore, Eustache Prudêncio grew up in the very heart of the so-called 'Brazilian' culture. The fact that he is both a descendant of the father of Don Francisco de Souza, a

13 The images referred to in this text are part of the articles 'From the bricolage of memory to the construction of the image itself among the Agudás of Benin' [Da bricolagem da memória à construção da própria imagem entre os agudás do Benim] (Guran 2002), available at http://www.afroasia.ufba.br/pdf/afroasia_n28_p45.pdf , and 'DIY of memory: oral and visual sources in the construction of Agudá identity' [Bricolagem da memória: fonts orais e visuais na construção da identidade agudá] (Guran 2013), available at http://www.historiaoral.org.br.

14 Agudás, in general, are very proud to maintain the original Portuguese pronunciation of their names. However, more and more, especially with the new generations, what we may find is French pronunciation of surnames and surnames of Brazilian origin.

15 Interview with Eustache Prudêncio on 6 February 1996 in Cotonou.

slave trader, and one of his 'collaborators' on his father's side, helps to make him a very significant example of this issue.

Moreover, having his portrait painted, as Gisèle Freund (1974, 11) observed, is 'one of those symbolic acts by which individuals of the ascendant class make visible to themselves and others their ascension and rank among those who enjoy social consideration'. This is particularly the case with Mr. Prudêncio's family portraits, where according to the Agudá habits, the characters are represented in the most European way possible (meaning the closest to the great Brazilian masters) and, therefore, the least African.[16]

It should be noted these three photographs were taken from a point that is below the eye level of the people photographed, which forcibly enhances the power of the image. Eustache Prudêncio chose for his salon a photo of himself taken on the occasion of a study period in France. This prestigious aspect – studying in France – is symbolically similar to his uncle's tall collar or his father's decoration. The representation of the self allows the 'Brazilians' to establish immediately a clear border marking their differences vis-à-vis the whole of society. The fact that these photos are on display in the entrance hall of the house clearly expresses the importance of keeping this difference very much in evidence from the beginning, and of always bolstering it.

This same method of self-representation using of an image of themselves with a marker of social prestige can be observed in the family photos of Mrs Patterson, born De Medeiros, great-granddaughter of Don Francisco Félix de Souza, Chachá I, and in the way she lets herself be photographed in the hall of her house in Porto Novo (see Guran 2002, 59). She is dressed in a Western-cut dress (although made of African fabric), her hair in European style, without braids or cloth on the head. Despite the technical limitations of the photograph, it can be seen that her skin colour is noticeably lighter than that of the African population in general, which is often the case among the Agudás.

In the image in question, we see the hall divided into two rooms: the living room, where Mrs Patterson is located, and the dining room, protected by a folding screen in the background, on the left side of the image. In the living room, whose entrance is on the right and the windows on the left, both outside the frame, it is possible to see a carpet that marks the place occupied by the armchairs (in the foreground) and by a coffee table. This table, covered by an embroidered tablecloth, is decorated with a vase of flowers picked, in fact, from the garden belonging to the house. Among the armchairs, there are other little tables like the one in the foreground, next to Mrs Patterson. On the noblest wall of the room, in front of

---

16   On the portraits of the nineteenth-century Brazilian aristocracy cf. Mauad (2008, 1997).

the armchairs, to the right of the picture, is the portrait of Mrs Patterson's paternal aunt, Cândida de Medeiros, with her husband and daughter, all elegantly dressed in the European fashion and arranged in the consecrated pose used to represent the bourgeois family of the early twentieth century (see Guran 2002, 60). This enlargement in black and white, in format 40 cm x 50 cm, was made in Paris around 1920 and yet is in perfect condition, which attests to its high quality.

Behind Mrs Patterson in the photo, one can see the portrait of her late husband in a suit and tie, arranged on a small piece of furniture where there is another flowerpot. The strict organisation of this domestic space, so different from a traditional African house and so similar to a wealthy Brazilian house from the beginning of the twentieth century, not only translates Brazilian identity but also indicates how this way of living every day is used socially.

Another photograph, shown in Mrs Patterson's living room (see Guran 2002, 62), gives us more information about her family history, and consequently about the construction of the 'Brazilian' identity, such as the images of Mr. Prudêncio in the living room. It shows her grandmother, Francisca de Medeiros, who was the youngest daughter of Don Francisco de Souza, with her son Cesário, father of Mrs. Patterson (the same one who is present), with his older brother Leopoldo in another photograph (see Guran 2002, 63), made in Paris years later, where the so-called 'white manners' are unmistakably explicit. This image of Mrs Francisca de Medeiros is a reproduction, originally dating from 1873 and retouched by the author, according to the technique of the time. The mere fact of portraying herself in nineteenth-century Africa sitting on a chair with her son on her knees already demonstrates a high standard of living and a conception of social life and its representation as absolutely European. Moreover, the lady in question presents herself 'as a white woman', that is, dressed in the Western style and not in the traditional way, with straightened hair, without braids or cloths in the African fashion, and with her head uncovered because she's inside the house. Little Cesário, of very light skin, dresses like a rich boy from nineteenth-century Brazilian society. In fact, the very scene of the photography, painted by the author, seeks to give the same impression of wealth and bourgeois sobriety that can be found in the photograph of the two brothers in Paris.

This representation of themselves in the 'Brazilian' fashion is present in all situations in which the Agudá identity is brought to the fore, being expressly used for this purpose. This is the case with the festivities of Our Lord of the Good End, the patron saint of the Agudás, with the Agudás' parade through the streets of Porto Novo on the eve of the celebration of the Mass for Our Lord of the Good End, which resembles a carnival parade in Brazil in the mid-twentieth century, including the use of the Brazilian national flag (see Guran 2013, 138 and 139). The parade is animated by songs in Portuguese and in Yoruba, whose words introduce the Brazilians' party and invite the population to join. The ladies dress in the 'Brazilian' fashion, that is, as a lady of Brazilian society of the nineteenth century (see Guran 2013, 134). In the parade there is a great puppet of the carnival of the city of Recife, which in Benin is called evocatively Ioiô or Papa Giganta.[17]

The construction of the Agudá image also occurs from a specific way of behaving socially, including how they greet each other, often with a resounding 'good morning' in Portuguese (see Guran 2002, 65).

The Times of Memory

Being Agudá in Benin today means sharing a common memory of a set of achievements and a way of being similar to that of a 'Brazilian'. To better understand this situation, we can divide the process of constructing this social identity into three successive periods.

The first one begins when the presence of Brazilian slave traders on the Coast becomes stronger, at the beginning of the nineteenth century. The slave trade was then banned and the Bahians did everything to ensure it would continue for a few more years. These Brazilian traffickers and merchants were whites who lived their own way and who married native women. They maintained commercial and political relations with the autochthonous population, who were assimilated through marriage to an extent. They were not very numerous despite their great economic and political importance, and they made their fortune and lived according to their own culture. They were white in a black society, their mestizo children were considered white like their parents, and they were all called (and everyone else called them) Agudás, a designation that dated back several generations.

A second important period begins with the massive arrival of former slaves, starting in 1835. They were black, but had 'white manners'. They discriminated against the natives, whom they considered 'savages', just as they were themselves rejected by them, as they continued to be seen as 'slaves' and were thus excluded.

The question of slavery is practically absent from school books in Benin and very often minimised in scholarly works on the ancient kingdom of Dahomey,[18] but it is nevertheless always present in social and personal relations. In fact, as

---

17 'Ioiô' is the colloquial form used in Brazil in the nineteenth century to designate a young slave owner. 'Giganta' is not unlike the Brazilian term 'gigante' which means someone of immeasurably tall stature, a giant.

18 A good example of this kind of attitude is the work of Le Danxomè, by Maurice Ahanhanzo Glèlè, member of the royal family, of the branch of King Glèlè, successor of Ghêzo.

C. Meillassoux (1986, 107) stresses, 'the capture (or the purchase that presupposes the capture) marks the slaves with an indestructible stigma'. Trafficking in the region had powered the economy for centuries, and slavery had been an enduring institution among all the peoples involved. Therefore, it is not surprising that social discrimination from having been a slave persists to this day in the relations of the Agudás among themselves and with other social groups.

All the 'Brazilians' that I interviewed throughout my research stated they had been pointed out and called 'slaves' in various everyday situations. It's pretty much the rule in school and in the market. In the realm of private life, on the contrary, explains the historian François de Medeiros, 'there is a tacit agreement not to speak of slave descent'.

The former slaves who returned had different ethnic origins and were only united through their common past spent in Brazil. In other words, what united them was the common memory of a lived social experience. This memory was translated into daily life, a way of being, and, above all, by a professional qualification in accordance with the new European cultural and economic parameters that were being imposed more and more in the country. They used white surnames and had as their model the white culture acquired in Brazil. This culture was a great asset and allowed them to associate themselves with the Bahian slave traders in the most modern economic activities. These activities, primarily based on the slave trade, have evolved towards more varied international and local trade, as well as the production and exploitation of local resources, such as palm or palm oil.

For society as a whole, they had 'white manners,' and they called themselves Catholics and spoke Portuguese. Their numbers – augmented by the native slaves at their service – became more significant and, as a result, they gradually acquired a greater weight in the demography of the region. They formed a community amongst themselves, in which the first whites and their mestizo descendants were a kind of elite. During the second half of the nineteenth century, they formed a society apart, basically inbreeding, and built a social identity assimilated to that of the first Brazilians. This identity was also reproduced through religion – they were basically Catholic, in spite of mixing with voodoo cults – and through school instruction. They set up schools where all children, boys and girls, learned to read and write in Portuguese, while Abomé's subjects were forbidden to attend classrooms.

The Agudá – at this time composed of descendants of slave traders, former slave returnees, their descendants and their slaves – are at the origin of practically all modern economic activity and the penetration of Western culture in the region. In fact, they represented the future when they first arrived, since European culture – that is, their 'white manners' – eventually imposed itself on everyone.

If we examine the Agudá culture of this second period more closely, we find that it is different from that of the first Brazilians. It is different in itself but, above all, its social function changes. The Bahian slave traders were white (and thus naturally different from the natives), so they had their own place in the autochthonous society. This place was secured by their economic alliance with the king of Dahomey, and was expressed symbolically by the role of the Chachá and other Brazilian figures in power.

The old returned slaves, on the contrary, were forced to invent a place for themselves in a society that did not accept them. There, they were both those who had already been expelled (i.e. sold as slaves) and foreigners (since, in addition, they came back completely different, with 'white manners'). The construction of a new social identity out of the memory of the time lived in Brazil was for them the means of inserting themselves in this society, in the same place that had already been established for whites. 'The notion of "foreigner"' – as Meillassoux explains (ibid, 105) – 'is common to all African populations. It is usually opposed to the notion of "man", that is, of "citizen", of "patrician", the person provided with all social prerogatives in the considered environment. [...] The alien must ally himself with a protector, his guarantor and his "witness" in the society where he penetrates, a previous bond that will allow the establishment of all the others. In the absence of this endorsement, in solitude, the foreigner is doomed to servitude'. In the situation under analysis, it is precisely this 'Brazilian' identity, already endorsed by King Ghezo (through his pact with the Chachá, Don Francisco Félix de Souza), and by other potentates, which guarantees the former returned slaves and provides effectiveness to their strategy of social insertion.

They become Agudás, but not exactly like the others. It is true they had their masters as models, and had roughly assimilated their culture (which was close to that of the first Agudás), but they also brought to Africa a certain culture developed in Brazil by the people and by slaves themselves. Thus, apart from architecture and the representation of the self, the most visible 'Brazilian' identity indicators date back to practices more closely related to slaves than to their masters in Brazil. This is the case with feijoada (originally a dish of the senzala, before turning into a Brazilian national dish), the feast of Our Lord of the Good End (initially a feast of Africans and Creoles from Bahia, before becoming an entire people's reason for devotion), and the folklore of Burrinha (a popular festival of folk character that was never really practised by the elites). Agudá culture, initially a European culture, was then enriched by aspects of a true Brazilian culture, as it was being built in Brazil itself.

The French colonial presence, imposing 'white manners' across the country, supported in a way the cultural choice of this mass of generic Africans newly returned from Brazil. Those who had left as slaves returned as masters, and, thus, as bearers of the culture that was being imposed on the country. It is at this moment that the opposition between the notions of 'civilisation / modernity' and 'primitivism / savagery' acquires new contours in the game of insertion of the former slaves into the local society.

Then, we come to the third period that is important in understanding the Agudá identity in Benin, which is the present period. In our day, the memory of the time lived in Brazil has given way to the memory of the achievements made in Benin. Similar to how the first memory had the function of allowing the insertion of these returned slaves into the local society, the second one also had a precise social function. In reality, the opposition 'slaves, imported people / savages' remains on the agenda of social interaction. It is from the memory of their achievements ('we have done everything in this country...') that the 'Brazilians' – excluded from office as slaves – defend the legitimacy of their place in today's Beninese society.

The relations between the Agudá and the French administration had various configurations. The 'Brazilians' were initially allies of the French, who used them as intermediaries in relation to the natives. From the outset, when the Porto Novo protectorate was set up in 1861, they strongly supported France against Great Britain (see Costa e Silva, 1989c, 61–62). The great families of Porto Novo, for example, came to participate directly, alongside the French, in the war effort against Behanzin. Ignacio Paraiso, the most important Agudá of Porto Novo, was the only African to sit on the colonial council since its installation. Several other 'Brazilians' were directly employed by the French administration at various levels (see Sanvi 1977). In a way, the 'Brazilians' still play this role as intermediaries, with small variations. In fact, they are unable to fully embrace their Agudá condition because they have established alliances with other ethnic groups through marriages, which leads them to a situation of integration within large, extended African families. Hence, their new condition as intermediaries.

However, as the French took control of the country, the 'Brazilians' were progressively removed from the most profitable economic activities. This was the case first with the wholesale trade and shortly after with the retail trade, both placed under the monopoly of French companies. The more solid Agudá traders were then led to bankruptcy.

The social and political influence of the 'Brazilians' truly fell into decline from 1946, when the political and economic life of Benin changed dramatically as a result of the new system of political representation in the Territorial Assembly and the French National Assembly. It is at this moment, as the Beninese historian Karl Emmanuel Augustt explains,[19] that 'Brazilians and mestizos in general, considered as assimilated to the colonial administration, are dislodged from power'. This trend was further accentuated on independence, when the Agudás, who were already traditionally considered foreigners, were then assimilated by the Beninese

---

19 Interview with K. E. Augustt, 4 September 1995, in Cotonou.

to the French as colonisers. 'They are accused of having helped the white man, they placed themselves from the beginning on the white side', summarises another Benin historian, Prof. Adrien Djivo.[20] Karin Urbain da Silva, the honorary consul of Brazil, points out there was a great 'reckoning' against the 'Brazilians' that lasted until 1972.[21] He referred to the Marxist regime of General Kérekou, when the Agudás were again discriminated against, and this time assimilated to the bourgeoisie. Despite the participation of some personalities in the nomenclature of the regime, the 'Brazilians' maintain that they were practically banished from public life in this period, 'victims of the same anticolonial fury that also tried to eliminate the traditional leadership'.

The process of democratisation installed in 1989 in Benin corresponds to a movement of revaluation of the traditional leadership, as well as of voodoo cults and other religious manifestations. An example of this is the international festival of voodoo arts and cultures called 'Ouidah 92', which took place in January 1993 (see Tall 1995a and 1995b), and the establishment of a national voodoo cult day to be celebrated in the month of January. The enthronement of Honoré de Souza as the eighth successor of D. Francisco Félix de Souza in October 1995, twenty-six years after the death of the last Chachá, is part of this movement aimed at valuing the political weight of traditional leaders, among them the Chachá.[22]

In this context, we can understand the importance of highly mediated public ceremonies that involved the enthronement of Chachá VIII. They reinforce the memory of achievements while symbolically reaffirming the primitive alliance that gave the Agudá people a place in Dahomean society. Moreover, at least for Abomé's court, the Chachá is effectively considered the representative of all 'Brazilians'.

The enthronement ceremony and the solemn visit of Chachá VIII to King Agoli-Agbo in Abomey soon afterwards, were carefully prepared to mediate a representation of the Agudá culture, with the clear objective of inscribing the figure of the Chachá as the main interlocutor of the community in the whole country (See photo in Guran 2002, 73). Mitô Honoré Feliciano Julião de ãouza, Chachá VIII, took over his functions while holding in his hands the sceptre that symbolises his power. It has on the handle the representation of an elephant, which refers to one of the

---

20 Interview with Prof. Djivo, 11 February 1996, in Djeffa.

21 Interview with Karim U. da Silva, 10 February 1996, in Porto Novo.

22 Interview with Émile Poisson, 23 September 1995, in Pahou: with Rachida de Souza, 27 August 1995, in Cotonou; and with Francisca Patterson, 12 February 1995, in Porto Novo. Mrs Patterson, in fact, even became a prisoner with several other 'Brazilians' under this regime, accused of counterrevolutionary activities.

nicknames of Don Francisco.[23] The elephant is also represented in the two sculptures that flank its throne, and in the enthronement he is flanked by bridesmaids – two twins from the De Souza family, whose natural condition assures them, according to tradition, of good luck – dressed in the 'Brazilian' fashion, using the standard fabric for the closest relatives of the Chachá. It should be noted that all members of the family next to the ceremonial throne are dressed in the European style, that is, the 'Brazilian' style.

In both the enthronement ceremony and the ceremonial visit to the king in Abomey shortly afterwards, it was very clear that the intention was to reinforce the memory of the achievements (marking the Agudá presence from the golden times of the Fon monarchy). At the same time, the primitive alliance (the blood pact between Don Francisco and Prince Kampke, future King Ghezo) was symbolically reaffirmed, assuring the Agudá a prestigious place in Dahomean society. It is worth noting that the Chachá is recognised in the court of Abomey as a brother of the king, as one who is on the same level as the king, and this equivalence was shown throughout the country on television (see Guran 2002, 75).

In conclusion, the main aspect to be highlighted is that the bricolage of a new ethnic identity from the memory of the time lived in slavery allowed the social insertion of the former slave returnees as citizens with full rights. In fact, this insertion was possible, on the one hand, because society as a whole was in the process of evolving in the direction of the culture brought by them and, on the other, because the admission of those excluded was absolutely necessary to make this evolution possible and more effective. The Agudás were first the intermediaries between the traditional societies and Western culture, soon to become the interpreters of the natives close to the colonial power and vice versa. Mixed and interwoven with traditional societies through marriage, they have also played the role of intermediaries within the different indigenous ethnic groups, always inscribing themselves as one of the main actors in the process of building a modern Benin.

BIBLIOGRAPHY

Almeida Prado, J. F., 1954 [1950]. Les relations de Bahia (Brésil) avec le Dahomey. *Revue d'Histoire des Colonies* [Paris], 41/143 (deuxième trimestre), 167–226. (Translated from the *Revista do Instituto Histórico e Geográfico Brasileiro*, Rio.)

23 Tradition says that, once, when the deposed king Andadozan met Chachá, who was walking in the palace beside Ghezo (who had deposed the king with the help of Chachá), he would have reviled the latter. At the time, Ghezo would have commented that the hyena growls, but cannot reach the elephant. Thus was born the nickname Ajinakou, one of the ceremonial names of Chachá I.

Appadurai, A., 2004. *The Post-colonial Backdrop*. Michigan: Gale Group.

Bourdieu, P., org., 1965. *Un art moyen. Essais sur les usages sociaux de la photographie*. Paris: Les Editions de Minuit.

Braga, Júlio Santana, 1968. Notas sobre o 'Quartier Brésil' no Daomé. *Afro-Ásia* [Salvador: Centro de Estudos Afro-Asiáticos/UFBa], 6/7.

Braga, Júlio Santana, 1970. Anciens esclaves brésiliens au Dahomey (Contributions à l'étude de la langue portugaise au Dahomey). *Etudes Dahoméennes* Nouvelle Série, Porto Novo.

Castillo, Lisa, 2011. Memory, Myth and History. In: Araújo, Ana Lúcia, *Paths of the Atlantic Slave Trade*. Cambria Press: New York.

Castro, Yída Pessoa de, 1965. Notícia de uma pesquisa em África. *Afro-Ásia* [Salvador: Centro de Estudos Afro-Asiáticos/UFBa], 1, 41–56.

Costa e Silva, Alberto, 1989a. Os sobrados brasileiros de Lagos. In: *O vício da África e outros vícios* [Lisbon: João Sá da Costa], 9–12.

Costa e Silva, Alberto, 1989b. Os habitantes brasileiros de Lagos. In: *O vício da África e outros vícios*, op. cit., 13–18.

Costa e Silva, Alberto, 1989c. As relações entre o Brasil e a África Negra, de 1922 à primeira guerra mundial. In: *O vício da África e outros vícios*, op. cit., 25–65.

Costa e Silva, Alberto, 1994. O Brasil, a África e o Atlântico no século XIX. *Studia* [Lisbon], 52, 195–220.

Costa e Silva, Alberto, 2003. *Um rio chamado Atlântico*. Rio de Janeiro: Nova Fronteira.

Costa e Silva, Alberto, 2004. *Francisco Felix de Souza: mercador de escravos*. Rio de Janeiro, Nova Fronteira/UERJ.

Cunha, Manuela Carneiro da, 1979. Etnicidade: da cultura residual mas irredutível. *Revista de cultura e política* [São Paulo], 1/1, 235–44.

Cunha, Manuela Carneiro da, 1985a. *Negros, estrangeiros – os escravos libertos e sua volta à África*. São Paulo: Brasiliense.

Cunha, Manuela Carneiro da, 1985b. Introdução in: Cunha, Mariano Carneiro da, *Da Senzala ao Sobrado*. São Paulo: Nobel/Edusp.

Edwards, E. and Hart, J., 2009. *Photographs Objects Histories*. London: Routledge.

Freund, G, 1974. *Photographie et société*. Paris: Seuil.

Freyre, Gilberto, 1990 [1962]. Acontece que são baianos. In: *Bahia e baianos*. Salvador: Fundação das Artes/Emp. Gráfica da Bahia [1st edn. in: *Problemas Brasileiros de Antropologia*. Rio de Janeiro: José Olympio].

Glèlè, Maurice Ahanahanzo, 1974. *Le Danxomè*. Paris: Nubia.

Goffman, E., 1973. *La mise en scène de la vie quotidienne*. Vol. 1: *La présentation de soi*, Paris: De Minuit.

Guran, Milton, 1998. Fotografar para descobrir, fotografar para contar. *Cadernos de Antropologia e Imagem*, Rio de Janeiro: UERJ, vol. 10.

Guran, Milton, 1996. Agoudas – Les 'Brésiliens' du Bénin – Enquête anthropologique et photographique. Thesis in Anthropology at l'École des Hautes Etudes en Sciences Sociales, Paris.

Guran, Milton, 2000. Agudás – os 'brasileiros' do Benim. Rio de Janeiro: Nova Fronteira/Gama Filho.

Guran, Milton, 2002. Da bricolagem da memória à construção da própria imagem entre os Agudás do Benim. *Afro-Ásia* [Salvador: Universidade Federal da Bahia], no. 28.

Guran, Milton, 2007. Du bricolage de la mémoire à la construction de l'identité sociale. Les Agoudas du Bénin. *Rue Descartes – Réflexion sur la Post-Colonie* [Paris: Collège International de Philosophie], no. 58, 2001/4.

Guran, Milton, 2010. Agoudas – Les 'brésiliens' du Bénin. Paris: La Dispute.

Guran, Milton, 2013. Bricolagem da memória: fontes orais e visuais na construção da identidade agudá. *Revista Brasileira de História Oral*, 16/1.

Guran. Milton, 2014. Identidade Agudá espelhada no tempo: fotografia como instrumento de pesquisa – um relato de experiência. *Boletim do Museu Paranaense Emílio Goeldi*. Ciências Humanas, Belém, 9/2, 557–65.

Hazoumé, Paul, 1937. *Le Pacte de Sang au Dahomey*. Paris: Institut d'Ethnologie.

Krasnowolski, Andrzej, 1987. *Les Afro-Brésiliens dans le processus de changement de la Côte des Esclaves*. Varsóvia: Académie Polonaise des Sciences, Centre de Recherches sur les Pays Hors d'Europe.

Law, Robin, 2004. *Ouidah – The Social History of a West African Slaving 'Port' 1727–1892*. Oxford: James Currey / Ohio University Press.

Lewicki, Tadeusz, 1967. Um afro-brasileiro introdutor da cultura de cana-deaçúcar e da indústria açucareira na Nigéria do Norte. *Afro-Ásia* [Salvador], 4/5, 53–57.

Lima, Mônica, 2013. Histórias entre margens: retornos de libertos para a África partindo do rio de Janeiro no século XIX. *Revista de História Comparada*. Rio de Janeiro, 7/1, 67–114.

Mauad, Ana Maria, 1997. Imagem e Auto-imagem do Império. In: Alencastro, Luis Felipe (org.) *História da Vida Privada no Brasil*, São Paulo: Companhia das Letras, vol. 2.

Mauad, Ana Maria, 2008. *Poses e Flagrantes: ensaios sobre história e fotografias*. Niterói: Eduff.

Meillassoux, Claude, 1986. *Anthropologie de l'esclavage. Le ventre de fer et d'argent*. Paris: Presses Universitaires de France.

Pinney, Christopher and Peterson, Nicolas, eds., 2005. *Photography's Other Histories*. Durham, NC: Duke University Press.

Rassinoux, Jean, 1987. *Dictionnaire Français-Fon*. Saint-Étienne (Fr.): Imprimerie Dumas.

Reis, João José, 1987 [1986], Rebelião escrava no Brasil – a história do levante dos malês (1835). São Paulo: Brasiliense.

Rodrigues, José Honório, 1962. The influence of Africa on Brazil and of Brazil on Africa. *Journal of African History*, 3/1, 49–67.

Rossi, David A., 1965. The career of Domingos Martinez in the Bright of Benin, 1933–64. *Journal of African History*, 6/1, 79–90.

Sanvi, Anne-Marie Clementine, 1977. Les métis et les Brésiliens dans la colonie du Dahomey 1880-1920. Master's dissertation in History. Cotonou: Université Nationale du Bénin.

Soumonni, Elisée, 2001. Some reflections on the Brazilian legacy in Dahomey. *Slavery and Abolition*, vol. 22, 42–60.

Souza, Simone de, 1992. *La famille De Souza du Bénin-Togo*. Cotonou: Les Éditions du Bénin.

Tall, Emmanuelle Kadya, 1995a. Dynamique des cultes voduns et du Christianisme Céleste au sud-Bénin. *Cahiers des Sciences Humaines*, 31/4, 797–823.

Tall, Emmanuelle Kadya, 1995b. De la démocracie et des cultes voduns au Bénin. *Cahiers d'Études Africaines*, 35/137, 195–208

Turner, Michel Jerry, 1975. Les Brésiliens – The impact of former Brazilian slaves upon Dahomey. Doctoral thesis in History. Boston: Boston University.

Verger, Pierre, 1953a. Influence du Brésil au Golfe du Bénin. *Les Afro-Américains – Mémoires de l'Institut Français de l'Afrique Noire* [Dakar], no. 27, 11–101.

Verger, Pierre, 1953b. Le culte des vodun d'Abomey aurait-il été apporté à Saint-Louis de Maranhon par la mère du roi Ghézo? *Les Afro-Américains – Mémoires de l'Institut Français de l'Afrique Noire* [Dakar], no. 27, 157–60.

Verger, Pierre, 1968. *Flux et reflux de la traite de nègres entre le Golfe du Bénin et Bahia de Todos os Santos du XVIIè au XIXè siècles*. Paris/La Haye: Mouton & Co.

Verger, Pierre Fatumbi, 1991. Entretien avec Emmanuel Garrides. *L'Ethnographie* (109), 167–78.

Verger, Pierre, 1992. *Os Libertos*. São Paulo: Corrupio.

Yai, Olabiyi B., 1997. Les 'agoudas' (afro-brésiliens) du golfe du Bénin – identité, apports, idéologie: essai de réinterpretation. *Lusotopie* [Bordeaux: Centre d'études d'Afrique, Institut d'Études Politiques de Bordeaux], vol. 4, 275–84.

Combating 'Modern Slavery' in Rhetoric and Practice

Joel Quirk

BIOGRAPHIY

Joel Quirk is a Full Professor and the Head of the Department of Political Studies, University of the Witwatersrand, South Africa. His research focuses on slavery and abolition, human mobility and human rights, repairing historical wrongs, social movements and contentious politics, and the history and politics of sub-Saharan Africa. Recent works include *The Anti-Slavery Project* (Penn, 2011), *International Orders in the Early Modern World* (Routledge, 2014, co-edited), *Mobility Makes States* (Penn, 2015, co-edited), and *The Invention of Contemporary Slavery* (UBC, in press, co-edited). He has also recently co-edited special issues/sections on 'Repairing Historical Wrongs' (*Social & Legal Studies*, 2012), 'Sampling Techniques in Johannesburg' (*Journal of Refugee Studies*, 2012), and the 'Politics of Numbers' (*Review of International Studies*, 2015). Joel has served as Rapporteur for the Scientific Committee since 2011, and is also an editor for *openDemocracy*'s 'Beyond Trafficking and Slavery' (https://www.opendemocracy.net/beyondslavery).

Introduction

Many different practices and problems have recently been classified as forms of 'slavery', or as 'modern slavery'. In one notorious example from Syria and Iraq, the systematic abuse of captured women and girls by Islamic State fighters has been described in terms of slave raiding and trading.[1] In another celebrated example from Brazil, local campaigners and officials working to combat the serious abuse of tens of thousands of migrant labourers by powerful rural landowners have similarly invoked the language of slavery.[2] Campaigners have also made an

---

1 Rukmini Callimachi, 'ISIS Enshrines a Theology of Rape', *New York Times*, 13 August 2015. Available at http://www.nytimes.com/2015/08/14/world/middleeast/isisenshrines- a-theology-of-rape.html?_r=0 (accessed 5 November 2016).

2 Leonardo Sakamoto, 'Using a "Dirty List" to Clean Up "Modern Slavery" in Brazil', open Democracy, 13 September 2016. Available at https://www.opendemocracy.net/beyond-slavery/lgscpd/leonardo-sakamoto/leonardosakamoto-yes (accessed 5 November 2016).

issue of 'World Cup slavery' in order to challenge the state-sponsored abuse of migrant workers building stadiums in Qatar.[3] In the less well-known case of North Korea, hundreds of thousands of enemies of the state endure inhuman conditions within a network of forced labour camps, which have in turn been described in terms of slavery.[4] All of these different examples have in turn contributed to a much larger political conversation. According to governments, political activists and international organisations, the category of 'slavery' can be applied to exploited workers on shrimp boats in South East Asia, Uzbeks forced to pick cotton by their government, child domestic workers in Haiti ('Restaveks') and West African sex workers in Europe, amongst others.[5]

This is a long and diverse list. Things quickly get even more complicated, however, since governments and activists generally agree that the category of 'slave' can only be legitimately applied to a specific subcategory of exceptional cases. These individual cases usually comprise only a small proportion of a much larger population. The logic here is hard to fault. Not all migrant workers, war captives, supply chain workers or other vulnerable populations have the same types of experiences. However, this case specific approach quickly creates tremendous analytical and practical difficulties when it comes to determining where slavery begins and ends.[6] In response to this challenge, a number of campaigners and governments have put together lists of 'signs', which have been specifically designed to help people to identify individual cases of slavery.[7] One recent example of such a list from the British government instructs concerned citizens to look out for the following 'signs of slavery': physical or psychological abuse; isolation; poor living

3 Greg Norman, 'Critics Call Foul as Qatar's 2022 World Cup City Built with "Slavery"', *Fox News*, 24 June 2016. Available at http://www.foxnews.com/sports/2016/06/24/criticscall-foul-as-qatars-2022-world-cup-city-built-with-slavery.html (accessed 5 November 2016).

4 James Griffiths, 'North Korea "Continues to Invest" in Nazi-Style Prison Camps', *CNN*, 30 November 2016. Available at http://edition.cnn.com/2016/11/30/asia/north-koreaprison-camps-new-satellite-images/ (accessed 5 November 2016).

5 See, for example, the *CNN Freedom Project*. Available at http://edition.cnn.com/specials/world/freedom-project (accessed 5 November 2016).

6 Annie Bunting and Joel Quirk, 'Contemporary Slavery as More than Rhetorical Strategy? The Politics and Ideology of a New Political Cause', in Annie Bunting and Joel Quirk (eds.), *Contemporary Slavery: Popular Rhetoric and Political Practice* (Vancouver: University of British Columbia Press, 2017).

7 'Spotting the Signs of Modern Slavery', *BBC Newsbeat*, 9 August 2016. Available at http://www.bbc.co.uk/newsbeat/article/37008846/spotting-the-signs-of-modern-slavery (accessed 5 November 2016).

conditions; few or no personal effects; restricted freedom of movement; unusual travel times; and reluctance to seek help.[8] While there is no question that these types of 'signs' can potentially provide evidence of real and significant problems and vulnerabilities, they are not particularly effective when it comes to drawing a clear and consistent line between slave and non-slave.

In a world that is increasingly divided between tremendous privilege and extreme poverty, we have no shortage of vulnerable individuals whose circumstances display many 'signs' of slavery. Few would dispute that 'physical or psychological abuse' is ubiquitous around the globe. Illegal migrants, whatever their working or living conditions, tend to be 'reluctant to seek help', since 'help' too often translates into deportation. They also frequently work according to 'unusual travel times', since they routinely labour under precarious and irregular conditions. Anyone who does not speak local languages or have local family or friends is likely to experience 'isolation'. Poor and vulnerable families typically have 'few or no personal effects' and endure 'poor living conditions'. The inhabitants of prisons and detention centres also have severely 'restricted freedom of movement'. Most of the signs of slavery that campaigners identify are ultimately symptoms of vulnerability, inequality and poverty. While these 'signs of slavery' may appear straightforward, it should become apparent upon further reflection that most people are talking about differences of degree, rather than differences of kind. In too many cases, 'modern slavery' ends up being little more than selective shorthand for 'worst of the worst'.[9]

It is here that conversations around slavery take on a strong political and ideological dimension. Drawing a line between 'slave' and 'free' is not simply a neutral or objective exercise, but it also invariably involves strategic calculations and political interests. Campaigners embrace the language of slavery in an attempt to harness the infamy and iconography of slavery and its legal abolition in order to both prioritise and dramatise all kinds of contemporary problems. The rhetorical strategy commonly involves a form of argument by analogy, wherein it is asserted that there is a substantive equivalence between historical slave systems (chiefly involving stylised images of transatlantic slavery) and more recent examples of exploitation, coercion and violence.[10] Many different actors have used this rhetor-

---

8 *Victims of Modern Slavery: Frontline Staff Guidance* (Home Office, 2016). Available at https://www.gov.uk/government/uploads/system/uploads/attachment_data/file/509326/victims-of-modern-slavery-frontline-staff-guidance-v3.pdf (accessed 5 November 2016).

9 Julia O'Connell Davidson, *Modern Slavery: The Margins of Freedom* (London: Palgrave Macmillan, 2015).

10 Ariel Gross, 'When Is the Time of Slavery? The History of Slavery in Contemporary Legal and Political Argument', *California Law Review*, 96/1 (2008), 283–321.

ical strategy in order to support larger arguments that specific sets of problems and practices should be regarded as exceptional cases of 'slavery', and should therefore be prioritised ahead of 'lesser' concerns. If we want to properly understand how slavery has been conceptualised and deployed, we need further historical guidance.

The Iconography of Transatlantic Slavery

Organised political opposition to slavery as a general institution emerged in response to the severe and systemic abuses that defined transatlantic slavery over nearly four centuries. As is well known, this far-reaching catastrophe began in (what became) Atlantic Africa, which experienced major transformations due to the political economy of enslavement that emerged due to rising European demand for slaves in the colonial Americas. This in turn led to the horrors of the 'Middle Passage' to the Americas, which involved a concentrated period of severe suffering, trauma and death. Enslaved Africans who were fortunate enough to survive this transcontinental forced migration were then subjected to an extremely exploitative and abusive slave regime that was principally defined on the basis of racial difference and ruthlessly structured around economic interests, economic calculations and emerging capitalist markets.[11] The emergence of organised political opposition to slavery was heavily influenced by these distinctive features. From the late eighteenth century onwards, the severe abuses which defined transatlantic slavery would come to be attributed to a clear-cut, economically exploitative and racially defined institution which could also be legally abolished, and thereby ostensibly ended. The pioneers of organised anti-slavery generally had no problem identifying who the slaves were – or how they differed from non-slaves – because slavery was a clearly demarcated legal category with a venerable historical pedigree. Despite the fact that not all Africans in the Americas were enslaved, the entrenched association between slavery and race further ensured that slavery was widely viewed as a discrete and easily identifiable category.

This clear differentiation between slave and non-slave only became sharper with the uptake of anti-slavery propaganda, which presented slavery as an unconscionable evil that was outside 'normal' (i.e. legitimate) practices and institutions, and thereby imbued the divide between slave and non-slave with a strong emotional and ideological resonance. While there were many facets to the overall case

---

11 See, for example, David Eltis and David Richardson, *Atlas of the Transatlantic Slave Trade*, (New Haven: Yale University Press, 2010), David Davis, *Inhuman Bondage: The Rise and Fall of Slavery in the New World*, (Oxford: Oxford University Press, 2006).

against slavery, there would be two themes in particular which stood out: the ownership of human beings and extreme dominion and exploitation. These twin themes have been fundamental to the case against slavery as a general institution, because they lay at the heart of arguments about what set slavery sharply apart from other practices and institutions. From an anti-slavery standpoint, it was both the legal right to buy, sell and own other human beings and the extreme brutality, mortality, exploitation and debasement that defined transatlantic slavery which ultimately rendered slavery fundamentally unacceptable. This was in contrast to the pro-slavery position, which (amongst other things) viewed slavery as natural, or normal, with slaves being collectively treated at least no worse than segments of the white working class of Europe or the Americas. While there were strengths and weaknesses to both of these perspectives, the remarkable success of organised anti-slavery over the course of the nineteenth century ultimately resolved this contest in favour of the abolitionists, thereby constructing slavery as a unique and exceptional category.[12]

This enduring connection between transatlantic slavery and the twin themes of human property and extreme exploitation has had profound consequences for efforts to conceptualise and classify both other historical slave systems and other forms of exploitation. Two interrelated themes can be identified here: (i) relational classification, and (ii) slavery and hierarchy. The first of these dynamics is concerned with classification by way of relational comparison, wherein the status and severity of various forms of exploitation tends to be primarily assessed in relation to the extent they are held to resemble (usually stylised images of) transatlantic slavery. As a number of scholars of slavery have observed, both historical and contemporary comparisons between transatlantic slavery and other slave systems and exploitative practices have most commonly been structured around crude assessments of 'good' or 'bad' treatment.[13] These relational comparisons between transatlantic slavery and other practices and institutions can be approached in two ways. One approach is concerned with distancing, with the underlying logic being that other slave systems and forms of exploitation were (or are) less 'severe' than transatlantic slavery, and should therefore be regarded as either lesser evils and perhaps even positive goods. A second variant focuses on equivalence, with the underlying logic being that other practices are just as bad as transatlantic slavery, and should therefore be classified as the worst of the worst.

---

12 Joel Quirk, *The Anti-Slavery Project: From the Slave Trade to Human Trafficking* (Philadelphia: Pennsylvania Press, 2011).

13 Igor Kopytoff, 'The Cultural Context of African Abolition', in Suzanne Miers and Richard Roberts (eds.), *The End of Slavery in Africa* (Madison: University of Wisconsin Press, 1998), 485–503.

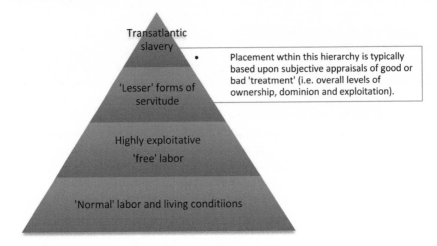

Fig. 1: Hierarchy and Relational Classifications

Both distancing and equivalence need to be understood and applied in relation to an underlying conception of hierarchy. Slavery is widely regarded as one of the worst forms of exploitation and abuse imaginable, and therefore occupies an exceptional position at the apex of a larger spectrum of exploitation, violence, vulnerability and abuse. This hierarchy can be visually represented in terms of a triangle (Fig. 1), with transatlantic slavery being located at the uppermost point, with other categories or 'levels' of exploitation and vulnerability being classified on the basis of perceptions of 'lesser' severity. For the purposes of illustration, the triangle below includes several other indicative categories: 'lesser' forms of servitude, exploitative 'free' labour, and 'normal' labour and living conditions. All three categories come with a great deal of ideological and historical baggage (hence the inverted commas). They should not be treated as neutral or stable descriptors, but should instead be approached as conceptual markers within a process of subjective appraisal. The width of the triangle at various intervals also speaks to popular perceptions of relative prevalence, with the idea (largely assumed, rather than actually tested) that slavery is both exceptional and rare, while 'free' labour is both less objectionable and more common. The key point is that relational comparisons between these sorts of categories exercise a major role in shaping how people think when they are faced with the question of how to classify either historical forms of bondage or contemporary forms of exploitation and abuse.

As we have seen, relational classifications can take one of two main forms: distancing and equivalence (Fig. 2). Distancing refers to various lines of argument that are deployed in order to support the overall conclusion that specific practices

Equivalence: just as bad as slavery
(i.e. the worst of the worst)

Distancing: not the same as slavery
(i.e. lesser evils or positive goods)

Fig. 2: Equivalence and Distancing

should be moved away from slavery, and therefore located lower down the triangle. They should not be regarded as slavery, or so this overall approach maintains, owing to essential differences. These differences can be either de jure (in law or policy) or de facto (in practice or substance). The case for distance frequently rests upon de jure arguments that strongly emphasises differences in law and policy, with government officials insisting that their preferred labour schemes (e.g. indentured labour, forced labour under colonial rule, current migrant labour schemes) cannot be regarded as equivalent to slavery because they have a very different legal and institutional status. Distancing is not confined to relational classifications between slavery and other practices and institutions, but can also extend to comparisons within the category of slavery itself. For example, many Spanish and Portuguese continue to proclaim that their national misdeeds in relation to the history of transatlantic slavery were much less objectionable than those of slave owners in the United States.[14] To make this argument, it is necessary to declare that some historical slave systems were comparatively 'mild' or 'benign', and therefore should not be equated or associated with the worst of the worst. As this example also helps to demonstrate, relational classification is rarely a neutral or objective exercise, but instead frequently involves various strategic efforts to minimise or excuse responsibility or culpability.

Equivalence provides a counterpoint to distancing. It refers to lines of argument that contribute to the overall conclusion that specific practices should be classified as the same as, or as bad as, transatlantic slavery, and should therefore be located at the apex of the triangle as examples of the worst of the worst. Specific practices and institutions can be regarded as forms of slavery, or so this overall approach maintains, owing to fundamental similarities. In this approach, the case for equivalence frequently rests upon a series of de facto arguments that strongly emphasise underlying similarities in lived experience. Specific cases of exploitation and abuse may not be formally or legally described as slavery, but

14 Marta Araújo and Silvia Rodríguez Maeso, 'Slavery and Racism as the "Wrongs" of (European) History: Reflections from a Study on Portuguese Textbooks', in Douglas Hamilton, Kate Hodgson, and Joel Quirk (eds.), *Slavery, Memory and Identity: National Representations and Global Legacies* (London: Pickering & Chatto, 2012).

their practical effects upon the relevant individuals involved are nonetheless regarded as being substantively the same. This logic of substantive equivalence has been foundational to recent and ongoing campaigns that have classified many different problems as forms of 'slavery' or as 'modern slavery'. Once again, it should be emphasised that these classifications are rarely neutral or objective, but instead frequently take the form of strategic efforts to both dramatise and prioritise specific political causes and issues.

As we have seen, the location of slavery at the apex of the triangle is ultimately founded upon a claim to exceptionality. This claim to exceptionality has all kinds of ideological and political effects. Campaigners who treat modern slavery as a unique and exceptional evil can tacitly end up minimising or otherwise normalising other 'lesser' abuses. Take, for example, the status that has been assigned to 'free' labour within the hierarchy in Fig. 1. When free labour is directly compared with slavery, it usually comes across very favourably, so any relational classification between the two is likely to have the effect of presenting free labour as both positive and desirable. Since campaigners against modern slavery specifically focus upon exceptional cases, they frequently end up excluding other 'normal' or 'lesser' problems from within their orbit of concern. This can in turn have the overall effect of legitimising or excusing larger practices and patterns of inequality, vulnerability and poverty that are said to fall short of 'true' or 'genuine' slavery. Instead of challenging larger global patterns of exploitation, violence and discrimination, campaigners against modern slavery typically focus more narrowly upon the worst of the worst. Within this framework, slavery is regarded as an exceptional problem within otherwise legitimate 'free' labour markets. As numerous scholars have demonstrated, there are currently hundreds of millions of 'free' labourers in the world today who endure terrible wages, precarious conditions, unsafe and unhealthy workspaces, sexual harassment and assault, and bullying and abuse. They may well be 'free' to leave, in the sense that they can quit their jobs and seek other options, but their precarious financial status is likely to make it very risky for them to quit, and their other available options may be no better. Whenever slavery is the benchmark against which other practices are measured, there will always be a risk of relational comparisons being used to minimise, excuse, or even legitimise all kinds of other problems.

Modern Slavery and the Politics of Exception

Conversations about modern slavery frequently begin with the 1926 Convention to Suppress the Slave Trade and Slavery, which was developed under the auspices of the League of Nations (and later taken over by the United Nations in 1953). In the aftermath of the Great War, the catalyst for action stemmed from concerns about slavery in Africa in general, and Abyssinia in particular. This eventually translated into the establishment of the Temporary Slavery Commission, a small group of predominantly European experts formed in 1924. Throughout the 1920s and 1930s, most attention focused upon the status of slavery and related forms of servitude in territories across Africa, Asia, and the Middle East.[15]

Despite working with limited and unreliable information, the final report of the Temporary Slavery Commission identified a number of territories where slavery remained an issue, including 'raids properly so called' on the 'borders of the Saharan desert' and in Abyssinia, the continuation of at least some slave trading in many parts of Africa, an 'open slave trade' in several Asia states, and the continuation of legal slavery in 'Thibet and Nepal, and in most of the Mohammedan States of the East, such as Afghanistan, the Hedjaz and other Arabian States'.[16] Establishing a precedent followed by subsequent League bodies, the strongest criticism was reserved for non-European governments, most notably Liberia and Abyssinia (Ethiopia), rather than European colonies, which were practising horrific forms of forced labour on an epic scale. When it came to colonial rule, the commission concluded that residual cases persisted – despite having been abolished in law – because 'the civilising influence of Colonial Powers, however energetic and vigilant they may be, cannot change completely in a few years the habits ingrained by centuries'.[17]

The commission was unable to settle upon a single definition of slavery. It instead divided its final report into thematic chapters, which included material devoted to 'Compulsory Labour' and 'Practices Restrictive On the Liberty of the Person'.[18] In the case of the latter, it was recognised that a number of practices, such as the acquisition of girls by payment of dowry, the abuse of adoption, and the manipulation of debt bondage could all degenerate into slavery, yet the relevant threshold between slavery and other 'restrictive' practices was not clearly articulated. As part of their submission to the commission, the premier non-governmental organisation focusing upon slavery – the Anti-Slavery and Aboriginal Protection Society (founded in 1839) – highlighted four areas of particular concern: (i) contract labour, (ii) forced labour, (iii) 'adoption', 'pledging', and do-

---

15 See, for example, Jean Allain, *The Slavery Conventions: The Travaux Préparatoires of the 1926 League of Nations Convention and the 1956 United Nations Convention* (Leiden: Martinus Nijhoff, 2008); Suzanne Miers, *Slavery in the Twentieth Century* (Walnut Creek, CA: Altamira Press, 2003).

16 Temporary Slavery Commission: Letter from the Chairman of the Commission to the President of the Council and Report of the Commission, League of Nations A.19.1925 VI, Geneva, 25 July 1925, 3, 4, 6, 14.

17 Ibid., 7.

18 Ibid., 8–12.

mestic slavery, and (iv) slavery. Emphasising the 'necessity of defining as a broad principle what practices may be said to-day to amount to modern slavery', the Society boldly – and ultimately rhetorically – suggested that 'any system in which force or fraud are exercised to secure control over the labourer for private ends partakes of slavery'.[19] This expansive approach was not welcome, since all colonial powers continued to make regular use of forced labour schemes involving the systematic exploitation and abuse of local 'natives'. While governments were keen to create distance, political activists instead insisted upon underlying equivalence.

The question of definitions would be chiefly addressed through the 1926 Slavery Convention, which took the decisive step of defining slavery as 'the status or condition of a person over whom any or all of the powers attaching to the right of ownership are exercised', and committed parties both 'to prevent and suppress the slave trade' and '[t]o bring about, progressively and as soon as possible, the complete abolition of slavery in all its forms'. Frustratingly, the precise nature of these forms was never clearly codified, so the burden chiefly fell upon signatories to the Convention to determine their new obligations. In the negotiations that preceded the final convention, the expansive terrain considered by the Temporary Commission was deliberately watered down. The preliminary draft of what eventually became the 1926 Convention contained a comparatively open-ended obligation to 'bring about progressively and as soon as possible the disappearance of slavery in every form, notably in the case of domestic slavery and similar conditions', but this was discarded during the negotiations which preceded the final convention, with the final text instead substituting the language of 'slavery in all its forms'.[20] This revision was ostensibly justified on the grounds that 'it was believed that such practices came within the definition of slavery', thereby rendering further elaboration redundant. As part of this justification, specific reference was made to 'domestic slavery', 'debt-slavery', 'the enslavement of persons disguised as the adoption of children', and 'the acquisition of girls by payment of dowry, etc.', but this list was immediately qualified by a further statement that 'even if these last practices do not come under the definition of slavery [...] they must be combated'.[21] This apparent ambiguity can be resolved by observing that

19 Temporary Slavery Commission, Communication of 20 May 1925 from the Anti-Slavery and Aborigines Protection Society, London, League of Nations, L/28029/23252, Geneva, 28 May 1925, 4, 7–8.

20 Convention Relating to Slavery and Proposed Amendments. Note by the Secretariat, League of Nations, A.VI/2/1926, 3.

21 Annex 20. Slavery Convention. Report of the Sixth Committee to the Assembly, League of Nations, A.104.1926.VI, 416.

the issue was not whether or not broad categories of servitude fall within the confines of the 1926 definition, but instead whether or not individual cases of bondage associated with these categories satisfy the exceptional threshold of 'powers attaching to the right of ownership'.

A good example of this distinction can be found in a further provision that obligates parties to 'take all necessary measures to prevent compulsory or forced labour from developing into conditions analogous to slavery'. This formula does not establish a substantive equivalence between slavery and forced labour in general, but instead recognises the fact that there may well be a subset of exceptional cases within the broader category of forced labour that might also satisfy the legally established criteria associated with slavery. This was always going to be a delicate topic, since colonial powers regularly made use of forced labour, and they were consequentially reluctant to take on any significant obligations in these areas. The topic nonetheless proved sufficiently prominent that it later found further expression in a separate convention via the International Labour Organisation devoted to forced labour in 1930. While obligations associated with this convention were heavily qualified by numerous exemptions, the parties involved were able to eventually agree to a definition of forced or compulsory labour that covered 'all work or service which is exacted from any person under the menace of any penalty and for which the said person has not offered himself voluntarily'.[22] While the legal definition of slavery remained unchanged, a complementary instrument covering new ground was introduced. Other instruments would follow.

The drafting of the 1926 Slavery Convention was heavily influenced by colonial politics, with European diplomats working to strategically minimise the scope of their international obligations in relation to legal slavery and its aftermath (with progressive rather than immediate abolition), forced labour for the state (which was widely held to be legitimate, albeit sometimes subject to abuse) and related forms of servitude and bondage (which were to be distinguished from 'true' slavery). These considerations also played an ongoing role in the way in which the 1926 convention was subsequently interpreted. Throughout the 1920s and 1930s, there was a concerted diplomatic effort to minimise the practical scope of the definition of slavery (unless a non-European government was the subject of inquiry), and to maintain as much distance as possible between slavery and forced labour for the state. These broader trends are reflected in the work of a further series of expert committees tasked by the League to examine slavery during the 1930s. These committees were fairly low-key affairs, with a small, exclusively European membership, limited mandate (forced labour was excluded), and no enforcement

---

22 C29 Forced Labour Convention, 1930, http://www.ilo.org/ilolex/cgilex/
convde.pl?C029.

powers. Much like earlier League inquiries into slavery, these committees focused upon territories where slavery remained legal, and upon territories in which slavery had only recently been abolished. In the case of the former, reports from this period habitually surveyed the handful of governments that still sanctioned slavery, or which had recently passed laws against slavery, but in many territories reliable information was scarce.

This was chiefly because the League was forced to heavily rely upon government submissions, which routinely proclaimed that slavery was no longer a significant problem. Some submissions took the form of blanket denials, but major colonial powers such as Britain and France tended to favour a more qualified stance, which involved cautiously acknowledging that residual cases continued in some colonies. There were two main variants to this overall approach. The first variant saw numerous qualifiers being placed alongside slavery. Examples taken from reports from 1935 and 1937 include references to 'natives living in [...] a servile state bordering on slavery', 'quasi-slaves', 'mild forms for slavery', 'semi-slaves', 'household captives', 'domestic serfs', 'voluntary slaves', or 'so-called slaves'.[23] Much like earlier slave-holders in the colonial Americas in the nineteenth century, colonial officials consistently sought to portray local slave systems as 'benign', or 'mild' in an effort to minimise complications and challenges associated with anti-slavery. In the second variant, this underlying logic was taken one step further with the suggestion that perhaps many of those involved 'were not really slaves at all', but instead belonged in some other category entirely.[24] In the absence of sustained critical scrutiny, too many of these deceptive statements were taken at face value, concealing widespread colonial complicity and abuse. This can once again be read as an attempt at distancing, with relational comparisons and classifications being involved in an attempt to redefine the practices in question as occupying lower positions within a larger hierarchy. The underlying message here was that these were not urgent or exceptional problems under colonial rule.

While historians of slavery generally agree that the overall prevalence of slavery in Africa, Asia and the Middle East declined over the first half of the twentieth century, there were still significant numbers of slaves and descendants of slaves who had yet to experience much in the way of change during the

---

23 Slavery. Report of the Advisory Committee of Experts: Second Session of the Committee, League of Nations, C.159.M.113, 1935, Geneva, 18 April 1935, 7, 10, 19, 23, Slavery. Report of the Advisory Committee of Experts: Third (Extraordinary) Session of the Committee, League of Nations, C.189(1).M.145. 1936.VI, Geneva, 15 May 1936, 17, 19.

24 Second Session of the Committee, ibid., 23.

1930s.[25] In theory, slaves were now free to leave, but this did not always work in practice due to ongoing surveillance, threats of retribution, socialisation and official complicity. In theory, ex-slaves were much the same as 'free servants', but in practice many continued to endure physical punishments, sexual abuse, economic exploitation, severe restrictions on movement, social discrimination and fragile family relationships. However much various apologists have sought to pretend otherwise, the still popular concept of 'benign' slavery has most commonly been associated with efforts to minimise or excuse complicity in all kinds of serious abuses. Furthermore, European colonial officials continued to make widespread use of forced labour schemes that were often unfavourably compared to earlier slave systems by individuals who had the misfortune of serving as both legal slaves and forced labourers for colonial conquerors.

In these challenging circumstances, the League experts unsurprisingly found it necessary to expend considerable energies upholding their preferred distinction between slavery and other forms of servitude or bondage. Despite a general agreement that other forms of bondage should be distinguished from 'slavery in the true sense of the word',[26] each report nonetheless included a separate section concerned with 'Practices Restrictive On the Liberty of the Person' (1932, 1935) or 'Other Institutions' (1936, 1937, 1938). Some of the main practices that featured in these sections were serfdom, debt bondage, marriage practices, domestic servitude by way of 'adoption' and pawnship (i.e. a system in which individuals were held in debt bondage as collateral for loans).[27] Despite a widespread recognition that these practices shared features with slavery, there was nonetheless a general consensus that 'proper' slavery should be prioritised, and that the 1926 definition should be narrowly applied.

This minimalist approach to slavery was gradually overshadowed by a more expansive vision over the course of the second half of the twentieth century. Under the auspices of the newly formed United Nations, conversations around slavery took on additional dimensions, resulting in a political landscape that saw many different forms of exploitation eventually (re)defined as 'contemporary forms of slavery', or 'modern slavery'. This process of redefinition was grounded in log-

25 See, for example, Benedetta Rossi (ed.), *Reconfiguring Slavery: West African Trajectories* (Liverpool: University of Liverpool Press, 2009); Susanne Miers and Richard Roberts (eds.), *The End of Slavery in Africa* (Madison: The University of Wisconsin Press, 1988).

26 Second Session of the Committee, 9.

27 Toyin Falola and Paul E. Lovejoy, 'Pawnship in Historical Perspective', in Toyin Falola and Paul E. Lovejoy (eds.), *Pawnship , Slavery, and Colonialism in Africa* (Trenton, NJ: Africa World Press, 2003), 1.

ics of substantive equivalence, with a key turning point being the 1956 Supplementary Convention on the Abolition of Slavery, the Slave Trade and Institutions and Practices Similar to Slavery. This Convention was presented as an attempt to 'augment' and 'intensify' efforts. Of particular interest is Article 1, which obligated parties to: take all practicable and necessary legislative and other measures to bring about progressively and as soon as possible the complete abolition or abandonment of the following institutions and practices, where they still exist and whether or not they are covered by the definition of slavery contained in Article 1 of the Slavery Convention signed at Geneva on 25 September 1926.

Four institutions and practices would be identified and defined as similar (but not necessarily equivalent) to slavery: debt bondage, serfdom, servile marriage and the transfer of persons under eighteen for the purpose of exploiting their labour. This new Convention deliberately side-lined the still contentious issue of forced labour for the state, which was instead moved into a separate channel under the auspices of the International Labour Organization. This was despite the ongoing use of forced labour in Communist Gulags and colonial territories, together with the recent horrors of Nazi forced labour schemes and the widespread use of forced prostitution (the so-called 'comfort' women) by Japanese military forces as part of their wartime policies in East Asia. Since forced labour directly implicated governments, the diplomats running things decided it would be expedient to again separate forced labour from slavery, resulting in a different diplomatic channel that culminated in the 1957 Forced Labour Convention.

More recent international agreements have built on the basic template established in 1956. There are three examples that are particularly prominent here. First, we have the 1998 Rome Statute of the International Criminal Court, which paved the way for a qualified capacity to charge individuals with the crime of enslavement, which was defined in terms of 'any or all of the powers attaching to the right of ownership over a person and includes the exercise of such power in the course of trafficking in persons', and also includes additional provisions pertaining to 'Rape, sexual slavery, enforced prostitution, forced pregnancy, enforced sterilisation, or any other form of sexual violence of comparable gravity'. Second, we have the 1999 Convention Concerning the Prohibition and Immediate Action for the Elimination of the Worst Forms of Child Labour, which aims to combat 'all forms of slavery or practices similar to slavery, such as the sale and trafficking of children, debt bondage and serfdom and forced or compulsory labour, including forced or compulsory recruitment of children for use in armed conflict'.

Finally, we have the 2000 United Nations Protocol to Prevent, Suppress and Punish Trafficking in Persons Especially Women and Children, which aims to combat 'the exploitation of the prostitution of others or other forms of sexual exploitation, forced labour or services, slavery or practices similar to slavery, servitude or the removal of organs'. Human trafficking occupies a particularly important position within this larger complex, because it has not only emerged as the dominant frame of reference used by governments and activists, but has also come to be used on an interchangeable basis with modern slavery. In addition to these three major instruments, we also have the 2011 Convention Concerning Decent Work for Domestic Workers, which contains provisions pertaining to 'the elimination of all forms of forced or compulsory labour', yet does not specifically mention slavery. Along similar lines, there is also the more recent 2014 Protocol to the Forced Labour Convention of 1930 (P029), which contains obligations to take 'effective measures for the identification, release, protection, recovery and rehabilitation of all victims of forced or compulsory labour', and to ensure that 'victims of forced or compulsory labour, irrespective of their presence or legal status in the national territory, have access to appropriate and effective remedies'.[28]

This brief snapshot should make it apparent that the category of slavery is now routinely found alongside a wide range of other related categories, the most significant of which are forced labour and human trafficking. While each of these categories means different things from a legal standpoint, the finer distinctions between them frequently get lost from a more practical and political standpoint. The specific attributes of historical slave systems rarely feature within recent conversations about 'modern slavery'. Instead, slavery frequently gets reduced to little more than shorthand for the worst of the worst, and therefore frequently displays many features associated with an empty signifier, or floating signifier. The parameters of slavery are not fixed or generally agreed, at least within the context of 'modern slavery' (or human trafficking), but can instead take on radically different interpretations and dimensions.

One of the underlying problems here is an enduring divide between rhetoric and practice. While all states and stakeholders are now ostensibly committed to the cause of combating modern slavery, this rhetoric tends to be little more than a shallow veneer that masks both different political agendas and tremendous variations in overall levels of interest and investment. During the late nineteenth century, the Portuguese government passed numerous anti-slavery laws in their African colonies that were chiefly understood by insiders to be 'só para o inglês ver', or 'just for the English to see'. Since these laws were geared towards alleviating outside pressure for reform, they accomplished little in the way of sub-

---

28 The text of these conventions and protocols is available here:
http://www.ohchr.org/EN/ProfessionalInterest/Pages/UniversalHumanRightsInstruments.aspx (accessed 5 November 2016).

stantive reform.[29] Much the same pattern applies in many parts of the world today, where governments have recently passed new legislation, but many of these laws are enforced either selectively or not at all.

The sheer variety and volume of 'modern slavery' also presents further practical and political challenges. According to one popular slogan from Not For Sale, a prominent non-governmental organisation based in the United States, their ultimate goal is to 'end slavery in our lifetime'. While this is undoubtedly a compelling slogan, we need to look beneath the rhetoric and ask what this actually looks like in reality. For historical anti-slavery activists, the cause of ending slavery involved targeting a clearly defined population whose status as slaves was heavily reliant on specific governments for sanction and support. For self-proclaimed 'modern-day abolitionists', the cause of ending slavery covers a tremendous range of practices and problems. While no list can ever be definitive, the goal of 'ending slavery in our lifetime' is most commonly understood in terms that require action in relation to the following themes:

- hereditary bondage and descent-based discrimination;
- prostitution and sexual exploitation;
- bonded labour (or debt bondage) and exploitation;
- migration and exploitation;
- child labour and exploitation;
- domestic labour and exploitation;
- global supply chains and exploitation;
- wartime captivity and wartime abuses;
- forced, servile and early marriage;
- forced labour by the state.

A number of examples have already been given of specific practices that fall within the rubric of some of the themes listed here. These are captive women and girls in Syria and Iraq (wartime captivity); migrant workers in Qatar (migration and exploitation); workers on shrimp boats in South East Asia (supply chains); and forced labour in North Korean Gulags (forced labour by the state). The now familiar challenges of identifying an exceptional subcategory of 'slaves' amongst a larger population also apply to other themes. There is no question that some married relationships display objectionable features, but it is not always clear when these features cross a line. There is no question that forms of hereditary bondage

---

29 James Duffy, *Question of Slavery* (Oxford: Clarendon Press, 1967); Eric Allina, *Slavery by Any Other Name: African Life under Company Rule in Colonial Mozambique* (Charlottesville: University of Virginia Press, 2012).

in places such as Mali, Mauritania and Niger display objectionable features, but it is by no means clear when specific cases can be classified as slavery, or should instead be primarily classified as forms of enduring discrimination on the basis of slave descent. Much the same can be said of sex workers, domestic labourers or working children. Combating 'modern slavery' not only requires us to clearly distinguish between slave and non-slave across different practices and population groups, but also to formulate interventions that specifically target a small subcategory of exceptional cases. This overall picture is in turn further complicated by the fact that people regularly move in and out of different types of situations and categories, so any interventions must also deal with the emergence of new cases.

It is at this juncture that political rhetoric frequently gives way to political reality. 'Modern-day abolitionists', such as Not For Sale, can't possibly take simultaneous action to target exceptional abuses against an amorphous subcategory of 'slaves' across all of these different practices and population groups. When push comes to shove, political activists and government agents only rarely concern themselves with the entire portfolio of these many different themes, and instead direct their energies in relation to specific themes and specific locations. In this context, we have three key themes in particular that stand out as focal points: prostitution, migration and supply chains. Since at least the 1990s, the vast majority of political interest and economic investment has been directed here (children have also attracted sustained interest in relation to these themes, but less so in relation to others).

The single most important theme has been prostitution and exploitation. Most interventions that take place under the rubric of combating modern slavery have focused upon forms of sex work, and most organisations that have emerged since the 1990s have prioritised sex work (and frequently only sex work). The main point of issue here is not so much slavery per se, but the legal status of prostitution, which recently emerged as a major talking point around the adoption of a new policy by Amnesty International in 2015 to regard sex-worker rights as human rights, and thereby advocate for the decriminalisation of sex work. Some activists and governments view all forms of commercial sex as a violation to be combated, and therefore advocate for policies that target the purchases and purveyors of commercial sex (although sex workers also frequently endure collateral damage from these policies as well). Other activists and governments instead view sex work as a legitimate activity that needs to be regulated to minimise and prevent abuse. This polarised debate has once again been marked by logics of distancing and equivalence, with sex workers and their allies trying to normalise their profession and present it as the same as any other, and their opponents seeking to combat further decriminalisation by establishing exceptional links with slavery.

The theme of migration and exploitation has been primarily understood in terms of movements across international borders, rather than internal movements within individual countries. International migration has become a major focal point for political debate in many parts of the world in recent years. Racism, xenophobia and nativism have all played major roles in the growth of political parties and political platforms, such as the remarkable rise of presidential candidate Donald Trump in the United States, whose signature policy platform is his desire to 'build a wall' with Mexico. As this example helps to demonstrate, the main focus has been migration by the citizens of a larger number of poor developing countries towards a minority of rich industrialised (and some oil-producing) countries. In this highly charged environment, 'modern slavery' has been put to a number of different political usages.

Instead of trying to help all migrants, governments and campaigners have once again sought to concentrate their energies upon a small number 'exceptional' cases of exploitation and abuse associated with migration. In this context, modern slavery (or human trafficking) has been incorporated into an established body of refugee law, with legal protections being awarded to specific individuals who satisfy relevant legal criteria as victims of slavery. While this may sound good in theory, it has ultimately proved to be subject to all kinds of problems in practice. A small number of exceptional victims have been given limited protections while a much larger migratory population remains subject to arrest, deportation, exploitation, vulnerability and abuse. Everything that doesn't count as 'exceptional' is tacitly regarded as 'normal', and it has become normal practice for governments to treat most migrants – both legal and illegal – horribly.

In a number of notorious cases, such as the ongoing refugee crisis in the Mediterranean, the language of modern slavery and human trafficking has been invoked by governments to both justify and legitimise policies that are primarily designed to make life even harder for migrants seeking sanctuary.

Efforts to combat modern slavery (or human trafficking) can sometimes look good on paper, but then end up doing more harm than good in practice. Researchers studying responses to trafficking have come to describe this disconnect between aims and outcomes in terms of 'collateral damage'. Research in many contexts has shown that government policies regularly inflict damage upon marginalised and vulnerable populations. Common examples include police abusing those they are supposed to assist, immigration systems mistreating migrants with impunity, and people who have been 'rescued' from modern slavery being subjected to forms of incarceration, exploitation and abuse. Instead of providing a solution, government agents can frequently end up making things worse. In the case of migration, the politics of 'exception' has too often translated into policies and practices that have focused on isolated individuals, rather than addressing collective vulnerabilities and abuses.

This selective focus on exceptional cases has also defined recent approaches to labour abuses in global supply chains. As is well known, the last three decades have seen multinational corporations engage in a 'race to the bottom', with many aspects of established production processes and supply chains being relocated to developing countries with lower wages, less regulation and less protection for workers. Viewed from a purely business standpoint, the main goal of the supply chain is to maximise corporate profits and to minimise political and legal liability for abuses or problems which occur within the supply chain. Corporations can exercise their market power to drive down costs per unit, since the producers they do business with have limited capacity to bargain for better returns or less demanding production cycles. This combination of low prices and high expectations means that companies further down the chain are under sustained pressure to rely upon precarious and highly exploited labour. Contracts get subcontracted and then subcontracted again, creating multiple layers between the original corporation and the worker who ultimately ends up producing the actual goods that are required. Corporations routinely insist upon a high degree of oversight and control when it comes to ensuring that the goods that are produced satisfy their expectations regarding product quality. However, they prefer to keep a strategic distance when it comes to exploitation and abuse of the workers actually producing their products.

Governments and corporations have been keen to depict serious abuses in global supply chains as isolated and deviant exceptions, which are chiefly perpetrated by 'a few bad apples'. This formula serves a number of strategically useful political purposes, because it narrowly assigns responsibly for labour abuses within supply chains to specific individuals, rather than viewing individual cases as symptoms of larger systemic problems and abuses that are central to the logic of supply chains as a global system of exploitation. According to this politics of exception, the key threshold for evaluating legitimate corporate conduct effectively amounts to corporations' not actively practising slavery. Other widespread forms of exploitation, vulnerability and abuse are once again pushed to the margins via the moral primacy assigned to slavery.

Concluding Remarks

Recent campaigns and conversations regarding modern slavery cannot be taken at face value, but instead need to be carefully evaluated from a political and historical standpoint. As we have seen, it is important to reflect upon how, why and where 'modern slavery' rhetoric aligns with other ideological, economic and political agendas, and what consequences can follow from these alignments. Rather than taking support for 'modern slavery' for granted, we need to reflect on how and why governments that are rhetorically committed to the cause continue to favour legal regimes and policy responses that promote forms of systemic abuse, vulnerability, discrimination and exploitation. Rather than treating slavery as a singular and exceptional category, we instead need to approach slavery as one of a number of manifestations of larger patterns of exploitation and exclusion. Rather than assuming that 'freedom' is always sharply differentiated from slavery, we instead take into account the ideological and political effects associated with declaring a person to be 'free', and the types of constraints that 'free' labour can gloss over.

Modern slavery can be best understood as a key site for political and ideological competition. This competition is particularly fierce whenever questions of classification take centre stage. On the one hand, we have a recurring tendency to attempt to create distance between slavery and other practices and problems by highlighting specific differences, particularly in relation to differential levels of treatment. On the other hand, we have a countervailing tendency to try and establish equivalence between slavery and other practices and problems by highlighting underlying similarities, resulting in claims that the practices in question should be regarded as the same as, or as bad as, transatlantic slavery. Whatever their other differences, both approaches accept that slavery should be regarded as the worst of the worst, and therefore constitutes an exceptional category occupying a clear position at the apex of a larger hierarchy. There are good reasons for the exceptional status accorded to slavery, especially in the context of the horrors of transatlantic slavery, but this elevated status can also have important political effects today. Conversations about modern slavery seek to draw a firm line between 'exceptional' and 'normal', with the latter half of the ledger being classified as either a lesser evil or a positive good. As we have seen, this politics of exception has proved to be strategically useful for governments, corporations and activists.

The International Slavery Museum

A Gateway to Memory, Identity, and Action

Richard Benjamin

BIOGRAPHY

Richard heads the International Slavery Museum team at National Museums Liverpool. He is responsible for the strategic development of the Museum, partnership work and research and supervises the acquisition of museum objects and collection policies. He is also the Co-Director of the Centre for the Study of International Slavery, a partnership between the University of Liverpool and National Museums Liverpool.

Richard gained a BA (Hons) degree in Community and Race Relations at Edge Hill College and then went on to complete an MA and PhD in Archaeology at the University of Liverpool. In 2002 he was a Visiting Research Scholar at the W. E. B. DuBois Institute of African and African American Research, Harvard University, and was appointed as the head of the International Slavery Museum in 2006. He is a Trustee of the Anthony Walker Foundation, a member of the International Scientific Committee of the UNESCO Slave Route Project and Commonwealth Association of Museums and a Governor of Edge Hill University.

ABSTRACT

The International Slavery Museum (ISM) is the only national museum in the world which deals with the subject of transatlantic slavery and its legacies. It is located in Liverpool, a city that was at the epicentre of the transatlantic slave trade. However, its remit includes other forms of slavery and enslavement, in particular, that which is related to modern forms of forced labour. As such the Museum has developed partnerships with human rights organisations and is now very much a campaigning museum. We believe that museums are not neutral; they need to be socially active and to fight for social justice, whilst at the same time offering pathways of engagement with complex and often difficult subjects.

Slavery Remembrance Day 2013, Walk of Remembrance
©National Museums Liverpool

Museum Background

ISM opened on 23 August 2007, the annual UNESCO International Day for the Remembrance of the Slave Trade and Its Abolition, in the year of the Bicentenary of the Abolition of the Slave Trade Act. Each year, National Museums Liverpool commemorates Slavery Remembrance Day with a series of events, including a memorial lecture culminating in a traditional libation on the world-famous Liverpool waterfront. The day pays homage to the many lives lost as a result of the transatlantic slave trade, it remembers Liverpool's role as the main European slaving port, and it also celebrates the survival and development of African and Caribbean cultures.

ISM is located on the third floor of the Merseyside Maritime Museum and is the successor to the Transatlantic Slavery Gallery, which opened in 1994. ISM is made up of three galleries: Life in West Africa, Enslavement and the Middle Passage, and Legacy.

- Life in West Africa – explores the story of Africa and its peoples, who although central to the story of transatlantic slavery, had a rich history and culture prior to the arrival of Europeans.

Slavery Remembrance Day 2013 wreath
© Dr. Richard Benjamin

- Enslavement and the Middle Passage – reveals the brutality and trauma suffered by enslaved Africans on the voyage across the Atlantic, and the oppression of their lives on plantations in the Americas and their fight for freedom.

- Legacy – details the continuing fight for freedom and equality; includes modern forms of slavery and enslavement, racism and discrimination and the achievements of the African Diaspora.

The Centre for the Study of International Slavery (CSIS), the main research arm of ISM – a partnership between the University of Liverpool and National Museums Liverpool – is a platform for research on slavery, enslavement and its legacies. Liverpool is a stimulating home for CSIS activities and holds its annual lecture in the iconic Dr Martin Luther King, Jr. Building, a listed building adjacent to the current display galleries. Speakers have included Guy Ryder, the Director-General of the International Labour Organization; Kevin Hyland, UK

Anti-Slavery Commissioner; and Professor Annette Gordon-Reed (Harvard Law School).

In 2009 ISM received an Honourable Mention by Koïchiro Matsuura, the UNESCO Director-General, as part of the UNESCO-Madanjeet Singh Prize for the Promotion of Tolerance and Non-Violence. Furthermore, in 2010, ISM coordinated the establishment of a new international museum initiative – the Federation of International Human Rights Museums (FIHRM) – which encourages museums that engage with sensitive and controversial human rights themes, such as transatlantic slavery, the Holocaust and other instances of genocide, to work together and share new thinking and initiatives.

Sensitive Histories

I will now discuss what the ISM team has learnt from developing exhibitions and permanent collections around subjects that have at times been regarded as the unrepresentable. I will also focus on the ethical and moral dimensions, which we had to negotiate when considering how we displayed and interpreted sensitive issues and sensitive objects. One might at first assume that an International Slavery Museum, located at the centre of a World Heritage site and only yards away from the dry docks where eighteenth-century slaver ships were repaired and fitted out, would focus solely on objects associated with the transatlantic slave trade, such as objects of physical restraint, shackles and whips. Such objects are of course central to the Museum's collection but we do not collect for the sake of collecting.

The ISM team has now created one of the first permanent modern slavery collections in the UK (and possibly globally). The first accessioned object within this newly developed collection strand (which sits alongside an established transatlantic slavery collection) was a series of photographs – of flats, brothels and massage parlours showing the reality of sex trafficking and prostitution – called *Missing,* by the artist Rachel Wilberforce. By 2010, the Museum had also acquired several slavery-related anklets from Anti-Slavery International which had been 'worn' by a young girl in Niger who was the victim a form of descent-based slavery. The anklets represent the importance of the work of ISM in developing its collections in modern slavery and supporting associated campaigns to fight it. Alongside the anklets we placed personal stories of the enslaved which humanised the object and individuals and as a result might make the visitor want to get involved (see Benjamin 2012, 191–93).

There are also occasions that the Museum is contacted by a member of the public who is in possession of an object which they don't want but rather than throw away realise there might be some educational opportunities to the object. For example, a Ku Klux Klan outfit was donated just weeks before we opened the Museum in 2007 (see Benjamin 2012, 188–90). The Ku Klux Klan outfit is a central

Anklet
©National Museums Liverpool

exhibit of the Legacy gallery which also includes objects and multimedia that depict racist and stereotypical imagery of Black people, scientific racism, far-right organisations in the United Kingdom such as the National Front and British National Party, and racist murders such as that of Anthony Walker in 2005 (Anthony Walker Foundation 2016). The ISM education space is now named after Anthony Walker, I am a trustee of the Anthony Walker Foundation, and members of Anthony's family have referred to the Anthony Walker Education Centre as 'my brother's room', which shows how important the Museum space has become to the Walker family; one could say it's also an example of place identity (see Uzzell 1996).

A sense of place and ownership of the Museum is very important and, although there is no homogenous Black community in Liverpool, there can be consolidating factors such as experience of racism and a belief in an ancestral connection with enslaved Africans. This sense of ownership of the Museum space can also be seen in the actual displays. The Black Achievers Wall was the suggestion of a leading Liverpool-born Black historian and is intended particularly for visitors who have little understanding of the transatlantic slave trade, an attempt at encouraging them not to leave the Museum and associate Black or African history solely with transatlantic slavery and enslavement. Does it achieve this? From personal experience, I believe it does. I met one community group from Birmingham which was made up of young Black men, and the group leader explained that the Black Achievers Wall was the starting point for their visit. It was their chosen gateway to the narrative of the Museum.

An example of this connection and feeling towards ISM can also be seen in the development and delivery of the Toxteth 1981 community photographic exhibition of the civil disturbances referred to as the 'Toxteth riots' or 'uprising' on display outside the Anthony Walker Education Centre from July 2011 to July

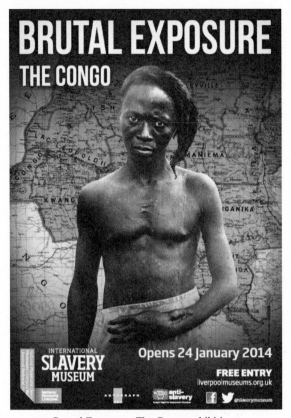

Brutal Exposure: The Congo exhibition
© National Museums Liverpool

2014. Members of the Merseyside Black History Month Group (MBHMG) approached ISM in 2011, as they wanted the exhibition to be displayed within ISM since it actively promotes anti-racist activities and projects and is a conduit to current events rather than simply displaying a static historical event. ISM was seen as an enabler museum, a museum that offers visitors the opportunity to engage with campaigns or initiatives rather than just being seen as a cathedral of objects (see Benjamin 2014).

Exhibitions

ISM has hosted an eclectic mix of exhibitions, including 'My life, my words' (2009), a display of videos and images exploring the lives and experiences of members of the Liverpool Black community; 'Beyond the Boundary' (2010),

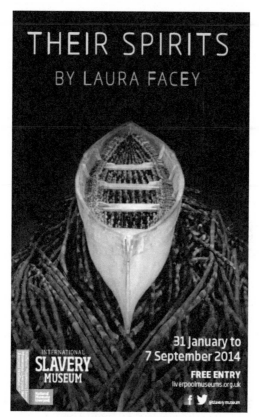

Their Spirits by Laura Facey
©National Museums Liverpool

which explored cricket, culture, class and politics; '42: Women of Sierra Leone' (2011), which focused on the strength and resilience of women in Sierra Leone whose life expectancy is around 42; and 'Liberty Bound: slavery in St Helena' (2014), an exhibition on the burial grounds containing the remains of 'liberated' Africans discovered and excavated in Rupert's Valley, St Helena.

In February 2014, we launched two new exhibitions: 'Their Spirits' by Laura Facey, and 'Brutal Exposure: the Congo.' 'Their Spirits' explores the journey taken by millions of enslaved Africans through an artistic interpretation of a cottonwood canoe, floating on dried sugar cane, which contains 1,357 resin miniatures of 'Redemption Song', a monument which stands in Emancipation Park in Kingston, Jamaica (International Slavery Museum 2014a). 'Brutal Exposure: the Congo' consists of photographs taken by missionary Alice Seeley Harris which document the exploitation and brutality in the Congo Free State, the fiefdom of

King Leopold II of Belgium, in one of the first human rights campaigns (see *King Leopold's Ghost – A story of greed, terror and heroism in colonial Africa* by Adam Hochschild).

As interesting as the subject is historically, fitting well with current displays within the Museum, such as our 'Impact on Africa' display case and interactive exhibit of the nineteenth-century 'Scramble for Africa', the fact that the exhibition would be an ideal opportunity to engage with members of the Liverpool French-speaking community was at the forefront of our thinking, as was the opportunity to highlight current campaigns centred on DR Congo. Being of value to the Congolese community in some way, both in Liverpool and in the DR Congo, of using the Museum to raise awareness, to stimulate debate and dialogue.

The exhibition was supported with associated events, for example, the panel discussion 'Congo: now and then' which had Vava Tampa from Save the Congo, Carron Mann, Policy Manager at Women for Women International and Petronelle Moanda from the Congolese Association of Merseyside discussing the Congo in the 1900s and present-day perceptions: an example of a contested past used to construct a dialogue in the present.

'Brutal Exposure: the Congo' (2014) follows in the footsteps of two earlier exhibitions within the Museum's Campaign Zone space, located within the Legacy gallery, which were developed with the express aim of hosting exhibitions which link to contemporary campaigns, with accompanying community and education programmes. 'Home Alone: end domestic slavery' (2010), was developed in partnership with Anti-Slavery International as part of an international campaign which led to the International Labour Organization's 2011 Convention No. 189 protecting rights for domestic workers (International Labour Organization 2014). This was followed by 'White Gold: the true cost of cotton' (2011), a collaboration with the Environmental Justice Foundation which highlighted the abuse of labour rights in the cotton industry, primarily in Uzbekistan. The Museum's exhibition 'Broken Lives: slavery in Modern India', which ran from June 2015 until December 2016, looked at the shocking experiences of India's Dalit community and was developed through a partnership with the Dalit Freedom Network. These exhibitions have given NGOs a platform to potentially reach thousands of people.

Education

To support the teaching of Britain's involvement in the transatlantic slave trade in the national curriculum in the UK, ISM has developed a number of learning resources for schools aimed at all age levels. The resources have been created as a classroom resource to support learning activities and visits to ISM. The 'History of Transatlantic Slave Trade and Abolition' teaching resource is aimed at key stage 2

Home Alone: End Domestic Slavery exhibition poster
©National Museums Liverpool

pupils (between the ages of seven and 11) and has been phenomenally successful. More recently the Museum has produced several educational resources that reflect current areas of research and collection development, such as the 'Contemporary Slavery' teachers' resource for key stage 3 students aged 11 to 14, in particular those studying Citizenship.

A practical response to the matter of what we call the legacies of transatlantic slavery, which is covered in our Legacy gallery at the Museum, was the development of our most recent educational resource, 'Legacies of Transatlantic Slavery: A teachers' guide to the Legacy gallery and object handling' session for key stage 3 and key stage 4 students (International Slavery Museum 2014b).

The resource looks at the development of racist ideologies and stereotyping, racist discrimination, ongoing forms of enslavement, financial gains made by European traders, and ongoing global issues of exploiting resources. Indeed the han-

Legacies of Transatlantic Slavery teachers' resource front page
© National Museums Liverpool

dling session includes a diverse array of objects, from a mobile phone, highlighting the dangerous and often illegal mining of minerals such as cobalt in DR Congo, to toothpaste with a grinning caricatured Black face peering out. The Legacies resource was born out necessity, in a city where changes in attitudes and actions are still needed.

Future

The next stage in the development of the International Slavery Museum will see it expand into the adjacent Dr Martin Luther King, Jr. Building (formerly known as the Dock Traffic Office and renamed in 2012 in the presence of Martin Luther King III, who gave that year's Slavery Remembrance Day memorial lecture). On 28 August 2013, we opened the ground floor of the building to commemorate the 50th anniversary of Dr Martin Luther King, Jr.'s "I Have a Dream"

'I Have a Dream' event in the Dr Martin Luther King, Jr. Building
© Dr. Richard Benjamin

speech which was delivered on 28 August 1963 at the Lincoln Memorial, Washington, D.C. When fully opened to the public, the building will accommodate a resource centre, a collections centre, and education and community spaces. The resource centre will give visitors access to slavery-related digital archives, as well as Black British and human rights multimedia. It will also enable visitors to research family and local history. The collections centre aims to exhibit all accessioned ISM collections in a publicly accessible and interactive storage and display area.

Conclusion

A museum which focuses on the subject of slavery and enslavement, historical or modern, must be prepared to tackle some sensitive issues in the development of collections, exhibitions and programming. However, through the sharing of ideas and experiences – such as the FIHRM initiative – museums can be socially aware, impactful and respectful.

ISM was born out of the Transatlantic Slavery Gallery but has expanded its remit to include other forms of slavery and enslavement, such as forced labour and trafficking for sexual exploitation. However, we must not lose touch with audiences, such as members of the Liverpool Black community, who still see ISM first and foremost as a museum of transatlantic slavery. As such we must continue to develop our transatlantic slavery collections when possible. Furthermore, the field of transatlantic slavery is not static and so CSIS is an important tool in highlighting this, particularly via its eclectic range of seminars (University of Liverpool 2014).

ISM already has some of the world's leading collections of slavery-related objects on display within our galleries. It has an active research programme, produces innovative educational materials, hosts diverse and challenging exhibitions and continues to support Slavery Remembrance Day. That said, we must not rest on our laurels; we must continue to speak for the millions of individuals who were traumatised and brutalised as part of the transatlantic slave trade, and we must actively campaign for those without a voice in the present. The Museum must also be at the centre of debate, discussion and action on topics such as reparations and movements like the Rhodes Must Fall campaign – some of the foremost issues of today. Having the opportunity to be a member of the International Scientific Committee for the Slave Route Project helps the Museum to do all of these things.

BIBLIOGRAPHY

Anthony Walker Foundation, 2016. About the Foundation. Accessed 24 March 2016. http://www.anthonywalkerfoundation.com/about-us.

Benjamin, Richard, 2014. The Museum as Enabler: Constructing and Contesting Futures. In: Francesca Lanz and Elena Montanari, eds., *Advancing Museum Practices*. Torino: Umberto Allemandi.

Benjamin, Richard, 2012. Museums and Sensitive Histories: The International Slavery Museum. In: Ana Lucia Araujo, ed., *Politics of Memory: Making Slavery Visible in the Public Space*. New York: Routledge.

Hochschild, Adam, 2006. *King Leopold's Ghost: A Story of Greed, Terror and Heroism in Colonial Africa*. Pan Books.

International Labour Organization, 2014. Ratifications of C189 - Domestic Workers Convention, 2011 (No. 189). Accessed 24 March 2016. http://www.ilo.org/dyn/normlex/en/f?p=1000:11300:0::NO::P11300_INSTRUMENT_ID:2551460.

International Slavery Museum, 2016a. Their Spirits. Accessed 24 March 2016. http://www.liverpoolmuseums.org.uk/ism/exhibitions/their-spirits/.

International Slavery Museum, 2016b. Schools and groups. Accessed 24 March 2016. http://www.liverpoolmuseums.org.uk/ism/learning/index.aspx. University of Liverpool. 2016. Welcome to the Centre for the Study of International Slavery. Accessed 24 March 2016. http://www.liv.ac.uk/csis/.

Uzzell, David, 1996. Creating place identity through heritage interpretation. *International Journal of Heritage Studies* 1/4, 219–28.

Issues in the Movement for Reparatory Justice for the Crimes of African Chattel Enslavement

Hilary McDonald Beckles

BIOGRAPHY

Sir Hilary McDonald Beckles is a historian, current vice-chancellor of the University of the West Indies and chair of the CARICOM Reparations Committee. His research fields are Afro-Caribbean History and Barbadian History. Among his publications are *Afro-Caribbean Women and Resistance to Slavery in Barbados* (London: Karnak House, 1988); *Liberties lost: the Indigenous Caribbean and Slave Systems* (with V. Shepherd, Cambridge University Press, 2004); *A History of Barbados* (CUP, 2006); *Britain's Black Debt: Reparations for Caribbean Slavery and Native Genocide* (University of the West Indies Press, 2012); and *Cricket without a Cause: Fall and Rise of the Mighty West Indian Test Cricketers* (Jamaica: Ian Randle Publishers, 2017).

The most expansive and impactful popular global movement of the twenty-first century will be the demand for reparative justice for the chattel enslavement of Africans in modernity, now recognised within the international political community as a crime against humanity. The globalisation of enslaved African labour within the project of European imperialism was responsible for the dispersion of over 20 million persons from the continent. This was the largest forced migration in human history.

Minor tributaries of enslaved African labour could be found in Asia, the Middle East and Europe, but the Atlantic Ocean was the primary portal through which these persons passed into the Americas from the late sixteenth century to the late nineteenth century. Chattel enslavement, or the commodification of persons through their transformation into non-human legal status, was the global norm for exported Africans. Criminal enrichment from the ownership and employment of enslaved persons powered the global economy centred on Western Europe until a series of emancipation laws in the nineteenth century terminated the system.

Everywhere that chattel slavery took root, it required extraordinary political mobilisation to uproot it, and to put in its place more enlightened social relations that institutionalised the concept of freedom. In all these 'liberated' societies, the emancipated communities called for reparative justice in multiple forms – social, psychological and material compensation.

Emancipation and the demand for reparations went together in public discourse but have not merged into a practical reality. Nowhere did the empowered elite consider that freed Africans had a right to reparations, even though the principle of compensation for wrongs was a part of their politics and jurisprudence. What in fact occurred was that slave owners received financial compensation from their own states for the loss of their property rights (i.e. in enslaved Africans) that followed from emancipation legislation.

The politics of reparation, the freed Africans discovered, was more about organised power than about social justice. Slave owners used their power in parliaments to extract compensation from taxpayers for the loss of enslaved persons. In the same parliaments, they won the argument that Africans were not entitled to reparations, nor were they deserving of it. Socially disenfranchised Africans could neither press legal claims nor participate in the parliamentary discourses. In all instances, European slave owners paid themselves reparations and denied the Africans any form of reparative justice. Even when the enslaved Africans liberated themselves by force of arms, as was the case in Haiti, the defeated French slave owners found a strategy to extract reparations from the liberated Africans. The French led a call for European solidarity in the face of African freedom. European governments formed a political coalition to deny the Haitian state legitimacy and recognition until it paid reparations to French slavers. On the twenty-first anniversary of the state in 1825, it agreed to pay French slavers 150 million gold francs as an act of reparative justice! European racial solidarity in the face of the African demand for freedom and reparative justice proved a potent force in the global politics of the nineteenth century.

The black demand for reparative justice never ceased, and remained a political element in the nineteenth and twentieth centuries. In the case of the British colonies, there was a major eruption in the early twentieth century, constituting by the 1930s a formal movement. These political conversations found expression in the pan-African campaign of Marcus Garvey and others, and served to define the grassroots nationalism incipient across the post-slavery world. It was this context that in 1937 led Arthur Lewis – half a century before he received a Nobel Prize in Economics – to point out that the matter of English and European reparations for slavery was yet to be addressed.

Pan-Africanists could find no sustainable way to frame the decolonisation agenda without reference to the reparative justice movement. Compensating for the crimes committed against Africans seemed a precursor to nation-building and racial reconciliation. The enormity of the crime seemed too large to be ignored, and too demanding of settlement to be brushed under the post-imperial carpet. The Europeans, nonetheless, tried to define it as a non-issue in their narrative of black freedom. In so doing, they reaffirmed political power as the determining force in defining the idea of social justice.

A century after European slave owners received reparative justice for losing their slave labour, blacks are still calling for justice as a legal right. The irony of this circumstance could be elevated to satire were it not for the palpable pain still associated with the criminality of slavery. Former slave-owning states remain adamant that blacks received full justice when slavery was abolished, and that the freedom they received was a reparative gift from generous and enlightened parliaments. Defining emancipation as a gift in full settlement of the crime was as absurd an argument as could be imagined within the imperial mentality, and reflects the depth of the racial resistance to the black claim to dignity and self-determination.

Indeed, the rise of pseudo-scientific racism within European nineteenth-century academic and political discourse focused upon the need to sustain black subjugation as a permanent feature of European modernity. Race rose to the surface of every aspect of European civilisation during and after the slavery regimes, and remained a powerful legacy at the onset of this new century. It took all of the nineteenth century to uproot the chattel slave systems from the Atlantic World, and all of the twentieth century to embrace the idea of black participation in parliamentary democracies as representatives and citizens. The twenty-first century is vibrating from the call to embrace black reparative justice as a right – and a reasonable one at that.

No subject has divided the global African community as sharply as the reparative justice movement. No issue has revealed the shallowness of African legal determination and Africa's political corruption as clearly. The middle passage that separated Africa and its American diaspora, and which bound them in bondage for four centuries, is as much a wall today as it was a bridge yesterday. The diaspora itself has been as fragmented as Africa, but within these fragments are shards that serve as swords in the absence of shields.

The first attempts to institutionalise the reparative justice movement took place in Abuja, Nigeria, when Chief Abiola formulated a master plan, which he funded, to transform the heart of Nigeria into the core of the African grandstand. In every respect a 1970s event, the gathering of African leaders, constituting a movement, was intended to transform the claim of past centuries into a cause for future generations.

Paramount on the agenda was the imperative to debunk the European claim that the transatlantic slave trade was primarily a business partnership between European and African commercial elites. Within European parliaments this argument has been used for centuries to minimise the immorality that haunts their political consciousness.

The effectiveness of this argument is to be found in its ability to keep African political leaders on the defensive with respect to the reparative justice movement. The accusation levelled against West African kings and chiefs – that they were equal partners in the crime against humanity – has been effective. Many leaders today use it as the basis for their inability to support their own civil societies' demands for reparative justice. Abiola's assembly in Abuja effectively crushed this myth by revealing that:

(i) Europeans entered West Africa and, with the force of massive military might, bent local societies into slave-supplying machines;

(ii) slave-trading corporations, armed and financed for war, were more powerful than most coastal states, and made them offers to gain their compliance or to make them disappear;

(iii) kings and rulers that complied were enriched at the expense of their societies, which rose up against them, creating a culture of resistance within all of West Africa;

(iv) only compliant states survived, while those that resisted were eradicated;

(v) West African economies were distorted and remade around the slave trade, which led to extreme militarisation and social instability;

(vi) European states sent out directives to assassinate African leaders who opposed them and to reward those who participated;

(vii) only the commercial crumbs accrued to the African collaborators, while the lion's share went to the merchants of London, Liverpool and Lisbon, and their investor partners.

The significance of this historical research was obvious; effectively used, it could have empowered elements of African political leadership. As a political strategy, however, it failed simply because most West African leaders have been devoid of the determination needed to participate in the movement. Posturing as participants while remaining passive has served to protect them from engaging in ways that would provide a foundation for post-colonial radicalism.

Meanwhile, in the diaspora, the movement remained at the grassroots level, providing civil liberties organisations with a clear view of the demand for completion of the decolonisation process. Implicit in the Caribbean context, for example, is the perception that reparative action represents the end point of the anti-colonial process – an end of 'the' history, so to speak!

But on the diaspora side of the divide, the discourse remained, until recently, pushed to the margins of the decolonisation agenda. In the USA, the civil rights movement did spawn a call for 'affirmative action', which, when implemented, was quietly referenced by the state as a form of national reparative justice.

The provision to African-Americans of specific forms of access to resources undoubtedly falls within the parameters of the narrative, though radical leaders of the civil rights movement share a different view. Consequently, there exists within the country an unsettled discussion as to whether reparative justice should or can embrace forty years of affirmative action. Those who demand that the promise of '40 acres and a mule' (which shaped the emancipation process at the end of the nineteenth century) be fulfilled see beyond this recent outreach to disenfranchised citizens.

In the Caribbean context, the black-led civil rights movement produced an altogether different result. It created black-managed national states in which democratic electoral processes produced black-majority parliaments. The descendants of the enslaved now 'rule' democratic states, and have been empowered with national constitutions to transform the lives of historically marginalised majorities. Despite this circumstance, the reparative justice movement found no support until 2015 within the official policy frameworks of governments. Civil society and official leadership could not converge on the subject, resulting in a public negation of the importance of the movement. Within the international community, however, the broader dimensions of the transatlantic slave trade were attracting attention as scientific scholarship on the subject served to shape political and diplomatic conversations about postmodernity. With the United Nations (UN), for example, the call for a global conversation about chattel slavery as a crime against humanity, and its role in the economic transformation of the 'West', gained traction across national and cultural terrains.

In many ways, the UN served as the official cover for vulnerable states to speak up on the legacies of slavery as inhibitors of development. Also, it created a dynamic context for scholars and diplomats to engage for the purpose of advancing the human rights causes set out within its Charter. The centring of these conversations within UNESCO was not unexpected, given its agenda relative to the cultural and educational landscapes where legacies remain impactful.

The conception of the International Slave Route Project, under UNESCO's auspices, is arguably the most obvious example of this intersection of scholarship, diplomacy and the discourse of development. The powerful impact of this project is felt globally, and in many ways it continues, after two decades, to shape the primary ways in which racial reconciliation across national and cultural boundaries is discussed.

The UN declaration that the transatlantic slave trade was indeed a crime against humanity emerged within the research traditions of this project. Critically, the declaration is read as the basis of a legal and political claim for reparations to be paid by those nations of the 'West' that were the primary financial beneficiaries of African global chattel bondage.

These discursive tributaries poured into the plenaries of the UN conference on race – the World Conference against Racism, Racial Discrimination, Xenophobia and Related Intolerance – held in Durban, South Africa, 2001. The world gathered to discuss historical crimes against humanity, primarily the transatlantic slave trade, and what should be done about its legacies. Reparations resided at the core of all concerns, and served as a lightning rod for nations to declare their positions.

First out was the USA, which made it explicit that the subject was not one it wished to discuss in international forums, causing it to pull out! The European Union, and 'West' group that included Japan and Australia, declared that their participation in the conference was dependent upon the removal of 'reparations' from the agenda. The Caribbean stood firm and refused to comply, though in the end a compromise was struck that the conference would retain the agenda item but that deliberations on the subject would be non-binding.

In the end, these conversations proved less relevant than originally imagined. More significant to the unfolding of the movement was the divide that developed between African states and the African diaspora. The refusal of African states to stand firm with the diaspora on pushing the reparations agenda represented at Durban was a rejection of the pan-African movement, which had been built upon the idea of ongoing, systemic diaspora support for Africa's liberation and development.

When African states voted with European states and the 'West' blocs on the motion that the transatlantic slave trade was not a crime when it was perpetrated and should therefore not attract reparations today, the blood in diaspora veins boiled and exploded in shame and rage. The diaspora, led by the Caribbean, stood resolute nonetheless, and refused to comply with the EU-African solidarity, and denounced the deal they had struck as a betrayal of global Africa.

Rejected in Durban by African leadership, the Caribbean reparations movement regrouped and refocused its energy on the need to persuade its governments to officially establish national and regional reparations commissions, representing solidarity between states and civil society, and to prepare for a future engagement with Europe and the 'West'. In 2013, CARICOM, the regional grouping of heads of government, agreed and established the CARICOM Reparations Commission, modelled on the CARICOM Initiative. A similar response is gradually taking shape in Brazil. It has been reported by the public media that CARICOM has called upon the slave-owning states of Europe to meet in an international summit in order to discuss the relationship between reparative justice and the development agenda of the Caribbean.

CARICOM has officially determined that Europe has a case to answer in terms of the crimes against humanity represented by African chattel enslavement and the genocide of indigenous people. This is a critical moment in the global development of the movement. It is here, finally, that African descendants have made an official commitment to pursue justice. Beyond the call for a global summit lies the option of the International Court of Justice.

BIBLIOGRAPHY

Hira, Sandew, 2014. *Decolonizing the Mind: 20 Questions and Answers about Reparation for Colonisation.* The Hague: Amrit Publishers.

Commissiong, David, 2016. *It's the Healing of the Nation: The Case for Reparations in an Era of Recession and Recolonisation.* Oistins, Barbados: Caribbean Chapters.

Beckles, Hilary, 2014. *Britain's Black Debt: Reparations Owed the Caribbean for African Enslavement and Native Genocide.* Kingston: University of the West Indies Press.

Coates, Ta-Nehisi, 2015. The Black family in the age of mass incarceration. *The Atlantic,* (October).

Robinson, Randall, 2000. *The Debt: What America Owes to Blacks.* New York: Dutton Books.

The Transatlantic Slave Trade and Slavery

The Psychic Inheritance

Rex Nettleford

Speech given at the UN Observance of the Commemoration of the 200th Anniversary of the Abolition of the Transatlantic Slave Trade, United Nations Headquarters, New York, Monday, 26 March 2007. http://www.thedominican.net/nettleford.pdf.

BIOGRAPHY

Rex Nettleford (1933–2010) was an academic, activist, choreographer, dancer, cofounder of Jamaica's National Dance Theatre Company and artistic director for the University Singers, University of the West Indies. He served as Vice-Chancellor of the University of the West Indies from 1998 to 2004 and was a long-standing member of the International Scientific Committee of the UNESCO Slave Route Project. Born in Falmouth, Jamaica, he received an honours degree in History at the University of the West Indies and an MPhil from Oxford University, where he held a Rhodes Scholarship. He subsequently received numerous awards and honorary degrees. His pioneering study of Rastafarianism, *The Rastafari Movement in Kingston, Jamaica* (1961) was one of many publications, including a collection of essays, *Mirror, Mirror: Identity, Race and Protest in Jamaica* (1970) and an edited edition of the speeches and writings of Norman Manley, *Manley and the New Jamaica* (1971). Among his most notable choreographies for the National Dance Theatre Company were *Pocomania* (1963), a re-enactment of a religious rural tradition that drew on African roots; *Recollections* (1965), which drew on the writings of Derek Walcott; and *The King Must Die* (1968), which paid tribute to American jazz drummer Art Blakey.

Introduction

I come from that part of the Americas – the Caribbean – which is arguably the living laboratory of the dynamism of the encounters between Africa and European foreign soil, and the encounters of both with the Native Americans who had inhabited the real estate of the Americas time out of mind, during periods of conquest and dehumanisation along with the corresponding process of struggle and resistance. For these purposes, north-east Brazil, with its iconic centre in Bahia, New Orleans, and all of that eastern littoral of North America referred to as Plantation America, constitute along with the island-Caribbean, the geo-cultural area that houses a civilisation with its own inner logic and inner consistency.

The advent of later arrivals into the Caribbean after the abolition – first, of the trade in enslaved Africans and later, of slavery itself – did not save them from labour exploitation. But those new arrivals did enter as free men and women into a society which by then had the promise of decency and civility informing human (if not an altogether humane) existence. This has been made distinctive by the cat-alytic role played by the African Presence in social formation within a psychic universe, a great part of which has been plunged, wittingly and unwittingly, into subterranean and submarine silence – to mix a metaphor. Mixed metaphors are, in any case, masks to hide real visages, audible decibels to mask the ultrasound or mute-buttons to impose that threatening silence which Jimmy Cliff, the reggae su-perstar and talented lyricist, characteristically described thus:

> You stole my history
> Destroyed my culture
> Cut out my tongue
> So I can't communicate
> Then you mediate
> And separate
> Hide my whole way of life
> So myself I should hate.

It is fitting that ones like us in the Caribbean Community (CARICOM) should be concerned with breaking the silence, that second most powerful act of oppres-sion which the African Presence in the Americas has suffered for the past 500 years along the Slave Route which UNESCO has wisely placed on its agenda of con-cerns, with a resolve to have action follow intention through efforts like this very Special Assembly of the parent body. Such are the acts that define the journey by those who, having been severed from ancestral homelands and suffered in exile on plantations, have survived and continue to struggle beyond survival.

The quest for delivery to humanity of the truth of what has evolved over the past half a millennium is all part of the exercise. It is a form of co-ordinated so-cial action and an effective way of tackling what has been arguably the greatest scourge of modern life. I refer to that which may well have been the culmination of some four centuries of obscenities perpetrated in the pursuit of material gain, fuelled by greed and the lust for power, and often under the guise of carrying out a civilising mission said to be divinely ordained and even earlier sanctified by papal edict.

The fight for land leading to wars and rumours of wars over time started with the occupation of newly 'discovered' spaces, which, as we know, were there before the Genoan Wanderer and his marauding successors, armed with papal papers, claimed the Americas and continued with the enslavement of millions torn from ancestral hearths and bulk-loaded across the Atlantic. This was followed by the systematic dehumanisation of a horrendously exploited labour force in the production of commodities for commercial profit as well as by the psychological conditioning of millions into stations of self-contempt bolstered by an enduring racism, underlying rigid class differentiation, and the habitual violation of human rights. These are but a few of the blots on human history that have left all of us legacies of the deepest concern in humankind's journey into the twenty-first century.

However, there are other legacies – legacies that are relegated to silence, but which in stubborn defiance speak, often through the intangible heritage of non-verbal communication, to the invincibility of the human spirit against all odds, to the ability of the human mind to exercise the intellect and imagination creatively for the advancement of human knowledge and aesthetic sensibility, to the refinement of ideas about individual rights and collective freedom giving rise to civil society and democratic governance, and to the exploration of the learning process to produce in the human being higher levels of tolerance in dealing with one other, manifested in mutual respect, human dignity, caring and compassion, despite temptations to embrace selfishness, dissembling and even strong doses of mean-spiritedness evident among ones of us. The contribution of the African Presence to all this is, without hubris or rancour, deserving of bold assertion, supported, to be sure, by painstaking investigation, critical analysis and decisively programmed dissemination – all part of the mission of UNESCO's Slave Route Project.

For all of us who tenant the Americas are the creatures of that awesome process of 'becoming' consequent on the historic encounters between diverse cultures from both sides of the Atlantic in circumstances that, for all their negative manifestations, have forged tolerance out of hate and suspicion, unity within diversity, and peace out of conflict and hostility. The ongoing struggle by those who seek recognition and status in human terms demands from all with the gift of knowledge and insight, the commitment of self in the continuing development of humankind. For stronger than war, which dehumanises, humiliates and destroys, is indeed the love of life. And the African Presence on the Route continues to speak of those gone, those living and those yet unborn – a celebratory incantation of a philosophy of life and of the hope-in-despair which has sustained survival in defiance of the transatlantic slave trade and slavery.

What we have learnt from history will have sharpened insights about ourselves in the process of cross-fertilisation which is the great art of humankind's 'becoming' out of the dynamism of the synthesising of contradictions. For this is the story of Africa-in-the-Americas for the past half a millennium. This, from ancient times to this day, is indeed the source and stuff of great literature, great art and great social structures, of sturdy crucibles of human understanding, of great intellectual achievement in science and the humanities. And all of this has taken place along the Slave Route of which we speak! And all of this has taken place, indeed, despite the stubborn persistence of the rules of representation which decree the denigration of things African, as well as a debilitating racism against all who carry the stain of Africa in their veins.

Lest we forget, that Presence, that African Presence, informed the ancestral pedigree of ancient Greece and Rome which Western civilisation has hijacked into its history with monopolistic fervour. In that Mediterranean crossroads civilisation, the treasures of cross-fertilisation gave to humanity the sort of creative energy which guaranteed humankind's capacity to live, die and live again. Within historical memory we again see that Presence playing its catalytic role in the Iberian Peninsula when the cross-pollination of cultures (the one from Africa included) gave rise to an expansiveness of thought that resulted in the so-called 'discovery' of the Americas and our own flowering into the vital source of 'crossroads' energy that this Hemisphere has been for modern humanity.

It is good for us to remember that the moment the European Iberians expelled the Moors and the Jews, Spain declined having lost its intellect and its imagination (as someone pungently and wickedly remarked). The enslaved and colonised Americas provided, as it were, a new arena for experimentation in inhuman exploitation, admittedly, but it was the relegation of hordes of humanity (themselves sources of creative energy) to margins of silence that was to render the Americas more impoverished than she might be. Thanks, however, to the resistance of those who would be silenced, the vitality and energy of the Hemisphere was to benefit. Neither total physical expulsion nor ethnic cleansing has been possible (since both modes of liquidation would have been unprofitable for slave owners and metropolitan masters), and the African Presence continues to make the impact where it most matters, in the enduring areas of language, religion, artistic manifestations and even kinship patterns, as well as in areas of ontology and cosmology rooted in the creative diversity that is now the global reality of our Third Millennium and has been the lived reality of the Caribbean and the wider Americas of which the Caribbean is an iconic integral part.

This is something that invites understanding and acknowledgement from the countries of modern Europe, which have been colonised in reverse, and their extension, white North America, where homogeneity has been considered a virtue among the power structures but which is now threatened by heterogeneity following on the breakdown of geographical boundaries with the advent of migrant hordes of different hue as well as a textured sensibility via galactic spheres. But, alas, the legacy of slavery and its fertiliser of a trade in African labour, continues.

I agree with the notion that 'there comes a time when the past ceases to be an alibi, and [that] … at the turn of the twentieth century [we] surely reached that point' (Fergal Keane: 'Time to wake up to the false dawn of Africa's renaissance' in *The Independent Weekend Review* [London], 13 March 1999, p. 3), but what I cannot agree with is the shrouding of critical elements like the brutality of the trade in enslaved Africans in a silence that would deny to hordes of humanity the fullest possible participation in all discourse that would attempt to define, determine and delineate the destiny of said hordes of humanity long relegated in that past to stations of humiliation, would-be psychic despair and non-personhood. Indeed, those who dare to ignore their history are doomed to repeat it. And the UNESCO Slave Route Project, in helping to prevent this, is clearly designed to identify all the deep social/cultural forces which have successfully conspired to prevent any such repetition, at least on the scale of that past or to deny history and us the long memory of that past. Hence the CARICOM Caribbean's deep involvement in the operations of the project ever since its inception in 1994 (and still today in its revitalised and restructured form). And that vision is what now fortuitously brings us here to challenge the validity of such past obscenities.

I have long had reason to address such obscenities elsewhere but in the context of the responsibilities of the African diaspora, which has helped to seminally shape the Americas but which is still being denied its historic and historical role in the growth and development of this Hemisphere and elsewhere. The African diaspora cries out for recognition and status in the new dispensation that goes by the name of globalisation which, from the perspective of ones like us in the ex-slave, post-colonial Caribbean, threatens to be a calculus of inequality rather than an opportunity to make a last dash towards universal human dignity and individual freedom in praxis.

Such dignity and freedom in praxis must continue to be on the agenda of concerns and positive action for the African diaspora in the new millennium. Crossing the boundary of thought to programmes of action that will benefit the millions that tenant the African diaspora is itself an imperative. Hence the need to incorporate designs for social living and a positive sense of self into the mainstream development strategies of the newly globalised world. The aim for diasporic Africa must be to help determine the mainstream and not merely to float along with the currents, wherever they may take one. The age-long struggle 'to be' and the working solutions providing life skills for survival and beyond, should be utilised to the hilt in sustaining the strengths of the diaspora and eliminating the weaknesses that have come to systematically plague progress and development.

So, one twenty-first century challenge for the African diaspora is to have the new globalisation veer away from inherited obscene habits of racialised division of the world into the rich industrialised North and the poor non-Caucasian South, the developed civilised world versus the two-thirds underdeveloped world, the [misnamed] Third World. That this is best done by the manifestation of achievement through the diaspora's exercise of the creative intellect and creative imagination is impatient of debate. But it must help replace the Cartesian-driven thought-system that declares that the show of emotion is a 'decline from thinking to feeling' with the diasporic reality that genuine creativity and intellectual rigour are not mutually exclusive and that the harmonisation of the two may well be the hope of a third-millennium world.

The abolition of the slave trade, including for all the reasons outlined in the Caribbean scholar Eric William's seminal *Capitalism and Slavery*, could not help but facilitate the re-humanisation of the offspring of the millions involuntarily and inhumanely lured/dragged from West Africa and the Congo across the Middle Passage. The mind, as the African diaspora has long known, can be a passionate organ too.

This is arguably a main point of the Reparation advocacy – by no means seeking a handout of £500 sterling per person to descendants of the oppressed, but rather positing serious investment, by countries which have been enriched by the heinous crime of the slave trade and slavery, in the human resource development of countries that suffered, preferably through the education and preparation of their young to enable them to cope with the inheritance of a continuing unjust world. And, above all, for them to be able to understand their own history and help plug the knowledge gap which the Honourable Representative from St. Vincent and the Grenadines so eloquently emphasised in the UN debate of last November. For as a well-known African proverb goes, 'until the lions have their own historians, tales of the hunt will always glorify the hunter'.

To cross the boundaries of hate, intolerance, discrimination, racial arrogance, class exclusivity, intellectual snobbery and cultural denigration, which constitute the legacy of that horrific past, the African diaspora must continue with its time-worn strategies of demarginalisation, reinforcing the intensity of the creative work through the expansion of communication arts serving humankind. Caribbean kweyol, sranan tonga of Suriname, and Jamaica Talk all legitimately speak to the African diasporic reality and help to substitute voice for the imposed silence of oppression. The choice of one's Creator, whether it be the Jah of the Rastafarians, Pentecostal versions of Jesus, African-American versions of Mohammed and Islam, the Orishas of Cuba's santeria, Brazil's candomblé, Trinidad's shango or the oguns of Haitian vodun must insist on the legitimacy accorded Christian and other orthodoxies in the spirit of that ecumenism which has forced the ritual of apology from Rome to Judaism and has the Graeco-Judaeo-Christian religious-cultural complex acknowledging the rightful existence of Hinduism, Buddhism and Shintoism, the great religions of the East. Heterogeneity as a guiding principle of human organisation is here the desired framework for peace – global, regional and local.

The gift of the grasp of the plurality and intertextuality of existence, though not exclusive to African diasporic experience, is the primary feature of that experience. The twenty-first century and the new millennium – through the accessibility by each segment of Planet Earth to every other at a moment's notice by way of the Internet, e-mail and electronic media – could benefit tremendously from such sense and sensibility to get the millennium's hopes for peace, security and the improvement of the social capital, fulfilled. Can the world without anguish accept itself as part this, part that, part the other but totally human, without one part of it trying to dominate the other? The idea of the Caribbean person being part-African, part-European, part-Asian, part-Native American but totally Caribbean is still a mystery to many in the North Atlantic, which has been spoiled by the very hegemonic control it has had over empires and faraway real estate for half a millennium – and with the indulgences of a trade in slaves, slavery and colonialism acting in tandem.

It is the full grasp of the creative diversity of all of humankind that provides the source for tolerance, generosity of spirit, forgiveness and respect for the Other that the new millennium will require if it is to house the brave new world with the human being as centre of the cosmos. It is the source, as well, of the patience needed for the human-scale development which all the grand objectives of United Nations declarations envision. That patience is honed in the habit of the African diasporic tenants who have had to negotiate their space over time and to find form on a playing field that has not been level, not since 1492 when Spain's Cristóbal Colón lost his way to Japan; not since 1562 when England's John Hawkins traded some surrogate beasts of burden (enslaved Africans) to the Spanish West Indies; not since 1807 when a mix of capitalistic self-interest and humanitarian impulse drove the British Parliament to enact the first step on the journey to restore decency to human life and living.

The African diaspora is for this reason more than equipped to enter the dialogue among civilisations, having seeded the germ of a civilisation itself, as if with the beneficence of retributive justice. Such dialogue, after all, is all about the quest for peace, tolerance, justice, liberty, sustainable development, trust, respect and human understanding and should not be seen as a threat but rather as a guarantee for peace.

Yet, even while I recommend this to our African diaspora and to the world as the guarantee of a safe and meaningful future, the experience of ages drives me back to some wise words uttered on 28 February 1968, which have been immortalised in the Bob Marley musical setting ironically entitled 'War' even while it hankers after peace:

'Until the philosophy which holds one race superior
and another inferior
is finally and permanently discredited and abandoned
Until the color of a man's skin is of no more significance
than the color of his eyes
Until the basic human rights are equally guaranteed to all
without regard to race ...
Until that day
The dream of lasting peace, world citizenship and the rule of international morality
will remain but a fleeting illusion to be pursued but never attained'!

Such, distinguished delegates, are the many boundaries left by the slave trade and slavery. Many rivers are indeed yet to be crossed, to take us all over to the right side of history and away from the obscenities of the slave trade and of slavery, as well as from the vile consequences that continue to plague far too much of humankind, depriving us all of decency and threatening our innate humanity.

The Harriet Tubman Series on the African Diaspora

Paul E. Lovejoy and Toyin Falola, eds., *Pawnship, Slavery and Colonialism in Africa*, 2003.

Donald G. Simpson, *Under the North Star: Black Communities in Upper Canada before Confederation (1867)*, 2005.

Paul E. Lovejoy, *Slavery, Commerce and Production in West Africa: Slave Society in the Sokoto Caliphate*, 2005.

José C. Curto and Renée Soulodre-La France, eds., *Africa and the Americas: Interconnections during the Slave Trade*, 2005.

Paul E. Lovejoy, *Ecology and Ethnography of Muslim Trade in West Africa*, 2005.

Naana Opoku-Agyemang, Paul E. Lovejoy and David Trotman, eds., *Africa and Trans-Atlantic Memories: Literary and Aesthetic Manifestations of Diaspora and History*, 2008.

Boubacar Barry, Livio Sansone, and Elisée Soumonni, eds., *Africa, Brazil, and the Construction of Trans-Atlantic Black Identities*, 2008.

Behnaz Asl Mirzai, Ismael Musah Montana, and Paul E. Lovejoy, eds., *Slavery, Islam and Diaspora*, 2009.

Carolyn Brown and Paul E. Lovejoy, eds., *Repercussions of the Atlantic Slave Trade: The Interior of the Bight of Biafra and the African Diaspora*, 2010.

Ute Röschenthaler, *Purchasing Culture in the Cross River Region of Cameroon and Nigeria*, 2011.

Ana Lucia Araujo, Mariana P. Candido and Paul E. Lovejoy, eds., *Crossing Memories: Slavery and African Diaspora*, 2011.

Edmund Abaka, *House of Slaves and "Door of No Return": Gold Coast Castles and Forts of the Atlantic Slave Trade*, 2012.

Christopher Innes, Annabel Rutherford, and Brigitte Bogar, eds. *Carnival: Theory and Practice*, 2012.

Paul E. Lovejoy and Benjamin P. Bowser, *The Transatlantic Slave Trade and Slavery*, 2012.

Audra A. Diptee & David V. Trotman, Eds. *Remembering Africa & Its Diasporas*, 2012.

Ehud R. Toledano, Ed. *African Communities in Asia and the Mediterranean*, 2012.

Joel Quirk and Darshan Vigneswaran, eds., *Slavery, Migration and Contemporary Bondage in Africa*, 2013.

Hakim Adi, *Pan-Africanism and Communism: The Communist International, Africa and the Diaspora, 1919-1939*, 2013.

Bruce L. Mouser, *American Colony on the Rio Pongo: The War of 1812, the Slave Trade, and the Proposed Settlement of African Americans, 1810-1830*, 2013.

Johnston Akuma-Kalu Njoku. *From Freedom to Freedom*, 2014.

Modesto Amegago. *African Drumming: The History and Continuity of African Drumming Traditions*, 2014.

Waibinte E. Wariboko. *Elem Kalabari of the Niger Delta: The Transition from Slave to Produce Trading under British Imperialism*, 2014.

Elisabeth Cunin & Odile Hoffmann, Eds. *Blackness & Mestizaje in Mexico & Central America*, 2014.

Paul E. Lovejoy and Suzanne Schwarz. *Slavery, Abolition and the Transition to Colonialism in Sierra Leone*, 2015.

Juanita De Barros and Sean Stilwell, eds., *Public Health and Colonialism in the British Imperial World*, 2015.

Dario Euraque and Yesenia Martinez. *The African Diaspora in the Educational Programs of Central America*, 2016.

Paul E. Lovejoy and Vanessa S. Oliveira, eds. *Slavery, Memory, Citizenship*, 2016.

Jennifer Lofkrantz & Olatunji Ojo, eds. *Ransoming, Captivity & Piracy in Africa and the Mediterranean*, 2016.

Meley Mulugetta. *Ethiopian Church Archives Collection: Volume 1: Ethiopian Manuscripts Digital Library, Codices 1–213*, 2017.

David Imbua, Paul Lovejoy & Ivor Miller, Eds. *Calabar on the Cross River: Historical and Cultural Studies*, 2017.

Alice Bellagamba, Sandra E. Greene, and Martin A. Klein, eds. *African Slaves, African Masters: Politics, Memories, Social Life*, 2017.

Myriam Cottias & Marie-Jeanne Rossignol. *Distant Ripples of the British Abolitionist Wave: Africa, Asia and the Americas*, 2017.

Abdoulaye Gueye & Johann Michel, eds. *A Stain on Our Past: Slavery and Memory*, 2018.

Behnaz A. Mirzai & Bonny Ibhawoh, eds. *Africa and Its Diasporas: Rethinking Struggles for Recognition and Empowerment*, 2019.

Philip Misevich. *Abolition and the Transformation of Atlantic Commerce in Southern Sierra Leone, 1790s to 1860s*, 2019.

Harriet Tubman Series